45th Edition  Warman's

Antiques &
Collectibles
2012

Mark F. Moran

Published by

Krause Publications, a division of F+W Media, Inc.
700 East State Street • Iola, WI 54990-0001
715-445-2214 • 888-457-2873
www.krausebooks.com

To order books or other products call toll-free 1-800-258-0929
or visit us online at www.krausebooks.com or www.Shop.Collect.com

ISSN 1076-1985

ISBN-13: 978-1-4402-1404-2
ISBN-10: 1-4402-1404-2

Cover Design by Wendy Wendt
Designed by Wendy Wendt
Edited by Mark F. Moran

Printed in China

ON THE COVER, CLOCKWISE FROM UPPER LEFT:

Electric Guitar, Gretsch Co., Brooklyn, N.Y., circa 1960, Country Gentleman Model, with case. Bridge pickup replaced with Lawrence Humbucking. Lead pickup surround cracked. **$889** *(Courtesy Skinner Inc.)*
Red-yellow bangle, one of a kind, slices of transparent red Bakelite laminated into yellow squares, also with apple-juice Bakelite; 1" wall, 1990s, signed Shultz. **$1,200** *(Courtesy Barbara Wood)*
John Berninger (American, 1897-1981), Untitled, oil on canvas (framed), signed, 25" x 20". **$5,185** *(Courtesy Rago Arts and Auction Center)*
French art glass footed goblet, Daum Frères, Nancy, France, circa 1895, marked Daum, Nancy, (cross of Lorraine), 7" x 7 1/2", patterned with a frieze of fieldmice in shades of red and orange over shaded and frosted sky. **$5,078** *(Courtesy Heritage Auction Galleries)*

Contents

OTHER WARMAN'S TITLES

Barbie™ Doll Field Guide
Bean Plush Field Guide
Bottles Field Guide
Buttons Field Guide
Carnival Glass
Civil War Collectibles
Coins and Paper Money
Depression Glass 5th Edition
Depression Glass Field Guide
Handbags Field Guide
Hot Wheels Field Guide
Jewelry 4th Edition
Jewelry Field Guide 2nd Edition
John Deere Collectibles
Kitschy Kitchen Collectibles Field Guide
Lunch Boxes Field Guide
McCoy Pottery 2nd Edition
Modern U.S. Coins Field Guide
Modernism Furniture and Accessories
North American Indian Artifacts
PEZ™ Field Guide
Political Collectibles
Precious Moments Field Guide
Rookwood Pottery
Roseville Pottery
Shoes Field Guide
Sterling Silver Flatware 2nd Edition
Tools Field Guide 2nd Edition
U.S. Coin Collecting
U.S. Coins & Currency Field Guide
U.S. Stamps Field Guide
Vietnam War Collectibles
Vintage Costume Jewelry
Vintage Jewelry
Vintage Quilts
Watches Field Guide 2nd Edition
Weller Pottery
World Coins Field Guide
World War II Collectibles 2nd Edition

Introduction

WELCOME TO THE NEW WARMAN'S GUIDE FOR 2012

The 45th edition of Warman's Antiques & Collectibles is better than ever, and continues our efforts to bring a fresh, 21st-century perspective to the collecting world.

Our list of auction houses features more than 70 businesses from coast to coast, covering hundreds of collecting categories. The number of consulting experts in various fields has also grown, and we have included new sections on both established and emerging collecting areas.

An important returning feature is a focus on the "Future of the Markets," advising collectors on the best places to invest:

Author Kathy Flood charts the future of jewelry categories. By her own admission, Flood "is a journalist who fell in love with jewelry while having her hair cut, when the salon's latest Vogue fell open on her lap to a page of Christmas tree brooches by Bulgari, Cartier and Mme. Belperron. Since then, her interests in jewelry have branched

Kathy Flood

out: She collects more widely, owns several Internet jewelry shops and has written about bijoux for newspapers and magazines across the country." She is the author of *Warman's Costume Jewelry Figurals* and the long-awaited fourth edition of *Warman's Jewelry*, whose editor she blames for her increasingly up-market taste in gems.

Catherine Saunders-Watson writes of the outlook for the antique-toy market, and interviews auctioneer Dan Morphy on the topic of mechanical

Catherine Saunders-Watson

banks. Saunders-Watson is president and CEO of The Saunders-Watson Group, a boutique public relations firm specializing in the antiques, auction and fine-art sector. Her 25-year background in antiques and fine art has included serving as

co-publisher of *Style Century Magazine,* editor of *Antique Trader,* national editor of *AntiqueWeek,* and as antiques columnist with the Times of London Group newspapers. In her latest venture in electronic media, she serves as editor-in-chief of *AuctionCentralNews. com* and *ToyCollectorMagazine.com.*

Andrew Truman

Andrew Truman joins the Warman's roster this edition to share information on "Door of Hope" dolls. Born and raised in Hallowell, Maine, whose main street has long been a center for antique shops, Truman gained a love early on for antique toys and advertising. He graduated in 1995 from the University of Oregon with a B.A. in English, and taught several years at a private school in Eugene, Ore. Truman returned to Maine in 1999 with his wife and three daughters and joined

Abigail Rutherford

James. D. Julia Inc. Auctioneer & Appraisers, Fairfield, Maine, the following year. Since that time he has helped make Julia's toy, doll and advertising division one of the tops in the country.

Our section on vintage clothing and couture has been expanded, and features prices realized and images from Leslie Hindman Auctioneers of Chicago, plus an overview of the market by Abigail

Rutherford, director of Director of Vintage Couture and Accessories at Leslie Hindman.

Rutherford, author of *Warman's Handbags Field Guide*, is the director of the Vintage Couture and Accessories Department at Leslie Hindman Auctioneers in Chicago. In the past five years, she has been responsible for amassing, appraising and authenticating all couture and accessories up for bid, helping to grow the department into one of the premier sources for these vintage pieces in the world. Rutherford also sits on the board of the Costume Council of the Chicago History Museum. Rutherford received a B.A. in Art History from Lafayette College in Easton, Pa.

Andrew Myers looks at the market for 18th-century French furniture. Myers writes extensively

about architecture, design and the fine and decorative arts for the Robb Report, the Modern Luxury family of magazines, 1stdibs.com, the online newspaper The Faster Times (www. thefastertimes.com), as well as a "catalog of shelter magazines too long (and boring) to mention."

Andrew Myers

"I write exclusively about beautiful things that I'm unlikely ever to be able to afford," he says, grumpily resolved. On good days, he tries to convince himself that he doesn't want all that "stuff" anyway. Myers grew up in Omaha, Neb., and studied at Stanford (undergrad) and UCLA (grad). Donation queries may be sent to adm10@mac. com.

Forrest Poston falls back on his experience with antiques whenever he "annoys the wrong administrator and loses his teaching job," so he spends most of his time as an antiques dealer. While looking for a collecting field that wasn't dominated by dealers

Forrest Poston

with deeper pockets, he discovered West German pottery and has been specializing in that area since 1999. His essays on that subject and others have been published in *Antique Week*, the *Journal of the American Art Pottery Association*, and *Northeast Journal*. His first auction hooked him in 1991, and the need to make room in the house soon moved him from collector to dealer, which led, of course,

to a more cluttered house. He credits his wife, Ginny, for "teaching me to see what I'm looking at."

Tom Deupree and Morrow Jones share their perspectives on the American snapshot, also known as vernacular photography.

Tom Deupree

Deupree has been a dealer in, and collector of, American folk art for the last 30 years. From the start his interest in this material led him to investigate its historical contexts, and the result of his curiosity is a large collection of vintage photographs of, for example, cigar store Indians in their original settings, long before anyone had ever heard of folk art or outsider art. Deupree's photography collection has expanded over the years and now also includes portraits, Native American subjects, panoramas and a good many "photo jokes," some calculated and some not.

Jones is a retired English and film-study teacher living in Connecticut, where he continues to add to his col-

Morrow Jones

lection of vintage snapshots, rereads the classics, and shoots video for non-profit organizations in New England. Jones's parallel interests in photography and folk art converged in the 1970's when he began to understand that old snapshots — then much harder to find than they are today — display the same humor, ingenuity and creative energy that have always informed American folk art. The search for interesting old pictures leads now to formal galleries, antique photo shows and the online auction service that's become a household word, but some of the best images still turn up in secondhand stores and tag sales.

"For the collector, the pleasure in finding great pictures is always tinged by the melancholy thought that somewhere there's a family that's lost track of its pictures," Jones said.

In the Beginning ...

Edwin G. Warman was an entrepreneur in Uniontown, Pa. He dabbled in several ventures, including ownership of a radio station. He was also an avid antiques collector who published his price listings in response to requests from friends and fellow collectors. The first modest price guide was published in 1948 as *Warman's Antiques and Their Current Prices*. It was a bold move. Until then, antiques were sold primarily through dealers, antiques shops and at auctions. The sellers and buyers negotiated prices and were forced to do their own research to determine fair prices. Under Warman's care, the price guide changed all that forever. Warman also published some specialized price guides for pattern glass and milk glass, as well as his "Oddities and Curiosities" editions, under the banner of the E.G. Warman Publishing Co.

Although the name varied slightly over the years, *Warman's Antiques and Their Current Prices* covered such collectible areas as mechanical banks, furniture and silver, just like the *Warman's* of today. His pages consisted of a brief statement about the topic, either relating to the history or perhaps the "collectibility" of the category. A listing of current prices was included, often containing a black and white photograph.

E.G. Warman died in 1979. His widow, Pat Warman, continued the tradition and completed work on the 15th edition after his death. The estate sold the E.G. Warman Publishing Co. to Stanley and Katherine Greene of Elkins Park, Pa., in 1981. Chilton Books bought the Warman Publishing Co. in the fall of 1989. With the 24th edition, Warman's was published under the Wallace-Homestead imprint. Krause Publications purchased both the Warman's and Wallace-Homestead imprints in 1997.

The Warman's Advantage

The Warman's Advantage manifests itself in several important ways in the 2012 edition. As we

Photo courtesy James D. Julia Auctioneers, Fairfield, Maine; www.JuliaAuctions.com

Door of Hope Child Doll, in colorful costume of rose-colored tunic with magenta vest and green braid trim, plaid trousers, gold hat with red pompom and pale orchid-colored slippers, 7" tall. **$690**

reviewed past volumes, we wanted to make this book as easy to use as possible. To that end, we've consolidated and reorganized how we present several key categories. Our new mantra is, "What is it first?"

For instance, an antique clock may also have an advertising component, an ethnic element (like black memorabilia), reflect a specific design theme (like Art Deco) and be made of cast iron. But first and foremost, it's a clock, and that's where you'll find it listed, even though there are other collecting areas involved.

There are a few categories that remain iconic in the collecting world. Coca-Cola collectibles cross many interests, as do folk art, Oriental antiques and Tiffany designs, to name just a few. These still have their own broad sections.

In addition to space memorabilia and western/cowboy collectibles, newly expanded sections include ceramics, jewelry, toys, lighting, Tiffany, photography and art glass.

Photo courtesy Heritage Auction Galleries, Dallas; www.HA.com

Henry James Soulen (American, 1888-1965), The Ukulele player (detail), gouache on board, 20' x 14", signed lower right. **$2,629**

Prices

The prices in this book have been established using the results of auction sales all across the country, and by tapping the resources of knowledgeable dealers and collectors. These values reflect not only current collector trends, but also the wider economy. The adage that "an antique (or collectible) is worth what someone will pay for it" still holds. A price guide measures value, but it also captures a moment in time, and sometimes that moment can pass very quickly.

Beginners should follow the same advice that all seasoned collectors will share: Make mistakes and learn from them; talk with other collectors and dealers; find reputable resources (including books and Web sites), and learn to invest wisely, buying the best examples you can afford.

Words of Thanks

This 45th edition of the Warman's guide is the best we've ever published. Dozens of auction houses have generously shared their resources, but a few deserve special recognition: Greg Belhorn, Belhorn Auction Services LLC, Columbus, Ohio; Andrew Truman, assisted by Lisa Oakes and Lisa Warren, at James D. Julia Auctioneers, Fairfield, Maine; Anthony Barnes at Rago Arts and Auction Center, Lambertville, N.J.; Karen Skinner at Skinner Inc., Boston; Heritage Auction Galleries, Dallas; Morphy Auctions, Denver, Pa.; Susan "BFF" Pinnell at Jeffrey S. Evans & Associates, Mount Crawford, Va.; Rebecca Weiss at Swann Auction Galleries, New York; and Abigail Rutherford at Leslie Hindman Auctioneers, Chicago. And special thanks to Catherine Saunders-Watson for her many contributions, friendship and support.

Read All About It

There are many fine publications that collectors and dealers may consult about antiques and collectibles in general. Space does not permit listing all of the national and regional publications in the antiques and collectibles field; this is a sampling:

• *Antique Trader*, published by Krause Publications, 700 E. State St., Iola, WI, 54990 – *www.antiquetrader.com*

• *Antique & The Arts Weekly*, 5 Church Hill Road, Newton, CT 06470 – *www.antiquesandthearts.com*

• *AntiqueWeek*, P.O. Box 90, Knightstown, IN 46148 – *www.antiqueweek.com*

• *Maine Antique Digest*, P.O. Box 358, Waldoboro, ME 04572 – *www.maineantiquedigest.com*

• *New England Antiques Journal*, 24 Water St., Palmer, MA 01069 – *www.antiquesjournal.com*

• *The Journal of Antiques and Collectibles*, P.O. Box 950, Sturbridge, MA 01566 – *www.journalofantiques.com*

• *Southeastern Antiquing & Collecting* magazine, P.O. Box 510, Acworth, GA 30101 – *www.go-star.com/antiquing*

Let us know what you think

We're always eager to hear what you think about this book and how we can improve it. Contact:

Mark F. Moran
Senior Editor, Antiques & Collectibles Books
Krause Publications
700 E. State St.
Iola, WI 54990-0001
715-445-2214, Ext. 13461
Mark.Moran@fwmedia.com

Visit an Antique Show

One of the best ways to enjoy the world of antiques and collectibles is to take the time to really explore an antiques show. Some areas, like Brimfield, Mass., and Manchester, N.H., turn into antique meccas for a few days each summer when dealers and collectors come for both specialized and general antiques shows, plus auctions.

Here are a few of our favorites:

Brimfield, Mass., shows, held three times a year in May, July and September, *www.brimfield.com.*

Round Top, Texas, antique shows, held spring and fall, *www.roundtop.com/antique1.htm*

Antiques Week in and around Manchester, N.H., held every August.

Palmer/Wirfs Antique & Collectible Shows, including the Portland, Ore., Expos, *www.palmerwirfs.com*

The Original Miami Beach Antique Show, *www.dmgantiqueshows.com*

Merchandise Mart International Antiques Fair, Chicago, *www.merchandisemart.com/chicagoantiques*

High Noon Western Americana Show & Auction, Phoenix, *www.highnoon.com*

Ask an Expert

Many contributors have proved invaluable in sharing their expertise during the compilation of the 45th edition of the Warman's guide. For more information on their specialties, call or visit their Web sites.

Caroline Ashleigh
Caroline Ashleigh Associates LLC
1000 S. Old Woodward, Suite 105
Birmingham, MI 48009-6734
248-792-2929
www.auctionyourart.com
Vintage Clothing, Couture and Accessories, Textiles, Western Wear

Al Bagdade
The Country Peasants
1325 N. State Parkway, Apt 15A
Chicago, IL 60610
312-397-1321
Quimper

Tim Chambers
Missouri Plain Folk
501 Hunter Ave
Sikeston, MO 63801-2115
573-471-6949
E-mail: plainfolk@charter.net
Folk Art

Noah Fleisher
E-mail: noah.fleisher@yahoo.com
Modernism

Reyne Haines
Reyne Gallery
4747 Research Forest Drive #180-274
The Woodlands, TX 77381
513-504-8159
www.reyne.com
E-mail: reyne@reyne.com
20th Century Decorative Arts, Lighting, Fine Jewelry, Wristwatches

Ted Hake
Hake's Americana & Collectibles Auctions
P.O. Box 1444
York, PA 17405
717-848-1333
E-mail: auction@hakes.com
Pop Culture, Disneyana, Political

Photo courtesy Skinner Inc.; www.SkinnerInc.com

Martin Brothers glazed stoneware Riverscape mantel vase, ex-Richard Wright collection.
$1,659

Photo courtesy Heritage Auction Galleries, Dallas; www.HA.com

Silvered brass Civil War-period Sheridan's Cavalry Corps Badge, 1 5/8" x 1 3/8". Separately affixed blue enamel center section with crossed sabers. Suspended from the name bar by small brass chains. Overall near-perfect condition, retaining 80% of the original silver finish. **$3,107**

Leslie Holms
Antique Purse Club of California
55 Ellenwood Ave.
Los Gatos, CA 95030
408-354-1626
E-mail: cree56@comcast.net
Antique handbags of all kinds

Mary P. Manion
Landmarks Gallery & Restoration Studio
231 N. 76th St.
Milwaukee, WI 53213
800-352-8892
www.landmarksgallery.com
Fine Art & Restoration

Mark F. Moran
Senior Editor, Antiques & Collectibles Books
Krause Publications
700 E. State St.
Iola, WI 54990-0001
715-445-2214, Ext. 13461
Mark.Moran@fwmedia.com
Folk Art, Fine Art, Americana

Suzanne Perrault
Perrault Rago Gallery
333 N. Main St.

Lambertville, NJ 08530
609-397-1802
www.ragoarts.com
E-mail: suzanne@ragoarts.com
Ceramics

David Rago
Rago Arts and Auction Center
333 N. Main St.
Lambertville, NJ 08530
609-397-9374
www.ragoarts.com
Art Pottery, Arts & Crafts

Dennis Raleigh Antiques & Folk Art
P.O. Box 745
Wiscasset, ME 04578
207-882-7821
3327 Cones Ct.
Midland, MI 48640
989-631-2603
www.dennisraleighantiques.com
E-mail: dgraleigh@verizon.net
Decoys, Silhouettes, Portrait Miniatures

Henry A. Taron
Tradewinds Antiques
P.O. Box 249
Manchester-By-The-Sea, MA 01944-0249
(978) 526-4085
www.tradewindsantiques.com
Canes

Andrew Truman
James D. Julia, Inc.
P.O. Box 830
Fairfield, ME 04937
207-453-7125
www.juliaauctions.net
E-mail: atruman@jamesdjulia.com
Toys, Dolls & Advertising

Auction Houses

Sanford Alderfer Auction & Appraisal
501 Fairgrounds Road
Hatfield, PA 19440
215-393-3000
www.alderferauction.com
Full service

American Bottle Auctions
2523 J St. Suite 203
Sacramento, CA 95816
800-806-7722
www.americanbottle.com
Antique bottles, jars

American Pottery Auction
Waasdorp Inc.
P. O. Box 434
Clarence, NY 14031
716-759-2361
www.antiques-stoneware.com
Stoneware, redware

American Sampler
P.O. 371
Barnesville, Md. 20838
301-972-6250
www.castirononline
Cast-iron bookends, doorstops

Antiques and Estate Auctioneers
44777 St. Route 18 E.
Wellington, OH 44090
440-647-4007
Fax: 440-647-4006
www.estateauctioneers.com
Full service

Auctions Neapolitan
1100 First Ave. S.
Naples, FL 34102
239-262-7333
www.auctionsneapolitan.com
Full service

Belhorn Auction Services LLC
P.O. Box 20211
Columbus, Ohio 43220
614-921-9441
www.belhorn.com
Full service, American art pottery

Bertoia Auctions
2141 DeMarco Drive
Vineland, NJ 08360
856-692-1881
www.bertoiaauctions.com
Toys, banks, holiday, doorstops

Brunk Auctions
P.O. Box 2135
Asheville, NC 28802
828-254-6846
www.brunkauctions.com
Full service

Caroline Ashleigh Associates LLC
1000 S. Old Woodward, Suite 105
Birmingham, MI 48009-6734
248-792-2929
www.auctionyourart.com
Full service, vintage clothing, couture and
    accessories, textiles, western wear

Clars Auction Gallery
5644 Telegraph Ave.
Oakland, CA 94609
888-339-7600
www.clars.com
Full service

Photo courtesy Heritage Auction Galleries, Dallas;
www.HA.com

*Archibald Knox For Liberty & Co., silver
hammered metal and enamel "Tudric" clock,
circa 1902-1905, impressed "English Pewter
01126/ Made By Liberty & Co", 8" x 12" x
3".* **$2,390**

Cowan's
6270 Este Ave.
Cincinnati, OH 45232
513-871-1670
www.cowanauctions.com
Full service, historic Americana, Native
American objects

Cyr Auction Co.
P.O. Box 1238
Gray, ME 04039
207-657-5253
www.cyrauction.com
Full service

Early Auction Co. LLC.
123 Main St.
Milford, OH 45150
513-831-4833
www.earlyauctionco.com
Art glass

Elder's Antiques
901 Tamiami Trail (US 41) S.
Nokomis, FL 34275
941-488-1005
www.eldersantiques.com
Full service

Greg Martin Auctions
660 Third St., Suite 100
San Francisco, CA 94107
800-509-1988
www.gregmartinauctions.com
Firearms, edged weapons, armor, Native
American objects

Grey Flannel
8 Moniebogue Lane
Westhampton Beach, NY 11978
631-288-7800
www.greyflannel.com
Sports jerseys, memorabilia

Guyette & Schmidt Inc.
P.O. Box 1170
24718 Beverly Road
St. Michaels, MD 21663
410-745-0485
www.guyetteandschmidt.com
Antique decoys

Photo courtesy Heritage Auction Galleries, Dallas; www.HA.com

*JFK, Ike, Mamie, Adlai, Rocky, and Dick: 6" advertising
button picturing all the top candidates of the 1950s.* **$717**

Hake's Americana & Collectibles Auctions
P.O. Box 1444
York, PA 17405
717-848-1333
www.hakes.com
Character collectibles, pop culture

Heritage Auctions Inc.
3500 Maple Ave., 17th Floor
Dallas, TX 75219-3941
800-872-6467
www.ha.com
Full service, coins, pop culture

iGavel Inc.
229 E. 120th St.
New York, NY 10035
866-iGavel6 or 212-289-5588
auction.igavel.com
Online auction, arts, antiques and collectibles

Ivey-Selkirk
7447 Forsyth Blvd.
Saint Louis, MO 63105
314-726-5515
www.iveyselkirk.com
Full service

Jackson's International
Auctioneers and Appraisers
2229 Lincoln St.
Cedar Falls, Iowa 50613

319-277-2256
www.jacksonsauction.com
Full service, religious and Russian objects,
postcards

James D. Julia Inc.
P.O. Box 830
Fairfield, ME 04937
207-453-7125
www.juliaauctions.net
Full service, toys, glass, lighting, firearms

Jeffrey S. Evans & Associates
2177 Green Valley Lane
Mount Crawford, VA 22841
540-434-3939
www.jeffreysevans.com
Full service, glass, lighting, Americana

John Moran Auctioneers Inc.
735 W. Woodbury Road
Altadena, CA 91001
626-793-1833
www.johnmoran.com
Full service, California art

Leigh Keno Auctions
127 E. 69th St.
New York, NY 10021
212-734-2381
www.kenoauctions.com
Fine antiques, decorative arts

Lang's Sporting Collectibles
663 Pleasant Valley Road
Waterville, NY 13480
315-841-4623
www.langsauction.com
Antique fishing tackle and memorabilia

Leslie Hindman Auctioneers
1338 W. Lake St.
Chicago, Il 60607
312-280-1212
www.lesliehindman.com
Full service

McMasters Harris Auction Co.
5855 John Glenn Hwy
P.O. Box 1755
Cambridge, OH 43725

740-432-7400
www.mcmastersharris.com
Dolls and accessories

Michael Ivankovich Auction Co.
P.O. Box 1536
Doylestown, PA 18901
215-345-6094
www.wnutting.com
Wallace Nutting objects

Leland Little Auctions & Estate Sales Ltd.
246 S. Nash St.
Hillsborough, NC 27278
919-644-1243
www.llauctions.com
Full Service

Litchfield County Auctions Inc.
425 Bantam Road (Route 202)
Litchfield, CT 06759
860-567-4661
212-724-0156
www.litchfieldcountyauctions.com
Full service

Photo courtesy Rago Arts and Auction Center, Lambertville, N.J.;
www.RagoArts.com

Pierre Le Faguays (French, 1892-1925), Archer (Tireur L'
Arc), bronze with brown and silver patinas and ivory on
marble base; Signed "LE FAGUAYS" on base; 26" x
23 3/4" x 5 1/2". **$18,300**

Morphy Auctions
2000 N. Reading Road
Denver, PA 17517
717-335-3435
www.morphyauctions.com
Toys, banks, advertising, pop culture

Mosby & Co. Auctions
905 West 7th St., #228
Frederick, MD 21701
301-304-0352
www.mosbyauctions.com
Mail, phone, Internet sales

New Orleans Auction Galleries Inc.
801 Magazine St.
New Orleans, LA 70130
800-501-0277
www.neworleansauction.com
Full service, Victorian

Noel Barrett Vintage Toys @ Auction
P.O. Box 300
Carversville, PA 18913
215-297 5109
www.noelbarrett.com
Toys, banks, holiday, advertising

Old Town Auctions
P.O. Box 91
Boonsboro, MD 21713
240-291-0114
301-416-2854
www.oldtownauctions.com
Toys, Advertising, Americana; no Internet sales

Old Toy Soldier Auctions USA
P.O. Box 13324
Pittsburgh, PA 15243
Ray Haradin
412-343-8733
800-349-8009
www.oldtoysoldierauctions.com

Old World Auctions
2155 W. Hwy 89A, Suite 206
Sedona, AZ 86336
800-664-7757
www.oldworldauctions.com
Maps, documents

Photo courtesy Rago Arts and Auction Center, Lambertville, N.J.;
www.RagoArts.com

Harvey Ellis (American, 1852-1904), untitled beach scene (detail), 1894, watercolor on paper (framed), signed and dated, 10 3/4" x 19 1/2" (sight). **$10,980**

Past Tyme Pleasures
39 California Ave., Suite 105
Pleasanton, CA 94566
925-484-6442
www.pasttyme1.com
Internet catalog auctions

Philip Weiss Auctions
1 Neil Court
Oceanside, NY 11572
516-594-0731
www.prwauctions.com
Full service, comic art

Pook & Pook Inc.
463 East Lancaster Ave.
Downingtown, PA 19335
610-629-0695
www.pookandpook.com
Full service, Americana

Professional Appraisers & Liquidators LLC
16 Lemington Court
Homosassa, FL 34446
800-542-3877
www.charliefudge.com
Full Service

Quinn's Auction Galleries
& Waverly Rare Books
431 N. Maple Ave.
Falls Church, VA 22046
703-532-5632
www.quinnsauction.com
www.waverlyauctions.com
Full service, rare books and prints

Rago Arts and Auction Center
333 N. Main St.
Lambertville, NJ 08530
609-397-9374
www.ragoarts.com
Arts & Crafts, modernism, fine art

Red Baron's Antiques Inc.
6450 Roswell Road
Atlanta, GA 30328
404-252-3770
www.redbaronsantiques.com
Full service, Victorian, architectural objects

Rich Penn Auctions
P.O. Box 1355
Waterloo, IA 50704
319-291-6688
www.richpennauctions.com
Advertising and country-store objects

Richard D. Hatch & Associates
913 Upward Road
Flat Rock, NC 28731
828-696-3440
www.richardhatchauctions.com
Full service

Robert Edward Auctions LLC
P.O. Box 7256
Watchung, NJ 07069
908-226-9900
www.robertedwardauctions.com
Baseball, sports memorabilia

Rock Island Auction Co.
4507 49th Ave.
Moline, IL 61265-7578
800-238-8022
www.rockislandauction.com
Firearms, edged weapons and accessories

St. Charles Gallery Inc.
1330 St. Charles Ave.
New Orleans, LA 70130
504-586-8733
www.stcharlesgallery.com
Full service, Victorian

Samuel T. Freeman & Co.
1808 Chestnut St.
Philadelphia, PA 19103
215-563-9275
www.freemansauction.com
Full service, Americana

Seeck Auctions
P.O. Box 377
Mason City, IA 50402
641-424-1116
www.seeckauction.com
Full service, carnival glass

Photo courtesy Rago Arts and Auction Center, Lambertville, N.J.; www.RagoArts.com

Pair of rattan chaises with adjustable backs, early 20th century, 36 1/2" x 30" x 71 1/4".
$1,464 pair

Skinner Inc.
357 Main St.
Bolton, MA 01740
978-779-6241
www.skinnerinc.com
Full service, Americana

Sloans and Kenyon
7034 Wisconsin Ave.
Chevy Chase, MD 20815
301-634-2344
www.sloansandkenyon.com
Full service

Slotin Folk Art
Folk Fest Inc.
5619 Ridgetop Drive
Gainesville, GA 30504
770-532-1115
www.slotinfolkart.com
Naïve and outsider art

Strawser Auctions
P.O. Box 332, 200 N. Main
Wolcottville, IN 46795
260-854-2859
www.strawserauctions.com
Full service, majolica, Fiesta ware

Swann Galleries Inc.
104 E. 25th St.
New York, NY 10010
212-254-4710
www.swanngalleries.com
Rare books, prints, photographs, posters

Theriault's
P.O. Box 151
Annapolis, MD 21404
800-638-0422
www.theriaults.com
Dolls and accessories

Tom Harris Auction Center
203 S. 18th Ave.
Marshalltown, IA 50158
641-754-4890
www.tomharrisauctions.com
Full service, clocks, watches

Photo courtesy Rago Arts and Auction Center, Lambertville, N.J.; www.RagoArts.com

Peter Max (American, b. 1937), four offset lithographs in colors: Top Cat (#19, shown), Captain Midnight (#12), Rainbow Lane (#14), The Coach With The Six Insides, 1967-68; 36" x 24" (sheet) each; Peter Max Poster Co., New York. **$600 set**

Tradewinds Antiques
P.O. Box 249
Manchester-By-The-Sea, MA 01944-0249
978-526-4085
www.tradewindsantiques.com
Canes

Treadway Gallery
2029 Madison Road
Cincinnati, OH 45208
513-321-6742
John Toomey Gallery
818 North Blvd.
Oak Park, IL 60301
708-383-5234
www.treadwaygallery.com
Arts & Crafts, modernism, fine art

Advertising

ADVERTISING

Commercial messages and displays have been found in the ruins of ancient Arabia. Egyptians used papyrus to create sales messages and wall posters, while lost-and-found advertising was common in ancient Greece and Rome. As printing developed in the 15th and 16th centuries, advertising expanded to include handbills. In the 17th century, advertisements started to appear in weekly newspapers in England.

Also see Coca-Cola, Folk Art, Posters, Toys.

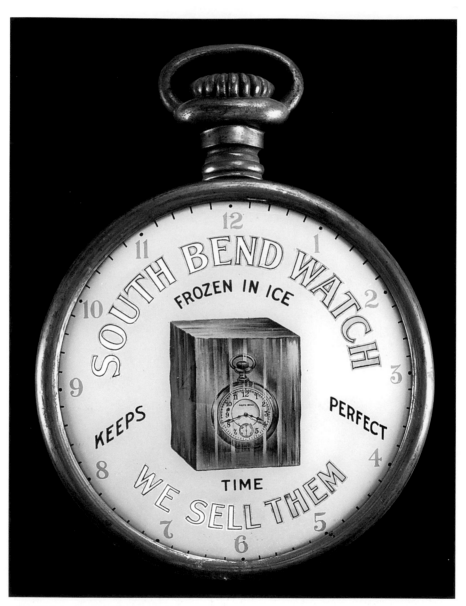

Photo courtesy James D. Julia Auctioneers, Fairfield, Maine; JamesDJulia.com

South Bend Watch countertop display, figural pocket watch light-up sign with a reverse-on-glass "dial" face depicting a watch frozen in a block of ice as testimony to its ability to take a licking and keep on ticking. Manufactured by the Cincinnati Sand Blast Co., includes a card from the C.C. Markham Jewelry Store, Guilford, Conn., where it originated. It is unusual that this piece comes with its original cowl and early white porcelain, wire-wrapped socket. Rarely seen with its complete back end, 12 1/2" x 17". Some loss of gilt to "bezel" but overall both the display and the reverse-on-glass paint are in very good condition. Electrical cord needs replacement. **$4,600**

Photo courtesy Skinner Inc., Boston; www.SkinnerInc.com

Broadside, "W.A. Snow Iron Works" Weather Vanes, Boston, late 19th century, black-printed broadside depicting a selection of the weathervanes offered by the maker, (creases), 35" x 24 1/2", in a contemporary aluminum frame.
$385

Photo courtesy James D. Julia Auctioneers, Fairfield, Maine; JamesDJulia.com

Rock Island Brewing Co. "Cross Country Beer" tin sign, early chromolithographed self-framed tin sign of two country gents placing a wager on the outcome of a cockfight, with the caption, "The Beer You Can Bet Your Money On," suggesting that the odds-on favorite for the day would be the stockpile of "Cross Country" beer seen in the background. The Rock Island Brewery of Rock Island, Ill. was founded in 1892 by the consolidation of the neighboring Huber Brewery, Raible & Stengle Brewery and the Atlantic Brewery; 20" x 24 1/2", faint vertical lines in the surface sheen and two small nail holes at bottom corners. **$1,298**

Brookfield Rye self-framed tin sign, attention-getting image of a beautiful woman in transparent negligee, in a classic Greek pose holding a bottle of Brookfield Rye. Lithographed by the Meek Co., 23" x 33". **$3,162**

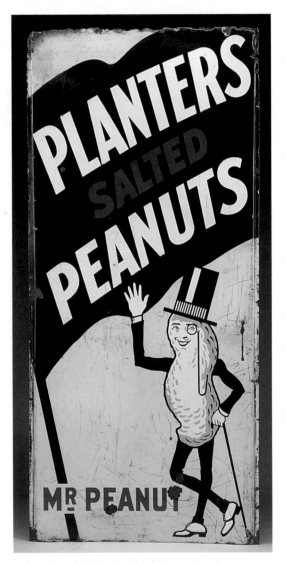

Photo courtesy James D. Julia Auctioneers, Fairfield, Maine; JamesDJulia.com

Planters Peanuts porcelain sign, rare sign used as an advertising panel in a "Highway Lighthouse." These lighthouses were found along roadways in the 1920s and '30s to alert motorists of roadway hazards that lay ahead. Constructed with a large blinking light atop a tall rectangular base, they proved too tempting a canvas for advertising companies to pass up. The Highway Lighthouse Co. had offices located in New York and Pittsburgh in the mid-1930s, 27 1/2" x 60 1/4". Scratches, scrapes and porcelain chips. The top has some corrosion and loss of metal. **$13,800**

Photo courtesy James D. Julia Auctioneers, Fairfield, Maine; JamesDJulia.com

George Wirdemann Brewing Co. tin sign, lithographed die-cut tin easel-back sign advertising Wiedemann's fine beers, depicting a scowling bespectacled curmudgeon reading a newspaper as two street urchins look on. The reverse of the sign has a tin support so the sign could be displayed on a store countertop. A few minor scratches, shallow corner bends and minor litho loss. **$800+**

Photo courtesy James D. Julia Auctioneers, Fairfield, Maine; JamesDJulia.com

Chero-Crush ceramic syrup dispenser, with a figural cherry body embossed with cherry boughs and "Chero-Crush" gilt script on both sides. Includes plunger-type pump with porcelain "button" at top, 13", some loss to gilt lettering and slight difference in hue on the sides. Professionally repaired (probably long ago) at the base where the pedestal foot had a radial crack. **$2,875**

Pre-1900 reverse-on-glass oval corner sign advertising Yuengling's brewery of Pottsville, Pa. **$6,600**

Hires Root Beer tin-on-cardboard sign, rare embossed oval illustration of soda fountain beauty set against a simulated wood grain background, 6 1/4" x 9 1/4", a few areas of surface rubbing and minor blemishes. **$1,035**

Photo courtesy James D. Julia Auctioneers, Fairfield, Maine; JamesDJulia.com

Inter-Woven Socks Trolley store display, early carved wood figural display promoting Inter-Woven Socks made to simulate the Toonerville Trolley. Complete with conductor and two passengers as well as luggage stacked atop trolley, 12"
x 17", some uniform wear and chips to paint finish. **$1,121**

Photo courtesy James D. Julia Auctioneers, Fairfield, Maine; JamesDJulia.com

Moxie cardboard floor display sign, uncommon die-cut store sign that would have been supported with a cardboard easel. Humorous illustration of the Moxie Boy resting on a pile of Moxie crates, being teased with a feather by the Moxie Girl. The caption reads: "Wake Up! Send a Case of Moxie To Our Home – Wouldn't That Tickle You?", 22 1/2" x 37", some edge chipping, good color. **$1,265**

Photo courtesy James D. Julia Auctioneers, Fairfield, Maine; JamesDJulia.com

Moxie 1911 tip tray with Moxie Boy die-cut, captioned "Our Idol". It was shipped flat from the factory and is intended to be bent at a right angle for display on the store counter. This example appears to be N.O.S. and has never been used, 6" x 11 3/4". **$632**

Photo courtesy James D. Julia Auctioneers, Fairfield, Maine; JamesDJulia.com

L.V. Orsinger's Ice Cream light shade, circa 1900, LaSalle, Ill., advertising light shade features two milk-glass panels that read, "Eat L.V. Orsinger's Ice Cream", set into a tin trapezoidal-shaped framework. Sides are embellished with decorative faceted colored glass jewels, 7 3/4" x 6 1/2" x 4", light overall pitting to the original painted black metal surface. **$575**

Crated papier-mâché advertising tiger, used either as a store display or parade figure. Circa 1900, depicting crouching tiger with mouth in a snarl on a molded, naturalistic base marked "Learbury Tiger," presumably for Learbury Clothiers, makers of fine men's suits in Syracuse, N.Y., and attributed to Old King Cole. Encased within original packing crate cage marked "Handle With Care This Box Contains Learbury Fashion Display", 76" x 30" x 29", small number of touch-ups to paint chips. **$3,737**

Walt Disney Vintage Advertisement/Club Membership Group (Disney, circa 1930s). Seven pieces of advertising and club membership ephemera. It includes a certificate to join the Mickey Mouse Globe-Trotters club, printed in red and black ink; a certificate to join the Mickey Mouse Good Teeth Brigade, printed in red and black ink, with a small 1/3" tear on the upper right corner; a full-color handbill, encouraging kids to "Be a ringmaster of your own Walt Disney Pinocchio Circus"; a die-cut Ringmaster top hat for the Pinocchio Circus, printed in black and red; a die-cut wall hanger/certificate to join the Mickey Mouse Globe-Trotters Club, printed in full-color; and two different die-cut cardboard ads for the free Mickey Mouse Scrap Book, both printed in full-color. **$262 all**

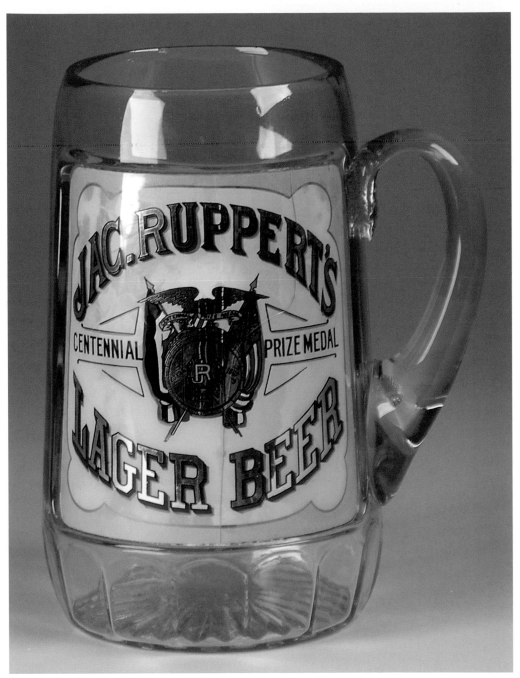

Photo courtesy James D. Julia Auctioneers, Fairfield, Maine; JamesDJulia.com

Ruppert's Lager Beer advertising mug, oversized glass backbar mug features a recessed panel and a curved reverse-on-glass advertisement for Jacob Ruppert's Lager Beer. Original manufacturer's label reads, "W.T. Murphy & Co., Manufacturers of Decorated Glassware, 72 Murray Street, New York", 10", reverse-on-glass label has one vertical crack.
$920

Philip Morris "Johnny" Bellhop die-cut floor display, captioned, "No Cigarette Hangover When you Smoke Philip Morris". A base has been built into which the sign dovetails, 18" x 45". "Johnny" has been broken just above the ankles; some white paint splatter and some paper loss and staining to the cardboard base. Die-cut portion of the sign likely began life with a cardboard easel on the back, but has since been mounted to a thin layer of birch plywood for support. **$172**

Hudnut Perfume lamp, has three reverse-painted panels depicting a woman and two children filling a basket with flowers. The advertising shade sits atop a cast-metal base with stylized leaf design and chain switch with acorn pull. The lid to the lamp contains a compartment in which perfume can be poured and the heat from the light bulb will cause it to evaporate, 20", finish on metal base has some wear and corrosion. **$1,035**

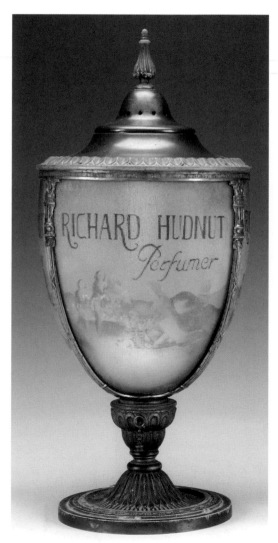

Photo courtesy Noel Barrett Antiques & Auctions Ltd., Carversville, Pa.; www.NoelBarrett.com

Blizzard Storm Front framed lithographed tin sign by The Vehicle Apron & Hood Co., which produced automobile storm aprons and covers, tire sleeves, etc., 15 1/2" x 11 1/2". **$4,600**

Photo courtesy Noel Barrett Antiques & Auctions Ltd., Carversville, Pa.; www.NoelBarrett.com

Double-sided lithographed tin die-cut flange sign advertising Pennsylvania Bicycle Tires, patent date June 7, 1907, 27 3/4" tall. **$9,200**

Photo courtesy James D. Julia Auctioneers, Fairfield, Maine; JamesDJulia.com

Aunt Jemima Pancake Flour cardboard premium toy, colorful die-cut advertising premium, circa 1905, from the Davis Milling Co., St. Joseph, Mo. Consists of a hinged, embossed cardboard 2-piece Aunt Jemima that was originally tethered to a die-cut box of pancake flour with a string. By pulling on the bottom of the string, Aunt Jemima would appear to be climbing a rope to reach the box of flour at the top, 6 1/2" x 13". Aunt Jemima is missing a small pin/grommet that held the top and bottom halves together; the original string and small guides that the string is threaded through are missing. Reverse of all three pieces has old glue residue. **$345**

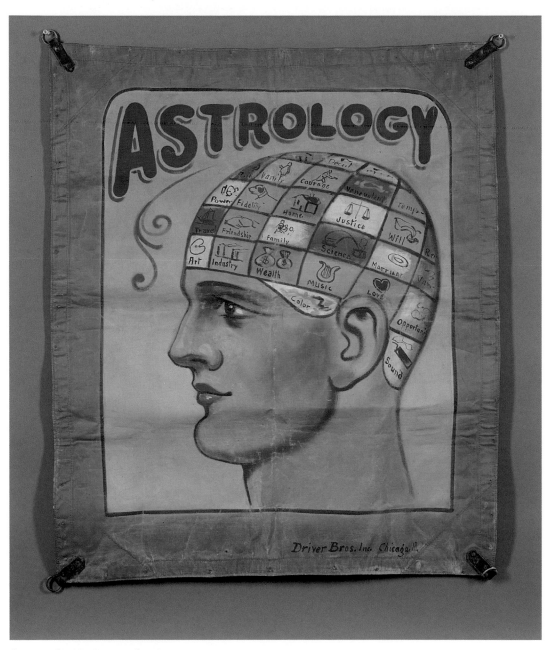

Photo courtesy Skinner Inc., Boston; www.SkinnerInc.com

Polychrome-painted canvas "Astrology" sideshow banner, Driver Bros. Inc. Chicago, early to mid-20th century, incorrectly titled, the banner painted with a man's head displays a phrenology diagram of the various mental faculties of the brain, 34" x 29". **$3,081**

Photo courtesy Skinner Inc., Boston; www.SkinnerInc.com

Painted tin fireworks advertising sign, American, mid-20th century, 8 1/4" x 28 1/2". Has three bullet holes, some rusty surface areas. **$533**

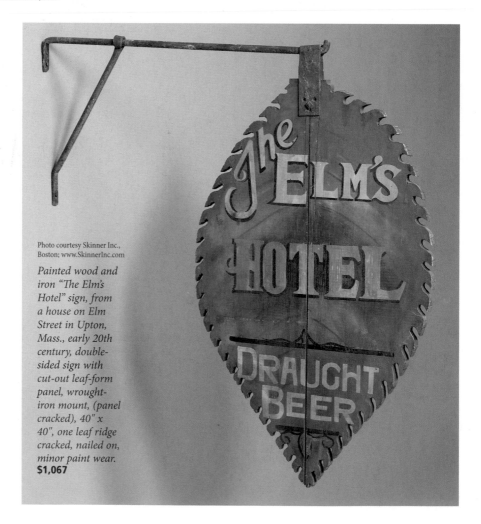

Photo courtesy Skinner Inc., Boston; www.SkinnerInc.com

Painted wood and iron "The Elm's Hotel" sign, from a house on Elm Street in Upton, Mass., early 20th century, double-sided sign with cut-out leaf-form panel, wrought-iron mount, (panel cracked), 40" x 40", one leaf ridge cracked, nailed on, minor paint wear. **$1,067**

Photo courtesy Skinner Inc., Boston; www.SkinnerInc.com

Painted tin boot and shoemaker's trade sign, American, late 19th century, double-sided painted tin panel, (minor paint wear, some dents on lower quarter), 20" x 14". **$237**

Photo courtesy Heritage Auction Galleries, Dallas; www.HA.com

Ulysses S. Grant bust advertising Empire Soap, dated 1885. Perhaps as a memorial, the Empire Soap Co. added "The Old Commander" brand to their soap line. Grant is depicted in his uniform much as he would have been seen during the war. The back has a copyright date of 1885 by Bernard Dreyfuss and is marked "Patent Applied For July 7,1885". The bust is 16.5" tall with only minor wear to its original paint. Many busts similar to this have surfaced but with no advertising connection. **$717**

Photo courtesy Morphy Auctions, Denver, Pa.; www.MorphyAuctions.com

Linen Rub-No-More sign, late 1800s. Mother elephant giving baby elephant a bath. Fashioned similarly to "pin the tail on the donkey" game, it is uncut and retains all of its original elephant tails, 38" x 42". **$1,852**

Photo courtesy Morphy Auctions, Denver, Pa.; www.MorphyAuctions.com

Tin Chinese laundry sign, double-sided, 34" x 22". **$161**

*JFK, Ike, Mamie,
Adlai, Rocky,
and Dick: 6"
advertising button
picturing all the
top candidates of
the 1950s.* **$717**

*Reverse-glass Red Rock
Ginger Ale sign, circa
1895, 6" x 8", pre-
Prohibition with chain
frame and suspension,
light fading.* **$298**

Cigar Cutter: Moss Agate Cigar countertop advertising. Cast iron, 6 1/4" x 6 1/2" high. The front plaque reads, "Smoke/ Moss Agate/ for Quality/ Riddle-Graff & Co. Delaware, O." The top reads, "Patented Oct. 7' 1902/ May 22' 06/ Aug. 7' 06". The underside is numbered "1092". Repainted. **$191**

Circa 1910 Mogul Egyptian Cigarettes advertising sign, 10" x 14". Dressed in flowing robes, clutching jeweled swords and smoking a cigarette, the cover model implores the tobacco enthusiast to join him for a smoke, and perhaps trade a few of the cards secreted within the Mogul packs; minor edge wear. **$251**

Photo courtesy Heritage Auction Galleries, Dallas; www.HA.com

Circa 1933 Goudey Gum advertising sign. A little sprite whispers in the ear of a young boy on this tin advertising sign from Goudey Gum Co. Boston - Chicago, light scratches, 7 1/2" x 15 1/2". **$286**

Photo courtesy Morphy Auctions, Denver, Pa.; www.MorphyAuctions.com

Tin Paul Jones Whiskey sign, minor oxidation, 14" x 19". **$1,053**

Photo courtesy Morphy Auctions, Denver, Pa.; www.MorphyAuctions.com

Rare store display for Weeden Engines, designed for a window display in the 1890s. An upright engine was shown as part of the display. The engine ran two lines of shafting to make the two cardboard blacksmiths weld a bar with their hammer blows. Engine not included, 10" x 17". **$1,092**

Photo courtesy Morphy Auctions, Denver, Pa.; www.MorphyAuctions.com

Whistle Soda sign, damage to left bottom, top and near handle, 33 1/2" x 25 1/2". **$126**

Photo courtesy Morphy Auctions, Denver, Pa.; www.MorphyAuctions.com

Stegmaier Brewing Co. tip tray. Circa 1905, Wilkes-Barre, Pa. Near mint, 4" diameter. **$258**

Photo courtesy Morphy Auctions, Denver, Pa.; www.MorphyAuctions.com

Woodward's Chocolates tip tray. Circa 1905, near Mint, 4" diameter. **$258**

Photo courtesy Morphy Auctions, Denver, Pa.; www.MorphyAuctions.com

Deacon Brown Phosphate Soda tip tray, Montgomery, Ala. Near mint, 6" diameter. **$1,610**

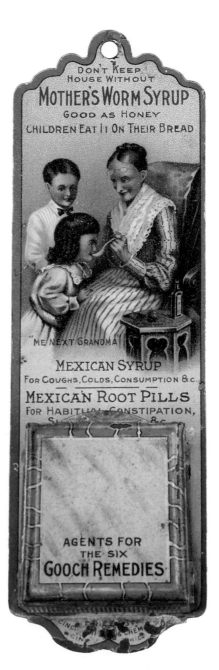

Photo courtesy Morphy Auctions, Denver, Pa.; www.MorphyAuctions.com

Mother's Worm Syrup tin match holder, with detailed image of a family on the front. Some light to moderate wear and scattered nicks and scrapes close to bottom, 3/4" x 2 1/4" x 6 1/4". **$1,100**

Photo courtesy Morphy Auctions, Denver, Pa.; www.MorphyAuctions.com

Sunbeam Bread die-cut standup sign, 1950s, cardboard, includes original display bread box. Near mint, 40" x 27". **$373**

ARCHITECTURAL ELEMENTS

Architectural elements, many of which are handcrafted, are those items that have been removed or salvaged from buildings, ships or gardens.

Beginning about 1840, decorative building styles began to feature carved wood and stone, stained glass, and ornate ironwork. At the same time, builders and manufacturers also began to use fancy doorknobs, doorplates, hinges, bells, window locks, shutter pulls and other decorative hardware as finishing touches on new homes and commercial buildings. Hardware was primarily produced from bronze, brass and iron, and doorknobs also were made from clear, colored and cut glass. Highly ornate hardware began appearing in the late 1860s and remained popular through the early 1900s. Figural pieces that featured animals, birds and heroic or mythological images were popular, as were ornate and graphic designs that complimented the many architectural styles that emerged in the late 19th century.

Photo courtesy Skinner Inc., Boston; www.SkinnerInc.com

Pair of continental carved wood architectural decorations, late 19th century, mahogany or walnut, formed as seated griffins holding shields, with acorn pendants, 38". **$474 pair**

Framed Classical Revival Adam-style architectural panel, first half 20th century, oil on canvas, painted with classical figures, urns, scrolls, and female herms holding an incense burner, in white painted frame, overall 55" x 14 3/4". **$948**

Set of six architectural leaded colored glass panels, two 38 1/4" x 30 1/4" and four 38 1/4" x 18 1/4". ......**$207 all**

Victorian, polychrome painted and turned wood architectural newel post, 43 1/4" x 4 1/2". **$504**

Painted wooden architectural model of an arbor, American, late 19th/early 20th century, 27 1/4" x 22". Loss at lower center, 3" x 1/4", small loss to molding on one column, two shrinkage cracks on arch. **$1,007**

Art

Photo courtesy Rago Arts and Auction Center, Lambertville, N.J.; www.RagoArts.com

Elizabeth O'Neill Verner (American, 1883-1979), Hagar, circa 1940, pastel on silk (framed), signed, 18 7/8" x 14 3/8". **$24,400**

Photo courtesy Rago Arts and Auction Center, Lambertville, N.J.; www.RagoArts.com

Harvey Ellis (American, 1852-1904), untitled beach scene, 1894, watercolor on paper (framed), signed and dated, 10 3/4" x 19 1/2" (sight). **$10,980**

Photo courtesy Rago Arts and Auction Center, Lambertville, N.J.; www.RagoArts.com

William Aiken Walker (American, 1838-1921), Male and Female with Corn Pipes; oil on board (framed separately), each signed, 9" x 4 3/4" each. **$20,740 pair**

Photo courtesy Rago Arts and Auction Center, Lambertville, N.J.; www.RagoArts.com

Andre Lhote (French, 1885-1962), untitled, 1909, oil on paper (framed), signed and dated, 10" x 12 7/8" (sight). **$4,880**

Photo courtesy Rago Arts and Auction Center, Lambertville, N.J.; www.RagoArts.com

Colin Campbell Cooper (American, 1856-1937), Grand Canyon Morning, oil on board (framed), signed, 10 1/2" x 13 5/8". **$3,660**

Maria Martinetti (Italian, 1864-?) Peasant With Pipe, watercolor portrait of a man with beard and tattered clothes standing against a stucco wall holding a pipe in one hand, a stick in the other. He holds his tattered blue jacket under his arm. Signed lower right, "Maria Martinetti Roma". Housed in its original gilt wood frame. Sight: 29 1/2" x 21 1/4". **$3,450**

Photo courtesy Rago Arts and Auction Center, Lambertville, N.J.; www.RagoArts.com

Joseph Barrett (American, b. 1935), Winter Road, oil on canvas (in artist frame), signed, 32" x 30". **$1,220**

Photo courtesy Rago Arts and Auction Center, Lambertville, N.J.; www.RagoArts.com

Thomas Hill (American, 1829-1908), Vernal Falls, Yosemite, 1899, oil on canvas (framed), signed and dated, 24" x 20".
$14,640

Photo courtesy Rago Arts and Auction Center, Lambertville, N.J.; www.RagoArts.com

Henry Bayley Snell (American, 1858-1943), A Summer Day, oil on canvas (framed), 18" x 24". **$3,965**

Photo courtesy Rago Arts and Auction Center, Lambertville, N.J.; www.RagoArts.com

William Francis Taylor (American, 1883-1970), Canal in the Summer, oil on board (framed), signed, 8" x 10". **$9,150**

Photo courtesy Rago Arts and Auction Center, Lambertville, N.J.; www.RagoArts.com

Theodore Saint-Amant Cunningham (American, 1899-?), untitled (Central Park), 1931, oil on board (framed), signed and dated, 8″ x 10″. **$1,830**

Photo courtesy Rago Arts and Auction Center, Lambertville, N.J.; www.RagoArts.com

Fern Isabel Coppedge (American, 1883-1951), Fishing Boats — Gloucester, oil on canvas (framed), signed, 20″ x 24″. **$18,300**

Joseph Stella (American, 1877-1946), Untitled, oil on canvas (framed), signed, 14" x 10 7/8". **$9,760**

Photo courtesy Rago Arts and Auction Center, Lambertville, N.J.; www.RagoArts.com

John R. Grabach (American, 1886-1981), Loading the Freighter, oil on board (framed), signed, 8" x 10 1/8". **$3,965**

Anton Vorauer (American, 1905-1985), N.Y. Harbor, 1959, oil on canvas, signed and dated, 24" x 36". **$2,440**

Photo courtesy Rago Arts and Auction Center, Lambertville, N.J.; www.RagoArts.com

Hendrik Jan Wolter (Dutch, 1873-1952), Untitled (Standing Nude), oil on canvas (in a carved and gilded period frame), signed, 39 7/8" x 28".
$18,300

Photo courtesy Rago Arts and Auction Center, Lambertville, N.J.; www.RagoArts.com

John Berninger (American, 1897-1981), Untitled, oil on canvas (framed), signed, 25" x 20".
$5,185

Photo courtesy Sanford Alderfer
Auction & Appraisal, Hatfield, Pa.;
www.AlderferAuction.com

Edward Willis Redfield (American, 1869-1965), Snow Scene, Center Bridge, Pa., oil on canvas, 22 1/2" x 25 1/2", signed lower right, "E.W. Redfield", with original bill of sale and Grand Central gallery label, in a Newcomb Macklin frame. **$163,800**

Photo courtesy Rago Arts and Auction Center, Lambertville, N.J.; www.RagoArts.com

Walt Francis Kuhn, (American, 1877-1949) Apples, 1933; Oil on canvas (Newcomb-Macklin frame); Signed and dated; 13" x 22", 22 1/4" x 31" (frame); Exhibition: Walt Kuhn Memorial Exhibition, Cincinnati Art Museum, Cincinnati, 1960 (label on verso). **$9,600**

Photo courtesy James D. Julia Auctioneers, Fairfield, Maine; www.JuliaAuctions.com

Jo Cantine (American, 1893-1987) Portrait of a Young Man In a Lincoln Rocker, oil on canvas half-size portrait shows a young man dressed in riding clothes seated sideways in an antique Lincoln rocker. The interior of the room shows a door, two chairs and a windowsill with pot. This is thought to be the artist's grandson. Signed bottom right "Jo Cantine 1934". Housed in a painted wood frame, 50" x 40". In-painting with evidence of creases. **$3,450**

Photo courtesy Rago Arts and Auction Center, Lambertville, N.J.; www.RagoArts.com

Joseph Meierhans (American, 1890-1980), Untitled, mixed media on Masonite (in artist's frame), signed, 31 7/8" x 27 7/8". **$976**

Photo courtesy Rago Arts and Auction Center, Lambertville, N.J.; www.RagoArts.com

Joseph Barrett (American, b. 1935), Deep Snow: Old Orchard, oil on canvas (in artist-made frame), signed and titled, 26" x 24". **$3,965**

George Armfield (British, 1808-1893), Sticking Together, oil on canvas scene shows a small black dog resting its chin on the back of a white and brown dog, both on alert for intruders. Signed lower right. Housed in an antique gesso decorated frame, 10" x 12". Relined, light craquelure. **$2,070**

Thomas Hewes Hinckley (American, 1813-1896), After The Hunt, two brown and white hunting dogs resting beside recently shot game birds. A rifle rests on a small tree limb beside a game bag. Signed lower left, "T H Hinckley 1849". Housed in a gold gesso decorated frame with liner. Relined on new stretcher with turnbuckle devices, some in-painting. **$13,225**

Basil Ivan Rakoczi (British, 1908-1979), The Lighthouse Boy, oil on canvasboard (framed), signed and titled, 16" x 12". **$2,806**

Artist unknown (English School, 19th Century), The Ferry Boat, oil on tin scene shows three children in a make-do boat flying British flag. The oldest boy poles the boat while another boy holds an infant. Their dog stands in water looking on while the father sleeps on the shore. Housed in a wood gilt frame, 11 3/4" x 23", some discolored varnish. **$632**

Photo courtesy James D. Julia Auctioneers, Fairfield, Maine; www.JuliaAuctions.com

John Norval Marchand (American, 1875-1921), Western Hunter, oil/gouache western scene shows a cowboy leaning over a ridge shooting at nearby game. His saddled horse stands beside him, all in a western mountain landscape. Signed lower right, "J N Marchand 1915". Housed in its original gesso decorated gilt frame, 9" x 11 1/2". **$2,185**

Photo courtesy James D. Julia Auctioneers, Fairfield, Maine; www.JuliaAuctions.com

Don Freeman (American, 1908-1978), "Sparing Partners at Gym in NYC", oil on canvas scene shows two men flexing their muscles facing each other. One is in flesh tones and the other in white tones, against a greenish background. Signed lower right "D.F.". Housed in a modern gilt-wood frame, 30" x 22", small puncture at center bottom. **$862**

Photo courtesy James D. Julia Auctioneers, Fairfield, Maine; www.JuliaAuctions.com

Margaret Anna Dobson (American, 1888-1981), California Dreaming, unsigned watercolor shows a beach scene with four young women under a red umbrella, a mother and child walk nearby. The watercolor is double sided having a California landscape with house on the reverse. Housed in a modern gilt molded wood frame having a linen and gilt liner with a glass front and back. Sight: 15 1/2" x 20 1/2". **$230**

Photo courtesy James D. Julia Auctioneers, Fairfield, Maine; www.JuliaAuctions.com

Artist unknown (Mid 20th Century), Children Playing by the Seaside, oil on canvas mounted to board, shows young children in the foreground with a C-shaped beach. Signed lower left "L.K.". Housed in a gesso decorated gilt frame with linen and gilt liner, 20" x 24". **$2,300**

Photo courtesy James D. Julia Auctioneers, Fairfield, Maine; www.JuliaAuctions.com

Sir John Hoppner R.A. (British, 1758-1810), Portrait Of Lady Charlotte Percy, Countess of Ashburnham. Large oil on canvas portrait of an elegant young woman seated in front of an alcove with landscape view. Housed in a period carved wood and gilt frame with gilt artist and sitter plaque, 50 1/4" x 40". Relined on new stretcher (stretcher marked "Produce of England",) minor in-painting, light craquelure. **$189,750**

Photo courtesy Leslie Hindman Auctioneers, Chicago; www.LeslieHindman.com

American School, 19th century, The Disagreement, oil on board, 17 3/4" x 21 1/4", in-painting throughout, surface dirt, numerous cracks to board, most prominent in background, wear to paint at edges, framed. **$1,708**

Photo courtesy Leslie Hindman Auctioneers, Chicago; www.LeslieHindman.com

American School, 19th century, Brother and Sisters, oil on canvas, 28 1/2" x 35", surface dirt, lined, in-painting in sky, visible repairs, framed. **$2,440**

Photo courtesy Leslie Hindman Auctioneers, Chicago; www.LeslieHindman.com

George Wesley Bellows (American, 1882-1925), Lady in a Green Dress, 1924, oil on canvas, 40" x 32", surface dirt, localized areas of craquelure most visible in orange paint, lower left and upper right corners; lined. Heavy amounts of in-painting in section of orange paint and immediately behind the sitter's right shoulder in the background. In-painting also visible in hair, forehead, face, neck and various areas of blouse; also in area of hands and background surrounding the left arm. **$91,500**

Photo courtesy Leslie Hindman Auctioneers, Chicago;
www.LeslieHindman.com

*Theodore Earl Butler (American, 1860-1936),
Two Women Bathing Baby, oil on canvas.
signed (lower right), 19" x 23 1/2", surface
dirt, localized areas of crquelure, in-painting
throughout background and in woman's hair
on right.* **$41,480**

Photo courtesy Leslie Hindman Auctioneers, Chicago;
www.LeslieHindman.com

*American School, 19th/20th century, Portrait
of a Lady, oil on canvas, 29" x 24", surface
dirt, extreme wear to edges, lined, specks
of paint loss in face, background and along
edges, small localized areas of craquelure,
oxidized varnish, in-painting in background,
dress and flowers, date appears to be
heightened, framed.* **$2,074**

Photo courtesy Leslie Hindman Auctioneers, Chicago; www.LeslieHindman.com

Schork, 20th century, Male Nude, oil on canvas, signed (upper right), 38" x 23", surface dirt, localized areas of craquelure, in-painting visible in areas of body definition, also background, lined, minor specks of paint loss, framed. **$3,172**

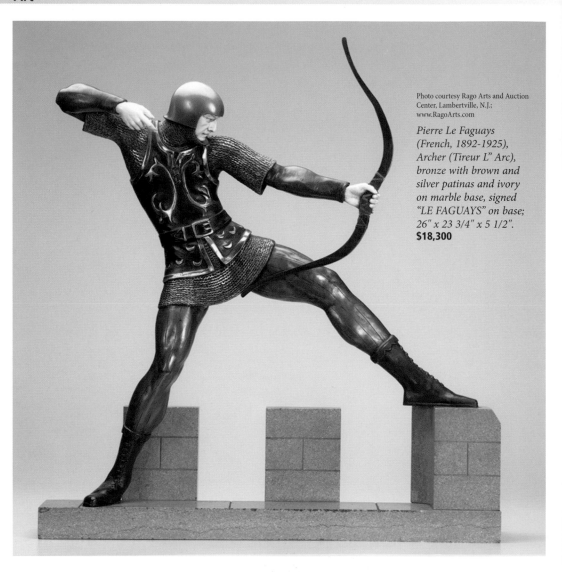

*Pierre Le Faguays
(French, 1892-1925),
Archer (Tireur L" Arc),
bronze with brown and
silver patinas and ivory
on marble base, signed
"LE FAGUAYS" on base;
26" x 23 3/4" x 5 1/2".*
$18,300

*Alexander Archipenko (Ukrainian/
American, 1887-1964), Floating Torso
(Variant), circa 1940, painted plaster,
inscribed.* **$30,500**

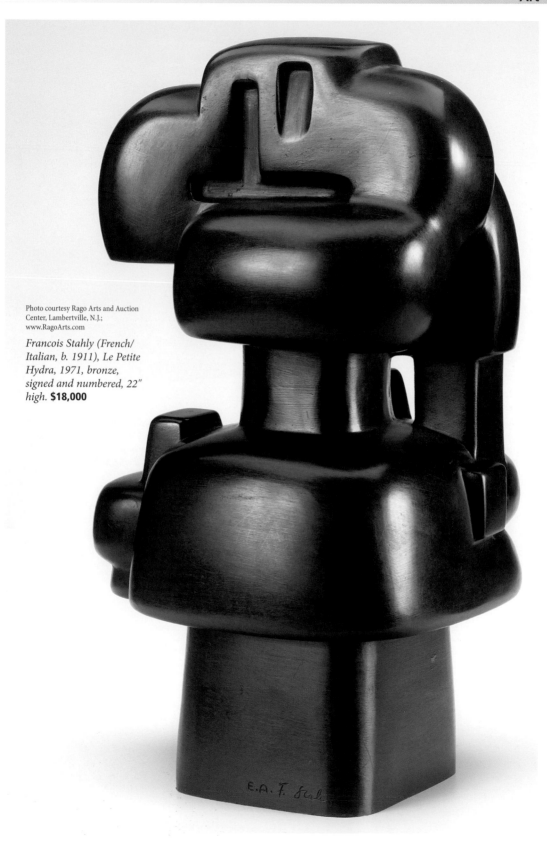

Photo courtesy Rago Arts and Auction Center, Lambertville, N.J.; www.RagoArts.com

Francois Stahly (French/ Italian, b. 1911), Le Petite Hydra, 1971, bronze, signed and numbered, 22" high. **$18,000**

Photo courtesy James D. Julia Auctioneers, Fairfield, Maine; www.JuliaAuctions.com

Theodore Baur (1835-1894), The Charging Buffalo, second half 19th century. Accompanied by an excerpt from a book that indicates the Meriden Britannia Co. commissioned Baur to execute this sculpture especially for the American Centennial. Signed in script "Theo Baur" under the right rear haunch, with no apparent foundry mark, 10 1/2" high, 17 3/4" in length and the green marble plinth measures 3/4" high, 15" in length, width 6 1/2". **$2,300**

Photo courtesy Rago Arts and Auction Center, Lambertville, N.J.; www.RagoArts.com

Leonard Baskin (American, 1922-2000), Head of Medea, 1981, bronze, signed "L.BASKIN" and stamped "(c) KENNEDY GALLERIES INC, N.Y., 2/3", 9 1/2" high (head), 48" base. **$5,795**

Burt Brent (b. 1939), Barn Owl Mask, bronze, No. 2 in an edition of 20, 5" x 10" x 10". **$2,800+**

Photo courtesy Rago Arts and Auction Center, Lambertville, N.J.; www.RagoArts.com

Edith Barretto Parsons (American, 1878-1956), two works of art: Untitled (Quiet Goat), bronze, signed "E.B.PARSONS (c)" and with foundry mark "GORHAM CO. FOUNDERS / OFES", 4 1/4" high; Untitled (Prancing Lamb), bronze, signed "E.B.PARSONS (c)" and with foundry mark "GORHAM CO. / OFOR", 4 5/8" high. **$1,220 pair**

Photo courtesy Rago Arts and Auction Center, Lambertville, N.J.; www.RagoArts.com

Bessie Onahotema Potter Vonnoh (American, 1872-1955), The Dance, 1908, bronze, signed "Bessie Potter Vonnoh No VI" with foundry mark "Roman Bronze Works NY", 12 3/8" high. **$17,080**

Daniel Chester French (American, 1850-1931), Seated Lincoln, 1915, bronze, signed "D.C. FRENCH/June 1915" with inscription "CAST FR/SCULPTORS PLASTER MAQUETTE", 10" high. **$8,540**

Photo courtesy Rago Arts and Auction Center, Lambertville, N.J.; www.RagoArts.com

Malvina Cornell Hoffman (American, 1885-1966), Kiki, bronze, signed "Malvina Hoffman" and with foundry mark "Alexis Rudier/Fondeur Paris", 7 3/4" high; accompanied by two books by Hoffman. **$3,660**

Photo courtesy Rago Arts and Auction Center, Lambertville, N.J.; www.RagoArts.com

Malvina Cornell Hoffman (American, 1887-1966), Column of Life, 1917, bronze, signed "(c) MALVINA HOFFMAN" and stamped "1917", 4 1/4" high. **$3,050**

*Bronze figural group,
after Antoine-Louis Barye
(1796-1875), depicting
Theseus battling the
Minotaur, raised on a
rectangular plinth base
inscribed BARYE, 32".*
$976

Photo courtesy Leslie Hindman Auctioneers, Chicago;
www.LeslieHindman.com

Continental bronze figural group, after Antoine-Louis Barye (1796-1875), depicting a Bedouin on horseback over a naturalistic ground, inscribed BARYE, mounted on an oval marble base, 27 1/2". **$1,342**

Harriet Whitney Frishmuth, (American, 1880-1980) "The Star," bronze sculpture modeled in 1918. The top edge of the base marked "Harriet W Frishmuth 1918 Gorham Co. Founders 0 505". Dark brown to black finish. The bronze depicts a standing nude woman with left arm and hand reaching straight up with head gazing up, with other hand and arm to the side. The bottom mounted to a square black marble base. Unknown edition, 19" overall. **$8,050**

Harriet Whitney Frishmuth, (American, 1880-1980) "The Vine," side of the bronze base "QBWS Gorham Co. Founders Harriet W Frishmuth 1921". The bronze depicting a nude woman leaning backwards with one hand outstretched holding a vine laden with grapes and the other hand behind her head. Mounted to a rectangular black marble base. Unknown edition, 12 1/2" overall. **$9,200**

Unknown artist, (European, circa 1900) Goddess of Wine, modeled as a female seated nude wearing a crown of grape vines, clutching a goblet in her left hand, supporting her resting head. She grasps a cluster of grapes in her extended right hand. Her legs are crossed, left leg against a spilled wine vessel. She is reclining against a leafy knoll on a discarded robe, the whole raised on a socle (a plain plinth that supports a wall), 15 1/2" x 13 1/2" x 11 1/2" d overall. Her head is seamed at the neck and is separated along this seam. **$1,437**

FUTURE OF THE MARKET: ANTIQUE FRAMING

By Eli Wilner

Eli Wilner & Co., New York

When I started collecting and studying period frames in earnest in the early 1980's, they were still being discarded with the daily trash. Learning about the frames then was an uphill struggle with little information readily available.

Today, nearly 25 years later, there is a growing body of scholarship available: books, videos, exhibition catalogs and essays.

Values noted are "current retail replacement values," or what a person can expect to pay if seeking such flames for artworks at a dealer in frames. As is true in most areas, the factors of condition, rarity and size are of key importance. A word about the market for period frames: it is important to recognize that it is an illiquid market—not one where auctions regularly take place and allow a wider value to be established. The wide margin between what a dealer will pay when purchasing frames for their inventory and what the frames may ultimately retail for is influenced by several factors unique to frames.

First: the frame size. There was little standardization in painting sizes during the 19th century, so few frames fit without alteration. Sensitive and competent alteration of period frames is a costly and labor-intensive process than must be executed properly for frame value to be maintained.

Second: Due in part to this size issue and also because of historically appropriate framing (the attempt to marry artworks with frames of the same period) a fine frame may languish in inventory for many years simply because the right confluence of factors hasn't occurred to allow the frame to be selected. (Indeed, some of our most spectacular frames have been in our inventory since I started the gallery.)

Third: There are nearly always restoration costs in order to put the frame in suitable condition.

Fourth: The market in fine period frames is inextricably entwined with the art market. The extraordinary prices achieved in frames correlates to the value of the paintings they can surround. If a client has just spent $200,000 or $300,000 on the Hudson River landscape of their dreams, it is not that far-fetched to understand that they are willing to pay as little as 10% of the cost of the painting on a fine period frame that will best complement and contain their prize. This cannot he emphasized enough. When assessing any period frame, you must look not only at what artwork it may be on at present, but also its inherent quality as a frame of its period, and

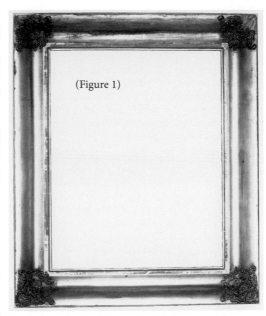

(Figure 1)

the quality of artwork it may be able to surround.

(Figure 1)

The style of American frames can be closely associated with trends in art, architecture, design and decorative trends, and as the swing of a pendulum, styles tended to shift from simple to elaborate and back again. In the early years of the 19th century when the simple elegance of Duncan Phyfe furniture reigned supreme, the primary sort of art being made was portraiture. For the simple dignified images produced, frames of simple cove moldings were made. If any ornament was used it was often a simple twist ornament in the cove and shells or leaves for corner embellishments. Other motifs from the Empire style — wreaths, palmettes and urns — occasionally appeared.

(Figure 2)

(Figure 2)

As the century progressed painting moved toward landscape, the celebration of what was seen as divinity expressed through the untamed American wilderness. Ornaments on frames of the l850's reflected elements in the compositions: naturalistic forms such as vines, flowers and berries proliferated. The simple rectangles of earlier years softened and frames frequently had softly projecting corners and centers, and oval openings. These features echoed the popular Belter furniture created during the Rococo Revival period.

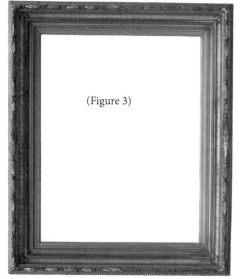

(Figure 3)

During the 1860's the pendulum swung back to a simpler style with the Renaissance Revival and the delight in neoclassical ornament. Soft undulant forms were replaced by the fluted cove design. The fluted cove was widely used and along with the laurel leaf and berry motif at the top edge, this form became the quintessential frame style for Hudson River landscapes.

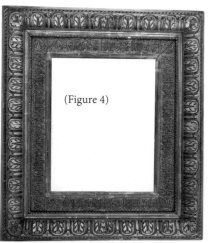

(Figure 4)

In the 1870's painting styles grew to include genre scenes and depictions of the exotic locales of the Near East.

Geometric motifs that echoed furniture and architecture in the artworks were employed. Moorish and Islamic pattern and calligraphy were used to embellish frames that enclosed scenes such as the interior of a mosque.

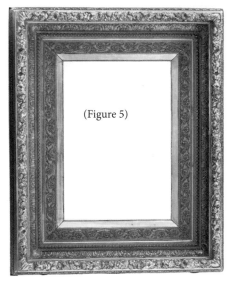

(Figure 5)

The 1880's signaled the height of Victorian eclecticism: There was no such thing as "too much of a good thing." During this time, frames were elaborately composed of many different patterns of ornament at once.

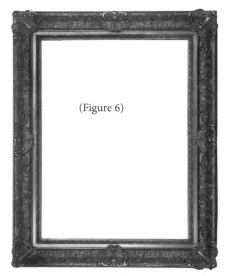

(Figure 6)

The French Barbizon style of frame (itself a design based on 17th century Louis XIII frames) gained popularity and was widely reinterpreted in America. This was also a time of widespread industrialization and frame manufacture was no exception. Machines were made that allowed pattern to be stamped onto lengths of molding that could he chopped and joined, and silver leaf was widely used as an alternative to gold at less expense.

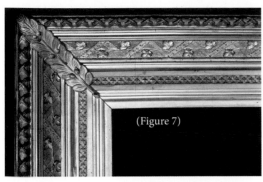

(Figure 7)

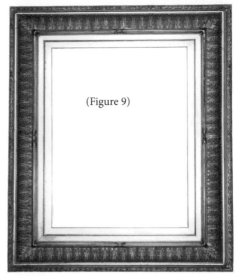

(Figure 9)

One of the results of this mass-manufacture was that ornament on frames was not carefully applied to resolve in a pleasing way. Patterns were joined together with jarring effect with little or no attention to form (Figure 7). Corner leaves that were made to mask the crude miters were made of pewter or lead and nailed on.

(Figure 8)

Eastlake-style frames also became popular with myriad variations available. The central characteristic that defines an American Eastlake-style frame is the incised design that usually appears at the corners. Painted surfaces emulating precious stone and black lacquer were popular surface treatments (Figure 8). Most of these frames were mass-produced to surround tintypes, the "everyman's portraiture" of the day, and this is why most of these frames are found in small formats and can still be found in antique shop and flea markets today.

(Figure 9)

The turn of the 19th to the 20th century saw the creation of some of America's most unique and elegant frame designs, especially those by Stanford White. Though White was an architect, his skill as a master of decorative interiors is legend, and his love of the Italian Renaissance informed his creations. White's list of friends reads like a veritable Who's Who of American artists of the day: Augustus Saint-Gaudens, Thomas Wilmer Dewing, Dwight Tryon, George DeForest Brush and Abbott Thayer to name a few. It was White who used the tabernacle-style frame to such dramatic effect, often adding many of his own stylistic embellishments.

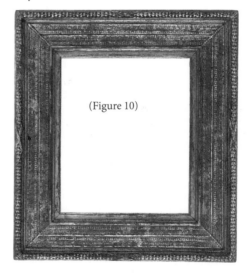

(Figure 10)

Due to White's untimely death in 1906 these frames are exceedingly rare. Some of White's designs were acquired by the Newcomb-Macklin Co. after his death and produced posthumously. These vary greatly in quality and must be taken case by case. Many of these posthumous frames are gilded with metal leaf rather than the superior gold leaf that White would have specified.

(Figure 11)

As American Impressionism took hold and artists were experimenting with new styles of brushwork and a new palette of color, a new style of frame for this new art was born. It is appropriate that this was introduced by an art-

(Figure 11)

ist. Hermann Dudley Murphy lived and worked in Boston and was greatly influenced by James McNeill Whistler, who was himself a frame reformer. Upon Murphy's return from his travels in Europe, he purchased the necessary materials and taught himself to carve and gild. In doing so, he began to create frames based on the Venetian cassetta-style frame, a profile characterized by a broad flat panel and raised inner and outer edges. Murphy's designs and those that followed are now widely referred to as American Impressionist-style frames.

(Figure 12)

(Figure 12)

In addition, after each frame was made, Murphy inscribed it, signaling that this, too, was an artwork worthy of a signature and a date.

(Figure 13)

(Figure 13)

Signed frames are always highly prized even when the maker is unknown. There were other makers who signed their frames, such as Charles Prendergast and Frederick Harer (Figure 13). During this period there was also a heightened interest in the tonalities of the gilded surface and many frames were finished in silver, various shades of gold leaf and the much more coppery-colored metal leaf to better complement the artworks they enclosed.

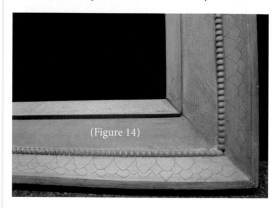

(Figure 14)

(Figure 14)

With the conclusion of World War I, the coming depression and an increasingly technologically oriented society, art changed again. In frames, gilding gave way to painted and manipulated surface treatments. American Modernist painters such as Arthur Dove created simple wood frames with copper accents. John Marin took mass-produced flames and made them his own by drawing, painting and carving on them. Though at first glance these frames appear crude, they are often integral to the overall artwork and create a dynamic presentation where the hand of the artist is powerfully present.

Key points to keep in mind when acquiring frames that are likely to increase in value are the same as in many fields (age, style, size, rarity). A frame in good condition with its original gilded surface is most desirable. It should also be of a style that is well suited to fine art. Frame values increase as they are paired with exceptional artworks. Lastly, if a frame has been altered, the alteration should be nearly impossible to detect. A clumsy alteration can destroy a great frame.

As frame studies advance and the market continues to evolve, I hope that we'll all continue to take a deeper look at the art of the frame.

For more information, contact Eli Wilner & Co., 1525 York Ave., New York, NY, 10028, *www.eliwilner.com*.

Reginald Marsh (American, 1898-1954), Minsky's New Gotham Chorus, circa 1930, etching (framed), numbered 34/100, 8 3/4" x 12" (image), 9 1/2" x 12 1/2" (sight). **$1,098**

Albert Durer (German, 1471-1528), Angles Restraining the Four Winds from The Apocalypse of St. John, 1497-98, etching, 15 1/2" x 11 1/8" (sheet). **$9,760**

Photo courtesy Rago Arts and Auction Center, Lambertville, N.J.; www.RagoArts.com

Rene Magritte (Belgian, 1898-1967), Le 16 Septembre, 1968, etching in colors, stamped signature and numbered 77/150, 5 7/8" x 4" (image), 11" x 8 5/8" (sheet). **$1,830**

John French Sloan (American, 1871-1951), The Lafayette, 1928, etching (in Meierhans frame), signed and marked "100 proofs", 7 3/4" x 9 3/4" (sight), 10" x 12" (frame). **$1,037**

Robert Indiana (American, 1928), Four, 1968, screenprint in colors (framed), signed and numbered 42/100, 24" x 24" (image), 28 3/8" x 28 3/8" (sight). **$960**

Photo courtesy Rago Arts and Auction Center, Lambertville, N.J.; www.RagoArts.com

Charles Turzak (American, 1899-1985), Grant Park, Chicago, 1931, woodcut on rice paper, signed, titled and numbered 43/50, 12" x 9 1/4" (image), 15 3/4" x 12 5/8" (sheet, irregular). **$1,464**

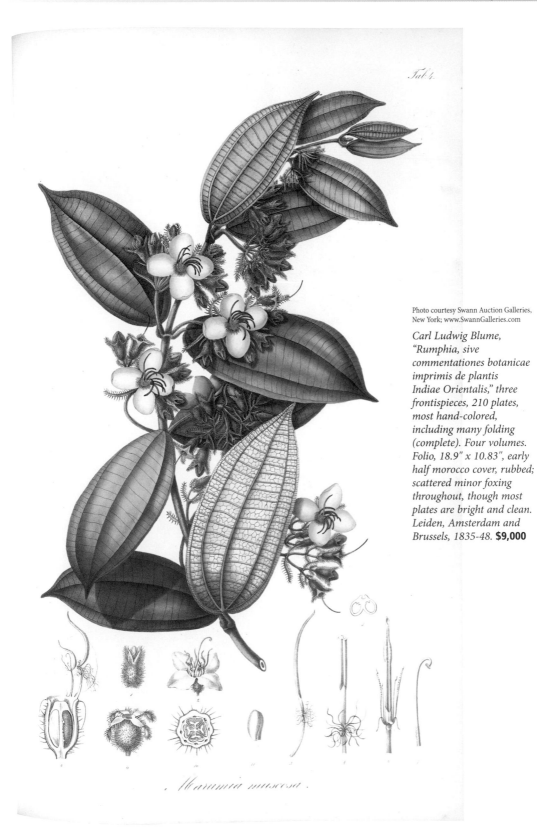

Carl Ludwig Blume, "Rumphia, sive commentationes botanicae imprimis de plantis Indiae Orientalis," three frontispieces, 210 plates, most hand-colored, including many folding (complete). Four volumes. Folio, 18.9" x 10.83", early half morocco cover, rubbed; scattered minor foxing throughout, though most plates are bright and clean. Leiden, Amsterdam and Brussels, 1835-48. **$9,000**

J.J. Grandville, Les Fleurs Animées. Two hand-colored additional titles, 50 hand-colored plates, two uncolored plates. Two volumes. Scattered minor foxing; plates quite bright and clean. Nouvelle Édition. Paris, 1867. **$1,000 set**

John James Audubon, Louisiana Tanager/Scarlet Tanager. Plate CCCLIV. Hand-colored engraved plate from the double-elephant-folio edition of "The Birds of America," on full sheet; matted and framed. Watermarked "J Whatman 1837." London: Havell, 1837. **$3,400**

Thomas Lord Busby, Costume of the Lower Orders of London, 24 hand-colored engraved plates, including frontispiece. Plates generally bright and clean, Fortune Teller plate stained. London, 1820. **$1,100 set**

Photo courtesy Swann Auction Galleries, New York; www.SwannGalleries.com

American Lithographic Co. archive of printer's progressive proofs of cigar labels, consisting of more than 500 folders, each folder representing successive proofs for a given label. Most folders have inked notes indicating the number of stones used, the colors, the location of the stones, and the date when they were ground flat. First decade 20th century. Taken together, there are thousands of labels in various states. **$13,000 all**

Photo courtesy Swann Auction Galleries, New York; www.SwannGalleries.com

John James Audubon, American Ptarmigan/ White-tailed Grous. Plate CCCCXVIII. Hand-colored engraved plate from the double-elephant-folio edition of "The Birds of America," on full folio sheet; repaired chip in each upper corner (far from image), some minor, removable marginal soiling; watermarked "J Whatman 1838." London: Havell, 1838. **$3,000**

Photo courtesy Heritage Auction Galleries, Dallas; www.HA.com

Gustave Baumann (German/American, 1881-1971), The Landmark, woodcut print on paper, 11 3/4" x 10 1/4", edition 87/100, signed in pencil lower right, Gustave Baumann. **$4,481**

ILLUSTRATION ART: THE "REAL ART OF AMERICA"

By Noah Fleisher

The late collector Charles Martignette – who died in early 2008 and left behind what is arguably the finest collection of illustration art ever assembled – once wrote of the form he loved so much: " … American illustration art was the real art of America."

It's hard to disagree with his assessment.

Spend a bit of time with the classic, bold imagery of American illustration art (roughly 1880-1960, give or take a decade on either side) and you'll quickly be won over. The men and women who populate the genre were among the greatest artistic talent of their day. From the early days of American illustration with Howard Pyle and the Brandywine luminaries, through its Golden Age with the likes of Norman Rockwell and J.C. Leyendecker, and into Mid-Century America with its iconic Gil Elvgren calendar girls and Alberto Vargas' Esquire gatefolds and Playboy drawings, they were simply plying their trades in an effort to make a living doing what they loved.

Noah Fleisher

This was no gilded age of great art patrons. It was a time of national growth and expansion, of the industrial revolution and World Wars, and without a mass media to instantly relay the everyday images of American lives, as we have today, Illustration Art became the default medium through which distilled – and often idealized – imagery spread. It was the advent of easily reproducible photography in the 1950s and 1960s that ultimately heralded the end of widespread illustration use.

There is barely enough room in these few pages to simply touch on the most basic aspects of Illustration Art, let alone effectively convey its full depth and meaning to the development of American pop culture and how the

Photo courtesy Heritage Auction Galleries, Dallas; www.HA.com

Gil Elvgren (American, 1914-1980), Bear Facts (A Modest Look; Bearback Rider), 1962, oil on canvas, 30" x 24", signed lower left; from the estate of Charles Martignette. Minor frame abrasion on right edge; 1" area of in-painting in upper left corner; framed to an overall size of 30 1/2" x 24 1/2". **$191,200.**

Valentine (American, 20th Century), Chick's Diner, gouache on board, 16 1/2" x 22 1/4", signed lower left; from the estate of Charles Martignette. Possible repair upper right corner. **$1,673**

American people ultimately viewed themselves.

If what you see in the pages that follow stirs the collector in you to do more, then you will have a long and satisfying journey of erudition and collecting ahead of you as you ply the ocean that is Illustration Art. If you simply like to look at great art that resolutely puts on no airs, then you'll have an equally satisfying side trip into some amazingly diverse art.

Three Types of Illustration Art

Pin-up and Glamour

This artwork was routinely done for calendars, cards and men's magazines. They present a decidedly romanticized view of the female form, one where a lady's modesty is usually compromised, whether by design or surprise. What is so powerful about the work is the range of innocence to sophistication across subjects, artists and time periods. There is always something more going on than you might think at first, so a deeper look is recommended.

The most popular examples of American Illustration Art you will see in the mainstream these days are bound to be Pin-up and Glamour, and those examples are likely to be by Gil Elvgren, maybe Alberto Vargas and occasionally a few other names: Earl Moran, Al Buell, Haddon

Sundblom, George Petty and Enoch Bolles, to name a few.

Gillette "Gil" Elvgren is the king of the form. Make no mistake: no American artist of the 1930s, 1940s and 1950s so captured the male imagination like Elvgren did with his girls on Brown & Bigelow calendars. The best examples of his work bring upwards of $250,000 today and his popularity only continues to grow as pieces of his greatest work make their way back into the collecting population with the disbursement at auction of Martignette's estate over the course of the next three years.

Mainstream Illustration

Four words: The Saturday Evening Post. There is almost no American alive who has not seen one of the iconic covers of this venerable publication, and it is the epitome of what "mainstream" illustration is. If you think of most any Norman Rockwell painting you'll have a prime example. Joseph Christian (J.C.) Leyendecker almost single-handedly defined American male style of the post-World War I era with his highly stylized and sharply painted Kuppenheimer Clothing ads. Other contemporaries – think John Clymer, N.C. Wyeth, Amos Sewell, Dean Cornwell, James Montgomery Flagg and Howard Chandler Christy – were the most famous, and prosperous, of this form.

These artists painted "everyday" life in America, and

their simple homespun scenes conveyed the enthusiasm and straightforwardness of the emerging post-Industrial Revolutionary world order, with America leading the way.

Before photography, before movies and television, there was only illustration to punctuate books, stories and magazines. As such, the diversity of subjects in this subset ranges from the aforementioned wholesome Mid-American scene to chaotic cityscapes, the Wild West, pirates on the high seas, historical and most anything you can think of in between. In sum, the possibilities for collecting are only limited by your passion and your bank account. The top pieces go for hundreds of thousands, if not millions of dollars, though a determined collector can still get decent examples for as little as a few hundred dollars, sometimes even less. With a few thousand to spend, the possibilities are greatly expanded.

Pulps, Pulp-like Fiction and Paperbacks

This subset is perhaps the most under-appreciated though easily the most fascinating aspect of this rapidly changing market. The publications that many of these paintings and drawings were done for were, literally, meant to be read once and thrown away; the paper upon which they were printed was the cheapest possible, as often was the content. It was not until at least a half-cen-tury later for the greatest artists of the genre that their original artwork started getting the attention it so richly deserves.

If the stories were mostly trashy, the art was strictly top notch, and holds up quite well today. Even with subjects that today are more kitschy than menacing, there is a wonderful noir irony that speaks to the American love of being entertained. Whether it's square-jawed toughs getting knocked out by trench-coated detectives, scenes of World War II battles, or sci-fi images of other-world battles of life and death, there is wonderful drama and movement present, and collectors respond viscerally to the work.

Unlike Mainstream and Pin-up Illustration, there is no one single name that dominates Pulp, Pulp-like Fiction and Paperback art. Names like Margaret Brundage, Norman Saunders, Hugh Joseph Ward, James Avati, Mort Künstler and Frank R. Paul have logged the highest prices, but there is still a great and affordable plethora of quality artists whose work can be had at good prices with just a little research and a healthy bit of patience.

Noah Fleisher, director of public relations for Heritage Auction Galleries in Dallas and former editor of *Antique Trader* magazine, has also written extensively for *New England Antiques Journal* and *Northeast Journal of Antiques and Art*.

Photo courtesy Heritage Auction Galleries, Dallas; www.HA.com

Joel Iskowitz (American, 20th Century), Never Cross a Vampire, oil on board, 19" x 15", signed lower left, this illustration appeared on both the hard cover and paperback editions of Stuart Kaminsky's Toby Peters mystery novel, Never Cross a Vampire. The hardcover was published by St. Martins Press in 1980, and the paperback was published by Mysterious Press in 1984; from the Estate of Charles Martignette. Minor scratches to varnish layer in upper right corner and in lower right curtain.
$2,151

Photo courtesy Heritage Auction Galleries, Dallas; www.HA.com

Frank Frazetta (American, 1928-2010), Warrior with Ball and Chain, Flashing Swords #1, paperback cover, 1973, oil on board, 23" x 19", signed lower right. One of the top Frazetta paintings in private hands, Warrior with Ball and Chain was purchased in a February 1993 Guernsey's auction, and according to its listing there, is one of the largest Frazetta covers ever painted. Fine paint loss in upper right and lower left corners; framed to an overall size of 38" x 34". Not examined out of frame. **$150,000**

Photo courtesy Heritage Auction Galleries, Dallas;
www.HA.com

*Alberto Vargas (American, 1896-
1982), 10 of Hearts, playing card
illustration, ink and watercolor on
paper, 16 1/2" x 10 1/2", signed
lower left; some color fading
and some light staining to the
background area at the left edge. Not
examined out of frame.* **$35,850**

Photo courtesy Heritage Auction Galleries, Dallas; www.HA.com

Andrew Loomis (American, 1892-1959), Dionne Quintuplets, Brown and Bigelow calendar illustration, circa 1944, oil on canvas, 32" x 42", signed lower right; slight scattered craquelure, commensurate with age. **$7,767**

Photo courtesy Heritage Auction Galleries, Dallas; www.HA.com

Artist unknown (20th Century), "This Boy Is the Star Runner," Cream of Wheat ad illustration for the Saturday Evening Post, 1926, gouache on board, 12" x 15"; linear accretion in upper left quadrant; slight toning of white border. **$507**

Photo courtesy Heritage Auction Galleries, Dallas; www.HA.com

Henry James Soulen (American, 1888-1965), The Ukulele Player, gouache on board, 20' x 14", signed lower right. **$2,629**

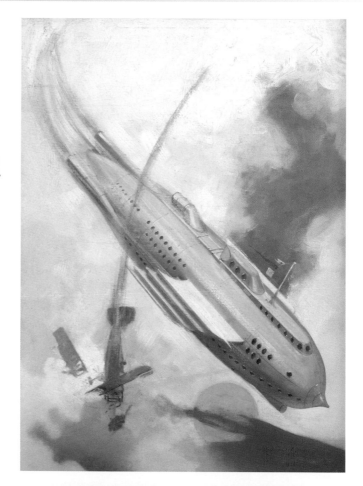

Photo courtesy Heritage Auction Galleries, Dallas; www.HA.com

Howard V. Brown (American, 1878-1945), Men From Space, Popular Magazine, pulp cover, December 1930, oil on canvas, 25 3/4" x 19", signed lower right; re-lined and restored. Horizontal creasing in canvas visible at the upper central and lower regions; in-painting along crease at top.
$16,132

Photo courtesy Heritage Auction Galleries, Dallas; www.HA.com

Hannes Bok (American, 1914-1964), Beyond Infinity, book cover, 1951, oil on board, 12' x 10 1/2", monogrammed lower left. Not examined outs of frame.
$3,346

Albert Hirschfeld (American, 1903-2003), Everything in the Garden, Sunday New York Times Arts and Leisure illustration, 1967, ink on board, 20 1/2" x 23", showing the cast of Edward Albee's Broadway show "Everything in the Garden," starring from left to right, Robert Moore, Barry Nelson, Beatrice Straight and Barbara Bell Geddes. Signed at the lower right, along with the number three, which represents the number of times the name of Hirschfeld's daughter, Nina, is hidden in the design. Not examined out of frame. **$3,107**

Joseph Christian Leyendecker (American, 1874-1951), Looks Good for '48, Amoco ad illustration, 1948, oil on canvas, 22" x 27", monogrammed lower left. The canvas has been cut down to eliminate the Amoco logo, and all of the advertising lettering was over-painted; a portion of the original lettering is underneath the white background. Not examined out of frame. **$20,315**

Photo courtesy Heritage Auction Galleries, Dallas; www.HA.com

James Montgomery Flagg (American, 1877-1960), Glamour Girl with Lipstick, circa 1930, watercolor on paper, 23" x 17", signed lower left. Flagg was known for his illustrations for Liberty, Cosmopolitan, College Humor and other magazines. Appointed military artist for New York State in World War I, he made 46 posters that were used by the U.S. Government. The best known is the poster featuring the character Uncle Sam and the words "I Want You". Not examined out of frame. **$2,031**

Photo courtesy Heritage Auction Galleries, Dallas; www.HA.com

Artist unknown (20th Century), Boiling Point, watercolor on board, 12 1/2" x 10 1/2". The painting has been varnished. There are glue stains in the borders. **$3,883**

Photo courtesy Heritage Auction Galleries, Dallas; www.HA.com

John Newton Howitt (American, 1885-1958), No Parking, oil on board, 26" x 20 1/2", signed lower left. Small areas of in-painting on parking sign; faint strengthening to light areas of painting. Not examined out of frame. **$1,792**

Walter Martin Baumhofer (American, 1904-1987), Second Sight, This Week Magazine illustration, oil on canvas, 23" x 20", signed lower right. Scattered staining and craquelure throughout the background, unframed. **$1,135**

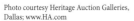

Ruehl Frederick Heckman (American, 1890-1942), Racing the Sun, 1934, oil on canvas, 32" x 24", signed lower right. Not examined out of frame. **$3,585**

Photo courtesy Heritage Auction Galleries, Dallas; www.HA.com

Howard Chandler Christy (American, 1872-1952), Amelia Earhart, Town and Country cover, Feb. 1, 1933, oil on canvas, 60" x 40", signed lower left. Relined, assorted minor in-painting in various spots throughout. More substantial in-painting in upper right corner background and bottom of dress. **$107,550**

AUTOGRAPHS

Autographs appear on an amazing array of objects: letters, photographs, books, cards, clothing, etc. Most collectors focus on a particular person, country or category, like movie stars, musicians or athletes.
Also see Sports Memorabilia.

Photo courtesy Swann Auction Galleries, New York; www.SwannGalleries.com

Color photograph signed by all seven members of the Columbia Space Shuttle mission STS-107, an official NASA lithograph showing each member of the crew in a space suit. Signed in the image, above the relevant portrait. Crew biographies printed on the back, approximately 8" x 10". **$8,500** *(All seven crew members died when Columbia was destroyed on re-entry on Feb. 1, 2003.)*

Photo courtesy Swann Auction Galleries, New York; www.SwannGalleries.com

Hans Christian Andersen, signed, "H.C. Andersen," carte-de-visite portrait by Georg E. Hansen, showing the Danish fairytale author seated at a desk holding an open book. Signed on the mount at bottom. Approximately 3 1/2" x 2 1/4" (image), framed. **$2,600**

Photos courtesy Heritage Auction Galleries, Dallas; www.HA.com

Myrna Loy signed photo, B&W 11" x 14", inscribed "To B.D. Burnes/Cordially," and signed by Loy in black fountain ink, with mild toning, light wear to the edges, and a crease to the top left corner. **$507**

John Quincy Adams, engraved portrait signed, one of the earliest signed presidential portraits, showing the President seated and with a furrowed brow. Boldly signed in the blank margin, top center. Approximately 2 1/4" x 2" (image), approximately 4 1/2" x 3 1/4" overall; faint marginal discoloration from prior matting, facsimile signature at bottom center; mounted and framed, circa 1825. ....**$11,000**

Otto Von Bismarck, photograph dated and signed, "Bismarck," large cabinet card vignette bust portrait by Loescher & Petsch, showing the "Iron Chancellor" in uniform. Signed in the image at bottom right. Photographer's imprint on mount at bottom. Approximately 11" x 7" (image), marginal staining at top and left edges of photograph, faint scattered foxing, 1885. ....**$1,300**

Johannes Brahms, photograph signed and inscribed, " ... with warm regards, J. Br.," in German, an informal image showing the composer at a point of greatness in both girth and fame, resting his head in his hand as he looks out a window. Inscribed on the mount below the image. Approximately 3 1/2" x 3" (image), approximately 5 1/4" x 4" overall; few unobtrusive scratches to photograph, circa 1894. ....**$3,000**

Lewis Carroll (Charles Lutwidge Dodgson), photograph inscribed to his sister, Mary Charlotte Collingwood ("M.C.C."), and with a signature "Lewis Carrol" [sic]. Carte-de-visite albumen oval bust self-portrait, showing the author wearing a dreamy expression. Inscribed on the back, top center, in purple ink. Approximately 2 1/4" x 1 3/4" (image), approximately 4" x 2 1/2" overall; slight bowing to mount, minor scattered soiling to back, circa 1875. Dodgson wrote in 1883 of his apprehension to release his portrait or autograph to any but his closest associates: "My constant aim is to remain, personally, unknown to the world; consequently I have always refused applications for photographs or autographs, as my features and handwriting belong to me as a private individual — and I often beg even my own private friends, who possess one or the other, not to put them into albums where strangers can see them." **$5,200**

Stephen Crane, photograph signed and inscribed, "To Mr Curtis Brown / With the regards of Stephen Crane / Hartwood, N.Y. January 27. '96," cabinet card bust portrait by Lundelius, showing the young author and journalist in a starched collar and tie. Inscribed on the back at top. Photographer's imprint on mount at bottom. Approximately 5 1/2" x 3 3/4" (image), approximately 6 1/2" x 4 1/4" overall; faint paperclip stain through signature, some minor scratches to photograph. Curtis Brown (1866-1945) was an editor at the New York Press between 1894 and 1898, where he shared responsibility for the publication of numerous stories by Crane. **$4,200**

Alfred Dreyfus, photograph postcard signed, "A Dreyfus," vignette bust portrait by C. Coquelin, showing him in uniform wearing the Legion of Honor medal. Signed in the blank margin at bottom left. Photographer's imprint at bottom right. Approximately 4 1/2" x 3" (image), approximately 5 1/2" x 3 1/2" overall, circa 1906. ....**$2,000**

George Herbert Walker Bush and Mikhail Sergeyevich Gorbachev, photo signed by both, showing each with one arm around the other and smiling at the 10-year-anniversary celebrations of the fall of the Berlin Wall. Approximately 11 1/2" x 8" overall. **$700**

Antonín Dvořák, large photograph signed and inscribed, in Czech, "To my dear compatriot and amazing friend Mrs. E. Rosewater / Omaha Neb. 4/9 1893 with fond remembrance, Antonín Dvořák," bust portrait by Spiess, showing the composer wearing a necktie printed with a horseshoe pattern. Inscribed on the mount below the image. Photographer's ink stamp on back. Approximately 19 1/2" x 15 1/2"(image), some discoloration to inscription area from prior matting, contemporary retouching to eyes and hair, some scattered loss to emulsion at edges, unobtrusive creases at left edge. Dvořák came to the United States in 1892 to "discover American music." From 1892 to 1895 he was director of the National Conservatory of Music of America, and spent most of 1893 in Spillville, Iowa. He took the occasion to visit the Czech-American communities in Chicago, Omaha and St. Paul, among others. This photograph was inscribed to the wife of Edward Rosewater, a Czech-born politician, who was also the founder and editor of the Omaha Bee. **$5,800**

Amelia Earhart, signed photograph, showing the smiling aviator in short sleeves standing before an airplane engine. Signed in the image at bottom center. Approximately 10" x 8"; mounted to a sheet trimmed to size. **$2,400**

David G. Farragut, photograph signed and inscribed, "With the comple- / ments of / Rear Admiral / D.G. Farragut / U.S. Navy," carte-de-visite 3/4-length portrait showing him standing in uniform. Famous for the cry,

"Damn the torpedoes, full speed ahead!" Inscribed on the back. Approximately 4" x 2 1/4" overall. 1862-64. ....**$750**

Sigmund Freud, large photograph signed and inscribed, "Sigm. Freud / 1925," bust portrait by Halberstadt, showing him without his eyeglasses looking directly into the camera. Signed in large characters in the image at bottom right. Photographer's blind stamp in image, lower left. Approximately 12" x 9"; sides trimmed, minor creases at corners. **$18,000**

George Gershwin, photograph signed and dated, bust portrait of the young composer in suit and tie. Signed in the image at right. Approximately 8" x 6"; mounted to a larger sheet, unobtrusive creases at top, short closed tear at top edge, 1935..**$2,000**

Ulysses S. Grant, signed photograph, "U.S. Grant," large cabinet card bust portrait by Taber, showing him in civilian attire. Signed on the mount below the image. Photographer's imprint on mount, lower right. Approximately 7 1/2" x 4 3/4" (image), tiny abrasion with loss to "t" of signature, scattered light foxing overall. **$1,800**

Victor Hugo, photograph signed and inscribed, "To my excellent / friend Mr. LeBar," in French, carte-de-visite vignette bust portrait by Garnier Arsene, showing him in an unbuttoned vest and coat. Inscribed in the image along bottom edge. With an inscription on the back by Hugo's friend: "Dear Mrs. Hammond, I give you with great pleasure this photograph given to me by the great poet. P.R. Le Ber. Guernsey, October 20 1867." Approximately 3 3/4" x 2 1/4" (image). **$1,400**

Henry James, photograph dated and signed, cabinet card vignette bust portrait by Elliott & Fry, showing the author in left profile. Signed in the image along bottom edge. Photographer's imprint on the mount at bottom. Approximately 5 1/2" x 4" (image), approximately 6 1/2" x 4 1/4" overall, March 1883. ....**$6,000**

Helen Keller, photograph signed and inscribed, "Sincerely Yours," in pencil, image by F. Garcia Monteiro, showing Keller and her assistant, Polly Thomson, seated in their home in Forest Hills, N.Y., with other guests, including Keller's teacher, Anne Sullivan Macy, seated in the rear center. Approximately 6 1/2" x 8 1/2" (image). **$2,400**

Photo courtesy Swann Auction Galleries, New York; www.SwannGalleries.com

Custer's Own Portrait of Officers of the Seventh Cavalry, photograph inscribed and signed "G.A.C." twice, in ink and pencil. An albumen print group portrait (by Orlando S. Goff), showing Custer and the officers under his command, and their wives. On the mount below the image, Custer has written, in ink, the name of each person in the group, adding, in pencil, "Names written in the order of the persons in the picture. G.A.C." On the back, in pencil, he notes, "Our house at Fort Lincoln, Dakota." Approximately 5" x 7 1/4" (image), 8" x 10" overall; minor toning at edges of mount, scattered minor foxing on verso. (Fort Lincoln, N.D., November 1873). **$20,000**

Abraham Lincoln, signed photograph, "A. Lincoln," carte-de-visite portrait by Gardner, showing the President seated, legs crossed, his left arm leaning on a book and holding a newspaper, his right hand holding his eyeglasses. Signed on the mount below the image. Photographer's imprint on back. Approximately 3" x 2 1/4" (image), approximately 3 1/2" x 2 1/2"; corners and top edge of mount slightly trimmed, discoloration from prior matting, minor scattered soiling. This image was taken early on Aug. 9, 1863, a Sunday, a time selected so as to avoid the unwanted attention of the curious. It is one of four images taken in the same instant, as Gardner employed a four-lens camera that allowed him to send each of the four parts of the negative to a different assistant in order to maximize production. John Hay made a note in his diary about the sitting: "I went down with the President to have his picture taken at Gardner's. He was in very good spirits." **$40,000**

Charles A. and Anne Morrow Lindbergh, photograph signed and inscribed by Charles, "For Doctor A.H. Ebeling / From Charles A. Lindbergh," and signed by Anne, full-length portrait showing the two standing beside each other. Inscribed in the image at bottom right. Approximately 8 1/2" x 6 1/2". **$850**

Louis Pasteur, photograph signed, "L. Pasteur," carte-de-visite bust portrait by A. Liebert, showing the chemist and microbiologist with short hair and beard. Signed on the mount below the image. Photographer's imprint on back.

Photo courtesy Swann Auction Galleries, New York; www.SwannGalleries.com

W.A. White and Sinclair Lewis, signed image by Alvord, showing the Nobel Prize-winning author and William Allen White facing each other. Additionally Signed and Inscribed by White: "For Harry Hanson / from W.A. White / Emporia Kansas / July 1926." Photographer's blind stamp in image, lower left. Approximately 9" x 7"; mounted to a card trimmed to size, slight silvering in dark areas. **$800**

Photos courtesy Heritage Auction Galleries, Dallas; www.HA.com

John Wayne signed yearbook, copy of the Glendale, Calif., Union High School 1924 Stylus yearbook autographed by junior class vice president John Wayne using his birth name, Marion Morrison. The yearbook is signed by Wayne in black ink on pages 121 (junior class intro page), and his football team photo can be found on page 159; with a fair amount of soiling and appreciable edge wear to the covers, pages in very good condition. **$1,314**

Approximately 3 1/2" x 2 1/4" (image), approximately 4" x 2 1/2"; matted and framed with an invitation to the 1904 ceremony inaugurating the monument to Pasteur in the Place de Breteuil. **$1,700**

Ivan Petrovich Pavlov, photograph signed, "Prof. Dr. I.P. Pavlov," showing the elderly psychologist and physiologist standing in a suit holding his hat and leaning on a cane. Signed in the image at bottom center. Approximately 10" x 7"; minor fading to signature, date and place inscribed in another hand at bottom right (Boston, August 1929). **$3,200**

Pablo Picasso, photograph postcard dated and signed, "Picasso," showing a close up of the artist holding a sculpture of a bird by its stone base. Inscribed in the image at bottom left. Approximately 4" x 5 3/4"; 3 pin-holes along top edge, bold signature, 1958. ....**$3,600**

Giacomo Puccini, photograph signed and 'nscribed, "A Monsieur de Forcounet / avec amitié et reconnaissance / Gia Puccini," bust portrait image by Ermini, showing the young composer in profile. Inscribed in the blank margin at bottom. Photographer's imprint in image, lower left. Approximately 7 1/2" x 5 1/4"; mounted to a card trimmed to size, some silvering in dark areas, mount slightly bowed, 1906. ....**$2,200**

Manfred Von Richthofen, the "Red Baron," photograph postcard signed, "Frhr. v. Richthofen / Rittmeister," showing the flying ace shaking hands with Ernst von Hoeppner, Commanding General of the German Air Service. Signed in the image, at bottom. Printed in the photograph, at bottom, is a caption, in German, "The commanding General of the German Air Service Ernst von Hoeppner congratulated by Captain Baron von Richthofen." Approximately 4 1/2" x 3 1/2"; minor fading to signature at points but rest bold.
.... **$3,000**

Franklin D. Roosevelt and the Mayo Brothers, photograph signed by Roosevelt, as President, and also by Charles Horace and William James Mayo ("C.H. Mayo" and "W.J. Mayo"), image showing the three seated in an automobile with the roof retracted during Roosevelt's visit to the Mayo Clinic in August of 1934. Signed in the blank margin below the image under the relevant portrait. Approximately 6" x 8 3/4" (image), approximately 8 1/2" x 11"; matted and framed, circa 1934. .... **$4,000**

Winfield Scott, photograph signed and inscribed, "This card is respectfully / inscribed to / Miss Van Horn-- / the friend of my family, / by her friend-- Winfield Scott / 1862," carte-de-visite portrait by Charles D. Fredricks, showing the elderly General seated in uniform and grasping his sword. Inscribed on the back. Approximately 3 1/2" x 2 1/4" (image), 1862. Scott (1786-1866) served in the War of 1812, commanded the Southern theater during the Mexican War, was promoted to Lieutenant General in 1855 — the first officer to attain that rank since George Washington. He was named General-in-Chief of the Union army at the start of the Civil War, and devised the "Anaconda Plan" to defeat Confederate forces. **$950**

Photo courtesy Swann Auction Galleries, New York; www.SwannGalleries.com

Christopher "Kit" Carson, carte-de-visite portrait by Brady, showing the soldier and frontiersman in civilian attire. Signed on the mount below the image. Photographer's full imprint on back. Approximately 3 1/4" x 2 1/4" (image), corners and top edge trimmed, minor scattered soiling. **$28,000**

William Tecumseh Sherman, photograph signed and inscribed, "W.T. Sherman / General / 1890," cabinet card bust portrait by Mora, showing the silver-bearded General in decorated uniform. Signed on the mount below the image. Photographer's imprint on mount at bottom. Approximately 5 1/2" x 4" (image), abrasion touching "G" of "General." **$3,600**

Robert Louis Stevenson, photograph signed and inscribed, "Mrs. Frank Hume / in memory of a first class liner, from / Robert Louis Stevenson," seated 3/4-length platinum portrait of the author leaning toward the camera. Signed on the mount below the image. Approximately 5 3/4" x 4" (image), even toning to mount and photograph, minor scattered staining to mount, mount and photograph are mounted to a larger card; matted and framed. A rare signed portrait of Stevenson (1850-1894). **$6,500**

Alfred Tennyson, photograph signed, "Tennyson," cabinet card bust portrait by Barraud, showing the poet in a large-brimmed hat and coat. Signed on the mount below the image. Photographer's full imprint on back. Approximately 5 1/2" x 4" (image). **$3,000**

Harry Truman, photograph signed and inscribed, "To Phil Regan with kindest regards / Harry Truman," as President, image showing him reciting the Oath of Office at his second inauguration. Inscribed in the image at bottom center. Additionally signed, vertically along bottom edge, by Dean Acheson, Justice William O. Douglas, Harry H. Vaughan, Chief Justice Fred M. Vinson, Sam Rayburn, Justice Stanley Reed, Carl Hayden and John W. McCormack. Approximately 11" x 14"; mounted to card trimmed to size; some fading to Hayden signature. Washington, 1949. ....**$1,500**

Giuseppe Verdi, photograph inscribed and signed, "G Verdi," in Italian, cabinet card image published by Bruckmann of a bust portrait painting, showing the composer in a heavy coat. Inscribed on the mount below the image. Approximately 5 1/2" x 4" (image), bottom of mount slightly trimmed, unobtrusive crease at upper right, remnants of prior mounting on back at top edge. July 1896.
....**$3,800**

Booker T. Washington, photograph postcard signed, portrait by Schumacher, showing him in a suit, seated, and looking into the camera. Signed in blank margin below the image. Approximately 5 1/2" x 3 1/4". **$1,900**

Daniel Webster, engraved portrait signed and inscribed, "To Dr. Benjamin Abbott; / from his affectionate Pupil, / Danl Webster. / April 1847," showing the Whig statesman looking upward slightly. Approximately 4 1/2" x 3 1/2" (image), approximately 9" x 6" overall; marginal discoloration from prior matting. April 1847. Inscribed to one of his teachers, the Headmaster of Phillips Exeter, where he briefly attended before going on to Dartmouth. **$4,000**

Oscar Wilde, photograph signed, cabinet card half-length portrait by Alfred Ellis, showing the poet in a typical pose, with a flower in his lapel and holding a cigarette. Signed in the image at bottom left with a flourish extending to mount. Photographer's full imprint on back. Approximately 5 1/2" x 4" (image), approximately 6 1/2" x 4 1/4" overall; minor fading to image, minor scattered soiling, even toning to mount, bold signature. **$10,000**

Photos courtesy Heritage Auction Galleries, Dallas; www.HA.com

James Dean signed yearbook. This copy of the 1948 Black and Gold yearbook for Fairmount (Ind.) High School features a Junior class photo of Dean. The book is signed "Jim Dean" in blue ink under his basketball photo in the Sports section, and is in overall good condition with moderate wear to the cover, which has detached from the contents of the book. Presented in a framed display box. **$1,673**

Photos courtesy Heritage Auction Galleries, Dallas; www.HA.com

Walt Disney autographed envelope, 3 1/4" x 5 1/2", signed in large script on one side, with some mild stains that do not overtly affect the signature. **$1,135**

Photos courtesy Heritage Auction Galleries, Dallas; www.HA.com

Samuel Clemens, signed albumen print, "Mark Twain" and "S. L. Clemens", with quotation and sentiment dated Sept. 28, 1900. Rare twice-signed photograph, 3" x 5 3/4", is mounted to an overall size of 5" x 8 1/4". Above the image, Clemens has written, "Truth is the most valuable thing we have. Let us economise it. Truly yours, Mark Twain" - a quotation from a chapter epigraph in "Pudd'nhead Wilson's New Calendar" in Twain's "Following the Equator" (1897). Twain's signature begins on the photo and ends on the backing. Below the photo, Clemens has written, "To Mr. Pinkhorn, with the compliments of S L. Clemens." The photographer's stamp is in three places (each a version of "H. Walter Barnett/ Park Side Hyde Park Corner/ London S.W."): in the lower right corner of the photo, below the photo, and on the back. **$2,629**

Charlie Chaplin signed photo. A vintage B&W 8" x 10" photo of the iconic silent era comedian, inscribed "With compliments to B.D. Burns", signed, and dated 1929 by Chaplin in black fountain ink, with some toning and mild edge wear. **$717**

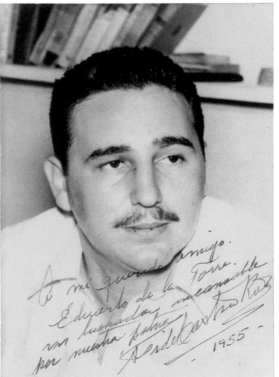

Fidel Castro, photograph signed, "Fidel Castro Ruz," and inscribed: "To my dear friend / Eduardo de la Torre, / a tireless fighter / for our country / 1955," in Spanish, bust portrait showing the young revolutionary clean-shaven except for a mustache. Signed in the image at bottom. Approximately 7" x 5"; slight silvering along top edge; owner's ink stamp on back: "Propiedad de Gaston Bernal." Castro was arrested in 1953 and sentenced to 15 years in prison for his part in an ill-fated attack on the Batista regime. He was released in 1955 and almost immediately went to Mexico and the United States to revive his movement, raise money and recruit supporters. This photo dates from that trip. **$3,000**

Photo courtesy Heritage Auction Galleries, Dallas; www.HA.com

Seventh Regiment of New York National Guard Gold Veteran's Badge, circa 1900, 1 3/8" x 1 1/2", gold and blue enamel, pin-back, unmarked. This three-dimensional gold badge has the famous 7th Regiment's motto "PRO PATRIA ET GLORIA" (For Country and Glory) on a garter with "7 / V / NG" in the center. **$180**

BADGES AND MEDALS

Badges and medals have been used for centuries to designate rank or official duties, to commemorate events and public observances, and even to mark the duties of slaves. Also see Political and Vietnam Collectibles.

Silver El Paso City Marshall's Badge, large silver shield-shaped badge 2 11/16" x 2 1/8". Stamped on front in zigzag pattern "CITY / MARSHALL / EL PASO". Back has an attached brass hinge pin and is marked in the upper right corner "COIN SILVER". Has a few nicks and scratches and retains a lightly tarnished finish. **$575**

Denver & Rio Grande Western Railroad Police Badge, ornate silver six-point star with balls on points, banners, special agent rank (no number), Colorado state seal center, modified pebble field; hallmarked "Blackington HI GLO". **$253**

Denver & Rio Grande Western Railroad Police Badge, circa 1962, 14K gold hand-engraved with ornate eagle on top showing swept wings, banners, chief special agent, gold and enamel train motif center, and "E" color diamond in the bottom, in glass-framed display reading, "Denver & Rio Grande Western Railroad, presented to Chief Special Agent William F. McCafferty, In Appreciation, Ca. 1934". With history on reverse. **$2,070**

Photo courtesy Heritage Auction Galleries, Dallas; www.HA.com

1813 Charleston Porter Slave Hire Badge. Number 300. A nearly flat octagonal tag with a hole at the top for suspension, approximately 2" x 2". John Joseph LaFar, a prominent Charleston silversmith, manufactured it; a very light "LAFAR" hallmark is punched on the back. The elements on the front are as follows (top to bottom): "CHARLESTON" in a crescent-shaped bar punch; "1813" bar punched; "PORTER" in a rectangular punch; "No" in a square punch (faint) followed by an incuse, and a hand-engraved "300". This is the last year in which numbers were engraved. From 1814 on, numbers were individually punched. The badge has been repaired where crimped above the word "PORTER" and at an elliptical area to the left of the "P". **$2,031**

Photo courtesy Heritage Auction Galleries, Dallas; www.HA.com

Silvered brass Civil War-period Sheridan's Cavalry Corps Badge, 1 5/8" x 1 3/8". Separately affixed blue enamel center section with crossed sabers. Suspended from the name bar by small brass chains. Overall near-perfect condition, retaining 80% of the original silver finish. **$3,107**

Photo courtesy Heritage Auction Galleries, Dallas; www.HA.com

World War I United States Army Air Service Non-Commissioned Officer Visor Hat Badge, 1 7/8", screwback, unmarked. This two-piece construction hat badge has a silvered bronze propeller and wing inside a brass wreath. Light wear to the silvered prop. **$215**

Photo courtesy Heritage Auction Galleries, Dallas; www.HA.com

Identification Badge of a Pennsylvanian Wounded at Gettysburg. Suspension badge with stamped battle honors belonged to an enlisted man who was wounded twice in battle before being captured and dying from the effects of prison life. The commercially produced, gray metal identification badge features a raised profile of Maj. Gen. Kearney in the shield at the top. Suspended from it by way of two rotating links is a 1 1/4" circular disk on which is stamped "Wm McCUTCHEON/ Co. B/ 105 REG/P V/ BROOKVILLE Pa" On the reverse is a raised leaf design with "WAR OF 1861" at the top. Under this, and filling the remaining space on the back, have been stamped "Yorktown/ Williamsburg/ Fair Oaks/ 7 Days/ Before Richmond/ Malvern Hill/ Bull Run/ Chantilly/ Fredericksburg/ Chancellorsville." **$4,182**

Photo courtesy Heritage Auction Galleries, Dallas; www.HA.com

Silver Civil War Corps/ ID badge of William H. Lewis, Co. C, 5th U.S. Artillery, wounded at Cold Harbor. Heavy silver 2d Corps trefoil, 9/10" x 9/10" with T-har pin back. Actually constructed from an English silver six pence coin with bust of Victoria, etc. on the reverse. Untouched condition. **$2,868**

Photo courtesy James D. Julia Auctions, Fairfield, Maine; www.jamesdjulia.com

Jockey tags, each round metal tag having a top section with round hole for hanging. Each has different color and geometric pattern to place outside the horse stall identifying the jockey's color. There are no marks as to manufacturer. Circa 1900-1910, each 4" diameter, 5 1/2" with hanging section, three have losses to enameling. **$632 all**

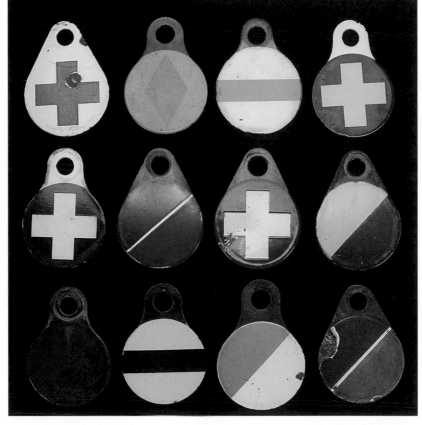

FUTURE OF THE MARKET: MECHANICAL BANKS

By Catherine Saunders-Watson

Within the entire realm of antique collecting, there is no category that can truthfully be described as "bulletproof," but mechanical banks come very close to it. Whether the bulls or the bears are in charge on Wall Street at any given time, history has shown that bank collectors pay them little mind and remain active throughout the ups and downs.

"They might slow down the pace at which they collect – maybe buying three good banks a year as opposed to five or six – but they don't stop collecting," said Dan Morphy, co-founder of Morphy Auctions and author of the book The Official Price Guide to Mechanical Banks.

Morphy cited a recent example in which a "very well-known collection" changed hands discreetly for several million dollars, seemingly oblivious to the worst economic recession America has experienced in 80 years. And even after the 9/11 tragedies brought American business to a standstill, Morphy said, a collection of mechanical banks was sold privately for $1.4 million.

"To some degree, mechanical banks are their own independent micro-economy," Morphy said. "They're not entirely immune to the whims of the financial markets, but they can really take a punch and stay on their feet better than any other type of antique I can think of."

"At the moment, the market for mechanical banks is as strong as it has ever been," he observed. "Even though we've all heard that the decision to buy antiques should never be based on the hope of one day making a profit, the type of person who is chasing banks right now is looking at it as an investment as much as a hobby. For that reason, today's mechanical bank collector is much more inclined to put his or her money into an example they think is going to be a sound investment. They're making their own rules."

Morphy believes the main catalyst that drives the mechanical-bank market and keeps the values buoyant in challenging times is the American legacy and social significance associated with many banks. "They do cross over as toys, but they're looked at with a different eye because there's a strong historical and folk-art side to them. Many of these banks are surviving witnesses to the most important events and social movements of the past century and a half. Some, which have a racially stereotypical theme, are tangible reminders of the injustices of a past era."

By far, the most valuable and sought-after banks are those made of cast iron or painted lead. Generally, American collectors prefer American-made examples, with some of the better-known manufacturers being J. & E. Stevens, Shepard Hardware and Kyser & Rex. The most desirable subjects in cast-iron banks are those that repre-sent an aspect of history, a Biblical theme, baseball, or an occupation, e.g., the Dentist bank, the Mason bank, etc.

European collectors are more attracted to lithographed-tin banks, and rarities in this classification, such as those made in the 1930s by Saalheimer & Strauss, can fetch a substantial price. A circa-1928 tin Mickey Mouse Accordion Player bank by the German manufacturer sold at Morphy's in 2007 for $48,875.

Morphy has handled his fair share of high-end banks, including those offered at the record-smashing $7.7 million auction in October 2007 of the Stephen and Marilyn Steckbeck Collection. Now widely acknowledged as the

Dan Morphy

highest-grossing toy auction ever held, the 492-lot sale surpassed the previously held record by a margin of more than $2.5 million. The result was reported to the Guinness Book of World Records.

The Steckbecks built their collection over a 53-year period and took a very pro-active approach in adding to it. Steve Steckbeck had pickers scouring several states on his behalf, and as his collection grew and he became more familiar with the better-quality banks, he made the natural transition that many bank collectors make as they grow more seasoned: he started to focus on acquiring only the rarest examples in the best possible condition. Steve and Marilyn's circa-1910 North Pole bank was one of the finest known (it sold for $149,500); and their turn of the century Kenton Hardware Mama Katzenjammer bank in superior, near-mint-plus condition, had actually been a manufacturer's showroom sample. It sold for $74,750. Almost every bank auctioned in that now-legendary sale had some sort of blue-chip provenance.

Mechanicals and money have always had a symbiotic connection, and not just the obvious one to be drawn from the fact that moneyboxes were created as store-houses for children's savings. They've always been viewed from an investment angle, even if it was just a few canny collectors who recognized the potential decades ago when the hobby was still in its formative years. The Steckbeck banks, for example, were featured over the years in a number of business and investment publications, including Forbes, Money and Wealth.

The Steckbecks' unrelenting efforts at networking, buying and selling resulted in a collection that contained spectacular examples from early collections of now-historic stature, e.g., those of financier Edwin Mosler, F.H. Griffith, Walter P. Chrysler and Andrew Emerine.

At the auction of the Steckbeck collection, successful bidders wrote checks that could have paid off many people's mortgages: $414,000 for a late-1880s Jonah and the Whale/Jonah Emerges bank, $287,500 for a circa-

1886 Mikado bank depicting an illusionist conducting a shell game, and $195,500 for a Roller Skating bank with a clever mechanism that propelled its skating figures.

The biggest buzz in the gallery was over the "politically incorrect" banks that had captured the attention of a CBS Sunday Morning film crew from New York. None of the crewmembers had ever seen 19th-century mechanical banks with cruel, racially stereotypical depictions of African-Americans and Chinese immigrant workers. In the end, the CBS producer, realizing how historically significant the banks were, chose to develop the entire segment around the valuable black-theme banks, later adding commentary – pro and con – from African-American historians.

Of the top 10 banks in the sale, two exhibited a black theme: the rare 1880s-vintage Charles A. Bailey painted-lead "Darky Fisherman," which sold for $287,500; and the circa-1888 J. & E. Stevens cast-iron "Darky and Watermelon," which reached $195,500. Another unbelievable indictment of our society 130 years ago was Charles A. Bailey's circa-1888 painted-lead "Chinaman in Boat" bank, which earned $103,500.

"By displaying banks of this type, collectors are not condoning the message that is inherent in them," said Morphy. "They are displaying a fragment of history that cannot be changed. Banks of this type are absolutely at the top of the most-wanted list with collectors who buy with investment in mind."

It's not just the old-timers who are collecting mechanical banks. Many new collectors are getting into the hobby, and a fair number of them are in their 20s. "We're definitely seeing new faces coming into the fold, and some are collectors of other types of antiques who've become interested in banks," Morphy said. "I just sold two banks for five figures to a buyer who got into it only a year ago."

While rarities can run into the hundreds of thousands of dollars, as confirmed by prices realized in the Steckbeck sale, there are many banks available in the $300 to $800 price range and probably more than 100 different models available in the under-$1,000 range. They may not be in pristine condition, but they are a good starting point and can always be upgraded.

An example would be the Darktown Battery bank, which merges the desirable themes of baseball and black Americana. If perfect, such a bank would run in the thousands of dollars, but a collector can acquire a perfectly acceptable example of this bank for around $500. It might have imperfections or issues with its paint or surface, or it might have been restored at some point in its life, but it's still very presentable and is a fine entry-level acquisition.

The key for beginners is to do as much research as possibly before diving in and making that first purchase. Because there are fakes and cleverly repaired banks out there, Morphy advises novices to "go to auctions, and hook up with someone trustworthy – a dealer who will be honest with you and steer you in the right direction." He cautions that the Internet is "a horrible way to buy – and I don't mean bidding in an auction online that is produced by a reputable auction house that knows and understands banks. That's just fine because you know whom you're dealing with and can ask questions. I mean buying 'blindly' from people you don't know who either intentionally or unintentionally might misrepresent a bank's authenticity and condition. Nine times out of 10, you're asking for trouble doing it that way." Morphy said it's better to pay an expert to advise you on whether or not to buy a particular bank that to buy on good faith alone.

An excellent way for potential bank collectors/investors to get started in the hobby is by joining the Mechanical Bank Collectors of America.

"I personally would sponsor anyone who wants to join that club; that's how important I think it is," Morphy said. The club holds an annual convention featuring informative seminars on a host of educational and practical topics, such as how to black-light banks to detect repairs. The group also maintains an excellent Web site whose members-only area contains a treasure trove of archival information, including articles written as far back as the 1930s. Membership in the MBCA is quite possibly the best investment any potential mechanical-bank collector will ever make. *www.mechanicalbanks. org.*

Photo courtesy Morphy Auctions, Denver, Pa.; www.MorphyAuctions.com

J. & E. Stevens, around 1907, the Clown, Harlequin and Columbine bank features an intricate action involving all three figures. As the columbine (harlequin's mistress in the Italian commedia dell'arte) dancer spins, the coin is deposited, ex-Stephen and Marilyn Steckbeck collection.
$103,500

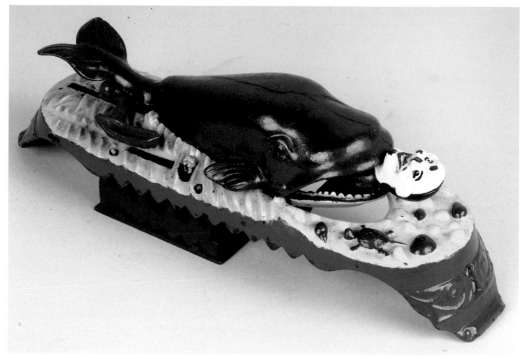

Photo courtesy Morphy Auctions, Denver, Pa; www.MorphyAuctions.com

Jonah & the Whale, J. & E. Stevens and Co. Cast iron, pedestal variation, extremely rare. One small break at tab by the back tail, which is common for this bank. Old repaint with some remnants of original paint. **$17,250**

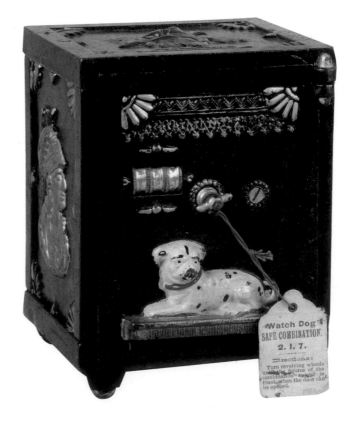

Photo courtesy Morphy Auctions, Denver, Pa; www.MorphyAuctions.com

Watch Dog Safe, cast iron, J. & E. Stevens and Co. Original, working condition. Original tag, bellows and drawer, 6". **$3,162**

Reproduction Alert. Reproductions, fakes and forgeries exist for many banks. Forgeries of some mechanical banks were made as early as 1937, so age alone is not a guarantee of authenticity.

Photo courtesy Morphy Auctions, Denver, Pa; www.MorphyAuctions.com

'Spise a Mule, cast iron, J. & E. Stevens and Co. bench variation. **$517**

Photo courtesy Morphy Auctions, Denver, Pa;
www.MorphyAuctions.com

*'Spise a Mule, cast iron, J. & E.
Stevens and Co., jockey-over
variation with brown base.* **$517**

Photo courtesy Morphy Auctions, Denver, Pa; www.MorphyAuctions.com

Mule in Barn, cast iron, J. & E. Stevens and Co. **$862**

Photo courtesy Morphy Auctions, Denver, Pa; www.MorphyAuctions.com

Trick Dog, cast iron, Shepard Hardware Co. Six-part base variation. All original. **$920**

Photo courtesy Morphy Auctions, Denver, Pa; www.MorphyAuctions.com

Armored Car still bank, cast iron, A.C. Williams, circa 1920s, rare. Original paint and solid gold-washed wheels, 4" x 6 1/2". **$1,955**

Photos courtesy Morphy Auctions, Denver, Pa; www.MorphyAuctions.com

Camel still bank, cast iron, A.C. Williams Co., 4 3/4". **$103**

Tammany Hall, J. & E. Stevens and Co. Brown-jacket variation. All original, including trap, 5 3/4". **$1,150**

Photo courtesy Morphy Auctions, Denver, Pa;
www.MorphyAuctions.com

*Tiger, tin mechanical, Saalheimer
and Strauss, with advertisement
for Lyons Toffee on back, 5 1/8".*
$12,075

Photo courtesy Morphy Auctions, Denver, Pa; www.MorphyAuctions.com

Main Street Trolley still bank, cast iron, A.C. Williams. Replaced wheels. **$80**

Photo courtesy Morphy Auctions, Denver, Pa.; www.MorphyAuctions.com

*Painted cast-iron lighthouse mechanical bank, 10 1/2",
working and all original.* **$11,000**

Photo courtesy Morphy Auctions, Denver, Pa.; www.MorphyAuctions.com

*Painted-lead still bank depicting Mickey Mouse on a
round of cheddar cheese, 5".* **$4,600**

Photo courtesy Noel Barrett Antiques & Auctions Ltd.,
Carversville, Pa.; www.NoelBarrett.com

*Scarce painted cast-iron still bank
with raised lettering to indicate the
building's name: Park Bank.* **$7,187**

Photo courtesy RSL Auction Co., Oldwick, N.J.; www.rslauctions.com

Only known example of J. & E. Stevens' cast-iron mechanical "Novelty" bank in a sea-foam green, cream, tan and red color motif. **$29,160**

Photo courtesy RSL Auction Co., Oldwick, N.J.; www.rslauctions.com

J. & E. Stevens Owl Turns Head cast-iron mechanical bank, circa 1880. **$23,085**

Photo courtesy RSL Auction Co., Oldwick, N.J.; www.rslauctions.com

Turtle cast-iron mechanical bank, Kilgore Mfg. Co., Westerville, Ohio, circa 1930. **$72,900**

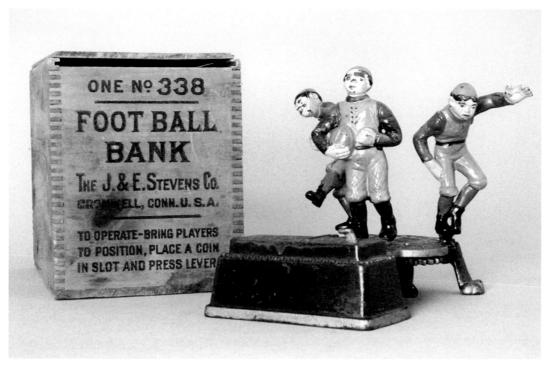

Photo courtesy RSL Auction Co., Oldwick, N.J.; www.rslauctions.com

J. & E. Stevens "Calamity" football cast-iron mechanical bank, circa 1905, with original wooden box. **$78,975**

Photo courtesy RSL Auction Co., Oldwick, N.J.; www.rslauctions.com

Butting Ram/Man Thumbs Nose cast-iron mechanical bank, circa 1895, made by Wagner & Zwiebel Machine Shop, Burlington, Wis. **$27,945**

Photo courtesy RSL Auction Co., Oldwick, N.J.; www.rslauctions.com

J. & E. Stevens Chief Big Moon cast-iron mechanical bank, circa 1899. **$42,310**

Photo courtesy RSL Auction Co., Oldwick, N.J.; www.rslauctions.com

Initiating First Degree cast-iron mechanical bank, circa 1880, manufactured by Mechanical Novelty Works of New Britain, Conn. **$60,850**

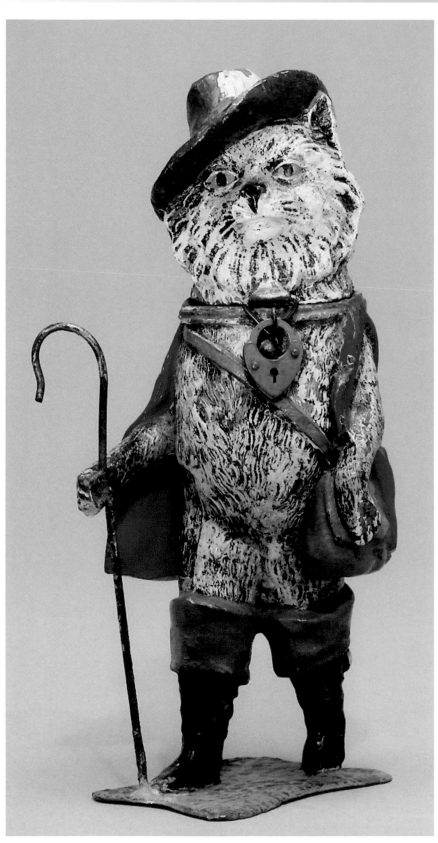

Photo courtesy RSL Auction Co.,
Oldwick, N.J.;
www.rslauctions.com

*German painted
spelter Puss 'n' Boots
with Staff bank, one
of only two known,
7 1/2".* **$12,757**

COMIC BOOKS

Publishers frequently reprint popular stories, even complete books, so the buyer must pay strict attention to the title, not just the portion printed in oversized letters on the front cover. If there is any doubt, look inside at the fine print on the bottom of the inside cover or first page. The correct title will be printed there in capital letters. Also note the dimensions of the comic book. Reprints often differ in size from the original. All photos courtesy Heritage Auction Galleries, Dallas; www.HA.com.

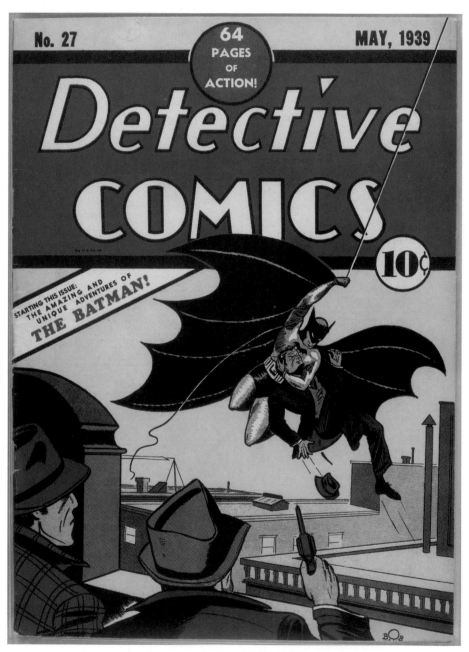

Detective Comics #27 (DC, 1939). CGC certification and grading: VF 8.0, off-white to white pages. "The Bat-Man" appeared in a six-page story that also introduced the character of Commissioner Gordon. The second-to-last panel revealed that this mysterious avenger was in fact Bruce Wayne, introduced earlier in the story. **$1.075 million**

Flash Comics #1 (January 1940), graded NM+ 9.6, off-white to white pages. One of the most important comic books of any age, Flash Comics #1 featured the origins and first appearances of the Flash, Hawkman, Shiera Sanders, the Whip, and Johnny Thunder. **$450,000**

Marvel Comics #1 "Pay Copy" (Timely, 1939), graded VF/NM 9.0, off-white pages. This is referred to as the pay copy or "payout copy" because it's the one used by the Lloyd Jacquet studio (aka Funnies Inc.), which produced the comic in its entirety for Timely, to record how much each contributor was paid, on which date and with which check number. **$227,050**

Action Comics #7 (DC, 1938), graded VF 8.0, off-white to white pages. Superman appeared on a comic book cover for just the second time here. **$143,400**

The Incredible Hulk #1 (Marvel, 1962) graded NM- 9.2, off-white pages. **$125,475**

Marvel Mystery Comics #9 (Timely, 1940) graded NM 9.4, off-white pages. **$107,550**

Detective Comics #38 Allentown pedigree (DC, 1940) CGC NM 9.4 Off-white pages. **$107,550**

Amazing Fantasy #15, "Biljo White copy" (Marvel, 1962) graded VF+ 8.5, off-white pages. (It originally belonged to Biljo White, one of the key figures in early comics fandom, who published the fanzine Batmunia. **$104,562**

The Human Torch #2 (#1) (Timely, 1940) graded NM 9.4, off-white pages. **$92,612**

More Fun Comics #52 (DC, 1940) graded NM- 9.2, off-white to white pages. **$89,625**

Sensation Comics #1 (DC, 1942) graded NM 9.4, off-white pages. The first appearance of the Amazing Amazon had been a just a month before in All Star Comics #8, and Wonder Woman's origin story continued from that issue. **$83,650**

Showcase #22 Green Lantern (DC, 1959) graded VF/NM 9.0, off-white pages. **$59,750**

Superman #6 (DC, 1940) graded VF+ 8.5, cream to off-white pages. **$56,762**

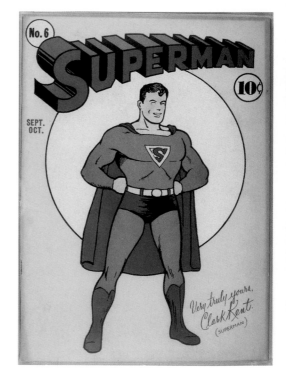

All Winners Comics #1 (Timely, 1941) graded NM+ 9.6, off-white to white pages. **$53,775**

Four Color (Series One) #16 Mickey Mouse (#1) (Dell, 1941) graded NM- 9.2, off-white to white pages. This is the first Mickey Mouse comic book. **$50,787**

Adventure Comics #40 (DC, 1939) graded FN/VF 7.0, cream to off-white pages. The debut of the Sandman in Adventure, this is the first superhero issue of one of DC's earliest and longest-running books. **$38,837**

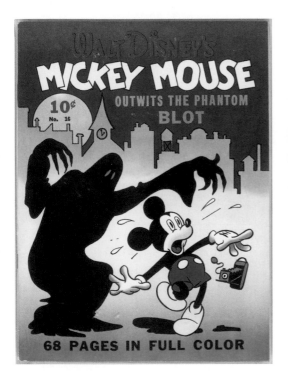

BOOKS, PAPERBACKS

The first mass-market, pocket-sized, paperback book printed in the U.S. was an edition of Pearl Buck's *The Good Earth*, produced by Pocket Books in late 1938, sold in New York City.

At first, paperbacks consisted entirely of reprints, but publishers soon began publishing original works. Genre categories began to emerge, and mass-market book covers reflected those categories. Mass-market paperbacks had an impact on slick magazines (slicks) and pulp magazines. The market for cheap magazines diminished when buyers went to cheap books instead. Authors also turned from magazines and began writing for the paperback market. Many pulp magazine cover artists were hired by paperback publishers to entice readers with their alluring artwork. Several well-known authors were published in paperback, including Arthur Miller and John Steinbeck, and some, like Dashiell Hammett, were published as paperback originals.

For more information and details on condition grades (values here are in three grades: good, very good and fine), consult *Antique Trader Collectible Paperbacks Price Guide* by Gary Lovisi, or visit *www.gryphonbooks.com*. Books in this year's edition of the guide come from Lovisi's *Bad Girls Need Love, Too — Pleasure Yourself With Pulp Fiction* (2010, Krause Publications).

Warped Women by Janet Pritchard, Uni Book #9, 1951, digest-size paperback. **$12-35-100**

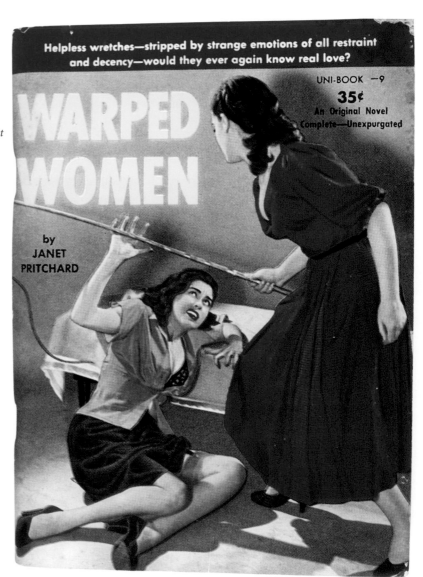

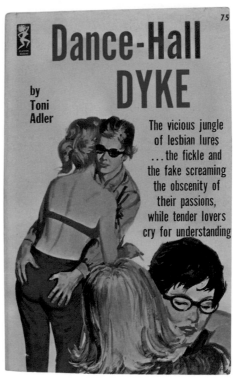

Girl-Crazy Professor by Florence Stonebraker, Croydon Book #46, 1953, digest-size paperback. **$9-22-55.**

Dance-Hall Dyke by Toni Adler, Playtime Book #699-S, 1964. Cover art by Robert Bonfils. **$12-25-55**

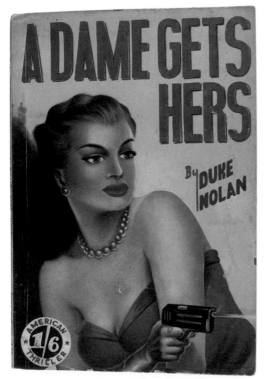

A Dame Gets Hers by Duke Nolan, Scion Books, 1952, UK digest-size paperback. **$15-55-125**

Office Hussy by John Hunter, Star Novels #767, 1957, digest-size paperback. **$12-35-75**

Rock 'N Roll Gal by Ernie Weatherall, Beacon Book #B379, 1957. Cover art by Owen Kampen. **$12-28-65**

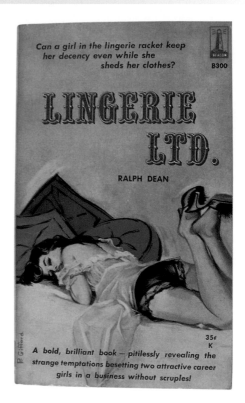

Lingerie Ltd. By Ralph Dean, Beacon Book #B300, 1960. Cover art by R. Gifford. **$9-15-35**

Knock On Any Head by Frank S. Miller, Vega Book #V-19, 1962. **$7-15-40**

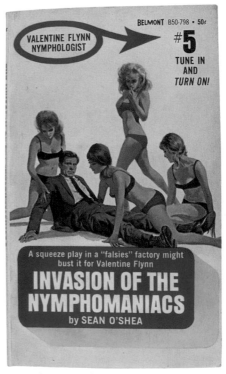

Invasion of The Nymphomaniacs by Sean O'Shea, Belmont Book #B50-798, 1967. **$9-15-35**

Sin Street by Dorine Manners, Pyramid Book #21, 1950.
$9-22-50

I Made My Bed by Celia Hye, Beacon Book #B188, 1958.
$7-15-35

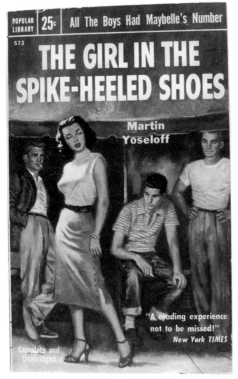

The Girl in The Spike-Heeled Shoes by Martin Yoseloff,
Popular Library #573, 1954. **$5-15-28**

The Stripper Died Dressed by Conrad Paul, Colin
Calhoun Magazine #8, circa 1952, Australian digest-size
magazine. Photo cover. **$10-25-65**

Run Tough, Run Hard by Carson Bingham, Monarch Book #487, 1964. Cover at by Ray Johnson. **$9-20-45**

Gorrila's Moll by Ben Sarto, Modern Fiction, circa 1952, UK digest-size paperback. Cover art by Leonard Potts. **$15-45-125**

Sex Racket by Mark Lucas, Tropic Book #928, 1966. **$9-16-35**

This Way For Hell by Spike Morelli, Leisure Library #7, 1952. Cover art by Reginald Heade. **$12-30-65**

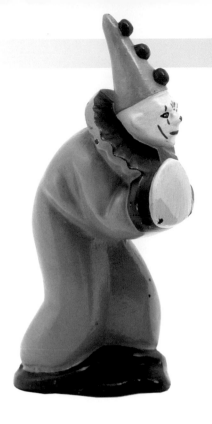

Photo courtesy Bertoia Auctions, Vineland, N.J.; www.BertoiaAuctions.com

Hubley clowns, rare, cleverly designed pieces, painted in vibrant colors, one clown appears to be pushing while the other holds hands behind back in propping up position, 6". **$805**

BOOKENDS

Unless otherwise indicated, listings in this section on cast-iron bookends come courtesy of John C. and Nancy Smith, owners of American Sampler, P.O. 371, Barnesville, Md. 20838; *www.castirononline*. The Smiths are also the authors of *The Doorstop Book — An Encyclopedia of Doorstop Collecting* (Schiffer, 2006).

Accordion Player, 6" x 4 1/2". Made by Hubley, cat. #497. Full-figure. .... **$200-$250**

Alamo, 4 1/4" x 6 1/2". Signed, "50th Anniversary, 1878-1928, Alamo Iron Works, San Antonio, Tex." ...... **$200-$300**

Amish Girl and Boy, 5 1/4" x 3 7/8". Made by John Wright. Background farm scene. .... **$50-$100**

Sitting Amish Boy and Girl, 4" x 4". Made by Wilton Products. .... **$200-$300**

Angelus (After Millet's Painting), 4 3/4" x 5". Signed on front of base, "Angelus". .... **$50-$100**

Art Deco Drape Woman, 6" x 5 1/4". Made by Hubley and numbered "73". .... **$100-$200**

Art Deco Nude Woman with Swan, 3 7/8" x 7 1/2". The swan's wings form a V. .... **$100-$200**

Art Deco Swaying Nude Woman, 4 1/2" x 6 3/4". Numbered "202". .... **$75-$150**

Art Deco "The Storm", 5 7/8" x 3 7/8". Made by Connecticut Foundry. Signed and dated, "The Storm, Copyright 1928". .... **$150-$250**

Art Deco Ballerina, 7 1/4" x 5". .... **$100-$200**

Art Deco Nude Woman Inside of Wreath, 5" x 4 1/2". Numbered "53". .... **$75-$150**

Art Deco Woman with Arched Back, 5 1/2" x 4 3/8". Numbered "154". .... **$75-$150**

Art Deco Woman with Drape, 6" x 4 3/4". Made by Creations. Marked "Copr. 130, C. Co., #217". .... **$75-$150**

Art Deco Swaying Nude Woman, 4 1/2" x 6 3/4". Numbered "202". .... **$75-$150**

Beaver with an O, 5" x 51/4". Logo for Oregon Sate. .... **$400-$500**

Bedouin, 5 3/4" x 5 1/4". Made by Hubley, cat. #418. Full-figure. .... **$200-$250**

Boston Terrier, 5 1/4" x 4 7/8". Signed "B&H" (Bradley and Hubbard). .... **$200-$300**

Boston Terrier on Base, 5" x 5 1/2". Made by Hubley, cat. #361. Full-figure. .... **$300-$400**

Boy & Girl Riding Rocking Horses, 5 1/2" x 5". Made by cjo (Judd Co.) and numbered "9690". .... **$500-$700**

Buccaneer, 5 3/4" x 4". Made by Hubley, cat. #420. Full-figure. .... **$100-$200**

Buffalo, 5 3/8" x 6 7/8". Signed, "Verona, Pat. Pend." .... **$200-$300**

Canadian Mounted Police, 6 3/8" x 4". Numbered "730". .... **$250-$350**

Cardinal (bird), 5 1/4" x 3". Made by Albany Fdry. Co. .... **$100-$200**

Children on Gate, 5 1/4" x 3 7/8". Made by Hubley. Numbered and artist signed, "© G.G.D. (Grace Drayton), #209, #210". .... **$300-$500**

Church and Coach, 5 1/2" x 4 1/8". Signed, "B&H" (Bradley and Hubbard). .... **$200-$300**

Clown, 6 1/4" x 3". Made by Hubley, cat. #32. ...... **$500-$700**

Conestoga Covered Wagon with Horses, 3 5/8" x 6 1/2". Signed and numbered, "Hubley, 378". ..... **$100-$200**

Conestoga Covered Wagon with Oxen, 2 7/8" x 6 1/8". Signed, dated and numbered, "Arion Hardware Co., copyright 1931, #1849". .... **$50-$150**

Conestoga Covered Wagon with Oxen, 6 1/8" x 6 1/4". Signed, "Cincinnati Artistic, Patent Appld. For". Marked on front of base, "Trecking West". .... **$100-$200**

Crowing Fantail Rooster, 6" x 5". Made by Creations Co. .... **$100-$200**

Cottage in Woods, 5 1/2" x 5". Made by Hubley and numbered "292". .... **$100-$200**

Cowboy, 6 1/2" x 5". Made by Hubley, cat. #495. Full-figure. .... **$200-$300**

Cowboy on Bucking Horse, 7 1/8" x 5 1/8". Signed, "Bronze Mfg.". .... **$250-$350**

Cowboy on Bucking Horse, 5 7/8" x 4 1/4". Signed and numbered, "© AC, 136". .... **$250-$350**

Cowboys Roping Steer, 4 3/4" x 5 1/8". Made by Hubley. .... **$100-$200**

Crane in the Bullrushes, 6 1/2" x 5". Made by Hubley, cat. #413. .... **$200-$300**

Dachshund, 4" x 8". Made by Hubley and numbered "355". .... **$500-$700**

Begging Scottie, 4" x 2 1/2". Signed, "Spencer, Guilford, Conn." **$200-$300**

Docile Jocelyn, the Donkey, 4 1/2" x 5". Made by Hubley, cat. #492. Full-figure. .... **$200-$250**

Doe, 5 3/4" x 4 1/4". Made by Hubley and numbered "399". .... **$300-$400**

Doe and Fawn, 4 1/2" x 5 1/2". Made by Hubley, cat. #494. Full-figure. .... **$150-$250**

Dog with Cat on Fence, 5 3/4" x 4 3/4". Made by Wilton Products. .... **$150-$250**

Dolly and Bobby with Puppy, 4 7/8" x 4 1/8". Made by Hubley. Signed and numbered, "Made in USA, 498". .... **$150-$250**

Eagle on Rocks with Spread Wings, 2 1/2" x 5". Made by Littco Products. Full-figure. .... **$75-$150**

Elephant, 4 3/4" x 5 1/4". Made by Creations Co. ... **$50-$100**

Elephant, 5 1/4" x 6 1/2". Signed, "Verona, Pat. Pend." .... **$150-$250**

Elephant, 5 5/8" x 6 1/2". Signed "B&H" (Bradley and Hubbard). .... **$300-$400**

Embossed Mixed Flowers in Basket, 5 5/8" x 4 7/8". Signed "B&H" (Bradley and Hubbard). .... **$150-$250**

Embossed Mixed Flowers in Urn, 3 7/8" x 5 1/2". Signed "B&H" (Bradley and Hubbard). .... **$100-$200**

End of the Trail, 6" x 5 1/4". Made by Hubley, cat. #372. Full-figure. .... **$250-$350**

English Tudor-Style Cottage, 5 3/4" x 4 1/2". .... **$100-$200**

Football Player, 5 1/2" x 6". Made by Hubley and numbered "416". .... **$300-$400**

Fireplace, 5 5/8" x 5 3/4". Made by National Foundry and numbered "147". .... **$75-$150**

Fish, 5 1/4" x 5". Made by Hubley, cat. #448. Full-figure. .... **$200-$250**

Fish, 6 1/2" x 4 1/2". Made by Littco Products. Full-figure. .... **$75-$150**

Gazelle, 6 1/2" x 5". Made by Hubley and numbered "410". .... **$150-$250**

German Shepherd on Base, 5 1/4" x 6". Made by Hubley, cat. #364. Full-figure. .... **$200-$300**

Bird on Branch, 4" x 4 7/8". Marked "Luca License". **$100-$200**

Photo courtesy Bertoia Auctions, Vineland, N.J.; www.BertoiaAuctions.com

Knight in archway, marked "The Travelers Convention Palm Beach Florida 1931" on reverse, stepped base leads to suited knight holding shield displaying crest of a griffin with prey in claws, marked "Gorham Co." on side of base, 7 5/8". **$316**

Girl Holding Dress, 5" x 4 3/4". Signed, "Albany Fdry. Co., 150". .... **$50-$150**

Hide and Seek, 6" x 5 3/4". Little girl playing hide and seek. .... **$200-$300**

Horse at Dutch Door, 4 3/4" x 3 1/4". Made by Hubley and numbered "2". .... **$150-$250**

Horse Head, 4 1/2" x 4". Made by Hubley. Belgian draft horse against brick wall surrounded by horseshoe. .... **$200-$300**

Hunter and Dog, 6 1/4" x 5". Made by Hubley, cat. #423. Full-figure. **$400-500**

Indian Brave on Horseback, 6" x 6". Made by Hubley. .... **$300-$500**

Indian Chief, 5" x 4 3/8". Made by Creations Co. .... **$75-$150**

Indian Planting Seeds, 3 3/8" x 4 1/2". .... **$100-$200**

Illinois Indian, 4 1/8" x 4 1/2". Signed and dated, "Shop Laboratorie – LaForce Bailey Sculpture, 1923". Mascot for University Illinois. .... **$100-$200**

John Alden & Priscilla, 7" x 2 3/8". Made by John Wright. Each signed, one "John Alden" and other "Priscilla". .... **$75-$150**

Kissing Dutch Boy and Girl, 4 3/4" x 4". Made by Hubley and numbered "332". .... **$100-$200**

Kneeling Kissing Asian Couple, 4 5/8" x 4 5/8". .... **$75-$150**

Lamb, 6 1/4" x 4 1/2". Made by Hubley, cat. #496. Full-figure. .... **$100-$200**

Laying Down Dromedary, 4 1/2" x 6 1/2". Made by Hubley, cat. #358. Full-figure. .... **$250-$350**

Lazy Pedro, 6 1/2" x 3". Made by Hubley, cat. #493. Full-figure. .... **$150-$250**

Lincoln Cabin, 3 7/8" x 4 7/8". Signed and numbered, "cjo (Judd Co.), 8678". .... **$100-$200**

Lion, 5 1/2" x 5". Signed, "Bronze Met, Copyright 1926". .... **$50-$150**

Man in Chair, 5 1/4" x 4 3/8". Signed, "B&H" (Bradley and Hubbard). .... **$300-$400**

Mixed Flowers in Hanging Basket, 7 3/4" x 6 3/8". Signed and numbered, "Albany Fdry. Co., 137". .... **$75-$150**

Mixed Flowers in Splint Basket, 5 5/8" x 3 1/2". Signed and numbered "Jersey, 30". .... **$75-$150**

Mount Vernon, 4" x 6 3/8". Made by Albany Fdry. Co. .... **$150-$250**

Owl, 5 1/8" x 6 1/2". Made by cjo (Judd Co.) and numbered "9729". .... **$150-$250**

Owl Perched Under Arch, 6" x 5 1/8". Signed "B&H" (Bradley and Hubbard). .... **$200-$300**

Parrot on Stump, 6 1/2" x 3 1/4". Signed, dated and numbered, "Albany Fdry. Co., 1922, #80". .... **$100-$200**

Owl on Branch, 5 1/2" x 3 1/2". Made by cjo (Judd Co.) and numbered "9890". **$150-$250**

Peacock, 6 1/8" x 4 1/2". Signed, "B&H" (Bradley and Hubbard). .... **$200-$300**

Pekingese, 5" x 5 1/4". Made by Hubley and numbered "366". .... **$400-$500**

Penguin, 5 3/4" x 3 3/8". Full-figure standing on square base. .... **$400-$500**

Pointer, 4" x 8". Made by Hubley and numbered "303". .... **$200-$300**

Pointer, 4 1/2" x 5 1/4". Made by Creations Co. ..... **$75-$150**

Pointer Bottle Opener, 5 1/4" x 3 7/8". Made by John Wright. .... **$100-$200**

Polar Bear, 3 1/2" x 6". Made by Hubley, cat. #370. Full-figure. .... **$300-$400**

Polo Player, 5 3/8" x 4 1/4". Made by Littco Products. .... **$100-$200**

Puppies in Barrel, 7" x 7 3/8". Made by Wilton Products. .... **$200-$300**

Quail, 5 1/2" x 5 3/4". Made by Hubley and numbered "461". Fred Everett designer. .... **$300-$500**

Raggedy Ann & Andy, 5 1/2" x 4". Signed "Copyright P.F. Volland Co., 1931". .... **$700-$1,000**

Sailboat, 5 3/4" x 5 1/2". Made by Hubley. Signed, "Made in USA". .... **$200-$300**

Scottie by Rose Fence, 6 3/4" x 4 1/2". Made by Hubley and numbered "430". .... **$200-$300**

Scottie by Lattice Fence, 6 3/8" x 4 3/4". Signed, "Kenco, Littlestown, PA., No. 20, Scotty". .... **$200-$300**

Scottie Leaning on Picket Fence, 6 1/4" x 4 1/4". .... **$100-$200**

Setter, 4 3/8" x 5 1/8". Signed "B&H" (Bradley and Hubbard). .... **$100-$200**

Setter, 5 1/4" x 6 1/4". Made by Hubley and numbered "281". .... **$250-$350**

Setter on Base, 5" x 8". Made by Hubley, cat. #363. Full-figure. .... **$200-$300**

Shakespeare's House, 4 5/8" x 5 3/4". Numbered "262". Marked on front of base, "Shakespeare's House, Stratford of Avon". .... **$50-$100**

*Parakeet Love Birds, 6" x 4 3/8". **$200-$300***

Sheik, 6 1/4" x 4 1/2". Made by Hubley, cat. #421. Full-figure. .... **$200-$250**

Ship, 4" x 4". Made by Albany Fdry. Co. .... **$50-$100**

Ship, 4 1/4" x 4 3/4". Signed, "Pirate Galleon, copyright". .... **$100-$200**

Ship, 5" x 5 1/4". Numbered "90620". .... **$75-$150**

Ship, 5 5/8" x 5 1/8". Signed, "English Galleon, Copr. 1928", with "Connecticut Fdry" logo. .... **$75-$150**

Ship Old Ironsides, 4" x 5 3/8". Signed "B&H" (Bradley and Hubbard). .... **$200-$300**

Sir Galahad, 5 7/8" x 4 3/8". Marked on front of base, "Sir Galahad". .... **$50-$100**

Sitting Boston Terrier Pup, 4 1/2" x 6". Made by Hubley, cat. #392. Full-figure. .... **$200-$300**

Sitting Cat, 6" x 4 3/4". Made by Creations Co. .... **$50-$100**

Sitting Scotty, 5" x 6". Made by Hubley, cat. #391. Full-figure. .... **$200-$250**

Sitting Sealyham, 4 1/2" x 6 1/2". Made by Hubley, cat. #426. Full-figure. .... **$200-$300**

*Great Dane, 6 1/4" x 6 3/4". Made by Hubley and numbered "354". **$300-$500***

Zebra, 4 3/4" x 6". Made by Hubley and numbered "2419". **$700-$1,000**

Sitting Wirehaired Fox Terrier, 4 3/4" x 6". Made by Hubley, cat. #390. Full-figure. ....**$200-$300**

Spread Winged Duck, 7" x 5 1/2". Made by Littco Products. Full-figure. ....**$75-$150**

Spirit of St. Louis Airplane, 4 7/8" x 4 3/4". Marked on front of base, "Spirit of St. Louis". ....**$200-$300**

Stage Coach with Horses, 4" x 7". Made by Hubley and numbered "379". ....**$100-$200**

Standing Boston Terrier Pup, 4 1/2" x 6". Made by Hubley, cat. #409. Full-figure. ....**$200-$300**

Standing Cocker Spaniel, 4 1/2" x 6 3/4". Made by Hubley, cat. #427. Full-figure. ....**$200-$300**

Standing Scottie, 4 3/8" x 5 3/8". Signed, "Spencer, Guilford, Conn." ....**$100-$200**

Standing Scotty, 5" x 6 1/2". Made by Hubley, cat. #408. Full-figure. ....**$200-$250**

Standing Sealyham, 4 3/4" x 5 1/8". Made by Hubley and numbered "52". ....**$300-$500**

Standing Wirehaired Fox Terrier, 5" x 6 1/2". Made by Hubley, cat. #407. Full-figure. ....**$200-$300**

St. Joseph's Parrish, 7 7/8" x 5". "Commemorating the 100th Anniversary of St. Joseph Parrish 1835-1935". ....**$300-$400**

The Thinker, 5" x 4 3/8". Made by Creations Co. ....**$50-$100**

The Whipper-in or Steeplechase, 5" x 4 3/4". Made by Hubley and numbered "415". ....**$250-$350**

Three Daisies with Bow, 5" x 3 1/2". ....**$200-$300**

Three Kittens in Basket, 4 5/8" x 5 5/8". Made by Wilton Products. ....**$150-$250**

Three Kittens on Book, 4 5/8" x 5 5/8". Signed "B&H" (Bradley and Hubbard). ....**$250-$350**

Three Singing Dog, 4 3/4" x 5". Made by Wilton Products. ....**$200-$300**

Totem Pole, 6" x 3". ....**$300-$500**

Water Lilies, 4 1/8" x 7 1/2". Signed and numbered, "Albany Fdry. Co., 52". ....**$150-$250**

Wirehaired Terrier, 5 1/8" x 5 1/2". Signed, "Spencer, Guilford, Conn." ....**$200-$300**

Wirehaired Terrier, 5 1/4" x 5 3/8". Made by Hubley and numbered "294". ....**$75-$150**

Wirehaired Terrier, 5 3/8" x 3 7/8". Signed "B&H" (Bradley and Hubbard). **$200-300**

Wirehaired Terrier, 5 5/8" x 5 1/2". Made by Hubley and numbered "351". ....**$200-$300**

Wirehaired Terrier on Base, 4 1/2" x 4 3/8". Made by Hubley, cat. #162. Full-figure. ....**$300-$400**

Wirehaired Terrier & Scottie, 4 3/4" x 5 3/8". Made by Hubley and numbered "263". ....**$200-$300**

Wolfhound, 6 5/8" x 3 5/8". Signed, "Spencer, Guilford, Conn." ....**$300-$500**

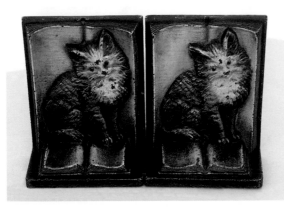

Sitting Kitten on Book, 4 7/8" x 3 3/4". Signed "B&H" (Bradley and Hubbard). **$300-$500**

CANES AND WALKING STICKS

Canes and walking sticks have existed through the ages, first as staffs or symbols of authority. They evolved into a fashion accessory that might incorporate carved ivory, precious metals, jewels, porcelain and enamel.

Canes have also been a favorite form of expression for folk artists, with intricate pictorial carving on shafts and handles.

Another category of interest to collectors features gadget canes or "system sticks" that contain hidden objects, from weapons to drinking flasks, telescopes, compasses and even musical instruments.

Photo courtesy Heritage Auction Galleries, Dallas; www.HA.com

Pistol Cane with Carved Wood Monkey Head Handle. The mechanism is an unusual variety of rim-fire pistol. The breech opens to the left side by pulling a spring-loaded hammer/lever. A cartridge is locked in place. The hammer is released by pushing a firing button on the right side. It appears that the pistol uses a 9mm rim-fire shot cartridge. The handle is a realistically carved monkey with a sterling collar. Originally the handle/pistol was disengaged by pushing a steel release button. The shaft included is a damaged replacement. One glass eye is missing. **$1,434**

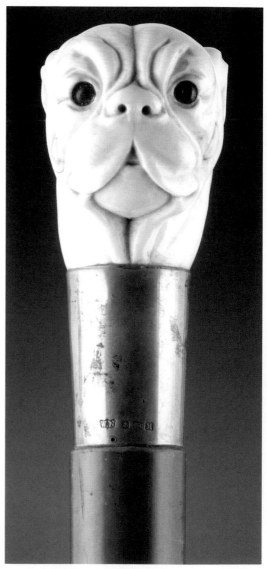

Photo courtesy Heritage Auction Galleries, Dallas; www.HA.com

Ivory-handle walking stick, the silver cuff by William Neale & Sons, Birmingham, England, 1937-1938, 39 5/8" long, carved ivory pug-head handle with red glass eyes, silver cuff and brass tip, overall good condition with minor wear to shaft. **$597**

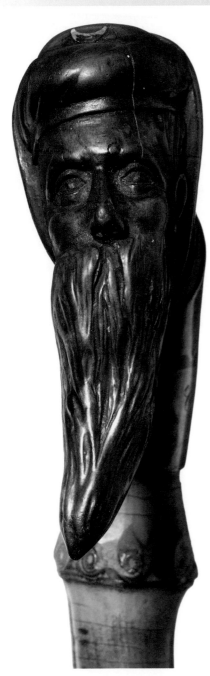

Photo courtesy Heritage Auction Galleries, Dallas; www.HA.com

Figural Cane owned by Lt. Charles DeRudio, 7th Cavalry, a survivor of the Battle of Little Bighorn. The bamboo shaft of this cane is mounted at the top with a carved Moor's head. The shaft and head are connected by an engraved fitted coin silver band that has the numeral "7" between crossed cavalry sabers and that reads, "25 June / 1876 / Captain C. C. de Rudio / U.S.A.". The flowing beard and mustache are similar to those worn by DeRudio. The turban has an inlaid silver crescent. The overall length of the cane is 35 1/2" and it retains the original ferrule. **$2,629**

Photo courtesy Heritage Auction Galleries, Dallas; www.HA.com

Walking Stick with ivory head of Ulysses S. Grant. Image shows Grant in civilian dress, with his name incused in block letters on the back of the neck. Appears to have been commercially produced. Original brass tip, dark brown hardwood shaft. The head measures 2 1/2", overall length 36". **$1,793**

Photos courtesy Heritage Auction Galleries, Dallas; www.HA.com

Presentation cane made of wood from Lincoln's log cabin. Ornate gold-finish head, engraved on both top and side. The side reads, "A stick from the log cabin built by A. Lincoln, J. and D. Hanks, in Macon County, Illinois. A.D. 1830." The top is engraved "Wm. B. Mills from J. & D. Hanks" (John and Dennis, son and father). Mills was elected Worshipful Master of the Charleston, Ill., Masonic Lodge in 1846. Upon Lincoln's assassination in 1865, the Lodge supported a statewide Masonic resolution denouncing the assassination and the president's assassin, and later made a donation to the Lincoln National Monument Fund. One small dent in the top, 34 1/2" long. **$6,572**

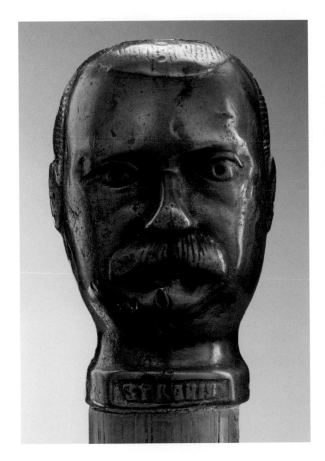

Photo courtesy Heritage Auction Galleries, Dallas; www.HA.com

Grover Cleveland walking stick with head of cast in brass rather than the typical pot metal. "St. Louis" in block letters below the chin. Probably issued for an exposition or presidential visit during Cleveland's two terms. Excellent condition. Brass top is 2 1/8" high, overall length 37". No protective metal tip, apparently as made. **$776**

Photo courtesy Heritage Auction Galleries, Dallas; www.HA.com

Theodore Roosevelt campaign walking stick. The metal knob has a 1 1/2" brass rimmed, sepia celluloid portrait button of Roosevelt affixed to the top. The wooden shaft is 32" from the top of the knob to the brass ferrule. The knob is marked, "American Badge Co. / Chicago". The celluloid is cracked and has light foxing. **$143**

Photos courtesy Heritage Auction Galleries, Dallas; www.HA.com

Cleveland & Thurman figural rooster head jugate cane, features the 1888 Democratic candidates, measuring 35" from head to tip. The 2 1/2" x 2" handle is in the form of a "stubby" rooster with enclosed portraits on opposite sides of Grover Cleveland and Allen Thurman. It is composed of silvered spelter or pot metal. There are light traces of the original silvering. The rooster's comb is lightly colored red and his crest gold. The shaft is composed of a soft wood, possibly birch. Complete with metal tip at the bottom. **$717**

Photos courtesy Heritage Auction Galleries, Dallas; www.HA.com

Violin Cane, handle screws on to the hardwood shaft, which contains a soundboard and fitted bow. The cane has a 1/2" nickel collar above the split. The shaft is 34 3/4" overall (including handle) and has a steel ferrule. Lightly marked "Made in Germany". The cane is missing the wood cover, the tuning key and a nickel set ring to secure the cover. **$1,792**

Ceramics

CERAMICS, AMERICAN

Also see Tiffany, Redware, Stoneware.

Photo courtesy Belhorn Auction Services LLC, Columbus, Ohio; www.Belhorn.com

Bulbous vase, from The Arts & Clay Co., 1997, in two-color matte glaze, inspired by Grueby Pottery. Signed SF and dated 1997 with the original paper label with the notation "1997 - No. 2". Mint. 9 1/2" x 6 7/8". **$138**

The Arts & Clay Co.

Two mini vases, from The Arts & Clay Co. in matte green with lighter green to yellow flower buds, inspired by Grueby Pottery. Each is marked with the original paper label with the notation "Mini." The vase bottoms are marked, but these markings are obscured by the paper labels. Mint. 3 1/8" and 3 5/8". .... **$86 pair**

Photo courtesy Belhorn Auction Services LLC, Columbus, Ohio; www.Belhorn.com

The Arts & Clay Co. Rhead-style vase with incised scenic decoration. Marked with original paper label and signed "A". Mint. 4 3/4". **$132**

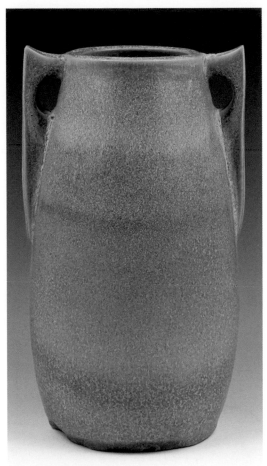

Photo courtesy Belhorn Auction Services LLC, Columbus, Ohio; www.Belhorn.com

The Arts & Clay Co. matte green Teco-style vase. Marked "A&C, A". Mint. 9 1/4". **$115**

The Arts & Clay Co., drip glaze vase in blue over dark green gloss. Signed "A". Mint. 4 7/8". **$80**
The Arts & Clay Co., vase with horse. Marked "Arts & Clay Company, A". Mint. 8 5/8". **$55**
The Arts & Clay Co., scarab paperweight with light tan gloss glaze. Marked with original paper label. Mint. 4 3/4". **$92**
The Arts & Clay Co., drip glaze vase in white over brown matte. Signed "A". Mint. 4 7/8".........................**$11**

Batchelder and Brown

Ernest Allan Batchelder founded the Batchelder Tile Co. in Pasadena, Calif., in 1909. He took on Frederick L. Brown as his partner, renaming the pottery Batchelder and Brown in 1912. The firm closed in 1932.

Batchelder, framed bird tile. Marked "Batchelder Los Angeles" and with Frankie Johnson Collection tag. There is a typical chip to the back side of the tile. Tile is 3 7/8" square in a 6 1/2" frame....................................$86

Burley, and Burley Winter

Several generations of the Burley and Winter families operated potteries in and around the Ohio communities of Crooksville, Zanesville and Mt. Sterling from the early 19th to the early 20th centuries.

Photo courtesy Belhorn Auction Services LLC, Columbus, Ohio; www.Belhorn.com

Burley Winter handled and lidded vessel in matte green over pumpkin. Unmarked, but there is a nearly perfect four-finger print to the bottom left by the pottery's glazer. Some very small nicks to the inner rim are hidden by the lid, 9" x 6 1/2". **$98**

Photo courtesy Belhorn Auction Services LLC, Columbus, Ohio; www.Belhorn.com

Burley Winter jardiniere. Marked "Burley Winter Crooksville O." Mint, 11" x 8". **$80**

Rose Cabat

Rose Cabat, born 1914, New York, is a Tucson, Ariz.-based potter known for her "feelies" — small, narrow-necked porcelain pots with soft glazes that feel feathery to the touch.

All photos courtesy Belhorn Auction Services LLC, Columbus, Ohio; www.Belhorn.com

Left, top to bottom:
Rose Cabat tapered Feelie in cream over blue with streaked highlights to the cream color. Marked 841 CABAT 40. Mint. 3". **$230**

Rose Cabat Feelie in cobalt blue with green streaks. Marked 841 Cabat 47. Mint. 2 1/2". **$209**

Rose Cabat squat Feelie in green over blue. Marked 841 CABAT 47. Mint. 2 1/4". **$431**

Below, top to bottom:
Rose Cabat ovoid Feelie in black with navy blue highlights around the neck. Marked 841 CABAT 11. Mint. 3 1/4". **$316**

Rose Cabat Feelie in black with turquoise neck. Unsigned, rare without markings, 2 7/8". **$316**

Camark

Camark Art Tile and Pottery Co. operated in Camden, Ark., from 1926 until the mid-1970s. Art director John Lessell created many of the firm's distinctive glazes.

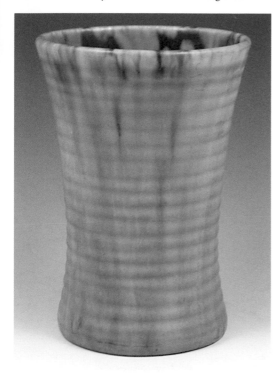

Photo courtesy Belhorn Auction Services LLC, Columbus, Ohio; www.Belhorn.com

Camark vase with horizontal ribs in matte green over blue. Marked Camark. Mint. 5 3/4". **$22**

Cincinnati Limoges

Mary Louise McLaughlin (1847-1939) was a ceramic painter and studio potter from Cincinnati. She was one of the originators of the art pottery movement that swept the United States. Her work was sometimes called "Cincinnati Limoges."

Cincinnati Limoges vase, with applied blackberry and floral decoration. Marked with an artist's cipher, "205, 1881". Typical small flakes, nicks and minor repairs to the design, 9 3/4". **$357**

Coultry, (early Cincinnati) Limoges flask vase with floral decorated. Signed "FH" and dated 1881 by the artist; 3/4" glaze chip to the side and a couple of other small nicks, 8 1/8". **$220**

Clark House Pottery

Clark House Pottery, Greenville, S.C., is operated by Bill and Pamela Clark and influenced by the Arts & Crafts movement of the early 1900s. In addition to original, hand-thrown and decorated art pottery, the Clarks produce wares in the style of George Ohr (1857-1918), the self-proclaimed "Mad Potter of Biloxi".

Clark House Pottery, swan handled vase in copper glaze. Marked "Clark House Pottery LLC, CHP, 10" and signed Clark. Mint. 11 1/2". **$52**

Clark House Pottery, vase in copper glaze made in the style of George Ohr's works. Signed Clark and marked "Clark House Pottery 09". Mint. 6". **$46**

Clark House Pottery, vase in gunmetal black glaze made in the style of George Ohr's works. Signed Clark and marked "Clark House Pottery 09". Mint. 4 3/4". **$34**

Clark House Pottery, "Mr. Waffles" vase in copper glaze. Marked "Clark House Pottery LLC, CHP, 10" and signed Clark. Mint. 7". **$60**

Clark House Pottery, squash vase in green lichen glaze. Marked "Clark House Pottery LLC, CHP, 09" and signed Clark. Mint. 3 1/2". **$80**

Clark House Pottery, single fold vase with beading in begonia glaze. Marked "Clark House Pottery LLC, CHP, 10" and signed Clark. Mint. 5 1/2". **$66**

Clark House Pottery, handled vase in copper glaze. Marked "CHP, 10" and signed Clark. Mint. 8 5/8".........**$138**

Clark House Pottery, flow pitcher in variegated glaze. Marked "Clark House Pottery LLC, CHP, 09" and signed Clark. Mint. 6". **$103**

Clark House Pottery, green squash blossom vase. Marked "Clark House Pottery LLC, CHP, 10" and signed Clark. Mint. 5 5/8". **$80**

Clark House Pottery, double-fold vase in begonia glaze. Marked "Clark House Pottery LLC, CHP, 09" and signed Clark. Mint. 4 3/4". **$46**

Clark House Pottery, chalice vase in brown lichen glaze. Marked "Clark House Pottery LLC, CHP, 0" and signed Clark. Mint. 7 1/2". **$115**

Clark House Pottery, handled vase in bursting purple glaze. Marked "Clark House Pottery LLC, CHP, 09" and signed Clark. Mint. 7 3/4". **$38**

Photo courtesy Belhorn Auction Services LLC, Columbus, Ohio; www.Belhorn.com

Clark House Pottery, tornado pitcher in copper glaze made in the style of George Ohr's works. Signed Clark and marked "Clark House Pottery 09". Mint. 6 3/4". **$34**

Clark House Pottery squash vase in begonia glaze. Marked "CHP, 10" and signed Clark. Mint. 4 5/8". **$98**

Clark House Pottery, butterfly handled vase in "Oil Slick" glaze. Marked "Clark House Pottery LLC, CHP, 09" and signed Clark. Mint. 7 1/2"...**$138**

Clark House Pottery, "Uplifting" vase in "Green Granite" glaze. Marked "Clark House Pottery LLC, CHP, 09" and signed Clark. Mint. 7 1/2"...**$176**

Clark House Pottery, totem vase in green moss glaze. Marked "CHP, 09" and signed Clark. Mint. 7 1/4"...........**$46**

Clark House Pottery, vase in copper glaze made in the style of George Ohr's works. Signed Clark and marked "Clark House Pottery 09". Mint. 4 5/8". **$46**

Clark House Pottery, creamer in begonia glaze. Marked "Clark House Pottery LLC, CHP, 10" and signed Clark. Mint. 3 1/2"..**$46**

Clark House Pottery, squat vase in copper glaze. Marked "Clark House Pottery LLC, CHP, 09" and signed Clark. Mint. 5 1/8" x 1 1/2". **$34**

Clark House Pottery, vase in copper glaze made in the style of George Ohr's works. Signed Clark and marked "Clark House Pottery 09". Mint. 6"...............................**$57**

Clark House Pottery, single-fold bowl in begonia glaze. Marked "Clark House Pottery LLC, CHP, 10" and signed Clark. Mint. 9 3/4" x 4". **$27**

Clark House Pottery, covered vase in green glaze. Marked "CHP, 10" and signed Clark. Mint. 7". **$44**

Clark House Pottery, "Uplifting" vase in green lichen glaze. Marked "Clark House Pottery LLC, CHP, 10" and signed Clark. Mint. 8 7/8". **$126**

*Clark House Pottery,
three-fold vase in
spotted glaze. Marked
"Clark House Pottery
LLC, CHP, 10" and
signed Clark. Mint.
5 1/2".* **$49**

*Clark House Pottery.
Double-fold vase in
green with spotted blue
glaze. Marked "Clark
House Pottery LLC,
CHP, 10" and signed
Clark. Mint. 5".* **$80**

Photo courtesy Belhorn Auction Services LLC, Columbus, Ohio; www.Belhorn.com

Clifton Indian Ware lidded teapot. Marked "Clifton 275". Mint. 3 3/4" x 8 3/4". **$71**

Clifton Art Pottery

The Clifton Art Pottery, Newark, N.J., was established by William A. Long, once associated with Lonhuda Pottery, and Fred Tschirner, a chemist.

Production consisted of two major lines: Crystal Patina, which resembled true porcelain with a subdued crystal-like glaze, and Indian Ware or Western Influence, an adaptation of the American Indians' unglazed and decorated pottery with a high-glazed black interior. Other lines included Robin's-Egg Blue and Tirrube. Robin's-Egg Blue is a variation of the Crystal Patina line, but in blue-green instead of straw-colored hues and with a less-prominent crushed-crystal effect in the glaze. Tirrube, which is often artist signed, features brightly colored, slip-decorated flowers on a terra-cotta ground.

Marks are incised or impressed. Early pieces may be dated and impressed with a shape number. Indian wares are identified by tribes.

Coors Pottery

Established by John J. Herold, formerly superintendent of the art pottery section at Roseville Pottery, in 1910 in Golden, Colo., financed by Adolph Coors Sr. The company was renamed Coors Porcelain in 1920, producing lines that included Rosebud, similar to Fiesta; Decalcomania, also resembling some of the Homer Laughlin patterns; MelloTone, similar to LuRay; plus a Golden Ivory. Pottery production ended after World War II.

Coors Pottery, vase in yellow matte with angled handles and horizontal ribs. Marked with Coors stamp. Mint. 8".
.... **$11**

Coors Pottery, circle vase in semi-gloss yellow. Marked with Coors stamp. Mint. 4 7/8". **$17**

Photo courtesy Belhorn Auction Services LLC, Columbus, Ohio; www.Belhorn.com

Coors Pottery, circle vase in matte blue. Marked with Coors stamp. Mint. 7 1/2". **$38**

Cowan Pottery

R. Guy Cowan was born in 1884 in East Liverpool, Ohio, and educated at the New York State School of Ceramics at Alfred. He founded the Cowan Pottery Studio in Lakewood, Ohio (a suburb of Cleveland) in 1912. The firm closed in 1931.

Photo courtesy Belhorn Auction Services LLC, Columbus, Ohio; www.Belhorn.com

Rare Cowan vase signed by Arthur E. Baggs from 1927. Hand thrown and simply glazed, this vase is a historical piece of Ohio's ceramic history. Having founded and built the highly successful Marblehead Pottery, Baggs moved to Ohio to work at Cowan and teach at the Cleveland School of Art. Soon after the production of this vase, Baggs went on to teach at The Ohio State University, which houses one of the oldest ceramics programs in the country. Marked with hand-incised RG Cowan mark and signed AEB in script with the date. There are a couple of insignificant scratches to the high-glaze finish on the body and a thin strip of roughness to the rim. 7 1/2". **$2,530**

Cowan, Sunbonnet Girl bookends with hand coloration in light blue and cream. While Sunbonnet Girls are not particularly rare, the color to this pair make them quite unusual. Unmarked. Mint. 7 1/8"............................ **$302 pair**

Cowan, #510 Gypsy Moth vase in Delft Blue. Partially marked with Cowan ink stamp and 510. Mint with a slight lean. 12 3/4". **$93**

Cowan, #653 wall pocket in Delphinium luster. Marked with COWAN ink stamp. Excellent condition. 8 1/2"...... **$88**

Cowan, #653 wall pocket in Marigold luster. Marked with COWAN ink stamp, 653 and 2.25 in crayon. Excellent condition. 8 1/2". **$60**

Cowan, #680 Heavenward nude flower figure in Original Ivory glaze. Marked with die-impressed circular Cowan, mark. Mint. 10 1/4"... **$352**

Cowan, #712 Repose Art Nouveau nude flower figure in Special Ivory glaze. Designed by R. Guy Cowan, circa 1926. Partially marked with die-impressed circular Cowan mark. Mint. 6 5/8". **$275**

Cowan, #715-A Seahorse fan vase in excellent October rutile glaze. Marked with die-impressed circular Cowan mark and 715A faintly in black. Mint and uncrazed. 7 1/8" x 6 1/2". **$110**

Cowan, #720 Swirl Dancer nude flower figure in Original Ivory glaze. Marked with die-impressed circular Cowan mark. Mint. 10 1/4". This form won 1st Prize at the 1926 Cleveland Museum of Art May Show.................... **$467**

Cowan, #720 Swirl Dancer nude flower figure in Special Ivory glaze. Marked with die-impressed circular Cowan mark. Mint. 10 1/4". **$632**

Cowan, #721 Laurel flower figure by R. Guy Cowan, in Special Ivory. Marked with die-impressed circular Cowan mark. Mint. 9 3/4". **$385**

Cowan, #733-B bowl with Turquoise high glaze interior and Special Ivory exterior. Marked with large die-impressed circular Cowan mark. Mint. 9 1/4" x 3 3/4".................... **$17**

Cowan, #755 vase in Egyptian Blue. Marked with die-impressed circular Cowan mark. Mint. 8 5/8". **$46**

Cowan, #932 vase in Cerise or Blush glaze. Marked COWAN in die-impressed block letters. Mint. 8"........................... **$88**

Cowan, 649-A vase in Fawn, a rutile crystalline glaze. Marked 649A in crayon and with die-impressed circular Cowan mark. Mint. 6 1/2". **$110**

Cowan, Awakening nude flower figure in Original Ivory glaze. Marked with die-impressed circular Cowan mark. Mint. 9".. **$412**

Cowan, bowl B-1 with four matching C-1 comports in April Green. All marked with die-impressed circular Cowan mark. Mint. Bowl is 11 1/4" x 2 3/8". Comports are 6 1/4". .... **$121 all**

Cowan, bowl in October lining Antique Green. Marked with large impressed RG Cowan mark. Mint with a couple of minor factory grinding nicks to the base edge. 18" x 2 3/4". **$40**

Cowan, bowl in Orchid lining Special Ivory. Marked with large impressed RG Cowan mark. Mint. 16 1/2" x 4 1/2". **$22**

Cowan, bowl in Persian Blue lining Orange Velour. Unmarked. Mint. 10 3/4" wide by 2 1/2"......................... **$22**

Cowan, D-3 Elephant Paperweight designed by Margaret Postgate (circa 1930) in black glaze. Marked with die-impressed circular Cowan mark and COWAN in die-impressed letters. Mint. 4 3/8" x 3 1/2"........................ **$330**

Cowan, D-3 Elephant Paperweight designed by Margaret Postgate (circa 1930) in excellent blue and turquoise glaze. Marked with die-impressed circular Cowan mark and COWAN in die-impressed letters. Mint. 4 3/8" x 3 1/2". **$440**

Cowan, Delphinium luster 554-B vase. Marked with circular Cowan ink stamp. Excellent condition. 11 1/2". **$66**

Cowan, Lakeware lotus bowl in Peacock. Marked Lakeware. Mint. 4 1/2" x 7 1/4". **$82**

Cowan, Lakeware vase in Peacock. Marked Lakeware and V-71. Excellent condition. 9"...................................... **$49**

Cowan, Larkspur vase. Marked with Cowan ink stamp. Excellent condition. 7 1/2"... **$27**

Photo courtesy Belhorn Auction Services LLC, Columbus, Ohio; www.Belhorn.com

Cowan, bowl in Azure Blue. Marked with die-impressed circular Cowan mark and COWAN in die-impressed letters. Mint. 11 1/4" x 2 1/4". **$55**

Pair of Cowan standing elephant Art Deco bookends in Primrose glaze. Designed by Margaret Postgate. Marked with die-impressed circular Cowan mark. Mint. 6 1/8". **$880**

Cowan, lobed bowl with foliage motif, a Wayland Gregory design, in matte Parchment green. Marked with die-impressed circular Cowan mark. Mint. 8 3/4" x 4 1/2". **$88**

Cowan, Logan vase, 649-B, in Antique Green rutile glaze. Marked with die-impressed circular Cowan mark. Mint. 8 3/8". **$121**

Cowan, Pterodactyl console bowl Special Ivory, lined in April Green. Marked with large die-impressed circular Cowan mark. Excellent condition. 14" x 4". **$44**

Cowan, Seahorse console set in Larkspur with strong iridescence. All marked. Excellent condition. Bowl is 16 1/4" x 5". Candleholders are 4 1/4". .... **$121 set**

Cowan, three-piece console set in Special Ivory with the bowl being lined in Turquoise. All three pieces marked. Mint. Bowl is 10 1/2" x 2 1/2". Candleholders are 2 1/8". .... **$60 set**

Cowan, V-2-D vase in with richly mottled Azure glaze. Marked with die-impressed circular Cowan mark. Mint. 5 3/4". **$60**

Cowan, V-30 vase in excellent Oriental Red glaze, with a semi-lustrous sheen. Marked with die-impressed circular Cowan mark and COWAN in die-impressed letters. Mint. 4 5/8". **$115**

Cowan, V-90 vase in uncommon Terra Cotta crackle glaze with separate black lid and base. Marked with die-impressed circular Cowan mark and COWAN in die-impressed letters and V-90. Mint. 13 3/4". **$632**

Cowan, vase #595 in gray and jade green velour glaze. Marked with COWAN ink stamp. Mint. 7 1/4". **$86**

Cowan, vase #620 in lustrous Larkspur glaze. Marked COWAN and 620. Excellent condition. 12 1/8". **$99**

Cowan, vase in Delphinium luster glaze with serpent handles. A drill hole to the bottom has been repaired, covering any markings that may be in place. 13". **$38**

Cowan, vase in Plum. Marked COWAN in impressed letters. Mint. 7". **$38**

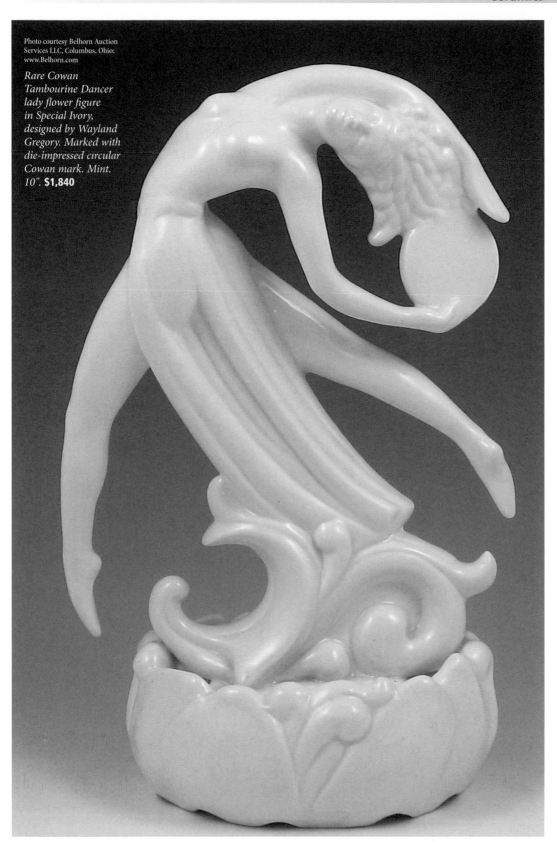

*Rare Cowan
Tambourine Dancer
lady flower figure
in Special Ivory,
designed by Wayland
Gregory. Marked with
die-impressed circular
Cowan mark. Mint.
10". **$1,840***

Cowan V-99 handled vase in Melon green designed by Viktor Schreckengost with drypoint decoration attributed to Whitney Atchley. Marked with die-impressed circular Cowan mark, COWAN in die-impressed letters and V99 in black crayon. Mint. 6". **$990**

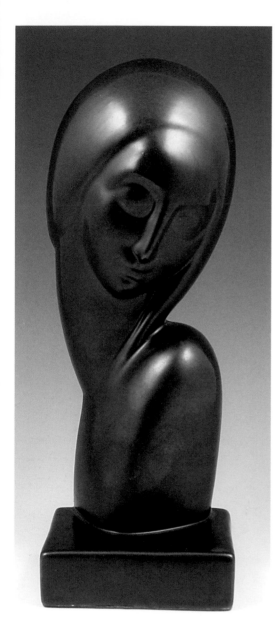

Rare Cowan Giulia figure, a limited edition, in black semi-matte glaze designed by A. Drexler Jacobson. Faintly marked with die-impressed circular Cowan mark. Mint. 9 7/8". **$1,210**

Cowan Art Deco figurine titled, "Introspection," finished in Oriental Red glaze. Designed by A. Drexler Jacobson, the glaze has obscured the typical Cowan and artist's marks on the plinth. Mint. 8 1/4". **$948**

Suzanne Crane

Suzanne Crane grew up in a family of botanists and bird-watchers in Wisconsin, but now lives in central Virginia, on the east side of the Blue Ridge Mountains. With her husband, Matthew, she opened Mud Dauber Pottery in Earlysville, Va., in 1997. She creates botanical-themed pottery and tiles.

Suzanne Crane tall lidded jar with fern motif, late 1990s, 10 1/2". **$600+**

Dedham Pottery

Alexander W. Robertson established a pottery in Chelsea, Mass., in about 1866. After his brother, Hugh Cornwall Robertson, joined him in 1868, the firm was called A. W. & H. C. Robertson. Their father, James Robertson, joined his sons in 1872, and the name Chelsea Keramic Art Works Robertson and Sons was used.

The pottery's initial products were simple flower and bean pots, but the firm quickly expanded its output to include a wide variety of artistic pottery. It produced a fine redware body used in classical forms, some with black backgrounds imitating ancient Greek and Apulian (an Iron and Bronze Age Greek colony) works. It experimented with under-glaze slip decoration on vases. The Chelsea Keramic Art Works also produced high-glazed vases, pitchers and plaques with a buff clay body, with either sculpted or molded applied decoration.

James Robertson died in 1880 and Alexander moved to California in 1884, leaving Hugh alone in Chelsea, where his experiments eventually yielded an imitation of the Chinese Ming-era blood-red glaze. Hugh's vases with that glaze were marked with an impressed "CKAW." Creating these red-glazed vases was expensive, and even though they received critical acclaim, the company declared bankruptcy in 1889.

Recapitalized by a circle of Boston art patrons in 1891, Hugh started the Chelsea Pottery U.S., which produced gray crackle-glazed dinnerware with cobalt-blue decorations, the rabbit pattern being the most popular.

The business moved to new facilities in Dedham, Mass., and began production in 1896 under the name Dedham Pottery. Hugh's son and grandson operated the business until it closed in 1943, by which time between 50 and 80 patterns had been produced.

The following marks help determine the approximate age of items:

• "Chelsea Keramic Art Works Robertson and Sons," impressed, 1874-1880.

• "CKAW," impressed, 1875-1889.

• "CPUS," impressed in a cloverleaf, 1891-1895.

• Foreshortened rabbit only, impressed, 1894-1896.

• Conventional rabbit with "Dedham Pottery" in square blue-stamped mark along with one impressed foreshortened rabbit, 1896-1928.

• Blue rabbit stamped mark, "reg. stamp" beneath, along with two impressed foreshortened rabbit marks, 1929-1943

Dedham Pottery "Polar Bear" Pattern Plate. Painted in dark blue with a border of polar bears on ice floes against a band of water. Stamped "Dedham Pottery" rabbit mark in under-glaze blue. 9 3/4" diameter. **$690**

Dedham Pottery Tri-Color "Rabbit" Pattern Plate. Painted in medium to dark blue with a border of crouching rabbits alternating with rare raised green decorated foliage. Impressed with "CPUS" mark (Chelsea Pottery US, circa 1881-1895). 8 5/8" diameter. **$8,190**

Dedham Pottery, "Elephant" Child's Mug And "Night And Morning" Pitcher. The 3 1/2" high child's mug in Elephant pattern, stamped with "DEDHAM POTTERY" blue rabbit mark. The 5" pitcher in Night and Morning pattern, stamped with "DEDHAM POTTERY/REGISTERED" blue rabbit mark. Mug with old professional repair to handle. Pitcher with flake on top edge near spout. .... **$468 pair**

Dedham Pottery, "Horse Chestnut" Pattern Steak Platter And Three Other Pieces. The first, a 14" oval platter in Horse Chestnut pattern. The second, a #1 Grape pattern 9" bowl. The third, an 8 1/2" Chick pattern plate. The fourth, a 5 1/2" Chick pattern bowl. All with the "DEDHAM POTTERY" rabbit mark in blue. The platter with some minor bubbling, all with normal crackle. .... **$3,335 all**

Six Dedham Pottery Butter Plates. Consisting of two Duck plates, one Horse Chestnut plate, one Iris plate, one Magnolia plate, and one Pond Lily plate. Four with impressed rabbit marks, and all with "DEDHAM POTTERY" rabbit marks in underglaze blue. Average diameter 6". Iris plate with worn glazing and minor discoloration, the Pond Lily with rim chips, glazing loss, and wear. **$300 all**

Dedham Pottery "Elephant And Baby" Pattern Plate. Painted in dark blue with a border of elephants walking with single calf following. Two impressed rabbit marks, also stamped "DEDHAM POTTERY REGISTERED" rabbit mark in under-glaze blue. 8 1/2" diameter. Flake in foot rim. **$805**

Dedham Pottery "Turtles" Pattern Plate. Painted in dark blue, the border with five pairs of turtles. Stamped "DEDHAM POTTERY" rabbit mark. 8 3/8" diameter. With 1/8" rim imperfection under glaze, small area of craquelure on underside of plate base. **$575**

Photo courtesy James D. Julia
Auctioneers, Fairfield, Maine;
www.JuliaAuctions.com

Unusual Dedham Pottery "Crested Duck" Pattern Plate. In medium blue, the border decorated with swimming ducks with crested heads in repeat, among rolling waves and water lilies. With impressed rabbit mark and the word "Dry" in under-glaze blue, 8 1/2" diameter. Minor foot rim flake. **$230**

Photo courtesy James D. Julia Auctioneers, Fairfield, Maine; www.JuliaAuctions.com

Dedham Pottery Pitcher, Eggcup And Creamer. Including a No. 14-size Rabbit pattern pitcher (6 1/2" h.) in the design of a No. 2 (with single blue line above rabbit band), a single eggcup in Elephant and Baby pattern (2 1/2" h.), and a Style of 1850 pattern pitcher with fluted shaped sides and leaf-tip handle (5" h.). Nominal glazing defects. **$1,404 all**

Photo courtesy James D. Julia Auctioneers, Fairfield, Maine; www.JuliaAuctions.com

Two Dedham Pottery "No. 2" Sugar Bowls. The first in Elephant And Baby pattern, the second in Elephant pattern. Each with lid and decorated with a dark blue border of striding elephants. Both with "DEDHAM POTTERY REGISTERED" rabbit mark in under-glaze blue. Each 3 1/2" overall h. x 4 1/4" diameter. **$1,380 both**

Photo courtesy James D. Julia Auctioneers, Fairfield, Maine; www.JuliaAuctions.com

Dedham Pottery "Elephant And Baby" Pattern Bowl. The No. 5 bowl with border painted in dark blue decorated with striding elephants and calf following, stamped with "DEDHAM POTTERY" rabbit mark in under-glaze blue. 5 1/4" diameter. Foot rim flake and glazing imperfections. **$690**

Photo courtesy James D. Julia Auctioneers, Fairfield, Maine; www.JuliaAuctions.com

Collection Of Dedham Pottery Cups And Saucers. Each cup-and-saucer set decorated in the following patterns: Elephant, Swan, Azalea, Magnolia, Duck, Iris, together with a Rabbit pattern demitasse set. All marked with "DEDHAM POTTERY" rabbit mark in under-glaze blue. Average c/s diameters 4" and 6" respectively. Demitasse set 2" and 4". **$1,035 all**

DOOR POTTERY

Door Pottery of Madison, Wis., was founded by Scott Draves in 2001, creating wares in the Arts & Crafts tradition.

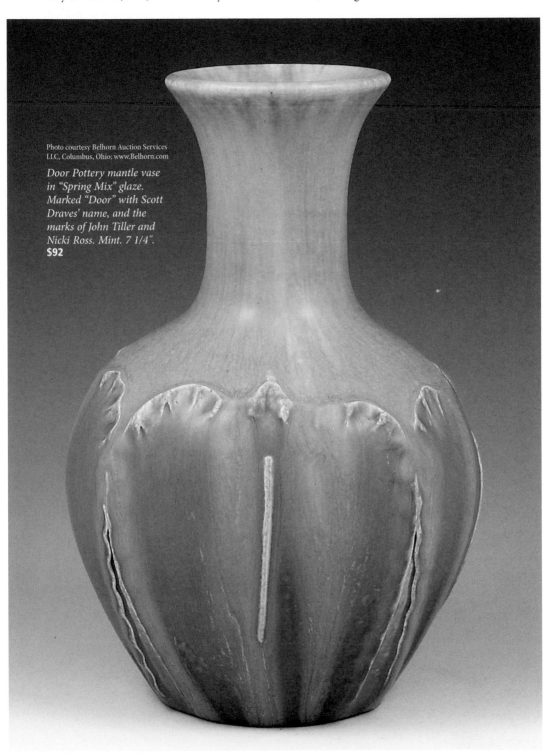

Photo courtesy Belhorn Auction Services
LLC, Columbus, Ohio; www.Belhorn.com

*Door Pottery mantle vase
in "Spring Mix" glaze.
Marked "Door" with Scott
Draves' name, and the
marks of John Tiller and
Nicki Ross. Mint. 7 1/4".*
$92

Fiesta

The Homer Laughlin China Co. introduced Fiesta, dinnerware in January 1936 at the Pottery and Glass Show in Pittsburgh. Frederick Rhead designed the pattern; Arthur Kraft and Bill Bensford molded it. Dr. A.V. Bleininger and H.W. Thiemecke developed the glazes.

The original five colors were red, dark blue, light green (with a trace of blue), brilliant yellow and ivory. A vigorous marketing campaign took place between 1939 and 1943. In mid-1937, turquoise was added. Red was removed in 1943 because some of the chemicals used to produce it were essential to the war effort; it did not reappear until 1959. In 1951, light green, dark blue and ivory were retired and forest green, rose, chartreuse and gray were added to the line. Other color changes took place in the late 1950s, including the addition of "medium green."

Fiesta, was redesigned in 1969 and discontinued about 1972. In 1986, Homer Laughlin reintroduced Fiesta. The new china body shrinks more than the old semi-vitreous and ironstone pieces, thus making the new pieces slightly smaller than the earlier pieces. The modern colors are also different in tone or hue, e.g., the cobalt blue is darker than the old blue.

Homer Laughlin has continued to introduce new colors in the popular Fiesta, pattern. It's important for collectors to understand when different colors were made.

Photo courtesy Belhorn Auction Services LLC, Columbus, Ohio; www.Belhorn.com

Door Pottery vase, with geese in the style of Paul Revere/ SEG pottery in matte green from 2004. Retired motif. Marked "Door", Scott Draves' name and Meyer. Mint. 7 1/4" x 8 1/4". **$276**

Door Pottery Curdled Fern Vase, in dark sage matte. Marked "Door" with Scott Draves' name, and the marks of John Tiller and Nicki Ross. Mint. 7 1/2". **$88**

Door Pottery Deco Vase, in cucumber green. Marked "Door" with Scott Draves' name, and the marks of John Tiller and Nicki Ross. Mint. 5 3/4". **$60**

Door Pottery Gingko cabinet vase, in "Spring Mix" glaze. Marked "Door" with Scott Draves' name, and the marks of John Tiller and Nicki Ross. Mint. 7". **$71**

Door Pottery Curled Fern vase, in cucumber green glaze. Marked "Door" with Scott Draves' name, and the marks of John Tiller and Nicki Ross. Mint. 6 1/4". **$132**

Door Pottery Tranquil Lines vase, in maple yellow glaze. Marked "Door" with Scott Draves' name, and the marks of John Tiller and Nicki Ross. Mint. 6 3/4". **$77**

Door Pottery handled cabinet vase, in cucumber green glaze. Marked "Door" with Scott Draves' name, and the marks of John Tiller and Nicki Ross. Mint. 5". **$82**

Door Pottery Paul Revere design vase, with nasturtiums. Marked "Door Pottery" (2008) with Scott Draves' name and JT. Mint. 6 1/8". **$69**

All Fiesta, listings and images in this edition come courtesy of Strawser Auction Group, Wolcottville, Ind., *www. strawserauctions.com,* facilitated by Artfact, *www.artfact. com.*

Fiesta, #1 mixing bowl lid, light green. **$190**
Fiesta, #1 mixing bowl, red. **$100**
Fiesta, #1 mixing bowl, yellow, inside rings, rim nick. **$50**
Fiesta, #2 mixing bowl lid, yellow, glaze nick. **$150**
Fiesta, #2 mixing bowl, cobalt, inside rings, rim nicks and wear to bottom. **$10**
Fiesta, #2 mixing bowl, light green, inside rings. **$50**
Fiesta, #3 mixing bowl lid, red, glaze nick. **$140**
Fiesta, #3 mixing bowl, cobalt. **$80**
Fiesta, #3 mixing bowl, light green. **$25**
Fiesta, #3 mixing bowl, yellow. **$55**
Fiesta, #4 mixing bowl lid, light green. **$250**
Fiesta, #4 mixing bowl, ivory. **$35**
Fiesta, #5 mixing bowl, turquoise. **$35**
Fiesta, #5 mixing bowl, yellow. **$40**
Fiesta, #6 mixing bowl, red, inside rings. **$90**
Fiesta, #6 mixing bowl, turquoise, glaze imperfection to bottom. **$45**
Fiesta, #7 mixing bowl, cobalt, inside rings, minor scratches to bottom. **$140**
Fiesta, #7 mixing bowl, red, wear to bottom, rim nicks. .. **$70**

Color Guide

Color Name	Color palette	Years of Production
Red	Reddish-orange	1936-43, 1959-72
Blue	Cobalt blue	1936-51
Ivory	Creamy yellow-white	1936-51
Yellow	Golden yellow	1936-69
Green	Light green	1936-51
Turquoise	Sky blue	1937-69
Rose	Dark dusky rose	1951-59
Chartreuse	Yellow-green	1951-59
Forest green	Dark hunter green	1951-59
Gray	Light gray	1951-59
Medium green	Deep bright green	1959-69
Antique gold	Dark butterscotch	1969-72
Turf green	Olive green	1969-72
Cobalt blue	Very dark blue, almost black	1986-
Rose	Bubblegum pink	1986-
White	Pearly white	1986-
Black	High gloss black	1986-
Apricot	Peach-beige	1986-98
Turquoise	Greenish-blue	1988-
Yellow	Pale yellow	1987-2002
Periwinkle blue	Pastel gray-blue	1989-
Sea mist green	Pastel light green	1991-
Lilac	Pastel violet	1993-95
Persimmon	Coral	1995-
Sapphire (Bloomingdale's exclusive)	Blue	1996-97
Chartreuse	More yellow than green	1997-99
Pearl gray	Similar to vintage gray, more transparent	1999-2001
Juniper green	Dark blue-green	1999-2001
Cinnabar	Brown-maroon	2000-
Sunflower	Muted yellow	2001-
Plum	Rich purple	2002-
Shamrock	Grassy green	2002-
Tangerine	Soft orange	2003-
Scarlet	Deep red	2004 -
Peacock	Rich light blue	2005 -
Heather	Muted burgundy	2006 - 2009
Evergreen	Dark green	2007 -
Ivory	Ivory	2008 -
Chocolate	Dark brown	2008 -
Lemongrass	Yellow green	2009 -
Marigold (75th Anniversary)	Rich yellow	2009-2010
Paprika	Cinnamon brown	2010-

Fiesta, #7 mixing bowl, turquoise. **$200**

Fiesta, 10 1/2" compartment plate group: cobalt, yellow, two turquoise, red and forest green, each with minor wear. ....**$25 all**

Fiesta, 10 1/2" compartment plate, chartreuse. **$10**

Fiesta, 10 1/2" compartment plate, gray. **$10**

Fiesta, 10 1/2" compartment plate, ivory. **$5**

Fiesta, 10 1/2" compartment plate, light green. **$20**

Fiesta, 10 1/2" compartment plate, rose. **$10**

Fiesta, 10 1/2" compartment plate, yellow. **$10**

Fiesta, 10" flower vase, ivory. **$350**

Fiesta, 10" flower vase, light green. **$170**

Fiesta, 10" flower vase, red. **$375**

Fiesta, 10" flower vase, turquoise. **$225**

Fiesta, 10" plate group, all 11 colors: medium green, gray, rose, forest green, chartreuse, red, cobalt, ivory, turquoise, light green and yellow. ....**$65 all**

Fiesta, 10" plate group: eight medium green, two with glaze misses. ....**$160 all**

Fiesta, 10" plate group: six chartreuse. ....**$40 all**

Fiesta, 10" plate group: six cobalt. ....**$15 all**

Fiesta, 10" plate group: six forest green. ....**$40 all**

Fiesta, 10" plate group: six gray. ....**$15 all**

Fiesta, 10" plate group: six ivory. ....**$15 all**

Fiesta, 10" plate group: six light green. ....**$15 all**

Fiesta, 10" plate group: six red. ....**$60 all**

Fiesta, 10" plate group: six rose. ....**$35 all**

Fiesta, 10" plate group: six turquoise. ....**$25 all**

Fiesta, 10" plate group: six yellow. ....**$10 all**

Fiesta, 11 3/4" fruit bowl, light green, rim nick. **$65**

Fiesta, 11 3/4" fruit bowl, red. **$100**

Fiesta, 12" compartment plate red and cobalt, minor nick to red. **$15**

Fiesta, 12" compartment plate, light green. **$20**

Fiesta, 12" compartment plate, yellow. **$15**

Fiesta, 12" comport, ivory. **$55**

Fiesta, 12" comport, red. **$95**

Fiesta, 12" comport, turquoise. **$50**

Fiesta, 12" flower vase, ivory. **$400**

Fiesta, 12" flower vase, turquoise. **$350**

Fiesta, bud vase with smoked brown/burnt glaze, unusual glaze. **$650**

Fiesta, carafe in experimental rose ebony color, no lid, chip to base, extremely rare. **$1,050**

Fiesta, 13" chop plate group, all six original colors, red, cobalt, ivory, turquoise, light green and yellow. ....**$35 all**

Fiesta, 13" chop plate, chartreuse. **$25**

Fiesta, 13" chop plate, forest green. **$10**

Fiesta, 13" chop plate, gray. **$5**

Fiesta, 13" chop plate, ivory. **$10**

Fiesta, 13" chop plate, medium green. **$110**

Fiesta, 13" chop plate, red. **$15**

Fiesta, 13" chop plate, rose. **$30**

Fiesta, 15" chop plate, chartreuse. **$10**

Fiesta, 15" chop plate, cobalt. **$10**

Fiesta, 15" chop plate, forest green. **$10**

Fiesta, 15" chop plate, gray. **$15**

Fiesta, 15" chop plate, ivory. **$10**

Fiesta, 15" chop plate, light green. **$5**

Fiesta, 15" chop plate, red. **$20**

Fiesta, 15" chop plate, rose. **$25**

Fiesta, 15" chop plate, turquoise and light green. **$20**

Fiesta, 15" chop plate, turquoise. **$35**

Fiesta, 15" chop plate, yellow. **$5**

Fiesta, 1955 green 10" calendar plate. **$15**

Fiesta, 1955 ivory 10" calendar plate. **$5**

Fiesta, 4 3/4" fruit bowl group, 10 colors: forest green, rose gray, chartreuse, red, cobalt, ivory, turquoise, light green and yellow. ....**$50 all**

Fiesta, 4 3/4" fruit bowl group, four turquoise. ....**$5 all**

Fiesta, 4 3/4" fruit bowl group, four yellow. ....**$5 all**

Fiesta, 4 3/4" fruit bowl group: ivory, turquoise, yellow, two gray, forest green, cobalt, chartreuse and rose. ....**$25 all**

Fiesta, 4 3/4" fruit bowl group: rose, two ivory, two yellow, light green and turquoise. ....**$20 all**

Fiesta, 4 3/4" fruit bowl, medium green. **$180**

Fiesta, 5 1/2" fruit bowl group: medium green, rose, forest green, chartreuse, red, two cobalt, ivory, turquoise, light green and yellow. ....**$80 all**

Fiesta, 5 1/2" fruit group: three yellow, turquoise, forest green and ivory. ....**$25 all**

Fiesta, 5 1/2" fruit, cobalt, "Lazarus 1851-1938 87th Anniversary." **$80**

Fiesta, 6" dessert bowl group, 50's colors: chartreuse, gray, rose, forest green, rim nick to forest green. ....**$35 all**

Fiesta, 10" plate group: five medium green. **$100 all**

Fiesta, 6" dessert bowl group: red, cobalt, turquoise, light green and yellow. ....$50 all
Fiesta, 6" dessert bowl, medium green. 160
Fiesta, 6" dessert bowl, rose. $15
Fiesta, 7" plate group, all 11 colors, medium green, chartreuse, forest green, gray, rose, red, cobalt, ivory, turquoise, light green and yellow. ....$50 all
Fiesta, 7" plate group: six chartreuse. ....$25 all
Fiesta, 7" plate group: six cobalt. ....$25 all
Fiesta, 7" plate group: six forest green. ....$25 all
Fiesta, 7" plate group: six ivory. ....$15 all
Fiesta, 7" plate group: six light green. ....$15 all
Fiesta, 7" plate group: six medium green. ....$45 all
Fiesta, 7" plate group: six red. ....$30 all
Fiesta, 7" plate group: six rose. ....$10 all
Fiesta, 7" plate group: six turquoise. ....$10 all
Fiesta, 7" plate group: six yellow. ....$10 all
Fiesta, 8 1/2" nappy bowl group, original six colors: red, cobalt, ivory, turquoise, light green and yellow. ....$35 all
Fiesta, 8 1/2" nappy bowl group: chartreuse, forest green and rose. ....$20 all

Fiesta, covered onion soup bowl, turquoise, rare. **$2,700**

Fiesta, 8 1/2" nappy bowl group: red, ivory, turquoise, yellow and light green. ....$15 all
Fiesta, 8 1/2" nappy bowl, ivory. $5
Fiesta, 8 1/2" nappy bowl, medium green. $30
Fiesta, 8 1/2" nappy bowl, rose. $5
Fiesta, 8" flower vase, ivory. $170
Fiesta, 8" flower vase, light green. $130
Fiesta, 8" flower vase, red. $250
Fiesta, 8" flower vase, turquoise, hairline. $35
Fiesta, 8" flower vase, yellow. $140
Fiesta, 9 1/2" nappy bowl, cobalt. $40
Fiesta, 9 1/2" nappy bowl, ivory. $35
Fiesta, 9 1/2" nappy bowl, light green. $35
Fiesta, 9 1/2" nappy bowl, red. $30
Fiesta, 9 1/2" nappy bowl, turquoise. $15
Fiesta, 9 1/2" nappy bowl, yellow. $35
Fiesta, 9" plate group: eight yellow. ....$10 all
Fiesta, 9" plate group: seven cobalt. ....$5 all
Fiesta, 9" trial plate in rare experimental caramel color, numbered #3431 on back. $375
Fiesta, ashtray, "Roosevelt Hotel in Pittsburgh, PA", red. .$90
Fiesta, ashtray, chartreuse. $30
Fiesta, ashtray, cobalt. $15
Fiesta, ashtray, forest green. $30
Fiesta, ashtray, gray. $10
Fiesta, ashtray, ivory. $25
Fiesta, ashtray, light green and turquoise. $30
Fiesta, ashtray, light green and yellow. $25
Fiesta, ashtray, light green. $10
Fiesta, ashtray, medium green. $130
Fiesta, bud vase, cobalt. $60
Fiesta, bud vase, ivory. $30
Fiesta, bud vase, light green. $25
Fiesta, bud vase, red. $25
Fiesta, bud vase, turquoise. $15
Fiesta, bud vase, yellow. $65
Fiesta, bulb candle holder with experimental gold glaze over light green, rare. $120
Fiesta, bulb candle holders, yellow. ....$40 pair
Fiesta, bulb candleholders, cobalt, nick to one. ....$35 pair

Fiesta, bulb candleholders, ivory. .... **$35 pair**
Fiesta, bulb candleholders, light green. .... **$40 pair**
Fiesta, bulb candleholders, three, red. .... **$65 all**
Fiesta, bulb candleholders, turquoise. .... **$35 pair**
Fiesta, carafe base, ivory. $45
Fiesta, carafe lid, turquoise, very minor nick to tip. $20
Fiesta, carafe, cobalt. $100
Fiesta, carafe, red. $95
Fiesta, carafe, turquoise. $120
Fiesta, casserole lid, forest green. $55
Fiesta, casserole lid, ivory. $20
Fiesta, casserole lid, medium green. $60
Fiesta, casserole lid, turquoise. $5
Fiesta, casserole lid, yellow. $20
Fiesta, casserole, gray. $80
Fiesta, casserole, medium green, rim chip to lid. $225
Fiesta, casserole, medium green, very minor rim glaze nick
    to base rim. $325
Fiesta, casserole, rose, rim glaze nick to base. $25
Fiesta, casserole, turquoise. $25
Fiesta, casserole, yellow. $70
Fiesta, coffee pot, cobalt, repair to finial. $20
Fiesta, coffee pot, cobalt. $70
Fiesta, coffee pot, ivory. $85
Fiesta, coffee pot, red. $100
Fiesta, coffee pot, turquoise, nick to finial. $15
Fiesta, coffee pot, yellow, nick to finial. $30
Fiesta, comport, light green. $50
Fiesta, comport, red. $50
Fiesta, covered onion soup bowl, cobalt, minor glaze nick to
    base handle. $150
Fiesta, covered onion soup bowl, ivory. $200
Fiesta, covered onion soup bowl, light green. $200
Fiesta, covered onion soup bowl, red, minor glaze nick to
    base handle. $275
Fiesta, covered onion soup bowl, yellow. $200
Fiesta, cream and sugar, chartreuse. .... **$40 both**
Fiesta, cream and sugar, gray. .... **$15 both**
Fiesta, cream and sugar, hairline to creamer, gray. ... **$5 both**
Fiesta, cream and sugar, medium green. .... **$150 both**
Fiesta, cream and sugar, minor nick to finial of sugar lid,
    medium green. .... **$60 both**

Fiesta, marmalade, red. **$160**

Fiesta, mustard, yellow. **$130**

Fiesta, cream and sugar, nick to lid finial, forest green.
    .... **$5 both**
Fiesta, cream and sugar, red. .... **$5 both**
Fiesta, cream and sugar, rose. .... **$10 both**
Fiesta, cream and sugar, turquoise. .... **$10 both**
Fiesta, cream soup group, original six colors: red, cobalt,
    ivory, turquoise, light green and yellow. .... **$180 all**
Fiesta, cream soup with metal handle, chartreuse. $45
Fiesta, cream soup with metal handle, rose. $60
Fiesta, cream soup, turquoise. $10
Fiesta, cup/saucer group, all 11 colors, medium green, gray,
    rose, forest green, chartreuse, red, cobalt, ivory, yellow,
    turquoise, and light green. .... **$45 all**
Fiesta, deep plate group, 50's colors: chartreuse, rose, gray
    and forest green. .... **$45 all**
Fiesta, deep plate group, original six colors: red, cobalt,
    ivory, turquoise, light green and yellow. .... **$80 all**
Fiesta, deep plate, medium green. $25
Fiesta, demitasse coffee pot lid, yellow. $60
Fiesta, demitasse coffee pot, ivory. $200
Fiesta, demitasse coffee pot, yellow. $150
Fiesta, demitasse cup/saucer, chartreuse. $140
Fiesta, demitasse cup/saucer, cobalt. $50
Fiesta, demitasse cup/saucer, forest green. $140
Fiesta, demitasse cup/saucer, gray. $150
Fiesta, demitasse cup/saucer, ivory. $50
Fiesta, demitasse cup/saucer, light green. $30
Fiesta, demitasse cup/saucer, red. $45
Fiesta, demitasse cup/saucer, rose. $160
Fiesta, demitasse cup/saucer, turquoise. $40
Fiesta, demitasse cup/saucer, yellow. $45
Fiesta, demitasse saucer, chartreuse, hairline. $10
Fiesta, demitasse saucer, forest green. $55
Fiesta, disk juice pitcher, celadon green. $85
Fiesta, disk juice pitcher, red. $325
Fiesta, disk juice pitcher, yellow. $5
Fiesta, disk water pitcher, chartreuse. $35
Fiesta, disk water pitcher, cobalt. $30
Fiesta, disk water pitcher, ivory. $35
Fiesta, disk water pitcher, light green. $35
Fiesta, disk water pitcher, minor nick, forest green. $10
Fiesta, disk water pitcher, red, minor nick. $25
Fiesta, disk water pitcher, turquoise. $25

Fiesta, tripod candleholders, red. **$225 pair**

Fiesta, eggcup group, original six colors: red, cobalt, ivory, turquoise, light green and yellow, nick to cobalt. ....**$100 all**

Fiesta, eggcup with experimental silver over light green glaze, rim flake, rare. **$50**

Fiesta, eggcup, chartreuse. **$45**

Fiesta, eggcup, cobalt. **$25**

Fiesta, eggcup, forest green. **$45**

Fiesta, eggcup, gray. **$50**

Fiesta, eggcup, rose. **$35**

Fiesta, figure-8 tray, turquoise. **$50**

Fiesta, French casserole, yellow. **$100**

Fiesta, footed salad bowl, red. **$300**

Fiesta, footed salad bowl, yellow. **$120**

Fiesta, go-along wood snack tray with fish toothpick holder. **$15**

Fiesta/Harlequin, teapot lid, turquoise. **$25**

Fiesta, ice-lip pitcher, cobalt. **$60**

Fiesta, ice-lip pitcher, light green. **$50**

Fiesta, ice-lip pitcher, yellow. **$45**

Fiesta, individual cream and sugar with cobalt figure-8 tray. ....**$55 set**

Fiesta, individual creamer, red. **$85**

Fiesta, individual salad bowl, medium green. **$25**

Fiesta, individual salad bowl, red. **$35**

Fiesta, individual salad bowl, turquoise. **$25**

Fiesta, medium teapot, medium green. **$600**

Fiesta, individual salad bowl, yellow. **$30**

Fiesta, ivory trial plate numbered #2779 on back. **$200**

Fiesta, juice tumbler group - original six colors: red, cobalt ivory, turquoise, light green and yellow. ....**$40 all**

Fiesta, juice tumbler group: red, cobalt, ivory, light green, yellow and rose. ....**$45 all**

Fiesta, juice tumbler, yellow. **$15**

Fiesta, Kitchen Kraft cake server, cobalt with label. **$80**

Fiesta, Kitchen Kraft covered jug, red, hairline to base. ...**$30**

Fiesta, Kitchen Kraft covered jug, yellow, rim repair to lid and nick to base. **$25**

Fiesta, Kitchen Kraft fork, light green. **$30**

Fiesta, Kitchen Kraft fork, light green. **$40**

Fiesta, Kitchen Kraft individual casserole, cobalt. **$40**

Fiesta, Kitchen Kraft individual casserole, light green. ...**$50**

Fiesta, Kitchen Kraft individual casserole, red. **$30**

Fiesta, Kitchen Kraft individual casserole, yellow. **$45**

Fiesta, Kitchen Kraft large and small casserole lids, red. ....**$10 pair**

Fiesta, Kitchen Kraft large covered jar lid, yellow. **$10**

Fiesta, Kitchen Kraft large covered jar, red. **$90**

Fiesta, Kitchen Kraft large covered jar, yellow. **$90**

Fiesta, Kitchen Kraft medium covered jar lid, red. **$40**

Fiesta, Kitchen Kraft Mexicana Oven Serve large mixing bowl, glaze imperfection in bottom of bowl. **$40**

Fiesta, Kitchen Kraft mixing bowls, small red, medium cobalt, minor nick to red. ....**$40 both**

Fiesta, Kitchen Kraft Oven Serve white small covered jar. **$80**

Fiesta, Kitchen Kraft range shakers, red. **$60**

Fiesta, Kitchen Kraft range shakers, yellow. **$45**

Fiesta, Kitchen Kraft red cake lifter and yellow cake plate. ....**$50 both**

Fiesta, Kitchen Kraft small covered jar, yellow. **$85**

Fiesta, Kitchen Kraft spoon, red. **$45**

Fiesta, Kitchen Kraft stacking set with red lid and one unit, light green and cobalt stacking units, minor nicks to each unit, lid in good condition. ....**$100 set**

Fiesta, Kitchen Kraft stacking units with red lid and one unit, yellow and light green stacking units, nick to yellow. ....**$140 all**

Fiesta, Kitchen Kraft stacking units, yellow and light green, nick to green. **$20**

Fiesta, large teapot lid, red. **$20**

Fiesta, large teapot, ivory. $35
Fiesta, large teapot, light green. $50
Fiesta, large teapot, red. $80
Fiesta, large teapot, turquoise. $40
Fiesta, light green eggcup, "Lazarus 1851-1940 89th
   Anniversary." $40
Fiesta, light green water tumbler, "Lazarus 1851-1941 90th
   Anniversary." $40
Fiesta, marmalade, light green, rim nick to base. $55
Fiesta, marmalade, turquoise. $100
Fiesta, marmalade, yellow. $110
Fiesta, medium green plate group: 10", 9" and 7". ...... $50 all
Fiesta, medium green trial 6" plate, numbered #20834 on
   back. $200
Fiesta, medium teapot lid, chartreuse. $30
Fiesta, medium teapot lid, forest green. $35
Fiesta, medium teapot lid, red. $35
Fiesta, medium teapot, chartreuse. $70
Fiesta, medium teapot, cobalt. $60
Fiesta, medium teapot, forest green. $60
Fiesta, medium teapot, gray. $55
Fiesta, medium teapot, ivory. $50
Fiesta, medium teapot, light green. $45
Fiesta, medium teapot, rose. $50
Fiesta, medium teapot, turquoise. $40
Fiesta, medium teapot, yellow. $40
Fiesta, Mexicana contemporary spoon and cake server.
   .... $50 both
Fiesta, Mexicana group: platter, two fruit bowls, cup/saucer,
   sauce boat and 6" plate. .... $75 all
Fiesta, mug group, 50's colors: forest green, chartreuse, rose
   and gray. .... $25 all
Fiesta, mug group, original six colors: red, cobalt, ivory,
   turquoise, light green and yellow. .... $45 all
Fiesta, mug, medium green. $55
Fiesta, mustard, light green. $75
Fiesta, mustard, red, minor rim nick to lid. $55
Fiesta, mustard, turquoise. $95
Fiesta, platter group, 50's colors, chartreuse, forest green,
   gray and rose. .... $25 all
Fiesta, platter group, six original colors, red, cobalt, ivory,
   turquoise, light green and yellow. .... $35 all
Fiesta, platter, ivory. $5

Fiesta, syrup pitcher, turquoise. **$130**

Fiesta, Kitchen Kraft medium covered jar, red with label.
$130

*Fiesta, relish tray, complete
all six colors: turquoise
tray, yellow center and red,
cobalt, ivory and light green
sides.* **$250**

Fiesta, platter, medium green. $50

Fiesta, platter, yellow. $5

Fiesta, Promotional casserole with yellow pie plate, cobalt casserole base and red lid. $80

Fiesta, red cream soup bowl with odd finish to handles. $30

Fiesta, red syrup tea container with cork and label, very rare. $300

Fiesta, relish tray center insert, cobalt. $25

Fiesta, relish tray center insert, turquoise. $25

Fiesta, relish tray center insert, yellow. $30

Fiesta, relish tray, complete all turquoise. $160

Fiesta, relish tray, complete all yellow. $200

Fiesta, relish tray, complete: red tray and one side, turquoise center, ivory, light green and cobalt sides. $170

Fiesta, salt/pepper, ivory. $5

Fiesta, salt/pepper, medium green. $45

Fiesta, salt/pepper, red and cobalt. $15

Fiesta, salt/pepper, red. $10

Fiesta, salt/pepper, yellow and ivory. $15

Fiesta, sauce boat, chartreuse. $25

Fiesta, sauce boat, cobalt. $35

Fiesta, sauce boat, forest green. $15

Fiesta, sauce boat, gray. $15

Fiesta, sauce boat, ivory. $15

Fiesta, sauce boat, light green. $30

Fiesta, sauce boat, red. $20

Fiesta, sauce boat, rose. $15

Fiesta, sauce boat, turquoise. $10

Fiesta, sauce boat, yellow. $20

Fiesta, stick-handle creamer, cobalt. $40

Fiesta, stick-handle creamer, light green. $20

Fiesta, stick-handle creamer, red. $25

Fiesta, stick-handle creamer, yellow. $25

Fiesta, sugar base in experimental "Lava Red" color with normal red lid, rare. $55

Fiesta, sugar lid, chartreuse. $20

Fiesta, sugar lid, ivory. $10

Fiesta, 12" flower vase, cobalt. **$400**

Fiesta, demitasse coffee pot, ivory with blue stripes, extremely rare. **$6,500**

Fiesta, sugar lid, medium green. $20

Fiesta, sugar lid, turquoise. $20

Fiesta, sugar with experimental silver over cobalt blue, rare.
....$140

Fiesta, sweets comport, cobalt. $50

Fiesta, sweets comport, ivory, marked HLC. $50

Fiesta, sweets comport, light green. $50

Fiesta, sweets comport, red, marked HLC. $60

Fiesta, sweets comport, red. $55

Fiesta, sweets comport, turquoise. $50

Fiesta, sweets comport, yellow, marked HLC. $45

Fiesta, syrup pitcher, cobalt. $140

Fiesta, syrup pitcher, ivory. $150

Fiesta, syrup pitcher, light green. $140

Fiesta, syrup pitcher, red. $170

Fiesta, syrup pitcher, yellow. $150

Fiesta, tidbit tray, three-tier: gray, chartreuse and rose. ..$45

Fiesta, tidbit tray, two-tier: turquoise and light green. $10

Fiesta, tripod candleholders, cobalt. ....**$170 pair**

Fiesta, tripod candleholders, ivory, nick to one. ....**$190 pair**

Fiesta, tripod candleholders, yellow. ....**$170 pair**

Fiesta, turquoise saucers (two) in original package.
....**$30 pair**

Fiesta, two-pint jug, chartreuse. $45

Fiesta, two-pint jug, forest green, nick to spout. $30

Fiesta, two-pint jug, ivory. $20

Fiesta, two-pint jug, red. $35

Fiesta, two-pint jug, rose. $35

Fiesta, two-pint jug, turquoise. $35

Fiesta, two-pint jug, yellow. $15

Fiesta, unlisted salad bowl, yellow. $70

Fiesta, water tumbler group, original six colors: red, cobalt, ivory, turquoise, light green and yellow. ....**$55 all**

Fiesta, water tumblers, turquoise and ivory. ....**$25 both**

Fiesta, World's Fair American Potter George Washington and Martha Washington jugs. ....**$110 pair**

Fiesta, yellow salt and pepper, employee invention, "Poor Ernie" and "Mac" under glaze. $100

Fiesta, Post 86 sapphire pyramid candle holder, rare trial piece, one of few known to exist. **$600**

Fiesta, Post 86 white 1986 experimental marmalade, rare. **$700**

Post 86

Fiesta, Post 86 2003 Conference Giveaway in baseball theme: teapot and 2 covered sugars, teapot is 1 of 40. .... **$100 all**

Fiesta, Post 86 chartreuse beverage set with dancing girl, NIB. **$35**

Fiesta, Post 86 chartreuse four-piece place setting with dinner plate, salad plate, mug and bowl, NIB. .... **$35 all**

Fiesta, Post 86 chartreuse medium vase, Millennium vase and bud vase, NIB. .... **$60 all**

Fiesta, Post 86 chartreuse wall plate clock, NIB. **$55**

Fiesta, Post 86 child's first tea set: teapot, two plates, two cups/saucers and cream/sugar, NIB. .... **$45 set**

Fiesta, Post 86 juniper set of five four-piece place settings with dinner and salad plates, mug and soup bowl. ... **$60 all**

Fiesta, Post 86 lilac beverage set. **65**

Fiesta, Post 86 lilac disc water pitcher. **$40**

Fiesta, Post 86 lilac teapot. **$50**

Fiesta, Post 86 pearl gray group: Millennium vase, eight napkin rings, two beverage sets, six chili bowls, AD cup/saucer, two mugs, pyramid candle holder, bread tray, 30 pieces. .... **$85 all**

Fiesta, Post 86 periwinkle disk water pitcher with Scottie dogs advertising Black and White Scotch. **$35**

Fiesta, Post 86 sapphire beverage set and serving tray. .... **$55 all**

Fiesta, Post 86 sapphire hostess tray, very rare, one of 12 known. **$350**

Fiesta, Post 86 turquoise salad bowl and three-piece utensil set. **$55**

Fiesta, Post 86 white Christmas group: two three-piece place settings, two salad plates and two bulb candleholders. .... **$60 all**

Fiesta, Post 86 sapphire mug, trial piece, one of about 24 known to exist. **$275**

Frankoma

John Frank was hired by the University of Oklahoma in 1927 to establish the school's first Ceramic Art Department. In 1933 he started his own business, Frank Potteries. His wife, Grace Lee, suggested that because it was Oklahoma's only commercial pottery, the company name should incorporate both their name and the state's name. The business became Frankoma Potteries, and moved to Sapulpa, a small town just southwest of Tulsa, in 1938. John Frank died in 1973, his wife in 1996. The business was sold in 1991 and is now operated by Joe Ragosta.

Photos courtesy Belhorn Auction Services LLC, Columbus, Ohio; www.Belhorn.com

Vintage Frankoma squat vase in mottled blue glaze. Marked "Frankoma". Mint. 5" x 6" wide. **$23**

Below: Early Frankoma Art Deco jug or pitcher and an Oklahoma National Youth Administration (NYA) cup. Both pieces are marked. Mint. 6 1/2" and 2 1/4". **$126 both**

Fulper Pottery Co.

The firm that became Fulper Pottery Co. of Flemington, N.J., originally made stoneware pottery and utilitarian wares beginning in the early 1800s. Fulper made art pottery from about 1909 to 1935.

The company's earliest artware was called the Vase-Kraft line (1910-1915). Its middle period (1915-1925) included some of the earlier shapes, but they also incorporated Oriental forms. Their glazing at this time was less consistent but more diverse. The last period (1925-1935) was characterized by Art Deco forms.

FULPER in a rectangle is known as the "ink mark" and dates from 1910-1915. The second mark, as shown, dates from 1915-1925; it was incised or in black ink. The final mark, FULPER, die-stamped, dates from about 1925 to 1935.

Fulper, bookend in blue Flambè. Unmarked, minute nicks to high points of the design. 4 5/8". **$77**

Fulper, bowl in blue Flambè over blue matte. Marked "Fulper", 8 3/4" diameter. **$46**

Fulper, bowl with brown and blue glaze treatment. Marked "Fulper", 6 1/4" diameter. **$57**

Fulper, bowl with handles in turquoise. Marked Fulper (incised). Deposits and stains to interior from use. 15 1/2" wide. **$44**

Fulper, bowl with light blue gloss interior and green, blue and white exterior. Marked with vertical Fulper ink stamp. Scratches and a spider line to the interior bottom that doesn't go through. 7 1/2" diameter. **$34**

Fulper, bowl with step handles. Marked "Fulper 857", 7 1/2" x 3 1/2". **$82**

Fulper, "canoe" vase in green over rose. Marked with vertical Fulper ink stamp. Mint. 6" x 3 1/2". **$69**

Fulper, bulbous vase with green over speckled brown glazes and buttresses around the rim. Marked with incised Fulper mark. Mint. 4 7/8". **$195**

Fulper, handled bowl. Marked "858 Fulper". Minute glaze pops or nicks to the edges of the piece. 9 1/2" x 4 1/2". ...**$80**

Fulper, handled fan vase in black and tan. Marked with vertical oval ink stamp. Mint. 6 1/4". **$66**

Fulper, low bowl in Flemington Green Flambè glaze. Marked with Fulper ink stamp. 9" x 2 1/8". **$23**

Fulper, vase in Flemington Green. Marked with incised vertical Fulper mark. Mint. 4 3/4". **$109**

Fulper, vase with brown and blue Flambè glaze. Marked with vertical Fulper ink stamp. Mint. 6". **$109**

Fulper, vase with green and blue Flambè over Famille Rose. Marked with incised vertical Fulper mark. Mint. 9 7/8". **$195**

Photo courtesy Belhorn Auction Services LLC, Columbus, Ohio; www.Belhorn.com

Fulper vase in Famille Rose glaze with four buttresses on a tapered form. Marked with remnants of two paper labels, 1/4" flake to the base. 8". **$241**

Photo courtesy Belhorn Auction Services LLC, Columbus, Ohio; www.Belhorn.com

Fulper handled vase with turquoise over amber glaze treatment. Marked with vertical Fulper mark, incised by hand, couple small factory grinding nicks to the edge of the base. 8 3/4". **$402**

Grueby Faience Co.

William Grueby was active in the ceramic industry for several years before he developed his own method of producing matte-glazed pottery and founded the Grueby Faience Co. of Boston in 1897.

The art pottery was hand thrown in natural shapes, hand molded and hand tooled. A variety of colored glazes, singly or in combinations, was produced, but green was the most popular. In 1908, the firm was divided into the Grueby Pottery Co. and the Grueby Faience and Tile Co. The Grueby Faience and Tile Co. made art tile until 1917, although its pottery production was phased out about 1910.

Photo courtesy Rago Arts and Auction Center, Lambertville, N.J.; www.RagoArts.com

Grueby, rare trivet tile with geese, professional restoration to minor edge chips, remnants of paper label, artist O.C. 9 1/2" square. **$7,320**

Photo courtesy Rago Arts and Auction Center, Lambertville, N.J.; www.RagoArts.com

Grueby large matte green vase with yellow blossoms, glaze run on buds, a few manganese glaze lines, circular Faience stamp, 20 and green triangle, 13" x 8". **$5,185**

Nan Hamilton

Potter Nan Hamilton founded Mudville Pottery in 1974 in Cambridge, Mass. It is now located in Somerville, Mass. Hamilton creates one-of-a-kind pieces, often with animal themes, especially Airedale motifs.

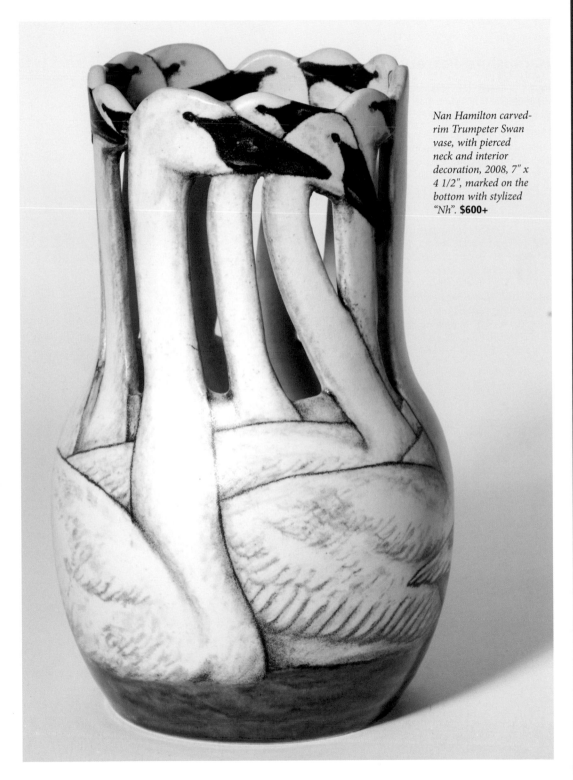

Nan Hamilton carved-rim Trumpeter Swan vase, with pierced neck and interior decoration, 2008, 7" x 4 1/2", marked on the bottom with stylized "Nh". **$600+**

Hampshire Pottery Co.

In 1871, James S. Taft founded the Hampshire Pottery Co. in Keene, N.H. Production began with redware and stoneware, followed by majolica in 1879.

Until World War I, the factory made an extensive line of utilitarian and artware, including souvenir items. After the war, the firm resumed operations, but made only hotel dinnerware and tiles. The company was dissolved in 1923.

Photos courtesy Belhorn Auction Services LLC, Columbus, Ohio; www.Belhorn.com

Arts & Crafts-style Hampshire vase in a matte blue glaze with feathered effect at the top of the vase. Marked with impressed "Hampshire Pottery 33" with an M in a circle and numbers in blue. Mint, 6 1/2". **$575**

Below: Early Hampshire squat vase in dark brown under a dark orange glaze. A souvenir piece, remnants of Portsmouth, N.H., in gold leaf remain. Marked "JST & CO KEENE NH", 1 5/8" x 4 1/4". **$110**

Hull Pottery Co.

In 1905, Addis E. Hull purchased the Acme Pottery Co. of Crooksville, Ohio. In 1917, the A.E. Hull Pottery Co. began making art pottery, novelties, stoneware and kitchenware, later including the famous Little Red Riding Hood line. Most items had a matte finish, with shades of pink and blue or brown predominating.

After a flood and fire in 1950, the factory reopened in 1952 as the Hull Pottery Co. New pieces, mostly with a glossy finish, were produced. The firm closed in 1985.

Pre-1950 vases are marked "Hull USA" or "Hull Art USA" on the bottom. Many also retain their paper labels. Post-1950 pieces are marked "Hull" in large script or "HULL" in block letters.

Each pattern has a distinctive letter or number, e.g., Wildflower has a "W" and a number; Water Lily, "L" and number; Poppy, numbers in the 600s; Orchid, in the 300s. Early stoneware pieces are marked with an "H."

Photo courtesy Belhorn Auction Services LLC, Columbus, Ohio; www.Belhorn.com

Hull Open Rose basket in pink and blue. Marked Hull USA 107-8". Mint, 8 3/8" x 7". **$110**

Photos courtesy Belhorn Auction Services LLC, Columbus, Ohio; www.Belhorn.com

Hull Wildflower pitcher in pink and blue. Marked Hull Art USA W-11-8 1/2". Mint, 8 3/4". **$92**
Below: Wildflower vase in pink and blue. Marked Hull Art USA W-9-8 1/2". Mint, 8 3/4". **$126**

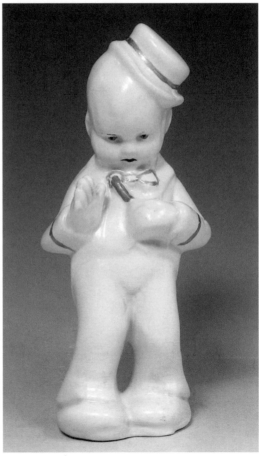

Photo courtesy Belhorn Auction Services LLC, Columbus, Ohio; www.Belhorn.com

Hull bandleader from the five-piece band. Unmarked. Mint, 6 3/8". **$40**

Jackson Pottery

Robert Jackson, Rock Island, Ill., has produced a variety of face jugs over the last two decades.

Set of three Robert Jackson face jugs: See No Evil, Hear No Evil, Speak No Evil, late 1990s, stamped "Jackson Pottery" and signed in script on the bottoms, artist commission, each 9 3/4". **$900+ set**

(Based on the 17th-century carving of the Three Wise Monkeys at Toshogu shrine, Nikko, Japan.)

Warren MacKenzie

Warren MacKenzie (b. 1924) is a craft potter living outside Stillwater, Minn. MacKenzie studied with Bernard Leach from 1949 to 1952. His simple, wheel-thrown functional pottery is heavily influenced by the oriental aesthetic of Shoji Hamada and Kanjiro Kawai. He taught at the University of Minnesota beginning in 1952, and is now a professor emeritus.

Warren MacKenzie trumpet vase with dome top, made in 2000, unsigned, 10". **$200+**

Marblehead

This hand-thrown pottery was first made in 1905 as part of a therapeutic program introduced by Dr. J. Hall for the patients confined to a sanitarium located in Marblehead, Mass. In 1916, production was removed from the hospital to another site. The factory continued under the directorship of Arthur E. Baggs until it closed in 1936. Most pieces found today are glazed with a smooth, porous, even finish in a single color. The most desirable pieces have a conventional design with one or more subordinate colors.

Marblehead, Arts & Crafts pitcher in matte green with dark band around the rim and handle. Marked with impressed ship mark and signed by the artist. Professionally restored handle and spout, 7 3/4"..........**$357**

Marblehead, flower pot-shaped vase in speckled brown. Marked with MP Ship mark. Mint, 5" x 6"......................**$60**

Marblehead, matte green squat vase with blue gloss interior. Marked with MP Ship mark. Mint, 3" x 5 1/2". **$275**

Marblehead, tray or underplate in shades of blue. Marked with impressed MP ship mark. Mint, 5 1/2" diameter. ...**$49**

Photo courtesy Belhorn Auction Services LLC, Columbus, Ohio; www.Belhorn.com

Marblehead hand-thrown pitcher signed by Arthur E. Baggs from 1936. Glazed in dark matte blue on the exterior with a lighter interior. Signed AEB by hand in script with the date. Mint, 7 3/4". **$550**

Photo courtesy Belhorn Auction Services LLC, Columbus, Ohio; www.Belhorn.com

Marblehead vase with Arts & Crafts flower and tree decoration. Finished in four colors with a blue semi-gloss interior. Marked with impressed ship mark. Invisible restoration to a rim chip, 3 1/2". **$1,092**

McCoy Pottery

The J. W. McCoy Pottery Co. was established in Roseville, Ohio, in September 1899. The early McCoy company produced both stoneware and some art pottery lines, including Rosewood. In October 1911, three potteries merged, creating the Brush-McCoy Pottery Co. This firm continued to produce the original McCoy lines and added several new art lines. Much of the early pottery is not marked.

In 1910, Nelson McCoy and his father, J. W. McCoy, founded the Nelson McCoy Sanitary Stoneware Co. In 1925, the McCoy family sold their interest in the Brush-McCoy Pottery Co. and started to expand and improve the Nelson McCoy Co. The new company produced stoneware, earthenware specialties, and artware.

Marks: The Nelson McCoy Co. made most of the pottery marked "McCoy."

J.W. McCoy Olympia vase, with rare cream-drip glaze overflow, early 1900s, marked 28, 5 1/4" h. **$80-$90**

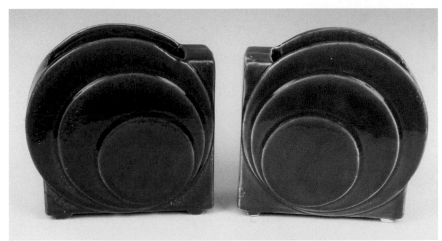

Two Disc vases in glossy cobalt blue and burgundy, 1940s, also found in yellow and white, USA mark, 6 3/4" h. **$40-$50 each**

Three Leaves and Berries fan vases, commonly found in aqua, pink, white and yellow; cobalt blue is hard to find, and the under-glaze decorated example at left is very rare; late 1930s or early '40s, McCoy USA or unmarked, 6" h, from left: **$75-$100; $50-$60; $30-$40.** *Beware of reproductions, which are lighter, have soft mold details, and thinner glazes.*

Sand Dollar vase in matte white, stoneware, 1940s, unmarked, also found in pastel colors, and brown and green, **$100-$125, depending on color.**

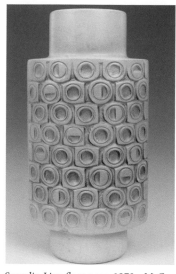

Scandia Line floor vase, 1970s, McCoy LCC mark, 14 1/2" h, **$25-$35**

Tall Scroll vase in matte green (often found in glossy tan-brown), late 1940s, USA mark, 14" h, **$50-$700**

From left: Grape vase in gold trim, 1950s, McCoy USA mark, also found with brown and green glazes, 9" h, **$40-$50.**
Sunburst gold vase, 1950s, faint McCoy USA mark, 6" h, **$30-$40**

From left: Tassel vase in glossy raspberry, 1930s, stoneware, unmarked, 8" h, **$25-$35.**
Flower pot with cold-paint decoration, 1940s, shield mark 10, 6" h, **$35-$45**

Matthew Metz

Matthew Metz (b. 1961) is a ceramic artist living and working in Alfred, N.Y. His pots are created from porcelain or a porcelainous clay body and salt glazed. His influences include Asian pottery traditions, Greek and Roman pots, early American decorative arts (quilts, face jugs) and other folk traditions. Metz uses a variety of techniques in developing the surfaces of his pots, including carving, drawing, and "sprigging."

Matthew Metz folk-influenced vase with carved faces, leaves, and pottery motifs, circa 2000, signed on the bottom, 10". **$350+**

Matthew Metz bowl with carved details of plant growing out of pot, circa 2000, signed on bottom, 9" diameter. **$200+**

Matthew Metz platter with carved details of face looking out of trees, late 1990s, signed on bottom, 14" diameter. **$1,200+**

Muncie Pottery

Muncie Pottery started production of art pottery in 1919 as the Muncie Clay Products Co. This Indiana firm used a variety of glazes ranging from quality matte glaze to high gloss, drip glazes. Some of the most sought-after Muncie Pottery examples include the Ruba Rombic and Spanish lines. Both of these scarce patterns were designed by Reuben Haley.

Muncie Pottery can be found both marked and unmarked. Marked examples are usually stamped "Muncie" and/or marked with molder/finisher marks. These marks include a combination of letters (A, B, D, E, K, and M) and numbers (I, II, 2, 3, 4 and 5) such as 2-B, D-3, etc. Muncie went out of business in 1939.

Muncie, vase with ruffled rim in gunmetal black. Marked MUNCIE and 2A. Mint, 5 3/4"..$57

Muncie, corset vase in Matte Blue over Rose. Marked I-B. Tight, short hairline to rim, 9 1/8".................................$46

Muncie, #119 corset vase in Matte White over Blue. Marked MUNCIE. Mint, 9"..$46

Muncie, bud vase in Matte Green over Rose. Marked IE. Mint with factory grinding chip to the edge of the base, 7 1/8"...$38

Muncie, vase with square rim in Matte White over Blue. Marked MUNCIE and IA. Mint, 7 1/2"............................$66

Muncie, vase in Matte Green over Pumpkin. Marked Muncie. Mint, 8 3/4"...$77

Muncie, vase in Matte Green over Rose. Marked I-K. Mint, 6"...$69

Muncie, fan vase in Matte Green over Pumpkin. Marked with an incised 4. Mint, 7 1/2" x 7 1/2". $49

Muncie, handled vases in Matte Green over Pumpkin, including a #420 with angled handles and a #143 with curved handles. Marked with an incised A and 4, respectively. Both are mint. The #420 does have a number of factory glaze bursts to the body and near the handles, 7 1/2" and 6 1/2". ....**$82 pair**

Muncie, vase with horizontal ridges in Matte Green over Pumpkin. Marked with an incised A. Some slightly darkened crazing, 7 1/4". $44

Muncie, vase in Peachskin glaze. Marked I-D. Mint with a few small grinding nicks to the edge of the base, 6 5/8". $63

Photo courtesy Belhorn Auction Services LLC, Columbus, Ohio; www.Belhorn.com

Muncie handled vase in Peachskin. Marked D-3. Mint with a couple of small factory grinding nicks to the base. 6 7/8". **$57**

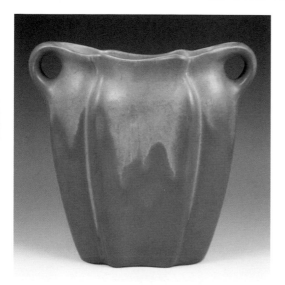

Photo courtesy Belhorn Auction Services LLC, Columbus, Ohio; www.Belhorn.com

Muncie #192 handled vase in Matte Green over Pumpkin glaze. Marked MUNCIE with an incised IA and 192-9 in black crayon. Mint, 9" x 9". **$71**

Photo courtesy Belhorn Auction Services LLC, Columbus, Ohio; www.Belhorn.com

Muncie #100 vase in Gloss Blue over Green. Unmarked. Mint, 8 3/8". **$52**

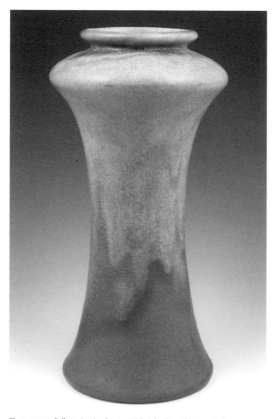

Photo courtesy Belhorn Auction Services LLC, Columbus, Ohio; www.Belhorn.com

Muncie #U-2 Matte Green over Rose vase. Marked with an incised 2B. Mint with some minor factory grinding nicks to the edge of the base, 11 5/8". **$121**

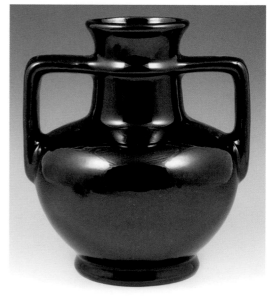

Photo courtesy Belhorn Auction Services LLC, Columbus, Ohio; www.Belhorn.com

Muncie handled vase in Gloss Black. Marked with I-E (incised), 7 1/2". **$11**

Newcomb College

The Sophie Newcomb Memorial College, an adjunct of Tulane University in New Orleans, was originated as a school to train local women in the decorative arts. While metalworking, painting and embroidery were among the classes taught, the production of handcrafted art pottery remains its most popular and collectible pursuit.

Pottery was made by the Newcomb women for nearly 50 years, with earlier work being the rarest and most valuable. This is characterized by glossy finishes and broad, flat-painted and modeled designs. More common, though still quite valuable, are the matte-glaze pieces, often depicting bayou scenes and native flora. All bear the impressed NC mark.

Photos courtesy Belhorn Auction Services LLC, Columbus, Ohio; www.Belhorn.com

Above: Paul Cox glaze effect cabinet vase. Cox was the Director of Newcomb College's School of Art from 1910 to 1918. Marked "The Paul E. Cox Pottery New Orleans Louisiana." Mint, 3 1/8" tall. **$99**

Left: Newcomb College cabinet vase with Art Nouveau decoration from 1925 by Sadie Irvine (artist) and Joseph Meyer (potter). Marked with NC logo, OV28 and JM and SI (both faint), short and light glaze scratch, 3 1/2". **$1,265**

Newcomb College, squat vessel with carved freesia decoration by Anna Frances Simpson from 1914. Marked with NC logo, "JM" for potter Joseph Meyer, GP34, 260, a circle C for buff clay and Simpson's mark. Mint, 5 3/4" x 3". **$1,725**

North Dakota School of Mines

The North Dakota School of Mines was established in 1890. Earle J. Babcock, a chemistry instructor, was impressed with the high purity level of North Dakota potter's clay. He tried to interest commercial potteries in the North Dakota clay, but had limited success.

In 1910, Babcock persuaded the school to establish a ceramics department. Margaret Cable, who studied under Charles Binns and Frederick H. Rhead, was appointed head. She remained until her retirement in 1949.

Decorative emphasis was placed on native themes, including flowers and animals. Art Nouveau, Art Deco and fairly plain pieces were made.

The pottery is often marked with a cobalt blue underglaze circle of the words "University of North Dakota/Grand Forks, N.D./Made at School of Mines/N.D. Clay." Some early pieces are marked only "U.N.D." or "U.N.D./Grand Forks, N.D." Most pieces are numbered (they can be dated from University records) and signed by both the instructor and student. Cable-signed pieces are the most desirable.

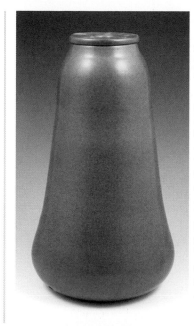

Photo courtesy Belhorn Auction Services LLC, Columbus, Ohio; www.Belhorn.com

UND School of Mines lamp base in blue matte from 1929. Marked with circular ink stamp and "Lila M. Argue Jan. 1929" (incised). There is a kiln kiss to the base, otherwise mint. The cap has a shallow flake to the underside, 10 3/4". **$99**

Photo courtesy Belhorn Auction Services LLC, Columbus, Ohio; www.Belhorn.com

UND School of Mines low bowl with ivory matte exterior and light blue gloss interior from 1944. Marked with circular UND stamp and signed "Gronbeck 3-31-44", 8 3/4" x 1 1/2" tall. **$99**

Photo courtesy Belhorn Auction Services LLC, Columbus, Ohio; www.Belhorn.com

UND School of Mines vase with cutout leaves, finished in a marbleized brown gloss glaze. Marked with UND circular stamp and "Minn" incised by the artist, 5 1/4" x 3 1/4". **$218**

George E. Ohr

Ohr pottery was produced by George E. Ohr in Biloxi, Miss. There is a discrepancy as to when he actually established his pottery; some say 1878, but Ohr's autobiography indicates 1883. In 1884, Ohr exhibited 600 pieces of his work, suggesting that he had been a potter for some time.

Ohr's techniques included twisting, crushing, folding, denting and crinkling thin-walled clay into odd, grotesque and sometimes graceful forms. His later pieces were often left unglazed.

In 1906, Ohr closed the pottery and stored more than 6,000 pieces as a legacy to his family. The entire collection remained in storage until it was rediscovered in 1972.

Today, Ohr is recognized as one of the leaders in the American art-pottery movement.

Much of Ohr's early work was signed with an impressed stamp including his name and location in block letters. His later work was often marked with the flowing script designation "G. E. Ohr."

Photo courtesy Rago Arts and Auction Center, Lambertville, N.J.; www.RagoArts.com

George Ohr dimpled vase in black speckled glaze, stamped G.E. OHR Biloxi, Miss., 4 1/2" x 3 1/2". **$2,074**

Photo courtesy Rago Arts and Auction Center, Lambertville, N.J.; www.RagoArts.com

George Ohr squat vessel in raspberry volcanic glaze, a couple minor flakes, stamped G.E. OHR, Biloxi, Miss., 2 1/4" x 4". **$5,795**

Overbeck Pottery

Four Overbeck sisters – Margaret, Hannah, Elizabeth and Mary Frances – established the Overbeck Pottery in their Cambridge City, Ind., home in 1911. Production ended with the death of Mary Frances in 1955.

Photo courtesy Rago Arts and Auction Center, Lambertville, N.J.; www.RagoArts.com

Overbeck early vase by Hannah and Elizabeth Overbeck with three panels carved and painted with owls on branches, in teals and purple against a brown ground. (A rare and early example decorated in the Arts & Crafts style, as opposed to the Art Deco influence more often seen.) Carved mark, OBK E H, 7 1/2" x 4". **$19,200**

Owens Pottery

J.B. Owens began making pottery in 1885 near Roseville, Ohio. In 1891, he built a plant in Zanesville and in 1897, began producing art pottery. After 1907, most of the firm's production centered on tiles.

Owens Pottery, employing many of the same artists and designs as its two cross-town rivals, Roseville and Weller, can appear similar to that of its competitors, e.g., Utopian (brown glaze), Lotus (light glaze) and Aqua Verde (green glaze).

There were a few techniques used exclusively at Owens. These included Red Flame ware (slip decoration under a high red glaze) and Mission (over-glaze, slip decorations in mineral colors) depicting Spanish Missions. Other specialties included Opalesce (semi-gloss designs in luster gold and orange) and Coralene (small beads affixed to the surface of the decorated vases).

Photos courtesy Belhorn Auction Services LLC, Columbus, Ohio; www.Belhorn.com

Top right: J.B. Owens Majolica jardiniere in blended green and blue glaze with griffins. Marked with raised J.B. Owens shield mark, 10 1/2" x 9". **$121**

Right: Owens Utopian ashtray or bowl with matches and a cigarette, signed "HL" by the artist. Marked "J.B. Owens Utopian 962", 3 1/4" x 1 7/8". **$103**

Below: Owens Matte Utopian jardiniere with tulip decoration and "pie crust" rim. Unmarked. Mint, 8" x 9 1/2". **$71**

Peters & Reed

J.D. Peters and Adam Reed founded their pottery in South Zanesville, Ohio, in 1900. Common flowerpots, jardiniéres and cooking wares comprised the majority of their early output. Occasionally, art pottery was attempted, but it was not until 1912 that their Moss Aztec line was introduced and widely accepted. Other art wares include Chromal, Landsun, Montene, Pereco and Persian.

Peters retired in 1921 and Reed changed the name of the firm to Zane Pottery Co.

Marked pieces of Peters & Reed pottery are extremely rare.

Peters & Reed, Moss Aztec tulip vase. Unmarked. Mint, 12"...**$172**

Peters & Reed, Wilse Blue hexagonal vase. Unmarked. Mint, 10 1/4"..**$63**

Peters & Reed, Scenic Landsun vase. Unmarked. Mint, 8 1/2". **$517**

Peters & Reed, Mirror Black cat doorstop. Unmarked open bottom. Loss to one ear and two large chips to the inner rim of the open base, 9 7/8"..............................**$23**

Peters & Reed, Wilse Blue vase. Unmarked, 6 3/4". **$11**

Peters & Reed, Landsun jardiniere. Unmarked. There is an unobtrusive age line to the underside, 7 1/2" x 6 1/4".....**$40**

Peters & Reed, Landsun bowl in blue and yellow. Marked with Zaneware impressed stamp. Some loose glaze and loss to the interior, 6 3/8" x 2".....................................**$11**

Peters & Reed, wall pocket in blue. Unmarked, 9".........**$63**

Photos courtesy Belhorn Auction Services LLC, Columbus, Ohio; www.Belhorn.com

Top right: Peters & Reed marbleized vase in green, blue and yellow tones. Unmarked. There is a factory kiln kiss to the side of the vase and scratches to the glaze, 8 3/4". **$103**

Right: Peters & Reed Shadow Ware pumpkin vase in blue and green drip over brownish orange. Mint, 8". **$178**

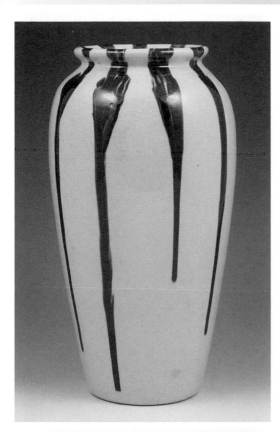

Photos courtesy Belhorn Auction Services LLC, Columbus, Ohio; www.Belhorn.com

Left: Peters & Reed Shadow Ware vase with elongated blue drip over a light yellowish cream body. Unmarked. Mint, 8 7/8". **$138**

Bottom left: Peters & Reed wall pocket in green. Unmarked, 9". **$104**

Below: Peters & Reed handled vase in dark blue high glaze. Unmarked, 14". **$44**

Red Wing, "Woman with Two Tubes," double bud vase No. 1175, designed by Charles Murphy, 1942, 10 1/2" h. **$700+**

RED WING POTTERY

The Red Wing pottery category includes several potteries from Red Wing, Minn. In 1868, David Hallem started Red Wing Stoneware Co., the first pottery with stoneware as its primary product. The Minnesota Stoneware Co. started in 1883. The North Star Stoneware Co. was in business from 1892 to 1896.

The Red Wing Stoneware Co. and the Minnesota Stoneware Co. merged in 1892. The new company, the Red Wing Union Stoneware Co., made stoneware until 1920 when it introduced a pottery line that it continued until the 1940s. In 1936, the name was changed to Red Wing Potteries, Inc. During the 1930s, this firm introduced several popular patterns of hand-painted dinnerware, which were distributed through department stores, mail-order catalogs, and gift-stamp centers. Dinnerware production declined in the 1950s and was replaced with hotel and restaurant china in the early 1960s. The plant closed in 1967.

Marks: Red Wing Stoneware Co. was the first firm to mark pieces with a red wing stamped under the glaze. The North Star Stoneware Co. used a raised star and the words "Red Wing" as its mark.

Red Wing vase with pink stylized leaves and yellow interior. Marked Red Wing 1203 USA. Mint, 10". **$22**

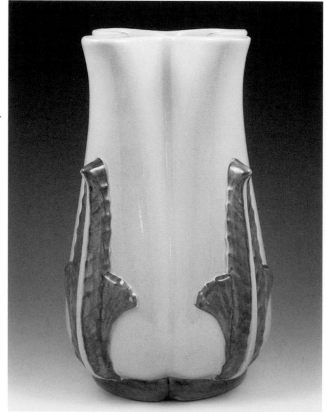

Country Garden dinner plate, 1953, from the Anniversary line, 11" diameter. **$10+**

Crazy Rhythm covered casserole, 1955, part of the Futura line, 11 1/2" wide, impressed mark, "Red Wing USA." **$25+**

Desert water pitcher, left, No. 252, 1952, part of the Fancy Free line, 10" tall, ink-stamped, "Red Wing Hand Painted." $50+

Caprice beverage server, 1952, part of the Fancy Free line, 10 1/2" tall, ink-stamped, "Red Wing Hand Painted." $60+

Coffee "Dripolators", two styles, late 1930s; left, 7 1/2" tall, impressed mark, "Red Wing"; right, No. 255, 6 3/4" tall, unmarked. $40+ each

Rookwood

Maria Longworth Nichols Storer of Cincinnati founded Rookwood Pottery in 1880. The name of the pottery came from her family estate, Rookwood, named for the crows that inhabited the grounds.

Though the Rookwood pottery filed for bankruptcy in 1941, it was soon reorganized under new management. Efforts at maintaining the pottery proved futile, and it was sold in 1956 and again in 1959. The pottery was moved to Starkville, Miss., in conjunction with the Herschede Clock Co. It finally ceased operating in 1967.

There are five elements to the Rookwood marking system: the clay or body mark, the size mark, the decorator mark, the date mark and the factory mark. The best way to date Rookwood art pottery is from factory marks.

From 1880 to 1882, the factory mark was the name "Rookwood" incised or painted on the base. Between 1881 and 1886, the firm name, address and year appeared in an oval. Beginning in 1886, the impressed "RP" monogram appeared and a flame mark was added for each year until 1900. After 1900, Roman numerals, indicating the last two digits of the year of production, were added at the bottom of the "RP" flame mark.

Rookwood, Art Deco vase from 1926 with floral design encircling the body and geometric band around the neck by William Hentschel. Marked with Rookwood logo, XXVI, the shape number 2903 and the artist's mark in black. There is a minute 3/16" nick to the outer rim, X'ed for no obvious reason, 9 3/4". **$299**

Rookwood, Arts & Crafts cabinet bowl from 1915 in matte blue with a touch of matte green at the top. Marked with Rookwood logo, XIV and the shape number 2159. Mint, 4 1/2" x 1 7/8". **$121**

Rookwood, Barbarosa stein from 2008 made for the Christian Moerlein Brewing Co. in Cincinnati. Includes original wood presentation box as well as information on the revival of the Rookwood Co. Marked with Rookwood logo, MMVIII and the number 10018. It is also signed in the mold by the team of artists at Rookwood. Mint and uncrazed, 7 5/8". (In 2006 the revived Rookwood Pottery Co. began to produce wares in Cincinnati again.) **$115**

Rookwood, early cup with cobalt blue floral decoration and gold highlights. Marked Rookwood ETK. Bruise with hairlines to the base with a factory stilt pull, 3 5/8". **$38**

Rookwood, grotesque face ashtray. Marked with Rookwood logo, 2457 and raised animal logo and the date, which is obscured by the glaze. Mint, 5 3/4". **$63**

Rookwood, handled vase in ivory matte from 1932. Marked with Rookwood logo, XXXII and the shape number 6254. Mint, 4 5/8". **$86**

Rookwood, ivory matte vase from 1937 with Art Nouveau design. Marked with Rookwood logo, XXXVII and the shape number 6510. Mint, 5". **$126**

Photo courtesy Belhorn Auction Services LLC, Columbus, Ohio; www.Belhorn.com

Rookwood decorated matte glaze vase with abstract floral decoration on a pink background by Sallie E. Coyne from 1930. Marked with Rookwood logo, XXX, the shape number 2721, a fan-shaped marked used during Rookwood's 50th year and the artist's mark in blue. Mint. The vase is X'ed, due to some glaze pooling at the base and subsequent factory grinding flakes, 6 1/8" tall. **$220**

Rookwood, ivory matte vase from 1940 with stylized leaves. Marked with Rookwood logo, XL and the shape number 2854. Mint, 4 1/2". **$55**

Rookwood, Jewel Porcelain vase with decoration of grape leaves and vines by William Hentschel from 1923. A drill hole to the bottom has been restored, requiring the marks to be reconstructed. They include the Rookwood logo, XXIII, the shape number 2528 and the artist's mark. The vase is uncrazed and without further damage or repairs, 8 1/8". **$374**

Rookwood, Limoges vase from 1883 with insects and bamboo-style foliage by Albert R. Valentien. Marked ROOKWOOD, 1883 with the shape number 97 and R for red clay. Also marked A.R.V. by the artist. Mint, 7 1/4" x 5 3/4". **$604**

Rookwood, matching pair of vases from 1946 with colorful leaves in high glaze decoration by Kay Ley. Marked with

Rookwood logo, XLVI, the shape number 922D and signed Ley. One is numbered 4542 while the other is 4543. Mint and uncrazed, 7 1/2". .... **$605 pair**

Rookwood, matte green creamer and sugar from 1926. Both are marked with Rookwood logo, XXVI and the shape number 547. Mint, 3 3/8" and 1 7/8". .... **$77 pair**

Rookwood, Scenic Vellum vase from 1925 by E.T. Hurley. Wooded scene with colorful, pink sky in the background. A drill hole to the bottom has been restored, requiring the marks to be reconstructed. They include the Rookwood logo, XXV, the shape number 2544, V for Vellum and the artist's mark. There are two tight, almost invisible 1" to 1 1/2" lines to the glaze that extend up from one the stilt marks on the underside of the base. 8". **$805**

Rookwood, Standard Glaze vase from 1898 with slender-neck form and floral decoration by Katherine Hickman. Marked with Rookwood logo with 12 flames, the shape number 806D and the artist's incised mark, 6 7/8". **$230**

Rookwood, Standard Glaze vase from 1900 with floral decoration by Josephine Zettel. Marked with Rookwood logo with 14 flames, 614F and the artist's incised mark, 6". **$357**

Rookwood, Standard Glaze vase from 1903 with dandelion decoration by Jeanette Swing. Marked with Rookwood logo, III, the shape number 906E and the artist's incised mark. A tight 3/4" hairline descends from the rim, 4 1/8" x 5". **$187**

Rookwood, Standard Glaze vase with berries and leaves by Lena Hanscom. Marked with Rookwood logo, II, the shape number 927F and the artist's initials. The vase has had an overspray applied, but it not apparent if this was due to a restoration, 5 1/2". **$110**

Rookwood, vase from 1928 in matte green over pink with floral motif. Marked with Rookwood logo, XXVIII and the shape number 1712. Mint, 9 1/4". **$385**

Rookwood, vase from 1928 in matte green over pink. Marked with Rookwood logo, XXVIII and the shape number 2139. Mint, 4 3/4". **$74**

Rookwood, vase from 1945 with bleeding heart design finished in Colonial Buff glaze. Marked with Rookwood logo, XLV and the shape number 6855. Mint, 10 1/2". **$88**

Rookwood, vase from 1951 in chartreuse gloss with molded lotus decoration. Marked with Rookwood logo, LI and the shape number 6833. Mint, 6 1/4". **$115**

Rookwood, vase from 1956 in turquoise gloss with molded lotus decoration. Marked with Rookwood logo, LVI, the shape number 6833 and Rookwood Cinti. Mint, 6 3/8". **$121**

Rookwood, vase in Double Vellum or decorated matte glaze with decoration of flowers and berries encircling the yellow body by C.S. Todd. Marked with Rookwood logo, date mark XX (1920), the shape number 892C and CST. Clean drill hole in the base, 9 1/4" tall. **$345**

Rookwood, vase in ivory matte with turquoise gloss lining from 1929. Marked with Rookwood logo, XXIX and the shape number 6098. Mint, 4 3/4". **$99**

Rookwood, vase with life-like floral decoration by Elizabeth Lincoln from 1903, finished in Standard Glaze. Marked with Rookwood logo, III, the shape number 939C and the artist's mark. There are two small abrasions to the

Photo courtesy Belhorn Auction Services LLC, Columbus, Ohio; www.Belhorn.com

Rookwood vase from 1925 by William E. Hentschel. Finished in Jewel Porcelain glaze, dark blue floral decor has been added to a turquoise background. Marked with Rookwood logo, XXV, shape number 2499A and the artist's mark. Mint and virtually uncrazed. X'ed due to factory grinding chips to glaze pooling at the base, 18 3/4" tall. **$1,150**

glaze and a few glaze scratches, X'ed, presumably due to the darkness of the piece, 8 1/4". **$207**

Rookwood, Z-line Arts & Crafts footed bowl from 1901 with incised design on the inside and finished in matte blue and green. Marked with Rookwood logo, 238Z and the incised initials "RCM" by an unknown artist. Mint, 7" x 2 5/8". **$546**

Roseville

In the late 1880s, a group of investors purchased the J.B. Owens Pottery in Roseville, Ohio, and made utilitarian stoneware items. In 1892, the firm was incorporated and joined by George F. Young, who became general manager. Four generations of the Young family controlled Roseville until the early 1950s.

Roseville Blackberry 573-6" double-handled vase. Unmarked. Mint, 6 1/4" x 6". **$253**

A series of acquisitions began: Midland Pottery of Roseville in 1898, Clark Stoneware Plant in Zanesville (formerly used by Peters and Reed), and Muskingum Stoneware (Mosaic Tile Co.) in Zanesville. In 1898, the offices also moved from Roseville to Zanesville.

In 1900, Roseville introduced Rozane, an art pottery. Rozane became a trade name to cover a large series of lines. The art lines were made in limited amounts after 1919.

The success of Roseville depended on its commercial lines, first developed by John J. Herald and Frederick Rhead in the first decades of the 1900s. In 1918, Frank Ferrell became art director and developed more than 80 lines of pottery. In the 1940s, a series of high-gloss glazes were tried in an attempt to revive certain lines. In 1952, Raymor dinnerware was produced. None of these changes brought economic success and in November 1954, Roseville was bought by the Mosaic Tile Co.

Also see *Cookie Jars.*

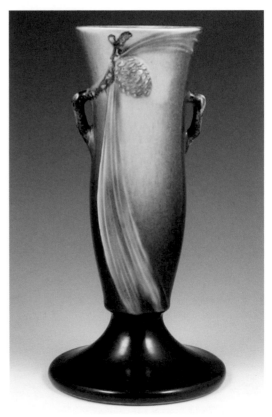

Roseville blue Pine Cone vase. Marked 705 in red crayon. Mint, 9 3/8". **$357**

Roseville Gardenia handled floor vase in green. Uncommon form. Marked Roseville USA 690-16". Spider line to bottom and a light one just above on the flowers, 16 3/8". **$230**

Photo courtesy Belhorn Auction Services LLC, Columbus, Ohio; www.Belhorn.com

Roseville Silhouette rose bowl in turquoise with molded nudes. Marked Roseville USA 742-6". Mint, 9" x 6". **$220**

Photo courtesy Belhorn Auction Services LLC, Columbus, Ohio; www.Belhorn.com

Roseville Montacello 564-9" vase in blue with handles. Unmarked. There is a restoration to what appears to be a hairline descending from the rim, 9 1/4". **$241**

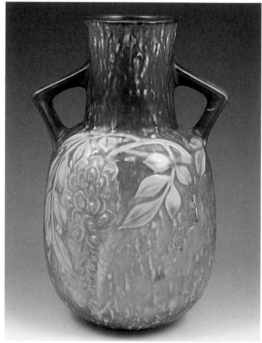

Photo courtesy Belhorn Auction Services LLC, Columbus, Ohio; www.Belhorn.com

Roseville Wisteria 638-9" bottle-necked vase with angular handles in brown. Unmarked. Mint, 9 1/4". **$385**

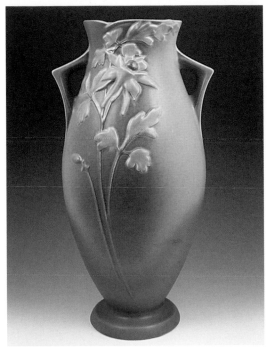

Photo courtesy Belhorn Auction Services LLC, Columbus, Ohio; www.Belhorn.com

Roseville Columbine floor vase in pink and green. Marked Roseville USA 27-16". Two rim chips have been professionally restored, 16 1/2". **$209**

Photo courtesy Belhorn Auction Services LLC, Columbus, Ohio; www.Belhorn.com

Roseville Laurel 667-6" vase in red with strong glaze treatment. Unmarked. Mint, 6 1/4". **$154**

Photo courtesy Belhorn Auction Services LLC, Columbus, Ohio; www.Belhorn.com

Large and scarce Roseville Carnelian I 1314-8" squat ewer in blue. Blue Rv ink stamp. Mint, 7 3/4" x 12". **$161**

Dean Schwarz

Dean Schwarz (b. 1938) is a ceramic artist, painter, writer and teacher from Cedar
Rapids, Iowa. While serving in the U.S.
Navy in the early 1960s, he used his shore
leaves to visit the studios of notable potters, including Shoji Hamada in Japan, and
Bauhaus-trained Marguerite Wildenhain
at Pond Farm near Guerneville, Calif. His
work is represented in numerous private
collections, and in the holdings of museums and universities around the world.

*Dean Schwarz vase (two views),
mid-1990s, 10 1/2".* **$350+**

Van Briggle

Artus Van Briggle, born in 1869, was a talented Ohio artist. He joined Rookwood in 1887 and studied in Paris under Rookwood's sponsorship from 1893 until 1896. In 1899, he moved to Colorado for his health and established his own pottery in Colorado Springs in 1901.

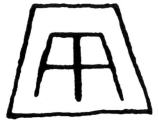

The Art Nouveau designs he had seen in France heavily influenced Van Briggle's work. He produced a wide variety of matte-glazed wares in this style. Colors varied. Artus died in 1904, but his wife, Anne, continued the pottery until 1912.

The "AA" mark, a date, and "Van Briggle" were incised on all pieces prior to 1907 and on some pieces into the 1920s. After 1920, "Colorado Springs, Colorado" or an abbreviation was added. Dated pieces are the most desirable.

Photo courtesy Belhorn Auction Services LLC, Columbus, Ohio; www.Belhorn.com

Van Briggle philodendron bowl with reticulated design in purple over blue matte. Marked Van Briggle with logo, Colo. Spgs. Colo. and the finisher's initials, AES. Mint, 5" x 4 1/4". **$71**

Photo courtesy Belhorn Auction Services LLC, Columbus, Ohio; www.Belhorn.com

Van Briggle floral plate made between 1907 and 1912 in red with gray overspray. Marked Van Briggle with logo, 17. Professionally restored, 8 1/4" diameter. $63

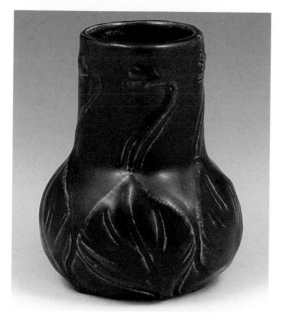

Photo courtesy Belhorn Auction Services LLC, Columbus, Ohio; www.Belhorn.com

Van Briggle vase from 1918 with Mulberry glaze and stylized leaf and floral design. Marked with the Van Briggle logo and the date. Two flakes to rim, 4". $241

Photo courtesy Belhorn Auction Services LLC, Columbus, Ohio; www.Belhorn.com

Van Briggle Lorelei vase in white matte with strong mold. Marked Van Briggle with logo, Colo Spgs, Colo and B by the finisher. Mint, 10 5/8". **$161**

Photo courtesy Belhorn Auction Services LLC, Columbus, Ohio; www.Belhorn.com

Van Briggle yucca vase from the 1920s in Mountain Craig. Marked Van Briggle with logo, USA. Mint, 4 1/8" x 5 1/2". **$109**

Weller

In 1872, Samuel A. Weller opened a small factory in Fultonham, near Zanesville, Ohio. There he produced utilitarian stoneware, such as milk pans and sewer tile. In 1882, he moved his facilities to Zanesville. In 1890, Weller built a new plant in the Putnam section of Zanesville along the tracks of the Cincinnati and Muskingum Railway. Additions followed in 1892 and 1894.

Weller entered into an agreement with William A. Long in 1894 to purchase the Lonhuda Faience Co., which had developed an art pottery line under the guidance of Laura A. Fry, formerly of Rookwood. Long left in 1895, but Weller continued to produce Lonhuda under the new name "Louwelsa." Replacing Long as art director was Charles Babcock Upjohn. He, along with Jacques Sicard, Frederick H. Rhead and Gazo Fudji, developed Weller's art pottery lines.

At the end of World War I, many prestige lines were discontinued and Weller concentrated on commercial wares. Rudolph Lorber joined the staff and designed lines such as Roma, Forest and Knifewood. In 1920, Weller purchased the plant of the Zanesville Art Pottery and claimed to produce more pottery than anyone else in the country.

Art pottery enjoyed a revival when the Hudson Line was introduced in the early 1920s. The 1920s also saw Coppertone, and Graystone Gardenware was added. However, the Depression forced the closing of the Putnam plant and one on Marietta Street in Zanesville. After World War II, inexpensive Japanese imports took over Weller's market. In 1947, Essex Wire Co. of Detroit bought the controlling stock, but early in 1948, operations ceased. Also see *Cookie Jars.*

Photo courtesy Belhorn Auction Services LLC, Columbus, Ohio; www.Belhorn.com

Unusual Weller Art Deco wall pocket with a face and finished in a semi-lustrous brown glaze. Marked Weller Pottery in script. Glaze nick to chin and repair to bottom point, 10 1/8". **$195**

Photo courtesy Belhorn Auction Services LLC, Columbus, Ohio; www.Belhorn.com

Weller Woodcraft footed bowl with squirrels. Good contrasting color. Marked with Weller Ware stamp. Mint, 7 1/2" x 3 3/4". **$172**

Photo courtesy Belhorn Auction Services LLC, Columbus, Ohio; www.Belhorn.com

Weller Kenova vase in matte olive green with a lizard, leaves and flowers. Marked only with an impressed 2. Mint, 6" tall. **$495**

Photo courtesy Belhorn Auction Services LLC, Columbus, Ohio; www.Belhorn.com

Weller Ardsley fish flower holder. Marked with Weller Ware stamp. Mint, 6 1/2" x 5". **$275**

Photo courtesy Belhorn Auction Services LLC, Columbus, Ohio; www.Belhorn.com

Weller white and decorated Hudson vase with bird on a branch, a scarce motif. Marked WELLER in block letters. Three hairlines descending from the rim ranging from faint to quite noticeable, 10". **$172**

Left: Weller Hudson vase by Sara Timberlake with slip-decorated daisies on a blue background. Signed ST and marked with Weller kiln stamp. Mint and uncrazed, 10 3/4". **$550**

Below: Weller Etna jardiniere with irises. Marked WELLER. Mint, 10 1/4" x 8 1/8". **$154**

Weller Brighton pheasant. Marked WELLER. Mint, 7" x 10". **$495**

REDWARE, STONEWARE

Also see Red Wing Pottery.

Redware

The availability of clay, the same used to make bricks and roof tiles, accounted for the great production of red earthenware pottery in the American colonies. Redware pieces are mainly utilitarian: bowls, crocks, jugs, etc.

Lead-glazed redware retained its reddish color, but a variety of colored glazes were obtained by the addition of metals to the basic glaze. Streaks and mottled splotches in redware items resulted from impurities in the clay and/or uneven firing temperatures.

Slipware is the term used to describe redware decorated by the application of slip, a semi-liquid paste made of clay. Slipwares were made in England, Germany and elsewhere in Europe for decades before becoming popular in the Pennsylvania German region and other areas in colonial America.

Photo courtesy Jeffrey S. Evans & Associates, Mt. Crawford, Va.; www.jeffreysevans.com

Earthenware bowl made for the Snow Hill Nunnery, lead single glazed, everted and collared rim, interior with slip-trailed green and cream decoration featuring a central six-point star. Attributed to John Bell, Waynesboro, Pa., mid-19th century, 10 1/2" diameter, with some expected light interior wear and scratching, small chip under the rim. **$11,500**

Extremely rare Suter Pottery, Rockingham Co., Va.-attributed earthenware tobacco jar with cover, lead and manganese glazed, squat conical form with a broad rim above a single incised ring, original cover with a button-like finial and sharp outer rim. Emanuel Suter's New Erection Pottery, possibly by John R. Suter, 1866-1890, 6 1/4", cover with a narrow 1 1/4" chip to outer rim. (This jar represents a previously unrecorded form of Suter Pottery. Its decorative glaze is not commonly seen on Suter pieces.) **$632**

Strasburg, Va., polychrome earthenware wash pitcher, lead, copper and manganese glazes over a slip wash, tall ovoid form with a multi-spur handle and pronounced foot. Probably J. Eberly & Co., late 19th century, 11 1/4" x 5 1/8", light 1 1/2" hairline at upper handle, one 1 1/2" area of glaze exfoliation and several other smaller spots, glazed over chip on spout as made. **$1,955**

Stoneware

Made from dense kaolin and commonly salt-glazed, stoneware was hand thrown and high fired to produce a simple, bold vitreous pottery. Stoneware crocks, jugs and jars were made to store food products and fill other utilitarian needs. These intended purposes dictated shape and design: solid, thick-walled forms with heavy rims, necks and handles and with little or no embellishment. Any decorations were usually simple: brushed cobalt oxide, incised, slip trailed, stamped or tooled.

Stoneware has been made for centuries. Early American settlers imported stoneware items at first. As English and European potters refined their earthenware, colonists began to produce their own wares.

By the late 18th century, stoneware was manufactured in all regions of the country. This industry flourished during the 19th century until glass fruit jars appeared and the use of refrigeration became widespread. By 1910, commercial production of salt-glazed stoneware was phased out.

Decorated stoneware pitcher, salt glazed exterior, approximately 2 gallons, baluster form with a squared rim, shoulder ring, and molded foot, brushed cobalt floral and leaf decorations, additional cobalt at the handle terminals, Albany-slip glazed interior. Probably Richard C. Remmey. Third quarter 19th century, 13" h. **$1,380**

Photo courtesy Jeffrey S. Evans & Associates, Mt. Crawford, Va.; www.jeffreysevans.com

Monumental Baltimore decorated stoneware storage jar, salt glazed, 10-gallon capacity mark, ovoid form with a square rim and one remaining vertical open strap handle, profuse brushed cobalt decoration on both sides consisting of a chain band above large flowering bushes flanked by two wheelbarrows under each handle. Second quarter 19th century 19", lacking one handle, 2" hairline off the rim. **$7,475**

Photo courtesy Jeffrey S. Evans & Associates, Mt. Crawford, Va.; www.jeffreysevans.com

Zigler Pottery, Timberville, Va., decorated stoneware jar, salt glazed, approximately 1 gallon, tall ovoid form with a bold rounded rim above multiple incised rings and two tab-like handles, brushed and slip-trailed cobalt tulip decoration on both sides, additional strong cobalt on rings and handles. John Zigler's Pottery, Timberville, Va., probably potted by Andrew Coffman, 1830-1850, 10". **$1,840**

CERAMICS, EUROPEAN

Select English, European Makers

The **Amphora Porcelain Works** was one of several pottery companies located in the Teplitz-Turn region of Bohemia in the late 19th and early 20th centuries. It is best known for art pottery, especially Art Nouveau and Art Deco pieces. Several markings were used, including the name and location of the pottery and the Imperial mark, which included a crown. Prior to World War I, Bohemia was part of the Austro-Hungarian Empire, so the word "Austria" may appear as part of the mark. After World War I, the word "Czechoslovakia" may be part of the mark.

Belleek is thin-bodied, ivory-colored, almost-iridescent porcelain, first made in 1857 in County Fermanagh, Ireland. Production continued until World War I, was discontinued for a period of time, and then resumed. The Shamrock pattern is most familiar, but many patterns were made, including Limpet, Tridacna and Grasses.

Several American firms made a Belleek-type porcelain. The first was Ott and Brewer Co. of Trenton, N.J., in 1884. Other firms producing this ware included The Ceramic Art Co. (1889), American Art China Works (1892), Columbian Art Co. (1893) and Lenox Inc. (1904). Irish Belleek bore specific marks during given time periods, which makes it relatively easy to date. Variations in mark color are important, as well as the symbols and words.

Capo-di-Monte: In 1743, King Charles of Naples established a soft-paste porcelain factory. The firm made figurines and dinnerware. In 1760, many of the workmen and most of the molds were moved to Buen Retiro, near Madrid, Spain. A new factory, which also made hard-paste porcelains, opened in Naples in 1771. In 1834, the Doccia factory in Florence purchased the molds and continued production in Italy.

Capo-di-Monte was copied well into the 20th century by makers in Hungary, Germany, France and Italy.

In 1749, **Josiah Spode** was apprenticed to Thomas Whieldon and in 1754 worked for William Banks in Stoke-on-Trent, Staffordshire, England. In the early 1760s, Spode started his own pottery, making cream-colored earthenware and blueprinted whiteware. In 1770, he returned to Banks' factory as master, purchasing it in 1776.

Spode pioneered the use of steam-powered, pottery-making machinery and mastered the art of transfer printing from copper plates. Spode opened a London shop in 1778 and sent William Copeland there in about 1784. A number of larger London locations followed. At the turn of the 18th century, Spode introduced bone china. In 1805, Josiah Spode II and William Copeland entered into a partnership for the London business. A series of partnerships between Josiah Spode II, Josiah Spode III and William Taylor Copeland resulted.

In 1833, Copeland acquired Spode's London operations and seven years later, the Stoke plants. William Taylor Copeland managed the business until his death in 1868. The firm remained in the hands of Copeland heirs. In 1923, the plant was electrified; other modernization followed.

In 1976, Spode merged with Worcester Royal Porcelain to become Royal Worcester Spode, Ltd.

Delftware is pottery with a soft, red-clay body and tin-enamel glaze. The white, dense, opaque color came from adding tin ash to lead glaze. The first examples had blue designs on a white ground. Polychrome examples followed.

The name originally applied to pottery made in the region around Delft, Holland, beginning in the 16th century and ending in the late 18th century. The tin used came from the Cornish mines in England. By the 17th and 18th centuries, English potters in London, Bristol and Liverpool were copying the glaze and designs. Some designs unique to English potters also developed.

Augustus II, Elector of Saxony and King of Poland, founded the Royal Saxon Porcelain Manufactory in the Albrechtsburg, **Meissen**, in 1710. Johann Frederick Boettger, an alchemist, and Tschirnhaus, a nobleman, experimented with kaolin from the Dresden area to produce porcelain. By 1720, the factory produced a whiter, hard-paste porcelain than that from the Far East. The factory experienced its golden age from the 1730s to the 1750s under the leadership of Samuel Stolzel, kiln master, and Johann Gregor Herold, enameler.

The Meissen factory was destroyed and looted by forces of Frederick the Great during the Seven Years' War (1756-1763). It was reopened, but never achieved its former greatness.

In the 19th century, the factory reissued some of its earlier forms. These later wares are called **"Dresden"** to differentiate them from the earlier examples. There were several other porcelain factories in the Dresden region

Photo courtesy Skinner Inc., Boston; www.SkinnerInc.com

Wedgwood Dragon Lustre Bowl, England, circa 1920, octagonal shape in pattern Z4825 with gilt Oriental dragons on a mottled orange/red exterior and mottled blue/purple interior, printed mark, 9″ diameter, 1″ hairline crack to rim. **$237**

Photo courtesy Skinner Inc., Boston; www.SkinnerInc.com

Wedgwood solid black Jasper Dancing Hours bowl, England, 20th century, applied white classical relief with running laurel border above figures, impressed mark, 7″ diameter, 6″ area of rim sprayed with rim chips repaired. **$119**

Photo courtesy Skinner Inc., Boston; www.SkinnerInc.com

Faience model of a recumbent lion, France, 19th century, modeled atop a rectangular base, blue enamel ground with white painted features and red enameling about the eyes, nose and mouth, 18 1/4" x 13 1/2", chipping to either ear, tongue, side of a nostril; surface chips to enamel at feet and base rim. **$711**

Photo courtesy Skinner Inc., Boston; www.SkinnerInc.com

Royal Crown Derby bone china cockerel, England, circa 1952, polychrome enamel decorated, modeled standing on a tree stump, printed mark, 11 3/4". **$207**

and their products also are grouped under the "Dresden" designation.

Many marks were used by the Meissen factory. The first was a pseudo-Oriental mark in a square. The famous crossed swords mark was adopted in 1724. A small dot between the hilts was used from 1763 to 1774, and a star between the hilts from 1774 to 1814. Two modern marks are swords with a hammer and sickle, and swords with a crown.

Gouda and the surrounding areas of Holland have been principal Dutch pottery centers for centuries. Originally, the potteries produced a simple utilitarian, tin-glazed Delft-type earthenware and the famous clay smoker's pipes.

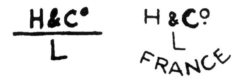

When pipe making declined in the early 1900s, Gouda turned to art pottery. Influenced by the Art Nouveau and Art Deco movements, artists expressed themselves with freeform and stylized designs in bold colors.

In 1842, American china importer David Haviland moved to Limoges, France, where he began manufacturing and decorating china specifically for the U.S. market. Haviland is synonymous with fine, white, translucent porcelain, although early hand-painted patterns were generally larger and darker colored on heavier whiteware blanks than were later ones.

Haviland revolutionized French china factories by both manufacturing the whiteware blank and decorating it at the same site. In addition, Haviland and Co. pioneered the use of decals in decorating china.

Haviland's sons, Charles Edward and Theodore, split the company in 1892. In 1936, Theodore opened an American division. In 1941, Theodore bought out Charles Edward's heirs and recombined both companies under the original name of H. and Co. The Haviland family sold the firm in 1981.

Charles Field Haviland, cousin of Charles Edward and Theodore, worked for and then, after his marriage in 1857, ran the Casseaux Works until 1882. Items continued to carry his name as decorator until 1941.

Thousands of Haviland patterns were made, but not con-

sistently named until after 1926. The similarities in many of the patterns make identification difficult. Numbers assigned by Arlene Schleiger and illustrated in her books have become the identification standard.

The **"KPM"** mark has been used separately and in conjunction with other symbols by many German porcelain manufacturers, among which are the Königliche Porzellan Manufactur in Meissen, 1720s; Königliche Porzellan Manufactur in Berlin, 1832-1847; and Krister Porzellan Manufactur in Waldenburg, mid-19th century.

Collectors now use the term KPM to refer to the high-quality porcelain produced in the Berlin area in the 18th and 19th centuries.

Creamware is a cream-colored earthenware created about 1750 by the potters of Staffordshire, England, which proved ideal for domestic ware. It was also known as "tortoiseshellware" or "Prattware" depending on the color of glaze used.

The most notable producer of creamware was Josiah Wedgwood. Around 1779, he was able to lighten the cream color to a bluish white and sold this product under the name "pearl ware." Wedgwood supplied his creamware to England's Queen Charlotte (1744-1818) and Russian Empress Catherine the Great (1729-1796), and used the trade name "Queen's ware."

The **Leeds Pottery** in Yorkshire, England, began production about 1758. Among its products was creamware that was competitive with that of Wedgwood. The original factory closed in 1820, but various subsequent owners continued until 1880. They made exceptional cream-colored ware, either plain, salt glazed or painted with colored enamels, and glazed and unglazed redware.

Early wares are unmarked. Later pieces are marked "Leeds Pottery," sometimes followed by "Hartley-Green and Co." or the letters "LP."

Liverpool is the name given to products made at several potteries in Liverpool, England, between 1750 and 1840. Seth and James Pennington and Richard Chaffers were among the early potters who made tin-enameled earthenware.

By the 1780s, tin-glazed earthenware gave way to cream-colored wares decorated with cobalt blue, enameled colors and blue or black transfers.

Bubbles and frequent clouding under the foot rims characterize the Liverpool glaze. By 1800, about 80 potteries were working in the town producing not only cream-ware, but soft paste, soapstone and bone porcelain.

The reproduction pieces have a crackled glaze and often age cracks have been artificially produced. When compared to genuine pieces, reproductions are thicker and heavier and have weaker transfers, grayish color (not as crisp and black), ecru or gray body color instead of cream, and crazing that does not spiral upward.

In 1793, Thomas Minton joined other entrepreneurs formed a partnership to build a small pottery at Stoke-on-Trent, Staffordshire, England. Production began in 1798 with blueprinted earthenware, mostly in the Willow pattern. In 1798, cream-colored earthenware and bone china were introduced.

A wide range of styles and wares was produced. Minton introduced porcelain figures in 1826, Parian wares in 1846, encaustic tiles in the late 1840s, and majolica wares in 1850. In 1883, the modern company was formed and called Mintons Limited. The "s" was dropped in 1968.

Many early pieces are unmarked or have a Sevres-type marking. The "ermine" mark was used in the early 19th century. Date codes can be found on tableware and majolica. The mark used between 1873 and 1911 was a small globe with a crown on top and the word "Minton."

Mocha decoration usually is found on utilitarian cream-ware and stoneware pieces and was produced through a simple chemical action. A color pigment of brown, blue, green or black was made acidic by an infusion of tobacco or hops. When the acidic colorant was applied in blobs to an alkaline ground, it reacted by spreading in feathery designs resembling sea plants. This type of decoration usually was supplemented with bands of light-colored slip.

Types of decoration vary greatly, from those done in a combination of motifs, such as Cat's Eye and Earth-worm, to a plain pink mug decorated with green ribbed bands. Most forms of mocha are hollow, e.g., mugs, jugs, bowls and shakers.

English potters made the vast majority of the pieces. Collectors group the wares into three chronological periods: 1780-1820, 1820-1840 and 1840-1880.

William Moorcroft was first employed as a potter by James Macintyre & Co. Ltd. of Burslem, Staffordshire, England, in 1897. He established the Moorcroft pottery in 1913.

The majority of the art pottery wares were hand thrown, resulting in a great variation among similarly styled pieces. Colors and marks are keys to determining age.

Walter Moorcroft, William's son, continued the business upon his father's death and made wares in the same style.

The company initially used an impressed mark, "Moorcroft, Burslem;" a signature mark, "W. Moorcroft" followed. Modern pieces are marked simply "Moorcroft," with export pieces also marked "Made in England."

In 1794, the Royal Bayreuth factory was founded in Tettau, Bavaria. Royal Bayreuth introduced its figural patterns in 1885. Designs of animals, people, fruits and vegetables decorated a wide array of tableware and inexpensive souvenir items.

Tapestry wares, in rose and other patterns, were made in the late 19th century. The surface of the pieces feel and look like woven cloth.

The Royal Bayreuth crest used to mark the wares varied in design and color.

Derby Crown Porcelain Co., established in 1875 in Derby, England, had no connection with earlier Derby factories that operated in the late 18th and early 19th centuries. In 1890, the company was appointed "Manufacturers of Porcelain to Her Majesty" (Queen Victoria) and since that date has been known as "Royal Crown Derby."

Most of these porcelains, both tableware and figural, were hand decorated. A variety of printing processes were used for additional adornment.

Derby porcelains from 1878 to 1890 carry only the standard crown printed mark. After 1891, the mark includes the "Royal Crown Derby" wording. In the 20th century, "Made in England" and "English Bone China" were added to the mark.

Doulton pottery began in 1815 under the direction of John Doulton at the Doulton & Watts pottery in Lambeth, England. Early output was limited to salt-glazed industrial stoneware. After John Watts retired in 1854, the firm became Doulton and Co., and production was expanded to include hand-decorated stoneware such as figurines, vases, dinnerware and flasks.

Photo courtesy Skinner Inc., Boston; www.SkinnerInc.com

Glazed stoneware puzzle jug, England, 19th century, translucent brown glaze to top rim and handle top, pierced neck, impressed verse, "Gentlemen drink & let your skill be tested & forfeit made if anything be wasted" and titled A. Baldwin, 7 1/2", two of the rim "teeth" restored. **$207**

Photos courtesy Skinner Inc., Boston;
www.SkinnerInc.com

*Top left: Staffordshire
earthenware character jug,
England, 19th century,
believed to depict the 19th
century cricketer W.G. Grace,
polychrome enamel decorated,
7 3/4".* **$119**

*Above: Faience bagpipe wall
vase, France, 19th century,
polychrome enamel decorated
with floral designs surrounding
a central theme with villagers
dancing, 16", glaze hairlines
to the top extending from the
ribbon, and to the horn. Chips
restored and slightly discolored
to rim of horn and to area
where horn meets the bag.* **$356**

*Left: KPM porcelain plaque
depicting the Duchess of
Devonshire as the Vestal
Virgin, Germany, late 19th
century, after the original by
Angelica Kauffmann, impressed
KPM and scepter, paper label
for "Henry Bucker, Painter
on China, 5 Pragerstrasse
Dresden", 9 3/8".* **$2,015**

In 1878, Doulton's son, Sir Henry Doulton, purchased Pinder Bourne & Co. in Burslem, Staffordshire. The companies became Doulton & Co., Ltd. in 1882. Decorated porcelain was added to Doulton's earthenware production in 1884.

Most Doulton figurines were produced at the Burslem plants, where they were made continuously from 1890 until 1978. After a short interruption, a new line of Doulton figurines was introduced in 1979.

Dickensware, in earthenware and porcelain, was introduced in 1908. The pieces were decorated with characters from Dickens' novels. Most of the line was withdrawn in the 1940s, except for plates, which continued to be made until 1974.

Character jugs, a 20th-century revival of early Toby models, were designed by Charles J. Noke for Doulton in the 1930s. Character jugs are limited to bust portraits, while Royal Doulton Toby jugs are full figured. The character jugs come in four sizes and feature fictional characters from Dickens, Shakespeare and other English and American novelists, as well as historical heroes. Marks on both character and Toby jugs must be carefully identified to determine dates and values.

Doulton's Rouge Flambé (Veined Sung) is a high-glazed, strong-colored ware.

Production of stoneware at Lambeth ceased in 1956.

Beginning in 1872, the "Royal Doulton" mark was used on all types of wares produced by the company.

Beginning in 1913, an "HN" number was assigned to each new Doulton figurine design. The "HN" numbers, which referred originally to Harry Nixon, a Doulton artist, were chronological until 1940, after which blocks of numbers were assigned to each modeler. From 1928 until 1954, a small number was placed to the right of the crown mark; this number, when added to 1927, gives the year of manufacture.

In 1751, the Worcester Porcelain Co., led by Dr. John Wall and William Davis, acquired the Bristol pottery of Benjamin Lund and moved it to Worcester. The first wares were painted blue under the glaze; soon thereafter decorating was accomplished by painting on the glaze in enamel colors. Among the most-famous 18th-century decorators were James Giles and Jeffery Hamet O'Neal. Transfer-print decoration was developed by the 1760s.

A series of partnerships took place after Davis' death in 1783: Flight (1783-1793); Flight & Barr (1793-1807); Barr, Flight & Barr (1807-1813); and Flight, Barr & Barr (1813-1840). In 1840, the factory was moved to Chamberlain & Co. in Diglis, Worcester. Decorative wares were discontinued. In 1852, W.H. Kerr and R.W. Binns formed a new company and revived the production of ornamental wares.

In 1862, the firm became the Royal Worcester Porcelain Co. Among the key modelers of the late 19th century were James Hadley, his three sons, and George Owen, an expert with pierced clay pieces. Royal Worcester absorbed the Grainger factory in 1889 and the James Had-

ley factory in 1905. Modern designers include Dorothy Doughty and Doris Lindner.

The principal patron of the French porcelain industry in early 18th-century France was Jeanne Antoinette Poisson, Marquise de Pompadour. She supported the Vincennes factory of Gilles and Robert Dubois and their successors in their attempt to make soft-paste porcelain in the 1740s. In 1753, she moved the porcelain operations to Sevres, near her home, Chateau de Bellevue.

The Sevres soft-paste formula used sand from Fontaine-bleau, salt, saltpeter, soda of Alicante, powdered alabaster, clay and soap.

In 1769, kaolin was discovered in France, and a hard-paste formula was developed. The baroque designs gave way to rococo, a style favored by Jeanne du Barry, Louis XV's next mistress. Louis XVI took little interest in Sevres, and many factories began to turn out counterfeits. In 1876, the factory was moved to St. Cloud and was eventually nationalized.

Louis XV allowed the firm to use the "double L" in its marks.

Spatterware generally was made of common earthenware, although occasionally creamware was used. The earliest English examples were made about 1780. The peak period of production was from 1810 to 1840. Firms known to have made spatterware are Adams, Barlow, and Harvey and Cotton.

The amount of spatter decoration varies from piece to piece. Some objects simply have decorated borders. These often were decorated with a brush, requiring several hundred touches per square inch to achieve the spatter effect. Other pieces have the entire surface covered with spatter. Marked pieces are rare.

Collectors today focus on the patterns—Cannon, Castle, Fort, Peafowl, Rainbow, Rose, Thistle, Schoolhouse, etc. The decoration on flatware is in the center of the piece; on hollow ware, it occurs on both sides.

WEDGWOOD

WEDGWOOD
c1759 - 1769

WEDGWOOD
c1900

Aesthetics and the colors of spatter are key to determining value. Blue and red are the most common colors; green, purple, and brown are in a middle group; black and yellow are scarce.

In 1754, Josiah Wedgwood and Thomas Whieldon of Fenton Vivian, Staffordshire, England, became partners in a pottery enterprise. Their products included marbled, agate, tortoiseshell, green glaze and Egyptian black wares. In 1759, Wedgwood opened his own pottery at the Ivy House works, Burslem, Staffordshire. In 1764, he moved to the Brick House (Bell Works) at Burslem. The pottery concentrated on utilitarian pieces.

Between 1766 and 1769, Wedgwood built the famous works at Etruria. Among the most-renowned products of this plant were the Empress Catherine of Russia dinner service (1774) and the Portland Vase (1790s). The firm also made caneware, unglazed earthenwares (drabwares), piecrust wares, variegated and marbled wares, black basalt (developed in 1768), Queen's or creamware, and Jasperware (perfected in 1774).

Bone china was produced under the direction of Josiah Wedgwood II between 1812 and 1822 and revived in 1878. Moonlight Luster was made from 1805 to 1815. Fairyland Luster began in 1920. All luster production ended in 1932.

A museum was established at the Etruria pottery in 1906. When Wedgwood moved to its modern plant at Barlaston, North Staffordshire, the museum was expanded.

Vilmos Zsolnay (1828-1900) assumed control of his brother's factory in Pécs, Hungary, in the mid-19th century. In 1899, Miklos, Vilmos' son, became manager. The firm still produces ceramic ware.

The early wares are highly ornamental, glazed and have a cream-colored ground. Eosin glaze, a deep, rich play of colors reminiscent of Tiffany's iridescent wares, received a gold medal at the 1900 Paris exhibition.

Originally, no trademark was used, but in 1878 the company began to use a blue mark depicting the five towers of the cathedral at Pécs. The initials "TJM" represent the names of Miklos' three children.

Ceramic styles produced by many makers—including Flow Blue, Majolica and Quimper—are found at the end of this section. *Also see Oriental Objects and Tiffany.*

Martinware Pottery

The Martin Brothers were pottery manufacturers in London, starting in 1873, and represent the transition from decorative Victorian ceramics to 20th-century studio pottery in England.

The four brothers (R. Wallace, Walter, Charles and Edwin) produced a distinctive type of stoneware pottery through the First World War, with limited work being produced until 1923 when the pottery closed. They were best known for their bird sculptures and bowls, vessels decorated with sea creatures, and tiles, fashioned in a whimsical but skillful style.

Robert Wallace Martin (1843–1923), had trained as a sculptor. Walter Martin (1857-1912) became the firm's specialist on the wheel, while Edwin Martin's (1860-1915) work included most of the fish and flower designs, and Charles Martin ran the shop. They worked mainly with a salt-glaze stoneware, a high-temperature firing method where salt was thrown into the kiln in order to fuse with the clay and give a surface that could be glassy or matt depending on the conditions of each firing. Colors included browns, greens, greys and blues, and this subdued palette is distinctive of Martinware.

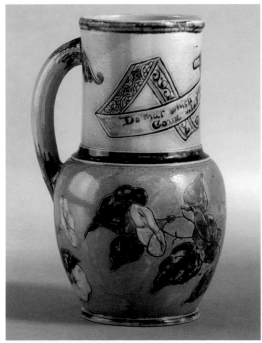

Photo courtesy Skinner Inc., Boston; www.SkinnerInc.com

Martin Brothers glazed stoneware milk pitcher, dated Aug. 21, 1882, small pinched spout and tall neck incised with an inscribed scroll with the motto, "Do that which you ought, come what may", body incised and molded in relief with blue morning glories and leafy vines, on a buff ground, R.W. Martin London & Southall mark, 8 5/8". ex-Richard Wright Collection. **$1,126**

Photo courtesy Skinner Inc., Boston;
www.SkinnerInc.com

Martin Brothers glazed stoneware mantel vase, dated January 1899, pinched neck above a rectangular body decorated with smirking cranes amidst foliage, Martin Bros. London & Southall mark, 9", ex-Richard Wright Collection. **$3,851**

Photo courtesy Skinner Inc., Boston; www.SkinnerInc.com

Martin Brothers glazed stoneware vase, circa 1885, slender neck decorated with flower heads and vines above a continuous scene of birds perched amidst apple blossom branches, circular foot, R.W. Martin & Bros. London and Southall mark, 9", ex-Richard Wright Collection. **$1,896**

Photo courtesy Skinner Inc., Boston; www.SkinnerInc.com

Martin Brothers brown glazed stoneware vase, 1906, undecorated wheel-turned ovoid shape, inscribed 5-1906 Martin Bros London & Southall, 7 3/4", ex-Richard Wright Collection. **$444**

Photo courtesy Skinner Inc., Boston; www.SkinnerInc.com

Martin Brothers glazed stoneware oil lamp, dated Dec. 13, 1881, in the Roman style with pierced handle and circular well, decorated with Greek key and three-leaved sprigs, on a brown ground, incised Martin London & Southall, 4 3/8" long, ex-Richard Wright Collection. **$593**

*Martin Brothers
glazed stoneware
rimmed plate, dated
1892, with overall
designs of daisies and
green foliage on a buff
ground, with London
and Southall mark, 7"
diameter, ex-Richard
Wright Collection.*
$1,126

*Martin Brothers glazed
stoneware miniature vase,
with flared lip and baluster
body, etched and raised
designs of white scrolling
foliage on a moss green
ground, 2 5/8", ex-Richard
Wright Collection.* **$326**

Photo courtesy Skinner Inc., Boston; www.SkinnerInc.com

*Martin Brothers salt-glazed stoneware vase, dated March 1889, pinched neck and globular body, incised with a continuous scene of lilies and leafy foliage on a buff ground, R.W. Martin & Brothers London & Southall mark, 13 1/4",
ex-Richard Wright Collection.* **$4,444**

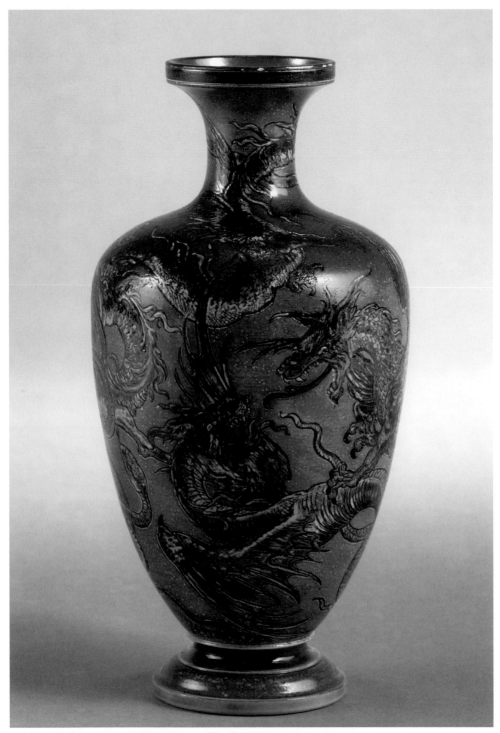

Photo courtesy Skinner Inc., Boston; www.SkinnerInc.com

Martin Brothers glazed stoneware baluster dragon vase, dated October 1892, high-shouldered, incised designs of fiercely fighting dragons and serpents, on a speckled brown ground, incised R.W. Martin & Bros. London & Southall mark, 9 5/8", ex-Richard Wright Collection. **$4,740**

Martin Brothers glazed stoneware angler fish-form water jug, dated March 1887, enamel glazed, finely carved and incised figure showing open mouth with carved teeth, wide eyes and scaled body with tail wrapped underneath, earth and cobalt blue tones, incised R.W. Martin & Bros. London & Southall mark, 9", ex-Richard Wright Collection. **$53,325**

Martin Brothers glazed stoneware fish vase, dated April 1883, with flared lip above two swan's neck handles and a band of cattails, globular body incised and molded with a scene of fantastical fish swimming amidst marine flora, incised R.W. Martin & Bros. London & Southall mark, 8 5/8", ex-Richard Wright Collection. **$8,295**

Photo courtesy Skinner Inc., Boston; www.SkinnerInc.com

Martin Brothers salt-glazed stoneware face jug (two views), dated January 1900, pinched spout and ear handle above a two-sided body showing a grinning face to both sides, R.W. Martin & Bros. London & Southall, 9 1/8", some scratching to face on one side and with light wear to points of highest relief; otherwise no chips, cracks or restorations. Some thin areas of glaze, but they could be intentional or kiln flaws, ex-Richard Wright Collection. **$11,258**

*Martin Brothers glazed
stoneware Barrister "Wally-
Bird" covered tobacco jar,
dated 1889 and signed on
cover and body, the bemused
bird with curved beak and
tilted slightly forward and
to the right, on an ebonized
wood base, overall 12 1/2",
small firing flaw to inner lip
of lid, ex-Richard Wright
Collection.* **$82,950**

Photo courtesy Skinner Inc., Boston; www.SkinnerInc.com

Martin Brothers stoneware "Wally-Bird" covered tobacco jar, both cover and base dated March 1888, enamel decorated, the inquisitive bird with head tilted to the left and with wings put back, all in tones of brown, blue and green, on an ebonized circular base, overall 14 1/8", slight and shallow 1/4" chip to back of head and a slight 1/8" chip along collar line of cover. Slight glaze roughness along top rim of base, ex-Richard Wright Collection. **$59,250**

Photo courtesy Skinner Inc., Boston;
www.SkinnerInc.com

Martin Brothers glazed stoneware fish jug (two views), dated July 1889, pinched spout and looped handle above a shaped body incised with a scene of fantastical fish, eels and alligator gars within a teeming marine environment, incised Martin Brothers London & Southall mark, 8 3/4", **$11,850**

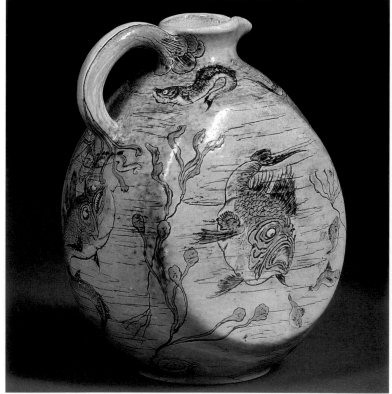

Ruscha's form 313, designed by Kurt Tschoerner and introduced in 1954, became one of the definitive West German forms and was produced until the company closed. The form was redesigned in the early to mid-1960s, probably to increase production numbers. The sleeker, more dramatic original form is on the right. Although the later form may not be as impressive, many of the later glazes are outstanding. Left, uncommon later glaze, **$245-$275;** *right, early glaze,* **$350-$400.**

FUTURE OF THE MARKET: WEST GERMAN ART POTTERY

By Forrest Poston

Over the past few years, more American antique shops and shows have begun including West German pottery, especially in the larger cities. However, it remains primarily an Internet collectible. This presents difficulties for collectors who are curious, but often only vaguely familiar with the subject, having heard the term, plus the phrase "fat lava" and perhaps a few company names. Few are aware of the range and depth in style and quality. Kevin Graham, one of the primary researchers, has so

Forrest Poston

far matched more than 13,000 form numbers with companies. Estimating an average of three sizes per form and three different glazes per form, and that's over 100,000 items a collector could find without a duplicate. Consider that some forms are already known in 50-100 glazes, and more form numbers are being attributed regularly, and the variations could easily top 200,000.

Collecting Approaches

The West German pottery field allows collectors to enjoy this pursuit whether money is fairly tight or just waiting to be spent on the right object. A large percentage of collectible West German items will never go over $100 and may be found under $50 with just a bit of effort. Collectors who like to buy often and build a collection quickly should be able to do just that if they enjoy variety.

Some lines offer slightly more refined options, such as trying to find all of the 50-60 glazes known on Ruscha form 313. For even more of a challenge, there are the nearly 200 versions of Scheurich form 271-22, or the over 200 versions of Scheurich 414-16. While those forms are easy to find, certain finishes range from uncommon to rare. It's also possible to find many of the glazes on a wide variety of forms, so collectors can search by form or by glaze.

Items made during the first part of the era (early 1950s) often had extensive handwork in the decoration, which is the usual meaning of "handarbeit" as part of the mark. Around 1965, companies moved toward glaze colors and chemistry for the effects, including the thick, often volcanic glazes now called "fat lava". All too often, fat lava is used as if synonymous with West German pottery, but even at its peak it remained a sub-category.

Companies

Almost 100 companies have been identified working during this era (1949-90), ranging from those well known before, such as Hutschenreuther, Karlsruhe and Rosenthal, to those that came and went within the West German era, such as Carstens Tönnieshof, Ceramano and Keto. In addition to the commercial potteries, studio potters enjoyed a matching creative rush, further extending the range of styles available to collectors.

Most of the companies focused on items that were widely marketable, but almost all of the companies made some superior items, and a few focused on smaller, higher-quality production. Of course, most successful designs were also imitated by other companies.

Photo courtesy of Kevin James Graham

Shape 271-22 was one of the first big successes for Scheurich. Designed by Heinz Siery and introduced in 1959, almost 200 different glazes have been discovered. Common glazes, **$25-$45;** *better,* **$50-$75;** *uncommon,* **$100-$125.**

These two Ruscha plates and plaque by Kiechle show the primary style for wall items from the mid-1950s into the early '60s. Also note the varying influences with stylized nature images, a strong Oriental influence in both style and subject, and the echo of Cubist and Art Deco styles. Toreador 7", uncommon, **$75-$100;** *Ruscha Mask, 5",* **$35-$50;** *Kiechle Monkeys, 13", rare,* **$275-$325.**

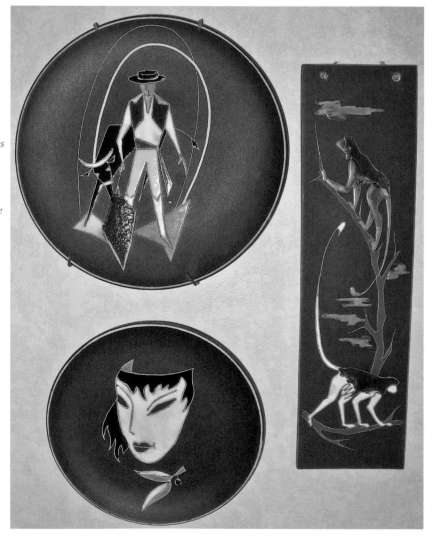

Collectors should pay particular attention to the proportions on items, since this will often make the difference between an item that pleases temporarily and one that endures. Many of the finishes on West German pottery, especially the fat lava/volcanic glazes, can obscure or overwhelm the form on first look. Some of the softer, more traditional glazes are actually as complex and pleasing as some of the more radical volcanic glazes.

As with most new collecting fields, it takes time to get a sense of where a given item falls within the quality range, and that's even more problematic with an Internet-based field such as West German pottery. Collectors should spend some time viewing various sites, some of which include large numbers of vases, for just such learning experiences. Unfortunately, few of the sites have done extensive work displaying better pieces in much quantity, and pricing is often too erratic to give a sense of relative quality, all of which has slowed the growth of the market.

Plaques and Hanging Plates

Several companies made wall art, but the master of plaques was Helmut Schaeffenacker. Motifs ranged from stylized animals to still lifes and highly abstract images. Items about 12" x 10" are most common, but Schaeffenacker produced some items over 24" and a few significantly larger. Karlsruhe also produced high quality, often large and thick plaques. Although they show up on the market less often, prices so far are lower than for similar Schaeffenacker items.

The largest producer of plaques and hanging plates was Ruscha, especially in the late 1950s and into the '60s. Earlier items feature a matte-black background with an incised and enameled decoration. Bird and horse motifs are common, especially in the 7" diameter size. Motifs such as clowns and bullfighting scenes are more difficult to find, while the most popular is the Hanns Welling design, "Paris." Although artists were working from a pattern, they were allowed a fair amount of leeway in adapting the design. This results in interesting variations but also a wide range in quality. Sizes 10" and larger are significantly more difficult to find, but they are known up to at least 13".

Many of the later Ruscha wall items are of lesser quality, but some large plaques featuring horses, or horse-and-chariot designs, are an exception. Another exception is the "mushroom" plaques or chargers, featuring raised discs in the center and a mottled glaze.

Keto, Kiechle and Ceramano also worked with the matte-black background and enamel designs. Most of the Keto work is average, but some designs, such as "Surreal," are striking exceptions. Kiechle work is of finer quality and more difficult to find, while the Ceramano items of this type are quite rare. They were done early in the company's history and often on Ruscha blanks.

Photo courtesy of Kevin James Graham

Scheurich typically used less dramatic forms while focusing on creative glazes. Mug-like form 414-16 is known in more than 200 glazes. The center version features a "fat lava" glaze. Common glazes, **$25-$45;** *better,* **$50-$75;** *uncommon,* **$100-$125**

Porcelain

Based on both style and period, a number of porcelain companies should be included under the West German pottery banner. Designs by Tapio Wirkkala and Martin Frey for Rosenthal, and by Heinrich Fuchs for Hutschenreuther, have already begun moving up in price. Items from Edelstein, Kerafina, Kaiser and Plankenhammer remain more affordable, but designs such as the fossil motifs by Kaiser justify more notice.

So far, most attention has been paid to the white-on-white designs, partly due to a push in the New York City market, but that has begun to stabilize. Other versions include strong bands of color, and the all-black versions, such as the Rosenthal "Porcelaine Noir" series, are among the most difficult to find.

Searching the Net

Collectors will still have trouble building a collection just through local shops, so the Internet will be a primary source for at least the near future. Numerous sites — from 1st dibs to Trocadero to Ruby Lane — have a variety of West German items. Identification of companies has improved significantly in just the past two years, but information beyond that remains scarce among dealers, which means prices vary from bargain to absurdly high. Although proportions and finer aspects of the decoration are hard for less-experienced collectors to determine from pictures, take time to look and to ask questions. Some dealers are learning more about this new field.

West German items are more widely available on European-based Web sites. Even on these sites, most of the items are lower to middle range, which is sometimes reflected in the price, sometimes not. Take note that shipping rates and time are significant factors when buying from Europe. When buying from sellers in Germany, purchasing multiple items can save even more on shipping than in most other countries, and the sellers are generally quite helpful in this regard.

A few key companies: Bay, Bückeburg, Carstens, Ceramano, Dümler & Breiden, ES Keramik, Hutschenreuther, Jasba, Karlsruhe, Otto, Ruscha, Schaeffenacker, Scheurich, Schlossberg, Silberdistel, Steuler, Ü (Uebelacker), van Daalen.

A few key designers: Heiner Balzar, Adele Bolz, Trude Carstens, Ursula Fesca, Otto Gerharz, Fridegart Glatzle, Willi Hack, Gerda Heuckeroth, Bodo Mans, A. Seide, Heinz Siery, Kurt Tschoerner, Hanns Welling, Cilli Wörsdörfer, Cari Zalloni, and Clare Zange.

These Carstens vases are form 1250, but they produced versions with varying proportions and with or without a handle. The mixed textures of the vase on the right show another common variation. West German items often have both visual and tactile combinations. Left, 18", $450-$500; right, 12", $250-$275.

Resources

Initial work, not surprisingly, was in German, including several works by Horst Makus, mostly out of print, which focus on the items from the earlier period, about 1950-1964. Dr. Michael Thomas published *Deutsche Keramik und Porcellane der 60er und 70er Jahre*, focusing on items from the 1960s and 70s. Work in English is still limited but growing. Mark Hill has now published the second edition of the exhibition catalog, "Fat Lava."

Collector Kevin James Graham's *West & East German Pottery: Marks and Form Numbers* is now available on CD, as is the book, *Spritzdecor to Fat Lava*.

One of the earliest Internet sources in English, and still the most extensive on the net, is the Gin-For's Odditiques site, which includes several essays, a page of marks and brief histories of several main companies, and several videos on identifying West German pottery. Visit *www.ginforsodditiques.com*.

Also visit Pottery and Glass (forum with an extensive threads on West German pottery, numerous pictures): *potteryandglass.forumandco.com*.

FLOW BLUE

Flow Blue is the name applied to china of cobalt blue and white, whose color, when fired in a kiln, produced a flowing or blurred effect. The color varies from dark royal cobalt blue to navy or steel blue. The flow may be very slight to a heavy blur, where the pattern cannot be easily recognized. The blue color does not permeate through the body of the china. The amount of flow on the back of a piece is determined by the position of the item in the "sagger" (a case of fire clay) during firing.

Known patterns of flow blue were first produced around 1830 in the Staffordshire area of England. Credit is generally given to Josiah Wedgwood, who worked in that area. Many other potters followed, including Alcock, Davenport, Grindley, Johnson Brothers, Meakin, Meigh and New Wharf. They were attempting to imitate the blue and white wares brought back by the ship captains of the tea trade. Early flow blue, 1830s to 1870s, was usually of the pearlware or ironstone variety. The later patterns, 1880s to 1900s, and the modern patterns after 1910, were of the more delicate semi-porcelains. Most flow blue was made in England but it was made in many other countries as well. Germany, Holland, France, Spain, Wales and Scotland are also known locations. Many patterns were made in the United States by several companies: Mercer, Warwick, Sterling and the Wheeling Pottery to name a few.

Gravy Boat and Covered Butter Dish. Dover Pattern by W.H. Grindley. Back stamp: Mark 1842. Circa 1891-1920's. **$206 both**

Collector's Note: The Flow Blue International Collectors' Club Inc. has studied new vs. reproduction flow blue. There are still areas of personal judgment as yet undetermined. The general rule has been "new" indicates recent or contemporary manufacture and "reproduction" is a copy of an older pattern. Problems arise when either are sold at "old" flow blue prices.

The club continues to inform members through its conventions, newsletters and the Web site: www.flowblue.com.

The following is a listing of "new" flow blue, produced since the 1960s.

Blossom: Ashworth Bros., Hanley, 1962. Washbowl and pitcher made for many years now.

Iris: By Dunn, Bennett, Burslem, has been reproduced in a full chamber set.

Romantic Flow Blue: Blakeney Pottery, 1970s. Resembles Watteau. The old patterns never had the words "flow blue" written on them.

Touraine: By Stanley, by far the most prolific reproduction made recently, in 2002. Again, the "England" is missing from the mark, and it is made in China. Nearly the entire dinnerware set has been made and is being sold.

Victoria Ware: Mark is of lion and uniform, but has paper label "Made in China," 1990s. Made in various patterns and designs, but the giveaway is the roughness on the bottoms, and much of it has a pea-green background.

Vinranka: Upsala-Ekeby, Sweden, 1967-1968. Now discontinued and highly collectible, a full dinnerware set.

Waldorf: By New Wharf, cups and saucers are found, but missing "England" from their mark and are made in China.

Floral pitchers (jugs) and teapots bearing a copied "T. Rathbone England" swan mark.

Williams-Sonoma and Cracker Barrel have released a vivid blue-and-white line. Both are made in China. One line is a simplified dahlia flower on white; the other has summer bouquets. Both are well made and readily available, just not old. The reproductions are more of a threat to collectors.

In all cases, regarding new pieces and reproductions, be aware of unglazed areas on the bottoms. The foot rings are rough and too white. The reproductions, particularly the Touraine, are heavier in weight, having a distinctive thick feel. The embossing isn't as crisp and the pieces are frequently slightly smaller in overall size than the originals.

Check the Flow Blue International Collectors' Club, Inc. Web site. Join the club, study the books available, and always work with a trusted dealer. Good dealers guarantee their merchandise and protect their customers.

Plate and Pitcher. These items have a brush-stroke pattern and were used between 1845-1860. Plate has two cracks with some discoloration and crazing, 9 1/4" d. Pitcher has many cracks with some repaired, 10" t. **$124 both**

Assorted Flow Blue Pieces Listed by Pattern

If the pattern is unknown, the maker is listed alphabetically. If the maker is unknown, the motif or form is listed alphabetically.

All flow blue listings and images in this edition of the Warman's guide come from Antiques and Estate Auctioneers, Wellington, Ohio; *www.estateauctioneers.com.*

Gravy Boat, with Underplate and Egg Cup. Aberdeen Pattern by E. Bourne & J.E. Leigh. Circa 1905-1910. All pieces have staining and crazing. Gravy boat and underplate show discoloration. Eggcup is unmarked with two hairline cracks and chip to outside rim edge. ..... **$26 all**

Plate, Saucer and Open Fruit Bowl. Alaska Pattern by W.H. Grindley. Back stamp: Mark 1842. Circa 1891. Plate shows crazing and some staining, 10" d. Bowl shows some wear with nick to inside rim and chip to outside rim. .... **$23 all**

Cup, Saucer and Bowl. Albany Pattern by Johnson Bros. Back stamp: Mark 2177. Circa 1900. Cup and bowl show crazing and bowl shows slight discoloration. .... **$50 all**

Plate, Creamer and Handleless Cup. Amoy Pattern by Davenport. Back stamp: Mark 1181A. Circa 1844. Plate shows some staining and crazing, 8 1/4" d. Creamer has crazing, repaired handle and hairline to foot. Cup has crazing and small nick to rim. .... **$62 all**

Large Open Vegetable Bowl, and Small Platter. Astoria Pattern by New Wharf Pottery. Back stamp: Mark 2886. Circa 1891. Bowl has 3 chips to back side of rim as well as a hairline. Also crazing and discoloration, 9 3/4" d. Platter has hairline on one end and shows wear, 9 1/4" x 12 1/2". .... **$26 both**

Cup and Saucer, plus Small Plate. AWA Pattern by P. Regout & Co. This is also the back stamp. Circa 1890. Small chip to inside rim of cup. .... **$23 all**

Large Soup Plate, and Handleless Cup. Beauties of China Pattern by Mellor, Venables & Co. Back stamp: Mark 2645 and impressed IRONSTONE. Circa 1851. Soup plate has fourteen paneled sides, 10 1/4" d with utensil marks and crazing. Handleless cup has a chip and a rough spot to the rim with discoloration to the base and crazing. ..... **$53 both**

Covered Butter Dish, and Soup Bowl. Candia by Cauldon Ltd. Back stamp: Cauldon used old Ridgway Belt Marks 821-22. Circa 1905-1910. Butter dish has crack to rim with some discoloration to base. Cover has crazing and some discoloration to inside edge. Soup bowl is 7 3/4" d with wear and discoloration to inside lip area. .... **$47 both**

Two Cups and Saucer, Cecil Pattern by F. Till & Son. Back stamp: Mark 3857. Circa 1891. Small nick on foot ring of saucer with crazing. One cup has small pinhead mark on one side of the handle. **$53**

Vegetable Bowl and Plates (2), Chinese Pattern by Allertons. Back stamp: Mark 88. Circa 1903-1912. Bowl has small nick to rim. One plate shows some wear while the other one looks hardly used. Both plates 9" d. .... **$12 all**

Tureen with Cover and Platter, Clyde Pattern by New Wharf Pottery. Back stamp: Mark 2886. Circa 1890-1894. Cover has small chip to rim with seven glaze pops on top. Tureen has hairline around one handle, 7 3/4" x 11 1/4". Platter has some staining on top of piece with a couple rough edges and two chips to rim, 12 1/4" x 16 1/4". All pieces have crazing. .... **$23 all**

Platter and Two Plates, Del Monte Pattern by Johnson Bros. Back stamp: Mark 2177 plus "England". Circa 1900. Platter is 8" x 10 1/2" with three small chips to back rim with wear marks. 10" d dinner plate with no chips or cracks noted but is does show wear. 9" d plate shows wear. ....**$29 all**

Handleless Cup, Saucer and Plate. Erford Pattern by James Edwards. Circa 1842-1851. Cup has chip to inside rim and chip to outside rim. Saucer has hairline on outside with discoloration to cup and saucer, and crazing to all three pieces. Plate is 10 1/4" d. ....**$18 all**

Dinner Plate and Smaller Plate, Excelsior Pattern by Thomas Fell. Back stamp: Mark 1534. Circa 1850. Large plate shows staining and crazing, 9 1/4" d. Small plate shows two tiny nicks to rim edge, 6 1/2" d. ....**$50 both**

Creamer and Dinner Plate, Fairy Villas Pattern by W. Adams & Co. Circa printed England indicates time after 1891. Creamer has hairline on handle with worn spots on handle, rim and feet. Dinner plate shows wear and crazing, 10 1/4" d. ....**$41 both**

Small Bowl and Plates (2), Fairy Villas Pattern by W. Adams & Co. Back stamp: Mark 31. Circa 1891. All three pieces show wear and one plate and bowl show crazing. Bowl 6 3/4" d. Plates 7 3/4" d. ....**$35 all**

Plate, Waste Bowl and Flow Green Waste Bowl. Festoon Pattern by W. Adams & Co. Back stamp: Mark 30. Circa 1891. Many spots on rim edge of plate where glaze is worn off and tiny hairline on rim with crazing, 9" d. One bowl has spots on rim edge where glaze is worn off and two tiny hairlines on rim with discoloration and crazing, 6" d. Flow green waste bowl has small stain in center bottom of bowl, 6" d. ....**$23 all**

Fish Plates (2), and Platter. Both plates show discoloration and crazing, 8 1/2" d. Platter shows some staining and crazing, 12" x 15 1/4". ....**$70 all**

Cup and Two Plates, Florida Pattern by W.H. Grindley. Back stamp: Mark 1842. Circa 1891. Cup has chip to outside rim. One plate has large crazing around center bouquet. 8" d. ....**$38 all**

Gravy Boat and Sauce Dish, Florida Pattern by Johnson Bros. Back stamp: Mark 2177. Circa 1900. Sauce dish has light crazing and creamer has hairline on rim. .....**$88 both**

Plate and Small Sauce Dish, Genovese Pattern by Edge, Malkin & Co. Back stamp: Mark 1445. Circa 1873. Plate shows discoloration and crazing, 9 1/4" d. Small sauce dish is very worn and crazed. ....**$12 both**

Small Vegetable Bowl and Bone Dish, Gironde Pattern by W.H. Grindley. Back stamp: Mark 1842. Circa 1891. Small chip repair on rim of bone dish and wear on both dishes...**$18 both**

Deep Saucer and Plates (2), Gotha Pattern by J. Heath. Back stamp: Gotha and J. H. contained in cartouche. Circa 1850-1860. Saucer shows loss of glaze around rim, staining, crazing and old factory crack. One plate has chip to outer rim edge and one plate shows staining, crazing and two chips/nicks below rim edge, 9 1/2" d. ....**$18 all**

Paneled Sugar Bowl with Lid, and Open Large Bowl. Both are Hong Kong Pattern by Charles Meigh. Back stamp: Unmarked but should be Mark 2618. Circa 1845. Two tiny chips to outside of sugar bowl and three chips to outside of lid. Bowl has small chip to foot ring and some

discoloration on inside. Bowl is 10 1/4" d and sugar bowl with lid is 7 1/2" t. ....**$26 both**

Gravy Boat, with Underplate and Butter Pat. Ideal Pattern by W.H. Grindley. Back stamp: Mark 1842. Circa 1893. Rd. No. 213154 on underplate and butter pat. Crazing on butter pat. ....**$23 both**

Waste Bowl and Saucer, Japanese Pattern by W. & B. Back stamp: Mark 4239. Circa 1875. Bowl shows wear and two stains inside with chip and hairline to outside rim edge. Saucer shows staining and crazing. ....**$12 both**

Base Bowl Tureen (Missing Cover) and a Cup, Killarney Pattern by New Wharf Pottery. Back stamp: Mark 2886 on both pieces. Circa 1891. Tureen has tiny chip just below outer rim. Tureen is 7" x 9". ....**$29 both**

Saucer, Plate and Platter. Lancaster Pattern by W. & E. Corn and New Wharf Pottery. Back stamp: W contained in diamond and Mark 2886. Circa 1891-1900. Plate shows staining and crazing, 8 3/4" d. Platter shows some stain spots and wear, 9" x 12 1/2". Saucer has small hairline on back. ....**$59 all**

Plate and Bowl, Leicester Pattern by Sampson Hancock & Sons. Back stamp: Mark 1933. Circa 1906-1912. Bowl is 3 1/2" h and 6" across with discoloration around inside rim and tiny flake to rim. 10" d dinner plate has discoloration and both pieces have crazing. ....**$26 both**

Covered Butter Dish, and Cup with Saucer. Linda Pattern by John Maddock & Sons, Ltd. Back stamp: Mark 2465. Circa 1896. Saucer has crazing. ....**$65 all**

Round Bowl and Oval Bowl, Lorne Pattern by W.H. Grindley. Back stamp: Mark 1842. Circa 1900. Round bowl shows small nick to rim edge with hairlines on bottom that

Pitcher. Unmarked. Circa 1890-1900. **$248**

Hand-Painted Pitcher. Back stamp: Set of initials under glaze and second set atop glaze. Date hand painted under glaze of 1893. 5 1/2" t. **$47**

do not go all the way through, 8" d. Oval bowl shows wear, 6 1/2" x 9". .... **$32 both**

Soup Bowls (2), Butter Pats (4) and Creamer. Luray Pattern by Bishop & Stonier. Back stamp: Mark 387. Circa 1899. Butter pats show crazing and two show some discoloration. Soup bowls show slight crazing to one.
.... **$59 all**

Open Vegetable Bowl and Plate, Lusitania Pattern by Alfred Colley Ltd. Back stamp: Mark 999. Circa 1910. Bowl shows wear and light staining with small nick to back side of rim, 9 1/4" d. Plate shows wear but not chips or cracks noted, 10" d. .... **$23 both**

Plate and Vegetable Bowl, Lyndhurst Pattern by W.H. Grindley. Back stamp: Mark 1842. Circa 1891. Both pieces show wear. Plate 9" d. Bowl 10" d. .... **$47 both**

Small Oval Platter and Oval Vegetable Bowl, Manhattan Pattern by Henry Alcock & Co. Back stamp: Mark 65. Circa 1891-1900. Vegetable bowl is 7" x 9 3/4". Platter is 8 1/2" x 12 1/2" with crazing and discoloration. .... **$35 both**

Soup Bowl and Small Sauce Dish, Marie Pattern by W.H. Grindley. Back stamp: Mark 1842. Circa 1891. Rd. No. 250387. Small sauce dish has tiny rim spot and bowl has chip under outside rim. Slight crazing in sauce dish.
.... **$29 both**

Cup and Saucer, and Small Serving Dish. Cup and Saucer are Medway Pattern by Alfred Meakin Ltd. Back stamp: Mark 2582. Circa 1897. Crazing to cup with tiny chip to foot rim. Small serving dish is Albemarle Pattern (same as Medway) by Alfred Meakin Ltd. Back stamp: Mark 2586. Circa 1891. Small chip to back edge of rim, 7" d. ...... **$20 all**

Plate and Platter, Neapolitan Pattern by Johnson Bros. Back stamp: Mark 2177. Circa 1900. Plate shows wear and

small chip to back of rim. Platter shows wear and two chips to back rim. Plate 7" d. Platter 10 3/4" x 14". .... **$29 both**

Gravy Boat with Underplate, and Covered Tureen. Oban Pattern by Alfred Meakin. Back stamp: Similar to Mark 2583. Circa 1891. Pieces have some staining and crazing. Small chip to inside lip of tureen. .... **$35 both**

Flat Bowl and Dinner Plate, Osborne Pattern by W.H. Grindley. Back stamp: Mark 1842. Circa 1900. Bowl shows staining and both pieces have crazing. Bowl 7 3/4" d. Plate 10" d. .... **$15 both**

Soup Plate and Sauce Dishes (2), Paris Pattern by Johnson Bros. Back stamp: Mark 2177. Circa 1900. Soup plate shows crazing. Sauce dishes show wear. .... **$18 all**

Shallow Bowl and Small Plate, brush-stroke pattern in the style of Petrus Regout, Dutch. Back stamp: in bowl, impressed "E", "F" and "9.L", in plate, impressed "F" and "AR". Circa 1891-1900. Both pieces have some staining and crazing. Bowl 9 1/4" d. Plate 7 3/4" d. .... **$65 both**

Plate, Bread Plate, Vegetable Bowl and Gravy Boat. Portman Pattern by W.H. Grindley. Back stamp: Mark 1842. Circa 1891. Small chip to back of vegetable bowl, three small chips to back of plate, discoloring and crazing on plate and bread plate. .... **$77 all**

Gravy Boat with Underplate, and Covered Tureen. Princess Pattern by Booths. Back stamp: Mark 451. Circa 1900-1915. Rd. No. 183173. Gravy Boat has crazing with small crack to rim and hairline with chip on bottom foot. Underplate shows some staining. Tureen shows crazing with light staining and hairline to inside lip of dish. Cover shows good repair to handle. .... **$12 both**

Milk Pitcher with Gold Trim. Clematis Pattern by Furnivals Ltd. Back stamp: 1653-5 Marks. Circa 1900. Reg. No.: Printed 362684, impressed 356048. **$153**

Chocolate Pot with Lid. Unmarked. Circa Probably 1890-1900. Excellent condition. **$242**

Cup and Saucer, Plate and Covered Vegetable Dish. Raleigh Pattern by Burgess & Leigh. Back stamp: Mark 717 & Mark 718. Circa 1906-1912. Reg. 393237 on Vegetable dish. Vegetable dish has crazing. Plate is 8 3/4" d with crazing and chip beneath outside of rim as well as a repair mark. Cup and saucer have crazing with a chip to foot of cup, hairline crack and discoloration. ....**$100 all**

Plate and Bone Dish, Richmond Pattern by Johnson Bros. Back stamp: Mark 2177. Circa 1900. Shows wear and crazing, 10" d. ....**$38 both**

Plate and Cup and Saucer, by Sampson Hancock & Son. Back stamp: Mark 1928. Circa 1891. Plate is 8 1/2" d and also marked, "Stoke on Trent" and "England". Saucer has tiny chip beneath outside of rim. Cup has factory flaws. ....**$29 all**

Plate with Cup and Saucer, Splendid Pattern by Societe Ceramique. Back stamp: Maastricht and Made in Holland. Circa 1900. Crazing and discoloration on plate with crazing on back side of saucer and faint hairline on inside of cup. Plate is 9" d. ....**$29 all**

Plate and Cereal Bowl, Somerset Pattern by W.H. Grindley. Back stamp: Mark 1843. Circa 1910-1914. Bowl has one spot of missing glaze, 7" d. Plate shows crazing. ....**$50 both**

Dinner Plate, Small Waste Bowl and Tall Fancy Pitcher. Taylor, Smith & Taylor Co. Back stamp: Mark #B. Circa 1899-1905. Pitcher is 9" tall and has crazing, unmarked. Plate is 9" d and has crazing and discoloration. Waste bowl has some rough edges. ....**$44 all**

Vegetable Bowl and Plate, bowl is Trent I Pattern by Wood & Son. Back stamp: Mark 4285. Circa 1891. Plate is Trent II Patter by Wood & Son. Back stamp: Mark 4285. Circa 1891-1895. Both 9" d. ....**$12 both**

Plate, Pattern is of fruit, flowers and butterfly by Cauldon. Back stamp: Cauldon printed and impressed. Circa 1891. Rgd. No. 183243. Plate shows wear and small chip to rim edge, 10 1/2" d. **$15**

Sugar (no lid) and Creamer, Vista Pattern by G.L. Ashworth & Bros. Ltd. Back stamp: Mark 2530 & Mason's. Circa 1891. Pieces have crazing but no chips or cracks, 4 1/4" t. ....**$12 pair**

Small Platter, Two Plates and Saucer. Waldorf Pattern by New Wharf Pottery. Back stamp: Mark 2886. Circa 1892. Plates are 9" d and show utensil marks. Platter is 9" x 10 3/4" and shows some wear. Saucer is 6" d. ....**$165 all**

Dresser Tray and Sauce Dish, Warwick China Co. with a Wild Rose pattern. Back stamp: Mark 38. Circa 1900. Chip to inside rim of dresser tray, 6" x 10 1/4" and crazing to sauce dish, 3" x 7 3/4". ....**$56 both**

Sauce and Serving Dish, York Pattern by W. & E. Corn. Back stamp: Mark 1113. Circa 1900-1904. Sauce dish shows some wear, 5 1/4" d. Serving dish shows discoloration and crazing along with some missing glaze on rim edges, 10" x 11 1/2". ....**$32 both**

Assorted Flow Blue Pieces Listed by Form

Gravy Boats

Flow Blue and Polychrome Gravy Boat, Derby Pattern by W.H. Grindley. Back stamp: Mark 1842. Circa 1891.
....**$65**

Gravy Boat and Underplate, Torbay Pattern by Bishop & Stonier. Back stamp: Mark 387. Circa 1900. Three chips on foot of gravy boat with some discoloration. Small spot on underplate rim missing glaze. **$12**

Teapot. Shapoo Pattern by Thomas Hughes. Back stamp: Printed initials plus pattern name in cartouche, Mark 2121. Circa 1860-1870. Spout lid is either replacement or heavily repaired. Spout has been restored. Small manufacturer's crease in handle. **$354**

Soup Plate. Indian Plant Pattern by Thomas Dimmock. Back stamp: Mark 1298 (Also marked Kaolin Ware and 'D'). Tiny chip on outer rim. 10 1/2" d. **$94**

Gravy Boat with Underplate, Grace Pattern by W.H. Grindley. Back stamp: Mark 1842. Circa 1897. Tray has two chips to rim and one chip beneath outside rim. Gravy boat has four chips to base, hairline on handle and light discoloration on spout. **$47**

Gravy Boat with Underplate, Hamilton Pattern by John Maddock & Sons. Back stamp: Mark 2464. Circa 1896. Gravy boat has hairline crack on inside that does go through to the outside with slight discoloration. Platter shows wear with some discolored blemishes on backside. 7 1/4" x 10 1/4". **$29**

Gravy Boat with Underplate, Olga Pattern by Ridgways. Back stamp: Mark 3312 or 3313. Circa 1905-1912. Some staining on both pieces. Gravy boat handle has two cracks, repaired. Crazing on both pieces. **$12**

Gravy Boat, Marguerite Pattern by W.H. Grindley. Back stamp: Mark 1842. Circa 1891. No chips or cracks noted but some crazing. **$23**

Gravy Boat, Verona Pattern by Ridgways. Back stamp: Mark 3313. Circa 1910. Has mended stress line at base of handle..............................**$29**

Creamers, Pitchers and Pots

Chocolate Pot with Lid, Abbey Pattern by George Jones & Sons. Back stamp: printed pattern name, "1790," potter and "England". Circa 1900. 6" t. **$47**

Creamer, Phoebe Pattern by Wedgwood & Co. Ltd. Back stamp: Mark 4059. Circa 1906. Small hairline on outside bowl as well as small crack that goes through to inside. **$12**

Large Milk Pitcher, Columbia Pattern by Clementson & Young. Unmarked. Circa 1846. Small hairline inside spout, 7 3/4" t. **$106**

Milk Pitcher, Azalia Pattern by J. Kent Ltd. Back stamp: Mark 2267, Except word Fenton instead of Longton. Circa 1913+. 7 1/4" t. **$118**

Milk Pitcher, Decoration includes three poppies. Unmarked. Circa 1900 or earlier. Some staining inside with discoloration and crazing throughout. 7 3/4" t. **$50**

Milk Pitcher, Osborne Pattern by W.H. Grindley. Back stamp: Mark 1842. Circa 1900, 6 3/4" t. **$195**

Milk Pitcher, with top and base trim of gold design and white/yellow enamel dot trim. Pattern not indicated but piece is by Keller & Guerin. Back stamp: K et G, Luneville, France. Circa 1900-1910. No chips or cracks but bit of enamel dots missing around the base design. Crazing. **$91**

Pitcher, decorated with cherubs and gold by Wheeling Pottery, U.S.A. Back stamp: La Belle China. Shows crazing. 8" t. **$124**

Small Cream Ewer, Astoria Pattern by Pitcairns Ltd. Back stamp: Mark 3052. Circa 1895. 3 1/2" t. **$59**

Tall Water Pitcher, Oxford Pattern by William Adderly & Co. Back stamp: Mark 48 and printed trademark #49 with W.A.A. & Co. Circa 1886-1905. 11 1/2" t. **$88**

Teapot with Lid, Lobelia Pattern by G. Phillips. Back stamp: Mark 3012. Circa 1845. Deep crack around base and hairline cracks inside and one outside. Some rough areas to finial. 9" t. **$59**

Plates

Advertising Plates (4), all plates have crazing. No chips or cracks noted. First plate is from the Cleveland Grocery Co., Groceries, Wall Paper, Fancy China, New London, Ohio, and has La Francaise Porcelain printed on back. Second plate is from J. H. Mollenkop, 1913, General Merchandise and also has La Francaise Porcelain printed on back. Third plate is unmarked and is Compliments of H.M. Rule, General Merchandise, Darlington, Ohio. Fourth plate is from Pittsburgh Commandery, 1898. Printed on back is Knowles, Taylor, Knowles, East Liverpool, Ohio, U.S.A. All plates are between 8" and 8 1/2" d. ....**$47 all**

Plate. Brush-stroke pattern with bluebells, and grapes and cherry border. Unmarked. Circa 1845-1865. Small nick to rim edge and crazing, 9 1/2" d. **$136**

Oval Platter. Venice Pattern by Upper Hanley Pottery Co. Back stamp: Mark 3929A. Circa 1900-1910. Reg. No. 354458 printed. 11 1/2" x 15 1/2". **$94**

Cake Plate, Gironde Pattern by W.H. Grindley. Back stamp: Mark 1842. Circa 1891. Reg. No. 293169. Some wear and crazing. 9 1/2" x 10 3/4". **$59**

Decorative Plates (2), Birds at Fountain/Exotic Birds Pattern, possibly by Josiah Wedgwood & Sons. Back stamp: imprinted "FN" and "ORD" and "1M". Marks could indicate October 1875. Outer edges of plates have pierced, open borders of vertical bars. Both plates have crazing. 8" d. .... **$23 pair**

Dessert/Cake Plate, with Molded Handles. Shusan Pattern by F. & R. Pratt & Co. Unmarked but matches Shusan, mark 3144. Circa 1855-65. Small chip to rim, 9" x 10". **$59**

Dinner Plate and Smaller Plate, Excelsior Pattern by Thomas Fell. Back stamp: Mark 1534. Circa 1850. Large plate shows staining and crazing, 9 1/4" d. Small plate shows two tiny nicks to rim edge, 6 1/2" d. ....**$50 both**

Dinner Plate, Agra Pattern by F. Winkle & Co. Back stamp: Mark 4214. Circa 1891. ....**$35**

Dinner Plate, Athens I Pattern by Charles Meigh. Back stamp: Mark 2618 or 2614A. Marked initials "C.M.". Circa 1840. Discoloration and crazing. 10 1/4" d. **$41**

Dinner Plate, Athol Pattern by Burgess & Leigh. Back stamp: Mark 718. Circa 1910. Rd. No. printed 324171, Rd. No. impressed 364190. Plate shows wear, 9 3/4" d. **$12**

Dinner Plate, Canton Pattern by John Maddock. Back stamp: Mark 2461. Circa 1850-1855. Shows wear and crazing, 9 1/2" d. **$18**

Dinner Plate, Coronet Pattern by Sampson Hancock & Sons. Back stamp: Mark 1933. Circa 1912. Reg. No.: 341031. 9" d. **$76**

Dinner Plate, Flora Pattern possibly by Cockson & Chetwynd. Back stamp: Mark 976. Circa 1867. Small chip to under side of rim and to foot rim. Has crazing and shows wear. 9 1/2" d. **$100**

Dinner Plate, Madras Pattern by Doulton & Co., Burslem, England. Back stamp: Mark 1832. Circa 1902. 10" d. **$29**

Dinner Plate, Vinranka, Percy Pattern by Gefle, made in Sweden. Back stamp: marked as stated prior and with circle containing three brick kilns belching smoke. Circa 1967 Modern. 10 1/4" d. **$18**

Flow Blue and Polychrome Plate, Bullfinch Pattern by Wedgwood. Back stamp: printed pattern name, Wedgwood, Etruria, England and impressed Wedgwood, plus others. 10 1/4" d. **$41**

Footed Cake Plate, Napier (Polychrome) Pattern by Wedgwood. Back stamp: FB cartouche containing pattern name and impressed WEDGWOOD and PEARL and gold painted number 2931. ....**$118**

Fourteen-Sided Plate, Arabesque Pattern by T.J. & J. Mayer. Back stamp: Mark 2570 (Also marked "Chinese Porcelain & Longport"). Circa 1850. Large chip to foot ring. 10 1/2" d. **$21**

Heavy Plate, Grandmother's Flowers Pattern by Elsmore & Forster. Back stamp: Unreadable impression in circular pattern. Circa 1850-1860. Plate has some roughness around the edge with heavy discoloration and crazing. 10" d. ... **$12**

Pedestal Cake/Tart Plate, by W.H. Grindley. Back stamp: Mark 1843 printed in green. Circa 1914-1925. 4 1/2" t x 10" w. Crazing around polychrome picture on inside of plate. **$41**

Plate with 10 Smaller Plates, Florida Pattern by Johnson Bros. Back stamp: Mark 2177. Circa 1900. Large plate has discoloration, cracks, chips and crazing, 9 1/2" d. Six of the smaller plates have crazing. The other four have chips and crazing, 7" d. ....**$65 all**

Plate with Six Panels, Nankin Pattern with impressed "Ironstone" on back. Circa 1845. 9 1/2" d with normal wear. **$38**

Covered Tureen. Mongolia Pattern by Johnson Bros. Back stamp: Mark 2177. Circa 1900. Dish has crazing. 9 1/2" x 11". **$366**

Plate, Chen-Si Pattern by John Meir. Back stamp: Marked I.M., Mark 2632. Circa 1835. 10 1/2" with hairline cracks, crazing and wear. **$29**

Plate, Chinese Pattern by Wedgwood. Back stamp: Mark 4088 and impressed "Wedgwood". Circa 1908-1910. Plate shows some wear, 8 1/4" d. **$23**

Plate, Chusan Pattern by J. Clementson. Back stamp: Mark 910a. Circa 1839-1864. Piece shows professional repair on rim. 9 1/4" d. **$12**

Plate, Elgar Pattern by Upper Hanley Pottery Co. Back stamp: Mark 3928-29A. Circa 1895-1910. Plate shows some crazing and tiny nick to back side of rim edge. 9" d. **$12**

Plate, Gladys Pattern by New Wharf Pottery. Back stamp: Mark 2883 (This mark doesn't contain the words "& Co." so may be other than Mark 2883). Circa 1891. Shows some wear, 9" d. **$18**

Plate, Ivanhoe Pattern by Wedgwood. Back stamp: Imprint of IVANHOE, WEDGWOOD and ETRURIA, ENGLAND. Circa 1901-1910. 10 1/4" d. **$35**

Plate, Paneled, 14-sided. Tonquin Pattern by W. Adams & Son. Back stamp: Mark 22. Circa 1845. Shows some wear and crazing, 8 1/2" d. **$100**

Plate, Scinde Pattern by J. & G. Alcock includes some decorative pattern on rear of plate as well. Back stamp: Mark 69, also impressed with "Oriental Stone". Circa 1840. Tiny chip to outside rim and does show crazing. 8 1/2" d. **$41**

Plate, Spanish Festivities Pattern by George Jones. Back stamp: Mark 2218. Circa 1891-1924. 9 1/4" d. **$32**

Plate, Water-Lilly Pattern by Wedgwood/Etruria England. 10" d. **$130**

Plates (2), Avon-Ware Pattern by Booths. Back stamp: Booths impressed. Circa 1880-1890. One plate has crazing. 9" d. .... **$41 pair**

Plates (2), Geisha Pattern by Upper Hanley Potteries Ltd. Back stamp: Mark 3929A. Circa 1901. One plate shows crazing and what looks like a repair. 9" d. **$18**

Plates (2), Hong Pattern by Petrus Regout & Co. Back stamp: P.R. also marked Maastricht. Circa 1900. Crow's foot on bottom of one plate and shows some wear, 8" d. Other plate 8 3/4" d. .... **$23 both**

Plates (2), Manilla Pattern by Podmore Walker & Co. Back stamp: Mark 3075 & Mark 3076. Circa 1845. Both plates are 10" d with crazing and normal wear. .... **$165 pair**

Plates (2), Osborne Pattern by Ridgways. Back stamp: Mark 3312. Circa 1905. Both plates have staining and crazing. 8" and 9" d. .... **$18 both**

Plates (2), Pelew Pattern by E. Challinor. Back stamp: Mark 855A. Circa 1840. Both plates show wear and crazing, 8 3/4" d. **$65**

Large Covered Sugar Bowl. Scinde Pattern by Thomas Walker. Unmarked. Circa 1847. Bowl has some discoloration inside and around outside bottom area. Tiny chips to rim of foot. Cover has large chip inside lip with some retouched areas. **$118**

Plates (2), Sobraon Pattern by Hill Pottery. Back stamp: Cartouche containing pattern name and one plate also has Hill Pottery print. Circa 1870-1880. Plates show wear, with crazing and slight discoloration, 10 1/2" d. .... **$94 pair**

Plates (2), The Temple Pattern by Podmore Walker. Back stamp: Mark 3080. Circa 1850. Both plates show wear and crazing. Large plate has large chip and nick to rim. Also nick to foot rim. 7" and 10 3/4" d. .... **$122 both**

Plates (2), Tokio Pattern by Johnson Bros. Back stamp: Mark 2179. Circa 1913. Plates show crazing. 7" d. **$38 pair**

Plates (3), Belport Pattern by John Maddock & Sons Ltd. Back stamp: Mark 2464. Circa 1896 - Two of the three plates also impressed with a crown above the initials "V" and "LX". Tiny chip to rim of third plate. 7" d. .... **$12 all**

Plates (3), Chapoo Pattern by J. Wedgwood. Back stamp: Mark 4276A. Circa 1850. Small plate has two small chips to foot rim, 4 1/4" d. Medium plate shows wear, crazing and small nick to rim edge, 6 1/4" d. Large plate shows wear, crazing and large chip to back of rim, 10 1/2" d. .... **$35 all**

Plates (3), Rock Pattern by E. Challinor or Masons. Back stamp: Cartouche containing pattern name. Circa 1850. Large plate is very worn with crazing, 9 1/2" d. Of the two smaller plates, one shows discoloration and one has staining to back and shows crazing, 6 1/4" d. .... **$59 all**

Plates (3), Somerset Pattern by W.H. Grindley. Back stamp: Mark 1842 & Mark 1843. Circa 1891 & 1910-1914. Medium plate 9" d has chip to rim, hairline crack and crazing. Large plate with Mark 1842. Back stamp shows wear and small chip to back side of plate beneath rim. Other large plate 10" d shows staining and crazing. .... **$23 all**

Plates (4), Pomona Pattern by E. M. Co. (Edge Malkin & Co.). Back stamp: Mark 1445 printed and Mark 1440 impressed. Circa 1880-1891. Plates show some staining and crazing. 8" d. .... **$12 all**

Plates (9), Touraine Pattern by Henry Alcock & Co. Back stamp: Mark 65. Circa 1898. Rd. No. 329815. Of the nine plates, three show staining and crazing and one has small nick to back side of rim, 9" d. .... **$65 all**

Small Plate, in Wire Basket. Decoration includes flowers with buds and leaves. Unmarked. Circa 1890. Plate is 5" and basket measures 8" x 11 1/2". **$53**

Soup Plate, Circassia Pattern by J. & G. Alcock. Back stamp: Mark 69. Circa 1840. Shows crazing and wear. Piece also impressed "ORIENTAL STONE". 10 1/2" d. **$18**

Soup Plate, Countess Pattern by T.R. & Co. Back stamp: Mark 3205. Circa 1912. Hairline on back, small stained area and crazing. **$15**

Soup Plate, Indiana Pattern by Wedgwood & Co. Back stamp: Mark 4055 impressed and Mark 4056 imprinted. Circa 1870. Two tiny chips and one small chip to top of rim, with some staining to back of plate. Shows some wear. 10 1/4" d. **$23**

Soup Plate, Spring Pattern by W.H. Grindley & Co. Back stamp: Mark 1842. Circa 1890-1891. .... **$15**

Soup Plate, Sylvan Pattern by T.C. Brown-Westhead, Moore & Co., Back stamp: Mark 684. Includes initials B.W.M. & Co. with letter "S" and No. "14". Circa 1900. Some crazing. **$23**

Soup Plates (3), Congo Pattern by Dudson Wilcox & Till Ltd. Back stamp: Mark 1412. Circa 1902-1926. One bowl has tiny nick to rim, two bowls have discoloration and all three bowls have crazing. .... **$12 all**

Platters

Deep Platter or Vegetable Dish, Keswick Pattern by Wood & Son. Back stamp: Mark 4285. Circa 1891-1898. 12" x 9". **$20**

Deep Platters or Vegetable Dishes, Keswick Pattern by Wood & Son. Back stamp: Mark 4285. Circa 1891-1898. Both platters/dishes show some wear but no chips or cracks noted. 9 1/2" x 12 1/4". .... **$23 both**

Eight-Sided Platter, Hong Kong Pattern by Charles Meigh. Back stamp: Unmarked with faint pattern name. Should be Mark 2618. Circa 1845. Some discoloration on back. 13 1/2" x 10 1/4". **$242**

Eight-Sided Platter, Kin Shan Pattern by Edward Challinor. Unmarked except for imprinted asterisk "*" on back with a blue "3". Circa 1855. Rim mark to right top corner that looks to have created stained crazing on back of plate. Normal wear. **$206**

Eight-Sided Platter, with a Deep Well. Castle Pattern. Circa 1850. Shows wear. 12 3/4" x 16 1/4". **$82**

Handleless Cup and Saucer. Chapoo Pattern by J. Wedgwood. Back stamp: Mark 4276A. Circa 1850. Crazing and small nick to cup foot rim. $82

Toothbrush Holder with Cover. Cover has three small air holes. Design is a Floral Dogwood Pattern by Copeland/Late Spode. Circa 1847-1867. Crazing with tiny nick to cover rim. **$94**

Large Oval Platter, Beaufort Pattern by W.H. Grindley. Back stamp: Mark 1842. Reg. No. 408448. Circa 1903. No chips or cracks noted but does have utensil marks. **$141**

Large Platter, Buccleuce Pattern. Back stamp: Cartouche containing pattern name. Circa 1845. Plate shows some staining with two chips and hairline to edge. 14 3/4" x 18 1/4". **$23**

Large Platter, Chatsworth Pattern by Ford & Sons. Back stamp: Mark 1585/1586. Circa 1893-1900. Plate has crazing. 13 3/4" x 18 3/4". **$29**

Large Platter, Chusan Pattern by J. Clementson. Back stamp: Mark 910A (Ironstone/Phoenix Bird & J. Clementson). Circa 1839-1864. Some discoloration but no chips or cracks. 12" x 16". **$283**

Large Platter, Dresden Pattern by Villeroy & Boch, (German). Back stamp: Mark 40. Circa 1900-1915. Some discoloration and crazing. 14 1/2" x 20 1/4". **$26**

Oval Platter, Clover Pattern by W.H. Grindley. Back stamp: Mark 1843. Circa 1914-1925. Couple small nicks on rim edge, 14 1/2" x 10 3/4". **$23**

Oval Platters (2), Sandringham Pattern by W. Adams & Co. Back stamp: Mark 30 and England. After 1891. Smaller platter has three small nicks to rim edge on back side, 8 1/4" x 11 1/4". Larger platter has two small nicks on rim edge, 9 1/4" x 12 1/4". ....**$41 both**

Platter by Burgess & Leigh, back stamp: Mark 715. Circa 1870, 16" x 13" with crazing, discoloration and a crack. **$15**

Platter, Alaska Pattern by W.H. Grindley. Back stamp: Mark 1842. Circa 1891. Platter shows wear, 7 1/2" x 10 1/4". ..**$47**

Platter, Alaska Pattern by W.H. Grindley. Back stamp: Mark 1842. Circa 1891. Platter shows wear, 10 1/4" x 14 1/4". **$76**

Platter, Alpha Pattern by Knowles, Taylor & Knowles (American). Circa 1890-1900. Piece shows slight wear, 11 3/4" x 15 1/4". **$35**

Platter, Andorra Pattern by Johnson Bros. Back stamp: Mark 2177. Circa 1901. Rd. No. is impressed on back. Shows some wear. 12" x 16". **$35**

Platter, Astral Pattern by W.H. Grindley. Back stamp: Mark 1842. Circa 1891 or a bit later. Reg. No. 426592. Three nicks to rim edge and crazing, 11 1/2" x 16 1/4". **$65**

Platter, Berlin Vase Pattern by I. Ridgway. Back stamp: printed design with pattern name and potter. Circa 1845-1850. Piece shows wear, staining, crazing, hairline crack and chip to rim edge. 10 1/2" x 12 3/4". **$12**

Platter, Clarendon Pattern by Henry Alcock & Co., Ltd. Back stamp: Mark 65. Normal surface wear, some discoloration and crazing. Small chip to rim or edge mark from the kiln rack, 11 3/4" x 16 1/4". **$35**

Platter, Dainty Pattern by John Maddock & Sons. Back stamp: Mark 2464. Circa 1896. Platter has crazing, 11 1/4" x 14 3/4". **$118**

Platter, Derby Pattern by W.H. Grindley. Back stamp: Mark 1842. Circa 1891. Small chip to back rim, 9" x 12". **$15**

Platter, Dorothy Pattern by Johnson Bros. Back stamp: Mark 2177. Circa 1900. Platter shows some wear with tiny chip to back side of rim. 12" x 16 1/4". **$41**

Platter, Dover Pattern by W.H. Grindley. Back stamp: Mark 1842. Circa 1891-1920's. 10 1/4" x 14". **$77**

Platter, Erie Pattern by Bourne & Leigh Ltd. Back stamp: F.B. J F.L. Circa 1900. Discoloration on front and back of platter with a couple tiny chips and some roughness to rim. Also some glazing. 12" x 16 1/4". **$29**

Platter, Flow Blue with Polychrome Chinoiserie with Lustre Chinese Pattern that is impressed "Ashworth". Back stamp: Mark 137. Circa 1862-1880. Shows wear from use with some roughness around outer edge. 11 1/2" x 14 1/4". **$18**

Platter, Gironde Pattern by W.H. Grindley. Back stamp: Mark 1842. Circa 1891. Shows some wear. 10 1/2" x 15". **$77**

Platter, Grace Pattern by W.H. Grindley. Back stamp: Mark 1842. Circa 1897. Some surface wear. 17" x 12". **$188**

Platter, Grosvenor Pattern by Moyatt Son & Co. Back stamp: Mark 2811. Circa 1907. Three small chips to plate edge. 14 3/4" x 18 1/2". **$47**

Platter, Grosvenor Pattern by Moyatt Son & Co. Back stamp: Mark 2811. Circa 1907. Three small chips to plate edge. 14 3/4" x 18 1/2". **$47**

Platter, Haddon Pattern by W.H. Grindley. Back stamp: Mark 1842. Circa 1891. Large chip to back side of end handle and small chips to back side of other end handle with tiny amount visible from the front. 12" x 8 1/2". **$26**

Platter, Kelvin Pattern by Alfred Meakin Ltd. Back stamp: Mark 2586. Circa 1891. 8 3/4" x 12 1/4". **$118**

Platter, Luray Pattern by Bishop & Stonier. Back stamp: Mark 387. Circa 1899. Reg. No. 227450. Two tiny chips to outside of rim. **$23**

Platter, Lyndhurst Pattern by W.H. Grindley. Back stamp: Mark 1842. Circa 1891. Piece shows wear with nick to rim edge. 11 1/2" x 15 3/4". **$82**

Platter, Medina Pattern by Jacob Furnival & Co. Back stamp: Mark 1643. Circa 1845-1870. Shows crazing. 10 1/2" x 13 1/2". $94

Platter, Nonpareil Pattern by Burgess & Leigh. Back stamp: Mark 712. Circa 1891. Small nick to inside lip. Shows wear. 10" x 12 1/4". $35

Platter, Oregon Pattern by T.J. & J. Mayer. Back stamp: Mark 2570, Longport. Circa 1845. Crazing and repairs to rim and center top surface. 9 1/2" x 12 1/2". $23

Platter, Osborne Pattern by W.H. Grindley. Back stamp: Mark 1842. Circa 1900, 10 1/4" x 14 1/4". $100

Platter, Peach (Royal) Pattern by Johnson Brothers. Back stamp: Mark 2177. Circa 1891-1900. 9 1/2" x 12 1/4" with wear from use. $71

Platter, Princess Pattern by Booths. Back stamp: Mark 451. Circa 1900-1915. Rd. No. 183173. Platter shows crazing. 12 1/2" x 16 1/2". $41

Platter, Regent Pattern by S. F. & Co. B. Ltd. Back stamp: Unmarked. Circa 1913-1939 or a bit later. Platter has crazing, 9 1/2" x 12 1/2". $23

Platter, Seville Pattern by New Wharf Pottery/Wood & Son. Back stamp: Pattern name and Wood & Son, mark 4285. Circa 1894. Platter is 10" x 14" with stain and crazing. $94

Platter, Shapoo Pattern by Thomas Hughes. Back stamp: Printed initials plus pattern name in cartouche, Mark 2121. Circa 1860-1870. 12 1/2" x 9 1/2" with utensil marks on top and crazing underneath. $165

Platter, Stafford Pattern by Ridgways. Back stamp: Mark 3313. Circa 1912. Platter shows some wear with tiny nick to rim. 10" x 14 1/2". $35

Platter, Torbrex Pattern by Wood & Sons. Back stamp: Wood & Sons. $12

Platter, Unknown Pattern Name by George Jones. Back stamp: Similar to Mark 2217 with unreadable impressed mark. Also, pattern name printed in oriental lettering. Circa 1873. Crazing and some staining. 16 1/2" x 20 1/4". $29

Platter, Venice Pattern by Johnson Bros. Back stamp: Mark 2177. Circa 1895. Rd. No. 250791 printed, 208597 embossed. Platter shows wear, 11 1/4" x 14 1/2". $76

Platter, Verona Pattern by Ridgways. Back stamp: Mark 3313. Circa 1910. 10 1/4" x 13 3/4". $82

Platter, Versailles Pattern by Furnivals. Back stamp: Mark 1651 printed and Mark 1650 impressed. Circa 1894. Platter shows some wear with a couple nicks to rim edge. $35

Platter, Windsor Pattern by C.H. & H., Tunstall England. Back stamp: shows a crown on top of a circular belt with England underneath, within belt is "Windsor" and in center of belt is C.H.&H. and Tunstall. Shows slight crazing, 10 1/2" x 14 1/2". $4

Platter, Yeddo Pattern by Arthur Wilkison. Back stamp: Mark 4170. Circa 1907. Tiny nick to rim. 12" x 16 1/2". $23

Tureens

Covered Oval Tureen, Flaxman Pattern by S.H. & S. Back stamp: Mark Similar to 1933. Circa 1912. Rd No. 479163 printed, Rd No. 479164 impressed. Tiny chip to inside lip and some crazing. $47

Covered Soup Tureen, Regent Pattern by S. F. & Co. B. Ltd. Back stamp: Unmarked. Circa 1913-1939 or a bit later. Handle on cover has been repaired. Bowl has crazing. 10" w. $26

Covered Tureen, Argyle Pattern by Wood & Son. Back stamp: Mark 4285. Circa 1900. Rd. No. 328742. No chips or cracks noted in cover or dish. Dish does have staining and crazing. $65

Covered Tureen, Dorothy Pattern by Wedgwood & Co. Back stamp: Mark 4057. Circa 1890-1900. May have repair to one handle. 6 1/2" x 8 1/2". $29

Covered Tureen, Lancaster Pattern by New Wharf Pottery. Back stamp: Mark 2886. Circa 1891. Tureen has large chip to rim of foot. $29

Covered Tureen, Windflower Pattern by Burgess & Leigh. Back stamp: Mark 717-718. Circa 1895-1896. Rd. No. 249191 printed and No. 236241 impressed. No. 249191 also printed on inside lid. Some crazing to bowl with faint hairline to inside of bowl. $88

Covered Tureen, Woodbine Pattern by Wood & Son. Lid has crack underneath with staining coming through to top and a chip to the inside lip. Also has good repair to top handle. $47

Deep Eight-Sided Cover for Large Tureen, Amoy Pattern by Davenport. Back stamp: Mark 1181A. Circa 1844. Some blemishes on the surface with crazing on inside, 9 1/4" w. $153

Oval Covered Tureen, Louise Pattern by W.H. Grindley. Circa 1891-1910. Rd. No. 269029. Just a tiny nick to inside cover lip. $29

Oval Sauce Tureen with Cover, Renown Pattern by Arthur Wilkinson Co. (Royal Staffordshire Pottery). Back stamp: Mark 4170. Circa 1907. Hairline cracks on bottom sides. Tiny hairline on inside of lid by spoon opening. 4 1/2" x 9". $12

Tureen with Cover, Loraine Pattern by Leighton Pottery. Back stamp: Mark 487. Circa 1930. Shows a little wear. 8" x 11". $35

Cake Plate with pierced handles. Unknown maker.
10 3/4" d. **$212**

Other Forms

Bone Dishes (2), Grace Pattern by W.H. Grindley. Back stamp: W.H. Grindley. Circa 1897. One has small discoloration. .... **$71 pair**

Bone Dishes (2), Rose Pattern by W.H. Grindley. Back stamp: Mark 1842. Circa 1893. Rd. No. 213117. Both pieces have crazing and hairline to rim edge. One piece has nick to rim edge and other piece has chip to rim edge and hairline to foot. .... **$29 pair**

Bone Dishes (5), LaBelle Pattern by Wheeling Pottery. Back stamp: Mark 28. Circa 1900. Crazing and discoloration. .... **$200 set**

Bowl, Cambridge Pattern by New Wharf Pottery. Back stamp: Mark 2886. Circa 1890-1894. 9 1/4" d with small, narrow chip beneath outside rim. **$32**

Bowl, Country Scenes Pattern. Back stamp: Country Scenes England with imprint of No. "214". Circa 1891. Signs of wear. 9" d. **$76**

Bowl, Lahore Pattern. Bowl shows wear. 9 1/4" d. **$71**

Bowl, Trilby Pattern by Wood and Son. Back stamp: Mark 4285. Circa 1907. Shows some wear and tiny chip to outside rim. 9 1/2" d. **$18**

Bowl, Violette Pattern by Keller & Guerin, Luneville, France. Circa 1891. .... **$12**

Bowl, Warwick China Co. with a Wild Rose pattern. Back stamp: Mark 38. Circa 1900. 8" d. **$41**

Celery Dish, Warwick Pansy Pattern by Warwick China Co., U.S.A. Circa 1900. Shows crazing and small chip to rim, 5 1/4" x 12 1/4". **$23**

Chamber Pot with Lid, Doreen Pattern by W.H. Grindley. Back stamp: Mark 1842. Circa 1891. .... **$177**

Cheese Keeper, Acme Pattern by Sampson Hancock & Sons. Back stamp: 1929 & 1929A. Circa 1900. Shows crazing and wear. **$71**

Compote, Byzantium Pattern by T.C. Brown-Westhead, Moore & Co., Cauldon, England. Back stamp: Mark 676. Circa 1900. Shows wear and roughness on edge of rim. 10" x 11". **$23**

Covered Chamber Pot, Kelmscott Pattern by F. Winkle & Co. (Colonial Pottery/Stoke England). Back stamp: Mark 4215. Circa 1890-1910. Chip on inside lip of cover and crazing on pot. **$15**

Covered Sardine Dish, Dish is 5" x 6" with a floral pattern. Unmarked. Type and style indicate date about 1880-1895. Chip to inside lip of cover. **$76**

Covered Soap Dish with Liner, Marseilles Pattern by W.H. Grindley & Co., England. Back stamp: like Mark 1842, but with England. Circa 1900-1914. Cover has some rough edges with staining on rim and lip. Some staining to inside of bowl. Liner has holes for draining. **$35**

Covered Sugar Bowl, Iris Pattern by A. Wilkinson/Royal Staffordshire Pottery. Back stamp: Mark 4170. Circa 1907. Cover has chip to inside lip with a crack and does have crazing. Bowl has some staining with a crack to handle and to inside lip. **$18**

Covered Sugar Bowl, Neapolitan Pattern by Johnson Bros. Back stamp: Mark 2177. Circa 1900. Bowl has hairline crack. **$47**

Covered Sugar Bowl, Wentworth Pattern by J. & G. Meakin. Back stamp: Mark 2602. Circa 1907. Bowl has small nick with faint hairline to inside lip. **$35**

Large Mug. Brush-stroke decorated with tulips, buds and leaves. Shows some wear and crazing. **$153**

Covered Vegetable Dish, Ormonde Pattern by Alfred Meakin. Unmarked. Circa 1891. Cover shows crazing but bowl does not, 9 1/2" x 10 1/4". **$41**

Covered Vegetable Dish, Raleigh Pattern by Burgess & Leigh. Back stamp: Mark 717-718. Circa 1906-1912. Rd. No. 393237. Shows some wear, crazing and hairline on inside corner lip. 7" x 11 1/2". **$65**

Cup and Saucer, Aldine Pattern by W.H. Grindley. Back stamp: Mark 1842. Circa 1891. Rd. No. 325874. Both pieces show some wear. **$12**

Cup and Saucer, Haddon Pattern by Libertas, Prussia. Back stamp: printed Libertas, Prussia. Circa 1891-1900. Short hairline on saucer rim and small nick to rim. Also crazing. **$12**

Cup and Saucer, Old Curiosity Shop Pattern by W.R.S. & Co. Back stamp: Mark 3309. Circa 1900. Cup shows wear, hairline from rim, some staining and both pieces show crazing. **$12**

Deep Bowl, Elsa Pattern by W. & E. Corn. Back stamp: Mark 1113. Circa 1891. Shows wear on inside and out. 8" d. **$26**

Deep Bowl, Jenny Lind Pattern by Arthur Wilkinson Ltd. Back stamp: Mark 4170. Circa 1895. This bowl shows some hairlines on bottom and crazing, 7 3/4" d. **$35**

Deep Oval Vegetable Dish, Marie Pattern by W.H. Grindley. Back stamp: Mark 1842. Circa 1891. Rd. No. 250387. Shows wear and tiny nick to outside rim edge, 6 3/4" x 9 1/4". **$29**

Dish, Columbia Pattern by Clementson & Young. Back stamp: Mark 911. Circa 1846. This dish has six pointed sides and a seventh side with embossed handle, 5 1/2" w. **$35**

Fancy Open Bowl, with Pierced Border. Decorated with grapes, leaves and blue roses by C. Tielsch & Co., Germany. Back stamp: "Made in Germany" and "C.T.C." with gold numbers hand written "7206/123". Also imprint of "J" and other mark that looks like "T". Small crack in border. 11 1/4" d. **$71**

Fourteen-Sided Paneled Waste Bowl, Calcutta Pattern by E. Challinor. Back stamp: Mark 835A. Circa 1845. Small chip to foot rim. **$59**

Handleless Cup and Saucer, Lozere Pattern by E. Challinor. Back stamp: Mark 835A. Circa 1850. Cup shows a tiny nick to rim and a couple tiny nicks to foot rim. Saucer shows crazing and staining with small chip to inside rim. **$35**

Large Bowl, Ceicel Pattern by Upper Hanley Pottery. Back stamp: Mark 3929A. Circa 1900-1910. 10" d with crazing and discoloration inside bottom. **$41**

Large Covered Cheese Dish, Unmarked except for large, blue "FB" inside cover. Circa: 1880-1890. ......**$118**

Large Covered Dish, Lily Pattern by W. Adams & Co. Back stamp: Mark 30. Circa 1891-1900. Cover has two small chips and one large chip to rim. Dish has chip to outside rim and tiny chip to tip of handle. Also has one hairline crack. **$29**

Large Covered Dish, Persian Pattern by Johnson Bros. Back stamp: Mark 2177. Circa 1902. Repair to inside rim of base. Crazing on base and lid. **$75**

Large Covered Vegetable Dish, Nonpareil Pattern by Burgess & Leigh. Back stamp: Mark 712. Circa 1891. Cover and base show crazing with small stain inside cover. 8 1/2" x 12". **$94**

Large Cup and Saucer, imprinted on inside of cup, "Take ye a cuppe o'kindnesse For auldlang syne." Back stamp: The Rowland & Marsellus Co. Staffordshire England. Circa 1905. Cup shows discoloration and crazing. Cup is 5 1/2" w. Saucer is 7 1/4" d. **$44**

Large Open Bowl, Delph Pattern by E. Bourne & J.E. Leigh. Circa 1905-1908. Bowl has some staining, crazing and a hairline crack, 10 1/2" d. **$12**

Large Vegetable Bowl, Fairy Villas Pattern by W. Adams Co. Circa: Printed England, indicates time after 1891. Bowl has 4 cracks, crazing and wear, 10 1/4" d. **$12**

Open Bowl, Beauty Roses Pattern by W.H. Grindley & Co, Back stamp: Mark 61. Circa 1914-1925. Reg. No. 690339. 12" d. **$15**

Oval Covered Vegetable Dish, Milan Pattern by W.H. Grindley. Back stamp: Mark 1842. Circa 1893. ......**$82**

Oval Vegetable Bowl, Navy Pattern by T. Till & Sons. Back stamp: Mark 3858. Circa 1891. Staining, crazing and a couple factory marks on rim, 7" x 9 3/4". **$32**

Oval Vegetable Bowl, Windflower Pattern by Burgess & Leigh. Back stamp: Mark 717-718. Circa 1895-1896. Small chip to glaze on outside rim, some staining and crazing. 7 1/4" x 9 3/4". **$23**

Polychrome Over-Painted Tea Set, this fancy five-piece tea set is thin porcelain, heavily molded and embossed with scrolls and flower forms on all parts. Includes small teapot and sugar bowl, both with covers; creamer and two handled cups. Each cup has a chip to the rim. Unmarked except for cross or plus sign on bottom of all pieces except teapot. ......**$236 set**

Twelve-Sided Deep Vegetable Bowl, Kenworth Pattern by Johnson Bros. Back stamp: Mark 2179. Circa 1900. Slight wear, 9 1/2" d. **$124**

Vase, decorated with fruit and gold trim. 10" with hairline in the base and a small chip to the rim. Unmarked. **$29**

Vase, Floral/Art Nouveau Pattern by Empire China (American). Back stamp: Empire China printed in gilt along with the No. 4138. Circa 1900-1915. 11 1/4" t. **$112**

Vase, Royal Pattern by William Adderly. Back stamp: Possibly Mark 49. Circa 1880. 8 3/4" t with some crazing. **$35**

Vegetable Bowl, Victoria Pattern by Wood & Sons. Back stamp: Mark 4285. Circa 1891. Small nick on rim with wear and some discoloration. 10 1/4" d. **$12**

Vegetable Bowls (3), Conway Pattern by New Wharf Pottery. Back stamp: Mark 2286. Circa 1891. First bowl shows wear and many blemishes on top surface. The second and third bowls have scalloped rims and both also show wear, 9" d. ......**$38 all**

Mulberry Ware

Mulberry, which can vary from almost black to a delicate purple, was a favorite in Victorian homes. Most of the English mulberry was made from the 1830s to the 1850s in Staffordshire. It was made by the same potters who were producing flow blue, often in the same patterns.

Bowl, Potter: Utzchneider & Co., Sarreguemines, France. Circa 19th Century. 6 1/4" bowl with couple stain spots on inside. **$29**

Dish Encased in Wire-ware Basket, Potter: Utzchneider & Co., Sarreguemines, France. Back stamp: Mark 'J'. 19th Century. Dish is 5 3/4" d with slight discoloration. Basket is 9 3/4" with some rust. **$29**

Ewers (2), Jeddo Pattern by W. Adams & Sons. Back stamp: Mark 22. Circa 1845-1850. 5 1/2" ewer has large chip to handle with crack that goes all the way around handle and small nick to top of handle. 6 1/4" ewer shows age wear, staining and crows foot on bottom. ......**$35 both**

Flow Purple Plates (2), Flora Pattern by Hulme & Booth. Back stamp: Hulme & Booth, Burslem (impressed) and pattern name printed. Circa 1840-1845. Small plate has staining and crazing, 6 1/2" d. Large plate 9 1/2" d. ......**$32 both**

Handled Cup, and Sixteen-Side Paneled Saucer. Jardiniere Pattern by Paul Utschneider & Co. Back stamp: U & C

Plate. Vincennes Pattern by John Alcock. Back stamp: Mark 67. Circa 1857. 10 1/2" d. **$165**

Sarraguemines, Mark 6 or Mark 14. Circa 1891. Cup has small chip to pedestal base. .... **$29 both**

Handleless Cup and Saucer, Flora Pattern by Thomas Walker. Back stamp: Unmarked. Circa 1845. Hairline crack in saucer. .... **$23 both**

Handleless Cup and Saucer, Kyber Pattern by John Meir (I. Meir). Back stamp: Mark 2639. Circa 1870. Cup has some discoloration. .... **$47 both**

Three Handleless Cups and Two Saucers, Vincennes Pattern by John Alcock. Back stamp: Mark 67. Circa 1857. One cup has two chips to rim, crack and some discoloration. One cup has crack and some discoloration. One saucer has hairline crack on bottom which does not go through to the top with small area of discoloration just below outside of rim. .... **$41 all**

Large Well and Tree Platter, Florentine Pattern by Thomas Dimmock. Back stamp: Mark 1298 with Kaolin Ware printed above. Circa 1844. Platter shows wear, staining, crazing, chips to foot edge, two hairlines on back with one on front that goes around rim to back. 15 3/4" x 19 1/2". **$29**

Miniature Sugar and Creamer, Unknown Pattern and no Back stamp. Bottom is marked with the letter "M". Circa 1845-1855. Creamer has large chip to spout and sugar has no lid. .... **$53 both**

Mulberry and Polychrome Plate, Jeddo Pattern by Beech & Hancock. Back stamp: Mark 312. Circa 1857-1876. Plate has staining and crazing but not chips or cracks noted. 10 3/4". **$59**

Mulberry and Polychrome Platter, Flower Vase Pattern by T. J. & J. Mayer. Back stamp: small impressed "FB". Circa 1843-1855. Crazing and discoloration with chip to outside rim. 14 3/4" x 18 1/4". **$29**

Oval Relish Dish, Albany Pattern by John & Robert Godwin. Back stamp: Unmarked. Circa 1834-1866. Crazing and two chips to foot rim. **$23**

Plate and Saucer, Fern and Tulip Brush-stroke Pattern. Potter unknown. Back stamp: impressed mark. Circa 1840-1855. Plate has a marble design by A. Shaw. Back stamp: Cartouche with potters name (check Mark 3497). Circa 1851-1856. Plate has crazing, 10" d. .... **$35 both**

Plate, Pelew Pattern by E. Challinor. Back stamp: Mark 855 A. Circa 1840. Some staining and crazing. 8 3/4" d. **$23**

Plates (2), Bochara Pattern by John Edwards. Back stamp: Mark 1449. Circa 1850. 9" d plate has tiny chip to rim and rough edges. The other plate is 8 1/2" d. Both have crazing and light discoloration. .... **$20 both**

Plates (2), Pelew Pattern by E. Challinor. Back stamp: Mark 855 A. Circa 1840. Both plates have crazing with slight staining. 9 3/4" d. **$29**

Plates (2), The Temple Pattern by Podmore Walker & Co. Back stamp: Mark 3080. Circa 1850. Both plates show wear, crazing and one plate has some staining, 9 3/4" d.

.... **$23 pair**

Plates (3), Foliage Pattern by Edward Walley. Back stamp: All have printed pattern name. Large plate has printed "W" and small plate has impressed "Ironstone China" and "R Walley". Circa 1850. 6 1/4" plate shows wear but not chips or cracks. 7 1/2" plate undamaged. 9 1/4" plate has crazing, some staining and hairline to back. .... **$29 all**

Plates (3), Rhone Scenery by T. J. & J. Mayer. Back stamp: Mark 2570-2571. Circa 1850. 8 1/2" d plate, 7 1/2" d plate and 6" d plate. 6" plate has hairline cracks and discoloration. .... **$23 all**

Platter, Athens Pattern by Charles Meigh. Back stamp: Mark 2618 or 2614A. Circa 1840. Platter has staining, crazing, nick to rim and inside lip, with many spots of glaze loss on backside. 14 1/2" x 18". **$35**

Platter, Killarney Pattern by New Wharf Pottery. Back stamp: Mark 2886. Circa 1891. Piece shows staining, crazing and small chip to rim. **$82**

Platter, Rhone Scenery by T. J. & J. Mayer. Back stamp: Mark 2570-2571. Circa 1850. Platter is 18" x 14" with light discoloration. **$118**

Mulberry (or Black Transfer) Covered Vegetable Bowl. Roses Pattern by Benjamin & Sampson Hancock. Back stamp: Mark 1922. Circa 1876-1881. Crazing, 6 1/4" x 12". **$112**

MAJOLICA

In 1851, California had been the nation's 31st state for only four months, and Millard Fillmore was U.S. president. Elisha Otis was perfecting his brake-equipped elevator, and Robert Bunsen was tinkering with the burner that would one day bear his name. Jenny Lind, the "Swedish Nightingale," toured America in a spectacle organized by P.T. Barnum; Nathaniel Hawthorne's *The Scarlet Letter* was being hailed by critics.

And an English potter was hoping that his new interpretation of a centuries-old style of ceramics would be well received at the "Great Exhibition of the Industries of All Nations" set to open May 1, 1851, in London's Hyde Park.

Potter Herbert Minton had high hopes for his display. His father, Thomas Minton, founded a pottery works in the mid-1790s in Stoke-on-Trent, Staffordshire. Herbert Minton had designed a "new" line of pottery, and his chemist, Leon Arnoux, had developed a process that resulted in vibrant, colorful glazes that came to be called "majolica."

Joseph Francois Leon Arnoux was born in Toulouse, France, in 1816, the son of a porcelain and earthenware manufacturer. Trained as an engineer, Arnoux also studied the making of encaustic tiles, and had been appointed Art Director at Minton's works in 1848. His job was to introduce and promote new products. Victorian fascination with the natural world prompted Arnoux to reintroduce the work of Bernard Palissy, whose naturalistic, bright-colored "Maiolica" wares had been created in the 16th century. But Arnoux used a thicker body to make pieces sturdier. This body was given a coating of opaque white glaze, which provided a surface for decoration.

Pieces were modeled in high relief, featuring butterflies and other insects, flowers and leaves, fruit, shells, animals and fish. Queen Victoria's endorsement of the new pottery prompted its acceptance by the general public.

Bernard Palissy (1510-1590) was an artist, writer and scientist, yet he is most celebrated for his ceramics, and for the development of enameled earthenware (also called faience, from the Italian city of Faenza), and for the exuberant plant and animal forms his work displayed.

Palissy was born in southwestern France. Around 1540, he moved to Saintes, north of Bordeaux, married and set up shop as a portrait painter. Legend has it that he was once shown an earthenware cup (probably of Italian origin), and was so attracted to its tin-based glaze that he decided to devote his time exclusively to enameling, despite having no previous knowledge of ceramics.

The tradition of tin-glazed and decorated earthenware is believed to have originated in the 9th century, somewhere in Persia. These wares moved along trade routes to the island of Majorca, a regular stop for trading vessels traveling between Spain and Italy. When the ceramics were imported into Italy, they came to be called "Maiolica."

George Jones monumental cobalt picket fence, daisy and wheat tall-size cheese keeper with branch handle, outstanding color and detail, professional hairline repair to cover, 12 1/2" h, 12" d. **$7,250**

Palissy eventually succeeded in creating brilliant enamel glazes. But after his death in 1590, his work was ignored for centuries. In the 19th century, private collectors and museums started acquiring original Renaissance pieces, and that helped to revive interest in traditional majolica.

When Minton introduced his wares at Philadelphia's 1876 Centennial Exhibition, American potters also began to produce majolica. The Griffen, Smith and Hill pottery of Phoenixville, Pa., produced some of the most collectable American majolica from 1879 to about 1893. The company was best known for the manufacture of "Etruscan Majolica" ware. Most pieces are marked with one of the two versions of their crest. However, some unmarked pottery can also be attributed to Griffen, Smith and Hill.

The Chesapeake Pottery in Baltimore made Clifton, a pattern featuring blackberries and, later, other types of fruit and flowers. This company also made Avalon Faience, a design imitating French faience.

Other Majolica Makers

John Adams & Co., Hanley, Stoke-on-Trent, Staffordshire, England, operated the Victoria Works, producing earthenware, jasperware, Parian, majolica, 1864-1873. (Collector's tip: Jasperware is a fine white stoneware originally produced by Josiah Wedgwood, often colored by metallic oxides with raised classical designs remaining white.)

Another Staffordshire pottery, Samuel Alcock & Co., Cobridge, 1828-1853; Burslem, 1830-1859, produced earthenware, china and Parian.

The W. & J.A. Bailey Alloa Pottery was founded in Alloa, the principal town in Clackmannanshire, located near Edinburgh, Scotland.

The Bevington family of potters worked in Hanley, Staffordshire, England, in the late 19th century.

W. Brownfield & Son, Burslem and Cobridge, Staffordshire, England, 1850-1891.

T.C. Brown-Westhead, Moore & Co., produced earthenware and porcelain at Hanley, Stoke-on-Trent, Staffordshire, from about 1862 to 1904.

The Choisy-le-Roi faience factory of Choisy-le-Roi, France, produced majolica from 1860 until 1910. The firm's wares are not always marked. The common mark is usually a black ink stamp "Choisy-le-Roi" pictured to the right with a large "HBm" which stands for Hippolyte Boulenger, a director at the pottery.

William T. Copeland & Sons pottery of Stoke-on-Trent, Staffordshire, England, began producing porcelain and earthenware in 1847. (Josiah Spode established a pottery at Stoke-on-Trent in 1770. In 1833, the firm was purchased by William Copeland and Thomas Garrett. In 1847, Copeland became the sole owner. W.T. Copeland & Sons continued until a 1976 merger when it became Royal Worcester Spode. Copeland majolica pieces are sometimes marked with an impressed "COPELAND," but many are unmarked.)

Jose A. Cunha, Caldas da Rainha, southern Portugal, also worked in the style of Bernard Palissy, the great French Renaissance potter.

Julius Dressler, Bela Czech Republic, company founded 1888, producing faience, majolica and porcelain. In

George Jones, "Underwater" majolica pitcher, with cobalt top, 9" h, outstanding color, an extremely rare piece. **$5,000**

1920, the name was changed to EPIAG. The firm closed about 1945.

Eureka Pottery was located in Trenton, N.J., circa 1883-1887.

Railway Pottery, established by S. Fielding & Co., Stoke, Stoke-on-Trent, Staffordshire, England, 1879.

There were two Thomas Forester potteries active in the late 19th century in Staffordshire, England. Some sources list the more famous of the two as Thomas Forester & Sons Ltd. at the Phoenix Works, Longton.

Established in the early 19th century, the Gien pottery works is located on the banks of France's Loire River near Orleans.

Joseph Holdcroft majolica ware was produced at Daisy Bank in Longton, Staffordshire, England, from 1870 to 1885. Items can be found marked with "J HOLDCROFT," but many pieces can only be attributed by the patterns and colors that are documented to have come from the Holdcroft potteries.

George Jones & Sons Ltd., Stoke, Staffordshire, started operation in about 1864 as George Jones and in 1873 became George Jones & Sons Ltd. The firm operated the Trent Potteries in Stoke-on-Trent (renamed "Crescent Potteries" in about 1907).

Majolica four-piece condiment set with bird shaker surrounded by snake, bird's-nest salt dip and tree-stump mustard pot and base with berries, rare form, repair to mustard pot and lid, 5 3/4" h. **$250**

In about 1877, Samuel Lear erected a small china works in Hanley, Staffordshire. Lear produced domestic china and, in addition, decorated all kinds of earthenware made by other manufacturers, including "spirit kegs."

In 1882, the firm expanded to include production of majolica, ivory-body earthenware and Wedgwood-type jasperware. The business closed in 1886.

Robert Charbonnier founded the Longchamp tile works in 1847 to make red clay tiles, but the factory soon started to produce majolica. Longchamp is known for its "barbotine" pieces (a paste of clay used in decorating coarse pottery in relief) made with vivid colors, especially oyster plates.

Hugo Lonitz operated in Haldensleben, Germany, from 1868-1886, and later Hugo Lonitz & Co., 1886-1904, producing household and decorative porcelain, earthenware and metalwares. Look for a mark of two entwined fish.

The Lunéville pottery was founded about 1728 by Jacques Chambrette in the city that bears its name, in the Alsace-Lorraine region of northeastern France. The firm became famous for its blue monochromatic and floral patterns. Around 1750, ceramist Paul-Louis Cyfflé introduced a pattern with animals and historical figures. Lunéville products range from hand-painted faience and majolica to pieces influenced by the Art Deco movement.

The Massier family began producing ceramics in Vallauris, France, in the mid-18th century.

François Maurice, School of Paris, active 1875-1885, also worked in the style of Bernard Palissy.

George Morley & Co., East Liverpool, Ohio, 1884-1891.

Morley & Co. Pottery was founded in 1879, Wellsville, Ohio, making graniteware and majolica.

Orchies, a majolica manufacturer in northern France near Lille, is also known under the mark "Moulin des Loups & Hamage," 1920s.

Faïencerie de Pornic is located near Quimper, France.

Quimper pottery has a long history. Tin-glazed, hand-

George Jones cobalt pitcher with monkey handle and floral motif, outstanding color and detail, 7", professional repair to spout. **$2,600**

painted pottery has been made in Quimper, France, since the late 17th century. The earliest firm, founded in 1685 by Jean Baptiste Bousquet, was known as HB Quimper. Another firm, founded in 1772 by Francois Eloury, was known as Porquier. A third firm, founded by Guillaume Dumaine in 1778, was known as HR or Henriot Quimper. All three companies made similar pottery decorated with designs of Breton peasants, and sea and flower motifs.

The Rörstrand factory made the first faience (tin-glazed earthenware) produced in Sweden. It was established in 1725 by Johann Wolff, near Stockholm.

Holdcroft cobalt majolica game tureen with fox and goose atop bed of ferns on cover on basket weave base with holly on branch feet with branch handles, 12 1/2" l, outstanding color and detail, professional rim repair to base. **$5,500**

Monumental Palissy-style 12-piece tea set made in Portugal, set includes coffee pot 10", teapot 8", creamer with lid 7", covered sugar 7" and four cups and saucers, each depicting cabbage leaves with snake handles and spouts, various professional repairs to high points, extremely rare to find a complete set. $5,750 set

The earthenware factory of Salins was established in 1857 in Salins-les-Bains, near the French border with Switzerland. Salins was awarded with the gold medal at the International Exhibition of Decorative Arts in Paris in 1912.

Sarreguemines wares are named for the city in the Lorraine region of northeastern France. The pottery was founded in 1790 by Nicholas-Henri Jacobi. For more than 100 years, it flourished under the direction of the Utzschneider family.

Wilhelm Schiller and Sons, Bodenbach, Bohemia, established 1885.

Thomas-Victor Sergent was one of the School of Paris ceramists of the late 19th century who was influenced by the works of Bernard Palissy.

St. Clement: Founded by Jacques Chambrette in Saint-Clément, France, in 1758. Chambrette also established works in Lunéville.

The St. Jean de Bretagne pottery works are located near Quimper, France.

Vallauris is a pottery center in southeastern France, near Cannes. Companies in production there include Massier and Foucard-Jourdan.

Victoria Pottery Co., Hanley, Staffordshire, England, 1895-1927.

Wardle & Co., established 1871 at Hanley, Staffordshire, England.

Josiah Wedgwood was born in Burslem, Staffordshire, England, on July 12, 1730, into a family with a long pottery tradition. At the age of nine, after the death of his father, he joined the family business. In 1759, he set up his own pottery works in Burslem. There he produced cream-colored earthenware that found favor with Queen

Charlotte. In 1762, she appointed him royal supplier of dinnerware. From the public sale of "Queen's Ware," as it came to be known, Wedgwood was able to build a production community in 1768, which he named Etruria, near Stoke-on-Trent, and a second factory equipped with tools and ovens of his own design. (Etruria is the ancient land of the Etruscans, in what is now northern Italy.)

Unless otherwise indicated, all majolica listings in this edition come courtesy of Strawser Auction Group, Wolcottville, Ind., *www.strawserauctions.com*, facilitated by Artfact, *www.artfact.com*.

Assorted Serving Pieces

Adams & Bromley, majolica cheese keeper with bull rushes and cow finial, rare form, 13" h, 12 1/2" d, professional rim repair to cover and base rim of base. **$2,100**

Banana leaf and basket-weave, majolica platter, 14". **$140**

Barrel-shaped creamer, with floral motif, 4 1/4". **$40**

Basket-weave and blackberry plate, 8 1/4", good color. **$45**

Basket-weave and floral, rustic cachepot, 7 1/2" h, 7 1/2" d, minor hairline. **$225**

Basket-weave and leaf, syrup pitcher with pewter top, 4 1/2". **$70**

Begonia leaf majolica platter, with basket-weave border, 12 1/2", minor hairline. **$160**

Begonia leaf, on brown ground pitcher, 8", professional spout repair. **$100**

Bird and fan, majolica platter with yellow ground and rope edge, minor wear, 14". **$50**

Bird on branch, syrup pitcher with pewter top, 4 3/4". **$90**

Bird on triple mottled leaf, majolica serving tray, 12" w. **$80**

Brownfield, game tureen in the form of a basket with a cover with rabbit handle and game birds and rabbits on bed of leaves and ferns, 11 1/2", professional hairline repair to cover and base, this is a rare form that came in two sizes and this is the larger of the two. **$1,050**

Brownfield, majolica figural owl pitcher with glass eyes, outstanding detail, rare, 13". **$400**

Cobalt bird on branch, majolica cheese keeper with floral finial, base and rim chips to cover and base, 7" h. **$400**

Cobalt majolica cachepot, with floral and fruit motif and ring handles, hairline to base, 8 1/4" h, 8 1/2" d. ...**$180**

Cobalt majolica covered butter dish, with bird handle, flowers and leaves. **$350**

Cobalt majolica, bird on branch and bull rush cheese keeper, 10" h, 10" d. **$500**

Cobalt wild rose, cheese keeper with branch handle, great color, 11" d, 12" d, minor nick to stand. **$500**

Copeland, oyster plate, six turquoise wells separated by brown picket fence surrounding cobalt center, 10 1/4", rare form, hairline to one well. **$850**

Copeland, shell jug with lady in shell riding dolphins on one side and lady in clouds on the other, each with lavender ground, ivy and grapes decorate top rim, base is surrounded with shells, professional rim repair, 10 1/2", great color and detail. **$200**

Dragonfly and fan, cobalt majolica pitcher, 7", chip to handle. **$90**

"Eat Thy Bread With Thankfulness", majolica begonia leaf bread tray, 12 3/4", professional rim repair, good color. **$140**

English figural, majolica teapot with Chinaman on melon with vine handle and spout, minor rim chip to teapot, 5" h. **$130**

Etruscan, classical plate with dog, 9". **$50**

Etruscan, cobalt majolica water lily sardine box with swan finial, good color, rim nicks to lid. **$300**

Etruscan, cobalt sunflower syrup pitcher with pewter top, 8". **$200**

Etruscan, daisy compote with brown ground, 9" d, 5" h. **$120**

Etruscan, daisy oval pickle dish, 8 1/2", hairline, crazing. **$75**

Etruscan, majolica cauliflower teapot, good color, minor interior chip to lid, 5 1/2" h. **$80**

Etruscan, majolica cobalt sunflower sauce dish or syrup pitcher tray, excellent color, 5". **$250**

Etruscan, majolica fern pitcher, 8 3/4", hairline, good color. **$120**

Etruscan, majolica fern pitcher, outstanding color and condition, 8 1/2". **$350**

Etruscan, morning glory cake stand with cobalt morning glory flowers, good color, 8 1/4" d, 4" h. **$130**

Etruscan, morning glory cake stand with white ground, good color and condition, 8" d, 4" h. **$90**

Etruscan, oak-leaf bread tray with pink border, 12", minor professional rim repair to back. **$130**

Etruscan, oak-leaf bread tray with pink border, 12". **$120**

Etruscan, pink sunflower majolica syrup pitcher with pewter top, 8", handle reattached. **$130**

Etruscan, shell and seaweed 14" platter, good color, minor rim nicks to back. **$275**

Etruscan, shell and seaweed 14" platter, rim chip and rim glaze nicks. **$110**

Etruscan, shell and seaweed 4" pitcher, good color, professional rim repair. **$85**

Etruscan, shell and seaweed butter pat without seaweed. **$160**

Etruscan, shell and seaweed cup and saucer. **$50**

Etruscan, shell and seaweed plate, good color, 8". **$100**

Etruscan, shell and seaweed shell-shaped sauce dish, good color. **$70**

Etruscan, strawberry and apple basket-weave plate, 9". ..**$90**

Etruscan, sunflower syrup pitcher with white ground and pewter top, 8", minor wear. **$130**

Eureka, bird and branch low compote, minor hairline, 9" d. **$80**

Fan-shaped majolica tray, with dragonfly on yellow ground, 10". **$150**

George Jones rare form game tureen in the form of a quail with seven chicks on bed of leaves and fern on cover, turquoise base is surrounded with rabbits among ferns and leaves with branch handles decorated with oak leaves and acorns, shape no. 3371, 14" l, professional repair to cover, extremely rare form great color and detail. **$27,500**

Minton monumental garden seat in the form of a monkey with coconut supporting cobalt pillow seat with yellow tassels, shape no. 589, 18" h, rare form, professional surface repair to seat. **$12,000**

Fern and floral plate, with turquoise border, hairline, 9 1/2". $50

Fielding, bird and fan turquoise majolica mustache cup and saucer, minor surface wear. $30

Fielding, bird and fan turquoise plate, nice color, 9 1/2". $80

Fielding, fan and scroll majolica teapot, repair to spout, chip to lid finial, 6". $45

Fielding, fan and scroll platter, nice color, 13". $140

Fielding, fan and scroll sardine box, lid handle reattached. $190

Fielding, fan and scroll with pebble ground majolica pitcher, minor wear to spout, 5". $100

Fielding, fish net and shells pitcher with red coral handle, 5 1/2", good color, hairline. $180

Fielding, fishnet and shells majolica cream pitcher with coral handle, minor surface wear, good color, 4 1/2". ..$160

Figural fish pitcher, 11", minor rim glaze wear. $40

Figural majolica monk pitcher, 6". $30

Figural owl pitcher, 10". $160

Figural parrot pitcher, with bamboo handle, 10 1/4" hairline. $120

Floral and leaf, turquoise majolica three-piece tea set with matching tray, good color, rare to find matching 15" tray. ....$225 set

Floral, single-handle majolica bowl with ribbon and bow handle, strong color, rare form, 9" d. $100

French face jug, "The Black Bill", shape no. 7891, 5 1/2". $50

French face jug, "The Scotsman", professional rim repair, 8 1/2". $30

French large majolica figural duck pitcher, with open-wing handle, 17", professional repair to duck's beak, rare size and form. $300

French Palissy-style, putto supporting shell compote, 14" h, 10" d, good detail. $750

George Jones, calla lily and bird monumental floor jardiniere, 22" w, 18 1/2" h, professional repair to leaves of feet, calla lily rims and rim of jardiniere, great color and detail. $2,200

George Jones, cheese keeper with pink ground and cow finial, 9" h, 12" d, great color, professional repair to cow's horns. $1,600

George Jones, chestnut leaf on napkin large serving tray with vine handle, 14 1/2" w, minor professional rim repair, rare to find in this size. $550

George Jones, chestnut leaf on napkin plate, 9". $190

George Jones, cobalt majolica daisy and wheat bowl, 6 1/2" d, great color and detail. $375

George Jones, cobalt majolica game tureen with partridge on bed of leaves and ferns on cover, base is decorated with rabbits, oak leaves, acorns, and ferns with branch handles, outstanding color and detail, 13" l. $6,500

George Jones, cobalt majolica plate with floral border, 9", excellent color. $225

George Jones, cobalt majolica wild rose pitcher, 5", outstanding color and detail. $500

George Jones, cobalt wine jug with putti, wine barrel, grapes and vine in relief, outstanding color and detail, 9", hairlines, rare form. $1,100

Minton monumental Blackamoor garden seat depicting a Blackamoor boy with lions skin over shoulders seated on green cushion with red/pink tassels supporting a similar cushion on his head with serves as the seat, shape no. 1225. **$7,500**

Majolica large French oval table center with painted portrait of lady and winged dragon handles, good detail, 16" l, 9" h.
$140

George Jones, crate sardine boat with three overlapping fish on bed of seaweed on cover, 9" l. **$550**

George Jones, empty-nest turquoise quail game dish, no. 3416, 13 1/2" l, large size, base has rabbits, oak leaves and acorns and ferns in relief, twig handles, great color and detail, professional repair to beak and one handle. ...**$8,000**

George Jones, figural compote with gun dog behind tree looking for quail under cover of leaves, oak tree trunk is supporting turquoise oval bowl with oak leaves and acorns decorating underside of bowl, 8" h, 10" w, professional repair to bowl rim. **$2,200**

George Jones, figural majolica salt with putto atop conch shell supported by dolphin, 7" h, professional rim repair to shell. **$650**

George Jones, figural salt in the form of a dove on a branch supporting a leaf, 3", professional repair to leaf tip and stem of leaf, rare form. **$850**

George Jones, figural salt in the form of green leaf surrounded by flowers and twigs with a branch handle supporting a white dove, rare form, 5" l, 3" h, professional repair to wing of bird. **$1,300**

George Jones, fox and leaf serving tray, good color and detail, 10" w, professional repair to fox ears. **$475**

George Jones, kingfisher bull rush and water lily serving tray, great color and detail, 12" l, hard to find form.
....**$2,850**

George Jones, majolica turquoise covered muffin server with butterfly finial handle, professional repair to finial, 11 1/2" d, 7" h, great color and detail, rare form. **$1,500**

George Jones, majolica turquoise oval pate box and tray with cow atop bed of wheat, good color, professional rim repair to cover, 7" w. **$1,000**

George Jones, majolica twin shell two-part server with coral handle, 12 1/2". **$150**

George Jones, platter with overlapping ferns and leaves, 14 1/2", great color and detail, professional repair to handles. **$1,150**

George Jones, set of four turquoise strawberry-pattern majolica plates, 8". ....**$850 set**

George Jones, set of three albino majolica strawberry spoons, 7 3/4" and 4 1/4" l. ....**$275 set**

George Jones, squirrel on chestnut leaf figural serving tray, 10 1/2" w, repair to squirrel's arms, good color and detail. **$425**

George Jones, strawberry server with bird and bird's nest cream and sugar, good color, 11" w. **$700**

George Jones, turquoise majolica apple blossom covered muffin server, 10 1/2" d, 5 1/2" h, great color and detail.
....**$1,200**

George Jones, turquoise majolica plate with oak leaves and fern border, 9", great color and detail, rare. **$475**

George Jones, turquoise majolica strawberry server without cream and sugar, 14 1/2", hairline. **$275**

George Jones, turquoise napkin strawberry server with pink cream and sugar, 14". **$550**

Holdcroft, basket-weave and dogwood turquoise majolica plate, 8 1/2". **$90**

Holdcroft, honeycomb majolica pitcher, minor rim glaze nick, 5 1/2". **$80**

Holdcroft, lily of the valley oval platter, rare form, 13", professional hairline repair. **$225**

Holdcroft, lily of the valley oval platter, rare form, 13".
....**$275**

Holdcroft, majolica melon-form, brown-ground cup and saucer with green vine handle, minor nick to base of cup.
....**$50**

Holdcroft, majolica pond lily pitcher, 4". **$120**

Holdcroft, majolica six-well oyster plate, cobalt ground, white wells with pink accent, great color, 10 3/4", hard form to find. **$500**

Holdcroft, majolica strawberry dish, crested with a bird handle, and decorated in pale green, ochre, white on blue ground and fitted at one end with receptacles for cream jug and sugar, 12", professional rim nick repair. **$325**

Holdcroft, majolica strawberry spoon, 8", minor nick to bowl of spoon, rare. **$225**

Holdcroft, mottled majolica fish and daisy plate, 8 1/2", rare color, surface wear. **$120**

Holdcroft, pond lily deep bowl with lily pad feet, 10 1/2" d.
....**$55**

Holdcroft, pond lily majolica ice cream tray with twisted vine handles, hairline and rim chip, 14". **$70**

Minton pair of three-light candelabra, each depicting two putti surrounding column with floral decor, cobalt ground, 16" h, 9 1/2" w, date code on both for 1878, minor professional repair to toes of one putto, very rare. **$4,000**

Large majolica round tray, with tree bark border decorated with oak leaves and acorns, 12". **$110**

Leaves and fern majolica platter, with yellow ground, 12", rim glaze wear. **$120**

Leaves and ferns plate, with basket-weave border, 8 3/4". **$50**

Leaves, fern and floral majolica tray with pink ground, attributed to George Jones, professional repair to handle, 11 1/2". **$110**

Luneville, asparagus plate, 9". **$30**

Majolica begonia leaf tray, good color, 11 1/2". **$70**

Majolica bread tray, with wheat border and cobalt center, "Eat Thy Bread With Thankfulness", 13". **$225**

Majolica cachepot, with floral and fern motif with mask handles, 7" h. **$130**

Majolica corn pitcher, 6 1/2". **$15**

Majolica corn pitcher, 7 1/2", brown leaf spout and handle. **$10**

Majolica corn pitcher, 8". **$35**

Majolica corn pitcher, 9". **$120**

Majolica corn platter, with ears of corn on yellow basket-weave ground and border of corn leaves, good color, 13". **$225**

Majolica corn tankard, 12 1/2". **$45**

Majolica dog and doghouse platter, 11". **$90**

Majolica Frie Onnaing, square floral pitcher, 7 1/2". ...**$50**

Majolica serving tray, with cobalt ground and squirrel handle, 10" w, minor rim surface wear. **$120**

Majolica serving tray, with turquoise ground and squirrel handle, 10" w. **$100**

Majolica serving tray, with yellow ground and squirrel handle, 10" w. **$120**

Majolica seven-piece corn tankard set, with 12" tankard (spout nick) and six 5" mugs. ....**$80 set**

Majolica shell plate, 7 3/4", hairline to back. **$40**

Majolica Toby platter, with yellow center and brown border, 11". **$20**

Majolica turquoise shaker, with floral motif, 3". **$50**

Majolica, continental chick egg basket, 6" d, hairline to base. **$150**

Majolica, corn covered jar, 7". **$35**

Majolica, figural bear bottle, rare form, 6 3/4" h. **$25**

Majolica, figural seated bear pitcher, 8". **$50**

Majolica, French figural monkey pitcher, 10 1/2". **$250**

Majolica, set of 12 French knife rests with fruits and vegetables in fitted case. ....**$275 set**

Majolica, shell and coral two-handle cake tray, 11", minor rim nick. **$100**

Majolica, sunflower platter with vine handles, nice color, 12". **$90**

Minton, asparagus server on stand, shape no. 1549, 10" l. **$500**

Minton, cobalt majolica bull rush square cachepot, hairline, nice color, 8 3/4" h, 8" w. **$400**

Minton, game tureen with rabbit, duck and quail on bed of ferns and leaves on cover with basket-weave base surrounded by oak leaves and acorns, 14" l, shape no. 668, professional rim repair to cover, hairline to base. **$750**

Minton, game tureen with rabbit, duck and quail on bed of leaves and fern on cover with basket base surrounded by oak leaves and acorns, professional repair to base, 13" l, professional hairline repair to base. **$700**

Minton, majolica cucumber tray depicting large green leaf with large yellow cucumber on rim, 14 1/2" l, 9" w, shape no. 1572, date code for 1870, professional rim chip repair, rare form. **$1,400**

Minton, majolica lily pitcher with burgundy ground, great color and detail, 8 3/4" h, professional spout repair, shape no. 1228. ....**$1,000**

Minton, majolica oyster plate with six turquoise wells and large cracker well on cobalt ground with yellow daisies, good color, minor glaze nick, 10". **$650**

Minton, majolica yellow six-well oyster plate, shape no. 1323, very rare color, 9", great color, minor hairline to one well. **$1,250**

Minton, merman supporting shell figural sweet-meat server, 7 1/2" h, 8 1/4" w, good detail, shape no. 1386, date code for 1869, professional rim repair to shell. **$650**

Minton, monumental turquoise floor jardiniere/urn, each handled modeled as a satyr seated holding garland of reeds, the sides molded in relief with two lady masks holding garlands of fruit and grain on a strap-work, four-sided base, shape no. 1340, professional repair to top rim of base top rim of jardiniere and other high points, 27" h, 27" w, originally from the Marilyn Karmason collection. **$4,800**

Minton, mottled majolica six-well oyster plate, shape no. 1323, 9". **$375**

Minton, sea-mist green six-well oyster plate, shape no. 1323, 9". **$300**

Minton, server in the form of a white rabbit on green leaf, 9" l, shape no. 1531, date code for 1869, good detail and color. **$1,150**

Minton, tavern jug with five figures in high relief, 10". **$700**

Minton, tower jug with hinged pewter and majolica cover with court jester, pitcher decorated with dancers in high relief, 13" h, professional repair to rim of lid, shape no. 1231. ....**$450**

Minton, turquoise majolica six-well oyster plate, shape no. 1323, 9", good color. **$425**

Mottled cobalt and yellow, eggcup basket with six eggcups, 9" l. ....**$225 set**

Multicolor figural fish pitcher, 9 3/4", strong color, hairline. **$130**

Oval majolica platter, with cobalt rim with wheat handles and mottled center, 12". **$100**

Oval majolica platter, with floral border with cobalt accents, 11". **$50**

Pair of dark green majolica geranium plates, 9" d. ....**$70 pair**

Pair of overlapping begonia leaf plates, 8 1/4" d. ....**$100 pair**

Passion flower, majolica plate with mottled center, 10 3/4" d. **$100**

Holdcroft majolica turquoise birds in flight over water lilies jardiniere and undertray, 8 1/2" h, outstanding colors. **$400**

Picket fence and leaves, majolica syrup pitcher with pewter top, 6 1/2". **$100**

Pineapple majolica, butter tub with cow on cover, nick to cow's horn, 6 1/2" d. **$225**

Pineapple pattern, majolica platter with cobalt center, 13". **$140**

Pineapple, majolica water carafe, 9". **$140**

Pond lily majolica plate, 8", good color. **$70**

Pond lily majolica, compote with three birds on base, 9 1/2" d, 6 1/2" h, rim chip. **$70**

Pond lily, on brown ground majolica platter, 13". **$150**

Royal Doulton, teapot from the Minton Archive Collection in the form of a Chinaman #302 of 2500 with original box. **$50**

Royal Doulton, teapot from the Minton Archive Collection in the form of a flat iron with cat and mouse, #39 of 2500. ....**$225**

Royal Doulton, teapot from the Minton Archive Collection in the form of a mushroom, #74 of 1000 with original box. **$150**

Royal Doulton, teapot from the Minton Archive Collection in the form of a turtle, #91 of 2500 with original box. ...**$50**

Royal Doulton, teapot from the Minton Archive Collection in the form of a fish, #39 of 2500 with original box. **$50**

Royal Doulton, teapot from the Minton Archive Collection in the form of a monkey with coconut, #1027 of 1793 with original box. **$120**

Royal Doulton, teapot from the Minton Archive Collection in the form of a cockerel, #77 of 2500 with original box. **$90**

Royal Doulton, teapot from the Minton Archive Collection in the form of a monkey and cockerel, #23 of 1000 with original box. **$225**

Royal Worcester, majolica jeweled cider jug with leaf spout, 10", professional spout and rim repair. **$50**

Royal Worcester, sweet-meat server in the form of a conch shell supported by white swan swimming with bull rushes and water lilies, good detail, 9". **$2,200**

Rustic majolica, two-part strawberry server with two birds, 14", rim repair. **$70**

Salins, asparagus cradle/platter with fern border, good color and detail, 13". **$130**

Samuel Alcock & Co., Palissy-style jug with snake wrapped around pitcher and frog on spout with vine handle, 10 1/2" h. **$900**

Samuel Lear, sunflower and urn diamond-shape majolica tray with lavender border, 10 1/2". **$100**

Sardine box, with three overlapping fish on cover and attached undertray, rim nicks to lid and base. **$190**

Sarreguemines, face jug, "John Bull," shape no. 3257, 7 1/2". **$110**

Sarreguemines, face jug, "Jolly Fellow," shape no. 3181, 8 1/2". **$60**

Sarreguemines, face jug, "Judge", shape no. 4502, 6 1/2". **$100**

Sarreguemines, face jug, "Puck," shape no. 653, 6 3/4". **$60**

Sarreguemines, face jug, "The English," shape no. 3210, 7 1/2". **$110**

Shells and fishnet, cobalt majolica pitcher with fish handle, 7". **$400**

Minton revolving oyster stand molded with 12 mottled oyster wells and floral center on base with shells surrounding bottom rim, shape no. 1355, date code for 1870, extremely rare form, 15 1/2" d, 4" h, professional repair to rim of tray. **$11,500**

Small majolica cheese keeper, with light green ground and panels of flowers and leaves separated by branches, 6 1/2" h, 8 1/2" d. $100

Small majolica pineapple creamer, minor rim nick, good color, 3 1/2". $20

Square majolica syrup pitcher, with pewter top and floral motif, 4 3/4". $60

St. Clement, asparagus set, platter and eight matching plates; platter 14 1/2", plates 10". $150

Stork in marsh, with flying fish overhead majolica pitcher with bamboo base, good color, 9". $350

Strawberry pattern, two-handle majolica tray, 9" d, professional hairline repair. $40

T.C. Brown-Westhead Moore & Co., cobalt moon flask vase with snake at base, putto on each side and butterfly finial on cover, 12" h, professional repair to leg and arm of one putto and to wing of butterfly. $1,400

T.C.Brown-Westhead Moore & Co., yellow ground pitcher with pink and white flower blossoms and branch handle, 8 1/4", professional rim and spout repair, rare form. $700

Tri-corner, owl and fan pitcher, good color, 8". $100

Turquoise majolica, picket fence cachepot with branch feet and handles, 8" h. $275

Turquoise strawberry, ribbon and bow basket-weave majolica platter, 13". $170

Wardle, bamboo and fern cachepot with elephant handles, rare form, 5 1/2" h, minor hairline. $200

Wardle, bamboo and fern pitcher, 9". 130

Wardle, bamboo and fern three-piece tea set with teapot, sugar and creamer, nicks, chips and hairlines. ...**$100 set**

Wardle, bird and fan majolica tray, 12", staining. $10

Water lily majolica, ice cream set with shell-handle tray with water lily center and five shell-handle water lily ice cream dishes; tray, 13", minor rim nick, rim chip to one sauce dish. ....$300 set

Wedgwood "Jumbo" Argenta cheese keeper, great color and detail, professional hairline repair to base. ...**$1,100**

Wedgwood Argenta, majolica bowl and stand with angels and cherubs, rim repair to bowl, rim chip and hairline to stand, 9" d. $50

Wedgwood Argenta, passion flower compote and seven matching plates, compote 5" h, 8 1/2" d, plates 8 1/2", hairlines to five plates. ....$325 set

Wedgwood, bird and fan Argenta creamer, 3 1/4", hairline. $60

Wedgwood, grape leaf and wicker oval tray with cobalt center, great color and detail, 12". $325

Wedgwood, majolica fruit and basket-weave sauce dish, 6 3/4". $110

Wedgwood, majolica grape and vine platter with turquoise ground, 12 1/2". $225

Wedgwood, majolica plate with strawberries, grapes and leaves with brown ground, 8 3/4". $150

Wedgwood, majolica strawberry server with green ground and matching green creamer and brown sugar with lid, minor rim surface wear. $225

Wedgwood, majolica turquoise plate with strawberries, grapes and leaves, great color, rim surface wear, 8 3/4". $190

Wedgwood, pair of Argenta majolica strawberry dishes, 6 3/4", hairline to one. ....$45 pair

Wedgwood, pineapple and fruit on turquoise basket-weave ground 9" plate, good color. $190

Wedgwood, shells and waves Argenta majolica pitcher, 5 1/2", factory hairline. $120

Wedgwood, strawberry, grape and leaf plate with yellow ground, 9", outstanding color and detail, professional rim chip repair to back. $250

Wedgwood, sunflower Argenta butter pat. $120

Wedgwood, turquoise and basket-weave lemon and fruit plate, 9", minor rim glaze nick. $190

Wedgwood, turquoise corn and poppy platter, great color, minor rim nick to back, 13". $350

Wedgwood, turquoise majolica platter with strawberries, grapes and leaves, 12". $225

Wheat and basket-weave, bread tray, "Eat Thy Bread With Thankfulness", 13". $180

Wilhelm Schiller & Son (W.S.&S.), figural majolica fish-form caviar server, shape no. 2869, 20" l. $50

Tobacco-Related Forms

Continental majolica car driver, with cigar and cap humidor, 6 1/2" h, hairline to base. $10

Continental, majolica oval plaque with scene of five Indians smoking peace pipe, rim nicks to back, 14". $110

Figural majolica match striker, with artist, 5", rim nick. $15

Indian chief majolica humidor, 5", chip to rim of lid. $10

Large full-figure majolica monk, on tree stump humidor, signed BB (Bernard Bloch), 10". $120

Large majolica Blackamor head humidor, 10 1/2". $130

Large majolica monk, with stein and baskets figural cigar holder with match striker, 10 1/2". $70

Majolica Amish man, with large hat humidor, 6 1/4". $25

Majolica bulldog on mat, with pitcher and bowl figural match striker, 7", minor nick. $150

Majolica cigar holder, with match striker in the form of an Indian Chief riding horse, chip to head feathers, hairline to horse on back, 7 1/4". $25

Majolica figural cigar holder, with match striker in the form of a dog seated on a bench, 6 1/4". $110

Majolica figural cigar holder, with match striker in the form of a bull dog standing in front of cigar and match holders, loss of leaf, repair to dog's tail and ear, 7". $25

Majolica figural cigar holder, with match striker in the form of a dog in front of doghouse, 6 1/2". $70

Majolica figural cigar holder, with match striker in the form of a dog with red hat in front of shed, repair to base, 5 1/2". $50

Majolica figural cigar holder, with match striker in the form of an elephant with tubs, 5 1/2". $100

Majolica figural cigar holder, with match striker in the form of a cowboy with rifle seated on rock, 8", minor nicks to hat. $80

Majolica figural cigar holder, with match striker in the form of Indian Chief on rocks, rim nicks, 6 1/4". $15

Majolica figural cigar holder, with match striker in the form of a reclining lady with umbrella in front of shed and tree stump, 5 1/2" h, nicks to umbrella, head re-attached, signed BB (Bernhard Bloch). $15

Majolica figural cigar holder, with match striker in the form of a Blackamoor atop log with baskets, head reattached, nicks to hat and rim, 7". $90

Majolica figural cigar holder, with match striker in the form of Blackamoor man seated with crates "Cuba Fina", rim chips, loss of man's foot, head reattached, 6". $70

Majolica figural cigar holder, with match striker in the form of Blackamoor with bundles of cigars, "Columbia All", rim nicks, 7". $25

Majolica figural cigar holder, with match striker in the form of Blackamoor in front of stone wall, minor rim repair, 5 1/2". $35

Majolica figural cigar holder, with match striker in the form of a Blackamoor riding an elephant, 7". $90

Majolica figural frog humidor, with red smoking jacket and pipe, 6 1/4", repair to base. $75

Majolica figural humidor, of a crouching frog with red smoking jacket, 5 1/2" h, rim repair to lid. $160

Majolica full-figure monk, with stein humidor, 6 1/2". $50

Majolica head humidor, of clown with spiked hair, 7", chip and nicks to lid. $50

Majolica head humidor, with green cap, 5". $15

Majolica humidor, of baby with bonnet, base nicks. ...$15

Majolica humidor, of lady with green scarf, 4 1/2", factory firing line. $30

Majolica humidor, of Scottish man with pipe, 6". $10

Majolica Indian maiden humidor, 4 3/4". $25

Majolica man, with blue hat and sideburns humidor, 5". $15

Majolica man, with cigar and hat with feather humidor, 5 1/4", minor nick to hat. $15

Majolica man, with cigar and multicolor hat humidor, 5 3/4". $10

Majolica man, with hunting hat, 5". $30

Majolica man, with pipe and blue hat humidor, 4 1/2". $10

Majolica match striker, cigar holder in the form of two pigs eating from trough, minor nick, 4 1/2". $90

Majolica match striker, with puppy on leaf, rim nick to leaf, 6" l. $40

Majolica military man humidor, 6 1/2". $35

Majolica monk figure, with bucket and raised hand, 9" h. $10

Majolica monk head humidor, 6". $25

Majolica monk, returning from wine cellar figural cigar holder with match striker, 7 1/2". $60

Majolica sailor, with beard and pipe humidor, 6". $15

Poet-Laval, French majolica rustic umbrella stand modeled as a tree stump with foliage, decorated with two woodpeckers watched by a cat, 24 1/2" h, circa 1890, high points professionally repaired. **$2,000**

Majolica sailor, with rain cap humidor, 4 1/2". **$10**

Majolica smoke set, with match striker in the form of a man playing mandolin, 7", minor nicks. **$10**

Majolica spittoon, with floral motif, 5". **$35**

Majolica, continental frog and floral match striker, frog is playing mandolin, 3" h, minor rim chip. **$120**

Monk head majolica humidor, 4 1/2". **$30**

Monk head majolica humidor, 7", minor nicks. **$10**

Monk head majolica humidor, 9". **$15**

Monk head, majolica wall hanging match striker, 4 1/2". **$50**

Monk majolica humidor, signed BB #8052, 5 1/2". **$45**

Monk with bottle of wine, cigar holder with match striker, 7 3/4", minor hairline. **$10**

Monk with stein, majolica match striker and cigar holder with lid, 8". **$25**

Sarreguemines, majolica tobacco jar with lid in a form of a monkey music lover playing piano, 9 1/2" long, rare to find with lid, circa 1880. ....**$1,550**

Singing man, playing mandolin figural match striker, 4 1/2". **$15**

Stork in marsh, with flying fish majolica spittoon with bamboo base, 6 1/2", minor chip to underside. **$180**

Sultan with pipe and purple cape, majolica humidor, 7 1/2", minor nicks to lid rim. **$60**

Other Forms

Banks and Thorley, basket-weave handled basket, 10" w, 6" h. **$150**

Bird on branch, basket with bamboo handle, 10" l, 6 1/2" h, good color. **$160**

Brownfield, rare figural majolica vase of boy holding on to horn of rearing ram while hiding behind tree, great color and detail, 11". **$1,700**

Brownfield, two-handle majolica vase with grape motif, 10 1/2", handle repair. **$25**

Continental sunflower basket, 4 1/2" h, minor interior rim nick. **$130**

Continental, ewer vase with dragon handle and portrait of lady, 9". **$15**

Continental, figural majolica planter of boy dressed as clown riding pig, 5 1/2". **$70**

Continental, majolica case shelf clock with New Haven clock works, rim nicks to case, 10 1/2". **$40**

Continental, majolica figural vase with lady standing beside tree, 12". **$10**

Continental, majolica figure of man with basket of fish and basket atop his head, 15" h. **$40**

Delphin Massier, table center in the form of a wishing well with bucket on chain and seven birds perched on and around wishing well, great color and detail, 13 1/2", professional repair to rim of small barrel, beaks of a couple bird. **$1,000**

English majolica spill vase, in the form of an elephant, 8", professional rim tip repair. **$325**

French figural flower vase, #1637, hairline to base, good color, 9". **$130**

French majolica floral wall pocket, with butterfly, great detail, one leaf reattached, 14". **$200**

Holdcroft, figure of Blackamoor female slave and baby "Freedom", 14", outstanding detail and an extremely rare form. **$2,700**

George Jones, bull rush and water lily pin tray with turquoise ground, great color and detail, 10", professional hairline repair. **$400**

George Jones, cobalt majolica ball-shaped vase supported by three frogs and decorated with insects and vine, 6", minor base nick. **$900**

George Jones, majolica cobalt dragonfly, swallow, water lily and bull rush garden seat, 19", outstanding color and detail. **$2,500**

George Jones, majolica figural warbler and nest menu holder, 5 1/2" h, great color and detail. **$1,000**

George Jones, Sphinx figural candlestick with cobalt accent on base, 8", professional repair to wing tips. **$600**

George Jones, warbler and nest vase, 9 1/4", professional repair to base and rim, good detail and color. **$950**

Holdcroft, majolica umbrella stand with stork with fish in mouth surrounded by bull rushes, 21". **$800**

Hugo Lonitz, majolica table center with two figures with carriage, great detail and color, 17" l, 15" h, repair to arm of one figure and jacket of the other, unusual form. **$150**

Large majolica monk, figural bell with stein, 10 3/4". **$25**

Mafra Portugal Palissy-style, wall pocket with moth and lizard on nest with heavy green grass, 8 1/4", minor glaze nick. **$275**

Majolica basket, with ribbon and bow on handle and floral motif to side, 7" h, 8 1/2" w. **$160**

Majolica figure, of lion lying on green marble-like base, 14" l, 9" h. **$1,200**

Majolica toothpick holder, with moth and butterfly, 1 1/2". **$120**

Majolica umbrella stand, with cobalt ground and panel with floral motif, good color and detail, 23". **$375**

Majolica wall pocket, with three cornucopias, 5 3/4". **$120**

Massier, iris-form figural vase with stem base, 13", nice color and detail, professional repair to leaf and flower petal rims. **$1,800**

Minton basket, with kitten at base playing with sock, rare form, great detail, 5 1/2" h, shape no. 2049, date code for 1876, professional repair to ear of cat. **$1,800**

Minton pair of spill vases, each in the form of a putto with basket, 10 1/2" h, hairline to basket, good color and detail. .... **$800 pair**

Minton, covered box in the form of a log with a beetle at each end decorated with ivy and supported by two small logs, shape no. 1604, date code for 1870, professional repair to rim of cover. **$2,300**

Minton, large floor jardiniere with ferns, morning glories, foxglove and leaves in high relief, 13" h, 19" w, shape no. 1056, date code for 1873. ....**$1,000**

Minton, majolica lavender bamboo garden seat with green ribbon and bow, 19", rare color, base chip to underside of garden seat. **$750**

Minton, majolica matchbox in the form of a crypt with man on cover, chip to hands of man, 4" l, rare form. **$600**

Minton, porcelain dove flower holder, hairline, 6". **$90**

Minton, posy holder in the form of a clamshell atop bed of rocks, shell and seaweed, shape no. 1560, 7", good color and detail. **$1,350**

Minton, table center in the form of a pair of rabbits hiding in ferns supporting turquoise cabbage leaf, shape no. 1451, date code for 1869, 9 1/2" l, 4 1/2" h, great color and detail, professional rim repair to cabbage. **$4,200**

Minton, table center in the form of two cherubs supporting tray with a pair of doves underneath, 10 3/4" l, 7" h, shape no. 930, date code for 1862. ....**$1,150**

Minton, table center in the form of two vintagers carrying tub on mottled and cobalt base , 11" h, 11" w. **$750**

Minton, table center with two putto carrying shell on mottled and cobalt base, 11" h, 11" w, professional repair to handle of shell. .... **$750 pair**

Monumental Caldas Palissy-style, plaque decorated with large carp in the center with pike, eel and roach on a profusion of leaves and surrounded by a frog and insects, 15 1/2", circa 1880. ....**$1,150**

Morley & Co., majolica figural dog doorstop, extremely rare, good color, minor hairline to base, 9 1/2" h. **$3,000**

Pair of bonnet wall pockets, with cobalt ribbon, applied flower and good detail, 13" h. .... **$600 pair**

Pair of cobalt majolica bull rush and swan, wall pockets, great color and detail, 10". ....**$1,000 pair**

Pair of continental figures, of man and women seated in chairs, woman playing mandolin with dog on lap and man playing violin with dog on pillow, 7" h, various repairs. .... **$25 pair**

Pair of French Limoges-style majolica table lamps, with bronze mounted base, top and handles, 21" h to top of vase portion of lamp, 37" overall, complete with matching lamp shades, professional repair to leaf and flower tips. .... **$750 pair**

Pair of French wall pockets, in the form of leaves with purple and yellow flowers and bird on vine, good detail, 10", professional repair to tips. .... **$750 pair**

Pair of majolica monkey figures, with young, 7 1/2" and 8". .... **$200 pair**

Pair of majolica table lamps, with hand-painted portraits of Victorian ladies, good detail, bases 12" h, 22" overall, repair to one. .... **$50 pair**

Holdcroft pair of monumental vases in the form of large swans with cobalt cornucopia vases surrounded by water lilies, great color and detail , 11 1/2" h, 10" w, rare form.
$5,250 pair

George Jones, "Punch" punch bowl with figure of Punch lying on back supporting large cobalt bowl surrounded by holly and berries, 10 1/2" d, 8 1/2" h, great color and detail.
$10,000

Rare majolica pipe, with claw-hold pipe bowl with silver cover, unusual form. **$225**

Royal Worcester, egg toothpick holder with two mice, nice detail, 2 1/2". **$600**

Royal Worcester, figure of putto with wine flask and grapes, 3" h, repair to one foot of putto. **$70**

Royal Worcester, majolica toothpick holder with picket-fence motif with snail and butterfly, 2 1/2" h. **$170**

Rustic jardiniere, in the form of tree trunk with floral and leaf motif and acorn handles, 11" h, 14" w. **$450**

Sarreguemines, double dolphin and shell figural majolica vase, 15", shape no. 948. .... **$450**

Sarreguemines, majolica fountain in the form of a turtle, 18 1/2" l, circa 1880, unusual form. **$600**

Table center, with nude lady seated in shells supported by dolphins on sea and rock base, 17" h, unusual form, professional rim repair to shells, creamware with cold painted majolica colors. **$200**

T.C. Brown-Westhead Moore & Co., cobalt majolica vase with bands of leaves tied with pink ribbon, 5 1/2".
.... **$50**

T.C. Brown-Westhead Moore & Co., turquoise and cobalt vase with fruit on one side and leaves on the other with ring handles , 12 1/2" h, great color, professional rim repair. **$850**

Thomas Sergent, bull's head wall pocket, 6". **$90**

Wedgwood, cobalt wicker basket with twig handles, great color, 11". **$400**

Wedgwood, pair of spill vases in the form of boy with wine glass and girl with flower, each seated with baskets, 6 1/2", repair to handle of boy's basket. .... **$550 pair**

Wilhelm Schiller & Son (WS&S), large urn with lady faces and high relief and mask handles on lavender ground, 18" h, chip to rim of one ladies bonnet, good detail. **$150**

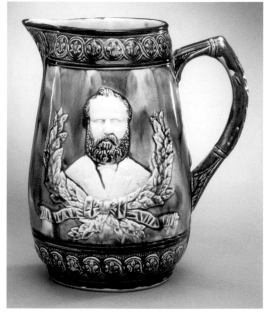

Photo courtesy Heritage Auction Galleries, Dallas; www.HA.com

Ulysses S. Grant Majolica Portrait Pitcher. This high relief bust of a more mature Grant in civilian dress probably dates from the period of his 1870s presidency, 9 7/8" in height. **$507**

Quimper

Quimper faience, dating back to the 17th century, is named for Quimper, a French town where numerous potteries were located. Several mergers resulted in the evolution of two major houses—the Jules Henriot and Hubaudière-Bousquet factories.

The peasant design first appeared in the 1860s, and many variations exist. Florals and geometrics, equally popular, also were produced in large quantities. During the 1920s, the Hubaudière-Bousquet factory introduced the Odetta line, which used a stone body and Art Deco decorations.

The two major houses merged in 1968, the products retaining the individual characteristics and marks of the originals. The concern suffered from labor problems in the 1980s and was purchased by an American group.

The "HR" and "HR Quimper" marks are found on Henriot pieces prior to 1922. The "Henriot Quimper" mark was used after 1922. The "HB" mark covers a long time span. Numbers or dots and dashes were added for inventory purposes and are found on later pieces. Most marks are in blue or black. Pieces ordered by department stores, such as Macy's and Carson Pirie Scott, carry the store mark along with the factory mark, making them less desirable to collectors.

Contributor: Al Bagdade.

Additional Terms:

A la touche border decor—single brush stroke to create floral

Breton Broderie decor—stylized blue and gold pattern inspired by a popular embroidery design often used on Breton costumes, dates from the 1920s.

Croisille—criss-cross pattern

Decor Riche border—acanthus leaves in two colors

Fleur-de-lys—the symbol of France.

Bud vases (two), 7 3/4", teardrop shape, male peasant with pipe or woman with basket, green and brown ground, blue acanthus base on yellow between orange stripes, blue and orange striped neck, red single-stroke florals on green stems on reverse, "HenRiot Quimper France" marks. **$700**

Holy water font, 8", fleur-de-lis shape, small peasant boy praying at yellow cross, blue jacket, green shirt, white trousers; scattered red, blue, and yellow stylized florals, blue chain rim, crest of Brittany at top, pierced for hanging, "HR" mark. **$250**

Plate, 7 1/4" diameter, fishing theme, front view of peasant woman with basket on each arm, red and orange-gold inner bands, border of red coral and yellow and green stylized snails, blue indented rim, "HB Quimper" mark. **$125**

Plate, 8 3/4" diameter, large yellow-centered blue and green petal sunflower in center, radiating blue dashes to border between green, red and yellow single-stroke flowers, border band of blue dot designs and stylized florals and red dash petals, blue rim, unmarked. **$175**

Plate, 13 1/2", square-on-square design, "HR Quimper" mark. **$295**

Plate, 9 1/4" diameter, three men in tavern scene, one seated, pouring wine, cider pitcher on table, light blue acanthus border on yellow ground, crest of Brittany at top, shaped rim, Porquier-Beau mark. **$1,250**

Plate, 9 7/8" diameter, well-painted peasant couple holding hands, dark blue acanthus border on light blue ground border, gold shaped rim with crest of Brittany at top, "HR Quimper" mark. **$750**

Platter, 13 1/2" x 10 1/4", male blowing horn, another playing bagpipes in forest setting, red and green flower border, scattered blue four-dot design, blue shaped rim, "HenRiot Quimper France" mark. **$450**

Porringer, 7 1/2" handle to handle, blue exotic bird with red and yellow accents, red and green side florals, blue and yellow striped inner border, red and green tab handles, pierced for hanging, unmarked, circa 1880. ....**$100**

Quintal, 4 7/8", seated peasant in gold-lobed frame on front, scattered red, yellow, blue and green scattered florals, center band of blue and gold herringbone pattern, blue and gold striped tubes, "HenRiot Quimper France" mark. **$150**

Salad bowl, 10" diameter, fluted body, blue and red exotic bird in center, light green cabbage roses, scattered red, yellow, blue, and green florals, band of red, yellow and green single-stroke florals on interior, blue fluted rim, blue outer band, "HB Quimper" mark. **$300**

Salt, 4 1/2", double, seated figural peasant woman with pipe, cobalt shawl, tan cap, blue dot yellow apron, brown wooden shoes, tan and black open basket at each side, "HB Quimper" mark, circa 1930. ....**$225**

Teapot, 5 1/2", bulbous, male peasant on front flanked by green, blue and red foliage, reverse with similar floral band, blue dash and gold wishbone handle, "HenRiot Quimper" mark. **$125**

Vase, 10 1/2", fleur-de-lis shape, front view of male peasant, red daisy and scattered typical florals on reverse, green, blue and yellow side panels wrapped in light blue striped band, crest of Brittany on spread base, "HR Quimper" on front. **$550**

Vase, teardrop shape, dancing peasant couple on front, crest of Quimper on neck, large pink peonies on reverse, band of dark blue acanthus on light blue band on neck, gold rim, large scroll handles with yellow and green accents, "HenRiot Quimper" mark. **$1,350**

COOKIE JARS

Cookie jars, colorful and often whimsical, are popular with collectors. They were made by almost every manufacturer in all types of materials. Figural character cookie jars are the most popular with collectors.

Cookie jars often were redesigned to reflect newer tastes. Hence, the same jar may be found in several different variations and these variations can affect the price.

Many cookie-jar shapes were manufactured by more than one company and, as a result, can be found with different marks. This often happened because of mergers. Molds also were traded and sold among companies.

Photos courtesy Belhorn Auction Services LLC, Columbus, Ohio; www.Belhorn.com

Right: Scarce Weller Mammy cookie jar. Marked "Weller Pottery Since 1872" and R by the finisher. Base is mint, lid has 3/16" chip and tight line to the bow, 11". **$575**

Below: Rick Wisecarver Cookstove Mammy cookie jar. The top is signed, "Special for Larry & Rita (Daniels) Oct/88 No. 1." The base is signed, "Wihoa's Original Cookie Classic by Rick Wisecarver R Sims No 1." Mint, 12" x 10". **$143**

Brush Humpty Dumpty cookie jar. Marked "Brush USA W-29". Mint, 11". **$82**

Roseville Water Lily lidded cookie jar in blue. Marked Roseville USA 1-8". Mint, 10 1/2". **$149**

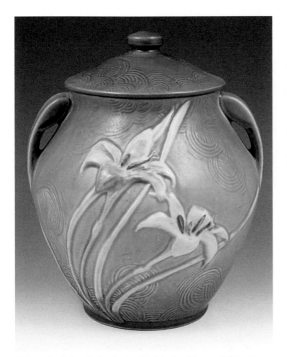

Roseville green Zephyr Lily lidded cookie jar. Marked Roseville USA 5-8". Mint, 10 1/2". **$207**

Roseville Magnolia lidded cookie jar in brown. Marked Roseville USA 2-8". Mint, 10 1/2". **$126**

CLOCKS

The clock is one of the oldest human inventions. The word clock (from the Latin word *clocca*, "bell"), suggests that it was the sound of bells that also characterized early timepieces.

The first mechanical clocks to be driven by weights and gears were invented by medieval Muslim engineers. The first geared mechanical clock was invented by an 11th century Arab engineer in Islamic Spain. The knowledge of weight-driven mechanical clocks produced by Muslim engineers was transmitted to other parts of Europe through Latin translations of Arabic and Spanish texts.

In the early 14th century, existing clock mechanisms that used water power were being adapted to take their driving power from falling weights. This power was controlled by some form of oscillating mechanism. This controlled release of power—the escapement—marks the beginning of the true mechanical clock.

Also see Modernism, Tiffany.

Photo courtesy Heritage Auction Galleries, Dallas; www.HA.com

Will Rogers Character Clock (United Clock Co., 1930s). Electric personality clock features three likenesses of the great American humorist: Will Rogers the radio star, humorist and movie star. Cast in base metals, it measures 12" x 14". Original light bulbs still in place. **$143**

Photo courtesy Heritage Auction Galleries, Dallas; www.HA.com

Archibald Knox for Liberty & Co., silver hammered metal and enamel "Tudric" clock, circa 1902-1905, impressed "English Pewter 01126/ Made By Liberty & Co", 8" x 12" x 3". **$2,390**

Photo courtesy Heritage Auction Galleries, Dallas; www.HA.com

Mickey Mouse alarm clock, Ingersoll, circa 1930s. Classic wind-up alarm clock with moving-head Mickey and pointing hands. Clock housing and base are painted green; listed on base as "Made in the U. S. A.", in style of later Bayard clock. **$69**

Photo courtesy Heritage Auction Galleries, Dallas; www.HA.com

Black man figure with clock, circa 1910. Made of cast spelter, the figure is a jolly African native sporting feathers on his head and pierced ears. His large belly holds the works of a 30-hour clock that is missing its glass and not functional. It is 12" tall and shows remnants of highlighted areas in gold with good patina. **$300**

Photo courtesy Heritage Auction Galleries, Dallas; www.HA.com

French tortoiseshell, brass and gilt bronze striking bracket clock, late 19th century, 49 1/2", the case with brass-inlaid tortoiseshell decoration and glazed side panels, the white enameled dial with Roman chapters and metal hands, the glazed door adorned with a gilt plaque depicting the goddess Amphitrite driving a chariot of seahorses. **$5,676**

Photo courtesy Heritage Auction Galleries, Dallas; www.HA.com

Cartier diamond, jade, pearl, coral and rock crystal "Mystery Clock," No. 202085. Case: upper mother-of pearl, coral and rock crystal case measuring 6" diameter with gold-set diamonds at the hour positions, silver and gold framework, atop a diamond-set, onyx and jade Oriental motif pedestal, jade and pearl base measuring 6" by 4 1/2" with coral-set silver feet, bottom sterling movement cover, 14 3/8". Dial: tapered yellow gold and black enamel hands with diamond-encrusted center. Movement: base-mounted 3/4-plate eight-day lever movement, 15 jewels, wound and set through the base, mono-metallic balance with circular gear-toothed regulator, gold finish to the plates. Signed, with original red and gold fitted box, movement signed Cartier, base signed Cartier N. 202085. (The mystery effect achieved by this timepiece has the clock hands seemingly floating in space without any connection to the movement. The hands are set on two clear revolving discs with toothed metal outer rims that are propelled by gears hidden in the outer clock frame.) **$155,350**

Photo courtesy Heritage Auction Galleries, Dallas; www.HA.com

Zachary Taylor mantel clock with reverse-on-glass portrait. From the 1830s through the 1850s, a number of companies produced clocks that incorporated reverse-on-glass portraits of presidents and statesmen into their design. Taylor's profile is flanked by draped American flags, while an eagle above clutches both the arrows of war and the olive branch of peace. Minor flaking on the original dial, and a few scattered paint flakes on the flags and eagle. Taylor's portrait has flaking on his white hair. The original maker's label inside indicates that the clock was made and sold by William S. Johnson of New York City. The works and pendulum are present, but not the weights; there is one broken hinge on the door, 19". **$1,135**

Photo courtesy Heritage Auction Galleries, Dallas; www.HA.com

Perfection Leather Oil Baird Advertising Clock. Although repainted some time ago, this Baird clock still has it's original dial and manufacturer's paper on the inside. Complete with pendulum, 18" x 31 1/2". **$2,031**

LeCoultre gilt brass and glass perpetual-motion Atmos clock, circa 1960s. Case: gilt brass glazed on four sides and the top, 9" x 8" x 6 1/2", stepped plinth base with canted corners, leveling screws and spirit level in the base, locking lever for the circular disc pendulum. Dial: white ring with golden Arabic numerals and applied dart indexes, golden Dauphine hands. Movement: 15 jewels, gilt with lever escapement, vacuum chamber winding the going barrel, annular tension pendulum, powered by barometric changes, signed LeCoultre. **$956**

Henri Marti mirrored glass, palmwood and chromium-plated brass mantel clock, circa 1925, 13". **$1,290**

Photo courtesy Heritage Auction Galleries, Dallas; www.HA.com

English painted and gilt wood tall-case clock, late 18th century; dial signed "John Burges Gosport", 86" x 19 1/2" x 10". The bonnet with shaped and arched crown over glazed door flanked by colonettes, waist with shaped door, raised on bracket feet, decorated all over in black paint with gilt chinoiserie motifs. **$4,182**

Photo courtesy James D. Julia Auctioneers, Fairfield, Maine; www.JuliaAuctions.com

Philadelphia Sheraton Tall Case Clock, Crowley & Farr. Circa 1823-1825. Figured mahogany example with molded swan's neck pediment terminating in rosettes centering a ball-and-spire brass finial, the astragal-glazed door flanked by free-standing rope-twist colonnettes, opening to the painted dial with moon phase aperture, the dial with paint-decorated and gilt Nautilus spandrels and shells, centering a Roman numeral dial marked with minutes, further centering a calendar aperture and subsidiary seconds dial, marked "Crowley & Farr / PHILAD,a". With winder, door keys, single brass finial, pendulum, and two weights, 8'4" h. x 15" throat w. x 9 1/2" d. **$2,875**

Photos courtesy Jeffrey S. Evans & Associates, Mt. Crawford, Va.; www.jeffreysevans.com

New Jersey Federal inlaid mahogany tall-case clock, unsigned, painted iron moon-phase dial and eight-day brass works, hood with broken-arch pediment, brass finials and reeded columns, waist with reeded quarter columns and inlaid ovals, string-inlaid base raised on replaced bracket feet. Weights and pendulum present. First quarter 19th century, 100" overall, base 9 1/2" x 20 1/2", top 10" x 20 7/8", with some small repairs to case. **$4,600**

Clothing
and Accessories

FUTURE OF THE MARKET: VINTAGE COUTURE AND ACCESSORIES

By Abigail Rutherford

Director of Vintage Couture and Accessories

Leslie Hindman Auctioneers, Chicago

In the face of an uncertain economy, the vintage couture category seems to have proven itself a sustainable collecting area, with strong prices and continual growth remaining constant. Here are some specific collecting categories where collectors should expect growth in the coming years.

Early 20th Century French Couture

This market has seen substantial and continual growth as a collecting category. Its impeccable hand-finished

Abigail Rutherford

craftsmanship, with rich and luxurious fabrics, have garnered strong prices. In a recent auction, a collection from Katharine Tiffany Abbott realized incredible prices against their original estimates. A French couture green velvet evening gown, without label but thought to be a Madeline Vionnet, realized $5,368 against an estimate of $200-$400. In that same collection of 31 French couture gowns, a pale blue day dress, also without label, with hand-sewn bird appliqués sold for $1,342 against an estimate of $200-$400.

One would assume that if the labels have been removed, it might devalue the garment. However, this is still a strong market. Collectors buying in the U.S. often find European labels have been removed at the time of purchase. Many buyers removed these to avoid customs charges when returning to the U.S. Look for couture techniques like hand-finished sewing with extreme attention to detail. Interior craftsmanship is just as incredible as the exterior, even including hand-sewn buttonholes. The fabrics are always of high quality and all embroideries and detailing will be hand finished, as well.

Mid-Century French Couture

This category has remained consistent and seems to have

**All images courtesy
Leslie Hindman Auctioneers;
www.LeslieHindman.com**

French couture green velvet evening gown, without label but thought to be a Madeline Vionnet, realized $5,368 against an estimate of $200-$400.

held its value. The 1940s, '50s and '60s were important historically for advances in fashion. The dawn of a post-war era created new and innovative silhouettes and will always be important as a collecting category.

Designers of importance in this time period are Christian Dior, Yves Saint Laurent, Chanel, Courreges, Balenciaga, Lanvin, Pierre Cardin and Givenchy. Recently at auction, a Pierre Cardin "Space Age" dress sold for $1,952 against an estimate of $300-$500. Another father of the Mod style, Andre Courreges, seems to have a strong following. A gray wool and white leather skirt suit sold for $1,830 against an estimate of $1,000-$2,000.

It is important that these are couture and not "prêt-a-porter" (ready to wear). Couture labels will always have a tape label with an identifying number on it. It is also important to be aware of "adaptation" labels. Adaptations are licensed copies that were not made by the designer, but rather the designer provided a pattern for someone else to make the garment. These usually say adaptation right on the label or words like "actualite" or "difuse."

American Classic

While French designers were the leading the lights in European fashion, there was a group of American designers revolutionizing the fashion scene here. Important postwar designers include Mainbocher, Valentina, Charles James and Norman Norell. All were an integral part of mid-century fashion. Charles James — known for his incredibly structured and feminine silhouettes — and Valentina were not as prolific as most designers within this time period and therefore quite collectible. An unlabeled, but authenticated, Charles James gown sold for $3,660 against an estimate of $2,000-$3,000. Similarly, a Valentina dress sold for $1,220 against an estimate of $500-$700. Norman Norell, known for his pared-down looks, has seen consistently strong prices realized for his evening wear. Most famous for his sequin "Mermaid" dress designs, in a recent auction, a green mermaid gown realized $2,440 against an estimate of $1,000-$2,000.

Masters

True pieces of art, both Chanel and Hermes accessories have consistently garnered great prices at auction and seem to have not slowed over the past decade. These will continue to realize excellent prices because of their incredible craftsmanship and rich history as fashion accessory houses. A mainstay in collecting will always be the Hermes classic bags: the Birkin, the Kelly, the Constance and the Le Trim. These constantly garner near-retail pricing as the supply for these bags is so limited. An Hermes Goatskin Kelly realized $6,710, basically the original price paid in the store in 2003, against an estimate of $3,000-$5,000. Chanel handbags can be applied to this same rule of thumb, especially the classic "2.55" bag. A Chanel black quilted leather bag recently sold for $2,928 against an estimate of $800-$1,200, again, what the owner originally paid for the bag in the 1980s.

French couture pale blue day dress with hand-sewn bird appliqués, sold for **$1,342** *against an estimate of $200-$400.*

Pierre Cardin "Space Age" dress sold for **$1,952** *against an estimate of $300-$500.*

Another area that has set record prices recently is Chanel costume jewelry, more specifically, when Maison Gripoix was commissioned by Chanel. Chanel-Gripoix pieces have "pate de verre" or "poured glass" detailing that is a complicated and meticulous art form, and designs from the 1970s, '80s and '90s have become hugely collectible. A Chanel-Gripoix red flower collar necklace recently set a record for Chanel costume jewelry at auction, realizing $6,710 against an estimate of $3,000-$5,000.

Newer Crop of Vintage, American, 1980s and '90s

While some people would not consider the 1980s and 90s vintage, there is a group of American designers from this time period that are important historically, offering a fresh take on contemporary fashion. Three designers in particular do not yet realize tremendous prices at auction, however the museum interest in these three has grown rapidly over the past year.

Marc Jacobs, while he was designing at Perry Ellis in the 1980s, has seen great momentum in prices recently.

Norell green mermaid gown realized **$2,440** *against an estimate of $1,000-$2,000.*

Courreges gray wool and white leather skirt suit sold for **$1,830** *against an estimate of $1,000-$2,000.*

His last "Grunge" collection was well loved by the trade press, but not by Perry Ellis. He was fired shortly after the collection was shown and now his final collections with Ellis seem to be at the top of the list for museum acquisitions.

Simultaneously in the 1980s, Stephen Sprouse was creating graffiti garments, designing just a few collections before he filed for bankruptcy. The rarity of these garments has created a strong market that will continue to

Valentina dress sold for **$1,220** *against an estimate of $500-$700.*

Unlabeled, but authenticated, two views of a Charles James gown, sold for **$3,660** *against an estimate of $2,000-$3,000.*

grow. A pink sequined graffiti dress (n) recently sold for $2,074 against an estimate of $1,000-$2,000.

The third is designer Donna Karan. Most notable for freeing the woman of the power suit, her "catsuit" knit ensembles that resonate with her invention of the body suit have garnered new interest recently. A black knit catsuit recently realized $335 against an estimate of $150-$250.

Another designer that is favored by museums is Norma Kamali. Well known for her alternative fabric choices, her "Sleeping Bag" coat and parachute material garments will be great investment pieces. Recently a sleeping bag coat realized $396 and a parachute ensemble realized $427, both hammering out below their auction estimate.

All of these items should begin to realize higher prices as museums acquisitions turn into retrospectives.

Newer Crop of Vintage, European, 1980s and '90s

Similar to their American counterparts, there are a few progressive European designers that have changed the landscape of fashion. Gianni Versace designs are highly coveted, especially the true avant-garde collections. Known for his over-the-top and flamboyant garments, his use of safety pins and bondage leather, silk hedonistic

prints and pop-cultural references have been garnering great and consistent prices over the past year. Recently a Versace "Warhol" Suit with all-over Marilyn Monroe faces sold for $1,220. Art references, like this Versace, in fashion seem to always be great investment pieces.

Similarly, both Moschino and Jean-Charles Castelbajac have seen strong prices for their garments recently. In a recent auction, a red jacket (q) with a Keith Haring depiction at back sold for $1,586. In addition, a Moschino Mondrian-style dress sold for $1,342.

A similar concept of commissioning artists to create capsule collections has brought Louis Vuitton an updated attitude. Both Stephen Sprouse and Takashi Murikami have been commission to create accessory collections, making those pieces quite collectible, as well. Recently a Stephen Sprouse for Vuitton bag sold for $1,830 against an estimate of $700-$900. Another area where fashion meets art is found in the more sculptural garments, like that of Thierry Mugler and Issey Miyake. Both designers have been gaining momentum over the past year. An Issey Miyake asymmetrical pleated dress sold for $1,342 against an estimate of $1,000-$2,000 while a "space age" Thierry Mugler dress sold for $1,586 against an estimate of $700-$900.

Hermes Goatskin Kelly realized **$6,710**, *basically the original price paid in the store, against an estimate of $3,000-$5,000.*

Chanel black quilted leather bag recently sold for **$2,928** *against an estimate of $800-$1,200, what the owner originally paid for the bag.*

Belt, Hermes, navy leather, Constance, 1972, gold hardware, blind stamp B. Stamped: Hermes. **$518**

Belt, Judith Leiber, green alligator, with a jeweled closure. Stamped: Judith Leiber. **$366**

Chanel-Gripoix red flower collar necklace recently set a record for Chanel costume jewelry at auction, realizing **$6,710** against an estimate of $3,000-$5,000.

Pink sequined graffiti dress recently sold for **$2,074** *against an estimate of $1,000-$2,000.*

Jean-Charles Castelbajac red jacket with a Keith Haring design at back sold for **$1,586**.

*Norma Kamali sleeping bag coat, above, realized **$396**, and her parachute ensemble, left, realized **$427**, both hammering below their auction estimates.*

*Versace "Warhol" Suit
with all-over Marilyn
Monroe faces sold for*
$1,220.

Donna Karan black knit catsuit recently realized **$335** *against an estimate of $150-$250.*

Moschino Mondrian-style dress sold for **$1,342**.

Stephen Sprouse for Louis Vuitton bag sold for **$1,830** *against an estimate of $700-$900.*

Issey Miyake asymmetrical pleated dress sold for **$1,342** *against an estimate of $1,000-$2,000.*

"Space age" Thierry Mugler dress sold for **$1,586** *against an estimate of $700-$900.*

SHOES

The shoes featured in this year's edition come courtesy of *Warman's Shoes Field Guide* by Caroline Ashleigh (Krause Publications, 2010). Ashleigh writes: "Today, owning a collection of great shoes in various styles and colors has gone from being considered a sign of excess to a rite of passage for the American woman. Take Carrie Bradshaw, for instance, of 'Sex and the City,' who mused about her wicked shoe craving: 'The fact is, sometimes it's hard to walk in a single woman's shoes. That's why we need really special ones now and then — to make the walk a little more fun.' "

Yves Saint Laurent, black and yellow stiletto platform sandals, 6" heels, circa 2008. **$800 each pair**

Nine West, black velvet sandals with gold trim and rivets, circa 2005. **$900**

Prada, purple velvet "tulip heel" sandals with ankle strap, circa 2008. **$900**

Louis Vuitton, black suede with gold leather trim stiletto evening sandals, circa 2007. **$800**

Prada, black suede with gold leather trim evening sandals with matching ankle cuff, circa 2008. **$800**

Pucci, black patent leather platform sandal with chunky heel and multicolored plastic disk detail on vamp, circa 2004. **$650**

Blue pearlized leather "Spring-O-Lator" sandals, circa 1950s. **$70**

Italian burgundy strappy sandals with gold and burgundy stiletto heel, circa 1970s. **$200**

Platinum mesh toe and ankle strap sandals with circular heel, circa 1980s. **$750**

Black velvet platform sandals with ankle strap, circa 1940. **$400**

Dolce and Gabbana, black leather ankle-strap sandals with stiletto heels and gold spur and chain detail, circa late 1990s. **$400**

Marc Jacobs, brown silk with gold leather detail and bronze-colored platform sandals, circa 2007. **$350**

Woven raffia sandals with applied flower detail and cork heels. Made in Italy, circa 1940s. **$60**

Red suede platform sandals, open toe, Thom McAn, circa 1970s. **$100-$150**

Connie, amber plastic sling back platform sandals with cutout wedge heel, circa 1977. **$150**

Manolo Blahnik, tan and black leather lace-up spectator stiletto sandals, circa 1998. **$500**

Photo courtesy Timeless Treasures, Manitowoc, Wis.

Late 1950s – early 1960s Herbert Levine classic pumps, purple suede with butterfly buckle. **$125-$250**

Photo courtesy Timeless Treasures, Manitowoc, Wis.

Early 1970s "Cover Girl" red and white Spectator platforms. **$125-$200**

COCA-COLA

Originally intended as a patent medicine when it was invented in the late 19th century by John Pemberton of Columbus, Ga., Coca-Cola was bought out by businessman Asa Griggs Candler, whose marketing tactics led Coke to its dominance of the world soft drink market throughout the 20th century.

The famous Coca-Cola logo was created by Pemberton's bookkeeper, Frank Mason Robinson, in 1885. It was Robinson who came up with the name, and he also chose the logo's distinctive cursive script.

Coca-Cola's advertising has had a significant impact on American culture, and is frequently credited with the "invention" of the modern image of Santa Claus as an old man in red-and-white garments.

Photo courtesy American Bottle Auctions, Sacramento, Calif.; www.AmericanBottle.com

Coca-Cola Pepsin Gum/ Manufactured By Franklin Mfg Co Richmond, Va., 10 1/2" with original glass lid, 1905-11. Counter display jar that held what apparently turned out to be not the most popular of the Coca-Cola products. Although it lasted a fair amount of time, by 1911 it was on its way out. By 1916 its competitors — such as Wrigley and Beechnut — began to cut into their profits. These are rare jars, especially in this condition. The top is perfect, and the jar itself has a couple minor scratches. A tough-to-find Coca-Cola item. **$1,000**

Photo courtesy American Bottle Auctions, Sacramento, Calif.; www.AmericanBottle.com

Coca-Cola Bottling Co., Cairo, Ill., 12". Fine condition seltzer made for Coca-Cola, with original metal spout. Paint is 100% intact and a few scratches are all that detract from this scarce seltzer. A tough one to find. **$300**

Photo courtesy American Bottle Auctions, Sacramento, Calif.; www.AmericanBottle.com

Coca-Cola Bottling Co., Las Vegas, one quart, 12". With painted picture of Boulder Dam. 12". Scarce Nevada seltzer with the Coca-Cola. **$550**

Photos courtesy Heritage Auction Galleries, Dallas; www.HA.com

1960's Coca-Cola baseball and football bottle cap collection (640 caps total). Baseball (180), highlighted by Amaro, Bouton, K. Boyer, Gibbs, Hamilton, Howard, Kranepool, Lewis, McGraw, Murcer, Pepitone, Peterson, C. Smith, J. Stephenson, Stottlemyre, Swoboda, and White. Football (460), highlighted by Baird, R. Baker, R. Brown, Carr, Case, DeLuca, Grantham, W. Hill, Katcavage, Larson, Lasky, Lockhart, Lynch, Maynard, McAdams, Morrall, Namath (3), Patton, Plunkett, Snell, Taliaferro, Timberlake, Blake Turner, J. Turner, Underwood, and Yearby. **$191 all**

Photo courtesy Heritage Auction Galleries, Dallas; www.HA.com

Coca-Cola 1915 Elaine Calendar. This paper litho is complete with original metal strip and full pad. Condition is strong overall in consideration of the color, and clarity of this example. The calendar has been rolled for some time and, due to rolling, there is a ripple effect from the center to the top. Slight toning of the paper from age and a rip along the area where the calendar is attached, 13" x 33". **$2,390**

Photo courtesy Heritage Auction Galleries, Dallas; www.HA.com

Coca-Cola 1917 Paper Calendar. Complete with original metal strip and a full pad. Two minor ripples are obvious toward the top from the calendar being rolled. Rarely found in excellent condition and complete, 12 3/4" x 31 1/3". **$3,900**

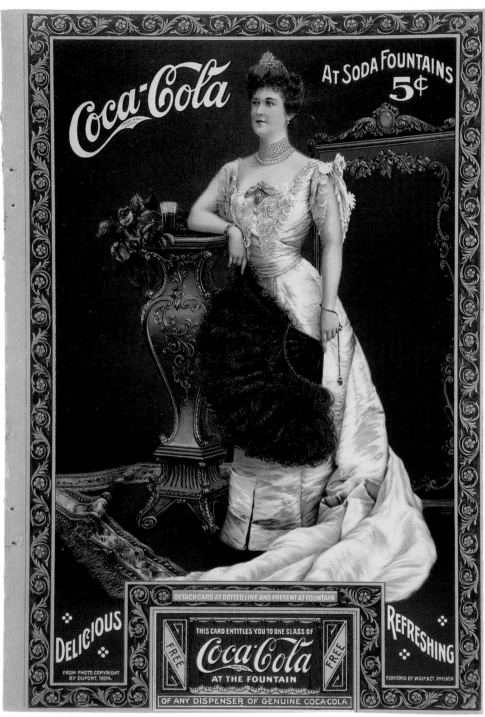

Photo courtesy Heritage Auction Galleries, Dallas; www.HA.com

Coca-Cola 1904 Lillian Nordica magazine insert with the undetached coupon at the bottom. This example does not appear to be trimmed and shows little or no wear. The holes used for binding the ad to the magazine remain in the left border, 6 1/4" x 9 1/2". **$179**

Photo courtesy Morphy Auctions, Denver, Pa.; www.MorphyAuctions.com

1903 Coca-Cola tip tray, 6". **$8,600**

Photo courtesy Heritage Auction Galleries, Dallas; www.HA.com

Two vintage Coca-Cola trays, one from 1932 with artwork by Hayden Hayden, and a 1938 tray. Both were lithographed by the American Art Works Inc of Coshocton, Ohio, each 10 1/2" x 13 1/4". **$300 pair**

Photo courtesy Heritage Auction Galleries, Dallas; www.HA.com

1925 Flapper Girl Coca-Cola Tray. Lithographed by American Art Works Co., this tray has several small surface imperfections. Edge wear to the rim is prevalent but not uncommon in this type of early tray. Fine condition. Size: 10 1/2" x 13 1/4". **$358**

Photo courtesy Heritage Auction Galleries, Dallas; www.HA.com

1941 Skater Girl Coca-Cola Tray, Made by the American Art Works in Coshocton, Ohio, this 10 1/2" x 13 1/4" serving tray pictures a girl seated on a log, relaxing with a bottle of Coke. Only very light wear in general. **$120**

Photo courtesy Heritage Auction Galleries, Dallas; www.HA.com

1927 Soda Jerk Coca-Cola tray, by American Art Works, Coshocton, Ohio. Light scuffing from normal use, 12 1/2" x 13 1/2".
$567

Photo courtesy Heritage Auction Galleries, Dallas; www.HA.com

Coca-Cola Farm Boy and Dog advertising tray, lithographed by American Art Works, Coshocton, Ohio. Normal wear as expected, 10 1/2″ x 13 1/4″. **$657**

Photo courtesy James D. Julia Auctioneers, Fairfield, Maine; www.JuliaAuctions.com

Vendo Model H81D Vending Machine. Holds 81 bottles and comes with a 10-cent coin mechanism. Shelves are adjustable. Produced mid- to late 1950s. 27" w x 16" d x 58" h. Unrestored working condition. **$1,265**

Photo courtesy James D. Julia Auctioneers, Fairfield, Maine; www.JuliaAuctions.com

1918 Coca-Cola Calendar. Summer beach scene illustration of two ladies enjoying their Coca-Cola refreshment. 13" w x 31 1/4" h. Some horizontal roll creasing. Retains original top metal band and full date pad. **$1,725**

Photo courtesy James D. Julia Auctioneers, Fairfield, Maine; www.JuliaAuctions.com

Smith-Miller Coca-Cola Delivery Truck. aka Smitty Toys. Los Angeles, Calif. Model 1-420. A 1953-54 GMC cab delivery truck with original Coca-Cola decals. Cab is cast aluminum with pressed-steel display bed. Wrapped cases as well as green bottles of probable later manufacture. 13" l. Toy and box in un-played-with condition. Decals are 100%, no chips or loss of paint. **$1,840**

Cooler Radio. 1950s tube radio in the shape of a miniature cooler. 12" w x 7 1/2" d x 10" h. Dial lights but no sound. **$402**

Counter-Top Vending Machine. This 10-cent Coke machine marked "Vendorlator" has original red and white Coca-Cola paint front, "Drink Coca-Cola Delicious and Refreshing". 27" h x 24" w x 18 1/2" d. **$977**

Photo courtesy Heritage Auction Galleries, Dallas; www.HA.com

1965-66 Coca-Cola hockey uncut panel complete set, 108 players in panel form. The presentation consists of six teams, Black Hawks, Bruins, Canadiens, Maple Leafs, Rangers and Red Wings. A total of 18 cards represent the 6 teams including a header card, which has information on receiving the N.H.L. Album. Some of the stars include Beliveau, Richard, Tremblay, Worsley, Ullman, Howe, Delvecchio, Pronovost, Kelly, Horton, Keon, Mahovlich, Sawchuk, Giacomin, Ratelle, Cheevers, Bucyk, Parent, Hall, Pilote, Esposito, B. Hull, and Mikita. Cards grade in the EX/MT to NM/MT range. **$478 set**

COIN-OPERATED DEVICES

Coin-operated devices fall into three main categories: amusement or arcade games, trade stimulators and vending machines.

Photo courtesy James D. Julia Auctioneers, Fairfield, Maine; www.jamesdjulia.com

5-Cent/25-Cent Caille Double with original music. All the original linkage is intact except wire rods to trip music. The crank on the side and the lever to deactivate music are still present. The original iron castings have substantial nickel plating and painted highlighting to head is almost all intact. The iron legs have little nickel left, which is typical and often times over the years the legs were painted silver. Dials are intact and in fine condition, original reverse glasses are present; one has three cracks, the others are intact and are flaking to blue background paint. Wood cabinet needs cleaning and some re-gluing. Lacking partial rounded molding around center dials and a few pieces of trim. Back doors are present with original locks; one door missing section of wood. Musical containment area is present including rear containment door. Approximately 47" x 14" x 63". Left-side handle plate is intact, handle missing. Mechanisms appear to be complete. Iron castings are intact and the only visible damage is a hairline crack in iron plate surrounding the right side coin head. **$80,500**

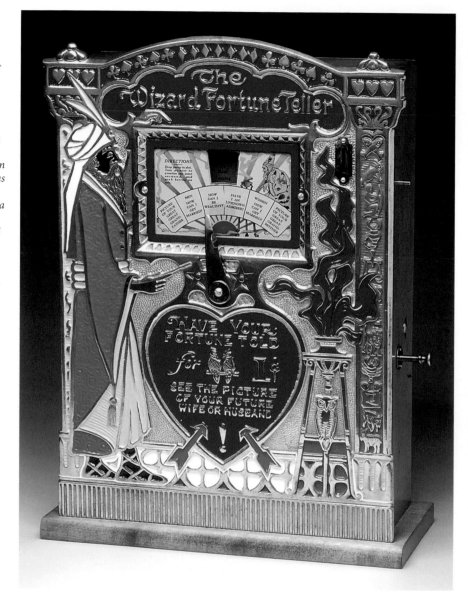

*Mills Wizard
Fortune Teller.
With Mills
trademark owl on
the front casting,
which is covered in
card symbols, signs
of the Zodiac,
flaming urn, and a
wise man/wizard.
Customer selected
the question;
upon depositing
a penny and
plunging the lever
on the right side
of the machine,
the answer
would appear.
Professionally
restored, 13 1/2"
x 6" x 18 1/2".*
$2,070

O.D. Jennings, 5-Cent Standard Chief Tic-Tac-Toe slot machine. Used in casinos, various social clubs, etc. from the early 1940s and produced in variety into the early 1960s. Nickel-plated castings with red highlights, visible jackpot, and a cast brass Indian's profile on the front. A unique feature to this machine is the Tic-Tac-Toe: A bar on the first reel in any visible position (one of three), a bar on the second reel in any position, and a bar on the third reel in any position would win the jackpot. Hence, the term Tic-Tac-Toe, 16" x 16" x 30". **$805**

Samuel Nafew, poker gambling machine. When a nickel is deposited and the lever depressed, the five rows of cards would flap about, stopping suddenly and a poker hand was visible to the player. Player would be rewarded with free cigars if he had a winning hand according to the award card at the top of the machine. In functional working condition with original iron castings and original award and direction

paper, 11 1/2" x 8 1/2" x 12 1/2". Overall very fine restored condition. Iron marquee has old damage/cracks with aged repair to rear. Lacking keys. **$2,875**

Caille "Banker" trade stimulator, an early 20th century gambling device frequently found in saloons, general sores, barbershops, etc. A hand of poker was "dealt" to the gambler in hopes of obtaining trade or cash for a winning hand. A nickel is deposited in the coin entry and the plunger/thumb lever pushed down would cause the five reels to spin and a new poker hand would appear. A fanciful front iron casting, upon close examination one can see the word "Banker" cast into the ornate design and also the trademark "CB" (Caille Brothers) also cast into the design. The cabinet, mounted on a swivel base, is constructed of quarter-sawn oak with a wooden back door (replaced) and on the top of the cabinet is an elaborate casting depicting two semi-nude women encasing the reward schedule for winning poker hands, 13" x 8" x 24". Rewards marquee is not original to the machine. **$2,300**

Mills "Two-Bit" Upright Dewey, patented in 1898, the Dewey was produced by Mills for 20+ years. A quarter, or up to six quarters, could be played. If all six slots were selected, player were guaranteed a winner. Rewards would be anywhere from 50 cents to $5. This is an earlier version with a paneled quarter-sawn oak cabinet and blackened copper oxide plated castings. The lithographed tin wheel is known as the "pie wedge" version. Original glass with mirror and reverse-painted "TWO BIT" is overall in very good condition with some flaking,: 66" x 29" x 18".
.... **$23,000**

Reliance novelty poker machine, a classic and ornate cast-iron card machine with an exposed mechanism. Upon depositing a penny in the slot and depressing the plunger, the five cylinders — each containing a number of cards that are spring-loaded — would spin and the player's poker

hand would appear, as well as the last coin played in lower right corner of front window. The iron castings other than the marquee are intact and in original nickel-plated finish. Front casting is embossed with "Reliance Novelty Co." and the original cash drawer at rear of machine is marked "Victor", 11" x 9" x 15". **$3,680**

Mills 5-Cent Futurity slot machine, a dial at the top of the machine is numbered from 1 to 10. Upon depositing a nickel, if the player did not win, the arrow moved upwards. If the player got the arrow to 10, he would be awarded ten nickels and the dial would reset to zero. Machine has an inordinate amount of cherries on the first and second reel, making it difficult for the player not to win, especially with the slim chance of advancing the arrow to 10. Original wood finish and some original orange paint to front castings. Later brown crackle paint enhancement to front castings. Mechanism is intact, operational, and complete, 16" x 16" x 30". **$3,220**

Photo courtesy James D. Julia Auctions, Fairfield, Maine; www.jamesdjulia.com

Seeburg Style "KT Special" Orchestrion. Produced from approximately 1918 until the late 1920s. This particular model has piano, xylophone, mandolin, base drum, snare drum, tympani (base drum attachment), cymbal, castanets, triangle, tambourine and Chinese wood block. According to Q. David Bowers (Encyclopedia of Automatic Instruments) this particular style was a top-of-the-line model with the most instruments of any cabinet-style orchestrion. Encased in a fancy veneered-oak cabinet with a leaded art glass front exposing a few of the instruments, 48 1/2" x 24 1/2" x 65 1/2". Art glass does have some cracks. **$12,650**

Encore coin-operated automated banjo. Features a banjo inside an elaborate oak case. When a coin is deposited, the banjo would play a tune. A paper roll similar to those used on player pianos was responsible for the action of the banjo. Curved metal "fingers" pluck away at the banjo. The cabinetry is oak with detailed inset panels, fancy trims and moldings, serpentine opening front, and cast-metal grilles in place on front and sides. Extremely rare, 83" x 26" x 24". Machine has had total overall restoration inside and out. Internal wood barrel covering the mechanics and music roll has been replaced. Wood panel at the rear of the machine is also of newer vintage. Machine is functional, but should be tuned. **$54,625**

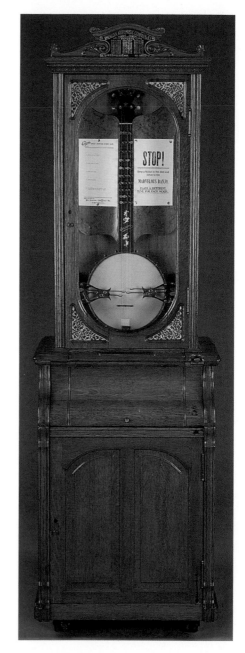

Mills 5-Cent Brownie slot machine, at the turn of the century the Palmer Cox Brownies were quite the rage, often used on a multitude of items ranging from soda bottles to rubber boots. Mills Novelty Co. produced this countertop gambling machine, which is in an oak cabinet, an elaborate tin litho dial with Brownie faces on the highest winning payout and a fancy cast-iron head accepting up to five coins. If all five slots were selected, a winner was guaranteed. However, varied pay amounts from 2-1 up to 20-1 depending on color chosen (red and black were a 2-to-1 payout). Green, the highest payout (20 to 1) had only 2 slices on the payout disc. Restored wooden cabinet and nickel-plated iron castings. The lithographed tin dial with the various colors is in near-mint condition, the machine is functional, 22" x 11 1/2" x 30". Replacement back door. **$6,037**

Caille Mayflower cast-iron trade stimulator, circa 1905, similar to the Caille Puritan. However this is a much rarer model and seldom found especially in all original condition, The main difference between the Caille Puritan and Mayflower is that this is a five-reel machine with card symbols, whereas Puritan is only a three-reel machine with either fruit symbols or numbers. The iron cabinet has a cast decoration on front and both sides and is in its original nickel-plated finish. A unique triangular coin entry head accepts only nickels; all other coins are rejected out the back base of coin entry head. The iron marquee with reward paper and mirrored back (operator could see cards as well) is intact and original. The rear door/drawer, which is marked "Puritan Machine Co. Detroit, Michigan", is intact with original lock and key present. Five-cent operation is smooth and the paper reel strips are in fine+ condition with only some minimal loss to first strip. A counter on the upper left front casting indicates amount of plays (27,109) registered and the serial number of this machine is 5038, 10" x 6 1/2" x 11". **$8,050**

O'Malley "Eclipse", gambling trade stimulator. A clockwork gambling device that was often found in saloons, general stores, etc. in the early 20th century. This unique machine contained within an oak cabinet with nickel trims has two arrows that spin when a penny is deposited in the slot. The player would add the total and then view the "award card" below. If a winning combination was obtained, the bartender/shopkeeper would reward the player with 5-cent cigars. Included is an original photograph of an O'Malley Eclipse on location in a general store, 12 1/2" x 6" x 19". Restored condition. Wooden back door is a later replacement. **$1,725**

Kelley "Improved", trade stimulator with gum vendor. Manufactured in the early 20th century for use in country stores, saloons, etc., this gambling device awarded the player a stick of gum every time he played. This subtle dispensing of gum navigated the gambling laws of the time, indicating that this was a mere gum vendor and not a gambling device. With five reels, two of which are blank, and the other three having various numbers, the concept

Photo courtesy James D. Julia Auctioneers, Fairfield, Maine; www.jamesdjulia.com

Groetchen "Poison This Rat" arcade machine. From the 1940s, featuring Hitler on the front facade. A penny is deposited and the player gets five "poison" pills to be dispensed to the Fuhrer in hopes of killing him off. The game uses slopes and runways to get the small red balls into Hitler's mouth. It retains much of its original finish and is in working order, 16 1/2" x 11" x 24". Couple of minor splits to wooden cabinet. Lacking original wooden back door. Original directions on interior panel. Needing additional small wooden pills/balls. **$7,475**

Photo courtesy James D. Julia Auctioneers, Fairfield, Maine; www.jamesdjulia.com

A.J. Stephens dice game. Circa 1930s, a player would deposit a nickel, depress the level, and watch the dice flip. Various award cards (four included) could be changed by the operator/ bartender. Displayed also would be the beer of choice that the player could win. Overall in as-found, original condition and finish. Glass possibly incorrect, 11" x 7 1/2" x 5" (excluding bottle and glass). Padlock lacking key. **$1,035**

being to total the numbers of the three reels and then view the award card to see if one was a winner. Originally there was a simple marquee (made of turned wire/rods) sitting atop the machine which is now missing. The oak cabinet has been refinished and iron castings have been re-plated. Oak-paneled back door is a quality replacement, 16 1/2" x 13 1/2" x 9". Reel strips are in good original condition, some staining and fading..**$1,667**

O.D. Jennings payout pinball machine, mid-1930s. With sportsman motif of ducks, rabbits, pheasants, squirrels, etc. One would shoot a ball in hopes of getting it into certain holes, winning six tokens and/or six nickels, depending on how the payout system was loaded. Unlike pinball machines of today, these early machines contained no flippers. A little minor twitching, a little shaking, or sheer luck would drop the ball into the appropriate

hole. These machines were easy to tilt and thus voided any possible reward/payout. Internally quite simple by nature, electric contacts indicated the holes in which the balls dropped. Thus the machine would "know" if two balls landed in the duck holes, winning three tokens. One could win only one reward, only the highest winning combination would pay out, 42" x 18" x 39". Overall pristine original condition. Two exterior aluminum leg caps have minor damage (repaired cracks). Small cashbox door possible replacement. Mechanics/electric untested. **$1,180**

Mutoscope monkey strength tester, from the 1940s, prevalent at arcades and amusement parks. As you stood on the iron base and pulled the handles upwards, the monkey would climb the coconut tree. The colored lights on the marquee would change from left to right as the monkey climbed higher. If you were a "strong man," the red light indicating 1,000 would glare brightly and the bell would ring. Obviously for the operator of this machine, it was a cash cow, as the kids would gather around, depositing coin after coin trying to outdo the others. Mechanics appear to be functional. Wooden cash drawer on side replaced with metal door, 90" tall. Coin entrance plaque is old but probable replacement. One-cent decals added to front facade of machine. **$4,025**

Nickel-drop payout gambling device, of unknown manufacture, but definitely from the first quarter of the 20th century, a somewhat complicated mechanism yet simple in concept. Similar to a Clawson "Crackerjacks,"

in which the coin would travel downwards through a series of pins and trip a lever releasing the coins in the visible pocket, this particular machine also has the nickel traveling down a series of pins and activating one of five levers. When a lever is activated there is an internal gear that advances, and every so often a token is dispensed and retrieved by the player on left side of machine. May be one of a kind. Internal plate holding the visible tokens in place has been replaced with a piece of sheet aluminum. Some sort of paper with directions and maker's name was originally behind the front glass panel, 17" x 11" x 19". Original wood finish to cabinet, split to domed top, otherwise minimal nick to cabinet. **$2,875**

Pulver's wooden cased "Yellow Kid" gum machine. A clockwork turn-of-the-century gum vendor features the Yellow Kid. Activated by a penny, the Yellow Kid bows, then turns to the gum column, raising his hand to his mouth and then turns back. A pot-metal head with original paint and a polished cotton gown (frail, fabric loss) adorn the Yellow Kid figure. Cabinet is constructed of oak with a glass front window and two smaller glass windows on either side. An oval brass tag is mounted to the front panel/door and all paper adorning the front window is original, 12" x 10 1/2" x 24 1/4". In as-found working condition with a couple minor splits to wood case, lacking lock on back door. **$10,350**

COINS

Collecting Modern U.S. Commemorative Coins

1982-S proof Washington silver half dollar. **$6.50**

For more information, see *The Instant Coin Collector* by Arlyn G. Sieber, 2009, Krause Publications.

Congress has authorized myriad commemorative coin series since 1982. Commemorative coins honor events, people, organizations or other things, and are authorized by law. They are official U.S. government issues and legal tender, but they are not intended to circulate. Instead, the U.S. Mint—at a premium above face value—sells them directly to collectors. Laws authorizing commemorative coins usually mandate that a certain amount of the purchase price benefit a group or event related to the coin's theme.

In terms of cost, collecting modern commemoratives is a step up from collecting coins from circulation at face value or buying them at shops or shows for a few dollars each.

The story behind the coins

The first U.S. commemorative coin was an 1892 half dollar for the Columbian Exposition. The exposition was held May 1-Oct. 30, 1893, in Chicago to commemorate the 400th anniversary of Columbus' arrival in the New World. The U.S. Mint struck 950,000 Columbian half dollars dated 1892 and more than 1.5 million dated 1893.

The Columbian half dollar opened the door to many other commemorative coins from the 1910s and continuing into the 1950s. Most were silver half dollars, but there was also an 1893 quarter (also for the Columbian Exposition), a number of gold dollars, two gold $2.50 coins and two gold $50 coins.

The coins were sold by the Mint at a premium above face value. Some commemorated state anniversaries or national themes, such as the U.S. Sesquicentennial in 1926.

There were no less than 18 commemorative half dollars issued in 1936 alone. Among them was an issue commemorating the 75th anniversary of the Battle of Gettysburg. Others, however, were of little national importance, such as issues for the Cincinnati Music Center and the centennial of Elgin, Ill.

Congress grew weary of U.S. coinage being used as local fundraisers, and the flow of commemorative coins slowed in the 1940s and '50s. The last issue among what are commonly called "early" commemoratives was a 1954 half dollar honoring Booker T. Washington and George Washington Carver.

A 28-year hiatus on commemorative coinage ensued until Congress authorized a half dollar in the traditional 90-percent-silver composition to honor the 250th anniversary of George Washington's birth in 1982. Thus began the "modern" commemoratives.

The Washington coin was a winner in many respects: First, its theme was of truly national significance and worthy of commemoration. Second, its design by Mint engraver Elizabeth Jones featured a striking depiction of Washington on horseback, a departure from the staid busts used for portraiture on coins since the Lincoln cent of 1909. The reverse, also designed by Jones, features a view of Washington's Mount Vernon home.

These factors, combined with the long break in commemorative coinage, made the coin popular with collectors. The Mint sold more than 2.2 million uncirculated versions ("D" mintmark) and almost 4.9 million proof versions ("S" mintmark).

1997-W proof Franklin Delano Roosevelt five dollar gold. **$565**

The first U.S. commemorative coin: 1892 Columbian Exposition half dollar (AU-50). **$18.50**

The proliferation of commemorative coins in the 1930s included a half dollar for the Cincinnati Music Center (AU-50). **$315**

Like the Columbian half dollar 90 years earlier, the George Washington half dollar opened the door to more commemorative coinage, and like the commemorative coinage of the 1930s, an undesirable proliferation resulted. The coins' themes in the 1990s weren't as localized as many of those in the 1930s, but commemorative coinage became an easy mark for senators and U.S. representatives looking to do a favor for a constituency, or for a fellow lawmaker by offering their vote for a commemorative coin program. Commemoratives could raise funds for a pet cause through surcharges on the Mint's sales of the coins, and a vote for a program went largely unnoticed by the general public.

The year 1994 alone brought five commemorative coin programs: World Cup soccer, National Prisoner of War Museum, U.S. Capitol Bicentennial, Vietnam Veterans Memorial and Women in Military Service Memorial. Although each theme had its virtues, the market for commemorative coins couldn't keep up with all the issues, and sales plummeted from the highs of the Washington half dollar and other early issues in the modern era.

In response, Congress passed the Commemorative Coin Reform Act of 1996. Among other provisions, it limits the number of commemorative themes to two per year. In addition, congressional proposals for commemorative coins must be reviewed by the Citizens Coinage Advisory Committee, which reports to the Treasury secretary. The 10-person committee consists of members from the general public and those with credentials in American history, sculpture and numismatics.

The last of the "early" commemoratives honored Booker T. Washington and George Washington Carver (AU-50). **$40**

1994 commemoratives included issues for World Cup soccer, National Prisoner of War Memorial, Bicentennial of the United States Capitol, Vietnam Veterans Memorial and the Women in Military Service Memorial.

1996-P proof Atlanta Olympics silver dollar, high-jumper design. **$60**

1988-W proof Olympiad gold five dollars. **$190**

Where to get them

Current-year commemoratives can be purchased directly from the U.S. Mint (www.usmint.gov). Issues from previous years can be purchased at shows, shops or through advertisements in hobby publications, such as Coins magazine.

Collecting strategies

A complete collection of every commemorative half dollar, silver dollar and gold coin issued since 1982 is a commendable but daunting goal for many collectors, especially beginners. Following are suggestions for getting started in collecting modern commemoratives, which can lead to expanding the collection in the future:

Collect what you like

If you see a modern commemorative coin and you like it, buy it. The coin may appeal to you because of its theme or design. Whatever the reason, if you like the coin and are willing to pay the asking price, it will make a great addition to your collection.

By denomination

A new collector may want to focus on just the commemorative half dollars issued since 1982 or just the silver dollars. With a good value guide in hand and more money to spend, a new collector could also venture into gold coins and select one or more of the many commemorative gold $5 coins.

By theme

Collectors of modern commemoratives can also focus on a particular theme that appeals to them, such as presidents, the Olympics or other sports, women or military themes. Again, collect what you like.

1990-P proof Eisenhower Centennial silver dollar. **$17**

1986-S proof Statue of Liberty Centennial clad half dollar. **$5.50**

1993-S proof Thomas Jefferson silver dollar. **$28**

As a complement to a circulating-coin collection

One or more commemorative coins can complement a collection of circulating coins with similar design themes. For example, a 1993 silver dollar commemorating the 250th anniversary of Thomas Jefferson's birth can complement a collection of Westward Journey nickels. A 1990 silver dollar commemorating the centennial of Dwight Eisenhower's birth can complement a collection of Eisenhower dollars.

By set

When selling a current-year commemorative series, the U.S. Mint often offers various sets containing individual coins in the series in uncirculated and proof versions. For example, the 1986 Statue of Liberty Centennial coin series consisted of a base-metal half dollar, silver dollar and gold $5. Various sets of the series offered by the Mint that year included a two-coin set consisting of an uncirculated silver dollar and clad half dollar; a three-coin set consisting of uncirculated versions of each coin; and a six-coin set consisting of proof and uncirculated versions of each coin.

These and sets of other series can be found in their original Mint packaging from online sellers, at shops and shows, and through advertisements in hobby publications such as Coins magazine.

How much?

Some of the least popular commemorative coins at the time of their issue are the most expensive on the secondary market today, and some of the most popular commemorative coins at the time of their issue are the most affordable today. Why? The least popular coins didn't sell as well, which resulted in lower mintages. Generally speaking, the scarcer coins are more valued by collectors, which increases demand and drives up their asking prices on the secondary market.

For example, the 1982 George Washington silver commemorative half dollar was popular and sold well at the time of issue. With millions of coins produced, either an uncirculated or proof example can be purchased for under $10.

1986-S proof Statue of Liberty Centennial silver dollar. **$13.50**

1986-W proof Statue of Liberty Centennial gold five dollars. **$190**

1993-S proof James Madison clad half dollar. **$16.50**

1996-S proof Atlanta Olympics clad half dollar, swimmer design. **$36**

1991-S proof Mount Rushmore Golden Anniversary clad half dollar. **$20**

In contrast, less than 50,000 uncirculated versions of the 1996 Atlanta Olympics commemorative clad half dollar with the swimmer design were produced. Expect to pay more than $150 for one on the secondary market.

Coin Prices magazine, available on many newsstands, provides a complete list of modern U.S. commemorative coins and a guide to current retail values.

Mintmarks

Modern U.S. commemorative coins have either a "P" mintmark for Philadelphia, "D" for Denver, "S" for San Francisco, or a "W" for West Point, N.Y. Mintmark location varies by coin.

Condition

Commemorative coins are specially handled and packaged at the mints. Thus, grading is less of a factor in purchasing and collecting them.

Still, check each coin before you purchase it or after you receive it in the mail. Make sure its surfaces are clean and free of scratches or other significant blemishes.

The U.S. Mint has a 30-day return policy for coins purchased directly from it. Mail-order dealers, such as those who advertise in Coins magazine, also offer return policies. Check individual ads for specific terms.

1989-S proof Bicentennial of the Congress silver dollar. **$18.50**

1997-S proof Jackie Robinson silver dollar. **$85**

1992-P proof Columbus Quincentenary silver dollar. **$39**

2004-P proof 125th Anniversary of the Light Bulb silver dollar.
$41

1995-S proof Civil War silver dollar. **$78**

How to store them

Keep commemorative coins in their original U.S. Mint packaging, whether purchased directly from the Mint or on the secondary market. The packaging is suitable for long-term storage and protects the coins from wear and blemishes that occur when handled directly.

Modern commemorative coin specs

Commemorative coins are struck in traditional specifications for the denomination and composition. Future issues may be subject to change from the specs listed.

Clad half dollars

Diameter: 30.6 millimeters.

Weight: 11.34 grams.

Composition: clad layers of 75-percent copper and 25-percent nickel bonded to a pure-copper core.

Silver half dollars

Diameter: 30.6 millimeters.

Weight: 12.5 grams.

Composition: 90-percent silver, 10-percent copper.

Actual silver weight: 0.3618 troy ounces.

Silver dollars

Diameter: 38.1 millimeters.

Weight: 26.73 grams.

Composition: 90-percent silver, 10-percent copper.

Actual silver weight: 0.76 troy ounces.

Gold $5

Diameter: 21.5 millimeters.

Weight: 8.359 grams.

Composition: 90-percent gold, 10-percent alloy.

Actual gold weight: 0.24 troy ounces.

Gold $10

Diameter: 27 millimeters.

Weight: 26.73 grams.

Composition: 90-percent gold, 10-percent alloy.

Actual gold weight: 0.484 troy ounces.

1999-W proof George Washington gold five dollars. **$475**

2006-P proof Benjamin Franklin Tercentenary silver dollar, Franklin portrait design. **$54**

1993-W James Madison gold five dollars. **$265**

2003-P proof First Flight Centennial gold 10 dollars. **$560**

DOORSTOPS

Decorative cast-iron doorstops date from around the turn of the 19th century, and have attracted collectors with their myriad depictions of flowers, people and animals. Beware of modern reproductions that simulate aged and worn paint. All photos are courtesy Bertoia Auctions, Vineland, N.J.; *www.BertoiaAuctions.com.*

Hubley Giraffe, strong overall original paint, 12 1/2" x 10". **$6,900**

Bradley & Hubbard squirrel on log, heavy casting, ornate overall details from fur to tree bark; original rubber bumpers (slightly worn) on reverse side, 10" x 11 1/2". **$2,875**

Nuydea Little Red Riding Hood and Wolf, embossed "Little Red Riding Hood" on reverse, strong overall casting details, rare, 7 1/2" x 9 1/2". **$1,610**

Little Red Riding Hood, rare flat-back style, engraved "Copyrighted 1930 Creation Co. Pat. No. 160," 4 7/8" x 8 3/4". **$1,093**

Screech Owl, cast iron, marked "cJo - 1287" on reverse, meticulously detailed and hand painted, 10 1/4" x 6". **$2,588**

Donald Duck, marked "© Walt Disney Productions 1971" on reverse; stop sign spins to reveal "Enter" on back side, 8 1/2". **$288**

Taylor Cook Penguin, cast iron, rare variation includes a wooden base and backing shaped to penguin's form, 5 1/4" x 9 1/2". **$1,955**

Duck With Top Hat, solid casting, rare, full figure painted in blue pants with black hat and shoes, 4 1/4" x 7 3/4". **$633**

Hubley Black Deco Dog, cast iron, whimsical full-figure Airedale with head cocked to side, 4 3/4" x 10 3/4". **$633**

Hubley Fox Terrier On Green Base, cast iron, flat-back example, 7 1/4" x 6 1/4". **$489**

Above: Hubley Bloodhound, rare, cast iron, painted in black and tan, 6" x 6 1/2". Chipping and touchup. **$690**

Right: French Bulldog, full-figure example posed in sitting position, 7 5/8" x 6 3/4". **$374**

Rabbit, full figure, facing left, realistic size and detail, 9" x 8 1/2". **$4,025**

Hubley Tulips and Hyacinths, no. 471, cast iron, handled wicker basket on black base, 6 1/4" x 9 1/2". **$288**

Hubley Roses in Cornucopia, no. 441, 9 1/8" x 10". **$230**

Bradley & Hubbard Huck Finn, flat-back style, retains one rubber bumper, 5 1/2" x 9 3/4". **$4,025**

Man On Break, rare, man smoking cigarette with knee bent up as if leaning against a wall, 7 3/4" x 4". **$1,610**

Caddy, hard to find, flat-back style, 6" x 8". **$2,588**

Colonial Boy, cast iron, standing with arm extended, double-sided example, 5 3/8" x 8 3/4". **$546**

FIREARMS

Laws regarding the sale of firearms, especially modern-era weapons, continue to evolve. Be sure to buy and sell firearms through auction houses and dealers properly licensed to transact business in this highly regulated area.

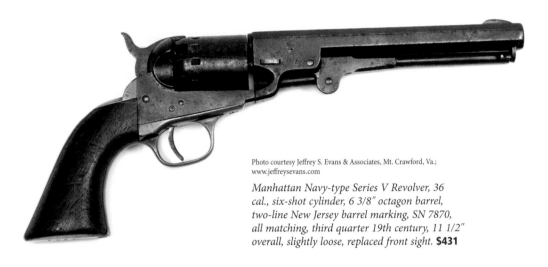

Photo courtesy Jeffrey S. Evans & Associates, Mt. Crawford, Va.; www.jeffreysevans.com

Manhattan Navy-type Series V Revolver, 36 cal., six-shot cylinder, 6 3/8" octagon barrel, two-line New Jersey barrel marking, SN 7870, all matching, third quarter 19th century, 11 1/2" overall, slightly loose, replaced front sight. **$431**

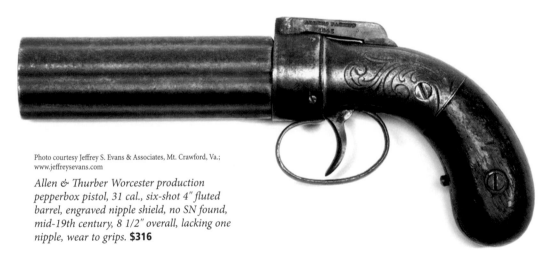

Photo courtesy Jeffrey S. Evans & Associates, Mt. Crawford, Va.; www.jeffreysevans.com

Allen & Thurber Worcester production pepperbox pistol, 31 cal., six-shot 4" fluted barrel, engraved nipple shield, no SN found, mid-19th century, 8 1/2" overall, lacking one nipple, wear to grips. **$316**

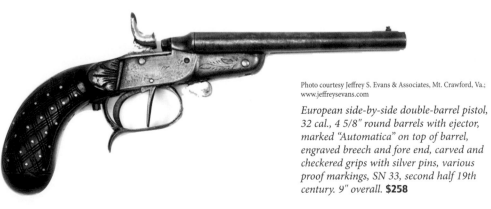

Photo courtesy Jeffrey S. Evans & Associates, Mt. Crawford, Va.; www.jeffreysevans.com

European side-by-side double-barrel pistol, 32 cal., 4 5/8" round barrels with ejector, marked "Automatica" on top of barrel, engraved breech and fore end, carved and checkered grips with silver pins, various proof markings, SN 33, second half 19th century. 9" overall. **$258**

Photo courtesy Jeffrey S. Evans & Associates, Mt. Crawford, Va.;
www.jeffreysevans.com

Rare 1861 Richmond "high hump" rifled musket, 58 cal., 40" round barrel secured by three barrel bands and marked with VP (broken-top) above eagle head and 1858, full humpback lock plate marked with "Richmond, VA" and "1861", iron butt plate, brass fore-end cap, sling swivels, long-range rear site, tulip-head swelled-shank cleaning rod.

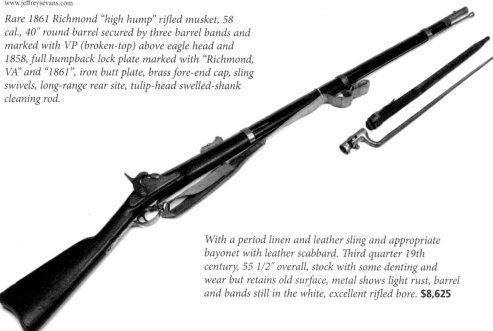

With a period linen and leather sling and appropriate bayonet with leather scabbard. Third quarter 19th century, 55 1/2" overall, stock with some denting and wear but retains old surface, metal shows light rust, barrel and bands still in the white, excellent rifled bore. **$8,625**

Photo courtesy Jeffrey S. Evans & Associates, Mt. Crawford, Va.; www.jeffreysevans.com

Model 1884 U.S. trapdoor rifle (two views), 29 1/2" round barrel secured by a single barrel band, lock plate marked with "1884" only, breechblock dated 1873, two-piece trigger guard, long-range rear site, inspectors initial cartouches with 1886 stamped on left side of stock, bayonet marked "US", lacking cleaning rod, no SN located. Fourth quarter 19th century 49" overall, lacking fore end cap, wear to stock, lightly pitted. **$373**

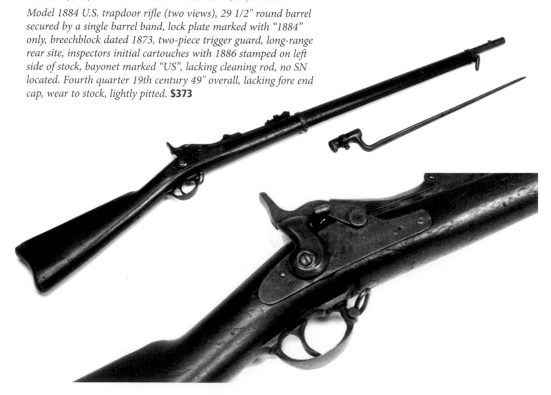

Hatfield Family percussion shotgun, 16 gauge, brass butt plate and trigger guard, original ramrod, no manufacturer's markings. Stock stamped with initials "G.N.H." five times, reportedly for George N. Hatfield of Kentucky. Along with copies of documents and a Confederate Service certificate for Hatfield. Second half 19th century. 52 1/2" overall, break to ramrod. **$345**

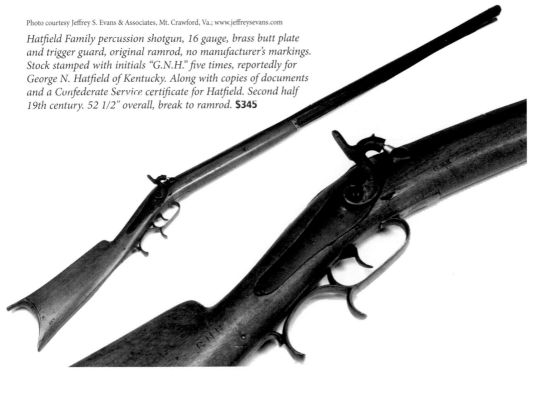

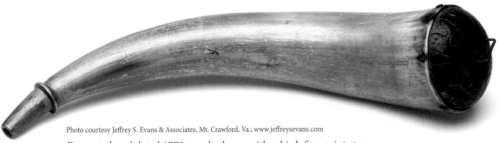

Decorated and dated 1773 powder horn, with a bird, five-point star, initials, and the date, the wooden cap carved with initials and the date within spaced hearts. Fourth quarter 18th century, 13". **$575**

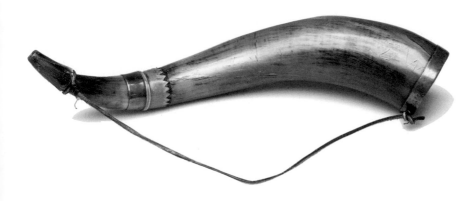

Photo Courtesy Heritage Auction Galleries, Dallas; www.HA.com

Remington .41 Caliber Rimfire "Double Derringer" Taken from the Person of one John Herbert Dillinger when arrested in Tucson, Arizona, Jan. 25, 1934. Dillinger, using the alias "Frank Sullivan," along with gang members Henry Pierpont, Russel Clark and Charles Makley, and their "molls," including Billie Frechette, were all arrested over a three-day period from Jan. 22-25, through a series of coordinated police raids, without a shot being fired. Upon being arrested, Dillinger was quoted as saying, "My God, how did you know I was in town? I'll be the laughing stock of the country! How could a hick-town police force ever suspect us." In reality, and unbeknownst to Dillinger, a local fireman, called to a fire in the hotel where some of the gang members were staying, recognized Russel Clark from his "wanted" picture in True Detective magazine, and alerted the local police. After their uneventful arrest, the gang members were all booked by the County Sheriff, John Belton, on fugitive warrants and held in the county jail. The next day the gang members were "put on display" to the curious public, and some 2,000 people trooped past their cells exchanging disparaging remarks. On Jan. 28, Arizona Governor B.B. Moeur signed extradition papers, and Dillinger was secretly flown to Indiana to face trial for murder. The rest of the gang was sent back to Ohio by train. Five weeks later, using a carved wooden pistol, Dillinger escaped from jail in Crown Point, Ind. Just four months later, on July 22, 1934, Dillinger was gunned down by FBI agents at the Biograph Theater in Chicago. 2009 was the 75th anniversary of Dillinger's death. The gun bears serial #L97255 and retains most of the original blue on screws, hammer and trigger, the balance with the original blue-gray matte finish mixing with gray patina. Perfect grips, mint bore, mechanically fine. The tip of the barrel-release lever is broken/missing. The hammer exhibits the late-circa-1930 detail of being grooved rather than knurled. The gun is accompanied by copies of the Tucson arrest reports on each of the fugitives (with the exception of Dillinger's which vanished many years ago). The property slips that accompany the reports list money, jewelry and vehicles with absolutely no mention of weapons. Apparently the Sheriff's Department already had plans for those, as two of the women were charged with possessing machine guns. This gun was concealed in Dillinger's sock when he was arrested by Sheriff John Belton, who presented the pistol to Evelyn B. Jenney, an attractive young widow, who was Deputy County Probation Officer and Secretary to Superior Court Judge Fred W. Fickett. Mrs. Jenney was the widow of William LeBaron Jenney Jr., who was the grandson of famed Chicago "Sky Scraper" architect William LeBaron Jenney. In 1949 she gave the gun to her son, William LeBaron Jenney III. Included with the gun are two notarized affidavits from Mr. Jenney, dated March 19, 1959, describing the gun, with serial number, and attesting to receiving the pistol from Sheriff Belton. The gun is accompanied by much additional research from the consignor, who was the purchaser of the gun from William LeBaron Jenney III on March 19, 1959. **$95,600**

AFFADAVIT

19 March,1959

The following described firearm was acquired by the undersigned as follows:

In the spring of 1933 one John Dillinger and gang was captured as the result of a fire which destroyed the Congress Hotel on Congress Street in Tucson,Arizona. He was taken into custody at the time by John Belton,Sheriff of Pima County,Jimmy Herron ,and Joe Rice of the Tucson Police force. The firearm below described was removed from the person of John Dillinger by Sheriff Belton and later presented to my mother,Evelyn Jenney Fields,who was then Secretary to Superior Court Judge Fred Fickett and also A'sst Probation Officer.
The firearm described below was presented to me in 1949 by Evelyn Jenney Fields.

Firearm:
Make: Remington Arms Co.,UMC,Utica,New York
Model: Derringer Pattern
Caliber: 41 Rimfire Derringer
Serial No. L 97255

The above is to the best of my knowledge a true and correct statement.

William LeB.Jenney

Subscribed and sworn to before me this _19th_ day of _March_,1959

Notary Public

My Commission Expires April 11, 1961

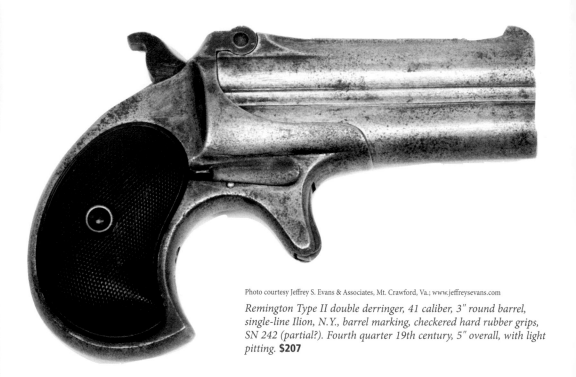

Remington Type II double derringer, 41 caliber, 3" round barrel, single-line Ilion, N.Y., barrel marking, checkered hard rubber grips, SN 242 (partial?). Fourth quarter 19th century, 5" overall, with light pitting. **$207**

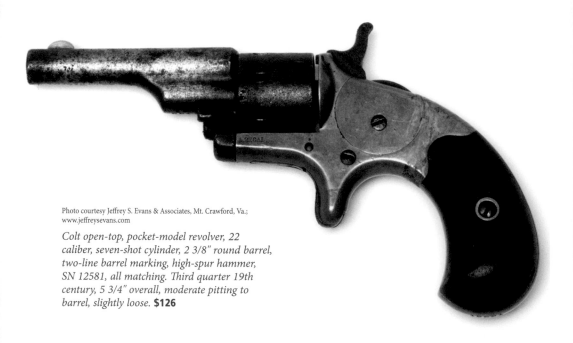

Colt open-top, pocket-model revolver, 22 caliber, seven-shot cylinder, 2 3/8" round barrel, two-line barrel marking, high-spur hammer, SN 12581, all matching. Third quarter 19th century, 5 3/4" overall, moderate pitting to barrel, slightly loose. **$126**

FIREPLACE EQUIPMENT

In colder climates throughout the world, the fireplace or hearth has traditionally been a central feature of the household. The sensation of direct heat, and the mesmerizing spectacle of a wood fire, make it a favored refuge at all times of the year.

Photo courtesy Heritage Auction Galleries, Dallas; www.HA.com

Louis XV-Style gilt bronze figural andirons, late 19th century 16 1/2" h, each cast as a rocaille scroll adorned with grapevines, supporting a nude cherub seated on a pedestal, one eating a bunch of grapes, and one holding a bunch of grapes and a chalice. **$717**

Photo courtesy Skinner Inc., Boston; www.SkinnerInc.com

English cast-iron and brass fireplace grate, late 18th century, cast-iron fireback with arched crest, cast with scene of Hercules carrying the Nimean lion, the curved front panel with scroll-pierced brass gallery, with four urn-shaped finials, 34 1/2" x 29 3/8". **$770**

Photo courtesy Heritage Auction Galleries, Dallas; www.HA.com

Wrought-iron andirons, attributed to Gustav Stickley, Eastwood, N.Y., circa 1900, 15 3/4" h x 21 1/2" l, with spade-shaped tops over four-sided shafts. One missing the back third of the piece. Surface wear and oxidation as appropriate to age and use. **$5,377**

Photo courtesy Leslie Hindman Auctioneers, Chicago; www.LeslieHindman.com

Dutch Baroque-style brass andirons (20 3/4"), baluster form, with an associated set of fireplace tools on stand. **$335 set**

Photos courtesy Skinner Inc., Boston; www.SkinnerInc.com

Red-painted, carved and turned fireplace mantel with paneled frieze, American, last half 19th century, 52 1/2" x 48". **$267**

Louis XV carved walnut and tapestry-inset firescreen, third quarter 18th century, the cartouche-shaped frame carved with C-scrolls and foliage on splayed trestle supports, the period Brussels tapestry panel depicting a satyr with a pipe, 39 1/2" x 24".

Cracked at upper left joint and with light worming throughout, age-typical minor defects. **$1,896**

FISHING, HUNTING EQUIPMENT

Bird Decoys

Carved wooden decoys, used to lure waterfowl to the hunter, have become widely recognized as an indigenous American folk-art form. Many decoys are from 1880 to 1930, when commercial gunners commonly hunted and used rigs of several hundred decoys. Fine carvers also worked through the 1930s and 1940s. Individuals and commercial decoy makers also carved fish decoys. The skill of the carver, rarity, type of bird, condition and age all affect the value.

All decoy photos come courtesy Guyette & Schmidt Inc., St. Michaels, Md.; *www.guyetteandschmidt.com.*

Mallard hen by Robert Elliston. **$100,625**

Canada goose by Nathan Cobb. **$74,750**

Blair School pintail drake. **$71,875**

Merganser drake by the Dodge Decoy Factory. **$57,500**

Bufflehead hen by Harry V. Shourds. **$48,875**

Stick-up Canada goose by Sam Soper. **$43,700**

Brant by Dave Watson. **$40,250**

Rigmate pair of mergansers by the Mason Decoy Factory. **$31,625 pair**

Two miniatures by Joseph Lincoln. **$6,613 pair**

*Pair of old squaw
by Mark English.*
$18,975 pair

*Mallard drake by
Charles Walker.*
$18,975

*Mallard hen by
Charles Perdew.*
$14,375

Black-bellied plover by John Dilley. **$37,375**

Dowitcher by William Bowman. **$37,375**

Robin snipe by Harry V. Shourds. **$27,600**

Sanderling or peep by Dave Watson. **$15,813**

Dunlin by the Mason Decoy Factory. **$11,500**

Willet by the Dodge Decoy Factory. **$8050**

Left: Duck call by Perry Hooker. **$17,250**

Bottom left: Duck call by G.D. Kinney. **$19,550**

Below: Duck call by Kinney & Harlow. **$20,700**

FISHING EQUIPMENT

Lures and Fish Decoys

All fishing-related photos courtesy Lang's Sporting Collectibles, Waterville, N.Y.; *www.LangsAuction.com.*

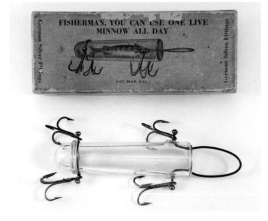

Above: Three Bite Em Baits, Warsaw, Ind., including red/ yellow/red, red/white/red and white/black/gold. **$234 all**

Top right: Detroit Glass Minnow Tube in picture box, 3 1/4" model with marked aluminum sliding cap, patented March 3, 1914, with a small factory air bubble in the glass at the tail end. Coming in its correct, scarce two-piece cardboard picture box, some fading, with edge wear and repaired corners to the box bottom. **$944**

Right: J.L. Clark's Expert Wooden Minnow, Rockford, Ill., measuring 3 3/4", rigged with type 2 detachable hooks, pointed holed props, blemish-free glass eyes, and reverse red hand-painted gill marks. With unmarked maroon box, typical of Clark Experts from this time. **$930**

Chautauqua Trolling Bait, patented Aug. 31, 1909, by Krantz & Smith of Jamestown, N.Y., measuring 3 5/8" with an overall length of 5 1/2", original box swivel, with scale finished silver body, detailed tail and head. With tarnished patina, complete with original red thread wraps on the spring-loaded single hooks, and just a trace of the red eye paint. Considered one of the top 10 greatest fishing lures of all time. **$3,835**

Woods Expert Minnow wood slide-top box, 5 1/2" x 2" x 1 1/4", with full paper side label, featuring both the March 17, 1903, and Dec. 23, 1903, patent dates, from the F.C. Woods & Co. Manufacturers, Alliance, Ohio. **$520**

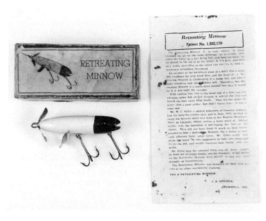

Above: *Hanson's Irresistible Minnow, 1919, Pittsburg, an extremely scarce diving bait, featuring two belly cup rigged treble hooks, a 3 5/8" gently tapering wood body, sharply slanted face with its signature "horn" protruding from the top of the head.* **$531**

Top left: *Florida Shinner, from Frostproof, Fla., and F.L.B. Flood, measuring 5", finished in brown back with silver scales, in the correct cardboard box with original fragile instruction flyer.* **$649**

Middle left: *Greider's Retreating Minnow in rare box, patent No. 1933170 was granted to Jethro A. Greider of Cromwell, Ind., on Oct. 31, 1933, for his unique bait. The 3 1/4" open-mouthed, wood-body minnow features a floppy nickel nose propeller, inserted belly plate, twin cup rigged treble hooks and glass eyes. Finished in red "tail"/ white body.. With few known examples of the two-piece cardboard picture box, 4 7/8" x 2 1/4" x 1 1/4". Included is the extremely rare original box insert, complete with a 1934 testimonial as to its fish-catching prowess.* **$3,450**

Bottom left: *Gruber's Glowurm Fish Lure, patented November 1920, by J.S. Gruber of Medical Lake, Wash., finished in yellow with green stripes, in the correct wood box. Also included is an unassembled, unfinished Glowurm.* **$265**

Below: *Howe's Vacuum Bass Bait, small size, finished in yellow with red/black and green spots, with Howe's patented swivel hook hangers, and gold-hinged tin box. The Baby Howe's Bass Bait is scarce, especially in this finish.* **$431**

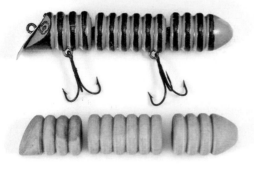

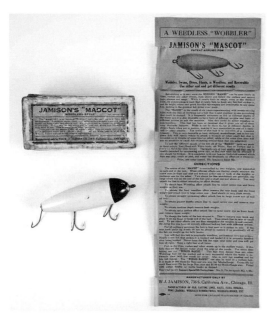

Rare Kimmich Mouse in box, from the Kimmich Bait Co. of Ellwood City, Pa., patented Jan. 22, 1929, finished in alternating olive green and red-striped head with blue bead eyes, and red and yellow striped deer hair body with white belly and marked diving lip, light damage to the bucktail body, in an unmarked two-piece cardboard box with fish logo and Kimmich Special marked lid and original insert tag. **$1,035**

Above: Jamison's Weedless Mascot, red head/white body with double line tie, cup rigging, belly and tail double hooks (1 broken), in its original, scarce two-piece cardboard box, "Pat Applied For," includes the original foldout paperwork with instructions. This is one of Jamison's scarcest packages. **$291**

Right: Lane's Wonder Wobbler store advertising card, patented March 13, 1920, from Charles Lane of Madrid, N.Y., finished in green with silver scales, marked diving lip, detailed metal tail, and original wire leader; hand sewn to an 8" x 12" countertop display card. **$531**

Quick-Change Bait, patent applied for, from Skvor & Co. of Cedar Rapids, Iowa, dating to about 1915, featuring six colors of both attractors and flies in their original box with double-sided foldout paperwork demonstrating its function as well as pointers and advantages of the Quick-Change Baits. There are only a few known examples of one of Iowa's better baits. **$225**

Reels

Early Julius Vom Hofe trout reel (two views). **$2,415** *(Reels from the early tackle supplier Abercrombie & Fitch may bring a premium with the A&F name applied.)*

Hardy Uniqua A&F reel (two views). **$196** *(Reels from the early tackle supplier Abercrombie & Fitch may bring a premium with the A&F name applied.)*

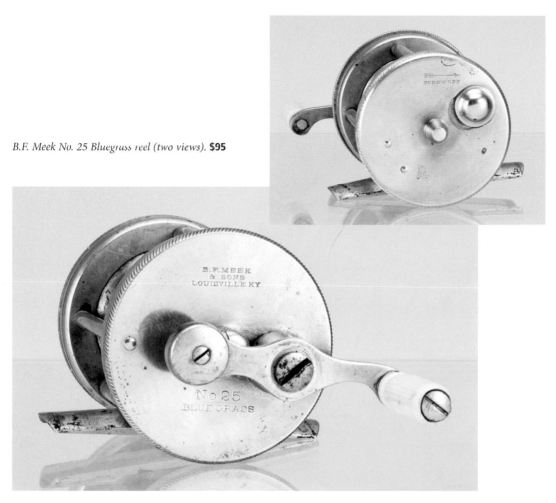

B.F. Meek No. 25 Bluegrass reel (two views). **$95**

Meek/Horton No. 4 reel (two views). **$213**

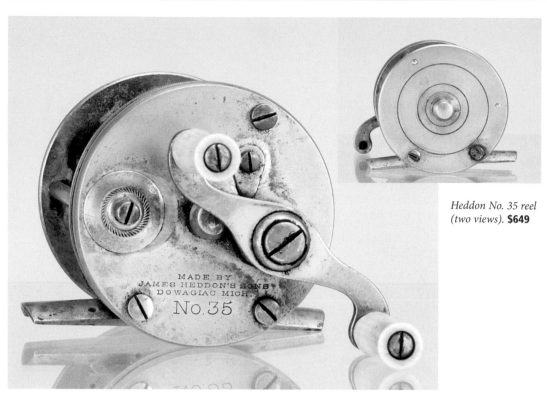

Heddon No. 35 reel (two views). **$649**

Heddon No. 45 reel in box (two views). **$502**

Rods

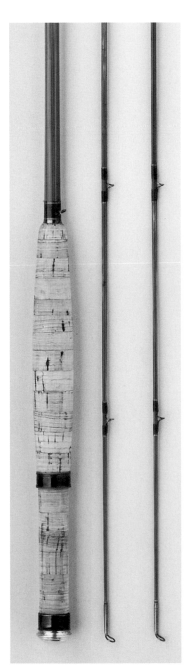

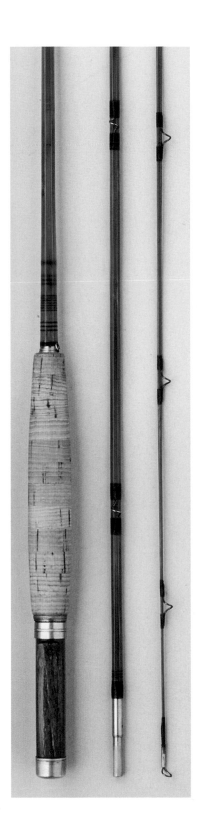

8′ Payne sold by Abercrombie & Fitch, with original bag and tube with silver label. **$2,588** (Rods may bring a premium with the A&F name applied.)

Right: 8′ F.E. Thomas, with its original green bag with tag, and Thomas tube with shield decal. **$1,416**

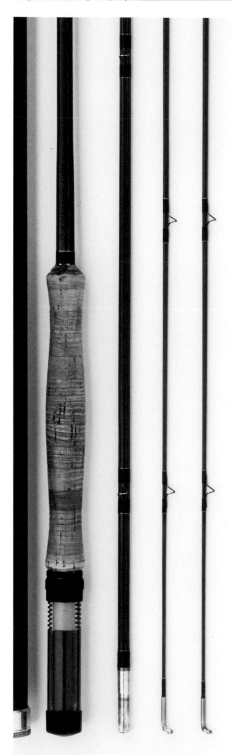

8 1/2' Phillipson 3/2 bamboo. **$546**

6 1/2' Orvis Deluxe, with the original plaid bag and black tube with early Orvis label. Sold by Abercrombie & Fitch. **$1,035**

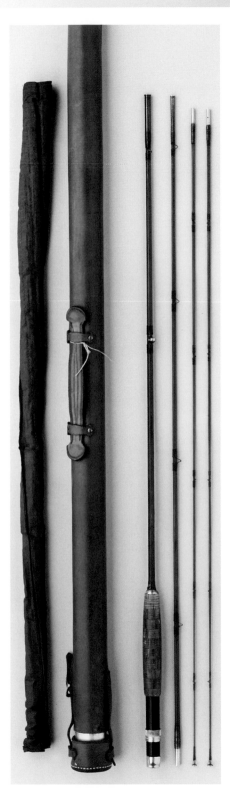

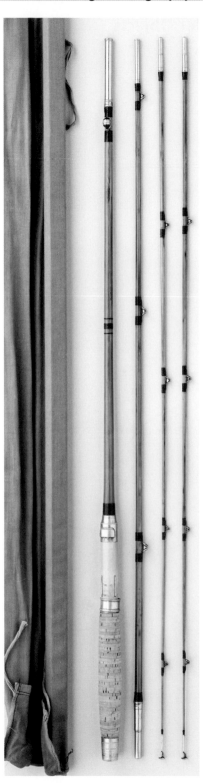

8' Hardy USA made for A&F, with the original bag and a stitched leather tube with broken strap. **$230**

7 1/2' Kosmic sold by A&F, complete with a bag and wooden tip protector. **$575**

Other Objects

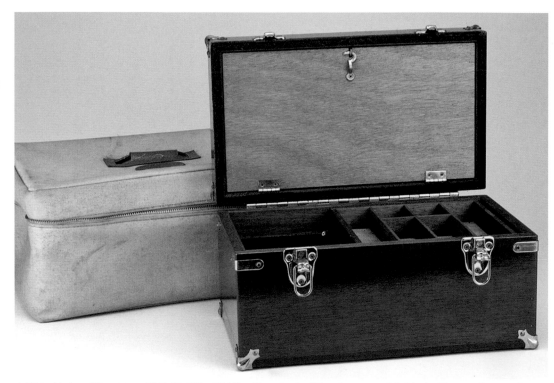

A&F tackle box, lift-out tray, 1945-65, 13" x 7 3/4" x 7", grained solid mahogany and finished with several coats of high-luster lacquer. Finished with brass corner protectors, piano hinge, latches and handle, with original custom-tailored canvas cover. **$767**

Early center-hole splint creel, bulbous form, and measuring just over 11" tall, minor wear, it features a canvas strap and original leather strap hangers. **$184**

Early wooden A&F line dryer, having a 9" wide spool consisting of eight spindles, mahogany, overall length of 12" not including the wooden handle, with circular A&F label, mild chipping. **$590**

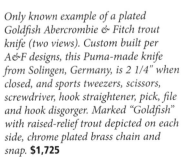

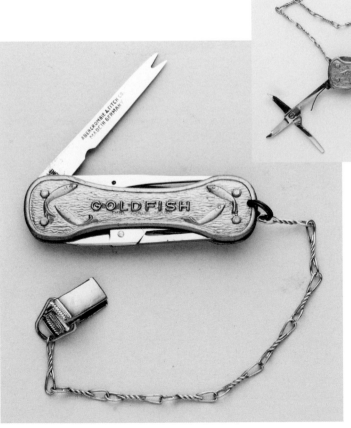

Only known example of a plated Goldfish Abercrombie & Fitch trout knife (two views). Custom built per A&F designs, this Puma-made knife from Solingen, Germany, is 2 1/4" when closed, and sports tweezers, scissors, screwdriver, hook straightener, pick, file and hook disgorger. Marked "Goldfish" with raised-relief trout depicted on each side, chrome plated brass chain and snap. **$1,725**

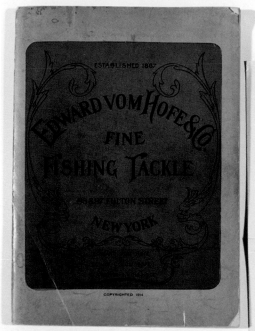

1914 Edward vom Hofe catalog, 167 pages plus blank order-form pages. Fine period illustrations of rods and reels, plus lures by Buel, Decker, Heddon, Wilson, Howe's, Jamison and more. Cover has some staining, a few light bends, and small corner loss, interior with light age discoloration, also includes a vom Hofe envelope, and full-page ad brochure detailing changes to the No. 501 and 521 reels. **$1,725**

1930s Oscar Peterson 8 7/8" fish decoy. **$272**

FLAGS

The first flags were used to assist military coordination on battlefields, and flags have since evolved into a general tool for signaling and identification, including semaphore. National flags are often patriotic symbols with varied and wide-ranging interpretations. Flags are also used for advertising or decorative purposes. The study of flags is known as "vexillology," from the Latin *vexillum* meaning flag or banner.

Photos courtesy James D. Julia Auctions, Fairfield, Maine; www.jamesdjulia.com

Sixteen-star American flag, identified as belonging to the USS Scorpion, from the War of 1812. The 16-star flag was first introduced in 1796 when Tennessee became a state. Few of these early flags with this star count are known today in any collections. Consists of four rows of four cotton stars in the canton, with double appliqué. The flag is hand sewn and made of loose wool bunting. On the hoist is inked in period script, "Scorpion", 34" x 49". Flag shows considerable use and wear. The blue canton shows much wear and losses including one or more early repairs to holes. There is "mothing" and staining; there are a couple of splotches of what appears to be blood. The selvage edge of the canton is missing. **$21,850**

Photo courtesy James D. Julia Auctions, Fairfield, Maine; www.jamesdjulia.com

Early 19th-century silk lithograph 26-star Decatur family flag. The 26 stars on the flag commemorate the state of Michigan, which came into the Union on July 4, 1837. This design, with the large star in the center, is referred to the "great star pattern" or "grand illuminary". Flags of this style and period from the Mexican War era are rare and seldom found. This is hand-stitched on both top and bottom edge, 29 1/2" x 19 1/2". The silk is delicate and there are some losses in the stripes, losses along the hoist and within the stars. **$6,900**

Photo courtesy James D. Julia Auctions, Fairfield, Maine; www.jamesdjulia.com

Thirteen-star bunting American flag with inscription on hoist, "A.R. Decatur", for Anna Rowell Philbrick Decatur; born in 1821, died in 1906. Anna married Commodore Stephen Decatur in 1848. At the outbreak of the Civil War he was a Commander in 1861, later a Captain in 1867 and eventually retiring as a Commodore. The flag has a canton arrangement of three rows of stars; four, five, four in configuration, 34 1/2" x 67". It exhibits various early repairs. **$8,050**

Civil War 34-star flag (1861-1863), introduced when Kansas became the 34th state. The flag has a wool bunting, the canvas hoist exhibits hand-sewn grommets, 24" x 52". It shows use and has scattered staining, soiling, "mothing" as well as a few separations. **$14,950**

Thirteen-star naval flag, white stars are hand sewn onto the blue canton with canvas hoist having brass grommets with two alternating red and white stripes. The name "ARP DECATUR" is written in period ink on the hoist, for Anna Rowell Philbrick Decatur, 53 1/2" x 97". Significant use and has scattered "mothing" throughout, stains and some discoloration. Portions of all stripes have been replaced long ago. **$2,875**

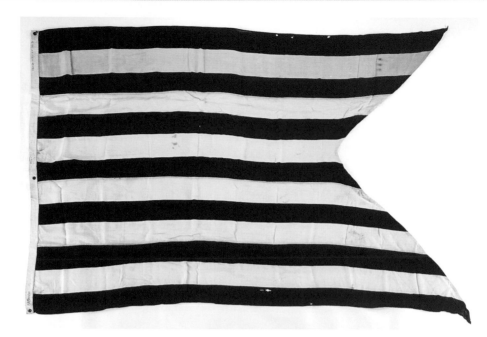

Photos courtesy James D. Julia Auctions, Fairfield, Maine; www.jamesdjulia.com

Four late-19th-century Spanish-American War-era flags along with three bunting flags. Descended through the Decatur family, including (1, top facing page) 45-star flag having wool bunting with alternating rows of eight and seven stars, 68" x 108"; (2, bottom facing page) 45-star flag, 52" x 88"; (3, above) three bunting flags include a naval designating flag, flown to show that an officer of that rank was aboard, 11 1/2" x 20", 22" x 35" and 70" x 107"; (4, top this page and middle facing page) two large naval-used pennants. They appear to be 19th century, one measures 48" x 17" and is a white and blue triangular pennant, hand sewn and could date as early as the Civil War. It is not a standard signal. The second flag measuring 107" x 74" is a swallowtail pennant consisting of 13 alternating red and white stripes. **$9,200 all**

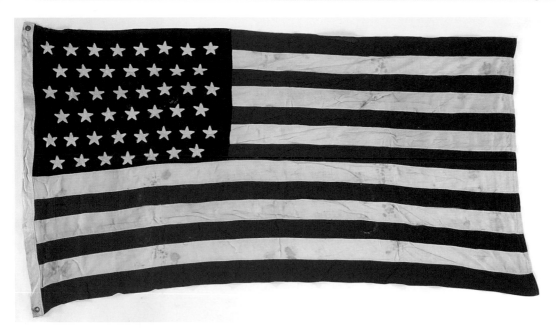

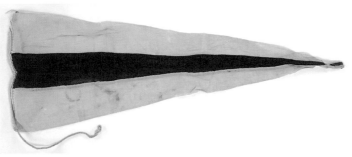

Folk Art

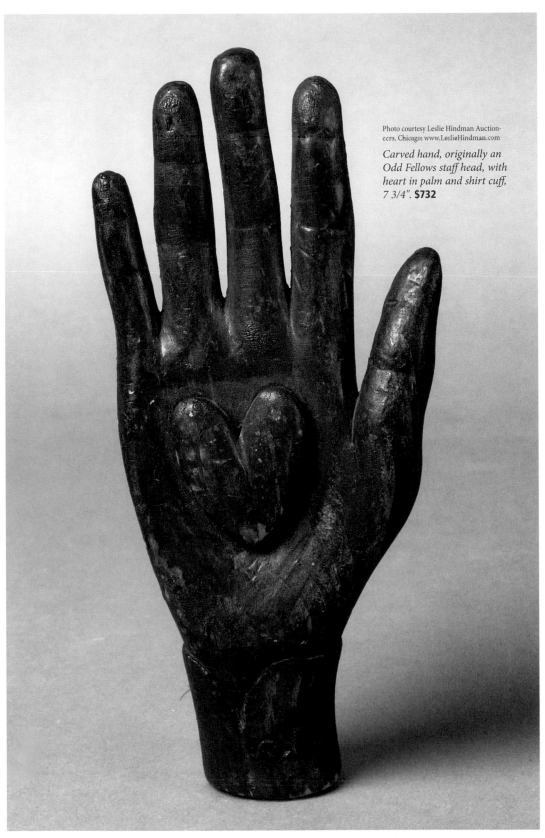

Carved hand, originally an Odd Fellows staff head, with heart in palm and shirt cuff, 7 3/4". **$732**

Photo courtesy Leslie Hindman Auctioneers,
Chicago; www.LeslieHindman.com

*Carved wood spoon rack,
geometric circle decoration over
a lidded compartment depicting
shaking hands, the interior
carved, "To Mary from Jack
1799", together with 23 pewter
spoons, 35 1/2".* **$457**

Photo courtesy James D. Julia Auctioneers, Fairfield, Maine;
www.jamesdjulia.com

*Carved pine fishmonger's trade sign,
first half 20th century, with remnants of
original paint and striated fins, retaining
original mounting brackets, 37" x 55 1/2".*
$1,725

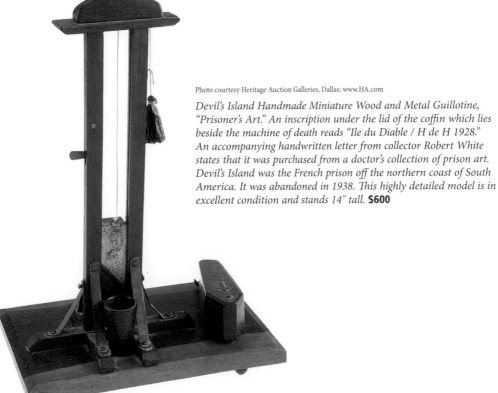

Photo courtesy Heritage Auction Galleries, Dallas; www.HA.com

*Devil's Island Handmade Miniature Wood and Metal Guillotine,
"Prisoner's Art." An inscription under the lid of the coffin which lies
beside the machine of death reads "Ile du Diable / H de H 1928."
An accompanying handwritten letter from collector Robert White
states that it was purchased from a doctor's collection of prison art.
Devil's Island was the French prison off the northern coast of South
America. It was abandoned in 1938. This highly detailed model is in
excellent condition and stands 14" tall.* **$600**

Photo courtesy Leslie Hindman Auctioneers, Chicago;
www.LeslieHindman.com

Sheet metal and bleached wood folk art cello, possibly a trade sign, of typical three-stringed form, 65". **$1,037**

Carved wood sculpture, depicting a seated dog with painted eyes, raised on a stump base, 63 1/4". **$1,037**

Folk art Victrola in carved-wood cabinet with floral and reptilian decoration. **$5,750.**

Photos courtesy Heritage Auction Galleries, Dallas; www.HA.com

Carved Civil War Pipe. Massive size and weight carved entirely by hand of burl wood. The front of the pipe is deeply carved with a full-spread-wing eagle with shield, holding a riband in its beak, "The Union Now And Forever". One side of the pipe is carved with an artillery piece with "64" on the barrel, doubtless referring to the date the pipe was made. The other side of the pipe depicts a mounted soldier. The back of the pipe is carved with the nude figure of a woman holding a riband inscribed "Liberty", the whole surrounded by a laurel wreath. The flat bottom of the pipe bears the incised carved legend, "Made In Camp Near Falmouth, Va. By Benj. G. Chapman 146 NYSV". The pipe is in perfect untouched condition, with no indication of having been smoked. Chapman enlisted in the 146th on Oct. 10, 1862, and served with the regiment until May 3, 1863, when he transferred to the Veteran Reserve Corps. The 146th, known as Garrard's Tigers, were, for a period, uniformed as Zouaves. The regiment was heavily engaged at Chancellorsville and Gettysburg during Chapman's term of service. Accompanied by a complete set of records. **$5,377**

Pineapple carving by Eugene "Nick" Nielsen (1921-2009), circa 1995, carved and painted pine board, inscribed on reverse "N.N.", 18" x 10" x 2". This is one of a series of pineapples that Nielsen carved in the 1980s and '90s, though it was unusual for him to paint them. He also carved three-dimensional fruit and vegetables. **$300+**

Photo courtesy James D. Julia Auctioneers, Fairfield, Maine; www.jamesdjulia.com

Grotesque Carved Folk Art Pine Center Table. Last quarter of the 19th Century. The rectangular tray top with serpentine and scalloped edging projecting above the heavily carved rectangular frieze, the corners carved with theatrical masks, one end carved with a fanciful crouching cat flanked by leaf tips, the opposing end carved with a fanciful leaping horse above a stag's head. One long side carved with a wide-eyed, winged, fanciful full moon mask among C and S scrolling volutes, the opposing long side with similar scrollwork centering a tornado-like funnel. The whole raised on exaggerated, tapering, cabriole legs with shell-carved knees and claw feet with knuckled toes. 28 1/2" h. x 39 1/2" l. x 26 1/2" d. With weathered and worn original white paint. Loss to tail of horse, some losses to toes, small knothole at end of top at edge. **$26,450**

Photo courtesy James D. Julia Auctioneers, Fairfield, Maine;
www.jamesdjulia.com

Grotesque Carved Folk Art Pine Console Table. Last quarter of the 19th Century. The rectangular tray top with wavy-molded edges above the conforming wide frieze fancifully carved with grotesque theatrical masks on the corners, the ends each carved with the face of a bearded gentleman. The front apron carved with a displayed eagle in high relief, flanked by two seated gentlemen wearing long coats and brimmed hats, further flanked by flags. The legs in the form of carved leaf-tip and scrolled corbels, raised on S-scrolled, knuckled, and acanthus-carved feet. 28 1/2" h. x 41" w. x 21 1/4" d. The top with heavily weathered surface and shrinkage crack through center. Original white paint, scrubbed on top, discolored on table base. Structural damages as follows: one leg missing on seated gentleman, half of one eagle foot missing, damages to two feet on table.
$25,300

Photos courtesy James D. Julia Auctioneers, Fairfield, Maine; www.jamesdjulia.com

Patriotic Carved Wood Figure of the "Goddess of Liberty". Last quarter 19th century. Carved and polychrome painted, she is depicted standing erect wearing a soft peaked "Liberty" cap, dressed in a full-length white tunic with rolled sleeves, draped in a red robe trimmed in gold. In her right hand she holds a sword, in her left a laurel wreath and federal shield, her sandaled feet showing beneath her robe. Carved standing on a square stepped plinth, further raised on a larger box plinth with canted sides, carved with swag draperies and mounted with carrying handles. 53" h. of statue. 71" overall h. 25" sq. base. This figure was originally discovered by Helena Penrose of New York City, who was a friend and colleague of Abby Aldridge Rockefeller in the pursuit of folk art during the 1930s and '40s. Penrose was an acknowledged authority and dealer on American folk art carvings, assisting in research with A.W. Pendergast in the compilation for Cigar Store Figures in American Folk Art, 1953 and also in Tuttle's et al Drawing on America's Past: Folk Art, Modernism and the Index of American Design. When Penrose sold the figure to a wealthy, avid antique collector, in the late 1940s/early '50s for a "significant" amount of money, she informed him that this figure originally resided in Tammany Hall in New York City before 1920. It was removed and was then present at the inauguration of President Harry Truman. Around the period of 1850 to 1900 there were likely a considerable number of similar patriotic goddess figures in use throughout the country, unlike cigar store figures which were manufactured in large numbers for purposes of business, these were likely far fewer in number and today only a handful survive. The entire surface was repainted some time ago, possibly done by Penrose in the 1940s when she acquired and sold this. Prior to repainting, the checks, cracks and separations were plastered, the largest of which were on the backside draped figure, however there were various other separations scattered over the figure, most nearly all of which have been re-gessoed prior to repaint. The cross-guard of the sword was also probably repainted at that time. The carvings on the base are original and the base appears to be original to the figure and has some old modifications on the interior. There are no modern restorations or repaint on any part of the figure. Note: This and other carved figures of their type were designed to be transported in parades and/or displayed in public or semi-public places, hence the installation of carrying handles on the primary plinth. This use also subjected these figures to stresses and torque from repeated moving and to extreme and frequent weather changes while out of doors. Any damages and subsequent restorations, including any areas of in-painting or repainting, whether of 19th- or 20th-century origin, were done for cosmetic reasons and not with the intent of disguising any element of this figure. **$143,750**

Photo courtesy Skinner Inc., Boston; www.SkinnerInc.com

Sand Picture in a Glass Bottle with American Eagle, Flag, and Urn of Flowers, Andrew Clemens, McGregor, Iowa, circa 1885, multicolored sand arranged in a glass bottle, one side of the bottle portraying an American eagle in flight, an American flag, and a banner reading "M.W. COLE," the reverse depicting a flower-filled urn, both designs flanked by several multicolored and shaped borders, 9 3/4" h. Note: Andrew Clemens was born in Dubuque, Iowa, in 1857. At the age of five he became deaf and mute after an illness. He earned his livelihood by painstakingly arranging colored sand to make pictures in glass bottles. The sand came from the naturally colored sandstone in the Pictured Rocks area of Iowa. He worked in McGregor, and for a short time he made and exhibited his work at South Side Museum, a dime museum in Chicago, Ill. He died in 1894 at the age of 37. **$7,110**

Photo courtesy Skinner Inc., Boston; www.SkinnerInc.com

Sand Picture in a Glass Bottle with Ship, Andrew Clemens, McGregor, Iowa, 1889, the multicolored sand arranged to show a foreshortened ship and distant vessels in a reserve on one side and the name and date "H.A. BAILEY 1889" flanked by multicolored geometric and marbled borders, (some sand shifting on upper border), 6 5/8" h. The cover is loose. Some substance was applied to the top sand surface prevent further shifting of sand. Note: Andrew Clemens was born in Dubuque, Iowa, in 1857. At the age of five he became deaf and mute after an illness. He earned his livelihood by painstakingly arranging colored sand to make pictures in glass bottles. The sand came from the naturally colored sandstone in the Pictured Rocks area of Iowa. He worked in McGregor, and for a short time he made and exhibited his work at South Side Museum, a dime museum in Chicago, Ill. He died in 1894 at the age of 37. **$1,896**

Carved walnut plaque showing a bird in a cherry tree, set against latticework and arches, circa 1860, untouched original finish, indications that it once was framed, approximately 10" x 10". **$800+**

Scrimshaw

Scrimshaw is the name given to handiwork created by whalers made from the by products of harvesting marine mammals. It is most commonly made out of the bones and teeth of sperm whales, the baleen of other whales, and the tusks of walruses. It takes the form of elaborate carvings of pictures and lettering on the surface of the bone or tooth, with the engravings highlighted using a pigment.

Warning: To avoid illegal ivory, contemporary collectors and dealers check provenance and deal only with other established and reputable sellers. Scrimshaw that is found to have an illegal source may be seized by customs officials worldwide.

Reproduction Alert: The biggest problem in the field is fakes, although there are some clues to spotting them. A hot needle will penetrate the plastics and resins used in reproductions, but not the authentic material. Ivory will not generate static electricity when rubbed, plastic will. Patina is not a good indicator; it has been faked by applying tea or tobacco juice.

Photo courtesy James D. Julia Auctioneers, Fairfield, Maine; www.jamesdjulia.com

Scrimshaw Whale's Tooth. Second half 19th century. Depicting an imperial robed figure standing above a coat of arms with crown, flanked by laurel leaves. 6" h. **$1,610**

Photo courtesy James D. Julia Auctioneers, Fairfield, Maine;
www.jamesdjulia.com

*Scrimshaw Whale's Tooth. Second half
19th century. With a depiction of the
battle between the U.S.S. Constitution
and the Guerriere, the opposing side
depicting a woman in period dress,
holding a book. 6" h.* **$2,990**

Weathervanes

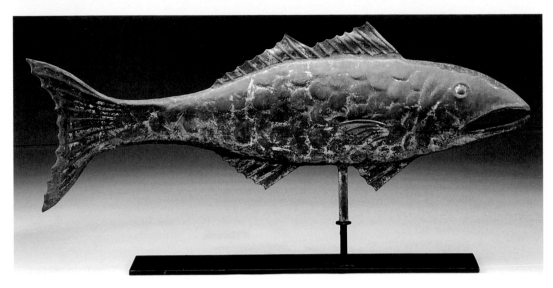

Photo courtesy James D. Julia Auctioneers, Fairfield, Maine; www.jamesdjulia.com

Molded copper codfish weathervane, late 19th/early 20th century, full-bodied example with original gilding, modeled with sheet copper fins and open mouth. With stand, vane only 11" x 26", shallow depression at base of right side of tail, two small dents beneath rear of dorsal fin. **$10,350**

Photo courtesy James D. Julia Auctioneers, Fairfield, Maine; www.jamesdjulia.com

Leaping stag weathervane, late 19th/early 20th century. Attributed to the Thomas W. Jones Co., New York. Full-bodied copper with zinc ears and antlers in a verdigris patina rendered in full stride, with a later wood stand, 16" x 30". Retains old original surfaces, a repaired bullet hole on the right side behind ribs, second bullet hole in mounting tube. Seam on rear of left rear leg with old repairs. Minor dent on left rear flank. Shallow dents along backbone. **$11,500**

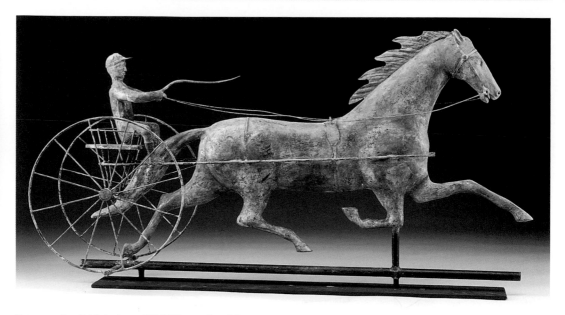

Photo courtesy James D. Julia Auctioneers, Fairfield, Maine; www.jamesdjulia.com

Horse and sulky weathervane, late 19th century, American, horse with zinc head and ears and sheet metal mane and harness, the rider depicted with outstretched arms and whip seated on a sheet copper sulky, 17" x 35 1/2". Retains original gilded surfaces with verdigris patina. A minor seam split on left foreleg of horse, minor 1/2" seam split alongside mane. **$4,025**

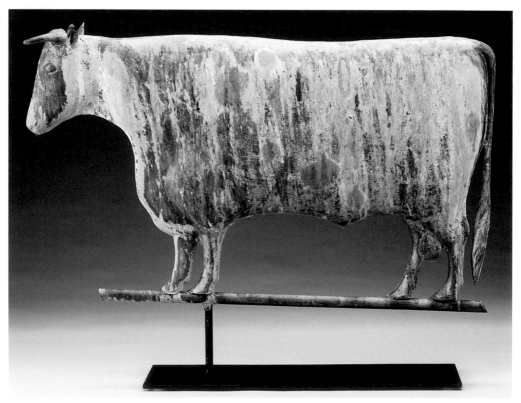

Photo courtesy James D. Julia Auctioneers, Fairfield, Maine; www.jamesdjulia.com

Bull weathervane, 19th Century. Molded copper with a long tail, applied horns and ears. Verdigris patina, 18" x 30". Two bullet holes. **$10,350**

Photo courtesy James D. Julia Auctioneers, Fairfield, Maine; www.jamesdjulia.com

Grasshopper weathervane, first half 20th century, molded copper with stylized antennae, legs and wings. It is weighted beneath the head, joined to the body by a screw. Overall with good verdigris patina and original gilding, 10 1/2" x 34 1/2". **$5,175**

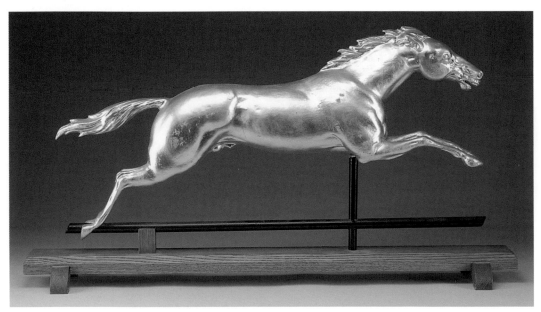

Photo courtesy James D. Julia Auctioneers, Fairfield, Maine; www.jamesdjulia.com

Jumping horse copper weathervane, early 20th century. Molded full-body gilt example with molded mane, tail and zinc head, 31" x 18". Has been re-gilded, now showing surface abrasions to gilding on both flanks. Evidence of small repairs beneath gilding. **$2,070**

Eagle weathervane, first quarter 20th century. Gilt-decorated molded copper eagle perched on a mid-banded ball joined to a weighted arrow with sheet copper feathers, 20" x 24", retains original gilded surfaces with losses to leading edges of wings and to back of neck, which is also dented. Other losses and imperfections to surfaces resulting from weathering. **$2,875**

Mule copper weathervane, late 19th, early 20th century. The full-bodied standing mule with sheet-copper ears and detailed mane, with dark mottled patina over original gilded surface, mounted on original tubular support. Rare. Overall 35" l. x 33" h. With minor dents and creases to ears. No repairs or restorations noted. **$117,300**

Furniture

FURNITURE AND ACCESSORIES

Furniture styles

Furniture styles can be determined by careful study and remembering what design elements each one embraces. To help understand what defines each period, here are some of the major design elements for each period.

William and Mary, 1690-1730: The style is named for the English King William of Orange and his consort, Mary. New colonists in America brought their English furniture traditions with them and tried to translate these styles using native woods. Their furniture was practical and sturdy. Lines of this furniture style tend to be crisp, while facades might be decorated with bold grains of walnut or maple veneers, framed by inlaid bands. Moldings and turnings are exaggerated in size. Turnings are baluster-shaped and the use of C-scrolls was quite common. Feet found in this period generally are round or oval. One exception to this is known as the Spanish foot, which flares to a scroll. Woods tend to be maple, walnut, white pine or southern yellow pine. One type of decoration that begins in the William and Mary period and extends through to Queen Anne and Chippendale styles is known as "japanning," referring to a lacquering process that combines ashes and varnish.

Queen Anne, 1720-1760: Evolution of this design style is from Queen Anne's court, 1702 to 1714, and lasted until the Revolution. This style of furniture is much more delicate than its predecessor. It was one way for the young Colonists to show their own unique style, with each regional area initiating special design elements. Forms tend to be attenuated in New England. Chair rails were more often mortised through the back legs when made in Philadelphia. New England furniture makers preferred pad feet, while the makers in Philadelphia used triffid feet. Makers in Connecticut and New York often preferred slipper and claw and ball feet. The most popular woods were walnut, poplar, cherry, and maple. Japanned

Photo courtesy Rago Arts and Auction, Lambertville, N.J.; www.RagoArts.com

William & Mary style walnut gate-leg drop-leaf table, 18th century, missing one spin-out leg, 28" x 41 1/2" x 22". **$305**

decoration tends to be in red, green and gilt, often on a blue-green field. A new furniture form of this period was the tilting tea table.

Chippendale, 1755-1790: This period is named for the famous English cabinetmaker, Thomas Chippendale, who wrote a book of furniture designs, *Gentlemen and Cabinet-Maker's Director*, published in 1754, 1755 and 1762. This book gave cabinetmakers real direction and they soon eagerly copied the styles presented. Chippendale was influenced by ancient cultures, such as the Romans, and Gothic influences. Look for Gothic arches, Chinese fretwork, columns, capitals, C-scrolls, S-scrolls, ribbons, flowers, leaves, scallop shells, gadrooning and acanthus leaves. The most popular wood used in this period was mahogany, with walnut, maple and cherry also present. Legs become straight and regional differences still existed in design elements, such as feet. Claw and ball feet become even larger and more decorative. Pennsylvania cabinetmakers used Marlborough feet, while other regions favored ogee bracket feet. One of the most popular forms of this period was a card table that sported five legs instead of the four of Queen Anne designs.

Federal (Hepplewhite), 1790-1815: This period reflects the growing patriotism felt in the young American states. Their desire to develop their own distinctive furniture style was apparent. Stylistically it also reflects the architectural style known as Federal, where balance and symmetry were extremely important. Woods used during this period were mahogany and mahogany veneer, but other native woods, such as maple, birch or satinwood, were used. Reflecting the architectural ornamentation of the period, inlays were popular, as was carving and even painted highlights. The motifs used for inlay included bellflowers, urns, festoons, acanthus leaves and pilasters, to name but a few. Inlaid bands and lines were also popular and often used in combination with other inlay. Legs of this period tend to be straight or tapered to the foot. The foot might be a simple extension of the leg, or bulbous or spade shaped. Two new furniture forms were created in this period. They are the sideboard and the worktable. Expect to find a little more comfort in chairs and sofas, but not very thick cushions or seats.

When a piece of furniture is made in England, or styled after an English example, it may be known as Hepplewhite. The time frame is the same. Robert Adam is credited with creating the style known as Hepplewhite during the 1760s and leading the form. Another English book heavily influenced the designers of the day. This one was by Alice Hepplewhite, and titled *The Cabinet Maker and Upholsterer's Guide*, published in 1788, 1789 and 1794.

Sheraton, 1790-1810: The style known as Sheraton closely resembles Federal. The lines are somewhat straighter and the designs plainer than Federal. Sheraton pieces are more closely associated with rural cabinetmakers. Woods would include mahogany, mahogany veneer, maple and pine, as well as other native woods. This period was heavily influenced by the work of Thomas Sheraton and his series of books, *The Cabinet Maker and Upholsterer's Drawing Book*, from 1791-1794, and his *The*

Dutch marquetry six-drawer chest, 19th century, losses to bottom of two feet, 62" x 41" x 19". **$2,806**

Cabinet Directory, 1803, and *The Cabinet-Maker, Upholsterer, and General Artist's Encyclopedia* of 1804.

Empire (Classical), 1805-1830: By the beginning of the 19th century, a new design style was emerging. Known as Empire, it had an emphasis on the classical world of Greece, Egypt and other ancient European influences. The American craftsmen began to incorporate more flowing patriotic motifs, such as eagles with spread wings. The basic wood used in the Empire period was mahogany. However, during this period, dark woods were so favored that often mahogany was painted black. Inlays were popular when made of ebony or maple veneer. The dark woods offset gilt highlights, as were the brass ormolu mountings often found in this period. The legs of this period are substantial and more flowing than those found in the Federal or Sheraton periods. Feet can be highly ornamental, as when they are carved to look like lion's paws, or plain when they extend to the floor with a swept leg. Regional differences in this style are very apparent, with New York City being the center of the design style, as it was also the center of fashion at the time.

New furniture forms of this period include the sleigh bed, with the headboard and footboard forming a graceful arch. Several new forms of tables also came into being, especially the sofa table. Because the architectural style of the Empire period used big, open rooms, the sofa was now allowed to be in the center of the room, with a table behind it. Former architectural periods found most furniture placed against the outside perimeter of the walls and brought forward to be used.

Victorian, 1830-1890: The Victorian period as it relates to furniture styles can be divided into several distinct styles. However, not every piece of furniture can be dated or definitely identified, so the generic term "Victorian" will apply to those pieces. Queen Victoria's reign affected the design styles of furniture, clothing and all sorts of items used in daily living. Her love of ornate styles is well known. When thinking of the general term, think of a cluttered environment, full of heavy furniture, and surrounded by plants, heavy fabrics and lots of china and glassware.

French Restoration, 1830-1850: This is the first sub-category of the Victoria era. This style is best simplified as the plainest of the Victorian styles. Lines tend to be sweeping, undulating curves. It is named for the style that was popular in France as the Bourbons tried to restore their claim to the French throne, from 1814 to 1848. The Empire (Classical) period influence is felt, but French Restoration lacks some of the ornamentation and fussiness of that period. Design motifs continue to reflect an interest in the classics of Greece and Egypt. Chair backs are styled with curved and concave crest rails, making them a little more comfortable than earlier straight-back chairs. The use of bolster pillows and more upholstery is starting to emerge. The style was only popular in clusters, but did entice makers from larger metropolitan areas, such as Boston and New Orleans, to embrace the style.

The Gothic Revival period, 1840-1860: This is relatively easy to identify for collectors. It is one of the few styles that celebrates elements found in the corresponding architectural themes: turrets, pointed arches and quatrefoils—designs found in 12th through 16th centuries that were adapted to this mid-century furniture style. The furniture shelving form known as an étagère was born in this period, allowing Victorians to have more room to display their treasured collections. Furniture that had mechanical parts was also embraced by the Victorians of this era. The woods preferred by makers of this period were walnut and oak, with some use of mahogany and rosewood. The scale used ranged from large and grand to small and petite. Carved details gave dimension and interest.

Rococo Revival, 1845-1870: This design style features the use of scrolls, either in a "C" shape or the more fluid "S" shape. Carved decoration in the form of scallop shells, leaves and flowers, particularly roses, and acanthus further add to the ornamentation of this style of furniture. Legs and feet of this form are cabriole or scrolling. Other than what might be needed structurally, it is often difficult to find a straight element in Rococo Revival furniture. The use of marble for tabletops was quite popular, but expect to find the corners shaped to conform to the overall scrolling form. To accomplish all this carving, walnut, rosewood, and mahogany were common choices. When lesser woods were used, they were often painted to reflect these more expensive woods. Some cast-iron elements can be found on furniture from this period, especially if it was cast as scrolls. The style began in France and England, but eventually migrated to America where it evolved into two other furniture styles, Naturalistic and Renaissance Revival.

Photo courtesy Jeffrey S. Evans & Associates, Mt. Crawford, Va.; www.jeffreysevans.com

Shenandoah Co., Va., painted hickory ladder-back armed rocking chair, three-slat back with crisply turned acorn finials, turned arms with button terminals, original thin rockers that appear to be oak, later woven twine seat. Old worn green paint over the original dark green painted surface. Attributed to the Fravel family shop(s), Woodstock, Va. Second quarter 19th century, 41" x 16 1/2". **$575**

Elizabethan, 1850-1915: This sub-category of the Victorian era is probably the most feminine-influenced style. It also makes use of the new machine-turned spools and spiral profiles that were fast becoming popular with furniture makers. New technology advancements allowed more machined parts to be generated. By adding flowers, either carved or painted, the furniture pieces of this era had a softness to them. Chair backs tend to be high and narrow, having a slight back tilt. Legs vary from straight to baluster-turned forms to spindle turned. This period of furniture design saw more usage of needlework upholstery and decoratively painted surfaces.

Louis XVI, 1850-1914: One period of the Victorian era that flies away with straight lines is Louis XVI. However, this furniture style is not austere; it is adorned with ovals, arches, applied medallions, wreaths, garlands, urns and other Victorian flourishes. As the period aged, more ornamentation became present on the finished furniture styles. Furniture of this time was made from more expensive woods, such as ebony or rosewood. Walnut was popular around the 1890s. Other dark woods were featured, often to contrast the lighter ornaments. Expect to find straight legs or fluted and slightly tapered legs.

Naturalistic, 1850-1914: This furniture period takes the scrolling effects of the Rococo Revival designs and adds more flowers and fruits to the styles. More detail is spent on the leaves—so much that one can tell if they are to represent grape, rose or oak leaves. Technology advances enhanced this design style, as manufacturers developed a way of laminating woods together. This layered effect was achieved by gluing thin layers together, with the grains running at right angles on each new layer. The thick panels created were then steamed in molds to create the illusion of carving. The woods used as a basis for the heavy ornamentation were mahogany, walnut and some rosewood. Upholstery of this period is often tufted, eliminating any large flat surface. The name of John Henry Belter is often connected with this period, for it was when he did some of his best design work. John and Joseph W. Meeks also enjoyed success with laminated furniture. Original labels bearing these names are sometimes found on furniture pieces from this period, giving further provenance.

Renaissance Revival, 1850-1880: Furniture made in this style period reflects how cabinetmakers interpreted 16th- and 17th-century designs. Their motifs range from curvilinear and florid early in the period to angular and almost severe by the end of the period. Dark woods, such as mahogany and walnut, were primary with some use of rosewood and ebony. Walnut veneer panels were a real favorite in the 1870s designs. Upholstery, usually of a more generous nature, was also often incorporated into this design style. Ornamentation and high relief carving included flowers, fruits, game, classical busts, acanthus scrolls, strapwork, tassels and masks. Architectural motifs, such as pilasters, columns, pediments, balusters and brackets, are another prominent design feature. Legs are usually cabriole or have substantial turned profiles.

Néo-Greek, 1855-1885: This design style easily merges with both the Louis XVI and Renaissance Revival. It is characterized by elements reminiscent of Greek architecture, such as pilasters, flutes, column, acanthus, foliate scrolls, Greek key motifs and anthemion high-relief carving. This style originated with the French, but was embraced by American furniture manufacturers. Woods are dark and often ebonized. Ornamentation may be gilded or bronzed. Legs tend to be curved to scrolled or cloven hoof feet.

Eastlake, 1870-1890: This design style is named for Charles Locke Eastlake, who wrote a popular book in 1872 called *Hints on Household Taste*. It was originally published in London. One of his principles was the relationship between function, form and craftsmanship. Shapes of furniture from this style tend to be more rectangular. Ornamentation was created through the use of brackets, grooves, chamfers and geometric designs. American furniture manufacturers were enthusiastic about this style, since it was so easy to adapt for mass production. Woods used were again dark, but more native woods, such as oak, maple and pine, were incorporated. Legs and chair backs are straighter, often with incised decoration.

Feet

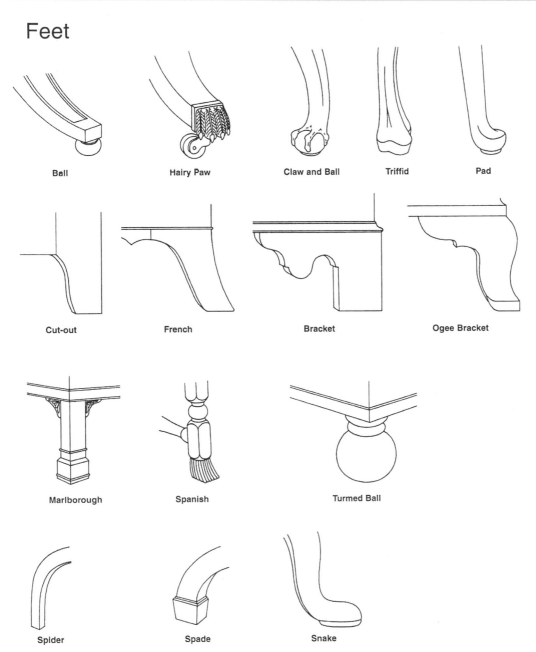

Ball

Hairy Paw

Claw and Ball

Triffid

Pad

Cut-out

French

Bracket

Ogee Bracket

Marlborough

Spanish

Turmed Ball

Spider

Spade

Snake

Art Furniture, 1880-1914: This period represents furniture designs gone mad, almost an "anything goes" school of thought. The style embraces both straight and angular with some pieces that are much more fluid, reflecting several earlier design periods. This era saw the wide usage of turned moldings and dark woods, but this time stained to imitate ebony and lacquer. The growing Oriental influence is seen in furniture from this period, including the use of bamboo, which was imported and included in the designs. Legs tend to be straight; feet tend to be small.

Arts & Crafts, 1895-1915: The Arts & Crafts period of furniture represents one of the strongest trends for cur-

rent collectors. Quality period Arts & Crafts furniture is available through most of the major auction houses. And, for those desiring the look, good quality modern furniture is also made in this style. The Arts & Crafts period furniture is generally rectilinear and a definite correlation is seen between form and function. The primary influences of this period were the Stickley brothers (especially Gustav, Leopold and John George), Elbert Hubbard, Frank Lloyd Wright and Harvey Ellis. Their furniture designs often overlapped into architectural and interior design, including rugs, textiles and other accessories. Wood used for Arts & Crafts furniture is primarily oak. Finishes were natural, fumed or painted. Hard-

Legs

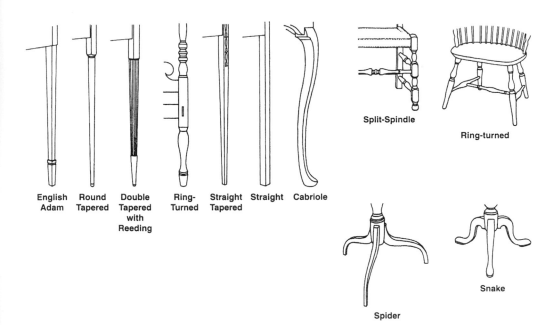

English Adam Round Tapered Double Tapered with Reeding Ring-Turned Straight Tapered Straight Cabriole

Split-Spindle

Ring-turned

Spider

Snake

Hardware

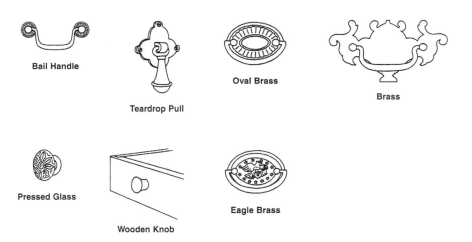

Bail Handle

Teardrop Pull

Oval Brass

Brass

Pressed Glass

Wooden Knob

Eagle Brass

ware was often made in copper. Legs are straight and feet are small, if present at all, as they were often a simple extension of the leg. Some inlay of natural materials was used, such as silver, copper and abalone shells.

Art Nouveau, 1896-1914: Just as the Art Nouveau period is known for women with long hair, flowers and curves, so is Art Nouveau furniture. The Paris Exposition of 1900 introduced furniture styles reflecting what was happening in the rest of the design world, such as jewelry and silver. This style of furniture was not warmly embraced, as the sweeping lines were not very conducive to mass production. The few manufacturers that did interpret it for their factories found interest to be slight in America. The French held it in higher esteem. Legs tend to be sweeping or cabriole. Upholstery becomes slimmer.

Art Deco, 1920-1945: The Paris *"L'Exposition International des Arts Décorative et Industriels Modernes"* became the mantra for designs of everything in this period. Lines are crisp, with some use of controlled curves. The Chrysler Building in New York City remains among the

Construction Details

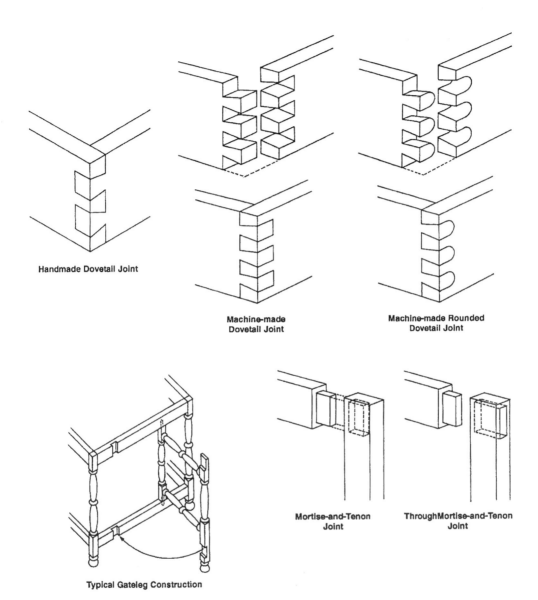

Handmade Dovetail Joint

Machine-made
Dovetail Joint

Machine-made Rounded
Dovetail Joint

Mortise-and-Tenon
Joint

ThroughMortise-and-Tenon
Joint

Typical Gateleg Construction

finest example of Art Deco architecture and those same straight lines and gentle curves are found in furniture. Makers used expensive materials, such as veneers, lacquered woods, glass and steel. The cocktail table first enters the furniture scene during this period. Upholstery can be vinyl or smooth fabrics. Legs are straight or slightly tapered; chair backs tend to be either low or extremely high.

Modernism, 1940-present: Furniture designed and produced during this period is distinctive, as it represents the usage of some new materials, like plastic, aluminum and molded laminates. The Bauhaus and also the Museum of Modern Art heavily influenced some designers. In 1940, the museum organized competitions for domestic furnishings. Designers Eero Saarien and Charles Eames won first prize for their designs. A new chair design combined the back, seat and arms together as one unit. Tables were designed that incorporated the top, pedestal and base as one. Shelf units were also designed in this manner.

Also see Folk Art, Modernism, Oriental Objects.

LOUIE LOUIE

18th- and 19th-century French and Continental Furniture

By Andrew Myers

Amble through The Wrightsman Galleries for French Decorative Arts in New York's Metropolitan Museum, gambol through Los Angeles' Getty Museum and its period 18th-century French rooms, or visit the Louis-Louis-Louis (XIV, XV, XVI) interiors in the hit 1988 film, "Dangerous Liaisons," and behold a French revolution that didn't involve the guillotine.

Andrew Myers

In all three you will find legions of small task-oriented tables (as night-stands, as well as for writing, sewing, reading, grooming and gaming); desks in a variety of configurations (flat, foldout or otherwise); commodes for storage and consoles for convenient surfaces. Often adorned with marquetry, marble, tortoise shell and exotic veneers, lacquered or porcelain panels, and fitted with gilt-bronze mounts and pulls, these pieces are in turn complemented by an army of upholstered, orthopedically sensitive, sinfully comfortable furniture.

The catalog, especially for sofas and chairs, is vast. To look at armchair designs singularly, exhaustively, would require reams. Some chairs have open arm rests (fauteuil); others come with wrap-around arm rests (bergère); still others boast wrap-around head-level wings (fauteuil en confessional); whereas a different leg-oriented variety is more concerned with length. Like a super-sized elongated bergère, chaises lounges stand alone; but if monsieur or madam wish to add a footboard then—voilà!—a duchesse; or, should the duchesse be divided lengthwise into two, even three pieces for greater versatility, then a duchesse brisée, or broken duchess. (Had we spoken of a fallen duchess we'd have to refer to comedies of manner and Molière, so let's stop.)

"Traditional," "old fashioned," "like my great aunt Ida's do-not-touch living room," the hipsters-than-thou might exclaim. But they would be wrong, because in its time, 18th-century French furniture defined the shockingly new, the avant-garde, the up-to-the-minute modern (indeed, in late 17th-century France it was called, simply, "the modern taste," a phrase ascribed to French furniture in the 18th century by none other than English cabinet-maker and furniture designer, Thomas Chippendale).

Consider what had come before. Since the early Renaissance, interiors had been created to reflect and reinforce social position, fostering an Age of Magnificence with an emphasis on presentation, appearance, and rituals replete with grandeur but devoid of commodité—the buzzword of the 18th century meaning both comfort and convenience. In these Baroque interiors, pieces of furniture were few. Storage of one's clothes and objects was relegated to a utilitarian chest; one of the only pieces not necessarily designed to be ambulatory (castle to castle or city to country) was the bed; and what little seating could be found was made of bare hardwood. Stools were usually foldable, allowing for mobility and easy storage, and the armchair, throne-like in its importance and scarcity, was usually un-upholstered (at most there was a cushion

Photo courtesy Heritage Auction Galleries, Dallas; www.HA.com

Louis XIV walnut commode, French early 18th century, rectangular top over a pair of short drawers carved with a cartouche, over two long drawers similarly carved, raised on bracket feet, 31 1/2" x 50" x 23 1/4". **$8,365**

Photo courtesy Heritage Auction Galleries, Dallas; www.HA.com

Louis XV-style mahogany canapé, Franch, late 19th century, foliate carved frame with a padded back and serpentine seat, on cabriole legs, upholstered in light blue silk, 43 1/2" x 76" x 27 1/2". **$2,868**

or thin layer of leather or tapestry), and always with a stiff back—encouraging the rigid etiquette and protocol of the era.

Indeed, the last time curves, seating and comfort had trysted was millennia earlier, in ancient Greece with klismos chairs the seating of choice (the Romans, by turn, introduced the chair as a symbol of power and importance, used for the public rather than private arena).

In "The Age of Comfort," scholar, professor and author Jean DeJean examines in detail the cultural, social, technological and political forces that fomented and shaped this aesthetic revolution. Suffice it to say these factors together laid the groundwork for what we today recognized as the "design industry," "the modern home," even "contemporary" pieces of furniture such as the sofa, the sectional, even the scourge of all aesthetes, the La-Z-Boy (OK, recliner).

Additionally, the era produced the first specialized rooms devoted to a single activity (sleeping! eating!) and the specialized furniture to fill them, as well as the first architect-designed pieces of furniture conceived not just for specific activities but specific interiors, too. As DeJean writes, referencing the iconic 18th-century furniture designer André Jacob Roubo, "the great furniture makers knew full well that the role furniture played in people's lives was changing dramatically and that with their designs, they were shaping the way people lived. Roubo explained that new kinds of furniture were being created every day 'in an attempt to respond to all the new needs that seem to pop up as soon as [furniture makers] are able to satisfy them.'"

To borrow a phrase associated with the Bauhaus and Modernism, in 18th-century furniture, form followed function. The new designs aided and abetted comfort and convenience, promoting reading, writing, study and intellectual exchange as much as relaxation, revelry, casual and—at least judging by the literature and engravings of the day—amorous interaction. Just as the Age of Comfort was both a creator and product of the Enlightenment, so was it also the parent of the most modern of concepts: Lifestyle.

Is it any wonder that for more than 100 years, from the latter part of the 17th century through 1815 and Waterloo, French taste and style held undisputed sway over all of Europe, with French furniture copied and collected from Lisbon to St. Petersburg? Is it any wonder, then, that 20th-century American collectors and connoisseurs collected Louis XIV, XV, XVI and Empire with Croesus-like cupidity?

Elsie de Wolfe, arguably the first professional interior designer in the United States, was not only a confirmed design Francophile (her particular penchant was neoclassical Louis XVI), she also filled the houses of industrial magnates such as Henry Clay Frick (including his mansion on East 70th Street in New York, now home to The Frick Collection of fine and decorative arts) with French 18th-century designs. In so doing, she did much to make fine French furniture (often called "FFF") an accepted, often preferred, choice for America's elite, from turn of the century robber barons to Wall Street's Masters of the Universe in the 1980s (Hello, John and Susan Gutfreund, lovers of the Louis as well as Second Empire).

Photo courtesy Heritage Auction Galleries, Dallas; www.HA.com

Louis XVI-style gilt wood armchairs, late 19th century, each with a serpentine crest rail carved with foliage, the shaped backrest padded and upholstered, with similarly carved padded arms on scrolled supports, over a padded and upholstered seat, the seat rail carved with a guilloche pattern, raised on tapering spiral fluted legs topped with acanthus, each 40" x 26" x 23". **$1,195 pair.**

Photo courtesy Heritage Auction Galleries, Dallas; www.HA.com

Louis XV-style walnut console with marble top, 19th Century, serpentine marble top with molded edge, above a conforming frieze set with three drawers, the knees with carved rocaille, raised on cabriole legs, the outer legs connected by carved floral stretchers, 42" x 81 1/2" x 24". **$5,975**

Given this history, one might expect current prices to be Upper East Side high. Such, however, is not the case—at least not necessarily. The reason has everything to do with the age-old, price-determining ratio of fashion/supply. In the 1980s and early 1990s, period rooms—everything from carpets and sconces—were the rage among the deep-pocketed design crown. Sale records were made, broken, and remade for "important" and rare pieces, and the category as a whole enjoyed a precipitous price rise. A bergère with, say, a royal provenance always attracts attention and commands a high price due to its extreme rarity; but middle-of-the-road pieces, aesthetically attractive but perhaps unstamped by the maker and/or with murky provenance, need the winds of fashion to propel its price onwards and upwards.

Over the last 15 years, design eclecticism (the mixing of styles and periods) has been the rage, the result being that prices for mid-level 18th-century French furniture have traded in a narrow range with little appreciation. A perusal of "Price Indices for Art, Stocks and Gold (Base=100=January 2004)" from the latest Art Market Report (or "The International Art Market 2007-2009, Trends in the Art Trade during Global Recession") commissioned by The European Fine Art Foundation and released in March, 2010, shows a five-year graph in which the line for French 18th-century furniture was categorically flat, with only a modest (approximately 10%) dip during the financial crisis of 2008-2009. By contrast, the lines for contemporary art, Modern art and European impressionists look like they've fallen off a cliff.

The graph, of course, represents an average from across the decorative spectrum. More specific examination reveals that over the last decade, the top tier for French 18th-century furniture has performed exceptionally well: the top 10 auction prices all were realized post 1999, with four of these since 2005 (nine out of the top 20 records have also been made since 2005). Tracking a singular piece of great importance reveals exceptional appreciation as well: During the Paris Biennale antiques show in 2004, while visiting a renowned Parisian dealer, I was shown a bureau plat that had belonged to Marie Antoinette, the last known desk of the French queen still in private hands. Its price was a cool $1 million. Back on the market, I understand it's now offered at just north of $2 million.

While the high and very high end has performed well, the middle has not—and here represents many a buying opportunity. To give but one example, lot No. 6 in Christie's April 20, 2010, "500 Years Decorative Arts Europe" sale was a pair of Louis XV fauteuils by master furniture maker Louis Cresson, circa 1750. Stamped "L.Cresson," covered in green and cream silk, and offered with linen slip covers, their estimate was $4,000-6,000, and their hammer price (including buyer's premium) $8,125. To summarize my discussions with several auction specialists, this represents substantial value with much room for appreciation, especially when the fashion for period rooms returns (I say when rather than if, as the penchant for period, when tracked over the last hundred or so years, is cyclical).

Photo courtesy Heritage Auction Galleries, Dallas; www.HA.com

Carved marble bust of Louis XIV on marble pedestal, French, Late 18th - Early 19th century, well-carved figure with flowing hair cascading over his shoulders wearing a ruffled lace collar and fur mantle, raised on a trapezoidal marble pedestal, 81" overall. **$10,755**

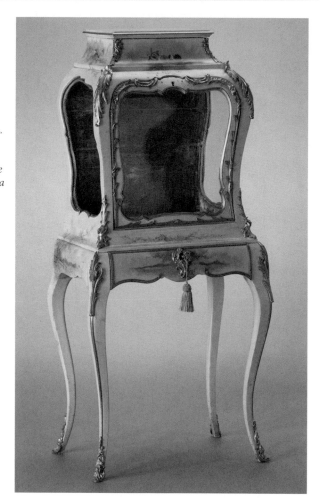

Louis XV-style painted wood and gilt bronze vitrine cabinet, probably Paris, circa 1880-1920, unmarked. The bombé-form vitrine cabinet raised on four cabriole legs with gilt bronze sabots, the shaped upper with glazed velvet-lined cabinet with hinged fall-front door over drawer with velvet covered slide, the cabinet with rocaille and scrolled acanthus leaf gilt bronze mounts, painted pale green with cherub, trophy and landscape decoration in imitation of Vernis Martin. Losses to painted surfaces, lock plate to fall-front door lacking, wear to velvet, 53 3/4" x 24" x 15 3/4". **$1,195**

Moving into the 19th century, the trajectory of Empire furniture mirrors its 18th-century cousin: the top tier having performed well, the middle far less so. Prices in general are less than for furniture of the previous century, and the base of collectors smaller. With its abundance of gilding and large scale, it is often the object of (as one specialist phrased it) "new money's" affection. Strength of pieces in the upper echelon was demonstrated in Sotheby's "Important French Furniture, Sculptures and Works of Art" sale in Paris on April 14, 2010, where lot No. 144, "An Exceptional Gilt-bronze Mounted Mahogany Secretaire, Empire, Attributed to Jacob-Desmalter, the Mounts Attributed to Pierre-Philippe Thomire," squashed its €100,000-150,000 estimate with a gavel price of €312,750 (including buyer's premium), about $444,000.

Furniture from the Charles X, Louis-Philippe and Second Empire periods have all enjoyed cycles of fashion, but prices do not generally approach those of the earlier periods—the exception being a personality-driven sale, such as the astronomical prices achieved for 19th-century French furniture in the November 2009 sale at Christie's Paris of 1,2000 pieces from the collection of Yves Saint-Laurent and Pierre Bergé, once housed in their country house, the Château Gabriel.

As far as German and Italian 18th- and 19th-century furniture, prices vary enormously. While several auction house specialists and antiques dealers agree that period Italian furniture can be easier to live with than the French "because they tend to be more decorative and don't impose a formality on the interior," market gauging is difficult due to limited supply. Ditto the scarcity of German furniture; as one specialist said, "Important pieces hardly ever appear." When they do, however, prices can be quite high indeed. One example, which I saw in the fall of 2009 at New York-based dealer Carlton Hobbs, is an incredibly rare secretaire à abattant, a metamorphic masterwork from circa 1790, possibly by Karl May, where a sleek neoclassical interior of polished mahogany with finely cast gilt-brass mounts is hidden by an exterior completely covered in cork and designed to resemble an architectural ruin. It's a magical masterwork of mechanized furniture, and a price well above $1 million.

In terms of value, price, room for appreciation, stability, safety—not to mention comfort and versatility—I would pay attention to mid-level 18th-century French pieces in good condition with clear provenance and minimal (if any) restoration. It's a buyer's market. Why not take advantage of it while it lasts?

Photos courtesy Carlton Hobbs, New York;
www.carltonhobbs.com

From New York-based dealer Carlton Hobbs, an incredibly rare secretaire à abattant, a metamorphic masterwork from circa 1790, possibly by Karl May, where a sleek neoclassical interior of polished mahogany with finely cast gilt-brass mounts is hidden by an exterior completely covered in cork and designed to resemble an architectural ruin. It's a magical masterwork of mechanized furniture, and a price well above **$1 million**.

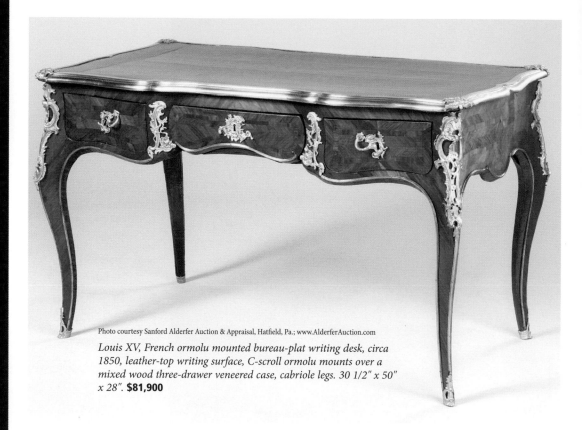

Photo courtesy Sanford Alderfer Auction & Appraisal, Hatfield, Pa.; www.AlderferAuction.com

Louis XV, French ormolu mounted bureau-plat writing desk, circa 1850, leather-top writing surface, C-scroll ormolu mounts over a mixed wood three-drawer veneered case, cabriole legs. 30 1/2" x 50" x 28". **$81,900**

Photo courtesy Rago Arts and Auctions, Lambertveile, N.J.; www.RagoArts.com

French parquetry-top dining room table, early 20th century, with refectory-style oak cabriole legs, 29 1/2" x 102 1/2" x 45", opens to 157". **$1,098**

Photo courtesy Rago Arts and Auctions, Lambertveile, N.J.;
www.RagoArts.com

*French chaise lounge, 19th century,
upholstered with painted frame, 34 3/4"
x 33 1/4" x 74 1/2".* **$671**

Photo courtesy James D. Julia Auctions, Fairfield, Maine; www.jamesdjulia.com

*Louis XV-style kingwood and burled walnut marble top commode, late 19th/early 20th century. Rectangular gray
Breschia marble top with rounded edges and serpentine front above the rectangular case with bombé sides and front
fitted with two long bombé drawers mounted with cast brass scrolling handles cast with leaf tips and bordered by
scrolling ormolu trim. Raised on out-swept angular legs with cast brass sabots and trim. The case with cross banding
overall centering burled veneered panels, 34 1/4" x 48" x 20", retains original cleaned finish and original marble.
Hardware and ormolu original.* **$1,500+**

Photos courtesy Leslie Hindman Auctioneers, Chicago;
www.LeslieHindman.com

*Above: Georgian-style lacquered cabinet on stand,
rectangular top over two doors decorated with
Chinoiserie scenes over a single drawer raised on
carved cabriole legs, 20th century, having minor
surface scratches typical of age and use, the back
panel is missing; retrofitted for shelves, 63" x 37" x
19 7/8".* **$457**

*Top right: Georgian-style vitrine cabinet on stand,
shaped cornice with Greek key decoration over the
two glazed doors, the base raised on cabriole legs.
Most likely 19th century, most glass is broken out,
framing around the glass with multiple repairs,
69 1/2" x 43 3/4" x 12 1/2".* **$793**

*Right: Georgian-style clerk's desk, having a hinged
slant-front writing surface over a paneled door
raised on carved claw and ball feet, 34 1/2" x 19" x
17 1/2".* **$275**

Photos courtesy Leslie Hindman Auctioneers, Chicago; www.LeslieHindman.com

Louis XVI-style painted bergere, having upholstered back, arms and seat raised on cabriole legs, 54 3/4" x 28 1/2" x 29". **$305**

William and Mary-style walnut low table, the oval galleried top raised on four baluster-form legs joined by shaped stretchers centered with a finial, 24 1/4" x 35" x 30 3/4". **$610**

Photo courtesy Jeffrey S. Evans & Associates, Mt. Crawford, Va.; www.jeffreysevans.com

New England highly figured tiger maple bedstead, featuring four boldly turned corner posts flanking turned rails and cutout boards, original side and end rails with holes for roping. Fitted with custom-made bedding. Second quarter 19th century, 48" x 51" x 75", some small chips to turnings, head rail dowels need repair, mattress with light stains. **$690**

Photo courtesy Jeffrey S. Evans & Associates, Mt. Crawford, Va.; www.jeffreysevans.com

Pennsylvania paint-decorated settee bench, triple back with three shaped tablets above three groups of six half spindles, solid-scroll arms, wide rolled-front plank seat, raised on eight turned legs joined by single stretchers. Original smoke-grained paint, yellow striping, and gold fruit stencils. Mid-19th century, 34" x 17 1/4" x 72". **$575**

Photo courtesy Leslie Hindman Auctioneers, Chicago; www.LeslieHindman.com

Gothic Revival half-tester bed, having carved canopy with pierced apron and corner brackets, raised on faceted columns flanking the headboard containing three lanceted arches with crocketed carving, the side rails and footboard having quatrefoil cartouches with the end posts of faceted columns with foliate form finials, 96" x 68" x 87". **$7,930**

Photo courtesy Leslie Hindman Auctioneers, Chicago; www.LeslieHindman.com

Gothic Revival walnut side chairs, the arched crest rails over gothic pierce-carved decoration above the upholstered trapezoidal seats, raised on turned and carved legs, each 41 1/4". One with crest reglued. The other with both rear blocks under seat replaced. Some looseness in joints. Normal surface wear (light nicks and scratches) throughout consistent with age and use. Fairly even finish. **$976 pair**

Photos courtesy Clars Auction Gallery, Oakland, Calif.; www.Clars.com

Marshall Laird, Los Angeles, Elizabethan-style carved oak server, circa 1920, the hand-planed top having a hinged left side above double doors featuring portrait panels over a frieze carved with grapes and acanthus leaves, on carved supports and box stretcher base, retaining maker's plaque, 37" h x 41" x 20" d. **$450**

Marshall Laird, Los Angeles, Elizabethan-style carved oak sideboard, circa 1920, with hand-planed and carved surface over conforming base with linen-fold side panels, three drawers with grape and vine carved motif, flanked by relief carved doors, the whole rising on turned legs with beaded stretchers, retaining Marshall Laird plaque, 36" h x 71" w x 21" d. **$475**

Photo courtesy Rago Arts and
Auctions, Lambertveile, N.J.;
www.RagoArts.com

*American Aesthetic
Movement armchairs,
circa 1880/1890, similar
to furniture associated
with or executed by
Louis Comfort Tiffany.
Sides, front, back and
stiles embellished with
glass mosaic. Vertical
stiles terminate in deeply
carved peacocks hooded
by their fully open tails.
In fragmentary condition,
the surviving springs,
stuffing, and cut velvet
upholstery original, each
37 3/4" x 29 3/4" x 28".*
$390,400 pair

Photos courtesy Jeffrey S. Evans & Associates, Mt. Crawford, Va.; www.jeffreysevans.com

Pennsylvania painted pine drysink, hinged top concealing a shallow well beside a single drawer, shaped backsplash, all above two fielded-panel doors, raised on simple cut-out feet. Pine and poplar secondary woods. Original painted surface with some enhancements. Mid 19th century, 37 1/2" x 18 1/2" x 49", several varmint holes and some small repairs/ restorations. **$920**

Southern yellow pine and poplar sideboard pie safe, featuring three drawers above four doors, each with a punched-tin panel, fielded-panel ends, all raised on four turned feet (not original). Yellow pine secondary wood. Lacking interior shelves. Mid 19th century, 43 1/2" x 20" x 64 1/2", with expected wear, stains and scratches, small patches to two drawer edges and associated rails. **$1,150**

Photos courtesy Jeffrey S. Evans & Associates, Mt. Crawford, Va.; www.jeffreysevans.com

Pennsylvania paint-decorated pine and popular blanket chest, hinged top with applied edge moldings, above a dovetailed case raised on applied dovetailed bracket feet. Interior with simple strap hinges, grab lock, and lidded till. Poplar secondary wood. Original ornamental painted surface. Second quarter 19th century, 23 1/4" x 23 1/2" x 50 5/8", some wear to top and moldings, feet with patches and repairs. **$747**

Pennsylvania Chippendale walnut bible box, hinged molded-edge top above a dovetailed case fitted with two lip-molded drawers, applied base moldings, raised on cut-out bracket feet that appear to be old replacements. Interior with original wrought-iron butterfly hinges and cabinet lock, brass hardware appears to be original. Yellow pine, poplar, and possibly white cedar secondary woods, rose-head nails throughout. Second half 18th century, 12 1/2" x 13" x 19 3/8". **$2,645**

Photos courtesy Jeffrey S. Evans & Associates, Mt. Crawford, Va.; www.jeffreysevans.com

Country pine and oak curved-back settle, cutout wing ends, beaded backboards, solid plank seat fitted with a contemporary cushion, center brace under seat. Retains an old dark surface. Late 18th/early 19th century, 56" x 16" x 83", with expected wear and old repairs, several separations to seat. **$546**

Virginia Late Classical mahogany sideboard, top featuring an applied backsplash with rail and spindle extensions, above three drawers and four doors flanked by applied ring-turned half columns, raised on turned feet. Pine and poplar secondary woods. Second quarter 19th century, 55 1/2" x 22 1/2" x 69". **$575**

Photos courtesy Jeffrey S. Evans & Associates, Mt. Crawford, Va.; www.jeffreysevans.com

Victorian walnut tilt-top center table, slightly oval top raised on a triple-column pedestal and cutout tripod base. Third quarter 19th century, as shown, 28 1/4" x 31 1/2" x 36 1/2".
$195

Victorian walnut and burl parlor table, molded-edge oval top raised on an ornate turned and carved base with center urn. Third quarter 19th century, 28" x 24 1/2" x 35 1/2".
$316

English walnut tavern table, having lobed top over triangular base, 19" x 40 1/2", minor surface scratches. **$671**

Neoclassical-style giltwood occasional table, the shaped rectangular onyx-inset top over the pierce carved frieze, raised on cabriole legs joined by stretchers centered with finial, 30" x 26 1/2" x 21". **$976**

Photo courtesy Leslie Hindman Auctioneers, Chicago; www.LeslieHindman.com

Irish mahogany game table, the shaped rectangular top opening to square, with fitted playing surface over a plain frieze, with carved cabriole legs ending in claw and ball feet, crackling with light chipping to veneer on frieze and top, one drawer support detached but present, normal light scratching and nicks consistent with age, 19th century or earlier, 28 1/2" x 33" x 16 1/4" (size closed). **$2,440**

Photo courtesy Jeffrey S. Evans & Associates, Mt. Crawford, Va.; www.jeffreysevans.com

Shenandoah Valley of Virginia walnut candlestand, fixed oval top raised on a turned pedestal and tripod base. Walnut secondary wood. Mid-19th century, 26 5/8" x 15 1/4" x 18 1/2", small patch and chip to top. **$402**

Photo courtesy Jeffrey S. Evans & Associates, Mt. Crawford, Va.; www.jeffreysevans.com

American rustic twig and burl plant stand, square well with applied random burl knots, raised on a twig and burl pedestal and legs. Late 19th/early 20th century, 30 1/2" x 8 1/2" x 15 1/4". **$345**

Photo courtesy Heritage Auction Galleries, Dallas; www.HA.com

Italian gilt-wood barometer, 20th Century, marked, "PALLADIO / HANDCARVED IN ITALY", 36 1/8", the circular dial inscribed "TEMPÊTE, Grande Pluie, PLUIE ou VENT, Variables, BEAU TEMPS, Beau Fixe, TRÈS-SEC", the case carved with acanthus leaves, surmounted by a ribboned basket of flowers, the tip of one acanthus leaf on the lower left side repaired. A few chips, cracks, and losses to the gilding throughout. Surface wear throughout. **$310**

Photo courtesy Heritage Auction Galleries, Dallas; www.HA.com

Carlo Bugatti boudoir mirror on stand, camelskin, walnut, ebonized wood, bone, pewter and punched copper, circa 1900. **$7,170**

Photo courtesy Heritage Auction Galleries, Dallas; www.HA.com

Italian mirrors, probably Venice, 20th century, unmarked, each 25 3/8" x 13 3/4", shield shape with beveled and cut conforming border, flaming urn-form finials, on black painted wood backs. **$717 pair**

Photo courtesy Heritage Auction Galleries, Dallas; www.HA.com

Nic Freres, wrought-iron mirror, circa 1925, 26" x 47". **$1,912**

Glass

ART GLASS

Also see Lighting, Perfume Containers, Tiffany.

Photo courtesy Heritage Auction Galleries, Dallas; www.HA.com

Continental enameled glass dressing set, Bohemian, circa 1935, unmarked, comprising atomizer, oval pin tray, pair of covered boxes and round tray (10 1/2"), decorated with enamel flowers on textured gilt ground. **$657**

Photo courtesy James D. Julia Auctioneers, Fairfield, Maine; www.JuliaAuctions.com

Bohemian Art Glass Bowl. Probably produced by Von Poschinger, features lightly iridized frosted glass body with purple threading and lightly stretched ruffled rim. 11" diameter. **$115**

Photo courtesy James D. Julia Auctioneers, Fairfield, Maine; www.JuliaAuctions.com

Kew Blas Decorated Vase. Cabinet vase has squat body with yellow to gold iridescent pulled-feather design against a creamy white background. The interior of the vase is finished with a bright gold iridescence. Signed on the underside within the polished pontil "Kew Blas". 3" t. **$115**

Photo courtesy Heritage Auction Galleries, Dallas; www.HA.com

Pair of French art glass vases, Morning and Evening, Legras & Cie, Saint-Denis, France, circa 1910, marked Legras, each 22 1/2" x 8" diameter, with painted landscapes, one on a ground of gold tones, its mate on a ground of violet tones. **$3,883 pair**

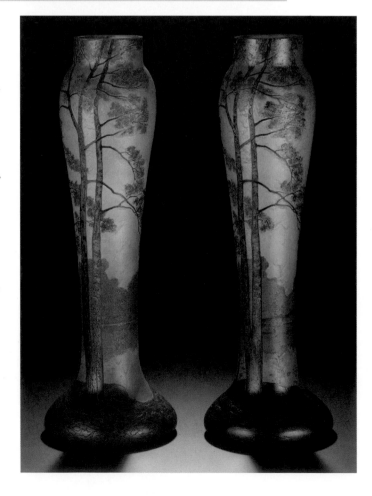

Photo courtesy James D. Julia Auctioneers, Fairfield, Maine; www.JuliaAuctions.com

Loetz Jack In The Pulpit Vase. Gold iridescent with stretched glass face with pink and green highlights. 12" t x 7 1/4" diameter of face. **$1,140**

Photo courtesy James D. Julia Auctioneers, Fairfield, Maine; www.JuliaAuctions.com

Loetz Decorated Vase. With platinum iridescent wave design against an amber background. The cylindrical body gives way to a slightly flaring lip. Unsigned. 6 1/8" t. **$517**

Photo courtesy James D. Julia Auctioneers, Fairfield, Maine; www.JuliaAuctions.com

Loetz Decorated Vase. With body of salmon at the lip shading to orange with a lightly iridescent wave pattern throughout the body. Vase is further highlighted with platinum and blue iridescent oval spots. Unsigned. 5 1/4" t. **$966**

Photo courtesy James D. Julia Auctioneers, Fairfield, Maine; www.JuliaAuctions.com

Loetz Gold Crater Vase. With deeply impressed moon crater design with rich gold iridescent finish showing pink and blue highlights. Unsigned. 3 1/4" t. **$180**

Photo courtesy Heritage Auction Galleries, Dallas; www.HA.com

French art glass vase, C. Schneider Glassworks, Epinay-sur-Seine, France, 1918-1933, marked Le Verre Francais (etched) 11 5/8″ x 8 5/8″, trumpet-form vase in brown cased, mottled and striated yellow-green cameo glass with stylized flying crane over grass frond decoration, minor scratching to rim and base. **$1,912**

Photo courtesy James D. Julia Auctioneers, Fairfield, Maine; www.JuliaAuctions.com

Steuben Blue Jade Vase. Large bulbous form with flaring rim, shape no. 6500. 6 1/2" t x 7 1/2" w. **$4,025**

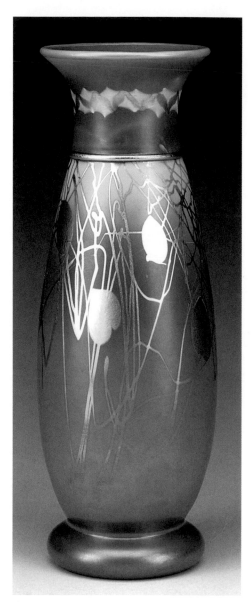

Photo courtesy James D. Julia Auctioneers, Fairfield, Maine; www.JuliaAuctions.com

Steuben Tyrian Vase. With gold iridescent leaf and vine design against a body shading from sea-foam green to rich bluish purple. The vase is finished with an applied neck with intarsia design and slightly flaring rim. Signed on the underside "Tyrian". 10" t. **$25,000**

Photo courtesy James D. Julia Auctioneers, Fairfield, Maine; www.JuliaAuctions.com

Steuben Acid Cut-Back Vase. Rose quartz vase has deep acid cut-back design in the Acanthus pattern with pink color and crackling. The vase is signed on the side with acid cut-back fleur de lis mark. 10 1/2" t. **$2,587**

Steuben Acid Cut-Back Vase. Green jade cut to alabaster in a Japanese pattern. Unsigned. 7" t x 7 1/2" diameter. **$920**

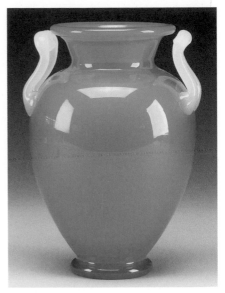

Steuben Green Jade Vase. With slightly flaring neck and rolled rim. The vase is finished with two applied alabaster "M" handles. Signed in center of polished pontil with acid etched script signature "Steuben". 10 1/4" t. **$1,380**

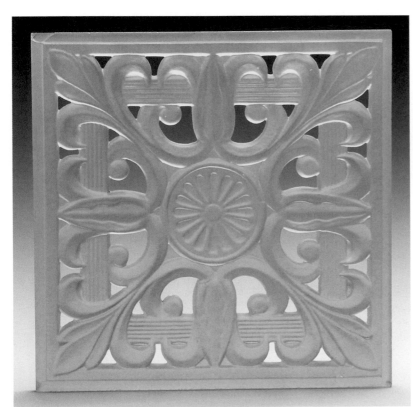

Steuben Cast Glass Grill. Made as a ventilation grate for a cruise liner. Bristol yellow and features a fleur de lis design in each corner with a spoked wheel in the center. 9 7/8" sq. Some minor fleabites and a bruise to the design with some slightly larger chips on the outside edge, which would be concealed if the grill was mounted. **$1,610**

*French art glass vase,
Daum Frères, Nancy,
France, circa 1900,
marked Daum, Nancy,
(cross of Lorraine)
12", with varied and
vibrant coloration, the
shaded orange ground
featuring a town scene
in one panel.* **$9,560**

French art glass footed goblet, Daum Frères, Nancy, France, circa 1895, marked Daum, Nancy, (cross of Lorraine), 7" x 7 1/2", patterned with a frieze of fieldmice in shades of red and orange over shaded and frosted sky. **$5,078**

French art glass box and cover, Daum Frères, Nancy, France, circa 1900, marked Daum, Nancy, (cross of Lorraine), 3 3/4" x 5 1/2", squared box with round cover patterned with conforming landscape of birch trees in naturalistic spring palette over frosted, opalescent pink ground. **$3,585**

Photo courtesy Heritage Auction Galleries, Dallas; www.HA.com

French art glass vase, Daum Freres, Nancy, France, circa 1910, marked DAUM, FRANCE, (cross of Lorraine), 11 3/4" x 4 3/4" x 3", with pattern of berried branches in dark mauve shades on dark blue and green modeled ground, surface showing multiple stress lines. **$310**

Daum Nancy Cameo and Enamel Floral Vase. With delicate blue enameled flowers and green foliage that rest against a mottled background of blue, purple and green. Signed on the underside "Daum Nancy" with the Cross of Lorraine in gold. 5" h. Minor enamel loss to stems. **$2,400**

Monumental Daum Nancy Cameo Vase. With decoration of swans and birch trees. Decoration adorns both from and back of the vase and is finished with enameled scene of islands and trees in the background. A superior example. Signed in enamel on the foot rim "Daum Nancy". 25 1/4" t. **$18,400**

Daum Nancy Art Deco Vase. With deep acid cut-back Art Deco design against a smoky gray glass. The design has a textured finish in contrast with the polished glass highlights. Signed on the underside with engraved "Daum Nancy France" with Cross of Lorraine. 4" t. **$460**

Photo courtesy James D. Julia Auctioneers, Fairfield, Maine; www.JuliaAuctions.com

Daum Nancy Cameo and Enameled Vase. Square vase is decorated on each side with a cameo poppy, stem and leaves against a mottled yellow shading to orange background. Each poppy, in various stages of bloom, is enameled with bright orange flowers and subtle green and brown stems and leaves. The foot of the vase is trimmed with a simple gold gilt line. Signed on the side in cameo "Daum Nancy" with the Cross of Lorraine.
4 3/4" t. **$4,200**

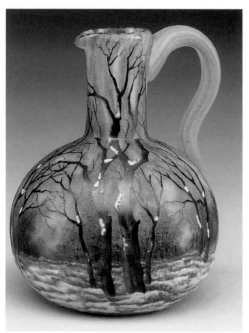

Photo courtesy James D. Julia Auctioneers, Fairfield, Maine; www.JuliaAuctions.com

Daum Nancy Cameo Cruet. Winter scene in rare shape. Signed in enamel on the underside "Daum Nancy" with Cross of Lorraine. 3" t. **$3,220**

Photo courtesy James D. Julia Auctioneers, Fairfield, Maine; www.JuliaAuctions.com

Daum Nancy Cameo Vase. Acid etched and enameled winter scene. Signed in enamel on the underside "Daum Nancy" with the Cross of Lorraine. 4" t. **$6,325**

Photo courtesy James D. Julia Auctioneers, Fairfield, Maine;
www.JuliaAuctions.com

Daum Nancy Snail Vase. Design of grapes, leaves and vines in autumn-colored vitreous glass against a mottled yellow, orange and brown background. The unusually large egg-shaped vase is finished with two applied glass snails (second view). Vase is signed on the side in cameo "Daum Nancy" with the Cross of Lorraine. 8 3/4" t. **$10,925**

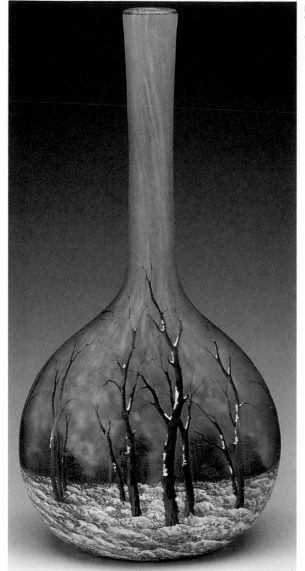

*Daum Nancy Cameo Vase. Winter scenic banjo vase.
Unusual shape. Signed in enamel on the underside
"Daum Nancy" with Cross of Lorraine. 12" t.* **$10,350**

*Daum Nancy Cameo Rose Bowl. Winter scenic
decoration, strongly colored and detailed.
Engraved signature "Daum Nancy" with Cross
of Lorraine on underside. 3 3/4" t x 5" diameter.*
$8,625

*Daum Nancy Cameo Vase. Canoe shape with acid-etched and enameled winter scene. Enameled signature on the
underside "Daum Nancy" with the Cross of Lorraine. 6 3/4" w.* **$6,325**

Photo courtesy James D. Julia Auctioneers, Fairfield, Maine; www.JuliaAuctions.com

Daum Nancy Rain Scene Vase. Extremely rare, square form is enameled with earthen-hued trees with green grass and foliage in the background. This design is set against a gray, rose and green ground. The "rain" effect is created by scoring the glass down to its transparency. Signed "Daum Nancy" with the Cross of Lorraine. 4 1/4" h. **$8,625**

Daum Nancy Cameo Vase. Spring scenic vase with acid-etched and enameled trees. Signed in enamel on the side "Daum Nancy" with the Cross of Lorraine. 10 1/2" h.
$6,325

Early Daum Cameo and Enameled Vase. Decorated with a large, central heavily enameled thistle and flower with gold highlights. The flower is set against an acid-etched background of creamy yellow shading to clear. The back and sides of the vase are decorated with all-over cameo thistle design with black enamel highlighting the stems and leaves with gold gilt thistle flowers and red enamel highlights. The vase is finished with an enameled floral band at the lip. Signed on the underside in red enamel "Daum Nancy" with the Cross of Lorraine. 8" h. Some minor wear to gilt trim on lip. **$5,750**

Photo courtesy James D. Julia Auctioneers, Fairfield, Maine; www.JuliaAuctions.com

Daum Nancy Cameo Vase. Acid etched and enameled pillow vase with red berries and green leaves on a yellow to brown mottled background. Vividly colored. Signed on the side in enamel "Daum Nancy France" with the Cross of Lorraine. 4 3/4" h. **$5,175**

Photo courtesy James D. Julia Auctioneers, Fairfield, Maine; www.JuliaAuctions.com

Daum Nancy Floral French Cameo Vase. Pillow-shaped vase has a frosted mottled ground which flows into a golden yellow hue. Accenting this is a pattern of violets enameled in purple with green foliage front and back. Signed "Daum Nancy" with Cross of Lorraine. 4 1/2" x 4 1/2". **$4,312**

Photo courtesy James D. Julia Auctioneers, Fairfield, Maine; www.JuliaAuctions.com

Daum Nancy Cameo and Enameled Floral Vase. Cornflowers in blue are accented by russet stamens with green foliage. This pattern wraps itself around the entire vase. The background glass is a softly mottled frost rose and green with an electric cobalt blue base. Signed "Daum Nancy" with the Cross of Lorraine. 3 3/4" h x 4" w. **$4,255**

Photo courtesy James D. Julia Auctioneers, Fairfield, Maine; www.JuliaAuctions.com

Daum Nancy Cameo Vase. Acid etched and enameled vase with red berries and green leaves on a yellow to brown mottled background. Vividly colored. Signed on the side in enamel "Daum Nancy France" with the Cross of Lorraine. 15 1/4" h. **$8,050**

Photo courtesy James D. Julia Auctioneers, Fairfield, Maine; www.JuliaAuctions.com

Daum Nancy French Cameo Berry Vase. Deep blue berry decoration with foliage in colors of amber and green atop a muted yellow mottled ground. Unusual tapered bulbous form. Signed "France" and also "Daum Nancy" in cameo with the Cross of Lorraine. 4 1/2" h. **$1,380**

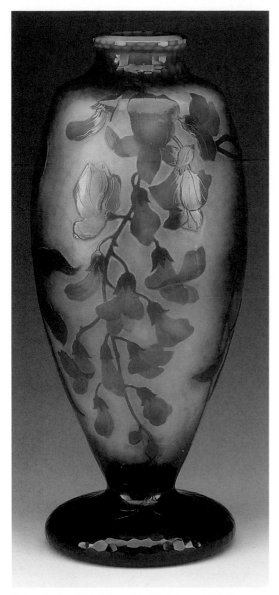

Daum Nancy Cameo Vase. Green acid-etched pendulous flowers on green to sky blue wheel-carved background and foot with simulated hammered texture, the entire vase fire-polished. Engraved signature on the underside "Daum Nancy" with the Cross of Lorraine enhanced with gilding. 11 3/4" h. **$8,400**

Daum Nancy Padded and Wheel-Carved Vase. Orange poppies on striated blue to green wheel-carved background with simulated hammered texture, brown and yellow mottled foot. Intaglio carved signature on the foot "Daum Nancy" with the Cross of Lorraine. 16 1/4" h. **$9,200**

Photo courtesy James D. Julia Auctioneers, Fairfield, Maine;
www.JuliaAuctions.com

*Daum Nancy Cameo and Applied Covered
Jar. Rare example with one green-gold applied
cabochon, one green applied insect and one
red applied leaf on body with acid-etched
maple leaves. The lid with applied and wheel-
carved handle with red applied insect on top
(second view). Signed on the underside with
engraved and gilded "Daum Nancy" with the
Cross of Lorraine. 4 1/2" h.* **$9,200**

Photo courtesy James D. Julia Auctioneers, Fairfield, Maine; www.JuliaAuctions.com

*Daum Nancy Cameo Vase. Padded and wheel-carved lavender and
brown iris flowers and buds on a frosted to chartreuse background
together with acid-etched, deep purple leaves. Acid etched signature
on the side "Daum Nancy" with the Cross of Lorraine. 12" h.* **$7,200**

Photo courtesy James D. Julia Auctioneers, Fairfield, Maine; www.JuliaAuctions.com

Daum Nancy Cameo Vase. Acid-etched green daffodils on wheel-carved green to frosted to green background with simulated hammered texture and foot with opalescent interior. Signed on the underside with engraved "Daum Nancy" with the Cross of Lorraine. 7 3/4" h. **$6,000**

Daum Nancy Cameo Vase. Single wheel-carved parrot tulip in shades of purple with wheel-carved leaves on a shaded clear to purple background with simulated hammered texture. Signed on the underside with engraved "Daum Nancy" with the Cross of Lorraine. 6" h. **$6,000**

Gallé Cameo Bowl. Red roses on yellow ground. Cameo signature on the side "Gallé". 8 1/2" w. Polishing on several of the pulled tips. **$2,040**

Photo courtesy James D. Julia Auctioneers, Fairfield, Maine; www.JuliaAuctions.com

Gallé Cameo Vase. Blue acid-etched Japanese peach blossoms with purple leaves and branches on a yellow ground. Windowpane technique behind the blue flowers. Acid-etched signature on the side "Gallé". 5" h. **$4,800**

Photo courtesy James D. Julia Auctioneers, Fairfield, Maine; www.JuliaAuctions.com

Gallé Cameo Vase. Burnt orange flowers and leaves on a shaded apricot and frosted ground. The entire vase is fire polished. Fancy engraved "Gallé" within a stylized flower on the underside. 7" h. **$2,880**

Gallé Cameo Vase. Red windowpane floral decoration on a yellow ground. Cameo signature on the side "Gallé". 8 1/4" h. **$6,000**

Gallé Cameo Vase. Salmon red windowpane floral decoration on a yellow ground. Teardrop form. Cameo signature on the side "Gallé". 9 3/4" h. **$3,600**

Gallé Fire-Polished French Cameo Vase. Background of frosted white shading to a soft blue/purple. The design is a cameo cutback of clematis flowers in various stages of bloom created in vibrant purple with hints of blue. This vase is completely fire-polished. Signed "Gallé" in cameo on side. 4 1/2" h. **$1,955**

Photo courtesy James D. Julia Auctioneers, Fairfield, Maine;
www.JuliaAuctions.com

*Gallé Cameo Verrerie Parlant Vase. Decoration
of an enameled reddish-brown and dark brown
bird in a snowy landscape with acid-etched
trees and snow and inscription "Dans les neiges
en fleur le jeune an souriait" ("In the snows in
flower the young year smiled") towards the top
of the vase. Acid-etched signature on the side of
the vase "Gallé". 13" h.* **$11,400**

Photo courtesy James D. Julia Auctioneers, Fairfield, Maine;
www.JuliaAuctions.com

*Gallé Rio De Genaro Cameo Vase. Highly detailed
tropical scenic vase with mountains and lake in
russet tones on buff colored background. Acid-
etched signature on the side "Gallé". 14 1/4" h.*
$9,600

Gallé Cameo Covered Box. Rare and fine decoration of two brown and blue dragonflies on the lid with blue water lilies and brown foliage on the body. Cameo signature on the lid (second view) and the side of the box "Gallé".
6 1/2" diameter. Two nicks to one leaf on the side of the box. **$7,475**

Gallé Cameo Vase. Early Crystallerie vase with acid-etched and heavily enameled gold and brown floral decoration on transparent green background with snowflake etching. Gilded highlights. Cameo signature on the side "Gallé" with gilded highlights to signature. 7" h. **$6,600**

Gallé Blown Out Cameo Vase. Blue gooseberries and purple leaves on strong yellow, shading to deep purple ground. Cameo signature on the side "Gallé". 9 1/2" h. **$9,775**

Gallé Cameo Vase. Large windowpane blue clematis flowers with lavender leaves and vines on an irregular yellow ground. 12 1/2" h. **$6,600**

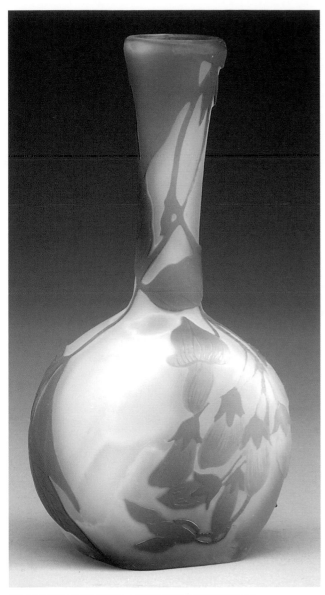

Photo courtesy James D. Julia Auctioneers, Fairfield, Maine; www.JuliaAuctions.com

Gallé Cameo Vase. Banjo form with lavender flowers and olive-colored leaves and branches on a shaded frosted to peach background. Acid-etched signature on the side "Gallé". 5 1/2" h. **$720**

Photo courtesy James D. Julia Auctioneers, Fairfield, Maine; www.JuliaAuctions.com

Gallé Lily Pond Vase. Cameo-cut lily pond design with lily pads floating in a pond with tall iris flowers extending up the length of the vase with brown stems and light blue flowers. Hovering beside the iris is a large, detailed dragonfly with brown body and blue wings. The pond scene gives way to subtle, almost indistinct trees in the background. The cameo decoration is all set against a background of subtle yellow shading to cream. The vase is finished with three seashells lightly acid cut into the foot. Signed within a lily pad with engraved signature "Gallé". 16 1/4" h. **$9,200**

Gallé French Cameo Fern Vase. Lemon-yellow ground, complemented by ferns and blossoms overall in a deep purple hue. The vase is of simple tapering form. Signed in cameo "Gallé". 7" h. **$840**

Gallé French Cameo Art Glass Vase. Classic form and flared upper rim. Background is frost to mottled green with a purple leaf and berry design prominent on the front of vase. Signed in cameo "Gallé". 6 1/4" h. **$690**

D'Argental French Cameo Vase. Soft yellow background and decorated with an all-over floral pattern in red. The red is carried down to the padded foot. Signed in cameo "D'Argental". 12" h. **$920**

Gallé French Cameo Vase. Multi-layered design depicts water lilies in various stages of bloom with pads and foliage set in water. This design is a deep purple hue and it is set against a yellow mottled to blue to purple ground. Signed "Gallé" in cameo. 7" h. **$1,680**

Decorchemont Pate De Verre Figure. Art Deco stylized fish in waves decoration in sienna shading on deep blue water. Marked on the side with impressed Decorchemont seal. 7 1/2" h. **$2,280**

Fenton Red Karnak Vase. Rich red, slightly iridescent body with an applied cobalt blue foot. The iridescence on the vase shows flashes of gold and blue. 5 3/4" t. **$1,150**

Le Verre Francais Monumental Cameo Vase. In the Cerises pattern with burnt orange cherries and leaves on a mauve background. Engraved signature "Le Verre Francis" on the foot rim as well as a candy cane on the foot rim. 17" h. **$4,200**

Photo courtesy James D. Julia Auctioneers, Fairfield, Maine; www.JuliaAuctions.com

Schneider Glass and Wrought Iron Vases. Large orange mottled glass vases are supported by dark purple glass saucer feet. Each vase rests in a wrought iron support of leaves and berries. Each is signed on the underside "France" in block letters. 16" h. **$690 pair**

Photo courtesy James D. Julia Auctioneers, Fairfield, Maine; www.JuliaAuctions.com

Harrach Guba Duck Jar. Done in the style of Royal Flemish with raised gold enameling separating geometric shapes of lightly frosted yellow and clear glass. Decorated with Guba-style ducks and finished with a decorated dome lid with a single Guba duck against gold filigree background. Signed on the underside with Harrach red propeller mark and "5233". 3 1/2" h. **$1,725**

Wheeling Peach Blow Morgan Vase. Maroon-red shading to a creamy amber with interior white lining. The vase is supported by its original glass Griffon holder. 10" h. Holder has chips to two of the feet. **$2,012**

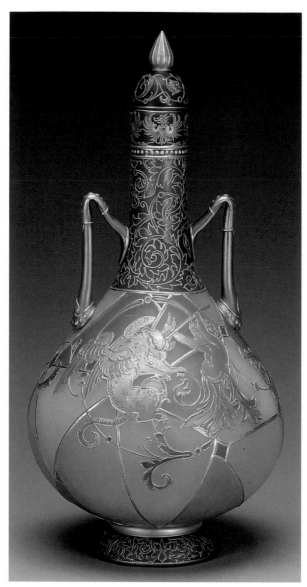

Royal Flemish Covered Jar. With gold gilt decoration of cherubs fighting mythological beasts on front and back. The neck of the jar is decorated with a swirling leaf design outlined in gold with a mauve background and the wide outer lip is decorated with stylized spread eagles in gold against a dark mauve background. The jar is further embellished with two delicate applied glass handles with gold gilt decoration. Topping the jar is its original glass stopper with gold vertically ribbed finial and swirling leaves against a dark mauve background. 15 1/2" h. Minor wear to gilt trim on lip. **$11,500**

Northwood Pull-Up Vase. Creamy tan colored body with purple pull-up design extending upward from the foot. The vase is finished with a cased blue interior and is marked on the underside "Patent". 7 1/4" h. **$1,725**

Stevens & Williams Pompeian Swirl Vase. Bulbous body with pinched waist with amber and dark red ribbing. Vase is cased with a bluish-white interior. 15 1/2" h.
$1,782

Moser Applied Decorated Vase. "Underwater" vase has three applied and decorated fish with enameled vegetation encircling the vase. Decoration is done against a smoky gray glass and the foot and lip are gilt. Unsigned. 8 1/4" h. Minor wear to gilt. **$920**

Photo courtesy James D. Julia Auctioneers, Fairfield, Maine; www.JuliaAuctions.com

Webb Cameo Sweet Meat. Six white wheel-carved butterflies on rose-red ground with applied metal rim, handle and lid. Unsigned. 5" diameter. **$1,200**

Photo courtesy James D. Julia Auctioneers, Fairfield, Maine; www.JuliaAuctions.com

Webb Cameo Vase. White wheel-carved morning glories on cerulean blue ground with matching butterfly (second view) on the reverse. 9" h. Minor nicks to foot rim. **$2,040**

Photo courtesy Heritage Auction Galleries, Dallas; www.HA.com

English cameo glass vase, Thomas Webb and Sons, Stourbridge, England, circa 1880, marked Thomas Webb & Sons, (butterfly), 9 1/2", patterned with trumpet lily in white and red over lemon ground, single cameo butterfly. **$2,629**

BOTTLES

Free-blown funnel-form utility bottle in bright yellow green, tapered circular body with a medium neck and applied sloping mouth, kick-up base with rough pontil mark. United States, probably New England, 1800-1840, 7 3/4". **$2,300**

Free-blown globular utility bottle, medium olive amber, short tapered neck with applied irregular lip, slight kick-up base with a rough pontil mark. Probably New England, 1780-1820, 10 1/2"; 8 3/4" diameter body, scattered light wear and light interior dirt. **$517**

Free-blown chestnut flask, bright grass green, flattened body with a medium tapered neck and an applied rounded lip, kick-up base with a rough pontil mark. Probably New England, 1780-1820, 9"; 5 1/2" diameter body, light to moderate scattered wear. **$862**

Free-blown demijohn, medium to deep olive green, thick tapered neck with an applied flat collar below the broken-off mouth, slight kick-up base without pontil mark. Probably 19th century, 17 1/2"; 12" diameter body, one partially burst surface bubble, roughness to mouth as made, interior dirt and residue. **$161.**

Photo courtesy Jeffrey S. Evans & Associates, Mt. Crawford, Va.; www.jeffreysevans.com

Pitkin-type pattern-molded flask, medium olive green, approximately half-pint, flattened ovoid form, 36 fine ribs swirled to the right, short neck with a plain mouth, kick-up base with a rough pontil mark. Probably New England, 1780-1820, 5 3/8"; 3 1/2" diameter body, minor wear to ribs. **$690**

Photo courtesy Jeffrey S. Evans & Associates, Mt. Crawford, Va.; www.jeffreysevans.com

Pattern-molded globular bottle, golden amber, molded with 20 ribs swirled slightly to the right, long neck with an applied sloping mouth, slight kick-up base with a rough pontil mark. Generally accepted as a product of the 20th century, 14 1/2"; 10" diameter body. **$69**

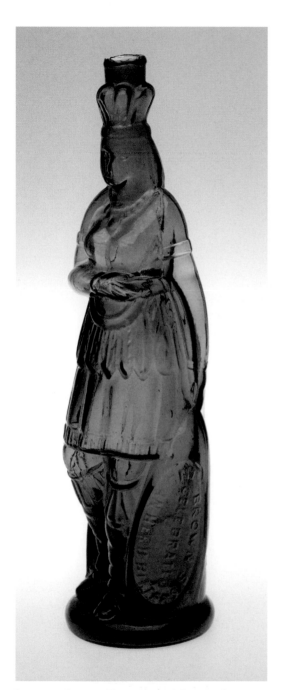

Blown-molded figural bottle, black amethyst, in the form of an old shoe with a toe worn through, embossed "Pat Apl'd For" under base, original metal screw cap, 1870-1900, 3 1/2" x 5 3/4". **$92**

"Brown's / Celebrated / Indian Herb Bitters" figural bottle, medium amber, additionally embossed "Patented / Feb 11. / 1868" on reverse, mouth with remnants of inward-folded lip, plain base, 1868-1880, 12 1/4", chipping to mouth. **$431**

Free-blown utility jar, light yellow green, crude cylindrical form with a sharp shoulder and rollover rim, slight kick-up base with a faint rough pontil mark, 19th century, 7" x 5", burst surface bubble at base. **$138**

PAPERWEIGHTS

New England Glass Co. crown paperweight with pink, yellow and blue twists separated by colored latticinio twists, topped by a central cane, slightly concave base with a small, rough pontil mark, 1850-1870, 2 1/16" diameter. **$460**

New England "Scrambled" paperweight, closely packed multi-color canes, concave base with a polished pontil mark. New England Glass Co. or Boston & Sandwich Glass Co., 1850-1887, 2 5/8" diameter, several small flakes to lower edge and a single shallow flake slightly off center of the crown. **$115**

New England clematis paperweight, 10-petal flower with three green leaves and a stem, dew-like controlled bubbles, all on a white latticinio ground, concave base with a polished pontil mark. New England Glass Co. or Boston & Sandwich Glass Co., 1850-1887, 2 5/8" diameter, light surface imperfections and spalls on the pontil mark. **$207**

New England fruit on latticinio ground paperweight with yellow, red, green and rose, containing five large pears, four large leaves, four cherries and four small leaves, dew-like air traps, concave base with polished pontil mark. New England Glass Co. or Boston & Sandwich Glass Co., 1853-1887, 2 7/8" diameter, some light surface scratches to crown. **$230**

Photo courtesy Jeffrey S. Evans & Associates, Mt. Crawford, Va.;
www.jeffreysevans.com

American fruit on latticinio ground paperweight with yellow, red, green and rose, containing five large fruits, three small fruits and three small leaves, dew-like air traps, partially polished base with rough pontil mark, 1850-1900, 2 7/8" diameter, chip and flakes under base. **$138**

Photo courtesy Jeffrey S. Evans & Associates, Mt. Crawford, Va.;
www.jeffreysevans.com

New England Glass Co. apple-form paperweight with deep rose to bright yellow, on a colorless circular base, 1875-1900, 3" diameter base, several small open bubbles. **$920**

ROLLING PINS

Free-blown Marbrie rolling pin, colorless with rose and white loops, knob-style handles, one with shear mark and the other with a rough open pontil mark. Boston & Sandwich Glass Co. and others, 1850-1870, 16 1/2", minor light wear. **$103**

Free-blown Potichomania decorated rolling pin, pale green, interior with original plaster coating and cutout hand-colored woodcuts, small knob handles with original plug in one end. United States or England, 1850-1890, 13". **$92**

Free-blown "Sailor's" rolling pin, cobalt blue, decorated with a vignette of a ship, crossed Union Jack flags, and "Unity & Love" within a gold border, small knob handles, one with an open rough pontil mark, along with a modern holder. England, 1860-1890, 14", hint of wear to decoration. **$126**

PILLAR-MOLDED GLASS

This heavily ribbed glassware was produced by blowing glass into full-sized ribbed molds and then finishing it by hand. The technique evolved from earlier "pattern molding" used on glass since ancient times, but in pillar-molded glass, the ribs are heavy and prominent. Most examples found in this country were produced in the Pittsburgh area from around 1850 to 1870, but similar English-made wares made before and after this period are also available.

Most American items were made from clear flint glass, and colored examples or pieces with colored strands in the ribs are rare and highly prized. Some collectors refer to this as "steamboat" glass, believing it was made to be used on American riverboats, but most likely it was used anywhere that a sturdy, relatively inexpensive glassware was needed, such as taverns and hotels.

Photo courtesy Jeffrey S. Evans & Associates, Mt. Crawford, Va.; www.jeffreysevans.com

Pair of extremely rare pillar-molded and pressed tulip vases, brilliant amethyst, each featuring a deep bowl with eight ribs and a gauffered rim, joined by a wafer to pressed hexagonal base with upper knop and flared foot. Attributed to the Boston & Sandwich Glass Co., 1850-1860, 10 1/2", one with a shallow sliver chip to rim. **$6,325 pair**

Photo courtesy Jeffrey S. Evans & Associates, Mt. Crawford, Va.; www.jeffreysevans.com

Extremely rare two-color pillar-molded, three-pint pitcher, lightly sanded alabaster/ clambroth with starch-blue ribs, waisted bulbous body with eight ribs and a bold applied handle featuring a wide tooled ridge, polished pontil mark. Probably New England, possibly Mt. Washington Glass Works, 1860-1880, 9", faint 1/4" rim check at upper handle juncture. **$1,150**

Photo courtesy Jeffrey S. Evans & Associates, Mt. Crawford, Va.; www.jeffreysevans.com

Pillar-molded cream pitcher in dull amethyst, 1850-1870. **$5,750**

Photo courtesy Jeffrey S. Evans & Associates, Mt. Crawford, Va.; www.jeffreysevans.com

Possibly unique gilt-decorated, pillar-molded vase or celery glass, vibrant powder blue opalescent, heavy deep bowl with eight pronounced ribs and a gauffered, cut and polished rim, applied to a short baluster-form stem and broad circular foot with a polished pontil mark. Featuring well-preserved extravagant gilt decorations often associated with presentation pieces. Possibly New England, 1860-1880, 9 1/2", light wear to gilding. **$3,737**

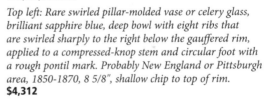

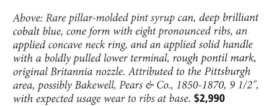

Photos courtesy Jeffrey S. Evans & Associates, Mt. Crawford, Va.; www.jeffreysevans.com

Top left: Rare swirled pillar-molded vase or celery glass, brilliant sapphire blue, deep bowl with eight ribs that are swirled sharply to the right below the gauffered rim, applied to a compressed-knop stem and circular foot with a rough pontil mark. Probably New England or Pittsburgh area, 1850-1870, 8 5/8", shallow chip to top of rim. **$4,312**

Above: Rare pillar-molded pint syrup can, deep brilliant cobalt blue, cone form with eight pronounced ribs, an applied concave neck ring, and an applied solid handle with a boldly pulled lower terminal, rough pontil mark, original Britannia nozzle. Attributed to the Pittsburgh area, possibly Bakewell, Pears & Co., 1850-1870, 9 1/2", with expected usage wear to ribs at base. **$2,990**

Left: Extremely rare pillar-molded cruet or molasses can, golden amber, bulbous-form body with eight pronounced ribs, a tooled spout, and an applied solid handle, rough pontil mark, original hollow ball stopper with open sheared end. Stopper sits somewhat loose because neither the stopper end nor the neck interior is ground for a tight fit. Attributed to the Pittsburgh area, 1840-1870, 9 1/2" overall, potstone near base showing a minute refraction, as made. **$2,530**

Photos courtesy Jeffrey S. Evans & Associates, Mt. Crawford, Va.; www.jeffreysevans.com

Right: Rare pillar-molded diminutive open compote, bright citron, deep bowl with eight pronounced ribs and a plain flared rim, raised on an applied hollow hourglass-form stem and circular foot with a polished pontil mark. United States or England, 1860-1880, 6", light usage wear. **$2,530**

Below: Rare pillar-molded vase or celery glass, bright apple green, deep bowl with eight pronounced ribs and a boldly gauffered rim, applied to a short baluster-form stem and circular foot with a rough pontil mark. United States or England, 1860-1880, 10 1/2", expected light usage wear. **$1,955**

Bottom right: Rare pillar-molded vase or celery glass, brilliant cased cranberry, deep bowl with eight ribs and a gauffered rim, applied to a colorless double-knop stem and circular foot with a rough pontil mark. United States or England, 1860-1880, 9 1/2". **$920**

FREE-BLOWN GLASS

Rare free-blown witch ball, ruby red, rough pontil mark with 1/4" opening. Boston & Sandwich Glass Co. and others, 1850-1880, 4" diameter, some scattered light wear. This example appears to have been blown from a single ruby gather and not cased. **$287**

Free-blown footed open sugar bowl, dull cobalt blue, deep bowl with plain rim, raised on an applied funnel foot with folded edge and a rough pontil mark. Probably England, 1780-1830, 4 1/8", light haze to interior bottom of bowl. **$149**

Photo courtesy Jeffrey S. Evans & Associates, Mt. Crawford, Va.; www.jeffreysevans.com

Rare blown polychrome-twist stem trick goblet, colorless double-walled bowl raised on an applied candy-stripe, opal-cased hollow stem, and a colorless broad foot, retains its original wax-sealed cork plug under base. Probably England, 1860-1880, 5 3/4". This goblet was originally filled through the base with an ale-like liquid, which would give the appearance that the goblet was full. The stem was cased in color to disguise the liquid-filled interior. Over time the original liquid has evaporated. **$316**

Free-blown striped diminutive flask, colorless with deep ruby and white tapes, flattened slightly ovoid form with a short neck, plain mouth, and rough pontil mark. United States or Europe, 1850-1890, 4 1/8". **$69**

Free-blown and pressed urn-form apothecary or show jar with cover, colorless, deep free-blown bowl raised on a simple pressed standard applied with a wafer, original pressed high-peak cover with factory polished inner rim. United States, 1860-1880, 16 1/2" overall.
.... **$126**

Free-blown footed cruet or molasses can, colorless, pyriform body with a tooled rim, applied hollow handle, and drawn foot with a rough pontil mark, original hollow stopper/cover with a flange shaped to cover the pour spout. Possibly Pittsburgh area, 1830-1860, 8 1/2" overall, light scattered wear. **$69**

Engraved free-blown footed ewer, colorless, applied ribbed strap handle and funnel foot with a rough pontil mark, stag and foliate decorations. Probably Germany, 1840-1860, 10 1/2". **$80**

Continental engraved free-blown goblet, colorless soda-lime glass, facet-base round funnel bowl decorated with figures and cartouches, reverse engraved "VIVAMUS - LAETI / DUM / FATA SINUNT" within a laurel wreath, raised on a faceted inverted baluster-form hollow stem and wide conical foot with a rough pontil mark. Fitted with a period engraved lead-glass cover with air beads, 18th century, 9". **$460**

Continental engraved free-blown goblet, colorless soda-lime glass, round funnel bowl decorated with two military inspired reserves within elaborate frames, titled "PACIS GERMANIAE" / 'RESTITVTAE MDCCXIV" and "MEDIIS CRESCEBAT IN ARMIS," raised on an inverted baluster-form hollow stem and wide foot with a rough pontil mark. Probably 19th century, 8". **$632**

English engraved free-blown wine glass, colorless lead glass, round funnel bowl decorated with a coat of arms and garlands, raised on a diamond-faceted stem and wide conical foot with a rough pontil mark. England, 18th or 19th century, 5 1/4". **$172**

Engraved and cut free-blown wine glass, colorless soda-lime glass, round funnel bowl decorated with swags and tassels, raised on a diamond-faceted stem and wide conical foot with a rough pontil mark. Probably Bohemia, 1780-1800, 5 3/4". **$92**

Engraved free-blown and pressed flute, tinted colorless soda-lime glass, deep conical bowl decorated with a band of sprigs above an all-over checkerboard and low flutes, raised on a pressed and polished octagonal foot with a polished base. Probably Bohemia, 1800-1820, 7 1/2", light flake and polishing to rim, two flakes under base, interior with scattered light residue. **$46**

Photo courtesy Jeffrey S. Evans & Associates, Mt. Crawford, Va.; www.jeffreysevans.com

Engraved free-blown flip glass, colorless soda-lime glass, decorated with a windmill, cottage, and coat of arms, rough pontil mark. Probably Bohemia, 1860-1890, 5 5/8". **$115**

Photo courtesy Jeffrey S. Evans & Associates, Mt. Crawford, Va.; www.jeffreysevans.com

Free-blown tall pitcher, blue green, unusual ovoid-form body with superimposed lily-pad decoration comprised of eight alternating tall and short fingers, cylindrical neck flared to a tooled double-rib rim, applied solid handle ending in a sheared and crimped tapered terminal made without a curl, all raised on an applied thick funnel foot with a wide rough pontil mark; possibly New Jersey or New York State. Probably 1850-1890, 8 3/4"; broken bubble to neck interior, expected light wear to medial body and high spots, some typical haziness to the glass. **$14,950**

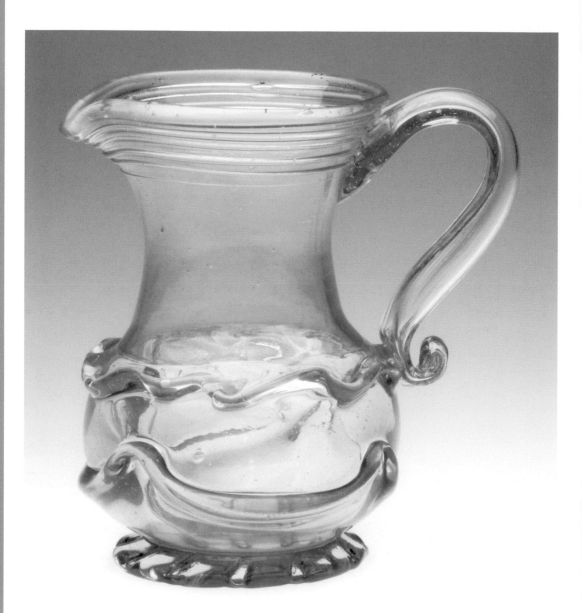

Photo courtesy Jeffrey S. Evans & Associates, Mt. Crawford, Va.; www.jeffreysevans.com

South Jersey free-blown and decorated pitcher, blue aquamarine, squat bulbous body with an applied wave-like shoulder band above a pulled, superimposed four-swag decoration around the base, gently tapering to a tall neck with applied threading below the boldly flared and tooled rim, applied hollow handle ending in a distinctive protruding curl, all raised on an applied, crimped foot with a rough pontil mark. Red painted "234" accession number under base, 1830-1850, 6 1/4". $6,900

Free-blown salver with applied cobalt rim edge and collar, circa 1850-1875, attributed to Bakewell, Pears & Co., Pittsburgh, 10 1/8" x 15 3/4". **$6,325**

Photos courtesy Jeffrey S. Evans & Associates, Mt. Crawford, Va.; www.jeffreysevans.com

Above: Free-blown and threaded vase or jar, deep blue green, slightly compressed bulbous urn-form body with a broad flared rim, applied threading from rim to upper shoulder, two bold applied strap-type handles, each with a medial rib, wide rough pontil mark. Attributed to New York State, probably the Saratoga Mountain Glass Works or the Redford Glass Works. 1845-1865, 6 3/4"; short vertical check to the outer edge of one handle curl which does not affect the terminal, resonance or body. **$8,625**

Photo courtesy Jeffrey S. Evans & Associates, Mt. Crawford, Va.; www.jeffreysevans.com

Pair of free-blown vases in sapphire blue, with an opalescent bloom, each baluster-form bowl with a folded rim, raised on an applied solid medial-knop stem and a bold trumpet foot, rough pontil mark to each base interior. Each exhibit the expected potstones, impurities, and striations to the glass; probably New England, 11 3/8" and 11 1/2", circa 1840-1860.
$3,450 pair

Photo courtesy Jeffrey S. Evans & Associates, Mt. Crawford, Va.; www.jeffreysevans.com

Free-blown enamel-twist-stem wine glass, light green, cup-shaped bowl on a hollow knop with three applied raspberry prunts, raised on a stem containing four heavy spiral threads outside gauze, and a domed foot with a small rough pontil mark; England, 1750-1775' 5 1/2", small ground spot to edge of foot. **$2,875**

Free-blown quart jug, ruby or ruby cased, bulbous form with an applied colorless handle and wide sloping foot with a rough pontil mark. Probably Sandwich Cooperative Glass Co., 1888-1891, 7 3/8", 1/2" scratch to body and light scratches to inner spout, numerous in-the-making imperfections to the body including striations and an annealing check at spout.
$402

RUBY-STAINED GLASS

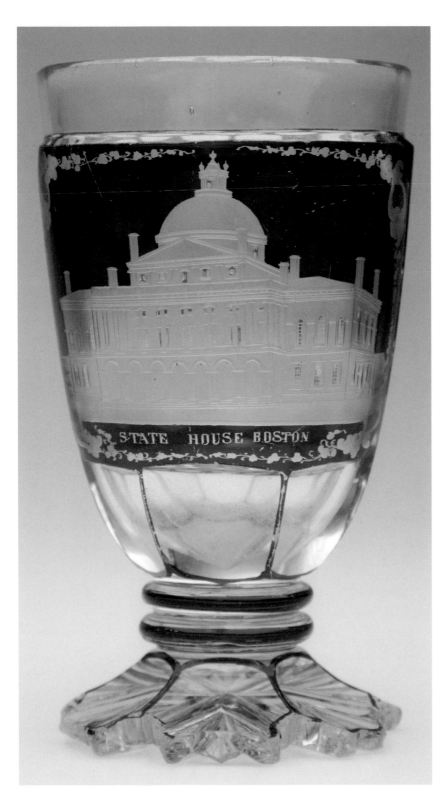

Americo-Bohemian ruby-stained footed tumbler with American view, circular form engraved on the front with the "STATE HOUSE BOSTON" within a vine border, cut punties on the reverse, raised on a complex-scallop foot. Probably Bohemia, 1840-1860, 5 1/2", moderate wear to interior and chipping to foot. **$1,725**

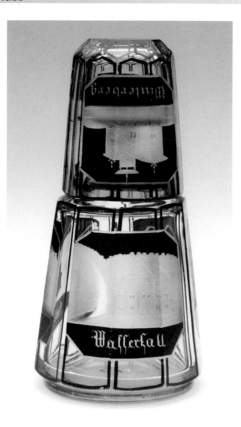

Photo courtesy Jeffrey S. Evans & Associates, Mt. Crawford, Va.; www.jeffreysevans.com

Above: Bohemian ruby-stained, cut and engraved diminutive souvenir tumble-up, colorless, panel cut decanter and shot-glass tumbler with five engraved views, titled "Winterberg," "Prebischth," "Wasserfall," "Prebischthor" and "Kuhstall," decanter with original stopper and polished base. Bohemia, 1850-1860, 5 1/4". **$69**

Top right: Ruby-stained, cut and engraved goblet, colorless, panel-cut bowl with alternating vintage decorated and plain panels, raised on a panel-cut baluster stem and scalloped foot. Probably Bohemia, 1850-1870, 6 1/2". **$80**

Right: Bohemian ruby-stained, cut and engraved souvenir footed beaker/tumbler, colorless with gilt rim, panel-cut body featuring four raised cartouches with engraved vignettes titled "Gesundheit" (health), "Gluck" (luck), "Verlangere z. leben" (long life), and "u. Freude" (joy), raised on a scalloped foot. Bohemia, 1840-1860, 5 1/2". **$92**

CUT OVERLAY GLASS

Photo courtesy Jeffrey S. Evans
& Associates, Mt. Crawford, Va.;
www.jeffreysevans.com

Cut overlay punty footed ewer, cobalt blue cut to colorless, urn form with a panel-cut neck, tri-corner rim, delicate applied strap handle with cased filament, and a groove-edge foot with a polished pontil mark. Possibly Boston & Sandwich Glass Co., 1865-1880, 10″, minor flake under the foot and several nicks to edge of foot. **$345**

Photo courtesy Jeffrey S. Evans & Associates, Mt. Crawford, Va.; www.jeffreysevans.com

Cut double overlay punty and quatrefoil flower stand/vase, rose cut to white cut to colorless with pristine gilt decoration, plain rimed short trumpet bowl on a wide foot, foliate and scroll ornamentations, factory-polished rim. Attributed to the Boston & Sandwich Glass Co., 1855-1887, 5 5/8". **$690**

Cut double overlay notch and oval newel post finial, rose cut to white cut to colorless, hollow ball form with flat polished top and an applied peg extension. Attributed to the Boston & Sandwich Glass Co., 1855-1887, 5 1/2″, slightly cloudy interior as made. **$805**

Collector's Note: In 1818, Deming Jarves was listed in the Boston directory as a glassmaker. That same year, he was appointed general manager of the newly formed New England Glass Co. In 1824, Jarves toured the glassmaking factories in Pittsburgh, left New England Glass and founded a glass factory in Sandwich, Mass.

Originally called the Sandwich Manufacturing Co., it was incorporated in April 1826 as the Boston & Sandwich Glass Co. The firm closed on Jan. 1, 1888.

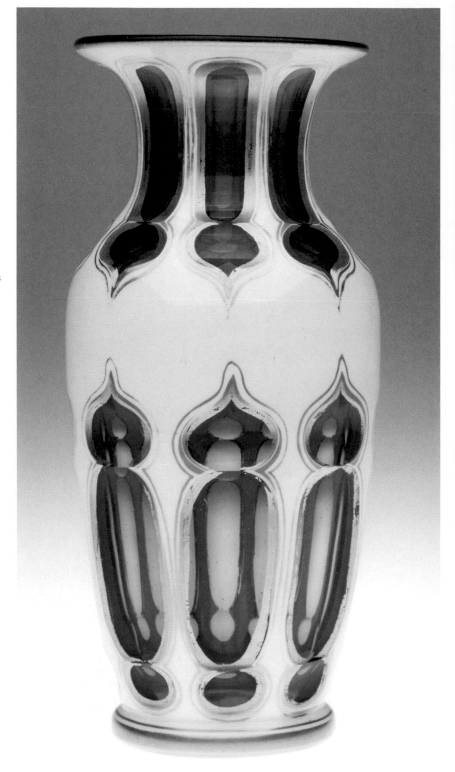

Photo courtesy Jeffrey S. Evans
& Associates, Mt. Crawford, Va.;
www.jeffreysevans.com

Cut overlay Moorish window vase, white cut to sapphire blue with gilt decoration, high-shoulder urn form, plain base with polished center. Probably Bohemia, 1850-1870, 7 3/4".
$138

Cut double overlay complex windows goblet, green cut to white cut to amber, bucket bowl raised on a panel-cut stem and a cased star and petal cut foot. Probably Europe, 1850-1880, 6 1/4".
$575

OPALINE GLASS

Photo courtesy Jeffrey S. Evans & Associates, Mt. Crawford, Va.; www.jeffreysevans.com

Opaline wash pitcher, translucent starch blue, baluster form with an applied strap handle displaying a factory-polished lower terminal, polished pontil mark. Probably France or England, 1860-1880, 12 1/2".
$138

Opaline snake decorated epergne, alabaster/clambroth with applied translucent green and gilt decoration, shallow-bowl compote with fluted rim and central trumpet vase with applied coiling snake, polished pontil mark under base. Trumpet plastered into bowl. Probably France, 1860-1880, 14 1/4" overall; bowl 10" diameter, several light scratches, expected wear to gilt.....................**$115**

Opaline Brocade/Spanish Lace syrup pitcher, blue opalescent, reeded transparent blue applied handle, period lid. Late 19th/early 20th century, 5 7/8" overall. Undamaged, lid with light rusting.....................**$488**

Opaline Brocade/Spanish Lace syrup pitcher, cranberry opalescent, reeded colorless applied handle, period lid. Late 19th/early 20th century, 6" overall. **$977**

Victorian opalescent glass sugar shakers, lot of two, colorless opalescent, consisting of Opaline Brocade/Spanish Lace and Ribbed Opal Lattice, period lids. Late 19th/early 20th century, 4 1/2" and 4 5/8" overall. Undamaged, lids with minor imperfections.....................**$184 pair**

Opaline Brocade / Spanish Lace squat mold water pitcher, blue opalescent, round crimped rim, transparent blue applied handle. Late 19th/early 20th century, 8 3/4".
.....................**$287**

Opaline Brocade / Spanish Lace water pitcher, blue opalescent, tri-corner crimped rim, transparent blue applied handle. Late 19th/early 20th century, 9 1/2", minute nick to lower terminal of handle.....................**$172**

Opaline Brocade / Spanish Lace celery vase, vaseline opalescent, tooled rim. Late 19th/early 20th century, 6 1/4".
.....................**$80**

Opaline Brocade / Spanish Lace cruet, cranberry opalescent, reeded colorless applied handle, non-original stopper. Late 19th/early 20th century, 7 3/4" overall.
.....................**$1,035**

Opaline wig stand, shaded rose and white, mushroom-cap top raised on a baluster-form stem and thick circular foot with a polished pontil mark. Probably France or England. 1860-1880, 7 3/4". **$172**

SALTS

Photo courtesy Jeffrey S. Evans & Associates, Mt. Crawford, Va.; www.jeffreysevans.com

Rare BT-2 "Pittsburgh" Steamboat pressed salt, medium to dark blue, embossed on stern, rope table ring. Attributed to the Stourbridge Flint Glass Works, Pittsburgh, 1830-1845, 1 1/2" x 1 7/8" x 3 5/8", inner-rim chip/spall at rear that only slightly affects the stern profile, inner-rim bruise and minor flaking, flake to keel. **$7,475**

Extremely Rare HL-4 "H. Clay" Steam Locomotive pressed salt, colorless, embossed under base, hairpin ends, on four scrolled feet. Boston & Sandwich Glass Co. or Midwestern, 1835-1845, 1 5/8" x 2" x 3 1/8", rim with two shallow chips and an under-fill to one shell, light flaking/mold roughness to corners and feet. **$2,645**

Rare BT-2 "Pittsburgh" Steamboat pressed salt, purple blue, embossed on stern, rope table ring. Attributed to the Stourbridge Flint Glass Works, Pittsburgh, 1830-1845, 1 1/2" x 1 7/8" x 3 1/2", moderate inner-rim chipping and roughness, none of which affects the profile, chip to left side of stern, slight under-fill to bowsprit. **$5,175**

Unlisted possibly unique PO-6 Peacock Eye oval pressed salt, deep fiery opalescent powder blue, scallop rim, eight-point star base. Boston & Sandwich Glass Co., 1830-1845, 1 1/2" x 2 7/8" x 3 7/8". **$2,645**

Extremely rare PO-6A Peacock Eye oval pressed salt, unlisted fiery opalescent brilliant cobalt blue with a mottled streak to interior, cavetto shows red in transmitted light, scallop rim, eight-point star base. Boston & Sandwich Glass Co., 1830-1845, 1 1/2" x 2 7/8" x 3 7/8", small area of light flaking/mold roughness to edge of base. **$1,265**

Rare GA-2 Gothic Arch pressed salt, opaque violet blue, even scallop rim, on four low feet. Boston & Sandwich Glass Co., 1835-1845, 1 5/8" x 2" x 2 3/4", some light flakes/spalls to top of rim, sliver chip to one corner below rim......**$2,300**

Rare LE-3 Lyre pressed salt, opalescent brilliant medium blue, shaped rim, on four scrolled feet. Boston & Sandwich Glass Co., 1835-1845, 1 7/8" x 1 7/8" x 3 1/8", minor flake to one corner scroll...**$3,105**

Extremely rare OG-1 Beaded Bull's Eye rectangular pressed salt, colorless, plain rim, resting on 12 bull's-eye feet. Probably Pittsburgh area, 1835-1845, 1 7/8" x 2 1/4" x 3 1/4", hint of mold roughness.....................................**$1,380**

Extremely rare SL-14 Shell And Hairpin pressed salt, deep brilliant purple blue, on four scrolled feet. Possibly Boston & Sandwich Glass Co., 1835-1850, 1 3/4" x 2" x 3 1/8", hint of mold roughness to inside of upper and lower scrolls. **$4,887**

Rare BF-1F Basket of Flowers pressed salt, opaque violet blue with slight mottling, one rim end tab is stippled, on four feet. Boston & Sandwich Glass Co., 1830-1840, 2" x 1 3/4" x 3", outer rim with two shallow chips and another to one corner, base with the loss of one corner scroll and minor flaking to feet. **$3,220**

Extremely rare CD-1 covered Peacock Eye pressed salt, colorless, base with serrated scallop and point rim, and two ropes inside table ring, cover with over-all stippling underneath, lacking underplate. Possibly Boston & Sandwich Glass Co., 1835-1850, 2 1/4" overall, base rim with the partial loss of three points along with scattered light flakes, foot with two shallow chips and several flakes, cover with a crack from rim to finial...........................**$2,185**

Extremely rare unlisted OL-12 Cornucopia And Scroll oval pressed salt, soft lavender, serrated large-scallop rim. Boston & Sandwich Glass Co., 1835-1850, 1 1/4" x 2 1/2" x 3 3/8", inner rim with a light bruise and a hint of mold roughness, base with a minor flake to outer edge...**$1,840**

Rare BT-2 "Pittsburgh" Steamboat pressed salt, colorless, embossed on stern, rope table ring. Attributed to the Stourbridge Flint Glass Works, Pittsburgh, 1830-1845, 1 1/2" x 1 7/8" x 3 5/8", rim with interior chips/roughness at wheels and stern that slightly affect the stern profile, light mold roughness and a minor flake to keel. **$920**

Rare BT-4D "Lafayet" Steamboat pressed salt, unlisted colorless, marked "B. &. S. / GLASS. / Co" on stern and "SANDWICH" on interior base. Boston & Sandwich Glass Co., 1830-1845, 1 1/2" x 1 7/8" x 3 5/8", rim with a top-edge flake and two areas of light chipping to interior. **$316**

Rare BT-4D "Lafayet" Steamboat pressed salt, unlisted colorless, marked "B. &. S. / GLASS. / Co" on stern and "SANDWICH" on interior base. Boston & Sandwich Glass Co., 1830-1845, 1 1/2" x 1 7/8" x 3 5/8", flake to top rim and light chipping/mold roughness to inner rim, chip to side of keel and table ring. **$172**

Rare BT-9 boat pressed salt, deep cobalt blue, plain rim and base. Boston & Sandwich Glass Co., 1835-1850, 1 3/4" x 2 1/8" x 3 7/8", a few spots of mold roughness to inner rim and bowsprit, strong light reveals an annealing check off the rim at one rear corner. **$632**

Rare EE-8 Eagle And Ship pressed salt, colorless, intricate foliate chain rim. Boston & Sandwich Glass Co., 1830-1845, 1 7/8" x 2 7/8", hint of mold roughness. **$747**

Unlisted extremely rare DI-17(B) divided pressed salt, deep cobalt blue, flat rim, rectangular form. Center divider is flat and only extends above the rim 1/16" Possibly New England area, 1830-1850, 1 5/8" x 2 1/8" x 3 1/4", minor base flakes. **$3,105**

Rare CT-1 Chariot pressed salt, strongly mottled silvery opaque powder blue, scallop and point rim. Boston & Sandwich Glass Co., 1835-1850, 1 3/4" x 2 1/8" x 2 7/8", rim with several light flakes, flake to one upper corner, scattered light flaking/mold roughness. **$632**

Rare CT-1 Chariot pressed salt, opaque shiny white with fiery opalescent rim and feet, scallop and point rim. Boston & Sandwich Glass Co., 1835-1850, 1 3/4" x 2 1/8" x 2 7/8", chip to one foot, scattered light flaking/mold roughness, short brownish annealing line above base as made. **$195**

Rare OL-11 Cornucopia And Shield pressed salt, deep cobalt blue, serrated large-scallop rim. Probably Boston & Sandwich Glass Co., 1830-1850, 1 3/8" x 2 3/8" x 3 1/4", inner rim chipping/mold roughness that does not affect the rim profile, several short annealing checks off rim at low points between scallops, which is commonly seen on this group of salts. **$488**

Rare SC-5 Scroll pressed salt, medium blue, on four scrolled feet. Possibly Boston & Sandwich Glass Co., 1835-1850, 1 3/4" x 1 5/8" x 3 1/4", light flaking/mold roughness to inner rim and inside of upper and lower scrolls, none of which affects the profile. **$316**

Photo courtesy Jeffrey S. Evans & Associates, Mt. Crawford, Va.; www.jeffreysevans.com

Extremely rare RP-3 round floral pressed salt, strongly mottled opaque powder to medium blue with scattered swirls of light silvery sheen, intricate foliate chain-top rim, 12-scallop foot. Boston & Sandwich Glass Co., 1835-1850, 2" x 3 1/8", two minute flakes under the rim which do not affect the profile. **$2,185**

Photo courtesy Jeffrey S. Evans & Associates, Mt. Crawford, Va.; www.jeffreysevans.com

Extremely rare OL-14 Star In Diamond oval pressed salt, medium amethyst, scalloped high-point rim. Probably Boston & Sandwich Glass Co., 1830-1850, 1 5/8" x 2 1/2" x 3 5/8", minor flake to one high point and a shallow chip to the interior of another. **$4,312**

Extremely rare OO-1 Octagon oblong pressed salt, unlisted deep brilliant amethyst, shaped rim, sunburst base. Boston & Sandwich Glass Co., 1835-1850, 1 5/8" x 2 3/8" x 3 3/8", foot with some light flakes to edges.................**$1,495**

Extremely rare OL-16A Strawberry Diamond and Swag oval pressed salt, medium fiery opalescent, scallop rim. Possibly Boston & Sandwich Glass Co., 1830-1850, 1 5/8" x 2 1/4" x 3 1/4", hint of mold roughness.
....**$373**

Extremely rare OL-16A Strawberry Diamond and Swag oval pressed salt, light opalescent, scallop rim. Possibly Boston & Sandwich Glass Co., 1830-1850, 1 5/8" x 2 1/4" x 3 1/4", light mold roughness to rim, light residue in base...**$316**

Rare OL-15 Beaded Strawberry Diamond oval pressed salt, deep brilliant purple blue, high and low point rim. Boston & Sandwich Glass Co., 1830-1850, 1 3/4" x 2 1/4" x 3 1/2", rim with the partial loss of two low points and two others lightly tipped. **$373**

Rare SD-9 Strawberry Diamond pressed salt, soft light blue, scallop and point rim. Boston & Sandwich Glass Co., 1828-1840, 2 1/8" x 2 1/8" x 2 3/4", single chip to one upper corner and a flake to one lower corner...............**$632**

Rare BB-1 Bird Bath And Cornucopia pressed salt, chalky opaque white with streaked and mottled impurities resembling marble, scallop and point rim, on four feet. Probably New England Glass Co., 1830-1850, 1 7/8" x 2" x 3 1/8", flake under one rim corner and few minute flakes.
....**$632**

Rare BF-1D Basket Of Flowers pressed salt, fiery opalescent, on four feet. Boston & Sandwich Glass Co., 1830-1840, 2" x 1 7/8" x 3 1/8", light flaking/mold roughness to feet. **$402**

Rare DI-11 Gothic Arch divided pressed salt, cobalt blue, on four scrolled feet. Probably France, 1830-1850, 1 3/4" x 1 7/8" x 4", overall light flaking and mold roughness, chip to bottom of one foot.........................**$632**

Rare MV-1B Mount Vernon pressed salt, brilliant cobalt blue scallop and point rim. Boston & Sandwich Glass Co. or Mount Vernon Glass Co., 1835-1850, 1 3/4" x 2 1/8" x 2 7/8", rim with only a few light interior flakes, chip to base removing one scallop. **$207**

Rare OP-17 Diamond and Quatrefoil oval pressed salt, fiery opalescent, complex rim, on four flared feet that are factory polished underneath to level. Possibly Boston & Sandwich Glass Co., 1835-1850, 2" x 2 5/8" x 3 1/2", rim with one interior chip and light mold roughness, feet with minor flaking/mold roughness. **$287**

Rare SD-16 Strawberry Diamond pressed salt, deep cobalt blue, scallop and point rim, crude eight-point star in base. Boston & Sandwich Glass Co., 1827-1840, 2" x 2 1/8" x 2 7/8", several shallow chips and moderate flaking to rim, flaking to one corner column, light mold roughness.
....**$316**

Unlisted extremely rare OO-12 variant Octagon oblong pressed salt, cobalt blue, serrated rim, with an inverted diamond base, thick heavy pressing. Possibly Boston & Sandwich Glass Co., 1835-1850, 1 1/4" x 2 1/4" x 3", inner rim with several light flakes, foot with several chips and flakes. **$402**

Rare NE-1A New England marked pressed salt, opaque white with areas of deep fiery opalescent, embossed under base, scallop and point rim. New England Glass Co., 1835-1850, 2" x 2 1/4" x 3", minor flake to the rim and a small chip to base. **$258**

Rare NE-1 variant New England marked pressed salt, strong fiery opalescent, embossed under base, scallop and point rim, with a much thinner rim showing only the lower section of the rim scrolls on the two ends, the side rims are lacking the scrolls. New England Glass Co., 1835-1850, 1 3/4" x 2 1/4" x 3", top of rim with one shallow chip and a flake. **$149**

Rare BH-1 Bee Hive pressed salt, colorless, scallop and point rim. New England Glass Co., 1830-1850, 1 7/8" x 2 1/8" x 3", rim with a chip to one scallop and light mold roughness. **$92**

Rare SL-1 Shell pressed salt, cobalt blue, shaped rim, waffle pattern under base. Possibly Boston & Sandwich Glass Co., 1835-1850, 1 5/8" x 2" x 3", base with a shallow chip to one end shell and two shallow chips and several flakes underneath. **$161**

Extremely rare OP-17 Diamond and Quatrefoil oval pressed salt, opaque light blue with subtle mottling, complex rim, on four flared feet. Possibly Boston & Sandwich Glass Co., 1830-1840, 2" x 2 5/8" x 3 1/2", loss of one foot, outer rim with two shallow chips and mold roughness. **$57**

Extremely rare SL-11 Shell pressed salt, unlisted soft medium blue, on four scrolled feet. Possibly Boston & Sandwich Glass Co., 1830-1845, 1 3/4" x 1 7/8" x 3 1/8", with two inner-rim chips and heavy overall roughness. **$103**

Unlisted BF-1 Basket of Flowers pressed salt, colorless, on four feet. Probably Boston & Sandwich Glass Co., 1830-1845, 2" x 1 7/8" x 3 1/8", rim with a shallow chip to one corner and the loss of one scroll tip, feet with one chip and light flaking. **$46**

Unlisted BS-3 Beaded Scroll and Basket of Flowers pressed salt, opalescent moonstone, on four scrolled feet, rayed star base, thick heavy pressing. Boston & Sandwich Glass Co., 1835-1845, 1 7/8" x 2" x 3 1/8", moderate flaking mold roughness to inner rim, half-inch annealing check in one corner. **$258**

Unlisted LE-2 Lyre pressed salt, colorless, on four scrolled feet. Unknown rarity. Boston & Sandwich Glass Co., 1835-1845,: 1 7/8" x 2" x 3 1/8", rim with a chip to one end scallop and a shallow interior chip, spall to the top of one cornucopia that probably occurred upon removal from mold. **$161**

Unlisted OO-25 variant Draped Panel Octagon oblong pressed salt, colorless, having pointed beads surrounding the upper rim, faintly molded base. Possibly Pittsburgh area, 1835-1850, 1 1/4" x 2 1/2" x 3 1/4", rim with moderate mold roughness and three chips under the outer flange. **$103**

Photo courtesy Jeffrey S. Evans & Associates, Mt. Crawford, Va.; www.jeffreysevans.com

Rare MV-1 Mount Vernon pressed salt, deep olive green, scallop and point rim. Probably Mount Vernon or Saratoga Glass Co., 1835-1850, 3/4" x 2" x 2 3/4", shallow chip to the outer edge of one corner, 1" annealing check off rim as made. **$1,035**

Photo courtesy Jeffrey S. Evans & Associates, Mt. Crawford, Va.; www.jeffreysevans.com

Unlisted BH-1 variant Bee Hive pressed salt, colorless, with tiny bees around the hive, scallop and point rim. New England Glass Co., 1830-1850, 2" x 2 1/8" x 3 1/8", minor flakes and a hint of mold roughness. **$805**

Unlisted PR-1(E) Peacock Eye round pressed salt, colorless, serrated scallop and point rim, the base features four concentric plain rings with a plain center. Boston & Sandwich Glass Co., 1830-1845, 1 1/2" x 3 1/8", moderate chipping to rim and foot......................................**$34**

Unlisted SL-8 Shell pressed salt, colorless, slightly shaped rim. Possibly New England area, 1835-1850, 1 1/2" x 1 7/8" x 2 3/4", light mold roughness to inner rim and foot, chip to side of foot...**$46**

Unlisted, possibly unique CN-1B Crown pressed salt, deep cobalt blue with an opalescent bloom to interior, on four scrolled feet. Boston & Sandwich Glass Co., 1830-1845, 2 1/8" x 2" x 3 1/8", light inner-rim flakes, one side with a chip to a lower corner and a reattached foot.................**$149**

Rare JY-1A Jersey pressed salt, light green, even scallop rim, 12-point star in base. Jersey Glass Co., 1835-1850, 1 5/8" x 2 1/8" x 3 1/8", each rim scallop with a flake or shallow chip, outer rim with one shallow chip. **$207**

Rare JY-2 Jersey marked pressed salt, colorless, embossed "JERSEY / GLASS. Co / nr.N.YORK" under base, scallop and point rim. Jersey Glass Co., 1835-1850, 1 7/8" x 2 1/4" x 3 1/8", two chips and overall flaking/mold roughness to rim, partial loss of two feet, light basal residue..**$195**

Rare OL-15 Beaded Strawberry Diamond oval pressed salt, slightly mottled blue fiery opalescent, high and low point rim. Boston & Sandwich Glass Co., 1830-

1850, 1 3/4" x 2 1/4" x 3 1/2", rim with the loss of one low point resulting in a 1" crack..**$115**

Rare OL-25 Oval pressed salt, light green, even scallop rim, rayed base. Unknown origin, 19th or 20th century, 1 1/4" x 2 1/2" x 4", rim with several light flakes and mold roughness, table ring with flaking/mold roughness......**$126**

Rare PP-1 Peacock Eye pedestal pressed salt, colorless, saw-tooth rim, bull's eye scallop lozenge-shape foot. Probably Pittsburgh area, 1830-1845, 2 5/8" x 2 5/6" x 3 3/4", rim with two shallow interior chips and light mold roughness, foot with a chip to one end causing the loss of an entire scallop...**$138**

Rare WN-1 Wagon pressed salt, colorless, rope rim, on four wheels. Possibly Boston & Sandwich Glass Co., 1835-1850, 2" x 2" x 3", each corner of the body exhibits heavy chipping/roughness, wheels also with chipping. **$195**

Rare GA-4 variant Gothic Arch and Heart pressed salt, opalescent medium blue, even scallop rim, on four bucket feet. Possibly Boston & Sandwich Glass Co., 1835-1845, 1 3/4" x 2" x 2 3/4", crack in one corner that probably occurred during manufacturing, rim with a spall and several flakes to top, chip to one medial corner............**$195**

Rare OG-10 Scrolling Acanthus Leaf rectangular pressed salt, colorless, shaped rim, on four short feet. Attributed to the Providence Flint Glass Co., 1835-1850, 1 5/8" x 2 1/4" x 3", rim with two top chips and moderate interior chipping/roughness, one chip to base edge........**$57**

Rare OG-2 Diamond Heart rectangular pressed salt, colorless, all-over ribbing, even scallop rim. Probably New England Glass Co., 1835-1850, 1 7/8" x 2 1/4" x 3 1/8", two tipped rim scallops...**$126**

Rare RD-8 round pressed salt, colorless, plain rim, waffle and dot base. Possibly Boston & Sandwich Glass Co., 1835-1850, 1 1/2" x 2 1/2", slightly rough fin as made.....**$46**

Rare SL-15 Shell pressed salt, colorless, on four scrolled feet, factory polished mold lines and under feet to level. United States or France. 1835-1850, 1 5/8" x 2" x 3 1/8", one inner-rim flake and light mold roughness to corners, small annealing check in one foot as made.................................**$69**

Rare SN-1B Stag's Horn pressed salt, cobalt blue, 32 rays under base. Possibly Boston & Sandwich Glass Co., 1835-1850, 1 5/8" x 1 7/8" x 3 1/8", scattered light flaking/mold roughness to rim and a shallow chip to one base corner..**$69**

Rare SN-1B Stag's Horn pressed salt, opaque clambroth, 32 rays under base. Possibly Boston & Sandwich Glass Co., 1835-1850, 1 3/4" x 1 7/8" x 3 1/8", light flakes to rim and base. **$115**

Scarce CT-1A Chariot pressed salt, colorless, scallop and point rim, a strongly and clearly pressed example that is 1/8" shorter than normal. Boston & Sandwich Glass Co., 1835-1850, 1 5/8" x 2 1/8" x 2 7/8", few minute flakes.
....**$115**

Scarce MV-1 Mount Vernon pressed salt, aquamarine, scallop and point rim. Probably Mount Vernon Glass Co., possibly Boston & Sandwich Glass Co., 1835-1850, 1 3/4" x 2 1/8" x 2 7/8", light interior-rim mold roughness and a minor flake to one base corner......................**$126**

Scarce PO-4 Peacock Eye oval pressed salt, colorless, scallop rim, 28 rays in base. Boston & Sandwich Glass Co., 1830-1845, 1 3/8" x 2 7/8" x 3 7/8", minute nick to inner rim. **$80**

Scarce SN-1B Stag's Horn pressed salt, medium amber, 26 rays under base. Possibly Boston & Sandwich Glass Co., 1835-1850,1 5/8" x 1 7/8" x 3 1/8", scattered light flaking/mold roughness to rim interior and a shallow chip below one base corner..**$57**

Rare BH-1 Bee Hive pressed salt, colorless, scallop and point rim. New England Glass Co., 1830-1850, 1 7/8" x 2 1/8" x 3", light flaking/mold roughness to rim and under base, moderate highpoint wear to sides. **$46**

Rare SL-1 Shell pressed salt, cobalt blue, shaped rim, waffle pattern under base. Possibly Boston & Sandwich Glass Co., 1835-1850, 1 5/8" x 2" x 3", rim with several shallow chips to interior and some light flaking/mold roughness, base with one tipped foot and light flaking.
....**$115**

Rare SC-5 Scroll pressed salt, medium blue, on four scrolled feet. Possibly Boston & Sandwich Glass Co., 1835-1850, 1 3/4" x 1 5/8" x 3 1/4", some light flaking/mold roughness to inside of upper and lower scrolls, none of which affects the profile, and a chip to the bottom of one foot..**$287**

Rare NE-1A New England marked pressed salt, opaque white with a hint of opalescence at rim, embossed under base, scallop and point rim. New England Glass Co., 1835-1850, 1 7/8" x 2 1/8" x 3", several shallow chips and flakes to rim, shallow chip to one upper and lower corner, several flakes under base. **$92**

Rare OO-1 Octagon oblong pressed salt, red amber, shaped rim, sunburst base. Boston & Sandwich Glass Co., 1835-1850, 1 5/8" x 2 3/8" x 3 1/4", inner rim with two shallow chips and a hint of mold roughness, top rim with two light flakes, base with a chip to side and flake underneath, interior residue. **$126**

Photo courtesy Jeffrey S. Evans & Associates, Mt. Crawford, Va.; www.jeffreysevans.com

Unlisted SL-2 Shell pressed salt, medium golden amber, shaped rim, raised table ring, fine prisms and diamonds under base. Possibly Boston & Sandwich Glass Co., 1835-1850, 1 3/4" x 2" x 3", loss of one base corner and a minor flake to another. **$92**

Photo courtesy Jeffrey S. Evans & Associates, Mt. Crawford, Va.; www.jeffreysevans.com

Scarce MV-1 Mount Vernon pressed salt, aquamarine, scallop and point rim. Probably Mount Vernon Glass Co., possibly Boston & Sandwich Glass Co., 1835-1850, 1 3/4" x 2 1/8" x 2 7/8". **$258**

Photo courtesy Jeffrey S. Evans & Associates, Mt. Crawford, Va.; www.jeffreysevans.com

PP-4A Peacock Eye pressed master salt in unlisted deep violet blue, circa 1830-1845. **$3,335**

Photo courtesy Jeffrey S. Evans & Associates, Mt. Crawford, Va.; www.jeffreysevans.com

Pattern-molded footed salt or bonnet glass, deep cobalt blue, double-ogee bowl molded with 16 vertical ribs, raised on a compressed knop and an applied circular foot with eight irregular scallops and a rough pontil mark. United States or England, 1810-1830, 2 1/2" x 2 3/8". **$460**

BLOWN-MOLD, PATTERN-MOLD, PRESSED GLASS

Engraved and pattern-molded flip glass, colorless soda-lime glass, molded with 18 basal flutes, so-called Stiegel decoration below the rim, rough pontil mark. Probably Bohemia, 1780-1820m 5 3/4", thin cloudy band at inner rim. **$115**

Unique pressed-loop nappy on a free-blown base, deep brilliant plum purple, nine-loop nappy with a slightly sagged bottom, applied to a solid baluster stem and a thick foot with a rough pontil mark. Inner rim of bowl with a narrow ledge but no indication of being fitted with a cover. Probably Pittsburgh area, 1850-1865, 5" x 7 3/8" overall, shallow chip to a loop below the rim, scattered interior wear. (The joining of pressed and blown elements in pattern glass of this period is seldom encountered. **$4,025**

Photo courtesy Jeffrey S. Evans & Associates, Mt. Crawford, Va.; www.jeffreysevans.com

Rare pair of pressed-loop vases, deep brilliant peacock green, each featuring a deep slender bowl with a gauffered six-flute rim, raised on a tall hexagonal double-knop stem and double-step foot, factory polished lower mold lines and under bases to level, single-piece construction. New England, 1850-1870, 10 1/4" and 10 1/2", minute flakes under one base.
$4,312 pair

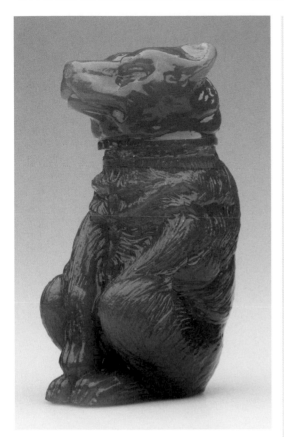

Rare pressed Chained Bear medium-size pomade jar, translucent starch blue, marked "X.BAZIN / PHILA" under base. Boston & Sandwich Glass Co., 1850-1870, 4 5/8", base rim with chipping to rear resulting in an 1/8" deep loss, cover with a chip to one ear and normal chipping and bruising to inner flange. **$2,990**

Rare pressed and blown Pine Tree And Shield compote, colorless, shallow bowl with a 20-scallop rim, raised on a blown double-knop stem and conical foot with a faint rough pontil mark, wafer construction. Boston & Sandwich Glass Co. or New England Glass Co., 1828-1835, 4", diameter rim 6 1/4", diameter foot 3 1/2", shallow spall to the interior of one scallop..**$690**

Rare pressed lacy Eagle And Constitution oval dish, colorless, the sides divided into eight stippled panels with alternating reserves of a shield-breast American eagle and a sailing ship believed to represent the USF Constitution, even scallop rim, rope surrounding the plain table ring. Possibly Boston & Sandwich Glass Co., 1830-1840, 1 1/2" x 3 7/8" x 6 1/4", shallow chip and several flakes to top rim and several shallow chips to outer rim...........................**$345**

Rare pressed Acorn And Oak Leaf plate, deep fiery opalescent, cavetto with four beaded rings and faint concentric rings surrounding a central five-petal rosette, reverse with fine concentric rings. New England, 1828-1835, 7" diameter, hint of mold roughness to a slight fin on the rim..**$316**

Scarce pressed lacy Peacock Eye covered mustard, colorless, standard cover with spoon slot, along with a 5 1/4" plate in a matching pattern that is often used as an underplate. Boston & Sandwich Glass Co., 1830-1845, 2 1/2" overall x 2 3/4", cover with a slight underfill and light flaking under the edge, plate with a light spall and normal flaking...**$195**

Extremely rare loop rectangular covered bowl on foot, colorless flint, 16-loop bowl with cross and spike device in base, applied with a crude wafer to a low hexagonal stem and circular foot, the cover, also with 16 loops, is surmounted by a dramatic heart-form finial. Probably Pittsburgh area, 1855-1870, 8 1/2" overall, diameter rim 5 1/2" x 8 3/4", base with two minor flakes to inner rim and another to foot, cover with minimal light flaking to rim. A previously unrecorded covered bowl with a seemingly unique finial...**$2,415**

Pressed toy flat iron, light bottle green, factory polished base and back. Boston & Sandwich Glass Co. and others, 1850-1870, 1" x 1 3/8", several flakes and a light bruise to base. **$184**

Photo courtesy Jeffrey S. Evans & Associates, Mt. Crawford, Va.; www.jeffreysevans.com

Lee/Rose No. 127 cup plate, deep amethyst with some small spots of cloudiness, plain rope rim, top only. Extremely rare, probably Pittsburgh, 1830-1845. 3" diameter, normal under-rim mold roughness. **$1,725**

Photo courtesy Jeffrey S. Evans & Associates, Mt. Crawford, Va.; www.jeffreysevans.com

Lee/Rose No. 148-A cup plate in soft blue, circa 1830-1845. **$1,955**

CARNIVAL GLASS

Photo courtesy Jeffrey S. Evans & Associates, Mt. Crawford, Va.; www.jeffreysevans.com

Northwood Rose show carnival glass plate, marigold, scallop edge. First half 20th century, 9 1/4" diameter, two minute areas of roughness. **$46**

Photo courtesy Jeffrey S. Evans & Associates, Mt. Crawford, Va.; www.jeffreysevans.com

Fenton Orange Tree carnival glass loving cup, blue, two handles, Peacock Tail on interior. First quarter 20th century, 5 3/4" x 3 3/8", minute nick to one handle. **$126**

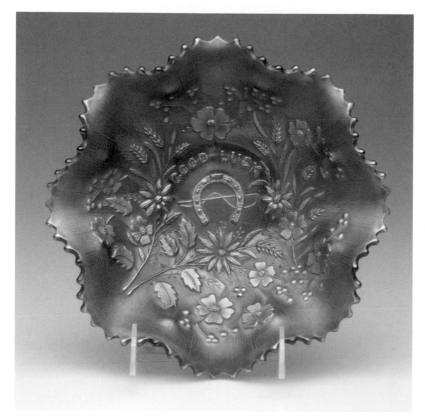

Photo courtesy Jeffrey S. Evans & Associates, Mt. Crawford, Va.; www.jeffreysevans.com

Northwood Good Luck carnival glass bowl, green piecrust rim, trademark under base. First quarter 20th century, 8 1/2" diameter overall. **$195**

Photo courtesy Jeffrey S. Evans & Associates, Mt. Crawford, Va.; www.jeffreysevans.com

Northwood Good Luck carnival glass bowl, amethyst, piecrust rim, trademark under base. First quarter 20th century, 8 1/2" diameter overall. **$172**

Photo courtesy Jeffrey S. Evans &
Associates, Mt. Crawford, Va.;
www.jeffreysevans.com

*Northwood Grape and
Cable carnival glass
hatpin holder, amethyst,
unmarked. First half 20th
century, 6 3/4".* **$149**

Fenton Art Glass

The Fenton Art Glass Co. was founded in 1905 by Frank L. Fenton and his brother, John W., in an old glass factory in Martins Ferry, Ohio. They initially sold hand-painted glass made by other manufacturers, but it wasn't long before they decided to produce their own glass. The new Fenton factory in Williamstown, W.V., opened on Jan. 2, 1907. Despite economic difficulties in their 100th-anniversary year, the firm remains in business and in family hands.

Also see Carnival Glass.

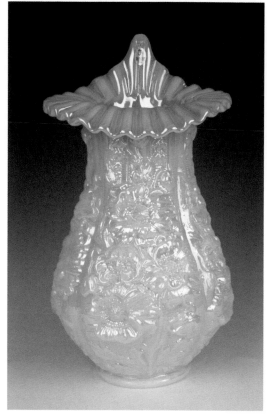

Fenton Iridescent Burmese Poppy Show Vase using an old Imperial mold, 2003, custom-made for Singleton Bailey, 13 3/4". **$100+**

Fenton Wheat vases, early 1980s, each 7 1/2", in overlay colors of, from left, Honey Amber, Wild Roase, Apple Green and Glacial Blue. **$30+ each**

Fenton Honeysuckle Opalescent lamp in Coin Dot, late 1940s, 16". **$125+**

Fenton French Opalescent three-horn epergne in Emerald Crest/Diamond Lace, 1949-55, 11". **$125+**

Fenton Chinese Yellow flared bowl with rolled rim, with Ebony glass base, mid-1920s, 11" diameter. **$80+**

Fenton, Robert Barber experimental off-hand vase in Hanging Hearts and Bittersweet glass, 1975-76, 10". **$250+**

Fenton Original Formula Carnival Glass pieces, amethyst base. Left: Persian Medallion chalice, 1972-73, 7" h, **$25+**
Right: Grape and Cable tobacco jar, 1969, 7 1/4" h, marked, "Preznick's Carnival Glass Museum–Lodi, Ohio 1969," **$80+**

Lalique

René Lalique (1860-1945) first gained prominence as a jewelry designer. Around 1900, he began experimenting with molded-glass brooches and pendants, often embellishing them with semiprecious stones. By 1905, he was devoting himself exclusively to the manufacture of glass articles. He produced many objects, especially vases, bowls and figurines, in the Art Nouveau and Art Deco styles.

Also see Perfume Containers.

Photo courtesy Heritage Auction Galleries, Dallas; www.HA.com

R. Lalique "Canard" topaz glass seal, designed 1925, engraved "R. Lalique France", 2 1/2". **$567**

R. Lalique, "Flora-Bella" blue glass bowl (two views), designed 1930, engraved "R. LALIQUE FRANCE", 15 3/8″ diameter. **$5,377**

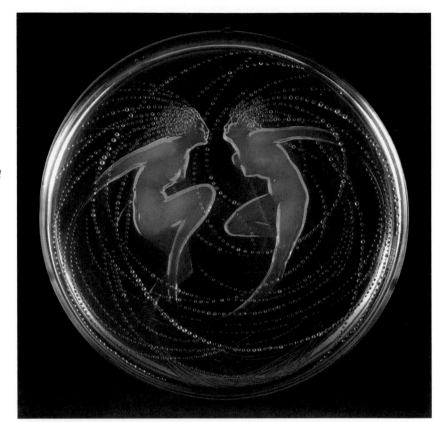

R. Lalique, "Deux Sirènes," opalescent glass covered box or bonbonnière, designed 1921, molded "R. LALIQUE", engraved "France No. 43", 10 1/4" diameter. **$2,629**

R. Lalique, "Cleones" amber glass box, designed 1921, impressed "R. LALIQUE", 7" diameter. **$717**

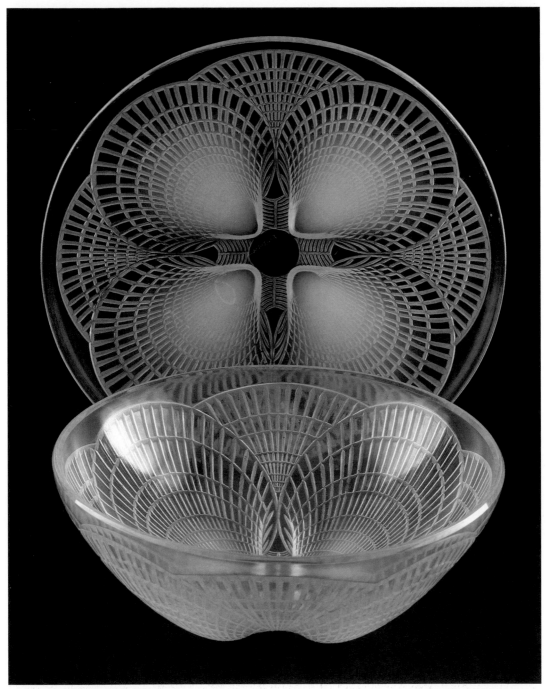

R. Lalique, "Coquilles" opalescent Glass bowl and plate, molded "R. LALIQUE", engraved "France", 9 1/2" diameter bowl, 10 1/2" diameter plate. **$657 pair**

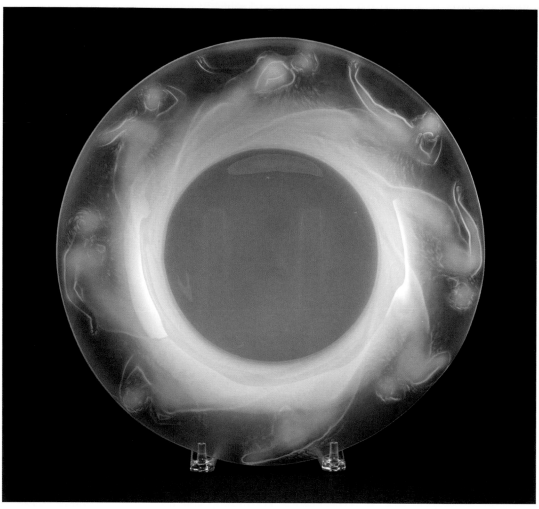

Photos courtesy Heritage Auction Galleries, Dallas; www.HA.com

R. Lalique, "Sirènes" white opalescent glass coupe (two views), designed 1920, engraved "R. Lalique France", 13 7/8"
diameter. **$8,365**

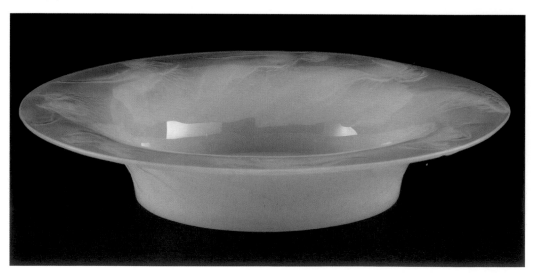

Photos courtesy Heritage Auction Galleries, Dallas; www.HA.com

R. Lalique, "Victoire" glass car mascot, designed 1928, molded "R. LALIQUE FRANCE", 10 3/8", mounted on a custom-made, hardwood base fitted with a modern chrome plated metal ring mount, comparable to fixtures used in the period. Second image shows mascot mounted on a 1935 Duesenberg. **$26,290**

Photo courtesy James D. Julia Auctioneers, Fairfield, Maine; www.JamesDJulia.com

R. Lalique Bacchus Vase. Decorated with a wide horizontal panel with deeply impressed design of satyrs sitting amongst heavy vegetation. The heavily decorated central band is finished in a gray patination and is bordered top and bottom by clear glass. Signed on the underside with etched block letters "R. Lalique France". 6 3/4" h. **$2,300**

Photo courtesy James D. Julia Auctioneers, Fairfield, Maine; www.JamesDJulia.com

R. Lalique Grignon Vase. Impressed all over with stylized wheat stalks and finished with a beautiful green patination. Vase is signed on the underside with lightly etched block letters "R. Lalique France". 7" h. **$1,840**

Photo courtesy James D. Julia Auctioneers, Fairfield, Maine; www.JamesDJulia.com

Lalique Coquilles Vase. Decorated with pressed design of overlapping seashells and finished with a light blue patination. Vase is signed on the underside with lightly etched script letters "Lalique". 7" h. **$1,610**

Photo courtesy James D. Julia Auctioneers, Fairfield, Maine; www.JamesDJulia.com

R. Lalique Bouchardon Vase. Simple bulbous body with applied pressed glass handles depicting a nude maiden holding a spray of flowers. The vase is done in smoky gray glass and is double signed on the underside with impressed block letters "R. Lalique" and engraved script signature "R. Lalique France". 4 3/4" h. One fleabite on edge of rim. **$4,025**

Photo courtesy James D. Julia Auctioneers, Fairfield, Maine; www.JamesDJulia.com

Lalique Bacchantes Vase. Decorated with Art Deco maidens surrounding the entire vase. Frosted with original sepia patina in the recesses. This model was produced from the 1920s to the present day, but this example dates from just after WWII. Signed "LALIQUE FRANCE" on the underside. 9 1/2" h. **$3,737**

Photo courtesy James D. Julia Auctioneers, Fairfield, Maine; www.JamesDJulia.com

R. Lalique Gobelet Six Figurines Vase. Deep olive green impressed with six vertical panels, each showing a different maiden in flowing gowns holding bouquets of flowers. Vase is signed on the underside with engraved block letters "R. Lalique". 7 1/2" h. Minor staining to bottom interior. **$3,795**

Photo courtesy James D. Julia Auctioneers, Fairfield, Maine; www.JamesDJulia.com

Lalique Scarabees Vase. Clear classic form vase has two small ear handles that support two rings with molded scarab design that carries a gray patination. 13″ h. Heat check at one handle. **$3,162**

Photo courtesy James D. Julia Auctioneers, Fairfield, Maine; www.JamesDJulia.com

R. Lalique Saint Francois Vase. Decorated with high-relief birds resting on leafy branches against a frosted background. The design is further enhanced with green patination and the vase is signed on the underside with etched block letters "R. Lalique France". 7" h. **$1,725**

R. Lalique Avallon Vase. Deeply impressed design of birds resting amongst cherry branches laden with fruit. The vase is finished with blue patination. Signed on the underside with acid-etched block signature "R. Lalique". 5 3/4" h. **$1,955**

Photo courtesy James D. Julia Auctioneers, Fairfield, Maine; www.JamesDJulia.com

R. Lalique Espalion Vase. With overlapping fern design covering the entire body of the vase. The vase is done in opalescent glass and is finished with a rich green patination. Signed on the underside with engraved script signature "R. Lalique France". 7 1/4" h. **$1,955**

Photo courtesy James D. Julia Auctioneers, Fairfield, Maine; www.JamesDJulia.com

R. Lalique Coqs Et Plumes. With strutting roosters with tail feathers extending to the top of the vase. The clear glass vase is finished with a blue patination and is signed on the underside with acid-etched block letters "R. Lalique". 6" h. **$1,610**

Photo courtesy Heritage Auction Galleries, Dallas; www.HA.com

René Lalique, clear frosted glass vase in the Bellecour pattern, Wingen-sur-Moder, France, circa 1927, marked "R Lalique France No. 993", 11 1/4", beak of one bird has been ground down. **$14,340**

Photo courtesy James D. Julia Auctioneers, Fairfield, Maine; www.JamesDJulia.com

R. Lalique Archers Vase. With a design of nude male archers shooting arrows at flocks of birds. The vase is finished in a satiny blue patination ending in a clear rim. Signed on the underside with etched script signature "R. Lalique France". 10 3/4" h. **$5,175**

Photo courtesy James D. Julia Auctioneers, Fairfield, Maine; www.JamesDJulia.com

R. Lalique Gros Scarabees Vase. All-over design of large scarabs against a gray patinated background. The vase is signed on the underside with engraved block letters "R. Lalique France". 11 1/2" h. **$7,200**

QUEZAL

The Quezal Art Glass Decorating Co., named for the quezal—a bird with brilliantly colored feathers found in tropical regions of the Americas—was organized in 1901 in Brooklyn, N.Y., by Martin Bach and Thomas Johnson, two disgruntled Tiffany workers. They soon hired Percy Britton and William Wiedebine, two more former Tiffany employees.

The first products, unmarked, were exact Tiffany imitations. Quezal pieces differ from Tiffany pieces in that they are more defined and the decorations are more visible and brighter. No new techniques were developed by Quezal.

Johnson left in 1905. T. Conrad Vahlsing, Bach's son-in-law, joined the firm in 1918, but left with Paul Frank in 1920 to form Lustre Art Glass Co., which in turn copied Quezal pieces. Martin Bach died in 1924, and by 1925, Quezal had ceased operations.

The "Quezal" trademark was first used in 1902 and placed on the base of vases and bowls and the rims of shades. The acid-etched or engraved letters vary in size and may be found in amber, black or gold. A printed label that includes an illustration of a quetzal was used briefly in 1907.

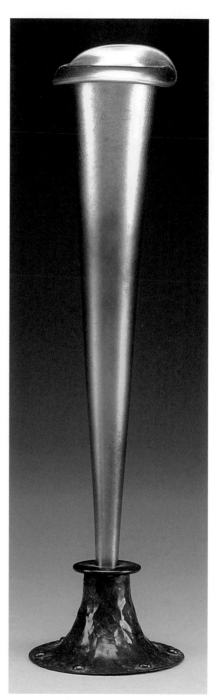

Photo courtesy James D. Julia Auctioneers, Fairfield, Maine; www.JamesDJulia.com

Quezal Flower-Form Vase. Flaring cylindrical shape with Jack in the Pulpit folded mouth resting in an Arts & Crafts hammered and patinated copper foot. Early engraved "Quezal" signature on the tip of the glass. 10 3/4" t. **$1,552**

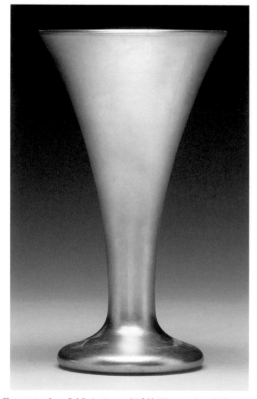

Photo courtesy James D. Julia Auctioneers, Fairfield, Maine; www.JamesDJulia.com

Quezal Trumpet Vase. With bright gold iridescent finish with a band of platinum iridescence at the foot. Vase is signed in the polished pontil "Quezal". 8 1/2" t. **$230**

Photo courtesy James D. Julia Auctioneers, Fairfield, Maine; www.JamesDJulia.com

Quezal Pulled Art Glass Vase. Simplistic Art Nouveau design consists of three pulled handles to top of bulbous shaped vase. Deep gold coloration has a soft magenta iridescence. Signed "Quezal" in script on pontil. 8" h. **$660**

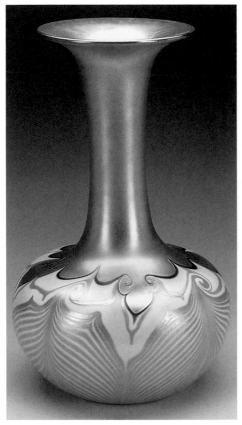

Photo courtesy James D. Julia Auctioneers, Fairfield, Maine; www.JamesDJulia.com

Quezal Silver Overlay Vase. Decorated with King Tut design with gold iridescence showing pink and blue iridescence. The vase is overlaid with an Art Nouveau floral design in sterling silver. The silver carries the Alvin Silver Co hallmark, "999/1000 Fine" and "Patented 49". Vase is signed on the underside in the polished pontil "Quezal" with a scroll beneath. 9 3/4" t. **$3,680**

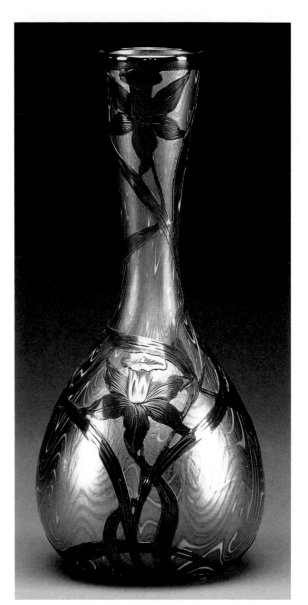

Photo courtesy James D. Julia Auctioneers, Fairfield, Maine; www.JamesDJulia.com

Quezal Decorated Vase. With bulbous body leading to long slender neck and flaring rim. The cream-colored background gives way to the gold iridescent neck, which is finished with a hooked-feather design at the shoulder. The gold iridescence on the neck has a strong green overtone with flashes of pink. Signed on the underside in the polished pontil "Quezal B952". 11" t. **$8,050**

GUITARS, BANJOS, MANDOLINS

The guitar has ancient roots and is used in a wide variety of musical styles. It typically has six strings, but four-, seven-, eight-, 10-, 11-, 12-, 13- and 18-string guitars also exist. The size and shape of the neck and the base of the guitar also vary. There are two main types of guitars, the electric guitar and the acoustic guitar. The banjo is a stringed instrument developed by enslaved Africans in the United States, adapted from several African instruments. The mandolin is part of the lute family (plucked, or strummed). It is descended from the mandore, a soprano lute. It usually has a body with a teardrop-shaped soundboard, or one which is essentially oval in shape, with a soundhole, or soundholes, of varying shapes which are open.

The instruments featured in this year's edition of the Warman's guide are all courtesy Skinner Inc., Boston and Marlborough, Mass.; *www.SkinnerInc.com.*

Mandolin, Gibson Mandolin-Guitar Co., Kalamazoo, circa 1923, Model F4, labeled GIBSON MANDOLIN STYLE F4, ..., etc., length of back 12 7/8", with case. Missing pick guard. surface scratches and abrasions. 1 cm chip in face of headstock. Fracture near upper treble body point, approx. 3 cm, fracture below body scroll, approx. 3 cm. Wear to upper edge, back of headstock. **$3,081**

Guitar, Gibson Mandolin-Guitar Co., Kalamazoo, circa 1924, Model L-2, labeled GIBSON STYLE, NUMBER 160403 IS HEREBY, GUARANTEED..., etc., length of back 18 15/16", width of lower bout 13 9/16", with case. Surface scratches and abrasions. **$948**

Ukulele, C.F. Martin & Co., Nazareth, Pa., circa 1920, Style 1, stamped internally CF MARTIN & CO, NAZARETH PA, and on the back of the peghead, length of back 9 3/8", with case. Surface scratches and abrasions. **$563**

Tiple, C.F. Martin & Co., Nazareth, Pa., circa 1931, stamped CF MARTIN & CO, NAZARETH PA on the center strip and on the back of the peghead, and T-17 and 46751 at the upper block, length of back 11 1/16", with case. Surface scratches and abrasions. **$830**

Harp guitar, Gibson Mandolin-Guitar Co., Kalamazoo, circa 1920, Style U, labeled GIBSON STYLE U, NUMBER 78381 IS HEREBY, GUARANTEED..., etc., GIBSON MANDOLIN GUITAR CO, MANUFACTURERS, KALAMAZOO MICH, USA, length of back 26 1/2", width of lower bout 18 1/2", with case. Surface scratches and abrasions, wear to back of neck. Fracture to peg head of sympathetic tenth string. **$3,081**

Guitar, Gibson Mandolin-Guitar Co., Kalamazoo, circa 1920, Style O, labeled GIBSON STYLE O, NUMBER 60358? IS HEREBY, GUARANTEED... etc..., GIBSON MANDOLIN-GUITAR CO, MANUFACTURERS, KALAMAZOO, MICH USA, length of back 17 3/4", width of lower bout 16 1/16", with case. Body clear coated. Surface scratches and abrasions. **$2,607**

Electric guitar, Gibson Inc., Kalamazoo, circa 1953, Model ES-175-D, labeled STYLE ES 175 D, GIBSON GUITAR, NUMBER A 15390 IS HEREBY, GUARANTEED..., etc., length of back 20 1/8", width of lower bout 16 1/16", with case. Later strap-hook at heel of neck, slight surface check, re-fretted. Surface scratches and abrasions. **$3,081**

Electric guitar, John D'Angelico, New York, 1955, Model Excel, stamped 1980, JOHN DANGELICO at the upper block, the bound peghead with D'ANGELICO NEW YORK and EXCEL pearl inlay, length of back 20 1/2", width of lower bout 16 7/8", with case. Replaced pickups, finish or hairline cracks near pickup switch, finish check, finish wear to back of neck, pickguard a replacement. Refretted with zero fret added. Two face cracks under tailpiece, one repaired. **$8,295**

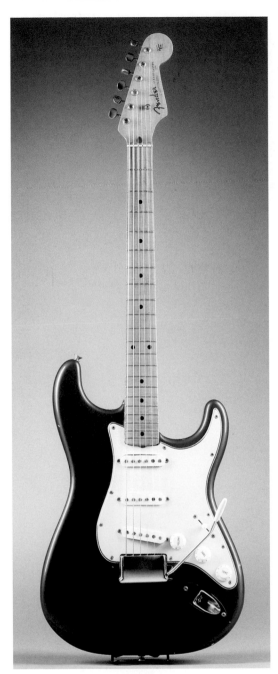

American Electric Guitar, Fender Electric Instruments, Fullerton, Calif., 1954, Model Stratocaster, labeled FENDER STRATOCASTER, WITH SYNCHRONIZED TREMOLO..., etc., and ORIGINAL CONTOUR BODY, PAT PEND on the headstock decals and stamped 1099 on the neck plate, (factory refinished in 1962 in "Lake Placid Blue"), length of back 15 3/4", with later 1962 case. Factory refinished in 1962, neck refinished with decals, body refinished in Lake Placid blue, pickguard replaced in 1962 with contemporary style. With original strap and polish cloth. Pot codes 250K, 304429. **$8,295**

American Electric Guitar, Gibson Inc., Kalamazoo, 1959, Model Les Paul Standard, Serial Number 9 1950, the mahogany back and neck, the painted headstock with GIBSON pearl inlay and LES PAUL MODEL silkscreen logo, the bound rosewood fingerboard with trapezoid pearl inlay, the carved two-piece maple top of irregular curl, the tune-o-matic bridge, stop tailpiece and all hardware original, the original "PAF" design double-coil humbucking pickups, the cherry sunburst finish, length of back 17 3/8", with original Les Paul Custom case. All hardware original. All electronics original and unmolested. **$237,000**

Tenor banjo, Weymann & Son, Philadelphia, circa 1930, labeled "WEYMANN, MANUFACTURED BY, WEYMANN & SON PHILA PA", serial number stamped on dowel stick, diameter of head 11", tarnish and mild corrosion to gold plating. **$5,925**

Mandola, Lyon & Healy, Chicago, circa 1920, labeled "MADE BY, LYON & HEALY, CHICAGO, MAKERS OF HIGHEST GRADE MUSICAL, INSTRUMENTS, SOLD UNDER OUR UNLIMITED GUARANTEE NO 2 STYLE A, LYON & HEALY", length of back 15", width of back 11 3/8", with original case. **$7,110**

Electric guitar, Gibson Inc., Kalamazoo, circa 1961, Model Les Paul, serial number 35361, cherry-red finish, two PAF humbucking pickups, Tune-o-matic bridge and stop tailpiece, sold with a color photograph of Andy Summers (The Police) holding the guitar. **$4,266**

American Banjo, Vega Co., Boston, circa 1921, Model Tubaphone #9, stamped on the dowel stick TUBAPHONE 45097, FAIRBANKS BANJO, MADE BY, THE VEGA COMPANY, BOSTON MASS, NO 9..., etc., and stamped 45097 on the inside rim, diameter of head 10 15/16", with later case. Very good condition. Later gold Grover tuners, Wear to fingerboard at first and second position. **$4,444**

Pair of American Mandolins, Gibson Mandolin-Guitar Co., Kalamazoo, 1926, Master Model F5, labeled THE GIBSON MASTER MODEL, STYLE F5 NUMBER 84264, IS HEREBY GUARANTEED...etc., the bound quartersawn back of strong narrow curl, the bound top of fine to medium grain, the sides of medium curl, the neck of strong medium curl, the bound peghead with THE GIBSON and "fern" pearl inlay, the bound ebony fingerboard with pearl dot inlay, the tailpiece and pickguard original, length of back 13 3/8". Master Model F5, labeled THE GIBSON MASTER MODEL F5 NUMBER 84265, IS HEREBY GUARANTEED...etc., the bound slab-cut back of irregular curl, the bound top of fine to medium grain, the sides of medium curl, the neck of strong medium curl, the bound peghead with THE GIBSON and "fern" pearl inlay, the bound ebony fingerboard with pearl dot inlay, the tailpiece and pickguard original, length of back 13 3/8". The original custom-built Artist double case with green velvet lining. Provenance: Robert L. Sharp. From the Sharp family archives; "As an agent for the Gibson Mandolin-Guitar Company in 1926, Robert L. Sharp ordered and purchased these twin F5 mandolins. He enjoyed playing these instruments in front of audiences in Memphis and Little Rock. If a mandolin string broke, he could reach down and pick up the twin without missing a note. These instruments became a part of the Sharp family, joining a guitar, mandocello, mandola, and ukulele all from Gibson in the late 20's and early 30's." Number 84265: minor chips to surface of top. Slightly distressed varnish surface on back, Medium fret ware, top five positions. Lost to gold plateing of tailpiece cover. Number 84264: replaced top bridge section, original in case, slightly distressed varnish surface on back, surface check to top, slight loss to gold plating on tailpiece cover. Case in good condition, distressed on edges. **$136,275 pair**

HALLOWEEN

The commercialization of Halloween in the United States did not start until the 20th century, beginning perhaps with Halloween postcards (featuring hundreds of designs) which were most popular between 1905 and 1915. Dennison Manufacturing Co., which published its first Hallowe'en catalog in 1909, and the Beistle Co. were pioneers in commercially made Halloween decorations, particularly die-cut paper items. German manufacturers specialized in Halloween figurines that were exported to the United States in the period between the world wars.

Mass-produced Halloween costumes did not appear in stores until the 1930s, and trick-or-treating did not become a fixture of the holiday until the 1940s.

For more information, see *Vintage Halloween Collectibles*, by Mark Ledenbach, 2007.

Mark Ledenback appeared on the Martha Stewart Show in the fall of 2008.

Photo courtesy Morphy Auctions, Denver, Pa.; www.MorphyAuctions.com

Halloween foot lantern, highly detailed papier-mache foot with a grinning mouth, a large protruding nose, and individual comical faces on each toe. The paper eyes and mouth are illuminated by a candle within foot (with original candle and candleholder), 7 1/2". **$10,350**

Photo courtesy Morphy Auctions, Denver, Pa.; www.MorphyAuctions.com

Halloween Devil Jack-O-Lantern, cardboard, original paper inserts, 8 3/4". **$690**

*Halloween cat figure squeaking mechanical toy
with pumpkin mask. Press chest and cat lowers
mask from face (below), 7".* **$1,725**

*Vegetable Halloween Man with movable glass eyes,
with radish arms, zucchini legs, walnut feet and watermelon head
with an expressive toothy grin. Clockwork mechanism contained
within head, activates eyes which move from right to left.
Simulated apron and vest cover vegetable body. Most likely the only
known example and probably originally used in a store as an trade
stimulator. Some in-painting to right arm, removable stem on top
of head was originally missing and one was recreated in papier-
mache, 17 1/2".* **$19,550**

Set of six celluloid Halloween nodders, prewar Japanese, rubber-band driven; includes one witch, one devil, one cat, and three pumpkin heads. New/old store stock, never used. Includes original box with original paper label, each 7". **$ 10,350**

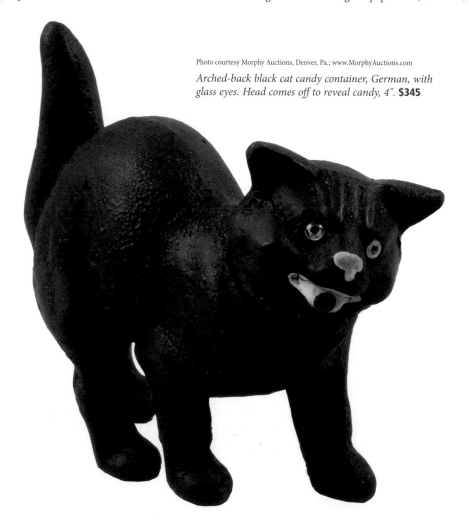

Arched-back black cat candy container, German, with glass eyes. Head comes off to reveal candy, 4". **$345**

Witch holding broom candy container, 7 1/2". **$2,300**

Skeleton sitting on watermelon candy container, German, closure on bottom, 4 1/2". **$373**

Composition witch driving automobile, extremely rare, wooden wheels, composition pumpkin hood ornament, cardboard car, 7". **$1,265**

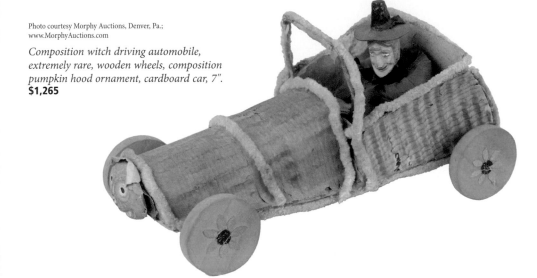

Jewelry

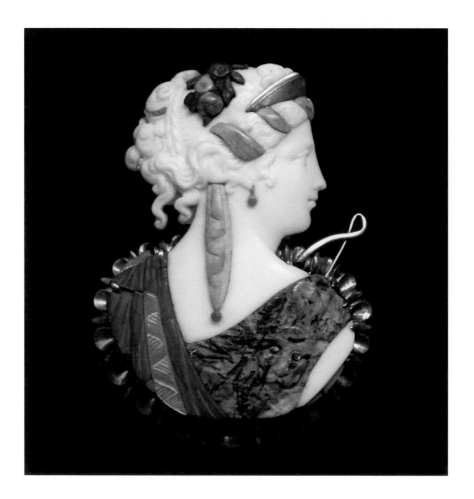

THE FUTURE OF THE MARKET: JEWELRY

By Kathy Flood

Musician Joni Mitchell once observed how differently we interact with the arts. "People shout at me from the audience, 'Sing *Chelsea Morning* again, Joni!,' but no one ever yelled at van Gogh, 'Hey, Vinnie, paint *The Starry Night* again.' " Similarly, we might prefer reading literature silently, alone in bed, but gather with gallery goers to get a glimpse of new paintings – and judge them loudly, to make our brilliant insights heard.

We respond to and interact with collectible objects, and they engage us, in their own unique ways, too, one category so different from another. Art collectors don't wear canvases around their necks, Civil War buffs don't match uniforms to their décor, doll devotees don't take their Dresden china out to dinner – but jewelry is another matter entirely. It's "out there," everywhere, highly visible in the public domain, for all to respond to immediately.

Predicting the future of the jewelry market is clear on one hand, but some of the forecast is far cloudier because it depends on … so many things. It often depends on what happens in the world.

Kathy Flood

For instance, who could have guessed in 2007 that in 2009, diamonds would be disparaged as a girl's past friend, or know the extent to which diamonds would fall out of favor and fashion? In light of the economic meltdown, these gems were suddenly deemed déclassé for their political incorrectness. Who imagined DeBeers would close two of its African mines to prevent even more ice melting all over a market flooded both by new diamonds – and old ones sold off by people suddenly strapped? Diamond values were forecast to drop by 20 to 60 percent. Yet was there any doubt the diamond would eventually rebound?

Who could have guessed pirates would cause panic on the open seas and at the same time spark a small passion for pirate pins?

The Scottish Terrier dog brooch became a huge best seller because of FDR's best friend, Fala, but would Obama's Bo engender the same fad?

Some things are unknowable and unpredictable.

The wearing (and not wearing) of the bling seriously affects jewelry's power in the present tense and alters its future. So, for instance, when best-actress nominee Helen Hunt took minimalism to the extreme in 1998, on the Oscar red carpet, wearing a severe up-do and plain-Jane strapless sheath adorned with … nothing, she plunged a stiletto into the heart of the jewelry market. What Gable did to undershirts and JFK to hats, Hunt did to jewelry that year, for nary a Harry Winston bauble nor Swarovski bib chilled her collarbone. (And if that wasn't bad enough, the costume-jewelry industry was already reeling, both from Chinese imports, and the American woman's sudden passion for beading jewelry – herself.) It was a far cry from the Eighties, when being heavily jeweled in either rhinestones or the real thing was pretty much de riguer. Resale prices then were stratospheric, with visitors from Germany and Japan only too happy to shell out boatloads of marks and yen from coast to coast. That was pre-Internet, so eager buyers were live and in person.

Compare the Hunt red-carpet incident with the more verdant pasture of 2009, when best-actress nominee Angelina Jolie arrived on the red carpet not only adorned with Brad Pitt, but the most sensational 65-carat Colombian emerald cocktail ring and 115-carat emerald earrings anyone had ever seen. Wealthy women might have lusted after the real thing, but the gorgeous greenery was also wanted by the Everywoman, so faceted glass was just fine.

Or, take the 20-million-plus viewers who tuned in to American Idol twice each week: they saw not only the brutal Brit's trademark T-shirt, but also judge Paula Abdul, drenched in jewels under an intense and loving spotlight. All that glitter was mesmerizing … and memorable. So we wanted some of it.

The tenor of the times affects jewelry trends, too, and sometimes those trends then evolve and harden. A preference on the part of collectors for signed jewelry (or at least jewelry with rock-solid, unimpeachable provenance if unsigned), might have started out as "signature snobbery" in the Eighties, but evolved to a form of self-protection by the end of the first decade of the 21st century. Collectors reasoned (or rationalized, if they felt guilt over their expenditures) that to recoup their money, or to know they were leaving something of real value as an inheritance, jewelry had to be connected to a name, and preferably a hot one. Jewelry lovers increasingly set out with rigorous determination to avoid anything merely beautiful or interesting. The economic downturn of 2009 made pure aesthetics seem an unaffordable luxury. Generally, goods had to be liquid to be any "good," and resale-ability was in a name. For example, one expert in Mexican silver mentioned even the most exquisitely made vintage pieces were almost impossible to sell if unmarked.

As recovery restores faith in investing, the final effect of the "panic" will be fascinating to study. Will Americans behave as our Depression-deflated ancestors did, socking money away and spending conservatively, or – after the deep and dismal recession, when all that virtual money was there one day and gone the next – will we crave more personal control over our earnings and even set out to enjoy what we have? If the latter, then Americans may catch up with Europeans, who are more likely with intention to include collectibles in their personal portfolios than we are. Obama of America spends his extracurricular energies on basketball; Sarkozy of France collects stamps. As noted in the London Evening Times, antiques and collectibles are part of the investment portfolio of many young British professionals: "One in six said they collected just as an investment. Eleven percent thought collections were as good an investment as stocks and bonds …" They said even if they didn't know how much they'd make, they felt confident they wouldn't lose money. Digging up antique gold and gemstones is a lot more fun than purchase orders for pharmaceuticals.

Jewelry is desirable for three reasons, and that won't change.

1. We buy for style's sake, to accessorize our fashions. When you're wearing something wonderful but want punctuation, a brilliantly designed $9.99 Deco ring at T.J. Maxx that resembles a Raymond Templier masterpiece is impossible to pass up.

2. Or we buy to wear and also purchase with an eye toward investment or resale. Before we plunk down $900 on an Iradj Moini moth brooch to make everyone envious at an elegant soiree, we want to be certain it will be worth more in a decade or hold its value (= forced savings) in the nearer future.

3. Or we buy purely as investment. Maybe you never wear necklaces, but recognize the value of a Sixties KJL creation that's dripping emerald pendants and just happens to close around the throat.

Jewelry also has some inherent qualities that assure an eternal sunshine of the golden kind, making it a reliable collecting destination where no one need be afraid of protracted darkness. An anagram is handy to help jewelry lovers remember why it's always OK to love and continue looking for more lariats and lavalieres:

(With a nod to Emeril): BAM!

B is for beauty. Jewelry is one of a limited group of collecting categories that has a two-way aesthetic. It, itself, is beautiful, yes, but also adds to the beauty and status of the wearer. Compare that with, say, guns and dolls. No one's toting his Derringers to a party to impress girls, and if you bring your baby Bru to brunch at the café, the stares won't be in admiration. Shimmering crystals glinting on a wrist or dangling from an earlobe, however, transfix and distract the gazes of onlookers and make them imagine you're even more beautiful than you are. Never underestimate the power of anything so pretty. Jewelry's got it, so jewelry's not going away.

A is for availability. (Ubiquity might be a better word, but it makes a bad anagram.) A character in Larry McMurtry's novel Cadillac Jack says, "Anything can be anywhere." That's true, but it's truest for costume jewelry. It's literally all over the place. Stop at any roadside retail dive connected to a filling station along a country highway … and you'll not only find vintage bracelets or brooches, but it's possible to discover a treasure – anywhere. A related "A" might be ad infinitum: there appears to be no end to the variety of this widely available commodity. About what other collectible object can you say: If you

Courtesy Janet Romanchik collection; photograph by Ann M. Pitman

Brooch, polychrome rhinestones, 1960s, unmarked DeLizza and Elster "Juliana" jewelry (verified), 2" x 2". **$150-$200**

look for it on any given day, you'll find something you've never seen before? That allure is almost electrifying.

M is for money. Costume jewelry can be acquired cheaply and some of it sold bullishly. It may take longer to turn a $1,000 profit on a $100 investment than it is to turn $3 into $30, but profit's definitely part of the picture, and that's useful for many more people than take advantage of it. Adolescents to octogenarians should develop a working knowledge of costume jewelry because it absolutely can help pay their bills, whether collegiate or pharmaceutical. The rap on costume jewelry is, unlike gold or precious gems, it has no inherent value. Detractors consider costume nothing short of fool's gold, and many view it as throwing money away on faddish junk. While they admit some costume jewelry possesses tremendous artistry and design integrity, they say it's in the eye of the beholder, so any given piece's appeal is less broad and its investment value less liquid. But very little money is required for entrée into the market for a new collector, and since costume jewelry sells regularly for hundreds and thousands of dollars, it's quite clear people consider it much more than base metal and glass.

S is for size. (Make that anagram "BAMS".) Jewelry's size is a huge factor in its appeal. Consider guns and dolls again. How much space does it take to house a hundred Winchester rifles … or Madame Alexanders? Collectors require major storage space for many categories. But 1,000 pieces of jewelry fit perfectly into a chest of drawers, manageable even for apartment dwellers. The psychological well-being of a collector is something else that should never be under-considered, so the feeling of not being burdened or over-crowded gives a lift to tender psyches rather than bringing on major depression in the face of cramped space.

For its beauty and value, jewelry bestows a great measure of joy on its wearers and bearers. Or, as I put it on T-shirts for a bijou bunch, "Life is cruel; buy jewels."

JEWELRY STYLES

Jewelry has been a part of every culture throughout time. It is often reflective of the times, as well as social and aesthetic movements, with each piece telling its own story through hidden clues that, when interpreted, will help solve the mysteries surrounding them. Jewelry is generally divided into periods and styles. Each period may have several styles, with some of the same styles and types of jewelry being made in both precious and non-precious materials. Additionally, there are recurring style revivals, which are interpretations of an earlier period. For example, the Egyptian Revival that took place in the early and late 1800s, and then again in the 1920s.

All jewelry in this year's edition comes courtesy *Warman's Jewelry 4th Edition* by Kathy Flood.

Georgian, 1760-1837. Fine jewelry from this period is quite desirable, but few good-quality pieces have found their way to auction in recent years. Sadly, much jewelry from this period has been lost.

Victorian, 1837-1901. Queen Victoria of England ascended the throne in 1837 and remained queen until her death in 1901. The Victorian period is a long and prolific one; abundant with many styles of jewelry. It warrants being divided into three sub-periods: Early or Romantic period dating from 1837-1860; Mid or Grand period dating from 1860-1880; and Late or Aesthetic period dating from 1880-1901.

Sentiment and romance were significant factors in Victorian jewelry. Often, jewelry and clothing represented love and affection, with symbolic motifs such as hearts, crosses, hands, flowers, anchors, doves, crowns, knots, stars, thistles, wheat, garlands, horseshoes and moons. The materials of the time were also abundant and varied. They included silver, gold, diamonds, onyx, glass, cameo, paste, carnelian, agate, coral, amber, garnet, emeralds, opals, pearls, peridot (a green gemstone), rubies, sapphires, marcasites, cut steel, enameling, tortoise shell, topaz, turquoise, bog oak, ivory, jet, hair, gutta percha and vulcanite.

Sentiments of love were often expressed in miniatures. Sometimes they were representative of deceased loved ones, but often the miniatures were of the living. Occasionally, the miniatures depicted landscapes, cherubs or religious themes.

Hair jewelry was a popular expression of love and sentiment. The hair of a loved one was placed in a special compartment in a brooch or a locket, or used to form a picture under a glass compartment. Later in the mid-19th century, pieces of jewelry were made completely of woven hair. Individual strands of hair would be woven together to create necklaces, watch chains, brooches, earrings and rings.

In 1861, Queen Victoria's husband, Prince Albert, died. The queen went into mourning for the rest of her life, and Victoria required that the royal court wear black. This atmosphere spread to the populace and created a demand for mourning jewelry.

Mourning jewelry is typically black. When it first came into fashion, it was made from jet, fossilized wood. By 1850, there were dozens of English workshops making jet brooches, lockets, bracelets and necklaces. As the supply of jet dwindled, other materials were used such as vulcanite, gutta percha, bog oak and French jet.

By the 1880s, the somber mourning jewelry was losing popularity. Fashions had changed and the clothing was simpler and had an air of delicacy. The Industrial Revolution, which had begun in the early part of the century, was now in full swing and machine-manufactured jewelry was affordable to the working class.

Edwardian, 1890-1920. The Edwardian period takes its name England's King Edward VII. Though he ascended the throne in 1901, he and his wife, Alexandria of Denmark, exerted influence over the period before and after his ascension. The 1890s was known as La Belle Epoque. This was a time known for ostentation and extravagance. As the years passed, jewelry became simpler and smaller. Instead of wearing one large brooch, women were often found wearing several small lapel pins.

Photo courtesy Alderfer Auction & Appraisal, Hatfield, Pa.; www.AlderferAuction.com

Swan pearl and enamel pendant, W. Bauscher, 14k gold, handmade pendant, Mabé pearl and enamel, 3", gold weight 11.3 grams. **$380**

In the early 1900s, platinum, diamonds and pearls were prevalent in the jewelry of the wealthy, while paste was being used by the masses to imitate the real thing. The styles were reminiscent of the neo-classical and rococo motifs. The jewelry was lacy and ornate, feminine and delicate.

Arts & Crafts, 1890-1920. The Arts & Crafts movement was focused on artisans and craftsmanship. There was a simplification of form where the material was secondary to the design. Guilds of artisans banded together. Some jewelry was mass-produced, but the most highly prized examples of this period are handmade and signed by their makers. The pieces were simple and at times abstract. They could be hammered, patinated and acid etched. Common materials were brass, bronze, copper, silver, blister pearls, freshwater pearls, turquoise, agate, opals, moonstones, coral, horn, ivory, base metals, amber, cabachon-cut garnets and amethysts.

Art Nouveau, 1895-1910. In 1895, Samuel Bing opened a shop called "Maison de lArt Nouveau" at 22 Rue de Provence in Paris. Art Nouveau designs in the jewelry were characterized by a sensuality that took on the forms of the female figure, butterflies, dragonflies, peacocks, snakes, wasps, swans, bats, orchids, irises and other exotic flowers. The lines used whiplash curves to create a feeling of lushness and opulence.

1920s-1930s. Costume jewelry began its steady ascent to popularity in the 1920s. Since it was relatively inexpensive to produce, there was mass production. The sizes and designs of the jewelry varied. Often, it was worn a few times, disposed of and then replaced with a new piece. It was thought of as expendable, a cheap throwaway to dress up an outfit. Costume jewelry became so popular that it was sold in both the upscale stores and the "five and dime."

During the 1920s, fashions were often accompanied by jewelry that drew on the Art Deco movement, which got its beginning in Paris at the "Exposition Internationale des Arts Décoratifs et Industriels Modernes" held in 1925. The idea behind this movement was that form follows function. The style was characterized by simple, straight, clean lines, stylized motifs and geometric shapes. Favored materials included chrome, rhodium, pot metal, glass, rhinestones, Bakelite and celluloid.

One designer who played an important role was Coco Chanel. Though previously reserved for evening wear, Chanel wore it during the day, making it fashionable for millions of other women to do so, too.

With the 1930s came the Depression and the advent of World War II. Perhaps in response to the gloom, designers began using enameling and brightly colored rhinestones to create whimsical birds, flowers, circus animals, bows, dogs and just about every other figural form imaginable.

Retro Modern, 1939-1950. Other jewelry designs of the 1940s were big and bold. Retro Modern had a more substantial feel to it and designers began using larger stones to enhance the dramatic pieces. The jewelry was stylized and exaggerated. Common motifs included flowing

Jewelry courtesy Didier Antiques, London; image by Adam Wide

Art Nouveau bat ring, 14k gold, circa 1900, J.F. Chatellier, New York. **$9,200**

scrolls, bows, ribbons, birds, animals, snakes, flowers and knots.

Sterling silver now became the metal of choice, often dipped in a gold wash known as vermeil.

Designers often incorporated patriotic themes of American flags, the V-sign, Uncle Sam's hat, airplanes, anchors and eagles.

Post-War Modern, 1945-1965. This was a movement that emphasized the artistic approach to jewelry making. It is also referred to as Mid-Century Modern. This approach was occurring at a time when the Beat Generation was prevalent. These avant-garde designers created jewelry that was handcrafted to illustrate the artist's own concepts and ideas. The materials often used were sterling, gold, copper, brass, enamel, cabochons, wood, quartz and amber.

1950s-1960s. The 1950s saw the rise of jewelry that was made purely of rhinestones: necklaces, bracelets, earrings and pins.

The focus of the early 1960s was on clean lines: pillbox hats and A-line dresses with short jackets were a mainstay for the conservative woman. The large, bold rhinestone pieces were no longer the must-have accessory. They were now replaced with smaller, more delicate gold-tone metal and faux pearls with only a hint of rhinestones.

At the other end of the spectrum was psychedelic-colored clothing, Nehru jackets, thigh-high miniskirts and go-go boots. These clothes were accessorized with beads, large metal pendants and occasionally big, bold rhinestones. By the late 1960s, there was a movement back to mother nature and the "hippie" look was born. Ethnic clothing, tie dye, long skirts, fringe and jeans were the prevalent style and the rhinestone had, for the most part, been left behind.

Mexican Silver, 1930-1970. Mexican silversmiths first made jewelry for tourists. The jewelry had pre-Hispanic and traditional Mexican motifs as well as some abstract modern designs. Artisans used silver, a combination of silver with brass or copper, alpaca, amethysts, malachite, obsidian, sodalite, tiger eye, turquoise, abalone, ebony, rosewood and enameling to create their original designs. While hundreds of artists set up their shops in the town of Taxco, Mexico, in the 30s and 40s creating a silversmith guild, there are only a relatively small number of well-known artisans who gained their reputation for their designs and craftsmanship.

Multi-Stone, diamond, Keshi pearl, gold enhancer-necklace, the ornately decorated enhancer features an oval-shaped pink tourmaline cabochon weighing 15.00 carats, enhanced by full-cut diamonds weighing a total of 2.10 carats, accented by a pear-shaped aquamarine weighing 11.30 carats, further enhanced by an oval-shaped ruby cabochon weighing 2.65 carats, further accented by baguette-cut sapphires weighing a total of 6.15 carats, set in 18k yellow gold. The pendant suspends from a necklace composed of Keshi pearls, forming 50 unknotted strands, completed by an 18k yellow gold clasp, accented by full-cut diamonds. Marked "S" for H. Stern. Gross weight 95.80 grams. Enhancer dimensions: 3 1/4" x 1 1/4", necklace 20". **$5,377**

Onyx, cultured pearl, gold brooch, features an oval-shaped onyx cameo, depicting a lady's profile, framed by cultured pearls, set in 14k yellow gold, completed by a pin stem and catch mechanism on the reverse, 1 3/4" x 1 1/2". **$717**

Natural pearl, diamond, white gold necklace, composed of pearls, ranging in size from 6.00 to 4.00mm, forming a single knotted strand, completed by a barrel clasp, featuring rose-cut diamonds, pavé set in 18k white gold, accented by mine-cut diamonds, 65". **$10,755**

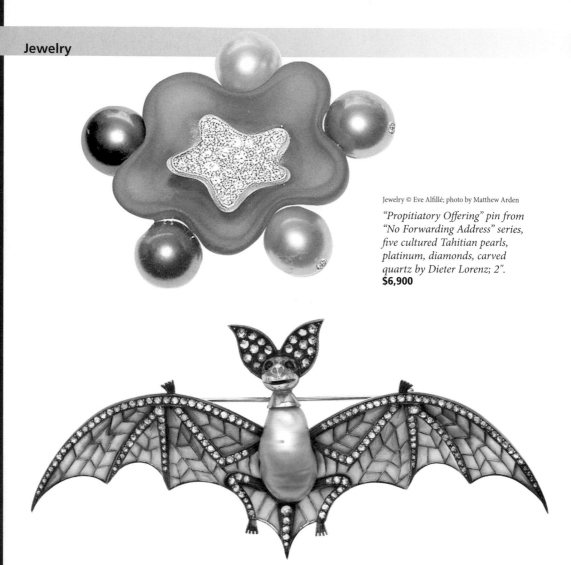

Jewelry © Eve Alfillé; photo by Matthew Arden

"Propitiatory Offering" pin from "No Forwarding Address" series, five cultured Tahitian pearls, platinum, diamonds, carved quartz by Dieter Lorenz; 2". **$6,900**

Photo courtesy Heritage Auction Galleries, Dallas; www.HA.com

South Seas cultured pearl, diamond, ruby, enamel, silver-topped gold brooch designed as a bat, features a South Seas cultured pearl measuring 21.00 x 12.00mm, highlighted by rose-cut diamonds, enhanced by ruby cabochon eyes, accented by plique-à-jour enamel, applied on silver-topped 18k yellow gold, completed by a pin stem and catch on the reverse, 4 1/4" x 2". **$3,585**

Courtesy Milky Way Jewels; Rocky Day photo

Walter Lampl jadeite brooch, 10k yellow gold, transitional styling combines elements of Edwardian and Art Deco design; apple-green oval-shaped jadeite cabochon of exceptional quality, marked W.L. and 10k, 1 3/4", 1925. **$340**

Jewelry courtesy Mason-Kay, Inc., image Zalephoto.com, L.A.

Ring, ice jade cabochon, 1/2", with citrine side stones, 18k white gold. **$2,250**

Jewelry courtesy Betty Ma; photo by John Acorda

Animal bracelet, two dragon heads, white mutton-fat nephrite jade bangle, nine carved balls as tails, mouths hold pearl; very rare; 2 1/2" diameter, 19th century.

Jewelry courtesy Mason-Kay, Inc., image Zalephoto.com, L.A.

Jade ring, two 1/3" pear-shape fine red jade cabochons, 18k white gold, .26 carats diamonds. **$2,950**

Jewelry courtesy Mason-Kay, Inc., image Zalephoto.com, L.A.

Necklace of fine lavender 1/2" jadeite beads. **$19,500**

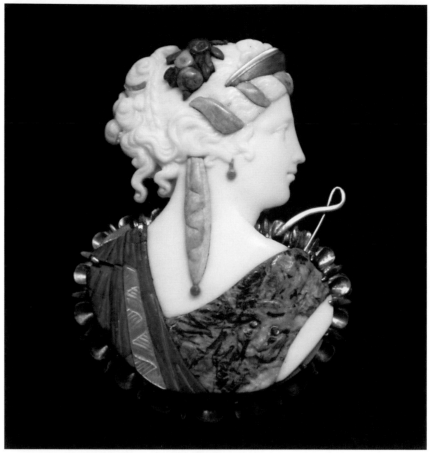

Jewelry courtesy Camelot Cameos and Antiques; photo by Kerry Davidson

Rare antique Commesso cameo of mythological goddess; using shell, coral, malachite, mother of pearl and mottled agate, incorporating multiple attributes of mythological goddesses, as well as Maenad (bacchante maiden). Base cameo is shell, different colored stones applied, exhibiting attributes of four different mythological figures, all rolled into one: fruits or flowers in hair associated with Flora; crown associated with Hera; animal pelt associated with Omphale or maenads; bow associated with Diana; 14k gold mount; Italian, circa 1870, 2 1/4". **$2,500**

Cameo courtesy Aesthetic Engineering Fine Jewels and Antiques; photo by Jacquelyn Babush

Cameo, "The Cupids Seller," lava carving with pierce work, 14k gold setting, 4 1/2", circa 1850 (with contemporary gold setting). **$2,800**

Jewelry courtesy Camelot Cameos and Antiques; photo by Kerry Davidson

Large hardstone cameo of Cupid (Eros) walking with a lion. This cameo is taken from a set of four bas-reliefs by Bertel Thorvaldsen depicting love's power over the elements. It shows love's power over the earth (represented by the lion). Rare subject, Italian, circa 1860, 18k gold and pearl pendant/brooch frame, carved in high relief, 2 1/2". **$6,500**

Photo courtesy Skinner Inc., Boston; www.SkinnerInc.com

Cameo, sardonyx and amethyst brooch, early 19th century, the work of Roman master Domenico Calabresi. In three layers, depicting Mars in a chariot drawn by two horses, with images of warring figures driven over clouds, the stone was set within a frame of circular-cut amethysts and purple rhinestones, all in 14k gold and silver mount, signed "(C)ALABRE(SI)". Damaged, loss of parts of the artist's signature. **$13,035.**

Jewelry courtesy CameoHeaven.com; photo by Jan Campbell

Cameo brooch, 1920s Flapper with her equine companion, carnelian helmet shell, 4-point diamond necklace set en habille, silver filigree, 1920, 1 1/2". **$1,595**

"Egret" locket, sterling silver, gold fill, rainbow moonstone and ancient mammoth ivory egret, designer Satya Linak, 2005, signed Zealandia Designs. **$285**

Photo courtesy Casco; www.cascosrl.it

Medusa cameo pendant brooch, hand-carved Mediterranean red coral (Corallium Rubrum), 18k yellow gold, 1 5/8", 1985, signed CP for carver Carlo Parlati II. **$2,400**

Jewelry courtesy Didier Antiques London; image by Adam Wide

W.S. Hadaway enamel on silver ship pendant, 2" drop, circa 1900, English. **$7,465**

Black hairwork set, necklace and bracelet, horsehair, metal charms (bracelet charm missing), unmarked, 15" and 7", 1880s-1900. **$400-$550 set**

Victorian mourning brooch, antique jet, varied shapes (diamonds, ovals, rounds), English, unmarked, 4", late 1800s. **$350**

Jewelry and image courtesy Linda Lombardo, Worn to Perfection on Ruby Lane

Hinged brass bracelet painted black with low-carat gold inlay, 1880s. **$150**

Jewelry and image courtesy Linda Lombardo, Worn to Perfection on Ruby Lane

Sash pin with large amethyst colored glass, circa 1900, 2 1/2". **$95**

Jewelry courtesy the Steve Fishbach Collection; photo by Linda Lombardo

European miniature portrait painting on enamel pin, circa 1880s, 18k gallery with diamonds, 1 5/8". **$2,500**

Art Deco gem-set devant de corsage, Boucheron, Paris, centering diamond-set scrolls among cabochon coral, lapis and jadeite leaves, 11.05 carats diamonds, platinum, palladium; 18k gold mount. Maison Boucheron was a major contributor toward the success of the 1925 Exposition Universelle, the defining event of the Art Deco period. **$189,600**

Art Deco guitar pendant necklace, rock crystal, labradorite and gold, suspending ribbed 18k rose gold guitar set with central frosted rock crystal tubular panel, black enamel trim to cylindrical labradorite, black enamel and 18k white gold base, 18k white gold brick link top; double-strand black silk cord, circa 1925, 25", adjustable; French assay marks and partial maker's mark, signed Gérard Sandoz. **$134,500**

Bracelet, diamond and ruby bangle, 18-karat yellow gold, six round old mine-cut diamonds (3.00 ct.), twelve 4.00 mm x 3.00 mm oval rubies, 63.2 grams. **$5,148**

© Christie's Images Ltd. 2009

Art Deco style figural brooch, sapphire, diamond and ruby squatting lion with sapphire cabochon head, collet-set diamond eyes and mouth, sculpted platinum whiskers extending a sculpted gold mane to circular single-cut diamond and calibré-cut sapphire body; mounted in platinum and gold, circa 1957, signed Yard (for Raymond Yard). **$43,750**

Art Deco brooch, triple-curtain chain fringe, varied-size crystal rose-cut rhinestones, antiqued-gold-finish base metal, filigree work, 3 1/4", 1940, signed Lidz Bros. N.Y. **$150**

Art Deco potted plant pendant necklace, copy of an original in diamonds, rubies, topaz and enamels, this of silver-plated metal, rhinestones, enameling and glass, calibré cuts in necklace, pendant 4", necklace 15", 1991, signed Art Deco 89, B325. **$750**

Courtesy GreatVintageJewelry.com; photo by Veronica McCullough

Modern cloisonné pendant, unusual geometric design with vibrant pearlescent metallic enamels trimmed in gold-plated metal, 1970s, unsigned, 2 1/2". **$75-$100**

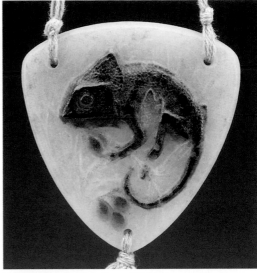

Photo courtesy James D. Julia Auctioneers, Fairfield, Maine; www.JuliaAuctions.com

Pendant, A. Walter Pate De Verre Iguana. Triangular-shaped butterscotch pendant features an iguana with green spots perched on a berry branch. Signed "AW" above its head. Pendant is suspended from a soft orange tasseled cord. Pendant is 2 1/2" w. **$1,150**

Courtesy GreatVintageJewelry.com; photo by Veronica McCullough

Vintage peacock pin, 1940-1950s, silver pot metal with glossy peacock-color enamels and faceted Marcasites. Unsigned, 2 3/8" x 5/8". **$85-$110**

Jewelry courtesy Barbara Wood, bwoodantique.
com; photos by Mary Cochran and Barbara
Wood

*Red-yellow bangle, unusual,
one of a kind, slices of
transparent red Bakelite
laminated into yellow squares,
also with apple-juice Bakelite;
1" wall, 1990s, signed Shultz.*
$1,200

*Bangle bracelet, four-color
laminate in Bakelite bangle
measuring 7/8" high, unsigned,
1930s.* **$450**

*Rainbow bangle bracelet, one of
a kind, multicolor (bright red,
clear, orange, apple juice) slices
of Bakelite, 1 1/4", chunky,
1990s, signed Shultz.* **$900**

Stacks of PVC tube bangle bracelets, multicolor with gold and silver trim, 2009, signed Petra Meiren. **$36-$49 each**

Jewelry courtesy Niki-Boden.com

Beetle brooch, synthetic material composite, iridescent foil, rhinestones, pearls, signed Niki Boden, 2000s, 3". **$75-$88**

Jewelry courtesy Past Perfection Vintage Costume Jewelry, PastPerfection.com

Dragon bracelet, heavy, ornate, with paneled box-link construction, fierce Asian dragon central motif of bone or ivory; accented with semi-precious stones; German attribution; 6 3/4" with 2 3/8" wall. **$500**

*Salvador Teran
Bracelet, sterling
silver, 7", hallmarked,
2" links, 83.6 grams.*
$650

*Evald Nielsen canoeist
silver brooch circa
1940s, 2 1/2", Danish.*
$1,120

*Silver fringe necklace by Alexander
Calder (1898-1976), untitled, hammered
silver on hemp cord, twisted silver bands
supporting a continuous fringe of stylized
silver musical notes; wedding gift to Mrs.
William B.F. Drew in 1940 from her
husband, who was best man and lifelong
friend of Calder; 1940, 20 1/2".* **$170,500**

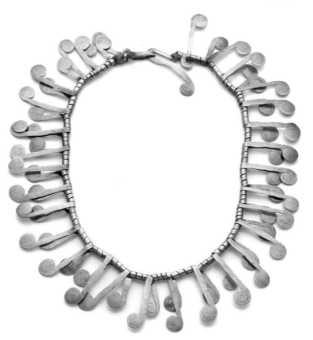

Photos courtesy Ann M. Pitman, insidethe-jewelrybox.com

Above: Trifari bracelet with aquamarine glass stones and chaton, tapered baguette and baguette clear stones, 7 1/2" x 1/2", marked with the crown Trifari mark. **$295-$350**

Left: Nearly life-size grapes bunch pin with beaded flowers and leaves, 5 1/2" x 3 1/2", by Ian Gielar for Stanley Hagler, with both applied tags. **$650 -$750**

Photos courtesy Ann M. Pitman, insidethe-jewelrybox.com

Below: Butler & Wilson rhinestone fruit clamper bracelet with tiny gold bee by the orange strawberry, signed inside the back of the apple. Bracelet is 1 1/2" tall. **$250-$300**

Jewelry courtesy Janet Romanchik; photo courtesy Ann M. Pitman

DeLizza & Elster show-stopping bracelet with heliotrope stones, from the early 1960s. **$400-$500**

Jewelry courtesy Nakamol Chicago,
nakamolchicago.com

*Vines couture necklace, coral and
leather, rhodium wire frame, 18",
N with Heart logo, 2009.* **$269**

Jewelry courtesy ValerieG.com; photo by Michael Gedziun

Belt buckle in Art Nouveau-style by Gripoix for Yves Saint Laurent couture show, paté de verre and 22k gold. One-of-a-kind creation, purchased from private collection of Madame Gripoix; 10", 1980s. **$2,500**

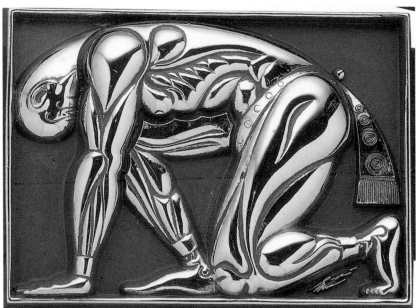

Photo courtesy Four Seasons Design Group, naturesmuseumstore.com

Art Deco Sampson and Delilah belt buckle, based on Erté's theatre design from the Famous Heroines act in 1926's George White's Scandals, later the Folies Bergére; finally made as a serigraph with embossing and foil stamping in 1980, then recreated as a buckle; handmade in America; silver, signed Erté, 1981, 2 3/4". **$350**

Jewelry courtesy ValerieG.com; photo by Michael Gedziun

Parrot trembler, riot of color featuring hand-soldered red, blue, green and yellow rhinestones on antiqued silver setting; wing trembles; feathers fringed; 2007, signed Bettina Von Walhof, 8 1/4". **$850**

Jewelry courtesy HeavenlyTreasures.com

Owl ring with golden mother of pearl crescent moon, 18k rose gold, 1.46 carat weight in 82 full-cut black diamonds, nine round white diamonds totaling .06 carats, 4mm pink tourmaline eyes totaling .57 carats, additional champagne diamonds on side of band, 7/8". **$1,995**

JUDAICA

Judaica is any object or text used to practice and observe Jewish commandments or traditions, or celebrate and portray its customs, philosophy and way of life.

All photos are courtesy Skinner Inc., Boston; www.SkinnerInc.com.

Silver and silver-gilt synagogue Ark-form Hanukkah lamp, Brody, dated 1787, with later duty stamp circa 1809-10, ark-form back plate with shell crest, over an upper panel with elaborate scrollwork, birds, and foliage, and a shelf supporting ewer for oil, all above a central panel flanked by twisted columns, the lower section formed as a shelf with eight dolphin-form oil lamps fronted by scrollwork and Hanukkah scene, 18 1/4". Note: Following the Eastern European style of ornate wooden Torah arks, elaborately carved and decorated to hold Torah scrolls, this form of lamp is characterized by bold scrollwork and vines, birds, and animals such as herons, squirrels and dolphins. Lamps of this elaborate and intricate form are particular to the region of Galicia. Shell crest is bent, it is lacking the two servant lamps, there is a crack between two of the silver dolphin-form fonts, the applied detail is lifted slightly in areas from the back plate, minor loss to the lower right of bottom crest. **$314,000**

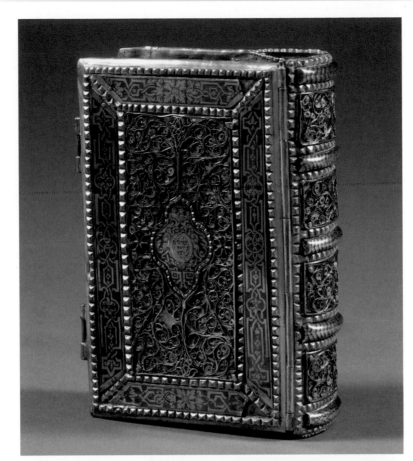

Galician silver, silver-gilt, filigree, and niello book binding, Krackow, early 19th century, tax stamp for Lwow (Lemberg), 1810-1824, rectangular form with applied niello (a black metallic alloy of sulfur, copper, silver and usually lead, used as an inlay on engraved metal) panels, filigree, enamelwork, and a cartouche inscribed in Hebrew, filigree hasps, (areas of loss to filigree, enamel loss, damages), 5 3/4". **$18,960**

Austro-Hungarian silver Etrog box, Vienna, dated 1831, rectangular form with hinged lid finely chased with flowers and foliage, concave body on molded base with anthemion and leaf-tip decoration, 5 3/4" long. **$889**

Top left: Bronze Judenstern hanging lamp, 19th century, turned support with star-form lamp above a drip-pan, with ratchet support (repaired), 22" overall. **$652**

Above: Early bronze Shabbat lamp, probably Germany, 17th century, star form with circular rimmed drip pan, 8". **$2,489**

Left: Russian silver sunflower-form spice container, Vilnius, circa 1865, maker's mark rubbed, formed as a flower head on a naturalistically cast stem with leaves, domed spreading circular foot, (minor losses), 8 1/2". **$13,035**

Russian silver presentation purse, Moscow, 1908-17, rectangular, lid applied with a rose-gold plaque engraved in Yiddish, with Art Nouveau engraved flower stems, underside engraved with names, and dated 1912, with green stone cabochon latch, link chain handle, purse 4 1/2" long. **$474**

Large Capo di Monte porcelain Passover Seder plate, Italy, 20th century, white ground embossed, transfer and hand painted with relevant scenes and Hebrew inscription, centered with a Star Of David, (small rim chip), 14 3/4". **$474**

Small Polish silver and silver-gilt Torah breastplate, apparently unmarked but dated 1756, arched form with crown suspending tassels over an ark enclosing the tablets, flanked by "jewel" mounted columns, with an inscribed and dated pendant, (wear, losses), 10 1/4". **$11,850**

Silver-gilt Torah breastplate, attributed to Georg Kahlert the Younger (active 1732-1773), Breslau, marked to perimeter with Russian "kokoshnik" mark 1896-1917, and Cyrillic maker's mark, arched form with the figures of Moses and Aaron flanking the tablets, within borders of stylized banding and foliage, the base with naturalistic detail and cartouches inscribed in Hebrew, (extensive repairs), 16". **$50,363**

Polish silver Torah crown, probably circa 1840, bearing only French swan import mark, openwork design of staves heavily cast and chased, and mounted throughout with stags, lions, birds, fruit and flowers, bells suspended from leaf tip, engraved townscapes to top, (losses), 13 1/4". **$65,175**

LIGHTING

Also see Modernism, Oriental, Tiffany.

Photo courtesy Jeffrey S. Evans & Associates, Mt. Crawford, Va.; www.jeffreysevans.com

Pair of pressed Loop/Leaf stand lamps in medium golden amber, each dome-top six-loop font featuring a lower double step and knop extension, raised on an octagonal baluster-form standard and square base, wafer construction. Pewter fine-line collars. Boston & Sandwich Glass Co. and possibly others, 1840-1860, 9 3/4", one with a minute flake to one loop and a shallow chip to the top edge of base, second with two light flakes to loops, a shallow chip to one upper base corner, and a chip/open bubble combination to the lower edge of base, both collars with a dent. **$6,900 pair**

Photo courtesy Jeffrey S. Evans & Associates, Mt. Crawford, Va.; www.jeffreysevans.com

*Pressed hexagonal candlestick in yellow amber and fiery opalescent, heavy urn-form socket with a pewter insert, raised on a knopped stem above a hexagonal standard terminating in a circular foot, waferless two-part construction. Probably Pittsburgh, 1850-1870, 9 1/2",
chip to a corner of the upper standard where the two halves are joined, likely occurred during manufacturing.* **$4,312**

Pressed Petal and Loop candlesticks in apple green, each six-petal socket with a hexagonal extension, raised on a hexagonal knop and seven-loop circular base with rough pontil mark, wafer construction. Boston & Sandwich Glass Co, 1840-1860, 7", each with a minor chip under the base, one with a fire-polished manufacturing chip under one socket petal and a small flake to the stem platform, the other with several minor flakes to the stem platform. **$4,887**

New England Glass Co. apple-form whimsy "sparking" lamp, deep rose to bright yellow, on a colorless circular base, original pewter collar and single-tube burner with cap and chain, 1850-1900, 4 3/4", ghost-like annealing crack under the base that does have depth but does not break the surface. This undoubtedly occurred when the apple and base were joined. (Small oil lamps were used in the 1800s to set the duration of a gentleman caller's visit. When the "sparking" lamp went out, so did he.) **$460**

Photo courtesy Jeffrey S. Evans & Associates,
Mt. Crawford, Va.; www.jeffreysevans.com

Rare free-blown and pressed whale oil lamp, sapphire blue and colorless, urn-shape font with later collar, applied with an annular wafer to a three-step circular standard and square foot with extended round corners, outer edges of foot with eight vertical ribs between each corner, base interior with prisms and a rough pontil mark. Boston & Sandwich Glass Co. and possibly others, 1830-1840, 7", single chip to the top of one base corner and a minor flake to another. **$3,105**

Photo courtesy Jeffrey S. Evans & Associates, Mt. Crawford, Va.; www.jeffreysevans.com

Rare pressed Acanthus Leaf fluid stand lamp, translucent jade green above alabaster/clambroth with a lightly sanded surface to base, dome-top font with 12 protruding petals below the shoulder and a short hexagonal extension with 12 beads below, raised on a 12-petal-top acanthus leaf standard and double-step square base beaded between the steps, wafer construction, brass fine-line collar. Boston & Sandwich Glass Co. and others, 1840-1860, 12 1/2", small professional restoration to one base corner. **$805**

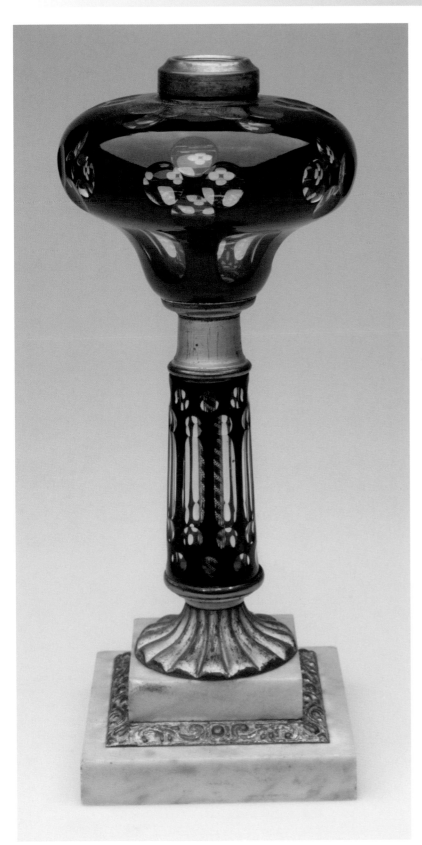

Photo courtesy Jeffrey S. Evans & Associates, Mt. Crawford, Va.; www.jeffreysevans.com

Rare cut overlay quatrefoil kerosene stand lamp, deep ruby cut to colorless squat inverted pyriform font with ovals cut on lower half, raised on a cobalt blue cut to colorless standard and a two-step marble base, the brass mounts retain much of their original gilding, no. 2 brass fine-line collar. Boston & Sandwich Glass Co., 1860-1880, 13", font shows some abrasions to lower ovals, base with a chip to one corner of marble. **$2,070**

Photo courtesy Jeffrey S. Evans & Associates, Mt. Crawford, Va.;
www.jeffreysevans.com

Rare pressed four-Printie Block whale oil or fluid stand lamp, amethyst, dome-top conical font with hexagonal knop extension, raised on a square two-tier monument base, wafer construction, factory polished under base to level, original pewter fine-line collar with a later soldered adapter. Boston & Sandwich Glass Co., 1840-1850, 9 1/2". **$2,185**

Photo courtesy Jeffrey S. Evans & Associates, Mt. Crawford, Va.; www.jeffreysevans.com

Pressed-loop whale oil or fluid stand lamps, brilliant sapphire blue, each featuring a dome-top six-loop font with lower extension, raised on an octagonal baluster-form standard and square base, original pewter fine-line collars. Probably Boston & Sandwich Glass Co., 1840-1860, 9 1/2", one with a chip to the side of one upper loop and marring to mouth of collar. **$1,840 pair**

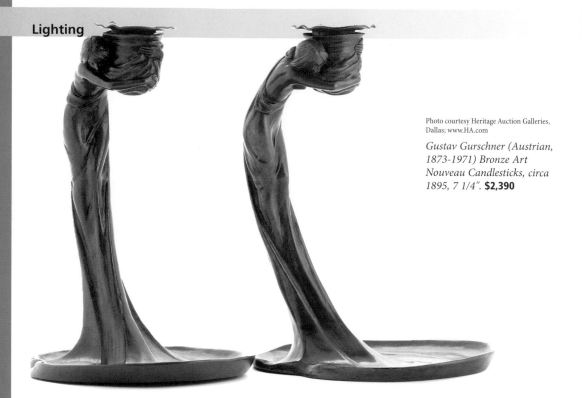

Gustav Gurschner (Austrian, 1873-1971) Bronze Art Nouveau Candlesticks, circa 1895, 7 1/4". **$2,390**

Duffner & Kimberly Peony Table Lamp. With red peony blossoms surrounding the entire bottom two-thirds of the shade. The upper third is done with a cream, yellow and tan background glass and the peony leaves are done in a bluish-green mottled glass (second view). The shade rests on a large bronze base with stylized leaves surrounding the foot and adorning the stem. The lamp is finished with a four-socket cluster and original Duffner heat cap with heart cutouts. The base is finished with a brown patina with strong green overtones. Shade is 24 1/2" diameter. Overall 32" h. A few tight hairlines. Base has some replacement socket parts. **$57,500**

Photo courtesy James D. Julia Auctioneers, Fairfield, Maine; www.JamesDJulia.com

Pairpoint Puffy Azalea Table Lamp. The stamens are an earthen color against the yellow centers (second view). The background is painted in a variety of greens. The shade is supported by a silver-plated base having three Art Nouveau stylized arms that support the ring, a single socket and a simple center shaft flowing into a padded bulbous base with four applied feet. Shade is signed on the exterior rim "The Pairpoint Corp July 9 1907". Base is signed "Pairpoint Mfg Co", a "P" in a diamond and "3033". Shade is 10" diameter. Overall 21" h. Minor wear to silver plate on base. **$17,250**

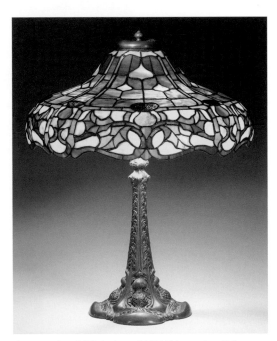

Photo courtesy James D. Julia Auctioneers, Fairfield, Maine; www.JamesDJulia.com

Duffner & Kimberly Thistle Table Lamp. Shade begins with striated earthen-hued geometric panels accented by green teardrops in the upper portion of the shade with purple textured glass accented in yellow, turquoise and blue glass on the apron. Irregular bordered shade is supported by a three-socket thistle base in high relief. Shade is 19" diameter. Overall 24" h. A few tight hairlines. **$10,350**

Daum Nancy Cameo Glass Night Light. Cameo cut-back shade of grapes and grape leaves in earthen hues on an orange to yellow mottled ground. The shade is supported by a wrought-iron base with complimentary berries and leaves. Shade is signed on the side in cameo "Daum Nancy" with Cross of Lorraine. 6 1/2" h. **$1,560**

Steuben Deco Luminaire Panel. Deeply impressed with figure of nude woman picking grapes. The grapevine and grapes extend around the outside edge of the panel. The panel is done in a rich green glass. The panel is housed in a contemporary oak table frame for display. Unsigned. Panel is 9" x 9 1/4". Overall in frame 11 1/2" h. Minor roughness to back edge. **$1,150**

Handel Cattail Table Lamp. With eight textured caramel-glass panels that are decorated with metal overlay design of cattails and foliage in green and brown. Shade is supported by a simple three-socket Handel Art Nouveau base. Overall chocolate brown patina finish. Shade is signed "Handel" on the ring and base is signed with a Handel cloth tag. Shade is 20" diameter. Overall 22" h. **$8,775**

Handel Treasure Island Table Lamp. Dome-shaped shade reverse painted with a decoration of palm trees, ocean and sailing ships against a moon-lit bay. The colors used are predominantly blues, greens and subtle earthen hues. Shade is signed "Handel 6391" on interior as well as "Handel Lamps" on the ring. Shade rests on a bronzed inverted trumpet-style, three-socket base complete with three acorn pull chains having brown patina. Shade is 18" diameter. **$14,400**

Photo courtesy James D. Julia Auctioneers, Fairfield, Maine; www.JamesDJulia.com

Handel Blue Chinese Pheasant Table Lamp. Shade has two Chinese pheasants painted in vibrant oranges, yellows, mauve, green and gray with minute detailing given to every aspect of the bird. The birds are set against a royal-blue background with green vertical stripes that represent the stylized foliage. Also decorating the shade are flowers painted in various shades of pink with yellow foliage and buds. The shade is completed with areas of gray and white to give it a three-dimensional effect. The shade is supported by a three-socket base with two gargoyle heads supporting rings. The shade rests atop an original Handel three-legged base with stylized leaf design at the termination of each leg. Base is finished with an original Handel heat cap with square cutout design and three-socket cluster. Shade is signed "Handel Lamps" on the aperture ring and is signed "Handel 2175 PAL" on the interior rim. Base is unsigned. Shade is 18" diameter. Overall 24" h. Minor blistering to finish on base. **$27,600**

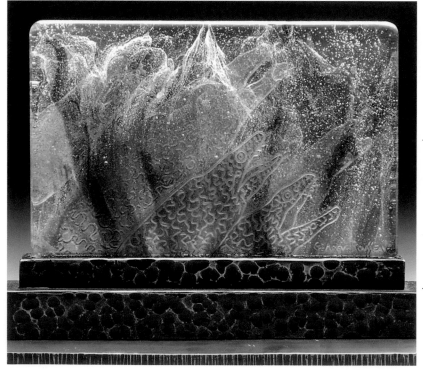

Photo courtesy James D. Julia Auctioneers, Fairfield, Maine; www.JamesDJulia.com

G. Argy Rousseau Luminaire. Depicts eel heads impressed into the luminaire panel on both front and back giving a three-dimensional feel to the luminaire. The glass panel has wispy colors of purple, pink and maroon against a clear background. The panel rests in original hammered metal stand with lighted interior. Panel is signed on the front "G. Argy-Rousseau France". Overall 9 1/4" w x 7" h. **$9,660**

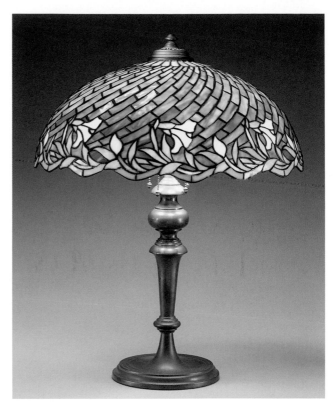

*Wilkinson Swirling Daffodil Table Lamp. Fully
leaded table lamp has a border of realistic
daffodils created in lemon yellow with green
foliage and border glass of tan. This decoration
is set against a swirl-effect leaded background
in amethyst glass that was a favorite of the
Wilkinson Company. This irregular-bordered
shade is supported by a four-socket base with
four acorn pulls. Base has an antique brass
finish and appears to be all original. Shade
is 20" diameter. Overall 26" h. Some tight
hairlines. Base has minor wear to patina.*
$11,500

*Gorham Leaded Table Lamp. Leaded shade
has rich red poppies extending around the
entire shade (second view). Butterflies in flight
surround the shoulder of the massive shade.
The shade rests on a bronze base with raised
poppy design in high relief at the four feet. The
bulging stem is also decorated with high-relief
poppies on two sides and butterflies on the other
two sides. The riser supports a large six-socket
cluster. The base is finished in a green patina.
Shade is 25" diameter. Overall 30" h. minor
wear to patina on base.* **$47,150**

Photo courtesy James D. Julia Auctioneers, Fairfield, Maine; www.JamesDJulia.com

Pairpoint Puffy Apple Tree Lamp. Background of rich green leaves with bluish highlights with pink apple blossoms surrounding green and red apples. The shade is further highlighted with a cluster of three bumblebees on one side and two butterflies on the opposing side. The shade rests on a Pairpoint tree-trunk base with four-arm spider and double-socket cluster. Shade is unsigned. Base is signed on underside "Pairpoint Mfg. Co." with a "P" inside a diamond and "3091". Shade is 16" diameter at the widest. Overall 21" t. **$32,200**

Photo courtesy James D. Julia Auctioneers, Fairfield, Maine; www.JamesDJulia.com

Photo courtesy James D. Julia Auctioneers, Fairfield, Maine; www.JamesDJulia.com

Decorated Webb Burmese Miniature Lamp. Peach-pink shading to yellow with enamel decoration including a branch with a bird. The base with peach to pink shading to yellow having an enamel decoration of flowering branches. Base is marked on the underside "Thos. Webb & Sons Queens Burmese Ware Patent". Foreign burner. 8 1/2" h. **$2,300**

Rainbow Cut-Glass Mini Lamp. SII-547. Strawberry pattern, yellow and pink coloring. Applied silver band with four ball feet around the base of the lamp. Hinks burner with signed "Hinks" chimney. 9 1/2" h. There are two minor imperfections in the cut design on the base, also one small imperfection in the cut on the shade. **$9,775**

Photo courtesy James D. Julia Auctioneers, Fairfield, Maine; www.JamesDJulia.com

Steuben Florentia Luminor. Paperweight design with green Florentia floral pattern on the interior with clear glass paperweight exterior with controlled-bubble decoration. The Florentia ball rests upon original Luminor base of black glass with round opening at the top exposing the bulb. 4 3/4" sq. Overall 7" t. **$2,645**

Photo courtesy James D. Julia Auctioneers, Fairfield, Maine; www.JamesDJulia.com

Miniature Hanging Lamp. SII-381. Brass frame and chain with side arms depicting birds sitting on tree branches. Removable font marked "LP Lamp Co Sample" and "83" in the center. Green transparent prisms. Cosmos pattern clear glass shade flashed green. Acorn burner. Overall 12" l. **$1,840**

Photo courtesy Rago Arts and Auction Center, Lambertville, N.J.; www.RagoArts.com

Shade, Handel, leaded glass with dogwood design and a graded checkered design on top. Marked Handel on inside of shade, 9" x 18 1/2" d. **$2,520**

Photo courtesy James D. Julia Auctioneers, Fairfield, Maine; www.JamesDJulia.com

Quezal Art Glass Shade. Snake skin dark green decorated shade with platinum iridescence. Unlined interior. Signed on the fitter rim with early engraved "Quezal" signature. 6 3/4" diameter. Minor wear to gold iridescence. **$3,600**

Photo courtesy James D. Julia Auctioneers, Fairfield, Maine; www.JamesDJulia.com

Steuben Art Glass Shade. Gold iridescent hearts and vines decoration on indigo blue iridescent background, with applied gold iridescent border. The shade has metal fitter. Unsigned. 10" diameter. **$4,600**

Quezal Art Glass Shade. Platinum pulled-feather decoration on dark green striped ground, gold iridescent interior. Early engraved signature "Quezal" on the fitter rim. 5" t x 2 1/4" fitter. **$1,610**

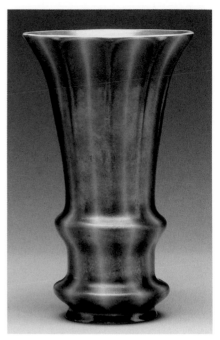

Durand Art Glass Shade. Oversized green optic ribbed art glass shade has unusual shape of elongated trumpet form decorated with gold interior and exterior having blue and pink highlights. 10" t with 3" fitter. **$1,092**

Decorated Bulb Shade. Clear glass form bulbs out to the end where it is decorated with a green pulled-feather pattern with gold trim on an ivory ground. The shade is completed with a metal collar. This style of shade is considered to be from the transitional period and is a rarity to still find. 6" t x 1 1/2" fitter. **$402**

MAPS

Throughout the ages, pictorial maps have been used to show the industries of a city, the attractions of a tourist town, the history of a region or its holy shrines. Ancient artifacts suggest that pictorial mapping has been around since recorded history began. "Here be dragons" is a mapping phrase used to denote dangerous or unexplored territories, in imitation of the medieval practice of putting sea serpents and other mythological creatures in blank areas of maps.

All photos courtesy Swann Auction Galleries, New York; www.SwannGalleries.com

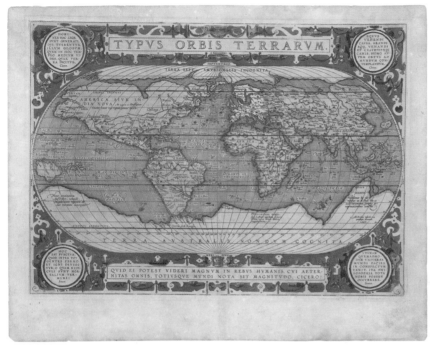

Abraham Ortelius, "Typus Orbis Terrarum," Antwerp, 1587. Double-page engraved world map, 14 3/8" x 19 1/2", wide margins, Latin text on reverse, hand-colored, mildly but evenly toned, some soiling in margins. **$3,800**

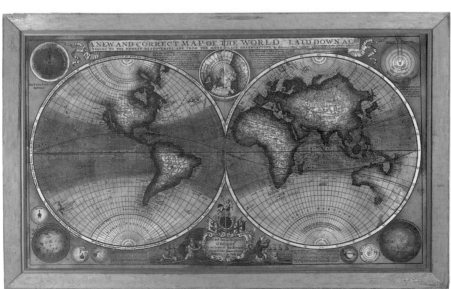

World map on glass by Herman Moll, 19th century, "A New and Correct Map of the World," double hemispheric, 22 1/2" x 38 1/2" sight size, vintage frame. A true curiosity, the process used for applying the map image to the glass is unclear. It may be some type of reverse painting technique. It is brightly colored and appears to have been created from 2 plates (?), as there is a central vertical line similar to the usual centerfold on double-page maps. The back of the glass is a patchwork of various applied colors. **$1,700**

Johann Baptist Homann, Kleiner Atlas Scholasticus. Nuremberg, circa 1725, 17 (of 18) hand-colored map sheets, lacking the map of Hungary/Greece (no. 17). Folio, 21 1/4" x 13 3/8", damp staining in lower corners throughout, heavier on the earlier maps, with some bleeding a short distance into the image, 5" tear on map of the Americas, chip along right edge of map of Russia, side margins trimmed close, other small scattered faults. **$3,400 set**

Willem and Jan Blaeu, "Terra Sancta quae en Sacris Terra Promissionis olim Palestina," Amsterdam, 1629, double-page engraved map, 15 1/8" x 19 7/8", wide margins, French text on reverse. **$700**

Cornelis Danckerts, "Insulae Americanae," Amsterdam, circa 1640, double-page engraved map, 19 7/8" x 23 1/4", ample margins. **$600**

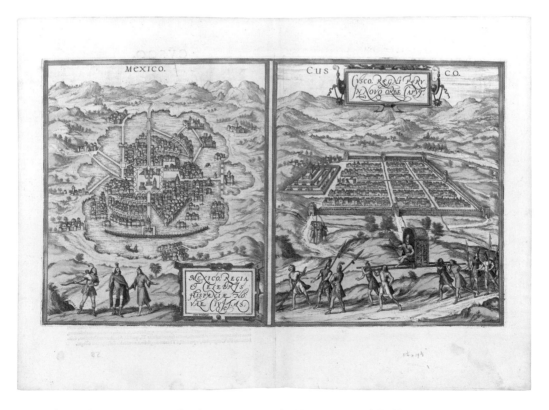

Braun and Hogenberg, "Mexico/Cusco," Cologne, circa 1572, double-page engraved double-image map, 10 7/8" x 19", wide margins, Latin text on reverse, matted. **$1,400**

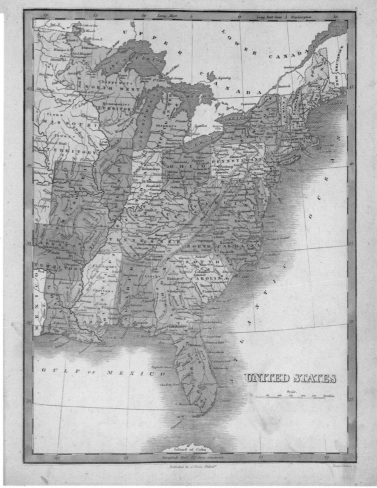

Anthony Finley, "A New General Atlas," Philadelphia, 1836, engraved title, 60 hand-colored engraved maps, colored table, and colored chart of mountains. Small folio, later buckram; lower corner of title chipped, scattered small tears and marginal chips, touching plate mark on several but away from images on all, scattered marginal staining. **$2,600 set**

Tobias Conrad Lotter, "Pensylvania Nova Jersey et Nova York," Augsburg, 1750, double-page engraved map, 23 1/4" x 19 7/8", wide margins, hand-colored and in outline; 7/8" piece lacking in right margin just above fold, inked note beneath the lower plate mark stating that the map was purchased in Munich in August 1933, some browning along fold; matted. **$900**

Modernism

Furniture

All photos are courtesy Rago Arts and Auction Center, Lambertville, N.J.; www.RagoArts.com.

Paul Evans, rare Skyline series sculpted steel and bronze dining table with octagonal plate glass top, 1970, signed "Paul Evans 70", base 42" x 42". **$32,940**

Paul Evans, sculpted bronze disc bar with interior cabinet, drawer and locking door, 1969, signed "PE 69", 72" x 72" x 19". **$15,860**

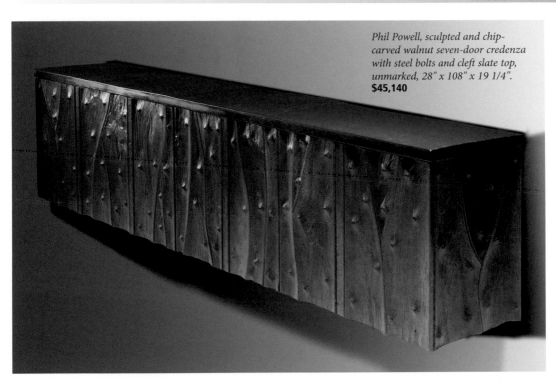

Phil Powell, sculpted and chip-carved walnut seven-door credenza with steel bolts and cleft slate top, unmarked, 28" x 108" x 19 1/4". **$45,140**

Vladimir Kagan, pair of barrel chairs with painted wood legs, unmarked, 31" x 30" x 36". **$6,100 pair**

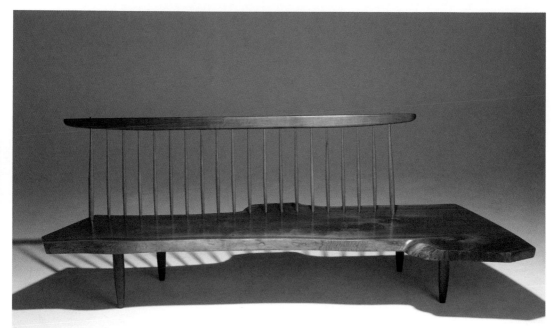

George Nakashima, figured walnut Conoid bench with hickory spindles, unmarked, 30" x 83" x 39". **$21,960**

George Nakashima, walnut Conoid dining table with four rosewood keys on book-matched top, signed with client's name, 28 3/4" x 46 1/2" x 72". **$25,620**

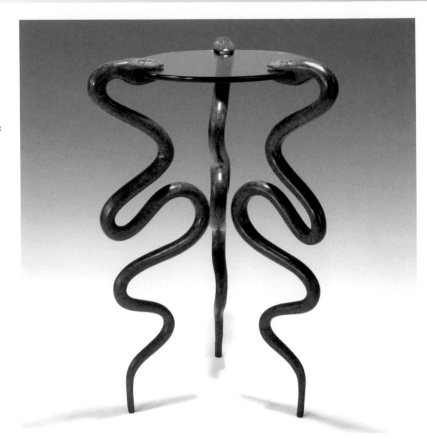

Judy Kensley McKie,
patinated bronze and glass
Serpent side table, 1997,
Inscribed "15 of 16", each
snake engraved "JKM 97"
and copyright, 31" x 21".
$31,720

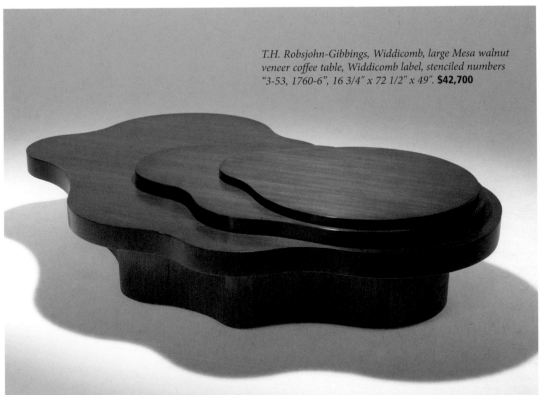

T.H. Robsjohn-Gibbings, Widdicomb, large Mesa walnut
veneer coffee table, Widdicomb label, stenciled numbers
"3-53, 1760-6", 16 3/4" x 72 1/2" x 49". **$42,700**

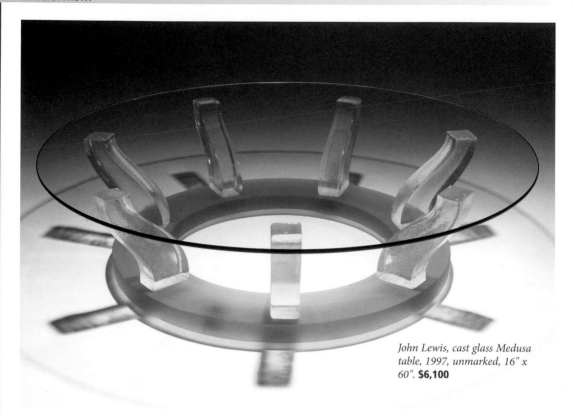

John Lewis, cast glass Medusa table, 1997, unmarked, 16" x 60". **$6,100**

Isamu Noguchi, Herman Miller, rare birch and aluminum Rudder coffee table (no. IN-52), circa 1949, unmarked, 15 1/4" x 50" x 35 1/2". **$7,930**

Osvaldo Borsani, Tecno, P40 lounge chair, marked, 31" x 27 3/4" x 58". **$2,928**

Charles and Ray Eames, Evans Plywood, Herman Miller, walnut LCW chair, late 1940s, remnants of an Evans Plywood Co. label, 26 1/4" x 22" x 23 1/2". **$1,586**

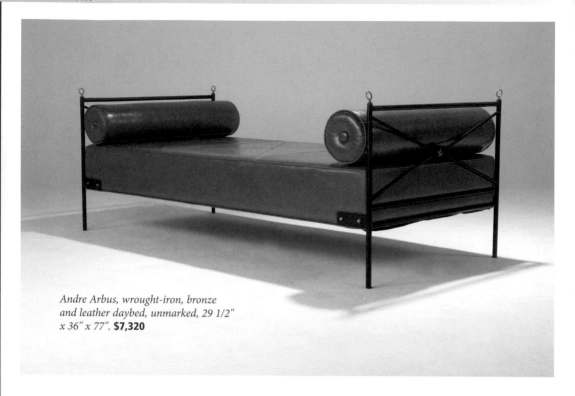

Andre Arbus, wrought-iron, bronze and leather daybed, unmarked, 29 1/2" x 36" x 77". **$7,320**

Alexander Calder, Bon-Art, cotton hammock, "Sun," signed "75 CA" and label on back, No. 3 of 100, 128" long. **$3,965**

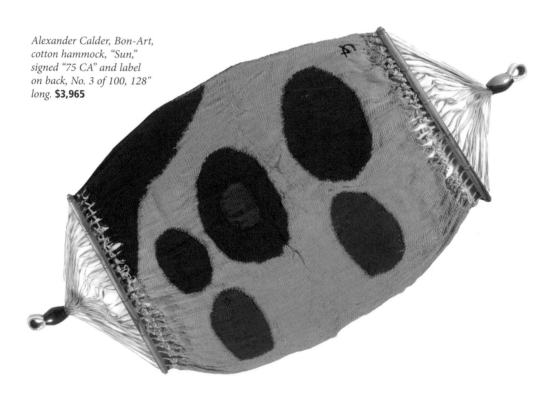

Wharton Esherick, cherry sheet-music stand, 1962, carved "WE 1962", 43 1/2" x 19 1/2" x 20 1/2". (An identical example is owned by the Metropolitan Museum of Art, New York.) **$48,800**

Alexander Calder, Bon-Art, maguey fiber tapestry, "# 9," 1974, Bon-Art label, woven "CA 74" and numbered 81 of 100 with copyright, 55 1/2" x 84". **$6,100**

Pedro Friedeberg, acrylic, pen and ink and carved wood wall relief sculpture, ink signature, 30" x 30" x 1". **$17,080**

Harry Bertoia, stainless steel Willow sculpture, unmarked, 45" x 11" square base.
$40,260

Josef Hoffman, Wiener Werkstatte, important brass on hammered copper vase, stamped "JH, MADE IN AUSTRIA", and "WIENER WERKSTATTE", 6 3/4" x 11 1/2".
$21,960

George Nelson, Howard Miller, large walnut "Spike" clock, Howard Miller label, 30" diameter. **$732**

Ignazio Gardella (attributed), Azucena (Italy), pair of brushed and enameled steel sconces, circa 1960, unmarked, each 17 1/4" x 13" x 6". **$1,098 pair**

Oriental

Chinese porcelain moon flask, late 19th/early 20th century, both sides of the flattened body painted with landscape reserves in bright enamels, the surrounding yellow ground of lotus blossoms and scrolling tendrils, a pair of zoomorphs applied to the shoulder, an apocryphal Jiaqing mark on the recessed base, 10 1/2". (Zoomorphism is the shaping of something in animal form or terms.) **$200**

All photos courtesy Clars Auction Gallery, Oakland, Calif.; www.Clars.com.

Below: Pair of Chinese polychrome enameled porcelain ovoid urns with covers, 20th century, the sharply tapering body finely painted in black and brightly colored enamels with two large figural reserves separated by fan- and leaf-form panels of foliage or scholar's objects, all on a dense spiral ground with stylized flowering tendrils above lappets encircling the flaring foot, the high shoulder with small reserves of further scholar's objects, the base with an apocryphal Kangxi mark, the high domical lids with a bud finial and decorated en suite, 15 1/2". **$425**

Chinese gilt and cloisonné enamel-decorated tripod censer, early 20th century, the globular body decorated with stylized lotus and scrolling tendrils on a turquoise ground and applied with a pair of gilt animal-mask and loose ring handles, further animal masks fronting the splayed supports, a gilt repoussé band of jeweled lappets encircling the waisted neck below the high reticulated domical lid with a fu-lion finial and decorated en suite (some repairs), 7 1/4". **$1,000**

Chinese large bronze tripod censer with silver inlay, of compressed globular form resting on three short cabriole-shaped supports and decorated with silver wire inlay of scholar's objects together with ribbon-tied flowers and auspicious emblems, further inlay on the wide everted rim surmounted by a pair of sinuous chilong-form (hornless dragon) handles (wear), 9 3/4" diameter. **$950**

Chinese jade (nephrite) inlaid hardwood table screen, the celadon-green jade plaque carved in high relief with a bodhisattva seated in royal ease clutching a ruyi scepter silhouetted against an incised ground with the russet skin incorporated as the sides of the cave, all framed by a tendril-pierced wood frame set above a free-standing base similarly decorated; jade, 4 1/4"; overall 13 3/4". **$650**

Japanese ivory and patinated bronze figure, Meiji period, featuring a Japanese farm girl seated next to her carrying basket with back straps, the ivory head well carved with demure features picked out with black and colored pigment and framed by a coiffure covered by a patterned scarf, further ivory employed for the hands and feet, the body and basket and base of dark patinated bronze, 5 3/4" x 7". **$250**

Left: Unframed Japanese woodblock print, by Utagawa Hiroshige (1797-1858), series Gojusan-tsugi meisho zue (Illustrations of the "Fifty-Three Stations, Famous Places"), known as the Tokaido tate-e edition, titled Sakanoshita (#49), signed Hiroshige-ga, with aratame and date seal (1855) and mark of the publisher Tsutaya (some toning, slightly soiled), 14 1/2" x 9 1/2". **$250**

Below: Japanese woodblock print album entitled "Suehiro Gojusan-tsugi" (Fan Tokaido), featuring 52 stations along the Tokaido road (missing Hodogaya #5) bracketed by Tokyo and Kyoto, each with aratame/date seal (1865) and publisher cartouche, the complete prints by Yoshitoshi (15), Hiroshige (10), Kuniteru (10), Sadahide (12), Yoshiiku (3), Kunisada II (3) and Kunichika (1), generally very good impressions and color, slight toning, a few stained/soiled; brocade cover worn, 14 1/4" x 9 1/2" each print. **$4,750 set**

Chinese gray pottery figure of a horse, Han Dynasty (206 BC-220 AD), the noble steed standing foursquare with head erect (restorations), with Plexiglas case, 11" horse. **$800**

Chinese jade carving of a Bactrian camel, fashioned with its long limbs tucked under its body with two small humps, the face framed by a long mane, the matrix of celadon hue with the skin incorporated into the carving, 3 3/4". **$120**

Sino-Tibetan gilt and copper-alloy figure of Vasudhara (the Buddhist bodhisattva of wealth, prosperity and abundance), 18th/19th century, the six-armed female tantric deity seated lalitasana (royal pose) with her right foot supported on a kalasa (water pot or jug) issuing from the lotus pedestal, one hand in the gift-granting gesture (varada mudra), the other displaying various attributes, the finely cast gilt face with an elaborate diadem fronting a tall chignon surmounted by a half-vajra (a ritual object), with silver accents (wear, resealed), 7 1/4". **$500**

Chinese Canton enamel-decorated snuff bottle, the double-conjoined body painted with reserves of children at play framed by a red ground with floral sprigs, the base bears mark "Qianlong nian zhi", 2 3/4". **$60**

Japanese Imari charger, the interior well centered by a kirin (a mythical beast) in shades of cobalt blue surrounded by polychrome enamel-painted bird-and-flower reserves alternating with abstract geometric panels, the rim with a narrow floral and geometric-patterned band, 16" diameter. **$90**

Japanese tinted ivory okimono of an elderly samurai, 20th century, standing in formal kami-shimo costume (a type of formal clothing) with brown-pigment enhanced pattern and holding a katana (long sword) in his right hand, a wakazashi (short sword) secured in his belt, signed Hozan (some losses), 6". **$300**

Chinese ivory vase, 20th century, of rouleau (small roll) form with a thick rolled rim above a cylindrical body carved with contorted dragons amid stylized clouds bounded by lappet bands, all supported on a foliate-accented pedestal base, 9 1/4". **$350**

Teapot, Chinese, "chicken blood" stone, faux bamboo, the rectangular body carved and incised as a bundle of bamboo secured by a twisted rope, a few stalks with leafy twigs, with a faux-bamboo curved spout and opposing loop handle, the fitted lid carved en suite, the bright red matrix with mushroom-colored inclusions, 5". **$450**

Left: Figure, Chinese, ivory carving, Guanyin, Qing Dynasty (1644–1911), portrayed as a beauty clothed in long robed with black-lacquered accents and holding an up-turned amphora to the front, further lacquer accents applied to the elaborate coiffure framing the smiling face (age cracks), with a footed wood stand, 6 1/2" excluding stand. **$650**

Center: Figure, Chinese, ivory carving, early 20th century, depicting a scholar standing in long robes secured by an ornate sash, his right hand suspending a large brush, the right holding a qin to one side of his youthful face framed by an official's cap, with stained accents and together with a tall wood stand carved as cresting waves, 11" excluding stand. **$500**

Right: Figure, Chinese, ivory carving, Qing Dynasty (1644–1911), well carved and incised as "Fu" of the three star immortals standing in long robes with a smiling child holding a peach cradled in his hands to the front, the bearded face with a gentle smile and framed by a soft cloth cap secured by ribbons suspended down the back, together with a carved wooden stand, 9 3/4" excluding stand. **$1,100**

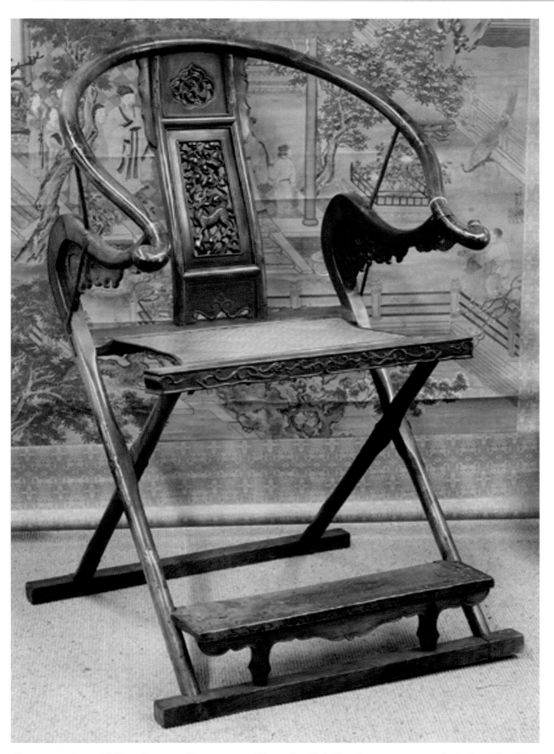

Chinese mixed-wood folding chair, possibly consisting of "huanghuali" (yellow flowering pear wood), the horseshoe form top rail with scroll terminals and suspending a back splat with a dragon in a lobed reserve above a panel reticulated with a double gourd above a majestic Qilin (mythological creature), the woven seat fronted by a beaded edge apron with confronted dragons, all on cross supports joined by metal pivots and with a hinged foot panel to the bottom (repairs), 43 1/2" x 28" x 28". **$4,000**

PERFUME CONTAINERS

The earliest known perfume containers date back more than 4,000 years. Knowledge of perfumery came to Europe as early as the 14th century, due partially to the spread of Islam. The Hungarians introduced the first modern perfume. Made of scented oils blended in an alcohol solution, it was made in 1370 at the command of Queen Elizabeth of Hungary and was known throughout Europe as "Hungary Water." *Also see Tiffany.*

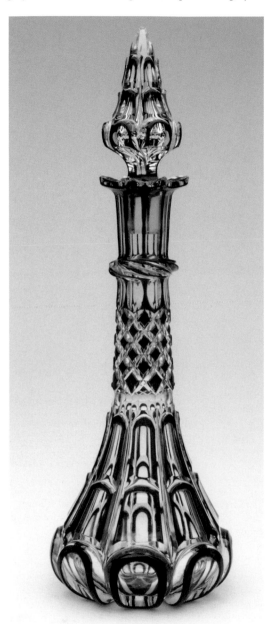

Photo courtesy Jeffrey S. Evans & Associates, Mt. Crawford, Va.; www.jeffreysevans.com

Cut overlay loop and diamond cologne bottle, blue cut to colorless, tall tapering cone form with a swirled neck ring, eight-point mouth, and flashed groove-cut base, original stopper. United States or Europe, 1850-1870, 11 1/2" overall. Bottle with a shallow chip to top of mouth, neck ring with a chip to one swirl, stopper with a flake to one loop. **$402**

Photo courtesy Jeffrey S. Evans & Associates, Mt. Crawford, Va.; www.jeffreysevans.com

Cut overlay flute cologne bottle, blue cut to colorless, compressed globular body with tall panel-cut neck, raised on an octagonal star-cut foot, original stopper numbered to match the bottle. United States or Europe, 1850-1870, 7" overall, minor flake under the foot. **$373**

Photos courtesy Jeffrey S. Evans & Associates, Mt. Crawford, Va.; www.jeffreysevans.com

Top left: Blown-molded, broad-rib cologne bottle, deep amethyst, bulbous bottle with 14 vertical ribs and a polished base, original facetted stopper numbered to match the bottle. United States, probably New England, 1850-1870, 5 3/4" overall. **$546**

Above: Paneled horizontal ovals cologne bottle, electric blue with ghost outlines of original gilt decoration, hexagonal bottle with panel-cut neck, factory polished mouth and base, original hexagonal air-trap stopper numbered to match the bottle. Possibly Boston & Sandwich Glass Co., 1845-1870, 6 3/4" overall, all-over light surface deterioration and interior residue, moderate bruise to stopper extension. **$575**

Left: Star and punty cologne bottle, canary yellow, hexagonal bottle produced from the same mold as the Boston & Sandwich Glass Co. stand lamp font, polished pontil mark, original panel-cut stopper numbered to match the bottle, 1840-1870, 7" overall, minute flake to shoulder ridge and one base point, stopper with numerous chips and flakes to top. **$218**

Photo courtesy Heritage Auction Galleries, Dallas; www.HA.com

English cameo glass scent bottle with silver mounts, attributed to Thomas Webb and Sons, Stourbridge, England, circa 1885, silver mounts by Gorham Manufacturing Co., Providence, R.I., 6", square, with white flora over ruby ground, the screw stopper chased with foliage, internal stopper missing, minor dents to silver top. **$956**

Silver and silver gilt perfume flask, Gorham Manufacturing Co., Providence, R.I., 1871 2 3/4" flask, 2.09 troy ounces. The circular flask with screw-top lid, gilt repoussé floral, insect and butterfly decoration to front on textured ground, side hoops connecting to 20-link chain with suspension loop, minor denting and losses to gilding. **$328**

Silver perfume flask, Gorham Manufacturing Co., Providence, R.I., circa 1875, 2 5/8" flask, 1.00 troy ounce. The egg-form perfume flask with screw-top lid, cast banded decoration and engraved stylized floral decoration on textured ground, side hoops connecting to chain with suspension loop, denting to body. **$328**

Photo courtesy Heritage Auction Galleries, Dallas; www.HA.com

Silver perfume flasks, Tiffany & Co., New York, circa 1890, 7 7/8" x 4 3/4", 27.71 troy ounces. The pair in the Cupids and Flowers or Princess Hatzfeldt pattern, of baluster form with projecting scrolled shoulder and flaring foot with cast and applied wave-and-leaf border, the sides with cast and applied, chased and repoussé groups of cherubs between trophies, the neck with chased and repoussé floral decoration and applied birds, twist-close lid with floral decoration, minor surface scratching, minor denting to lids and bases. **$4,182 pair**

Photo courtesy Heritage Auction Galleries, Dallas; www.HA.com

French art glass fleurette perfumes, René Lalique, Wingen-sur-Moder, France, circa 1912, marked "R. Lalique France" (engraved) and "LALIQUE" (molded) "France" (engraved), 6 1/8" x 3" x 3", with original sepia patina, one stopper frozen with chip to underside. **$537 pair**

Photo courtesy James D. Julia Auctioneers, Fairfield, Maine; www.JuliaAuctions.com

R. Lalique Perfume Bottle. Artichoke design impressed around entire body of the bottle with a matching pressed floral stopper. The bottle is finished in a rich green patination and is double signed on the underside with impressed block letters "R. Lalique France" and engraved script signature "R. Lalique France 515". 3 1/4" h. **$1,140**

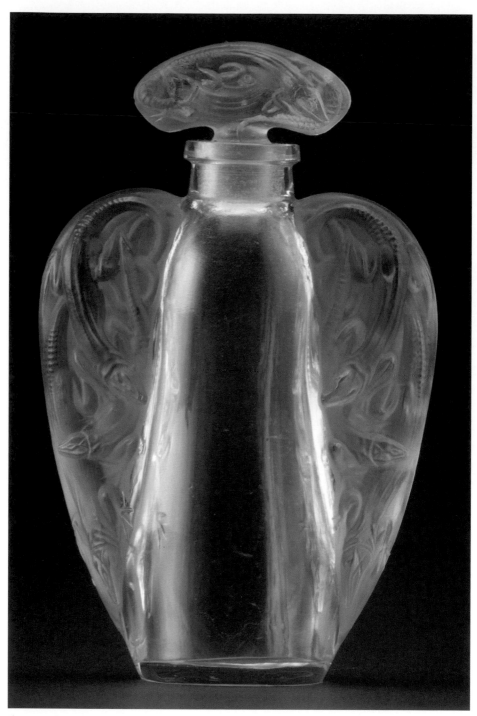

Photo courtesy Heritage Auction Galleries, Dallas; www.HA.com

*R. Lalique, "Lézards" frosted and clear glass perfume bottle, designed 1912, engraved "R. Lalique",
4 1/4".* **$11,950**

Photo courtesy Heritage Auction Galleries, Dallas; www.HA.com

R. Lalique, "Au Coeur des Calices" frosted blue glass perfume bottle (stopper frozen), made for Coty, designed 1913, impressed "Au Coeur des Calices, Coty, LALIQUE", with gold label, 2 1/2". **$7,170**

Photo courtesy Heritage Auction Galleries, Dallas; www.HA.com

R. Lalique, "Pavots d'Argent" glass perfume bottle, created for Roger & Gallet, designed 1927, molded "R. LALIQUE", 3 1/8". **$478**

PHONOGRAPHS

Thomas Alva Edison conceived the principle of recording and reproducing sound between May and July 1877 as a by product of his efforts to play back recorded telegraph messages and to automate speech sounds for transmission by telephone. He announced his invention of the first phonograph, a device for recording and replaying sound, on Nov. 21, 1877. Edison's early phonographs recorded onto a tinfoil sheet cylinder using an up-down motion of the stylus.

All photos are courtesy Skinner Inc., Boston. www.SkinnerInc.com.

Hand-cranked Berliner Gramophone, with 7" turntable, clamp, Clark-Johnson sound box no. J8092, oak traveling arm on turned ebonized pillar, belt drive from celluloid crank-wheel to friction wheel, metal parts with original bronzed finish, oak base stamped "E. Berliner Gramophone" and patent dates from 1887-1895, metal plaque (below) of Berliner Gramophone Co., Philadelphia, straight-flared black horn and leather elbow, base 9 1/2" x 15 1/2", (wear on bronzed finish, later sound box), and Berliner 7" record No. 1731, "She Never Did Anything Twice" by Dan M. Quinn. (Note: This was the first Berliner Gramophone manufactured in America, from late 1894. A smaller model, for 5" records, had been made in Germany as a toy from 1890.) **$9,480**

Disc Graphophone by the Columbia Phonograph Co., New York, oak case with turned quarter columns and maker's decal on front, 6 1/2" turntable, 10" arm and reproducer both with maker's name, hand crank and horn, 8 3/4" x 5".
$474

Century, table model disc phonograph with Century reproducer, made in Utica, N.Y. $50

Child's Genola, "green" phonograph complete with nursery rhyme graphics. $275

Columbia, Graphophone Model BC "20th Century" with 6" mandrel, correct large brass bell horn and floor crane. $1,000

Columbia, Model Q cylinder phonograph with lid and -two color morning glory horn. $300

Columbia, Type "BG" mahogany cylinder phonograph with 6" mandrel, Lyre reproducer and flowered "searchlight" horn. $1,100

Edison, Amberola "Model B-5" cylinder phonograph in mahogany cabinet, SN-638. ....$600

Edison, Diamond Disc "B-150" floor model phonograph in mahogany case, SN-SM387. ....$160

Edison, Fireside (Model A) cylinder phonograph with "H" reproducer, SN-97285. ....$375

Edison, Home cylinder phonograph with "C" reproducer and repeater, with adjustable crane and nickel 11-panel morning glory horn, SN-H232660. ....$1,000

Edison, Standard "four-Latch" cylinder phonograph with "C" reproducer, SN-523477. ....$500

Edison, Standard "Model D" cylinder unit with cygnet horn and "H" reproducer, SN-648826. ....$550

Edison, Standard "Model VIII" cylinder phonograph with black cygnet horn, SN-2166, scarce. $700

Edison, Standard cylinder phonograph with "Combination K" reproducer, crane, crank and flowered morning glory horn, SN-711550D. There is also a celluloid tag on the machine, "Eastern Talking Machine Company, 177 Tremont St., Boston, Massachusetts". $600

Edison, two-latch Standard cylinder phonograph with early Automatic reproducer, SN-S15194. ....$550

Pathé, Model 11I, table model disc phonograph with interior horn, SN-15984. ....$50

Perfektone, floor phonograph with Perfektone reproducer in a Heywood Wakefield wicker cabinet. $550

Standard, Model A table model disc machine with rear mount red morning glory horn and Analyzing reproducer. $350

Standard, Style X table model disc phonograph with front red morning glory horn, complete. $275

Tonalic, Sonora ("Clear As A Bell") floor model phonograph in walnut case. $350

Victor II, "Humpback" disc phonograph with oak replica spear-tip horn made in Michigan. The machine has a Victrola No. 2 reproducer, SN-2565. ....$1,400

Victor III, disc phonograph with red repainted floral morning glory horn, SN-405491C. $550

Victor V, disc phonograph with wooden horn made of Spruce, SN-25994. ....$1,600

Victor XVI, oak case floor model phonograph with gold Victor No. 2 reproducer. The unit has all of the record albums, SN-162764. ....$1,700

Victrola XVII, mahogany disc phonograph with gold Victrola No. 2 reproducer. $600

Victor, "Schoolhouse" VV-XXV disc phonograph with oak wood horn, SN-2716A, lid missing. $1,600

Edison Model B Home Phonograph, H201563, oak case stenciled Edison Home Phonograph with domed lid, single spring, iron bedplate with maker's plaque, gilt lining and signed "Trade Mark Thomas A. Edison", straight horn and crane mount, model C reproducer, crank and approximately 36 brown and black wax cylinders, base 16 1/2" x 9". Phonograph in playing condition, crane mount is modern, many of the cylinders are useable with some mildew. **$533**

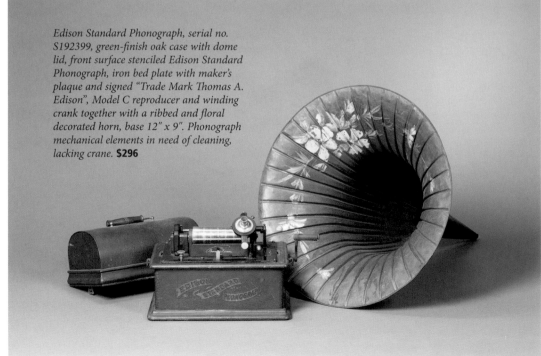

Edison Standard Phonograph, serial no. S192399, green-finish oak case with dome lid, front surface stenciled Edison Standard Phonograph, iron bed plate with maker's plaque and signed "Trade Mark Thomas A. Edison", Model C reproducer and winding crank together with a ribbed and floral decorated horn, base 12" x 9". Phonograph mechanical elements in need of cleaning, lacking crane. **$296**

FUTURE OF THE MARKET: THE AMERICAN SNAPSHOT

Tom Deupree   *Morrow Jones*

By Tom Deupree and Morrow Jones

Have you ever seen baskets of snapshots in an antique mall and wondered why they're there? Your first reaction might be: Who wants someone else's memories? But if you have some time, you might flip through the basket or, if you're lucky, through an entire album that has somehow gotten away from the family that made it. You'll find no end of couples standing on front sidewalks staring at the camera, Halloween costumes, new babies, fishing trophies ...

One picture catches your eye, though. There's a quirky aspect to it. Maybe couples are dancing on a frozen pond. Maybe the women are wearing men's clothes, and the men women's clothes. Maybe the light is unusual or the composition striking. The fact that you have singled out this photo for closer inspection means you may be ready to become a collector.

You would then ask yourself: How are these photos valued? What's a fair price to pay?

The short answer lies in the law of supply and demand, and demand for interesting snapshots has been increasing. Vintage snapshots have become collectible for three reasons. First, even the best pictures are still relatively cheap. Second, the lowly snapshot has been the subject of at least half a dozen critical books and an equal number of museum shows. Third, more people are becoming sophisticated and aggressive in their pursuit of the best examples. And there is almost certainly a fourth reason: As our American lives become more challenging, we become nostalgic for our American past.

Supply is harder to measure. While we collectors bemoan the declining number of good snapshots, growing awareness of the value of the snapshot should mean that many photos once headed for the dump will now find their way to the marketplace.

As you browse for antiques, ask dealers if they ever have any old photographs or photograph albums. The more often that question is asked, the more likely it is that you will be able to build collections.

We are probably looking at three generations here, and the customary thing would be to line them up, step back 10 feet, and shoot. Instead we have a game of checkers, and we immediately get a strong sense of the pleasure the three of them take in the game and in each other's company.

All images courtesy the Jones-Deupree Collection.

Humor is one of the defining qualities in folk art generally, and it shows up frequently in vintage snapshots.

The Place of the Snapshot in the World of Photography

It can be more difficult than you might expect to define the term "snapshot" and, with that definition in mind, to go looking for the kinds of photographs you might collect. Some collectors, gallery owners, and museum curators favor the term "anonymous photographs," a term that doesn't separate everyday snapshots from the work of equally anonymous press photographers and studio photographers. Some use the term "found photographs," and some speak of "vernacular photography."

It might seem reasonable to start by separating the work of amateur photographers from that of professional photographers, but in practice this distinction can be hard to apply. In a practical sense, then, the would-be collector should be prepared to cast a wide net, should be willing to look over any and all old pictures dealers may have in their shops or their booths. They should also be willing to range freely over the categories eBay has created for auctions of photographic images. (We'll return to the subject of eBay later in this article.)

If you find that you're struck as much by formal portraits from the later 19th century as you are by deckle-edged, drug-store prints from the period 1920-1960, you should pursue both. What matters, what makes this whole undertaking worthwhile, is the moment when you find an old picture that speaks to you, stirs a memory, opens your eyes, makes you laugh, or breaks your heart.

The broad outlines of the history of photography are well known to many people, but a quick refresher course won't be out of place here. We live in a culture of photographic images, so much so that we tend to forget that until about 150 years ago, only the wealthy could surround themselves with images — painted images, in this case — of themselves, their family members and their surroundings. The invention of photography in the early 1800s would ultimately permit ordinary people to make their own pictures, but not immediately. In its infancy, the new medium was dominated by professionals who had the technical skills, the resources and the stamina to set themselves up as photographers.

By the 1890s, with the introduction of the ready-to-use Kodak, amateurs with no special training and no commercial aspirations could take photographs. The simple box camera, roll film and convenient photo-finishing made photography affordable for the masses. At first thousands, then millions, of people had cameras. As the Kodak ads of the time put it, "You press the button, we do the rest."

For our culture as a whole, the results were profoundly transformational. Democratic technology had opened up for everyone a means of expression and validation once reserved for the few. Photographs in an album or in a box under the bed gave people the means to document their own lives.

Amateur pictures often have an amateurish quality, but the best of them express — without pretense or affectation — feelings that we all recognize. They capture a moment in time or make a comment on the human condition, and the beauty of it is that these amateur photographers, as often as not, didn't anticipate the results they were getting. They just snapped the picture.

But, among all the photos in that basket or album you're leafing through, only a few will stand out. How do you pick out the good ones from the routine ones of dogs doing tricks, Christmas trees and picnics on the beach?

What Makes a Good Snapshot?

If your interest in old pictures is limited to a single subject, you don't actually need to confront the whole question of the cultural and artistic value of casual photographs. You know what you're looking for. We know people who collect in this way, saying: "Find us some birthday cakes, pit bulls, or cigar store Indians and call us. We'll make some money."

There is an active market in topical collecting, but topical photos aren't necessarily good snapshots, and more people are narrowing their searches, not by subject but by qualities in the pictures that are easier to show than they are to explain.

What makes a good snapshot, then? What makes one of these pictures ordinary and the other extraordinary?

There are several qualities to look for in these old pictures, attributes that confer both artistic value and monetary value. First, there's the element of humor, of whimsy. Humor is one of the defining qualities in folk art generally, and it shows up frequently in vintage snapshots.

Second, there's technique. Photographic technique involves framing, composition, the use of light and shadow, and perspective. The best vernacular photos show a technical skill that in many cases must have been as much good luck as good management. Most casual photographers stand too far away from their subjects; some of them manage to decapitate their subjects; many of them fail to notice intruding telephone poles and shadows.

Following some obscure inspiration, though, a few amateur photographers put their cameras and their subjects in exactly the right places. In their pictures the arrangement of lines and shapes is pleasing to the eye, and we realize immediately that this is a pleasure most snapshots don't give.

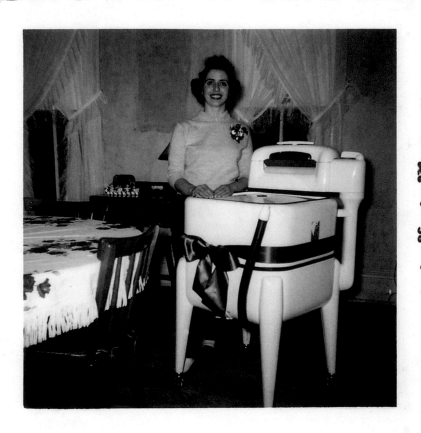

Snapshots may also be statements of the owners' pride in having achieved a certain standard of living, and the box camera gave them a way to express that pride.

At the other extreme there are snapshots in which the technique is so terrible that the pictures take on a certain charm despite the fingertips over the lens. We're now taught never to have our shadows in the picture, yet these folks, freshly armed with early Kodaks, thought so much of their shadowy pictures that they preserved them in albums, the memory being greater than the shot. How revealing is that?

Third, the writing on vintage pictures or the damage they have sustained will sometimes give them an appeal they might otherwise lack. Some photographers — or family members charged with keeping track of family pictures — carefully identified every picture in their albums, but some people wrote right on their prints. Some even did hand coloring. This kind of engagement with the image is fun to see in our tidy digital age.

Fourth, there are old pictures that deliver to us intact an unrehearsed, intimate moment or perception. Most snapshots were taken, and are still taken, of predictable subjects. Most were, and are, set up in predictable ways. The sameness is such that two families might almost exchange photo albums and not know the difference. They'd still be looking at prom dresses, birthday cakes, new cars, sunsets over the lake, and so on.

Subjects not on the standard short list immediately get our attention, especially when they afford us a glimpse into the life and times of the photographer.

In our own searches we've found straight-ahead pictures of cars, radios, television sets, living room sets, and even one washing machine. You might want to categorize such pictures as topical —washing machine collectors? — but the point is that these aren't just pictures of possessions. They're statements of the owners' pride in having achieved a certain standard of living, and the box camera gave them a way to express that pride. We've all felt that way about something, but perhaps we're so used to a surfeit of consumer goods that we've forgotten the perception behind these pictures.

Finally, there's the nostalgia that draws us into old photographs. The long dresses, the touring cars, the wide front porches, the prices on the signs in old lunchrooms, the bicycles with huge front wheels — so much in these images evokes a past that we want to believe in.

But we're responding to more than just the physical details of American life as it used to be. We're seeing and sensing the values of those vanished days, personal and social values. We respond to and collect snapshots that might be seen as making up a kind of collective American family album. They help us understand our past and, therefore, our present. The best old pictures have something to say to us, as well as something to show us.

A photograph is more than visual information. It freezes a moment in time, a glimpse of the way things were, and, we hope, the way things still are. The best of these pictures tell more than a narrow story. They say something about the human condition and life itself. When you can look at a snapshot and say, "I've been there — I know the

There's the nostalgia that draws us into old photographs. The long dresses, the touring cars, the wide front porches, the prices on the signs in old lunchrooms, the bicycles with huge front wheels — so much in these images evokes a past that we want to believe in. As for the budding collector, once you've seen a puppy stuffed in a cowboy boot, there's no turning back.

feeling," you are looking at a photo that is superior to the others in the basket and ought to be preserved.

Reading Snapshots

We don't generally expect snapshots to hold more than personal or family interest. We turn to the snapshots in our photograph albums to confirm — or, at times perhaps, to create — our memories of childhood, of houses and holidays, of aunts and uncles and cousins and classmates not seen for years. We certainly don't expect the discoveries associated with the experience of art, but a few snapshots do, in fact, yield such discoveries — if we look closely.

In the culture of our day, we are surrounded by a superabundance of pictures, most of them taken and published for commercial purposes. There is little novelty in these pictures, and we have grown lazy in our encounters with them.

To make the disclosures vernacular images are capable of making, they deserve more than a cursory glance, more than the second we are apt to give them.

Cautions and Pitfalls for the Snapshot Collector

The first thing to be said under this heading is that Internet auctions like eBay have transformed the collecting of early photographs. Before eBay we simply kept our eyes open in antique shops, antique malls and secondhand stores. Most visits to all three produced nothing. It was a rare dealer who saw the cultural and potential monetary value of old pictures.

As we all know, the quest is part of the fun of collecting, and we wouldn't discourage anyone from pulling off the highway at the next group mall, but while more dealers now have the idea, you shouldn't get your hopes up too high. Even when there are snapshots to look through, there are many more mediocre ones than there are interesting ones. Today, though, without leaving the couch you can browse scores or hundreds or thousands of old photographs.

At any given moment there may be as many as 100,000 listings on eBay under the broad heading of "Photographic Images." Down the left-hand side of that opening page, there are all kinds of ways to narrow the search. You can hope to be more efficient by picking a cutoff date ("pre-1950"), by picking particular subject matter, a price range, a size range, a photographic genre and so on.

The catch is that not all sellers seem to understand or follow these distinctions. You'll have to experiment with search parameters to see what works for you, but don't be surprised if you find snapshots keeping company with newspaper and wire service photos, Hollywood publicity stills, commercial photo postcards, photo negatives, photo booth strips, photogravure, and corporate publicity shots. With a little practice, you'll be able to sort it all out without spending every weekend in front of the computer.

The goal is to build a "watch list" of dealers who sell what you're interested in. Bookmark their sites or add them to your favorites on eBay.

Here are a few general principles to bear in mind:

Some snapshots are quite small, in some cases no bigger than 1" x 1 1/2". It's hard to appreciate the detail in such small images unless they're scanned and enlarged, as they generally are by eBay sellers; it's also hard to display such small images.

Distinguish between vintage prints and modern reprints. (There are online sellers who pirate the images of other sellers and may or may not disclose that their pictures are, in fact, digital copies and not prints from back in the day.)

Don't worry too much about condition. Don't bypass photos that have been written on. It may be the writing that makes them interesting. There are other condition issues — tears, repairs, tape and album paper residue, stains, fading, silvering — that don't really detract from old snapshots as long as the content is still mostly there.

Albums are tempting, but beware. Most times, there are only a few great pictures in a single album. If you are buying albums with the intent to break up and resell, understand the work involved in separating and scanning the individual photos.

Subjects not on the standard short list immediately get our attention, especially when they afford us a glimpse into the life and times of the photographer.

Prices and Resources

Prices are rising as the demand rises, but even the good old snapshots are affordable, especially compared to finds you might make in other fields of collecting. Ordinary subjects done in an ordinary way should cost no more than a couple of dollars; rarer subjects done in an uninspired way should be in the $5-$10 range. A common subject treated more personally and more artistically, but in a small print, gets us to the next level, $5-$20. Common subjects in larger prints are on the next plateau. Unusual subjects treated in a striking way can fetch tens of dollars — or a dollar or two from a dealer who really isn't familiar with the photo market or the qualities that separate the pedestrian from the extraordinary. It's difficult to classify unique objects by price. Some old photographs — Hollywood publicity pictures, for example — were duplicated in quantity, and in such cases you could seek some guidance in auction records, but virtually every snapshot is unique, not necessarily interesting. But unique.

Web Sites

www.vernacular-photography.org

www.squareamerica.com

www.thefoundphoto.com

www.accidentalmysteries.com

There are both physical galleries and online galleries offering vintage snapshots for sale, and in fact, many galleries are as easy to browse online as they would be in person. We highly recommend the Robert Tat Gallery (www.roberttat.com), project b (www.projectb.com), Be-hold (www.be-hold.com/content/HomeFrame.html), and the Fraenkel Gallery (www.fraenkelgallery.com), see "Photographer Unknown".

Using eBay

To get your bearings in the world of eBay vintage photo auctions, we encourage you to consult eBay's collectible photo shopping guides. These guides help to clear up some of the confusion surrounding photo terms and genres, and they give appropriate warnings about reprints that are not identified as reprints. (To find these guides, you'll have to drill down: At the very bottom of any eBay page, you'll find a link to "eBay Reviews;" at the bottom of the right-hand column on "Guides" click on "Collectibles." Once you're there click on "Photographic Images" in the box on the left.)

Obviously, no list of eBay sellers can be anything but highly selective, and such a list may go out of date sooner rather than later. The following are dealers from whom we have bought online or at vintage photography shows or both: ClancysClassics, snapshotmaven, houseofmirth, XPRESSYOURSELF, All-Vintage-Photographs. (These are the dealers' eBay names; to find their stores you have to do an "Advanced Search." Look for the link close to the top of any eBay page; on the Advanced Search page, use the "By Seller" option.)

Suggested Reading

Robert Flynn Johnson, *Anonymous: Enigmatic Images from Unknown Photographers* (2005)

Stacey McCarroll Cutshaw and Ross Barrett, *In the Vernacular: Photography of the Everyday* (2008)

Sarah Greenough, Diane Waggoner, Sarah Kennel, Matthew S. Witkovsky, *The Art of the American Snapshot, 1888-1978* (2007)

Marvin Heiferman, *Now is Then: Snapshots from the Maresca Collection* (2007)

Michel Frizot and Cedric de Veigy, *Photo trouvée* (2007)

A photograph is more than visual information. It freezes a moment in time, a glimpse of the way things were, and, we hope, the way things still are. The best of these pictures tell more than a narrow story. They say something about the human condition and life itself. When you can look at a snapshot and say, "I've been there — I know the feeling," you are looking at a photo that ought to be preserved.

A stoic grandmother on a motorcycle is one thing. On the right is a witty snapshot in which the photographer's shadow is a member of the family.

Homeward bound

In recent years we've been told again and again that we live in a deeply divided country, that we live not in one country but in red states or blue states. It's time to take a longer, wider view of things, and great old snapshots culled from several generations of American family picture-taking can help in a small way to restore our sense of perspective. In themselves, taken one by one, these snapshots are a pleasure to look at, but taken together they may also serve to remind us of some important, permanent American values: humor, forthrightness, energy, ingenuity, devotion to family and love of country.

PHOTOGRAPHY, GENERAL

Modern photographic images date back to the 1820s with the development of chemical photography. The first permanent photograph was an image produced in 1826 by the French inventor Nicéphore Niépce. However, the picture took eight hours to expose, so he went about trying to find a new process. Working in conjunction with Louis Daguerre, they experimented with silver compounds based on a Johann Heinrich Schultz discovery in 1724 that a silver and chalk mixture darkens when exposed to light. Niépce died in 1833, but Daguerre continued the work, eventually culminating with the development of the daguerreotype in 1837.

Many advances in photographic glass plates and printing were made all through the 19th century. In 1884, American George Eastman developed the technology to replace photographic plates, leading to the technology used by film cameras today.

Eastman patented a photographic medium that used a photo-emulsion coated on paper rolls. The invention of roll film greatly sped up the process of recording multiple images.

Also see Autographs.

Berenice Abbott, (American, 1898-1991) Stone and William Streets, 1936, From Berenice Abbott, Retrospective, 1982; gelatin silver print (printed later); Signed and numbered 13/40; 23 3/8" x 18 3/8" (sheet). **$3,600**

Berenice Abbott, (American, 1898-1991) Portrait of John Sloan, 1940s; gelatin silver print (printed 1960s); Signed; 14 7/8" x 13 5/8" (sheet). **$1,680**

Berenice Abbott, (American, 1898-1991) Princess Eugene Murat, circa 1928, from Berenice Abbott; gelatin silver print (printed 1976); Signed and numbered 25/50; 13 1/2" x 10 1/2" (sheet). **$360**

Berenice Abbott, (American, 1898-1991) Eugene Atget, 1927, from Berenice Abbott; gelatin silver print (printed later); Signed and numbered 25/50; 13 1/4" x 10 3/8" (sheet). **$3,120**

Ansel Easton Adams, (American, 1902-1984) Gottardo Piazzoni in His Studio, San Francisco (image 10), circa 1932, from Portfolio VI; gelatin silver print (printed 1974); Signed, dated, titled and numbered 81/110; 15 3/4" x 19 1/2" (sheet). **$2,280**

Ansel Easton Adams, (American, 1902-1984) White Post and Spandrel, Columbia, California (image 7), 1953, From Portfolio VI; gelatin silver print (printed 1974); Signed, dated, titled and numbered 81/110; 19 1/2" x 15 3/4" (sheet). **$2,520**

Ansel Easton Adams, (American, 1902-1984) Nasturtiums, Big Sur, Calif., 1951; gelatin silver print (printed 1970s); Signed, titled and with studio stamp; 13 3/4" x 10 3/4" (sheet). **$4,800**

Ansel Easton Adams, (American, 1902-1984) Half Dome, Merced River, Winter, circa 1938, From Photographs of Yosemite; gelatin silver print (printed circa 1970); Signed, titled and with studio stamp; 7 5/8" x 9 5/8" (sheet). **$4,500**

Edward K. Alenius, (Finnish/American, 1892-1950) Manhattan, circa 1930; gelatin silver print (printed circa 1930); 13 1/2" x 10 3/8" (sheet). **$480**

Eugene Atget, (French, 1857-1927) Lampshade Seller, circa 1900; gelatin silver print (printed 1956 by Berenice Abbott); Titled, dated and inscribed; 8 1/4" x 6 1/2" (sheet). **$1,320**

Eduard Baldus, (French, 1813-1889) Untitled (View of the Seine, Paris), circa 1800s; Albumen print; Stamped; 8 3/8" x 11 1/4" (sheet). **$360**

Photo courtesy Rago Arts and Auction Center, Lambertville, N.J.: www.RagoArts.com

Berenice Abbott (American, 1898-1991) James Joyce (image 2), circa 1920, from Berenice Abbott; gelatin silver print (printed 1976); Signed and numbered 29/50; 10 3/8" x 13 3/4" (sheet). **$2,280**

Ruth Bernhard, (German/American, 1905-2006) Doll's Head, 1936; gelatin silver print (printed later); Signed, titled and dated; 7 1/4" x 9 1/2" (sheet). **$2,160**

Felix Bonfils, (French, 1831-1885) Place du Marche a Jaffa (Marketplace at Jaffa), circa 1870s; Albumen print; 8 1/2" x 10 7/8" (sheet). **$120**

Edouard Boubat, (French, 1923-1999) Inde, 1964; gelatin silver print; Signed, titled and dated; 11 7/8" x 15 3/8" (sheet). **$1,560**

Margaret Bourke-White, (American, 1904-1971) Shaking Down Slag, 1930; gelatin silver print (printed 1930); Titled with studio stamps; 13 3/8" x 9 1/4" (sheet). **$3,120**

Margaret Bourke-White, (American, 1904-1971) Italy - Details of Locking Bridge in Place, circa 1944; gelatin silver print (printed circa 1944); Signed; 10 3/8" x 10 3/8" (sheet). **$1,560**

Brassai, (Romanian/French, 1899-1984) Brassai: A Portfolio of Ten Photographs, 1973; Portfolio of 10 gelatin silver prints; Signed, dated and numbered Artist Proof 3/5 from an edition of 50; Various sizes, 21" x 17" x 1 1/4" (portfolio)..**$48,000**

Adolphe Braun, (French, 1812-1877) Panorama from Murreu, circa 1860s; Albumen print; Titled; 8 3/4" x 19" (sheet). **$240**

Manuel Alvarez Bravo, (Mexican, 1902-2002) Montana Negra, Nube Blanca (Black Mountain, White Cloud) (image 10), 1974, from The Manuel Alvarez Bravo Platinum Portfolio, 1980; Platinum print (printed 1980); Signed; 10" x 12" (sheet). **$1,800**

Manuel Alvarez Bravo, (Mexican, 1902-2002) Calabazay Caracol (Squash and Snail) (image 2), 1929, from The Manuel Alvarez Bravo Platinum Portfolio, 1980; Platinum print (printed 1980); Signed; 10" x 7 3/4" (sheet)........**$2,520**

Frederic Brenner, (French, b. 1959) Dans le quartier hongrois de Mea Shearim, 1979; gelatin silver print (printed later); Signed; 12" x 16" (sheet). **$360**

Paul Auguste Briol, (American, 1889-1969) Untitled, 1930s; gelatin silver print (printed 1930s); Signed; 7 1/2" x 9 1/2" (sheet). **$540**

Esther Bubley, (American, 1921-1998) Brazilian Street Scene, Ouro Preto, 1957; gelatin silver print (printed 1957); Signed, dated and titled; 11" x 13 7/8" (sheet). **$1,800**

Harry Callahan, (American, 1912-1999) Siena, 1968; gelatin silver print (printed circa 1968); Signed; 6" x 6" (sheet)..**$3,600**

Harry Callahan, (American, 1912-1999) Detroit, 1942; gelatin silver print (printed circa 1970); Signed; 5" x 7" (sheet). **$4,800**

Camera Work Issue No. 3, July 1903; Magazine with photogravures (incomplete); Including 8 images by Clarence H. White (5), John Francis Strauss (1), Joseph T. Keiley (1) and Alvin Langdon Coburn (1); 11 3/4" x 8 1/2" x 1/2"; Publisher: Alfred Steiglitz, New York. **$960**

Camera Work Issue No. 5, Jan. 1904; Magazine with photogravures (complete); Including 8 images by Robert Demachy (6), Prescott Adamson (1) and Frank Eugene (1); 11 3/4" x 8 1/2" x 1/2"; Publisher: Alfred Steiglitz, New York. **$570**

Camera Work Issue No. 19, July 1907; Magazine with photogravures (complete); Including 6 images by J. Craig Annan (5) and Eduard J. Steichen (1); 11 3/4" x 8 1/2" x 1/2"; Publisher: Alfred Steiglitz, New York. **$720**

Camera Work Issue No. 20, Oct. 1907; Magazine with photogravures (incomplete); Including 9 images by George H. Seeley (6) and Alfred Steiglitz (3); 11 3/4" x 8 1/2" x 1/2"; Publisher: Alfred Steiglitz, New York. **$2,280**

Camera Work Issue No. 25, Jan. 1909; Magazine with photogravures (incomplete); Including 9 images by Annie W. Brigman (5), Ema Spencer (1), Yarnall Abbott (1) and Frank Eugene (2); 11 3/4" x 8 1/2" x 1/2"; Publisher: Alfred Steiglitz, New York. **$1,020**

Camera Work Issue No. 28, October 1909; Magazine with photogravures (complete); Including 10 images

by David Octavius Hill (6), George Davison (1), Paul B. Haviland (1), Marshall R. Kernochan (1) and Alvin Langdon Coburn (1); 11 3/4" x 8 1/2" x 1/2"; Publisher: Alfred Steiglitz, New York. **$600**

Paul Caponigro, (American, b. 1932) Nahant, MA, 1958; gelatin silver print; Signed; 6 3/8" x 5 1/2" (sheet). ...**$1,080**

Keith Carter, (American, b. 1948) Megan, Jefferson County, 1988; gelatin silver print; Signed, dated and titled; 20" x 16" (sheet). **$570**

Henri Cartier-Bresson, (French, 1908-2004) Mexico, 1963; gelatin silver exhibition print (printed circa 1963); 9 1/4" x 13 1/2" (sheet). **$6,000**

William Clift, (American, b. 1944) Reflection: Old St. Louis County Courthouse, St. Louis, MO, 1976, from County Courthouses: A Portfolio of 6 Prints; gelatin silver print; Signed; 13" x 15 3/4" (sheet). **$1,560**

Alvin Langdon Coburn, (American/British, 1882-1966) Untitled (Landscape), 1910s; Photogravure; Signed; 15 3/8" x 11 1/4" (sheet). **$2,280**

Gordon Coster, (American, 1906-1988) Untitled, 1930s; gelatin silver print (printed circa 1930s); Titled illegibly with studio stamp; 14" x 11" (sheet). **$480**

Bruce Cratsley, (American, 1944-1998) Louvre Window, Paris, 1980; gelatin silver print (printed circa 1980); Signed, dated and titled; 9 1/2" x 9 1/2" (sheet). **$300**

Ralston Crawford, (American, 1906-1978) Interior View of Station, Newark, 1942; gelatin silver print (printed circa

Photo courtesy Rago Arts and Auction Center, Lambertville, N.J.; www.RagoArts.com

Wolf von dem Bussche (German, b. 1934) Totem: The Papago Legend of the Creation of the Giant Cactus, Called Saguardo, 1993; Portfolio of 12 gelatin silver prints; each signed, dated, titled and numbered 6/44; 22" x 17 7/8" (sheet) each; Publisher: Three Plowshares, 1993. **$4,800 all**

Photo courtesy Rago Arts and Auction Center, Lambertville, N.J.; www.RagoArts.com

Imogen Cunningham (American, 1883-1976) Triangles, 1928; gelatin silver print (printed later); Signed and dated with photographer's label; 3 3/4" x 2 3/4" (sheet). **$9,000**

1942); with estate stamp; 3 1/4" x 4 1/2" (sheet); Exhibition: "Ralston Crawford," Whitney Museum of American Art, New York, 1985. ....**$3,000**

Edward S. Curtis, (American, 1868-1952) Volume 8: The Nez, Wallawalla, Umatilla, Cayuse, and the Chinookan Tribes, 1911, From The North American Indian; Unbound volume including 67 of the original 77 photogravures; 12 3/4" x 9 5/8" (sheet) each; Printer: The Plimpton Press, Norwood, MA; Publisher: Edward Sheriff Curtis, Seattle; Engraver: John Andrew & Son, Boston, MA. **$3,000**

Edward S. Curtis, (American, 1868-1952) Untitled (Wood Carrier), circa 1908; Platinum print (printed circa 1908); Signed with blind stamp; 5 7/8" x 7 7/8" (sheet). **$2,400**

Edward S. Curtis, (American, 1868-1952) Modern Designs in Washo Basketry (Plate 542), 1924; Photogravure on vellum; 17 3/4" x 21 3/4" (sheet). **$1,020**

Louise Dahl-Wolfe, (American, 1895-1989) Untitled (Nude), circa 1937; gelatin silver print (printed circa 1937); Dated with studio stamp; 12 3/4" x 10 3/8" (sheet). ...**$2,520**

Judy Dater, (American, b. 1941) Imogen and Twinka at Yosemite, 1974; gelatin silver print (printed 1974); Signed, titled and dated with studio stamp; 9 5/8" x 7 5/8" (sheet). **$4,800**

Liliane De Cock, (American, b. 1939) Evening, Taos, New Mexico, 1970; gelatin silver print; Signed; 20" x 24" (sheet). **$570**

Jed Devine, (American, b. 1944) Untitled; Palladium print; Signed; 10 3/4" x 9" (sheet). **$660**

Robert Doisneau, (French, 1912-1994) Jacques Tati et Sa Bicyclette, 1949; gelatin silver print (printed 1980); Signed, dated, titled and numbered 3/3; 24" x 20" (sheet). **$1,560**

Robert Doisneau, (French, 1912-1994) Portraits, 1943-1971; Portfolio of 15 gelatin silver prints (printed 1984); Signed and numbered 5/50; 16" x 20" (sheet) each.
....**$12,000 all**

Frantisek Drtikol, (Czechoslovakian, 1883-1961) Untitled, 1923; gelatin silver print (printed circa 1923); with blind stamp; 10" x 7 1/2" (sheet). **$1,800**

Walker Evans, (American, 1903-1975) Untitled, 1970s; SX-70 Polaroid print; 4 1/4" x 3 3/8" (sheet). **$3,120**

Walker Evans, (American, 1903-1975) Doorway, 204 West 13th Street, New York City (image 10 of 15), circa 1931, from Walker Evans: Selected Photographs, 1974; gelatin silver print (printed 1974); Signed and numbered 71/75; 11 1/8" x 8 3/4" (sheet); Publisher: Double Elephant Press, New York, 1974. ....**$1,800**

Adolf Fassbender, (American, 1884-1980) Today, World's Fair, 1938; Silver bromide print (printed circa 1938); Signed and titled; 17" x 14" (sheet). **$2,280**

Louis Faurer, (American, 1916-2001) Freudian Handclasp, New York City, 1948; gelatin silver print (printed 1980); Signed, dated and titled; 14" x 11" (sheet). **$2,160**

Nat Fein, (American, 1914-2000) Aqueduct Race Track, 1940s; gelatin silver print (additional gelatin silver print adhered to verso); Signed, dated and titled; 10 3/4" x 12 1/2" (sheet). **$1,560**

Andreas Feininger, (French/American, 1907-1999) Jewish Shop on the Lower East Side, Manhattan, circa 1940; gelatin silver print (printed later); Signed; 14" x 10 3/4" (sheet)..**$1,800**

Larry Fink, (American, b. 1941) Graduation - Bangor High School, Pa., June 1977; gelatin silver print (printed 1983); Signed, dated and titled; 16" x 20" (sheet). **$1,080**

Photo courtesy Rago Arts and Auction Center, Lambertville, N.J.; www.RagoArts.com

Elliott Erwitt (American, b. 1928) Venice (image 7 of 10), 1965, From A Portfolio of Ten Photographs; gelatin silver print (printed 1974); Signed; 13 1/2" x 9 1/8" (sheet). **$1,080**

Photo courtesy Rago Arts and Auction Center, Lambertville, N.J.; www.RagoArts.com

Eikoh Hosoe (Japanese, b. 1933) Embrace #15, 1970; gelatin silver print (printed circa 1970); Signed and titled with blind stamp; 8" x 10" (sheet). **$2,640**

Larry Fink, (American, b. 1941) English Speaking Union N.Y.C., December 1975; gelatin silver print (printed 1983); Signed, dated and titled; 14" x 14" (sheet). **$1,140**

Neil H. Folberg, (American, b. 1950) Zalman Kleinman Painting in His Studio, Brooklyn, 1975; gelatin silver print; Signed, dated and titled; 11" x 14" (sheet). **$480**

Francis Frith, (British, 1822-1898) Athens, circa 1870; Albumen print; Titled; 6 1/4" x 8 1/4" (sheet). **$510**

Allen Ginsberg, (American, 1926-1997) View out my Kitchen Window, 1987; gelatin silver print (printed circa 1987); Signed, dated and titled; 14" x 11" (sheet). **$3,900**

Allen Ginsberg, (American, 1926-1997) Paul Bowles Preparing Tea at Christopher Wanklyn's House, Marrakesh, Morocco, July 20, 1961; gelatin silver print (printed later); Signed, dated and inscribed; 16" x 20" (sheet). **$1,200**

William Paul Gottlieb, (American, 1917-2006) Duke Ellington, circa 1948; gelatin silver print (printed later); Signed and titled; 14" x 11" (sheet). **$360**

Lois Greenfield, (American, b. 1949) Daniel Ezralow and Ashley Roland, 1988; gelatin silver print; Signed, titled and numbered 5/50; 20" x 16" (sheet). **$1,080**

F. Bedrich Grunzweig, (American, b. 1910) Washington Square Arch, New York, 1965; gelatin silver print (printed later); Signed; 20" x 16" (sheet). **$1,200**

F. Bedrich Grunzweig, (American, b. 1910) The Midtown Elevated, New York, 1954-55; gelatin silver print (printed later); Signed, dated and inscribed; 19 7/8" x 15 7/8" (sheet). **$3,240**

Philippe Halsman, (American, 1906-1979) Two works of art: Edward Albee, 1961; gelatin silver print; Dated and titled with studio stamp; 13 7/8" x 10 7/8" (sheet); Woody Allen; gelatin silver print; Titled with studio stamp; 10 1/2" x 10 5/8" (sheet). ....**$1,200 both**

Philippe Halsman, (American, 1906-1979) Untitled; Four gelatin silver prints; Each with studio stamp; 10" x 8" (sheet) each. ....**$1,800 all**

Eugene V. Harris, (American, 20th Century) Peruvian Flute Player, 1955; gelatin silver print (printed circa 1955); with Collier's Encyclopedia Art Department stamp; 9 1/4" x 7 1/4" (sheet); Note: From the cover of "Family of Man" by Edward Steichen, Museum of Modern Art, 1955. .....**$4,500**

George E. Hurrell, (American, 1904-1992) Raymond Navarro, 1930s; gelatin silver print (printed circa 1930s); Signed and titled with studio, Sid Avery copyright and The Avery Collection stamps; 13 3/8" x 10 5/8" (sheet). ...**$2,640**

Izis (Izis Bidermanas), (French, 1911-1980) Paris - quai de l' Horloge, 1946; gelatin silver print (printed 1970s); Signed, titled, dated and inscribed with studio stamp; 11 5/8" x 9" (sheet). **$960**

William Henry Jackson, attributed (American, 1843-1942) Untitled, circa 1870s; Process unknown; 16 5/8" x 21" (sheet). **$1,200**

Japanese (19th-20th Century) Two albums, including 72 hand-colored albumen prints; Many titled in negative; 10 1/2" x 13 3/4" x 1" and 9 3/4" x 12 1/4" x 1 1/4" (overall). ....**$2,040 both**

Constantin Joffe (20th Century) Untitled, 1947; gelatin silver print (printed circa 1947); with artist's Vogue studio stamp and Conde Nast publication stamp; 14" x 11" (sheet). **$840**

Photo courtesy Rago Arts and Auction Center, Lambertville, N.J.; www.RagoArts.com

Photographer Unknown (possibly Alvin Langdon Coburn, 1882-1966) George Bernard Shaw, circa 1905; gelatin silver print; Inscribed (possibly titled); 9 3/4" x 8" (sheet). **$300**

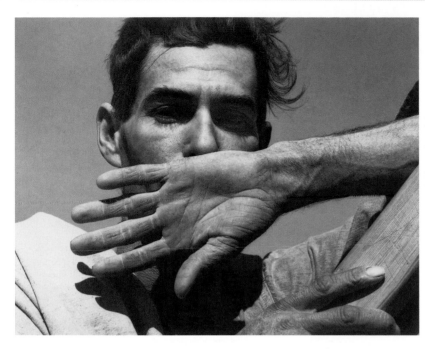

Dorothea Lange (American, 1895-1965) Migratory Cotton Picker, Eloy, Arizona, 1940; gelatin silver print (printed later); 13" x 16" (sheet). **$9,000**

Yousuf Karsh, (Canadian, 1908-2002) Georgia O'Keeffe, 1950s; gelatin silver print; Signed and titled; 23 3/4" x 20" (sheet). **$6,000**

Clarence Kennedy, (American, 1892-1972) Untitled (XXXIV); gelatin silver print; 6 1/2" x 10 3/8" (sheet). .**$180**

Andre Kertesz, (Hungarian/American, 1894-1985) Melancholic Tulip, February 10, 1939; gelatin silver print (printed later); Signed, dated, titled and numbered 26/150; 13 7/8" x 10 7/8" (sheet). **$4,200**

Andre Kertesz, (Hungarian/American, 1894-1985) Untitled, 1959; gelatin silver print (printed circa 1959); Dated and with studio stamp; 10" x 8" (sheet). **$1,440**

Andre Kertesz, (Hungarian/American, 1894-1985) Swimming, Duna Haraszti (image 3), Sept. 14, 1919, From Portfolio: Andre Kertesz, Volume I, 1913-1929; gelatin silver print (printed 1973); Signed and dated; Number 9 from an edition of 50; 9 3/4" x 7 3/4" (sheet); Publisher: Light, New York, NY. **$3,000**

Manuel Komroff, (American, 1890-1974) E.E. Cummings; Vintage gelatin silver print; Titled and inscribed with studio stamp; 8 1/2" x 6 1/2" (sheet). **$420**

Dorothea Lange, (American, 1895-1965) Road Leading to Small Farm in Northern Oregon, Irrison, Morrow County, Oregon, October 1939; gelatin silver print (printed circa 1939); Titled and dated with Farm Security Administration credit stamp; 8" x 10" (sheet). **$3,900**

Dorothea Lange, (American, 1895-1965) Ditched, Stalled and Stranded, San Joaquin Valley, California, 1936; gelatin silver print (printed later); 16" x 13 3/4" (sheet) irregular. **$4,200**

Jacques Henri Lartigue, (French, 1894-1986) Woman with Fox Fur, Avenue des Acacias, 1911; gelatin silver print (printed before 1973); Signed, dated and inscribed to Dan Berley; 11 3/4" x 15 3/4" (sheet). **$6,600**

Danny Lyon, (American, b. 1942) Untitled, circa 1969, from Conversations With the Dead; gelatin silver print (printed 1970s); Signed; 11" x 14" (sheet). **$2,040**

Wendell MacRae, (American, 1896-1980) Builder's Dream, circa 1935; gelatin silver print (printed circa 1935); Signed and titled with studio stamp; 17 7/8" x 13 7/8" (sheet). **$600**

Reginald Marsh, (British, 20th Century) The Steps of St. Paul's, 1926; gelatin silver print (printed circa 1926); Signed, dated, titled and inscribed; 8 1/2" x 11 1/2" (sheet). **$540**

Ray K. Metzker, (American, b. 1931) Untitled, 1983; gelatin silver print (printed 1983); Signed, and numbered 4/30; 13 7/8" x 10 7/8" (sheet). **$7,200**

Ray K. Metzker, (American, b. 1931) Philadelphia, From City Whispers, 1982; gelatin silver print (printed circa 1982); Signed and numbered 6/30; 10 7/8" x 14" (sheet). **$4,800**

Joel Meyerowitz, (American, b. 1938) House Without Walls: Blue Sky, 1991; C-print; Signed, dated, titled and numbered 58/100; 11" x 14" (sheet). **$1,560**

Lisette Model, (American, 1901-1983) Fashion Show, Hotel Pierre, New York, 1940-46; gelatin silver print (printed later); Signed and numbered 61/75; 15 3/4" x 19 1/2" (sheet). **$5,400**

Denny Moers, (American, b. 1953) Hallway #2, 1979; Toned gelatin silver print; Signed, dated and titled; 17" x 15" (sheet). **$240**

Inge Morath, (Austrian, 1923-2002) Saul Steinberg with Nose Mask, Manhattan, 1966; gelatin silver print (printed circa 1966); Signed, dated and titled; 14" x 11" (sheet). **$5,700**

Barbara Morgan, (American, 1900-1992) Merce Cunningham, "Root of the Unfocus," 1944; gelatin silver print (printed circa 1970); Signed, dated and titled with artist's copyright stamp; 7 7/8" x 9 5/8" (sheet). **$660**

Arnold Newman, (American, 1918-2006) Untitled, 1941; gelatin silver print (printed circa 1948); Signed, dated and inscribed; 5 7/8" x 9 5/8" (sheet). **$2,640**

Beaumont Newhall, (American, 1908-1993) Edward Weston, Carmel, California, 1940; gelatin silver print (printed 1993); Signed, dated and titled with studio stamp; 11 3/8" x 8 7/8" (sheet). **$600**

Janine Niepce, (French, b. 1921) Le chat de la concierge, Rue de Tournon, Paris, 1956; gelatin silver print (printed 1970s); Signed, dated and titled; 15 3/4" x 11 3/4" (sheet). **$1,020**

Ferdinando Ongania, (Italian, 1842-1911) Streets and Canals of Venice and in the Islands of the Lagoons, circa 1896-1899; Album including 85 gravures and 15 engravings; Haverhill Public Library blind stamp and stamp; 23 1/4" x 16" x 1 3/4" (album); Publisher: Ferdinando Ongania, Venice. ....**$1,680 all**

Photographer Unknown, (Late 19th Century) Two works of art: Gargoyle, Paris, Notre Dame, 1870s; Albumen print; 10 5/8" x 8" (sheet); Gargoyle, Paris, Notre Dame, 1870s; Albumen print; 10 5/8" x 8" (sheet). ....**$660 pair**

Photographer Unknown, (19th-20th Century) Views of Italy; Album of 84 albumen prints; Many titled in the negative; Album measures 11 1/2" x 14 1/4" x 1 3/4", print sizes vary. ....**$480 all**

Photographer Unknown, (19th-20th Century) Two Photography Albums (New York City and Environs), circa 1900; gelatin silver prints; Inscribed and dated; Each print approximately 3 1/2" x 4 1/2" (sight), each album approximately 11" x 14 1/2" x 2". ....**$480 both**

Eliot Porter, (American, 1901-1990) River Edge at Sunset, Below Piute Rapids, San Juan, Colorado, May 24, 1962; Dye-transfer print; Signed; 13 5/8" x 10 3/4" (sheet). **$3,900**

Edward Quigley, (American, 1898-1977) Untitled (Philadelphia), 1938; gelatin silver print (printed circa 1938); with studio stamp; 3 5/8" x 3 1/4" (sheet). **$1,680**

John Rawlings, (American, 1912-1970) Nude Study, circa 1966; gelatin silver print (printed circa 1966); with studio stamp; 12 3/4" x 9 1/2" (sheet). **$600**

Albert Renger-Patzsch, (German, 1897-1966) Hainbuchen-Kruppelwuches, Holstein, circa 1950; gelatin silver print (printed 1950s); Dated and titled with studio stamps and Galerie Wilde Koln stamp; 15 1/8" x 11 1/8" (sheet)..**$1,200**

Wynn Richards, (American, 1888-1960) Dotted Glassware, circa 1930; gelatin silver print (printed circa 1930); 7 5/8" x 9 1/2" (sheet). **$480**

Walter Rosenblum, (American, 1919-2000) Women with Carriage, Pitt Street, New York, 1938; gelatin silver print (printed later); Signed, dated and titled; 10 7/8" x 13 7/8" (sheet). **$1,800**

Sanford Roth, (American, 1906-1962) Untitled, circa 1950; Vintage gelatin silver print; 8" x 10" (sheet). **$480**

Arthur Rothstein, (American, 1915-1985) Three works of art: Agate, Nebraska, 1939; gelatin silver print (printed 1981); Signed, titled and with publisher's blind stamp; Edition 16/50; 11" x 14" (sheet); John Dudeck, Dalton, New York, 1937; gelatin silver print (printed 1981); Signed and with publisher's blind stamp; Edition 16/50; 11" x 14" (sheet); Young Coal Miner, Wales, 1947; gelatin silver print (printed 1981); Signed and with publisher's blind stamp; Edition 16/50; 14" x 11" (sheet); Publisher: Hyperion Press, New York. ....**$1,200 all**

Eva Rubinstein, (American, b. 1933) Italy, 1973; gelatin silver print; Signed, dated and titled; 8 1/2" x 6 1/4" (sheet). **$330**

George Segal, (American, 1924-2000) Sequence: New York/New Jersey: Window display, St. Marks Place, New York, 1990-1990, 1991; gelatin silver print (printed later); Signed and numbered with copyright stamp; 16" x 20" (sheet)..**$540**

Tomio Seike, (Japanese, b. 1943) Rue Saint Honore, 1992; Toned gelatin silver print (printed 1997); Signed, dated,

Sebastiao Salgado (Brazilian, b. 1944) Three Coal Miners, India, 1989; gelatin silver print; Signed, dated, titled and numbered; 19 1/8" x 23 1/8" (sheet).
$3,900

Photo courtesy Rago Arts and Auction Center, Lambertville, N.J.: www.RagoArts.com

August Sander (German, 1876-1964) Pastry Cook, 1928; Oversized gelatin silver print (printed circa 1980 by Gunther Sander); with "Aug. Sander, Lindenthal, Koln" blindstamp; 16 1/2" x 12" (sheet). **$9,000**

titled, numbered 22/30 with studio stamp; 13 1/2" x 10 1/2" (sheet). **$1,440**

Stephen Shore, (American, b. 1947) U.S.1, Arundel, Maine, July 17, 1974; C-print (printed circa 1974); Signed, dated, titled and inscribed; 10" x 12" (sheet). **$5,700**

Jeanloup Sieff, (French, 1933-2000) Cabines de Gair, 1972, Gelatin silver print (printed circa 1972); Signed, dated and titled; 12" x 16" (sheet). **$1,800**

Clara Estelle Sipprell, (Canadian/American, 1885-1975) Along the Gaspe Peninsula, 1920; Silver bromide print (printed circa 1920); Signed, dated and titled; 7 1/4" x 9 1/4" (sheet). **$420**

Clara Estelle Sipprell, (Canadian/American, 1885-1975) Street in Sarajevo, Yugoslavia, 1924; Silver bromide print (printed circa 1924); Signed, dated and titled; 7 3/8" x 9 1/2" (sheet). **$330**

Aaron Siskind, (American, 1903-1991) North Carolina 30, 1951; gelatin silver print (printed later); Signed, titled and dated; 14" x 11" (sheet). **$3,600**

Aaron Siskind, (American, 1903-1991) Chicago 224, 1953; gelatin silver print (printed circa 1955); Signed and dated with Art Institute of Chicago curatorial stamp; 11 3/4" x 10 7/8" (sheet). **$3,900**

Aaron Siskind, (American, 1903-1991) Chicago, 1952; gelatin silver print (printed circa 1955); Signed and dated with Art Institute of Chicago curatorial stamp; 10 1/2" x 13 1/8" (sheet). **$4,200**

W. Eugene Smith, (American, 1918-1978) Untitled; gelatin silver print; Signed; 8 1/2" x 10 7/8" (sheet). **$3,000**

Frederick Sommer, (Italian/American, 1905-1999) Virgin and Child with Saint Anne and the Infant St. John, 1966; gelatin silver print; Signed, dated and titled; 14" x 11" (sheet). **$4,800**

Edward Steichen, (American, 1879-1973) In Memoriam, New York, 1904; gelatin silver print (printed 1950s); Inscribed; 8 7/8" x 7" (sheet). **$7,200**

Edward Steichen, (American, 1879-1973) The George Washington Bridge, New York, 1931; gelatin silver print (printed circa 1931); Signed and titled; 9 3/8" x 7 1/2" (sheet). **$10,800**

Ralph Steiner, (American, 1899-1986) Three works of art: Lollipop, circa 1924; gelatin silver print; 4 3/4" x 3 5/8" (sheet); Typewriter Keys, 1921-22; gelatin silver print; 7 7/8" x 6" (sheet); Carnovsky and Lee Strasberg, 1936; gelatin silver print; 9 3/8" x 7 1/2" (sheet). ....**$1,920 all**

Ralph Steiner, (American, 1899-1986) Untitled, circa 1930; gelatin silver print; Signed; 4 3/8" x 10 3/8" (sheet). **$1,440**

Alfred Stieglitz, (American, 1864-1946) Portrait of John Marin, circa 1913; waxed platinum print; 9 1/2" x 7 1/2" (sheet). **$16,800**

William James Stillman, (American, 1828-1901) Greece, circa 1870; Carbon print; 9 1/2" x 7 1/4" (sheet). **$1,020**

Paul Strand, (American, 1890-1976) Photograph - New York, 1917, from Camera Work, June 1917; Photogravure (printed circa 1917); 9" x 6 1/2" (image). **$3,120**

Paul Strand, (American, 1890-1976) The Mexican Portfolio, 1932-33; Portfolio of 20 photogravures (printed 1967); Signed and numbered 233/1000; 15 3/4" x 12 3/4" (sheet) each, 17" x 13 1/4" x 1 1/4" (overall); Publisher: Da Capo Press, New York, 1967. ....**$2,040**

Photo courtesy Rago Arts and Auction Center, Lambertville, N.J.: www.RagoArts.com

Roman Vishniac (Russian, 1897-1990) Albert Einstein in Princeton, circa 1941; gelatin silver print; Signed, titled and inscribed; 13 1/2" x 10 3/4" (sheet). **$1,200**

*F.S. Lincoln (1894-1976)
Upshot of Stairway,
Paris Apartment House,
Architect: Mallet-Stevens,
circa 1930; gelatin silver
print (printed circa 1930);
Signed and titled with
studio stamp; 13 1/4" x
10 3/8" (sheet).* **$3,360**

Karl Struss, (American, 1886-1981) Flatiron Building, Twilight, 1912; gelatin silver print (printed circa 1912); 4 1/2" x 3 5/8" (sheet). **$2,880**

Josef Sudek, (Czechoslovakian, 1896-1976) St. Guy's Cathedral, Prague, circa 1948; gelatin silver print (printed circa 1948); with studio stamp; 9 1/4" x 6 1/4" (sheet). **$3,480**

Frank Meadow Sutcliffe, after (British, 1853-1941) Water Rats, 1886; gelatin silver print (printed later); Stamped; 12" x 15" (sheet). **$1,080**

Edmund Teske, (American, 1911-1996) Image of Young Man and Brooklyn Bridge Combined, 1973; gelatin silver print; Signed, dated and titled; 9 3/4" x 9 3/8" (sheet). **$900**

George Andrew Tice, (American, b. 1938) Oak Tree, Holmdel, N.J., 1970; Selenium-toned gelatin silver print (printed 1970); Signed, dated and titled; 15 3/8" x 19 1/2" (sheet). **$3,600**

Karen Truax, (American, b. 1946) Painted Woman, 1970s; Hand-colored and painted gelatin silver print; Signed and titled; 13 1/8" x 8 7/8" (sheet). **$240**

Jerry N. Uelsmann, (American, b. 1934) Portfolio, 1959-1971; Portfolio of 9 gelatin silver prints (print 1 missing); Signed, titled, dated and numbered Artist Proof 1/5 from an edition of 25; Various size prints, 21" x 17" x 1 3/4" (portfolio). ....**$12,000 all**

Doris Ullman, (American, 1884-1934) Standing Woman with Basket, from Roll Jordan Roll (Deluxe Edition); Photogravure; 8 3/8" x 6 1/2" (image). **$900**

Irving Underhill, (American, 1872-1960) 60 Wall Tower, 1932; gelatin silver print (printed circa 1932); Signed, titled, and dated in negative; 13 3/8" x 10 1/2" (sheet). **$360**

Burk Uzzle, (American, b. 1938) Untitled, 1969; gelatin silver print; with studio stamp; 11" x 14" (sheet). **$540**

John Vachon, (American, 1914-1975) Cincinnati, Ohio, circa 1940; gelatin silver print (printed circa 1940); Titled with Farm Security Administration stamp; 10" x 8" (sheet). **$480**

Various Photographers, Group of five Woodbury types from Galerie Contemporaine, Paris, circa 1870. Including portraits of: Zola, Sylvestre, Dumas, Delacroix and Garnier; Various sizes, largest: 9 3/8" x 7 1/2" (image). .... **$600 all**

Roman Vishniac, (Russian, 1897-1990) A Rabbi Carrying His Books, 1938; gelatin silver print (printed circa 1977); Signed; 12 1/2" x 10 3/8" (sheet). **$2,160**

Brett Weston, (American, 1911-1993) Nine photographs from the portfolio "New York: Twelve Photographs": Forty-Seventh Street (image 2), Brownstone in the Fifties (image 3), Church Door, Bowery (image 4), Brooklyn Bridge (image 6), Church- Brooklyn Outskirts (image 8), Washington Square (image 9), Sutton Place (image 10), End of Forty-Second Street (image 11), Manhattan Courtyard (image 12), gelatin silver prints (printed circa 1951) with folio; Each signed and stamped; From an edition of 50; 9 1/2" x 7 5/8" (sheet) each; Printer: Adrian Wilson, San Francisco (cases by Perry Davis, San Francisco).
....**$12,000 all**

Edward Weston, (American, 1886-1958) Cyprus, Point Lobos (image 5), 1929, From Edward Weston Portfolio, 1971; gelatin silver print (printed 1971 by Cole Weston); Signed, titled and dated by Cole Weston, numbered 44/50 with Edward Weston signature stamp; 7 1/2" x 9 3/8"

(sheet); Publisher: Witkin-Berley, New York, NY, 1971.
....**$1,320**

Edward Weston, (American, 1886-1958) Dante's View, 1938; gelatin silver print (printed later by Cole Weston); Signed by Cole Weston; 7 1/2" x 9 3/8" (sheet). **$1,560**

Geoff Winningham, (American, b. 1943) Houston Wrestler, 1971, from A Texas Dozen; gelatin silver print (printed circa 1971); Signed, dated and titled; 16" x 20" (sheet). **$510**

Garry Winogrand, (American, 1928-1984) Untitled, circa 1969; gelatin silver print; 11" x 14" (sheet). **$3,120**

Marion Post Wolcott, (American, 1910-1990) Car Attempting to go up Creek Bed, 1940; gelatin silver print (printed circa 1970 from original negative); Titled and dated with Library of Congress stamp; 8" x 10" (sheet).
....**$180**

Paul J. Woolf, (American, 1899-1985) Museum of Natural History Park, circa 1935; gelatin silver print (printed circa 1935); Titled with studio stamp, copyright stamp and Frederic Lewis Agency stamp; 8" x 10" (sheet). **$720**

Don Worth, (American, b. 1924) Tree and Fog, San Francisco, 1962; gelatin silver print (printed circa 1962); Signed, dated and titled; 9 5/8" x 7 5/8" (sheet). **$1,440**

CAMERAS

Photo courtesy Skinner Inc., Boston; www.SkinnerInc.com

Mahogany view camera, with Duplex lens, patent date Nov. 22, 1886, and brass tube marked "R.& J. Beck, No. 2391 W.H. Walmsley & Co." with F-stop adjustment, leather carrying case, together with a black and white panoramic view of Leominster, Mass. **$444**

Photo courtesy Skinner Inc., Boston; www.SkinnerInc.com

Leicaflex SLR 35mm camera and five Leitz Lenses, Germany, the camera marked "Leitz Wetzlar Germany" and "1258728" together with five bayonet-fit Leitz lenses, 35 mm 1:2.8, 50 mm 1:2, 90 mm 1:2.8, 135 mm 1:2.8, and 180 mm 1:2.8, polarizing filters and cases. **$889 all**

Photo courtesy Skinner Inc., Boston; www.SkinnerInc.com

Nikon Model F 35mm camera, no. 6442445 with Nikkor-S f/1.4 58mm lens, hood and leather case. (Note: This camera was owned and used by Theodore Miller Edison, West Orange, N.J., the youngest son of Thomas Edison. **$415**

Photo courtesy Skinner Inc., Boston; www.SkinnerInc.com

Leica M3 No. 966314 camera, with Summicron 1:2/50 lens No. 1607966 screw-fit, range finder, meter and leather case.
$1,126

Photo courtesy Skinner Inc., Boston; www.SkinnerInc.com

Leica IIIf camera No. 724162, chrome, red-scale, delayed-timer, with a Leitz Summcron f/2.5cm lens no. 1190853, in maker's ever-ready case; Pocket Leica Book and non-Leitz outfit case. Scuff marks top and base plates, fine scratches on the upper element. **$593**

POLITICAL ITEMS

Initially, American political-campaign souvenirs were created to celebrate victories. Items issued during a campaign to show support for a candidate were actively being distributed in the William Henry Harrison election of 1840.

For more information, consult *Warman's Political Collectibles* by Dr. Enoch L. Nappen, 2008. *Also see Posters.*

Photo courtesy Heritage Auction Galleries, Dallas; www.HA.com

George Washington 1800-dated leather fire bucket. The principal hand-painted decoration is a funerary urn with a large "W" on the side, resting on a pedestal marked "1800". Above is the slogan, "Protection in Danger," while on either side are "No." and "2," probably the fire brigade's unit number. On a streamer below is the name of the fireman who used it. The last name "Thompson" is clear, while the first name, which appears to be "Jeremiah," has partially eroded over the years. Washington died in December of 1799, so the majority of such memorial items were produced in and often dated 1800. The original integral leather handle has broken off at the top rim, 12 1/2" x 8 1/2". **$2,390**

Photo courtesy Heritage Auction Galleries, Dallas; www.HA.com

Martin Van Buren wall plaque incorporating hand-painted miniatures on ivory. Possibly made in Europe for sale in America at the time of Van Buren's presidency, it shows him along with four Founding Fathers: Washington, Adams, Jefferson and Madison. Each portrait is hand-painted on ivory, measuring 2" x 1 5/8", protected by a thin domed glass cover. All are signed by the artists. This may well have been a custom order for presentation purposes. It is encased in an openwork brass frame with original hanging loop, measuring 6 3/4" x 8 1/2". Slight deterioration of the blue fabric background along the edge and scattered staining of the cloth. **$10,157**

Photo courtesy Heritage Auction Galleries, Dallas; www.HA.com

William Henry Harrison 1840 silk flag banner. Harrison's bust is enclosed in a rectangle and in the background is a drapery similar to that seen on the single-portrait Currier political prints. The legend below Harrison's name is punctuated by an unusual military vignette with a flag. The red dye has faded but the flag is complete, with original borders on all four sides, and has no significant damage. There are several small partial separations and two small areas of fabric loss at the beginning of the word "Tippecanoe", 26" x 23 1/2" sight. **$33,460**

Abraham Lincoln large ambrotype portrait badge from the 1860 campaign. It features the "Cooper Union" image of Lincoln, taken by Matthew Brady when Lincoln gave a campaign speech at that New York landmark. On the back is a cardboard insert with "For President, Hon. Abraham Lincoln", as well as advertising for the manufacturer, Geo. Clark Jr. & Co. of Boston. There are evenly scattered, light moisture marks in the fields, which give the appearance of light soiling, 2 5/8" x 2 1/8". **$9,560**

Stephen A. Douglas 1860 campaign ferrotype, uses the scarcest of the three Douglas portraits, based on a Brady image. The portrait is surrounded by concentric plain and rope brass borders, and set into a colorful red, white and blue rosette for wearing, with ribbon bearing the slogan "UNION" in gold letters. Ferro is 18mm, rosette 2" diameter. **$657**

Photo courtesy Heritage Auction Galleries, Dallas; www.HA.com

Theodore Roosevelt "San Juan Hill" campaign button. Shows Teddy in Rough Rider uniform on horseback atop San Juan Hill. His Spanish-American war exploits, which had propelled Roosevelt to the governorship of New York and the vice presidency, still resounded in the 1904 campaign, 1 1/4". **$1,015**

Photo courtesy Heritage Auction Galleries, Dallas; www.HA.com

William Jennings Bryan 1908 celluloid. Found in both brown, cream and color-tinted versions, both the 1 1/4" celluloid and the leather fob are in near-mint condition. **$776**

POSTCARDS

John P. Charlton of Philadelphia patented the postcard in 1861, selling the rights to H.L. Lipman, whose postcards, complete with a decorated border, were labeled "Lipman's postal card." Within a decade, European countries were also producing postcards.

The United States Postal Service began issuing pre-stamped postal cards in 1873. The postal cards came about because the public was looking for an easier way to send quick notes. The USPS was the only establishment allowed to print postcards, and it held its monopoly until May 19, 1898, when Congress passed the Private Mailing Card Act.

Initially, the United States government prohibited private companies from calling their products "postcards," so they were known as "souvenir cards." Although this prohibition was rescinded in 1901, it was not until 1908 that people were permitted to write on the address side of a postcard.

Photo courtesy Heritage Auction Galleries, Dallas; www.HA.com

Fillmore concert postcard group (Bill Graham, 1966-67). Set of six unused postcards, Jefferson Airplane, Yardbirds/ Doors, Doors/Procol Harum, Doors/Big Brother/Jefferson Airplane/Chuck Berry and others, and Jefferson Airplane/Big Brother. All are near mint. **$179 all**

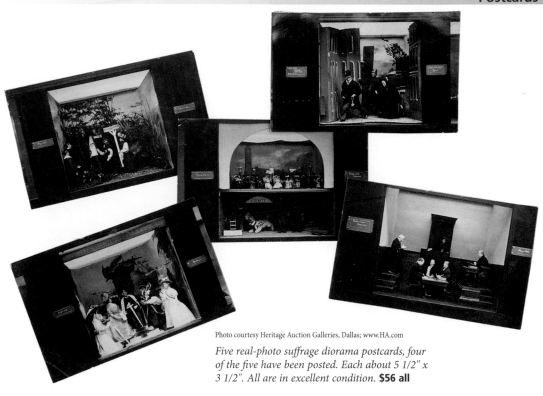

Five real-photo suffrage diorama postcards, four of the five have been posted. Each about 5 1/2" x 3 1/2". All are in excellent condition. **$56 all**

Sixteen English color comic suffrage postcards. Each about 5 1/2" x 3 1/2" and all in very good condition. **$221 all**

Photo courtesy Heritage Auction Galleries, Dallas; www.HA.com

Coolidge, Edison, Ford, and Firestone real-photo postcard, 5 1/2" x 3 1/4", unused, Aug. 19, 1924, Plymouth, Vt. The postcard pictures Harvey Firestone, President Coolidge, Henry Ford, Thomas Edison, Russell Firestone, Mrs. Grace Coolidge and Colonel John Coolidge, the president's father. **$54**

Photo courtesy Heritage Auction Galleries, Dallas; www.HA.com

1909 St. Paul Gophers real-photo postcard. The 1909 World's Colored Champions, a label the club bestowed upon itself after challenging and defeating Rube Foster's Leland Giants that year. The Gophers disbanded after its first and only season. Edge and corner wear. **$1,673**

Photo courtesy Heritage Auction Galleries, Dallas; www.HA.com

1930s movie-star postcards (18), 3 1/2" x 5 1/2", includes Hoot Gibson, Shirley Temple (4), Clara Bow, Greta Garbo, Claudette Colbert, Buster Keaton, Harold Lloyd and many more. Unrestored with bright color and a clean overall appearance. **$39 all**

POSTERS

The advancement of printing techniques in the 18th century —including lithography, which was invented in 1796 by the German Alois Senefelder—allowed for cheap mass production and printing of posters. The invention of lithography was soon followed by chromolithography, which allowed for mass editions of posters illustrated in vibrant colors.

By the 1890s, chromolithography had spread throughout Europe. A number of noted artists created poster art in this period, foremost amongst them Henri de Toulouse-Lautrec and Jules Chéret. Chéret is considered to be the "father" of advertisement placards. He was a pencil artist and a scene decorator, who founded a small lithography office in Paris in 1866. He used striking characters, contrast and bright colors, and created more than 1,000 advertisements, primarily for exhibitions, theatres and products. The industry soon attracted the service of many aspiring painters who needed a source of revenue to support themselves.

Photo courtesy Swann Auction Galleries, New York; www.SwannGalleries.com

Ludwig Hohlwein (1874-1949) Direct China Cotton Importers, circa 1910, 32" x 23", Vereinigte Druckereien & Kunstanstalten, Munich. This is one of two images Hohlwein created for the New Hampshire-based company. **$3,200**

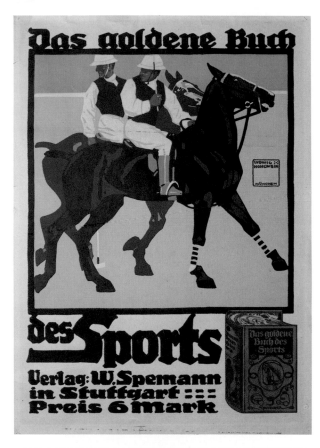

Ludwig Hohlwein (1874-1949) Das Goldene Buch Des Sports, 1910, 24 1/2" x 17 1/4", G. Shuh, Munich, pinholes in corners and margins; staining in image. **$1,900**

Rolf Stoll (1892-1978) Bal Dynamique. 1929, 21 3/4" x 16", Crane-Howard Litho. Co. Little biographical information exists on Stoll. His few paintings in public institutions (The Cleveland Museum of Art) show a far less dramatic and graphic flair than his posters. His suggestive, sophisticated Art Deco-inspired images for the Kokoon Club are infused with an energy, passion, flair and a hedonistic spirit that elevate them to a unique position within the world of pre-World War II American graphics. **$2,800**

Photo courtesy Swann Auction Galleries, New York; www.SwannGalleries.com

Franz von Stuck (1863-1928) Internationale Hygiene Ausstellung Dresden, 1911, 35 1/2" x 23 1/2", Leutert & Schneidewind, Dresden, creases and wrinkles in margins and image. A painter, architect and graphic designer, von Stuck was a founding member of the Munich Secession in 1893, and a cartoonist for the magazine Jugend. This image, which perhaps had its roots in Masonic imagery, was extremely popular and resonated throughout the German graphic landscape: It was stolen by a cigarette company, cartooned in Die Lustige Blatter and later, in 1930, was revamped by Billy Petzold for the same exhibition. This is the larger format. A smaller version was printed by Meisenbach Riffarth & Co., Berlin. **$2,800**

Photo courtesy Heritage Auction Galleries, Dallas; www.HA.com

1860 Currier & Ives "Grand National Banner" print with Stephen Douglas and Herschel Johnson. Part of a series that included every presidential ticket from 1844 through 1876. This 1860 design picturing the "Little Giant" and his running mate is one of the tougher to find. With subtle overall light aging, 10" x 13 3/4". **$3,107**

Photo courtesy Heritage Auction Galleries, Dallas; www.HA.com

Breckinridge & Lane: Extremely rare Currier & Ives "Grand National Banner" campaign poster. Currier published this series of prints for every presidential ticket from 1844 through 1876. The rarest is this 1860 issue for the candidates of the traditional Democratic Party. Fine condition with ample borders, which exhibit a hint of the age browning typically seen on these Grand National Banners. Slight irregularity along the upper portion of the right edge, and a tiny piece missing from the border at the upper right hand corner, 13 3/4" x 9 7/8". **$23,900**

*Toyonosuke Kurozumi
(1908-1955), Osaka
Railways/Kansai Lines,
circa 1935, 42 1/4" x
30", repaired tears and
abrasions in margins and
image. Advertising new
schedules with more trains
traveling to Sakurai and
Wakayama, Kurozumi
presents information in a
minimal way, employing a
station clock, crossing gates
and a plume of smoke from
an engine.* **$1,600**

*Raymond Gid (1905-
2000), Duncan Yo-Yo.
1930, 31 1/2" x 23 3/4",
Bedos, Paris. Duncan yo-
yos hit the market in 1929
and quickly became an
international sensation.
Gid's design, using only
two colors, encapsulates
the sheer joy of the toy
through three simplistic
characters, who are not
only playing with them,
but are embodiments of the
yo-yo itself. Their heads,
each with one large eye,
look like yo-yos, and even
the letters dance. A rare
mixture of Art Deco and
humor.* **$7,500**

Photo courtesy Swann Auction Galleries, New York; www.SwannGalleries.com

Unknown Designer, Chrysler, 1938, 49 1/2" x 38", minor restoration and creases along vertical and horizontal folds. Depiction of a Chrysler Imperial against a radiant cityscape. It is unusual that such a bright image, infused with pre-war optimism for such a prominent American company, should be unrecorded. **$4,200**

Sandor (Alexander Raymond Katz, 1895-1974), Chicago World's Fair, 1934, 39 1/2" x 26 1/4", Goes Litho, minor restoration at edges; expertly repaired, unobtrusive tears in margins. The Chicago World's Fair marked the first time that neon lights were used extensively, and this poster reflects the novelty, energy and brightness of the many displays. Born in Hungary, Katz was a prominent Jewish artist who worked extensively on WPA projects including murals, illustrations and stained glass. **$2,800**

Phil Von Phul (Dates Unknown) Stamp Out the Axis, circa 1941, 14" x 11", minor creasing in corners; light staining in image. Silk-screen on board. Between the time the United States entered World War II and 1943, when the WPA was terminated, many of the WPA artists turned their hands towards propaganda, producing some "vivid and effective" images. An impressive, but little-known, series of images emerged from the 13th Naval District in Seattle. Each of the images in this series is numbered (here it is 33), indicating that many more of these were produced than seem to have survived. Previously unrecorded. Not in the Library of Congress. **$1,500**

Photo courtesy Swann Auction Galleries, New York; www.SwannGalleries.com

Milton Glaser (1929 -) Bob Dylan, 1966, 33" x 22", sharp vertical and horizontal folds, as issued; minor abrasions and pencil marks in image. This is certainly the most famous posters designed by Milton Glaser and one of the most recognized images of post-war American pop culture. This poster was printed in huge quantities and inserted in record albums (Dylan's Greatest Hits, 1967). However, it seems that after being pinned up in college dorm rooms, they were discarded, and have now become quite scarce. **$1,300**

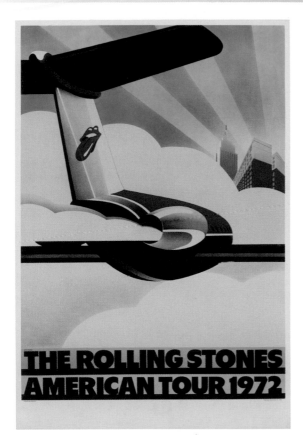

John Pashe (Dates Unknown) The Rolling Stones American Tour, 1972, 37 3/4" x 25 1/4", Sunday Promotions Inc., minor restoration in margins; abrasions in image. Pashe designed The Rolling Stones' iconic "tongue and lip" logo in 1971, as well as four concert posters between 1970 and 1974. Each of his posters for the band is a paean to the Art Deco transportation designs of the 1920s and '30s, reinterpreted with a post-Haight Ashbury flourish. **$900**

Peter Max (1937 -), Toulouse Lautrec, 1967, 36" x 24", Peter Max Printing Corp. Max was one of the earliest, and certainly the most enduring, of the psychedelic artists in the 1960s, and among the most prolific creators of decorative posters, all of which bore his distinctive strong pop colors and ornate decorative patterns. **$1,200**

MOVIE POSTERS, LOBBY CARDS AND STILLS

Photo courtesy Heritage Auction Galleries, Dallas; www.HA.com

The Silver Streak (RKO, 1934). One Sheet (27" x 41"). Not to be confused with the Gene Wilder version, this film featured future B Western star Charles Starrett designing a revolutionary new passenger train capable of speeds over 100 miles per hour. Excitement mounts as he has to prove his train's worth by delivering emergency medical supplies across the country. This poster has pinholes in the corners, tears at the edges, tape on the reverse, a Dutch censor stamp in the bottom right corner, and creases to the right border and top right and bottom left corners. **$717**

Photo courtesy Heritage Auction Galleries, Dallas; www.HA.com

Lifeboat (20th Century Fox, 1944). Title Lobby Card (11" x 14"). Some smudging in the borders, corner bends in the bottom and top left, creasing in the right side, and a small tear in the right border. **$776**

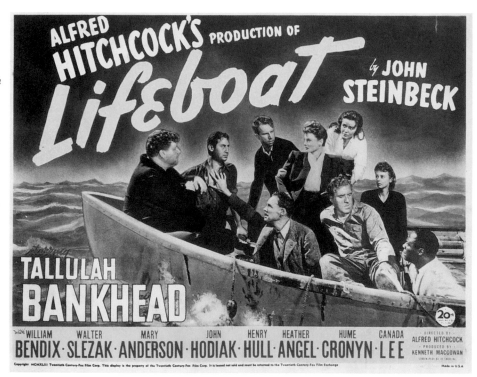

Photo courtesy Heritage Auction Galleries, Dallas; www.HA.com

The She-Devil (Fox, 1918). Three Sheet (41" x 81"). Between 1914 and 1926, Theda Bara made more than 40 films, nearly all of which are now considered lost following a fire at Fox Studios' New Jersey-based nitrate film storage vault in 1937. Only three complete pictures remain, as well as a handful of brief fragments. The She-Devil, one of Bara's lost films, was reportedly a solid effort, featuring Bara as the fiery Spanish girl Lolette. Professional restoration, on Linen. **$3,883**

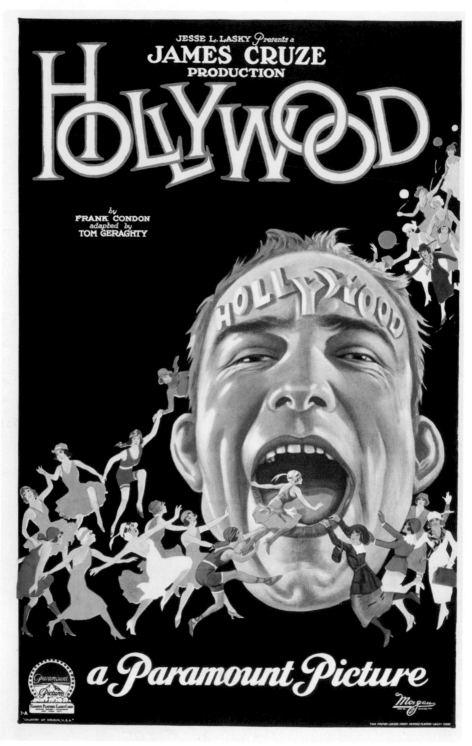

Photo courtesy Heritage Auction Galleries, Dallas; www.HA.com

Hollywood (Paramount, 1923). One Sheet (27" x 41") Style A. Star cameos in this silent film include Mary Astor, William Boyd, Charles Chaplin, Bebe Daniels, Cecil B. DeMille, Douglas Fairbanks, Sid Grauman, Alan Hale, William S. Hart, Jack Holt, Pola Negri, Anna Q. Nilsson, Charles Ogle, Mary Pickford, Zasu Pitts, Will Rogers, Gloria Swanson, and Ben Turpin. In perhaps the most poignant cameo of all, Roscoe "Fatty" Arbuckle appears briefly as an unemployed actor, standing forlornly in a casting line, unable to get work. Professional restoration on Linen. **$89,625**

Photo courtesy Heritage Auction Galleries, Dallas; www.HA.com

Bride of the Monster (Filmmakers Releasing, 1956). Half Sheet (22" x 28"). Director Edward D. Wood's biggest budget film, and the only one that proved financially successful in its original release, this picture also marked Lugosi's last starring role in a feature film. As with all of Wood's films, paper advertising is scarce and highly collectible. This half-sheet had a vertical crease in the right side, tears in the top border, wrinkling overall, a small area of surface paper loss in the bottom, pinholes in the corners, a missing top left corner, edge wear, and a bottom right corner bend. Professional restoration. **$776**

Photo courtesy Heritage Auction Galleries, Dallas; www.HA.com

The Bride of Frankenstein (Universal, 1935). Herald (7" x 9 1/2"). This small single-fold handout has a couple of tiny edge tears and a crease on the front cover. There is a small date inked on the backside. **$1,195**

Photo courtesy Heritage Auction Galleries, Dallas; www.HA.com

Flash Gordon's Trip to Mars (Universal, 1938). One Sheet (27" x 41") Chapter 1 -- "New Worlds to Conquer." After the success of the first Flash Gordon serial in 1936, Universal knew they had a winner on their hands, and went ahead with production on this sequel, with the action switched to Mars (rather than Mongo), to take advantage of the Red Planet hysteria caused by Orson Welles' infamous radio broadcast. Buster Crabbe is back as Flash, as is Charles Middleton as the evil dictator, Ming the Merciless, and Jean Rogers as Dale Arden. Professional restoration, on Linen. **$1,434**

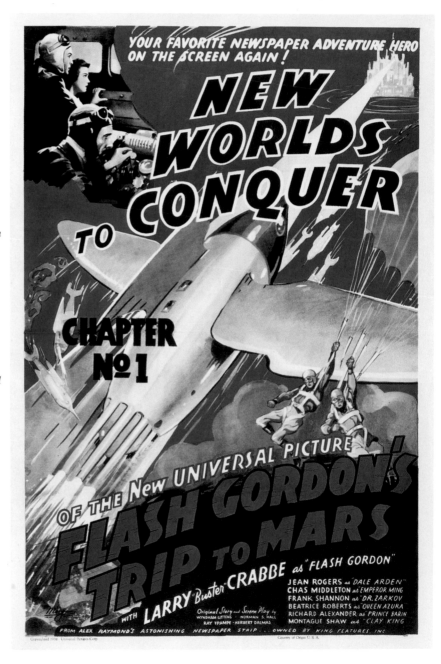

Photo courtesy Swann Auction Galleries, New York; www.SwannGalleries.com

Attributed to Josef Fenneker (1895-1956), The Dance of Death, 1919, 54 1/2" x 41", restoration along vertical and horizontal folds; minor restoration in margins. Fenneker designed more than 300 movie posters. His recognizable style drew largely on German Expressionism combined with a flair for aesthetic decadence. Written by Fritz Lang, "Totentanz" is considered by the Internet Movie Database to be a " lost film (in which) a beautiful dancer's sexual allure is used by an evil cripple to entice men to their deaths. Falling in love with one of the potential victims, she is told by the cripple that he will set her free if her lover, actually a murderer himself, survives and escapes a bizarre labyrinth which runs beneath the cripple's house" (www.imdb.com). Even without a signature, this poster is clearly the work of Fenneker. Although another image by Fenneker for this film exists, this particular version is previously unrecorded. **$4,400**

RECORDS

With the advent of the more sophisticated recording materials, earlier phonograph records became collectors' items. Condition is critical. As with many types of collectibles, a grading scale has been developed.

Mint (M): Perfect condition, no flaws, scratches or scuffs in the grooves. The cardboard jacket will be crisp.

Near Mint (NM) or Mint-Minus (M-): The record will be close to perfect, with no marks in the grooves. The label will be clean, not marked, or scuffed. There will be no ring wear on the record or album cover.

Very Good Plus (VG+): Used for a record that has been played, but well taken care of. Slight scuffle or warps to the grooves is acceptable as long as it does not affect the sound. A faint ring wear discoloration is acceptable. The jacket may appear slightly worn, especially on the edges.

Very Good (VG): Used to describe a record that has some pronounced defects, as does the cover. The record will still play well. This usually is the lowest grade acceptable to a serious collector. Most records listed in price guides are of this grade.

Good (G): This category of record will be playable, but probably will have loss to the sound quality. The cover might be marked or torn.

Poor or Fair (P, F): Record is damaged, may be difficult to play. The cover will be damaged, usually marked, dirty or torn.

Note: Most records, especially popular recordings, have a value of less than $3. Picture sleeves will generally increase values, and often have an independent value.

Hank Williams, Honky-tonkin', MGM E-3412, 1957. **$100**

Dee Dee Sharp, It's Mashed Potato Time, Cameo C-1018, 1962. **$60**

Jerry Lee Lewis, Jerry Lee Lewis, Sun SLP-1230, 1958. **$200**

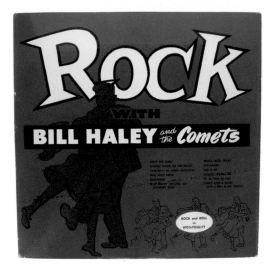

Little Richard, Little Richard, RCA Camden CAL-420, 1956. **$200**

Bill Haley and the Comets, Rock with, Somerset P-4600, 1958. **$150**

Buddy Holly, Buddy Holly, Coral CRL 57210, 1964. **$100**

Ray Charles, Country and Western meets Rhythm and Blues, ABC-Paramount ABC-520, 1965. **$20**

James Brown, Mighty Instrumentals, King 961, 1966. **$100**

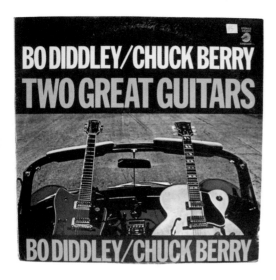

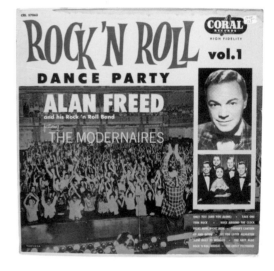

Dion, Alone With, Laurie LLP 2004, 1960. **$200**

Bo Diddley/Chuck Berry, Two Great Guitars, Checker LP 2991, 1964. **$60**

Alan Freed, Rock 'n Roll Dance Party, Coral CRL 57063, 1956. **$150**

Frank Zappa, Sleep Dirt, Discreet/Warner DSK 2292, 1978. **$15**

Atomic Rooster, In Hearing of, Elektra EKS-74109, 1971. **$20**

Roger Daltrey, Daltrey, Track 328, 1973. **$12**

Molly Hatchet, Molly Hatchet, Epic JE 35347, 1978. **$6**

The Moody Blues, Every Good Boy Deserves Favour, Threshold THS 5, 1971. **$15**

Peter Gabriel, So, Geffen GHS 24088, 1986. **$10**

Jethro Tull, Thick as a Brick, Chrysalis CHR 1003, 1973. **$12**

SALT AND PEPPERSHAKERS

Rare, unique and decorative salt and peppershakers have become such popular collector's items over the years that many shaker sets are produced for the sole purpose of being a collectible and are rarely used to hold seasonings.

Salt and peppershakers can be found in nearly every conceivable shape and size and are made in a variety of materials including wood, metal, ceramics, glass, and plastics. They are abundant, colorful, fun, span almost every theme, and best of all, they're often inexpensive.

For more information, see *Antique Trader Salt and Pepper Shaker Price Guide* by Mark F. Moran, 2008.

American Bisque

The American Bisque Pottery Co. of Williamstown, W.V., was founded in 1919 to produce china doll heads, which had become difficult to import from Germany during World War I. Production expanded to include cookie jars, bowls, serving dishes, ashtrays and kitchenwares. The company closed in 1983.

Teddy bears, with gold trim, 1950s, 3 1/4". **$50+**

Teddy bears, 1950s, 3 1/4". **$30+**

Chicks, with gold trim, 1950s, 3 1/4". **$50+**

Cows, 1950s, souvenir of Chicago, 3 1/4". **$30+**

Hocking Glass Co./Anchor Hocking Glass Corp.

Hocking Glass Co. was established in 1905, and named for the river that runs through Lancaster, Ohio. Its first factory was known as the Black Cat because of the haze of carbon dust that hung in the air. In 1937, the Anchor Cap and Closure Corp. merged with Hocking Glass to become Anchor Hocking Glass Corp. The word "Glass" was dropped from the company's name in 1969. The firm's headquarters are still in Lancaster.

Anchor Hocking Glass Corp., Manhattan pattern, late 1930s to early '40s, 2 5/8". **$20+**

Anchor Hocking Glass Corp., Queen Mary pattern, late 1930s to early '40s, 2 5/8". **$20+**

Anchor Hocking Glass Corp., Royal Ruby, 1940s-60s, 3 3/4". No established value.

Hocking Glass Co., yellow Block Optic pattern, footed, circa 1930, 4 1/4". **$80+**

Hocking Glass Co., green Squat Block Optic pattern, circa 1930, 3". **$90+**

Cambridge Glass Co.

The Cambridge (Ohio) Glass Co. began production in 1902. The firm initially used the molds of other companies to make table sets, jugs, bowls, jars, tumblers and lamps. In the 1930s, about 700 people were employed. The company closed in 1954, and after several attempts to reopen, Imperial Glass Co. of Bellaire, Ohio, bought the Cambridge molds in 1960.

Amber glass with crystal handled tray, 1930s; shakers 2 3/4", tray 5 1/4". **$50+ set**

Caprice pattern, Moonlight Blue, 1940s-50s, 3". **$50+**

Ball form in amethyst glass, with Farber Bros. metal bases, 1940s. **$30+**

Decagon pattern, footed, in Bluebell, 1926-30s, 4 1/4". **$70+**

Dutch children, 4". **$40+**

Ceramic Arts Studio

Ceramic Arts Studio of Madison, Wis., produced decorative figurines, wall plaques, shakers and head vases from 1942 until the business closed in 1956. Artist Betty Harrington designed more than 800 figurines for the company.

Asian children, 4 1/2". **$40+**

"Wee People" German children, 3 1/3" and 3". **$50+**

"Wee People" French children, 3 1/4". **$60+**

"Wee People" Indian children, 3 1/4" and 3". **$30+**

Consolidated Lamp & Glass Co.

The Consolidated Lamp & Glass Co. of Coraopolis, Pa., was founded in 1894. The company made lamps, tableware and art glass. In 1928, the firm introduced the "Ruba Rombic" line of Art Deco glassware. The factory was destroyed by fire in 1963.

Bulging Petal pattern, marbleized pastel, late 1800s, 2 1/2". **$60+**

Cord and Tassel pattern, marbleized pastel, late 1800s, 2". **$80+**

Guttate pattern, ruby overlay, later version of an old Consolidated mold, 3 1/4". **$50+**

Leaf Layers pattern, late 1800s, 2 1/2" diameter. **$80+**

SILVER (STERLING)

Silver has been known since ancient times and has long been valued as a precious metal, used to make ornaments, jewelry, tableware and utensils, and coins. Following are select objects from *Warman's Sterling Silver Flatware, 2nd Edition*, by Phil Dreis.

Also see Lighting.

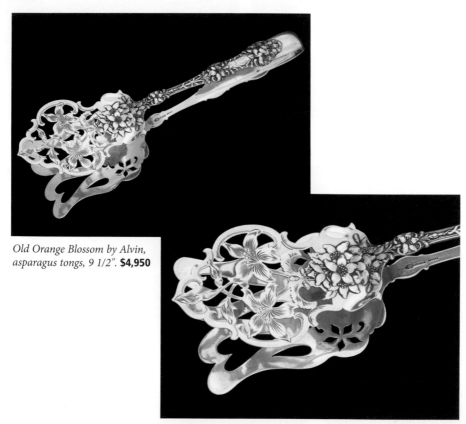

Old Orange Blossom by Alvin, asparagus tongs, 9 1/2". **$4,950**

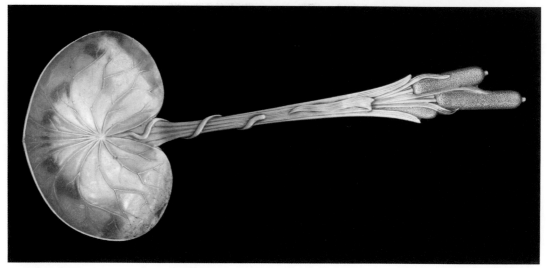

Cattails by Durgin, sauce ladle, 5 1/2". **$695**

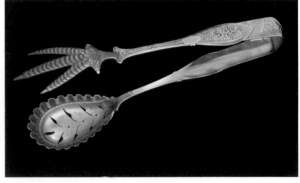

Calla Lily by Whiting, ice cream server, 10 1/2". **$1,295**

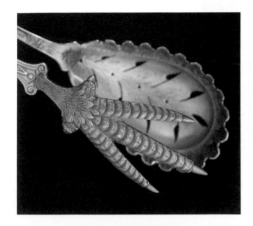

Montezuma by George W. Shiebler & Co., ice tongs, 9 1/2". **$695**

Strasbourg by Gorham, cheese knife with pick, 7 7/8". **$279**

Lily by Whiting, cucumber server. **$495**

Lady's by Gorham, sauce ladle with bucket bowl, 6 1/2". **$795**

Bird's Nest by Gorham, ice cream spoon, 5 7/8".
$1,295

Fuchsia by Whiting, sugar sifter,
8 1/4". **$1,295**

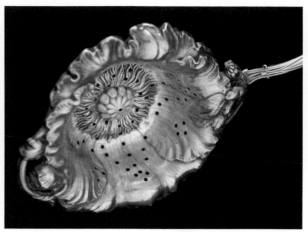

La Parisienne by Reed & Barton, tea strainer. **$495**

Chrysanthemum by Tiffany & Co., fish server, pierced with seahorses, French style. **$17,500**

Les Cinq Fleurs by Reed & Barton, pierced asparagus server. **$495**

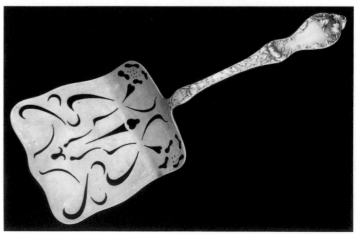

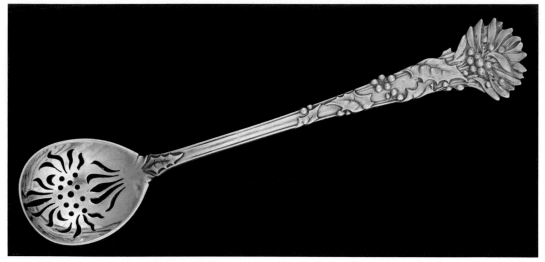

Holly by Tiffany & Co., pierced olive spoon. **$650**

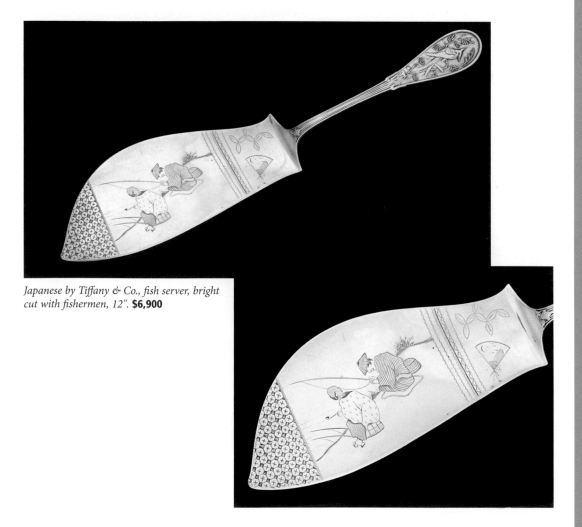

Japanese by Tiffany & Co., fish server, bright cut with fishermen, 12". **$6,900**

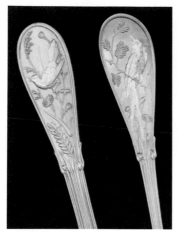

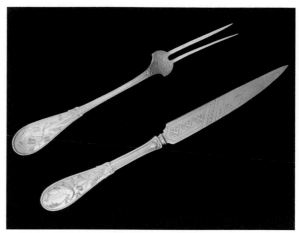

Japanese by Tiffany & Co., gilt fruit knife and fruit fork, bright cut. **$2,650**

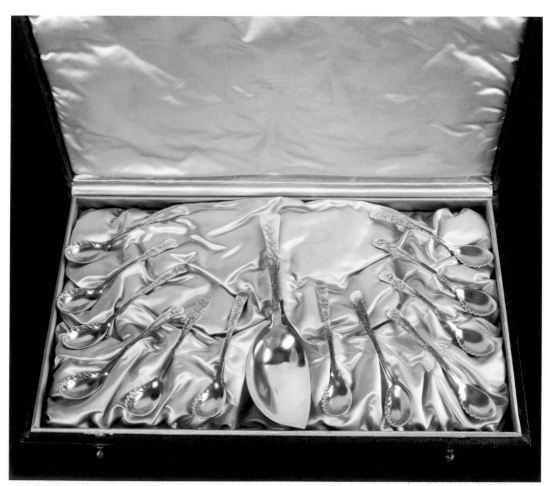

Lap Over Edge, acid-etched by Tiffany & Co., sorbet set in fitted box. **$8,900**

SPACE: COLLECTING'S FINAL FRONTIER?

By Noah Fleisher

Human conquest of the cosmos has the ability to inspire humans like little else and, in the brief time we've been slipping these surly bonds, we've done remarkably well, all things considered. In the cosmic sense this span but a blink of blink. We've walked on the moon, sent craft to mars to explore the surface, sent satellites hurtling headlong into the unknown of the Milky Way beyond our system and we've taken pictures of the beginning of time. These are but baby steps for which future generations will be grateful because they will enjoy the fruits of this early labor.

Noah Fleisher

Little wonder then that the pieces, parts, ephemera and personal memorabilia associated with America's space program – the men and women who, in large part, made science fiction a reality – have made collectors of all sorts sit up and take notice.

"The supply of the really important items is certainly finite," said Howard Weinberger, Senior Space Consultant for Heritage Auction Galleries in Dallas, and CEO of Asset Alternatives. "The old saying is that if you collected all the personal items from the six missions that landed on the moon, all of it would fit in a small suitcase."

Weinberger is talking about the cream of the crop, the things that the Apollo astronauts took special pains with to make sure they were on the lunar surface and spent time in the vacuum of space. The rest of the field – from souvenir patches, parts and models, autographs and well beyond – has as much room for variance of budget as a collector could wish and a plethora of material that – like the very subject it covers – can sometimes seem infinite.

Unlike so many categories of collecting, the market for Space is still being established. The subject has long been popular, but the ability to get the very best of The Right Stuff was not there until recently, as many of the astronauts – or their families, if they've passed on – have realized the value, both historic and financial, of their accomplishments. The more that the remaining original astronauts release key pieces of their extra-terrestrial lives, the more established the market will become.

One of the most important things Space collecting has going for it is its appeal, said Weinberger. The steady increase in prices at auction in the three years he's been working with Heritage shows just how broad this appeal is.

"I think it's a function of the fact that people are now aware that these items can be bought," said Weinberger, who is among the few with the connections to bring the choicest pieces to auction. "The genre is unique because the demographic, in my opinion, is among the top three to five potential demographics for collecting."

Meaning there's almost no soul on this planet that doesn't know about, and isn't at least peripherally fascinated by, space travel.

"Show a baseball card, a comic book or a regional American quilt to a woman in Asia," Weinberger said, "and it won't translate. If you go back to 1969, to Apollo 11 and the first moon landing, you have the entire planet watching. Everybody remembers where they were when Neil Armstrong walked on the moon, or when Allan Sheppard went up with Mercury."

The broad scope of potential buyers is indeed as varied as the material, as a few minutes with the following pages will show. As the field sorts itself out, it is tough to break down into categories. The astronauts, and all the workers at NASA – from the men who walked on the moon to the guys that swept up at the end of the day – were all aware from the beginning of the historic nature of their pursuit – and it potential value.

This prospective worth, then, necessitates at least an attempt at breaking the hobby into categories. According to Weinberger, this is not something that should be done by item type, but rather by mission type and purpose.

"There's not a lot of the very best stuff, so there is a hierarchy of sorts that has evolved," he said. "The highest rung is for items that actually landed on moon and went

Buzz Aldrin's 1923-S Peace Silver Dollar Flown on the Moon Mission Aboard Apollo 11. This was part of his Personal Preference Kit (PPK). Accompanied by a signed letter of authenticity from him. **$31,070**

Mercury 7 Type M Astronaut's Test Gloves worn by John Glenn and Wally Schirra. Two 11" x 4" aluminized nylon gloves manufactured by the B.F. Goodrich Co. for NASA during the agency's testing of the Mercury Astronauts' spacesuits. Both gloves include an internal cloth Project Mercury label. One glove has the name "Glenn" and one "Shirra" (sic) written in black marker inside the aluminum fittings. **$7,170 both**

on the surface. Then it's something that landed on the moon but didn't leave capsule. After that it's memorabilia that flew to the moon but only stayed in orbit. From there it's about things that flew in space, things that were strictly in earth orbit and things that didn't fly in space but are of a personal nature belonging to the astronauts, or having their autographs."

Within these several categories, however, again there can be a striking difference in price depending on the name and the program it's associated with.

Whatever level a collector is looking at to get into the market for Space memorabilia, the most important thing is authenticity, especially at the high end. In fact, Weinberger said, if it comes from an astronaut's personal collection, a signature and/or a letter of authentication is of paramount importance.

"No matter what it is, even if it's purchased personally from an astronaut, it has to be certified," he said. "The most desirable certification is having the signature on the item itself. If it has that, and a letter as well, then so much

the better."

The most important thing to get started is not a broad general knowledge of what's out there, but to simply have a passion for it no matter how much cash you can put in. You can buy autographs, first-day covers or specially minted Robbins medals that flew on every Apollo mission. You can spend a few hundred or a few hundred thousand; either way, it's an accessible market.

"You can start with something basic," Weinberger said. "The overall amount of memorabilia related to space is endless."

It's a good thing, then, that the enthusiasm of collectors, especially for something as inspiring as space travel, seems to be equally as endless.

Noah Fleisher is a media and public relations liaison for Heritage Auction Galleries in Dallas, and former editor of Antique Trader magazine.

All listings and images courtesy Heritage Auction Galleries, Dallas; *www.HA.com*

U.S. Flag Carried on the Moon by Neil Armstrong, affixed to a 12" x 14" wooden shield plaque, flag is 6" x 3 3/4" and an Apollo 11 patch, covered in clear plastic. The 5" x 3" metallic plaque affixed certifies that "This flag was carried on the moon by/ astronaut Neil Armstrong/ on July 20, 1969/ and presented to/ Joe D. Garino Jr./ by/ The Apollo 11 Astronauts." As Armstrong set foot on the lunar surface, he carried this flag. Accompanied by a signed certificate of authentication from Garino verifying its provenance. **$56,763**

Buzz Aldrin's Apollo 11 Slide Rule, Flown to the Moon. A Pickett Model N600-ES (Eye Saver) Log Speed Rule, 6" with 22 five-inch scales. Flown to the moon aboard Apollo 11 by Aldrin. Very fine condition. Accompanied by a signed letter of authenticity from him. **$77,675**

Space Shuttle Columbia Commander John Young's Flight Suit Patches, Worn on the First Shuttle Mission, directly from his Personal Collection, Certified and Signed on the Display Frame. On the paper backing of the frame, Young has written: "Patches From My Suit Flown Aboard STS-1. John Young". **$56,762**

Apollo 8 Flown CMP Checklist, Directly from the Personal Collection of Mission Command Module Pilot James Lovell, Certified and Signed. Lovell has certified and signed the front: "James Lovell Flown". With normal wear and light soiling. **$47,800**

Apollo 13-Flown, Lunar Module Spacecraft Identification Plate Display Directly from the Personal Collection of Mission Commander James Lovell, certified and signed. A metal plate 5 1/4" x 1 3/4" mounted to a 10" x 11" wooden display plaque beneath a metal die-cut representation of the lunar module and an engraved brass plate with the words: APOLLO XIII LUNAR MODULE – 7, "FAREWELL AQUARIUS, AND WE THANK YOU" – Capt. J. Lovell - F. Haise - J. Swigert Jr. At the top left of this wooden plaque, Lovell has written in silver: "From the personal collection of James Lovell". On the back, he has written: "Apollo 13 Lunar Module/ name plate -- removed/ prior to jettison LM./ James Lovell."............**$47,800**

Apollo 10, Complete Lunar Module-Flown Rendezvous Checklist with Original Signed Snoopy Sketch by Charles Schulz. Twenty-nine numbered card stock pages of 8 1/4" x 10 1/2", three-hole punched, and bound with rings inside heavier boards. Just inside is an additional card stock leaf containing a full-page black-felt-tip drawing of Snoopy. Drawn and signed by Schulz, Snoopy is shown in his "flying ace" goggles and scarf (along with a space helmet); sitting atop his "Sopwith Camel" (doghouse). Snoopy was the semi-official nickname given to the lunar module (the command module was called Charlie Brown). From the personal collection of Captain Gene Cernan accompanied by written authentication by Cernan. **$41,825**

1969 Omega Speedmaster, Professional Apollo XI Commemorative Watch, Serial No. 9. 18K Gold Presented to Him by the Omega Watch Co, Signed on Case and Box. Inscribed on the back: "ASTRONAUT JOHN W. YOUNG- to mark man's conquest of space with time, through time, on time GEMINI 3 & 10 - APOLLO 10 No 9". The Omega Speedmaster chronograph, often known as the "Moonwatch," was first manufactured in 1957 and has a long history with NASA. There are numerous photos available showing astronauts wearing their NASA-issue Omega Speedmasters during various spaceflights and moon landings. **$38,837**

Apollo Bracelet, Containing All 11 Flown Silver Robbins Medallions from the personal collection of astronaut Paul J. Weitz. Individual serial numbers as follows: Apollo 7 (#197); Apollo 8 (#254); Apollo 9 (#320); Apollo 10 (#225); Apollo 11 (#139); Apollo 12 (#243); Apollo 13 (# 371, made from flown metal); Apollo 14 (#118); Apollo 15 (#116); Apollo 16 (#55); and Apollo 17 (#F42). A handwritten and

BUZZ ALDRIN, HANDWRITTEN NOTES AND SCRIPTURES FLOWN TO THE SURFACE OF THE MOON

Front and verso of a 3" x 5" buff-colored lightweight card, one horizontal fold affecting some text. The astronauts of the Apollo 8 mission were so inspired by their view of the earth from moon orbit the previous Christmas Eve that they read the biblical account of the creation story from Genesis. Noted atheist Madalyn Murray O'Hair brought suit against NASA over this Bible reading, asking the courts to ban any further such activity.

Though the courts eventually rejected the suit, NASA was quite nervous about further religious activities throughout the rest of the Apollo program. Buzz Aldrin, a Christian and an elder at the Webster, Texas, Presbyterian Church, wished to express his personal faith and give thanks to God by the taking of the Holy Communion on the moon. His church furnished him with the wine and wafer, which he stowed secretly in his kit. He described the activity in his book Return to Earth (Bantam Books, 1973): "During the first idle moment in the LM before eating our snack, I reached into my personal preference kit and pulled out two small packages which had been specially prepared at my request. One contained a small amount of wine, the other a small wafer. With them and a small chalice from the kit, I took communion on the moon, reading to myself from a small card I carried on which I had written the portion of the Book of John used in the traditional communion ceremony."

He had wanted to read the scripture back to earth, but NASA requested that he not do so. Instead, he read from this card, on which is written: "Houston This is Eagle The LM Pilot speaking. I would like to request a few moments of silence. Over. I would like to invite each person listening in, wherever and whomever he may be, to contemplate for a moment the events of the past few hours and to give thanks in his own individual way - - My way shall be by partaking of the elements of Holy Communion." His fellow astronaut, Neil Armstrong, watched but did not partake.

The verses he would have liked to have read are found at the top of the other side of this handwritten card: "An [sic] Jesus said, 'I am the vine, you are the branches. Whoever remains in me, and I in him, will bear much fruit; for you can do nothing without me.' [John 15:5]". There are additional, and appropriate, verses beneath in a different ink that Aldrin did actually quote three days later during a TV broadcast by the astronauts aboard Columbia the evening before they splashed down safely in the Pacific. He writes: "Psalm 8: v. 3,4 'When I consider thy heavens, the work of thy fingers, the moon and the stars, which thou has ordained; What is man that thou art mindful of him? And the Son of Man, that thou visitest Him?'"

From the personal collection of Dr. Buzz Aldrin and also accompanied by a signed letter of authenticity from him. **$179,250**

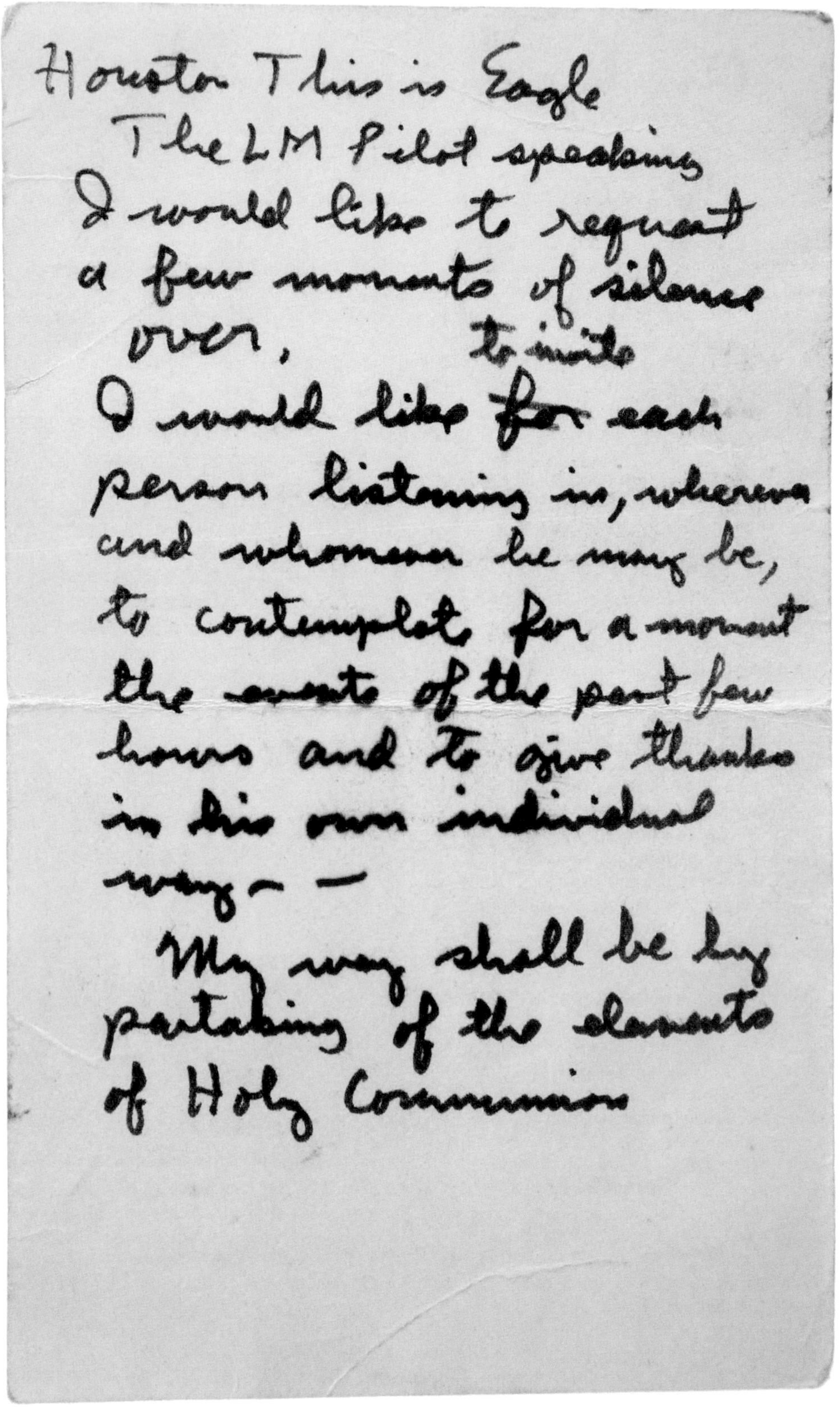

Houston This is Eagle
The LM Pilot speaking
I would like to request
a few moments of silence
over,   to invite
I would like for each
person listening in, wherever
and whomever he may be,
to contemplate for a moment
the events of the past few
hours and to give thanks
in his own individual
way — —
My way shall be by
partaking of the elements
of Holy Communion

signed letter of authenticity from Paul Weitz is included. **$37,344**

Apollo 16, Lunar Module Flown Needle-Nose Pliers from the collection of Lunar Module Pilot Charles M. Duke Jr., overall length 5". These pliers were flown to the moon aboard the Lunar Module Orion and used on the lunar surface during April 16-27, 1972. From the collection of Charles M. Duke, Jr., who has included a handwritten and signed letter of certification verifying its provenance. **$33,460**

Apollo 17, Command Module Flown Flight Plan, Volumes I and II, Both signed by and from the personal collection of Mission Commander Gene Cernan. Two separate books, each one is 8 1/2" x 10 1/2", printed on cardstock, and bound between two heavier boards with three binder rings. Cernan has certified and signed each: Volume I- "Flown to the Moon Apollo XVII Gene Cernan" and Volume II- "Flown on Apollo XVII Gene Cernan." **$33,460**

Apollo 8, Flown Update Book Signed by and from the Personal Collection of Mission Command Module Pilot James Lovell. This 5 1/2" x 8", 200+-page book, printed on cardstock and bound between stiff covers with two binder rings, is titled "APOLLO 8 UPDATES". Certified and signed on the cover by Lovell: "James Lovell Flown on Apollo 8". **$33,460**

Apollo 16, Lunar Module Flown Spacecraft Identification Plate Display Directly from the Personal Collection of Mission Commander John Young, Certified and Signed. A metal plaque of 5 1/4" x 1 3/4" mounted to a 10" x 11" wooden display plaque beneath a metal die-cut representation of the lunar module and an engraved brass plate. At the bottom of this wooden plaque, Young has written in silver: "Plaque Flown on Apollo XVI John Young". **$33,460**

Buzz Aldrin's Space Flown Cutting Tool, Used on the Apollo 11 Mission, with original Velcro still attached. Measuring 8" in length, this stainless steel hand tool was used on the lunar module by Buzz Aldrin on Apollo 11. From the personal collection of Dr. Buzz Aldrin and accompanied by a signed letter of authenticity from him. **$31,070**

Buzz Aldrin, Apollo 11 Space Flown Book by Robert Goddard. The small leather-bound book, The Autobiography of Robert Hutchings Goddard: Father of the Space Age, Early Years to 1927 (Worchester, Mass.: Achille J. St. Onge, 1966), is 2" x 3" and has 85 gilt-edged pages. The book is inscribed in pencil, "Flown on Apollo 11 July 16-24-'69 E.E. Aldrin Jr. (signed) Buzz Aldrin." The book was published to commemorate the 40th anniversary of Goddard's first liquid propellant rocket. There were 1,926 copies printed, of which this is number 659. The book was carried on Apollo 11 by Buzz Aldrin as a favor to his father and as a token of respect for Goddard, the "Father of Modern Rocketry." Accompanied by a signed letter of authenticity from Aldrin. **$29,875**

Buzz Aldrin's Original Gemini 12 Space Suit Patches, originally presented to his parents for Christmas in 1966. Framed 16 1/2" x 13 1/2" with printed text, "These articles were worn on the space suit of Astronaut Edwin E. Aldrin, Jr. during the historic flight of Gemini XII in November, 1966." To the left of that is a handwritten inscription, "To Mother & Dad With a grateful son's love, Buzz Christmas 1966." **$29,875**

Apollo 11 Flown Robbins Silver Medallion, Serial Number 188, from the collection of astronaut Charles M. Duke Jr., 25mm, with the mission dates engraved on the reverse. From the collection of Charles M. Duke, Jr., with a handwritten and signed letter of certification verifying its provenance. **$28,680**

Apollo 17, Lunar Module Flown Lunar Rover Malfunction Procedures Checklist Card, signed by and from the personal collection of Mission Commander Gene Cernan, with smudges of lunar dust. **$28,680**

Apollo 13-Flown CSM Systems Data Checklist, from the personal collection of Mission Commander James Lovell, certified and signed. An 8 1/2" x 10 1/2" book of approximately 100 pages including dozens of multi-page pull-out schematic diagrams, bound with three binder

Apollo 10 Command Module Pilot John Young's Flown Space Suit Patches (four) Directly from his Personal Collection, certified and signed on the display frame. A 10" x 17" framed display containing all four pressure suit patches from the May 18-26, 1969, Apollo 10 mission, a dress rehearsal for the first manned lunar landing. On the paper backing of the frame, Young has written: "I certify that these 4 patches were on my Apollo 10 Pressure Suit when I went to the MOON. John Young". **$31,070**

Apollo 11 Signed and Flown Commemorative Cover with Notation. Neil Armstrong, Michael Collins and Buzz Aldrin have all signed in blue felt-tip this NASA Manned Spacecraft Center Stamp Club Official Commemorative Cover of the First Manned Lunar Exploration with a colorful cachet of two astronauts on the lunar surface. From the personal collection of Dr. Buzz Aldrin and accompanied by a signed letter of authenticity from him. $26,290

rings between two heavyweight covers. Rare in complete form. **$28,680**

Apollo 14, Lunar Module Antares Flown American Flag, signed by Edgar Mitchell. The Apollo 14 Lunar Module (LM) Antares was the third crewed vehicle to land on the moon. The flag was carried by LM Pilot Edgar Mitchell during the Apollo 14 mission. Inscribed and signed: "Flown to the Lunar surface aboard Antares - Feb. 5, 1971. Edgar Mitchell, Apollo 14 LMP". The flag is accompanied by two certificates of authenticity - one handwritten and one typed - by Ed Mitchell on his personal Apollo 14 letterhead.
....**$26,290**

Apollo 17-Flown, Robbins Sterling Silver Medallion, obtained by Astronaut Joseph P. Kerwin as a member of the Astronaut Flight Office. The 35mm medal, with the serial number 38, was flown aboard Apollo 17, the 11th manned space mission in the NASA Apollo program. There were only 80 Apollo 17-flown silver Robbins medals. From the collection of Joseph P. Kerwin M.D., who has included a signed letter of certification verifying its provenance.
....**$26,290**

Gene Cernan's Apollo 17 Lunar Module-Flown Fisher AG-7 Space Pen, used during the flight and actually carried by Cernan in a spacesuit pocket onto the surface of the moon. From the personal collection of Captain Gene Cernan accompanied by written authentication by Cernan. **$23,900**

Gemini 10, Mission Commander John Young's Flown Space Suit Patches (three) directly from his personal collection, certified and signed on the display frame. On the paper backing of the frame, Young has written: "I certify that these patches flew on my pressure suit on Gemini 10. John Young". **$23,900**

Apollo 17-Flown, Omega Stainless Steel Speedmaster Professional Watch and Flown-Metal Attachment directly from the personal collection of Mission Command Module Pilot Ron Evans, certified and signed. Included is a signed letter of certification from Jan Evans (Mrs. Ron Evans).
....**$23,900**

Apollo 15, Lunar Module-Flown Miniature Lunar Rover License Plate certified by Mission Commander Dave Scott. A 1 1/4" x 3/4" mini Moon 1971 license plate numbered

"LRV 001." Novaspace Galleries Certificate of Authenticity signed by Dave Scott included. **$21,510**

Gene Cernan's Apollo 17 Lunar Module-Flown Sunglasses, and Beta Cloth Case. Manufactured by American Optical, 5 1/2" size, 1-10 12K GF, with a NASA part number of "SEB12100033-201" and serial number of "60" printed on the right earpiece. These sunglasses were worn by Cernan during the final mission to the moon in December 1972. From the personal collection of Captain Gene Cernan accompanied by written authentication by Cernan. **$20,315**

Apollo 14, Lunar Module-Flown Portable Utility Light as presented by Mission Commander Alan Shepard to Support Crew Member William Pogue. Portable light of approximately 2 1/4" x 2 1/4" x 1 1/2" plus mounting bracket and attached coiled electrical cord. The light is accompanied by a signed ASF Certificate of Authenticity from Edgar Mitchell. **$20,315**

Original Russian Sokol Spacesuit, Sokol (Falcon) Type KV-1 or KV-2 as manufactured by the Zvezda company.
....**$17,925**

Apollo 8-Flown, Unopened Bottle of Coronet Brandy from the personal collection of Mission Command Module Pilot James Lovell. A two-ounce, still-sealed bottle of Coronet VSQ California Grape Brandy, 100 proof, that was included in Lovell's holiday dinner aboard the Apollo 8 spacecraft during its historic journey on Christmas 1968. The second signed letter of authenticity from Lovell on his letterhead states: "I hereby certify that this bottle of brandy was part of the Christmas Day dinner on board the Apollo 8 spacecraft. Apollo 8 circled the moon on December 25, 1968. This bottle of brandy is from my personal collection of space artifacts and has been in my possession since the mission." **$17,925**

Apollo 13-Flown, Pair of "Booties" from the personal collection of Mission Commander James Lovell. This lot includes a signed letter of authenticity from Lovell stating, "[These] Internal flight suit beta cloth booties - worn during flight of Apollo 13 [were] flown on board the Apollo 13 Command Module Odyssey during its perilous flight around the moon April 11-17, 1970." **$17,925**

Apollo 17, Lunar Module-Flown Commander's Armrest signed by and from the personal collection of Mission

Commander Gene Cernan. This metal, right-side armrest has overall dimensions of 7 1/4" x 10 3/4" x 7" including brackets. There is a label on the top, "Pull Down Armrest to Release From Stowed Position", around which Cernan has certified and signed: "LM CDR Arm Rest - LM/ Flown as part of Apollo XVII Lunar Module Challenger Gene Cernan." **$14,340**

Apollo 17, Lunar Module-Flown LM Water Gun and Filter from the personal collection of Mission Commander Gene Cernan. This was used aboard the Lunar Module Challenger during three days on the surface of the moon, allowing astronauts Gene Cernan and Harrison Schmitt to drink clean water and to prepare their meals. Certified and signed by Cernan: "Flown to the Lunar Surface on Apollo XVII Gene Cernan." **$14,340**

Apollo 11, Lunar Landing Astronauts signed photograph. Official NASA photograph of the Apollo 11 lunar landing signed "Buzz Aldrin" and "Neil Armstrong", 9 3/4" x 8", April 22, 1983. ....**$13,145**

Apollo 17-Flown, Beta Cloth Lunar Module Astronaut Preference Kit belonging to Apollo 17 Commander Gene Cernan. An off-white bag of approximately 4" x 8" x 1 1/2" with a drawstring top and original red wax seal. From the personal collection of Captain Gene Cernan accompanied by written authentication by Cernan. **$11,950**

Apollo 8-Flown, Flashlight from the personal collection of Mission Command Module Pilot James Lovell. A heavy, brass-milled two-cell flashlight, 5" in length and with a maximum diameter of 1". The original batteries are still inside. Includes a signed letter of authenticity from Lovell on his letterhead. **$10,157**

Apollo 16, Lunar Module-Flown Mechanical Pencil directly from the personal collection of Mission Commander John Young. Includes a signed letter of certification from John Young. **$10,157**

Apollo 16, Lunar Module-Flown Engraved Spoon, directly from the personal collection of Mission Commander John Young. Engraved on the handle. Letter of certification from John Young included. **$10,157**

Apollo 12, Lunar Module-Flown Paperweight with Lunar Surface Experiments Package Emblem. The Apollo Lunar Surface Experiments Package (ALSEP) comprised a set of scientific instruments placed by the astronauts at the landing site of each of the five Apollo Moon missions following Apollo 11 (Apollos 12, 14, 15, 16, and 17). Designed and built by Bendix Aerospace of Ann Arbor, Mich., the instruments were designed to run autonomously after the astronauts left and to make long-term studies of the lunar environment. Bendix designed a number of small silver emblems, depicting an astronaut carrying the ALSEP, to be carried into space and returned for use as mementos. From the collection of Richard Gordon. **$9,560**

Large Section of Apollo 11-Flown "Kapton Foil", from Buzz Aldrin's personal collection. Measures approximately 8 1/4" x 2". Accompanied by a signed letter of authenticity from him. **$8,962**

Apollo 16-Flown, Hand Tools (three) directly from the personal collection of Mission Commander John Young. All three of these items flew on Apollo 16 to the moon and back during its 11-day mission, April 16-27, 1972. Includes letter of certification from John Young. ....**$8,962 all**

Apollo 17, Command Module-Flown Pan Camera Spring Pin directly from the personal collection of Mission Command Module Pilot Ron Evans, certified. A steel pin 3 3/4" long overall including a 1 1/2" round ring at top, still with its spring action, and engraved "AVDEL PUSH PULL/ MS17990C310". Letter of certification from Jan Evans (Mrs. Ron Evans) included. **$8,365**

Neil Armstrong, Michael Collins, and Edwin E. Aldrin, Jr. First on the Moon. A Voyage with Neil Armstrong, Michael Collins, Edwin E. Aldrin Jr. Written with Gene Farmer and Dora Jane Hamblin. Epilogue by Arthur C. Clarke. Boston: Little, Brown and Co., (1970). First edition. Inscribed and signed on the half-title page: "To Joseph Sakmyster- With Best Wishes Neil Armstrong", and signed "Buzz Aldrin" and "Michael Collins". Octavo. xiii, 434 pages. Black and white illustrations. Signed certificate of authenticity from Space Coast Cover Service included. **$7,767**

Apollo 10, Lunar Module-Flown Spotlight and Power Cord. From the personal collection of Captain Gene Cernan accompanied by written authentication by Cernan.
....**$7,767**

Apollo 13-Flown, Spacesuit Repair Kit signed by and from the personal collection of Mission Commander James Lovell. This Beta cloth kit with Velcro closures is 6" x 4 3/4" x 1" when folded and 13" x 14" overall when opened out. Lovell has certified and signed the outside front. **$7,767**

NEIL A. ARMSTRONG

Neil Armstrong Color Spacesuit Photo signed but not inscribed, the "smiling" pose. An 8" x 10" NASA lithographed print showing the Apollo 11 Commander, helmet off, in front of a large image of the moon. He has signed boldly in blue felt-tip on his white spacesuit beneath the American flag patch. **$8,365**

Apollo 17, Command Module-Flown Lunar Orbit Chart "A" signed by and from the personal collection of Mission Commander Gene Cernan. **$7,767**

Apollo 8-Flown, Mismatched Pair of Cufflinks directly from the personal collection of Mission Command Module Pilot James Lovell. **$7,170**

Apollo 14, Command Module-Flown Optics Handhold. Once owned by astronaut Stuart Roosa, this piece of the Apollo 14 Command Module Kitty Hawk was presented to a friend as a gift. **$7,170**

Neil Armstrong Autograph Letter, signed "Neil," on right half of photocopy of article, one page, 8 1/2" x 11". From the collection of former physical trainer of the astronauts, Joe Garino. Accompanied by a signed certificate of authentication from Garino verifying its provenance. **$6,573**

Gemini 4-Flown, 1902 U.S. $2.50 Gold Coin originally from the collection of Mission Command Pilot Jim McDivitt, NGC Certified. This gold quarter-eagle was carried along on the Gemini 4 mission, the first U.S. multi-day flight, and the one in which Ed White performed the first American EVA (extra-vehicular activity). **$5,377**

Apollo 16, Lunar and Command Module-Flown Metal Comb used by Charles Duke. It remained on the surface of the moon for almost 72 hours and was exposed to the vacuum of space on each of the three EVAs. From the collection of Charles M. Duke Jr., who has included a handwritten and signed Letter of certification verifying its provenance. **$5,138**

Yuri Gagarin, Inscribed and Signed Photograph. Printed black and white and is inscribed and signed by him in purple ink. **$5,078**

Apollo 16-Flown, Toothbrush with Original Pouch directly from the personal collection of Mission Commander John Young. This was Young's personal toothbrush on man's fifth moon-landing mission, April 16-27, 1972. With signed letter of certification from John Young. **$5,078**

Apollo 14, Command Module Flown American Flag directly from the personal Collection of Mission Lunar Module Pilot Edgar Mitchell, certified and signed. Includes signed letter of certification from Dr. Mitchell on his personal letterhead. **$4,780**

Skylab I (SL-2), Robbins Gold Medallion with Skylab-Flown Emerald directly from the collection of Astronaut Paul Weitz. **$4,780**

Two Apollo 16, Command Module-Flown Freeze Dried Food Packets from the collection of Lunar Module Pilot Charles M. Duke Jr. One packet of four sugar cookie cubes, and one packet of six strawberry cubes. From the collection of Charles M. Duke Jr., with a handwritten letter of certification. **$4,780**

Buzz Aldrin, Signed Lunar Plastic Relief Map Showing the Apollo 11 Landing Site. Dr. Aldrin has signed at the top in the Mare Tranquillatis (Sea of Tranquility): "Apollo XI Landing Site/ Buzz Aldrin." **$4,481**

Roll of 70mm Images from the Apollo 11 Mission, containing dozens of full-color images taken prior to landing on the Moon. This first-generation duplicate was owned by Buzz Aldrin and includes numerous views of the Earth from space, photos of the astronauts, the command

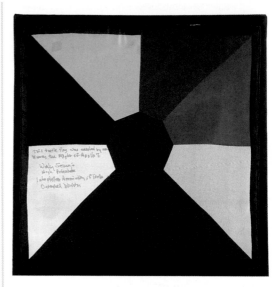

Apollo 7 Flown Turtle Flag Signed By Wally Schirra, the Imperial Potentate of the Interstellar Association of Turtles. Membership in this group has been sought by other astronauts since the Apollo years. Signed by Wally Schirra. **$3,585**

module, the lunar module and close-ups of the lunar surface. **$5,676**

Apollo 11, Command Module-Flown Heat Shield Ablater Plugs (14) in Acrylic. Included is a collectSPACE.com statement of provenance. **$4,481**

Neil Armstrong, Buzz Aldrin, Wernher von Braun, and others: Signed 1970 Banquet Program. Approximately 20 signatures total including several of major aeronautic executives. **$4,183**

Apollo 8-Flown, Heat Shield Ablative Plug in Plastic. Likely removed by a technician working on the command module after its return to Earth. **$3,884**

Apollo 11, The First Moon Landing - Group of 33 Original NASA Photographs. From the collection of the former physical trainer of the astronauts, Joe Garino, accompanied by a signed certificate of authentication. **$3,884**

Invitation to attend a Space Shuttle Launch, with STS-1 Pilot Bob Crippen. **$3,585**

Space Shuttle Columbia (STS-3)-Flown Ascent Checklist, with added notations, used by crew members Jack Lousma and Charles G. Fullerton during the March 22-30, 1982, mission. From the collection of Jack Lousma, with handwritten letter of certification. **$3,586**

Neil Armstrong, First Step on the Moon Photo, signed. A 10" x 8" official NASA B&W photo, with caption on verso. **$3,346**

Apollo 13-Flown, Custom Communication Ear Plugs from the personal collection of Mission Commander James Lovell. Includes a signed letter of authenticity from Lovell on his letterhead. **$3,107**

Colonel Buzz Aldrin, United States Air Force, Flyer's Summer Coveralls. Worn by Aldrin at a reunion of the

22nd Fighter Squadron, a unit where he flew F-100 Super Sabres as a flight commander. From the personal collection of Dr. Buzz Aldrin and accompanied by a signed letter of authenticity from him. **$3,107**

Apollo 14, Command Module Kittyhawk-Flown Stitched Cloth Mission Emblem. From the collection of Edgar D. Mitchell, Sc.D., with signed typed letter of certification and a handwritten letter. **$2,987**

Gemini Foldout Desktop Cockpit Control Training Aide, directly from the personal collection of Gemini 3 and 10 Astronaut John Young, certified and signed. .**$2,988**

Gemini Program Reentry Control System Thruster, Rocketdyne SE-6. Neil Armstrong fired the RCS thrusters to regain enough command of the spacecraft to make an emergency landing only 10 hours into the mission. ..**$2,032**

Neil Armstrong Signed Moon Globe, with special notations of all landing sites made by man. **$1,256**

Lunar Receiving Lab Squeegee, he squeegee is accompanied by 2" spring that appears to fit into the hollowed squeegee handle. The spring package bears a NASA tag indicating that it was last "Cleaned for Service" on July 30, 1971, five months after the last astronauts were quarantined in the LRL. **$1,195**

Headset, Pacific Plantronics Spencomm, as used by Apollo and Skylab astronauts. **$1,195**

Neil Armstrong, Signed Baseball, very rare. **$856**

Apollo 17, Crew-Signed Large Color Challenger Photo directly from the collection of Mission Command Module Pilot Ron Evans. Evans took this photo as he inspected the lunar module during the rendezvous before docking. ..**$837**

Apollo 17, Crew-Signed Large Color "Tracy's Rock" Photo directly from the collection of Mission Command Module Pilot Ron Evans. This rock formation, also known as Split Rock or the Station Six Boulder, was visited and studied by Schmitt and Cernan on their third lunar EVA. Tracy is the name of Gene Cernan's daughter. **$777**

Neil Armstrong "First Man on the Moon" Stamp Sheet, Signed. A full sheet of thirty-two 10-cent U.S. airmail stamps (Scott #C76) signed "Neil Armstrong" at the very edge of the right selvage, just above "Mr. Zip." **$628**

Large Assortment of Astronaut-Signed Christmas Cards, various sizes on card stock. From the collection of former physical trainer of the astronauts, Joe Garino, accompanied by a signed certificate of authentication. **$478**

Gemini Titan-6 First Day Cover, Signed by Schirra and Stafford. Postmarked Dec. 15, 1965, Cape Canaveral, Fla. **$448**

NASA Camera Control Unit, metallic, rectangular cube-shaped device, 4" x 4" x 2 1/2", manufactured by the Mitchell Camera Corp. Two small NASA "Property of U.S. Government" metallic plates affixed. **$287**

Apollo "Snoopy", 1969 Moon Landing Commemorative Medallion. From the collection of former physical trainer of the astronauts, Joe Garino, with a signed certificate of authentication. **$287**

John Young's Personal ID Badge, for the Space Shuttle External Tanks Assembly Plant. Directly from his personal collection, certified and signed. **$287**

Gemini 8 Mission Report, from the estate of Dr. D. Owen Coons, Chief of NASA's Manned Spacecraft Center Medical Office. **$263**

Skylab Oxygen Tank Art, Glass Paperweight by Correia, 3" in diameter, in fitted walnut box. The paperweight is signed on the bottom "Correia" and "1985 Limited Edition WCLSYB 337/1000". **$263**

Sally Ride and Richard Truly, signed photographs. ....**$168 both**

Space-Worn International Space Station Underwear and Socks, made for U.S. astronaut C. Michael Foale. **$155**

1963 Popsicle Space Card #7, The Seven Astronauts. Slabbed by PA Sports and graded EX - MT 6. ....**$96**

Framed Display, of 27 NASA and Space Exploration souvenir patches. ....**$72 set**

First Day Cover, and Color Litho of First Space Shuttle Crew. ....**$72 both**

Alan Shepard and Deke Slayton, Moon Shot: The Inside Story of America's Race to the Moon. Introduction by Neil Armstrong. Atlanta: Turner Publishing, Inc., 1994. First edition. Inscribed and signed by Alan Shepard in black marker on the title page. Octavo. 383 pages. **$54**

Nine Astronaut Signatures, including Charles D. Gemar, Jim Wetherbee, Steve Oswald, Carl Meade, Michael Baker, and Brian Duffy. Each signature is on or near a space related stamp mounted on a 5" x 3" card. **$42**

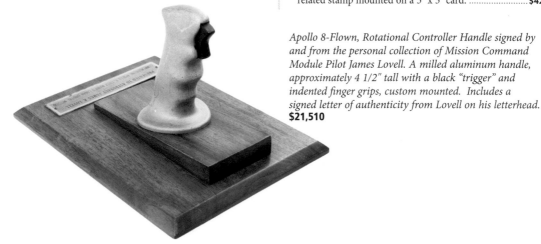

Apollo 8-Flown, Rotational Controller Handle signed by and from the personal collection of Mission Command Module Pilot James Lovell. A milled aluminum handle, approximately 4 1/2" tall with a black "trigger" and indented finger grips, custom mounted. Includes a signed letter of authenticity from Lovell on his letterhead. **$21,510**

SPORTS MEMORABILIA

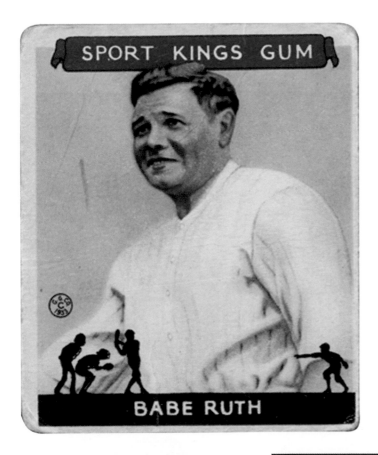

The grading of sports memorabilia, especially baseball cards, has reached such a level of detail that space does not allow for an in-depth discussion of it here. For more information, visit Collect.com Auctions, www.collect.com/auctions.

Also see Autographs, Toys.

1933 Goudey Sport Kings single of Babe Ruth, has seen some better days, and has been graded poor. It's a little off center, has some creases and rounded corners. **$585**

Below: 1915 Cracker Jack single (front and back) of Nap Lajoie grades in poor condition due to severely rounded corners and a pencil notation at the bottom, which has been mostly erased. **$181**

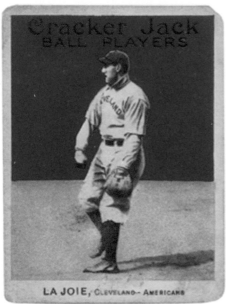

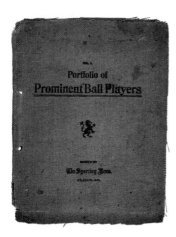

1898-99 National Copper Plate Co. Portraits Complete Set of 50 with Original Book. This set may well be the sole surviving complete set of 1898-99 National Copper Plate Co. baseball player pictures in existence. Once in a great while, a single picture shows up at auction and it's usually in lower grade. This complete set arrives looking very similar to the issued condition 110 years ago and even includes the original binder in which the cards were issued and which preserved their uniformly superior state of preservation. For more than half of the players on the checklist, this appearance is their first, if not their only, appearance on a collectible. This is the earliest memorabilia depiction of Jimmy Collins, Elmer Flick, Willie Keeler, Bobby Wallace, Vic Willis and, most significantly, Honus Wagner. **$52,650**

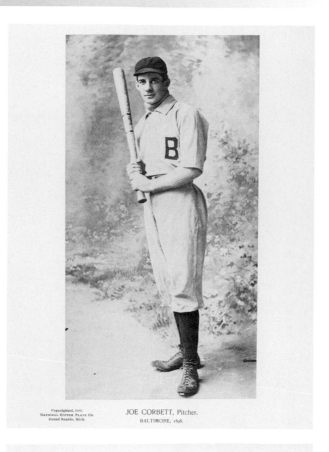

Copyrighted, 1898.
NATIONAL COPPER PLATE CO.
Grand Rapids, Mich.

JOE CORBETT, Pitcher.
BALTIMORE, 1898.

Copyrighted 1898.
National Copper Plate Co.

S. L. THOMPSON, Right Fielder.
PHILADELPHIA, 1898.

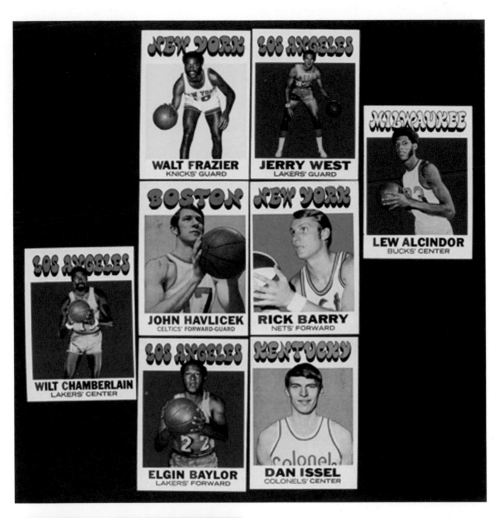

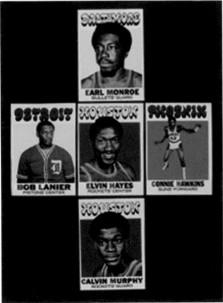

1971-72 Topps Basketball lot of 165 cards plus 13 stickers, virtually all cards coming in at near-mint condition, a description that also applies to Alcindor, Chamberlain, West, Havlicek, Baylor, Barry and Issel, plus Monroe, Frazier, Hayes, Hawkins, Lanier and Murphy, to name the headliners. Cards are devoid of print dots or other defects, all but a half dozen are decently centered, and there are many Hall of Famers. **$269 all**

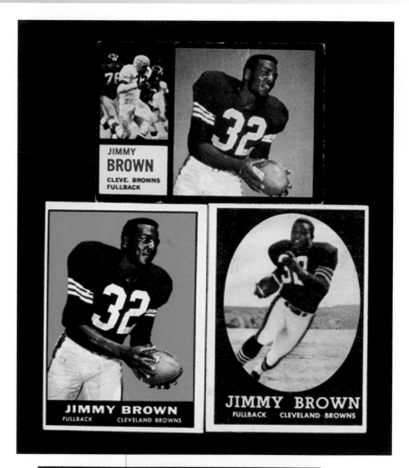

Jim Brown Topps cards (three), including rookie card from 1958; 1961 with the cobalt blue background; and 1962 card No. 28. **$269 all**

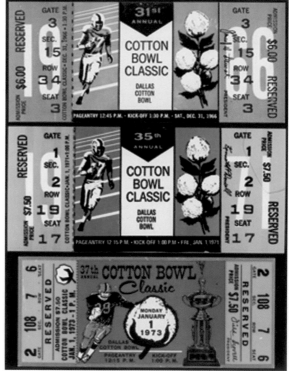

Cotton Bowl full tickets from 1966, 1971 and 1973, fine condition. The 1971 ticket has a pencil marking on the top right corner, while the others show only minor surface wear and are considered near mint. **$117 set**

Brett Favre bobblehead signed by Favre in black Sharpie across his chest and shoulder. The bobblehead was given out by MBNA and has a certificate of authenticity and Favre hologram. **$122**

BRETT FAVRE

Signed hockey puck collection of eight, Bobby Hull signed three Chicago Blackhawk pucks, and Stan Mikita signed two Blackhawk pucks. Other Hall of Fame signatures include Andy Bathgate and Harry Howell, both on New York Rangers pucks with their induction year inscribed. The final puck is signed by what looks like #6 Izotti on a Blackhawk puck. **$140 all**

Floyd Patterson has signed this pair of Everlast boxing gloves with black Sharpie. The typical bleeding of the signature is not present on either glove, with both signatures bold and clear. Patterson has also added an "Olympic Champion 1952" inscription to both. **$293**

TEXTILES

Including needlework and quilts.

Photo courtesy Jeffrey S. Evans & Associates, Mt. Crawford, Va.; www.jeffreysevans.com

Richardson Family 19th-century needlework sampler, probably New Hampshire, silk on linen, central landscape reserve featuring a weathervane-topped academy-like structure flanked by a colonnade, and with a small cottage in the foreground, inscribed "Charlotte Richardson's sampler wrought in the 11th year of her age" across the lower edge, never framed. Second quarter 19th century, 22" x 17". **$8,050**

Photo courtesy Jeffrey S. Evans & Associates, Mt. Crawford, Va.; www.jeffreysevans.com

1819 New England needlework sampler, silk on linen, lower half featuring a two-story house flanked by trees, animals, and a basket, inscribed "Glsey Flints sampler aged 10. In virtuous ways I will spend my days 1819", not framed. First quarter 19th century, 9" x 18". **$1,610**

Photo courtesy Jeffrey S. Evans & Associates, Mt. Crawford, Va.; www.jeffreysevans.com

1824 Cornish, N.H., Richardson Family needlework sampler, silk on linen, lower landscape featuring a two-story house flanked by a small structure, an arbor, a mother sheep and her two frolicking lambs, along with various trees, bushes and flowers, inscribed "Sarah Richardson Cornish, Aug. 4th 1824 made in the 9th year of her age under the care of Sukey Comin (Cumings)", a four-line religious verse above the lower landscape, never framed. First quarter 19th century, 17" x 18". **$4,887**

Photo courtesy Jeffrey S. Evans & Associates, Mt. Crawford, Va.; www.jeffreysevans.com

19th-century Richardson Family needlework sampler, probably New Hampshire, silk on linen, inscribed "Sophia L Richardson wrought in the 12th year of her age under the instruction of Joann Cumings" above a four-line verse, a flowering vine, and two trees, never framed. Second quarter 19th century, 15 1/2" x 17 1/2". **$1,725**

Photo courtesy Jeffrey S. Evans & Associates, Mt. Crawford, Va.; www.jeffreysevans.com

Mid-Atlantic potted-tulip pattern appliquéd quilt, consisting of 12 tulip blocks within a repeated tulip border, silhouette hand quilting, three-panel backing. Probably first quarter 20th century, 96" x 77", 1/2" L-shape tear in one corner, light toning to folds on reverse, several small light stains. **$546**

Photo courtesy James D. Julia Auctioneers, Fairfield, Maine; www.JuliaAuctions.com

Lone Star Quilt With Dark Blue Background, Lancaster County, Pa. Circa 1875. Maker unknown. With eight satellite stars. The large star is pieced from 17 rows of diamonds (each point has 81 diamonds). All fabrics are solid cottons in cheddar, light yellow, red, light pink, medium blue and indigo blue. The background is a dark blue. The large red border has inner border of triangles in light yellow, light pink, cheddar and red. Hand quilted with eight stitches per inch, outlined 1/8" from seams of diamonds. Background is quilted in a hanging grid; large border has a triple cable. Quilt has a thin cotton batting, a hand-sewn light pink binding, and a large turkey-red paisley cotton print back. 82" x 84". **$3,162**

Photo courtesy James D. Julia Auctioneers, Fairfield, Maine; www.JuliaAuctions.com

Four-Block Appliqué Quilt With Eagles And Roses Border, Southeast Pennsylvania. Dated 1856. Maker unknown. Construction of quilt is four 33″ appliquéd blocks in center with 13 1/2″ border. Appliqué blocks have intertwined stems with flowers and pomegranates. Each block has three tiny birds appliquéd on the vines. In the center is a star surrounded by four butterflies. Border has eight (displayed) eagles with shields above crossed (laurel) leaves. Center of each border has quarter-moon shape appliqué, with bouquets of roses in the corners. Quilted in white thread at 12 stitches per inch. All appliqué shapes are outlined in the background, veins quilted on large leaves. Background quilted with various small motifs including pineapples, scissors, flowers, stars, leaves, crossed spoons, pitchers and many hearts. One border with the initials "LH" and "SAH" quilted on either side of the moon shape, with the date "1856" above the moon and intertwined hearts below it. Two houses are quilted in the center near the star. Fabric is all solid cottons in green, turkey red, yellow, cheddar and blue (in the shields). Batting is thin cotton, white matching front. Edge finish is a separate 1/4″ green binding, hand applied. 94″ x 94 1/2″. Faded. Stains throughout. **$2,587**

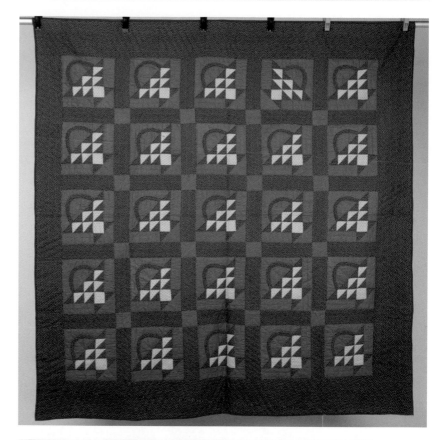

Photo courtesy Jeffrey S. Evans & Associates, Mt. Crawford, Va.; www.jeffreysevans.com

Mid-Atlantic basket-pattern pieced quilt, yellow, green and bubble-gum pink print fabrics, simple hand quilting, raspberry pattern print backing in four panels. Late 19th/early 20th century, 80" x 82 1/2". **$316**

Photo courtesy Jeffrey S. Evans & Associates, Mt. Crawford, Va.; www. jeffreysevans.com

Virginia Rosebud-type pattern appliquéd quilt, red and green print fabrics, 16 full blocks and four half blocks with allover tiny block hand quilting, white backing in three panels. (Another nearly identical example of this quilt has a history of ownership in the Shenandoah Valley.) Second half 19th century, 82" x 92", minute losses to the red prints, moderate spotting and some stains. **$287**

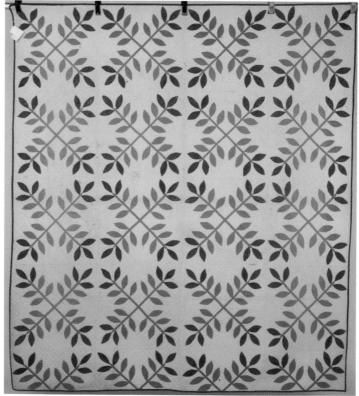

Tiffany

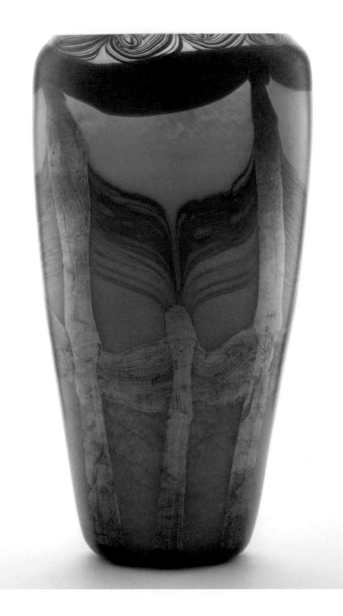

Tiffany & Co. was founded by Charles Lewis Tiffany (1812-1902) and Teddy Young in New York City in 1837 as a "stationery and fancy goods emporium." The store initially sold a wide variety of stationery items, and operated as Tiffany, Young and Ellis in lower Manhattan. The name was shortened to Tiffany & Co. in 1853, and the firm's emphasis on jewelry was established.

The first Tiffany catalog, known as the "Blue Book," was published in 1845. It is still being published today.

In 1862 Tiffany & Co. supplied the Union Army with swords, flags and surgical implements.

Charles' son, Louis Comfort Tiffany (1848-1933) was an American artist and designer who worked in the decorative arts and is best known for his work in stained glass. Louis established Tiffany Glass Co. in 1885, and in 1902 it became known as the Tiffany Studios.

Photo courtesy Heritage Auction Galleries, Dallas; www.HA.com

Rare Kilpatrick Cavalry Division badge by Tiffany. This emblem bears the design adopted by Gen. Judson Kilpatrick's cavalry corps, circa 1864. The yellow metal badge measures about 1 1/4" x 1 1/2" and consists of a spread-wing eagle surmounting a red painted swallowtail banner suspended from a short spear-point staff. Across the top of the banner, in relief, are three yellow stars and a yellow riband. Under the riband is a plain yellow swallowtail guidon on a staff. The reverse is marked "Tiffany & Co." and retains the complete T-bar pin fastener. **$3,883**

Photo courtesy James D. Julia Auctioneers, Fairfield, Maine; www.JuliaAuctions.com

Tiffany Studios Abalone Frame. Calendar-style bronze frame in the Abalone pattern with gold finish. Tiffany originally created this design to represent a grape pattern and used the abalone disc to form the design. Signed on the underside "Tiffany Studios New York 1166". 6 1/2" x 5 3/4". Opening: 3 1/4" x 2 1/4" h. One abalone disc missing. **$1,680**

Photo courtesy James D. Julia Auctioneers, Fairfield, Maine; www.JuliaAuctions.com

Tiffany Studios Blown-Glass Candelabra. Six-arm candelabra is made of bronze and has patina finish of brown with hints of green and red. From the oval-shaped platform base arises a single center stem with three candle cups on either side. Each of these candle cups has green blown-glass ornamentation and a bobeche. In the center stem of the candlestick rests a Tiffany snuffer that is concealed when in place. Signed on the underside "Tiffany Studios New York 1648". 15" x 21". One tight hairline to blown glass and one blown glass insert is slightly different color. **$6,900**

Photo courtesy Heritage Auction Galleries, Dallas; www.HA.com

Tiffany Studios picture frame, circa 1906, in the Grapevine pattern with green and white opalescent glass, easel back, 7 3/8" x 8 3/4". **$1,673**

Photo courtesy James D. Julia Auctioneers, Fairfield, Maine; www.JuliaAuctions.com

Tiffany Studios Grapevine Carriage Clock. Signed "Tiffany & Co." on the face and "Tiffany Studios New York 877" on underside as well as "Made in France" on the mechanism. 5" h. Some crazing lines to the clock face. **$6,900**

Photo courtesy James D. Julia Auctioneers, Fairfield, Maine; www.JuliaAuctions.com

Tiffany Blue Favrile Cabinet Vase. Blue iridescence at the foot shading to platinum iridescence at the shoulder and neck. Signed on the bottom "L.C.T. D3473". 2 1/2" h. minor scratches to iridescence. **$805**

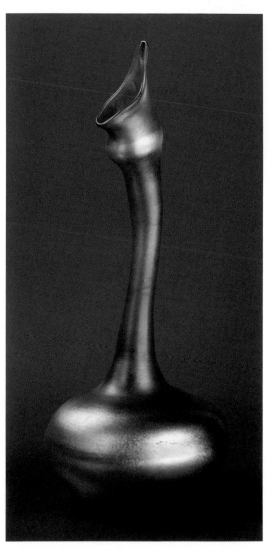

Photo courtesy Heritage Auction Galleries, Dallas; www.HA.com

Tiffany Studios rose-water sprinkler, circa 1900, goose-neck form in iridescent Favrile glass with pink undertones, marked "L.C. Tiffany - Favrile W2714", 10" x 4". **$5,078**

Photo courtesy James D. Julia Auctioneers, Fairfield, Maine;
www.JuliaAuctions.com

Tiffany Studios Fireball Lamp. One of two known examples. Exceptional early Tiffany Studios leaded orb shade has flame design in mottled red and orange glass against a textured green and brown swirled background. The flames are made up of numerous types of glass, including heavily rippled to lightly textured, giving the effect of dancing flames when lit. The shade rests atop a bronze saucer base with single socket. Base is finished with rich brown patina with green highlights. Shade and base are unsigned. Shade is 12" diameter. Overall 15" h. Few tight hairlines. **$48,875**

Photo courtesy Heritage Auction Galleries, Dallas; www.HA.com

Tiffany Studios, nine Favrile glass tiles, circa 1900, four with molded "PAT. APPL'D. FOR", largest 4" square, four tiles with chips to the prongs on the reverse. **$1,195 all**

Tiffany Studios Lemon Leaf Table Lamp. Heavily mottled apple-green background glass with heavily mottled maize-colored lemon-leaf band. Shade is signed "Tiffany Studios New York 1470". Base is signed "Tiffany Studios New York 531". Original patina on base and shade. Shade is 18" diameter. Overall 25 1/2" h. Some tight hairlines primarily in lower border with no missing glass. Slight lead separation in one small area where lemon-leaf band meets lower geometric bands. Slight dent in heat cap. **$17,250**

Tiffany Studios Ruffled Bowl. Deep gold iridescent finish with magenta, blue and pink highlights. Signed on the underside "L.C.T.". 4 1/2" diameter. **$287**

*Tiffany Studios Geometric
Table Lamp. Colors of
butterscotch and caramel
striated with white. Shade
is supported by a Colonial-
style, four-socket base with
inverted saucer foot. Shade is
signed "Tiffany Studios NY
1469". Base is marked "Tiffany
Studios New York 532". Shade
is 18" diameter. Overall 25" h.
Base has replaced pull chains
and has been cleaned down to
copper finish.* **$8,050**

*Tiffany Studios Footed Candy
Dish. With applied gold
iridescent border on opaque blue
body and foot. Scratched in "59"
on the underside. 6" diameter.
Multiple chips to foot rim, some
scratches on interior.* **$60**

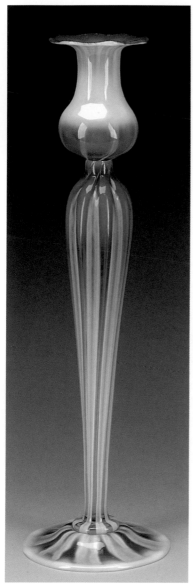

Photo courtesy James D. Julia Auctioneers, Fairfield, Maine; www.JuliaAuctions.com

Tiffany Pastel Tulip Candlestick. With raspberry opalescent cup applied to blue-to-green opalescent stem with white pulled striping and applied raspberry foot with opalescent ribbing. Signed on the underside "1845 L.C. Tiffany-Favrile". 16" t. **$6,612**

Photo courtesy James D. Julia Auctioneers, Fairfield, Maine; www.JuliaAuctions.com

Tiffany Studios Nautilus Lamp. Natural shell shade on a patina harp base with additional hook on the underside for possible wall hanging as well as five ball feet. Impressed on underside "403 Tiffany Studios New York". 12 1/2" h. Minor wear to patina. **$6,900**

Photo courtesy James D. Julia Auctioneers, Fairfield, Maine;
www.JuliaAuctions.com

Tiffany Reactive Glass Shade. Green and orange flame design extending from the foot to near the rim. The smokey gray body of the shade has a slightly swirling rib running vertically. When shade is lit in a darkened room, it appears like a dancing flame. Shade is unsigned. 5" t x 2 1/4" fitter. **$4,025**

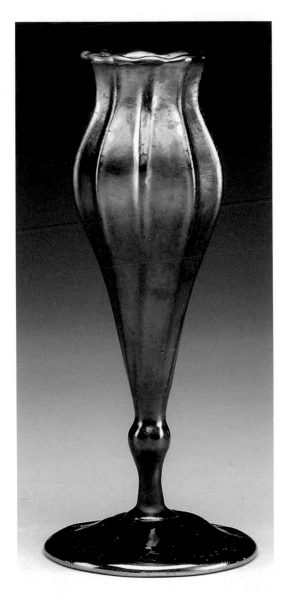

Photo courtesy James D. Julia Auctioneers, Fairfield, Maine; www.JuliaAuctions.com

Tiffany Studios Mini Flower-Form Vase. Blue iridescent with vertical ribbing and applied foot. Irregular iridescence to top quarter of the vase shading down to deep purple mirror iridescence on the foot. Engraved signature "7311N 1522 L.C. Tiffany-Inc Favrile" on the underside. 6 1/4" t. **$2,400**

Photo courtesy James D. Julia Auctioneers, Fairfield, Maine;
www.JuliaAuctions.com

Tiffany Studios Art Glass Shade. Vertical ribbing and deep gold with purple and blue iridescence. Shade is finished with a gently scalloped border. Signed "L.C.T. Favrile" in rim. 2 1/4" fitter x 4 3/4" h. **$862**

Tiffany Studios Flower-Form Vase. Pulled-feather vase on opalescent ground with everted rim and decorated foot. Engraved signature "L.C. Tiffany Favrile 539A". 11 1/4" h. Some staining to the interior.
$3,680

Tiffany Studios Lily & Prism Chandelier. With six gold lily shades and 19 prisms in colors of oyster, gold, amber and green with a deep iridescence over the lilies and complimentary prisms. All of this Tiffany glass surrounds a decorated stalactite Tiffany shade with deep vertical ribbing and a hooked-feather pattern. The shade is supported by a bronze collar, three chains and hooks. The shades are supported by a Moorish-style bronze hanging fixture with openwork at the top, medallions of roping above six lily shade holders, nineteen prism hooks and a single stem for the stalactite shade. Further accenting this lamp, alternating between the prisms, are 19 beaded chains that end in bronze balls. This entire lamp is supported by a bronze decorated ceiling cap, chain and S hook. Stalactite shade is signed "S323" and one lily shade is signed "L.C.T. Favrile" and another is signed "L.C.T." and the remainder are unsigned. Overall 42" l. Some parts are authentic while other parts are exact replications of Tiffany Studios hardware. Three lily shades have broken fitter rims, one has roughness to fitter rim. Stalactite shade has chips to fitter rim that are concealed when in place. All prisms either have chips or are cracked. **$32,775**

Photo courtesy James D. Julia Auctioneers, Fairfield, Maine; www.JuliaAuctions.com

Tiffany Studios Favrile Desk Lamp. Gold Favrile shade with rainbow iridescent finish with stretched edge. The cased white-lined shade is supported by a three-arm, leaf-decorated base with a statuary finish. The lamp is completed with a top cap in a patina finish. Shade is signed on the fitter "L.C.T. Favrile" and base is signed on the underside "Tiffany Studios New York 426". Shade is 7" diameter. Overall 14" t. **$4,200**

Photo courtesy James D. Julia Auctioneers, Fairfield, Maine; www.JuliaAuctions.com

Tiffany Stalactite Hanger. Shade has gold iridescent hooked-feather design extending from the bottom of the shade. There is an additional hooked-feather design descending from the fitter. Design is set against a lighter gold iridescent background of the vertically ribbed body of the shade. Interior of the shade has a light chartreuse color. Shade is unsigned and numbered "L2400". It is suspended from three chains attached to hooks on a center light post which terminates to a ceiling cap having beaded rim. The bronze replacement hardware is finished in a rich brown patina with strong red and green highlights. Shade is 8" l x 6" diameter x 4 3/4" fitter. Overall 24" h. **$7,187**

Photo courtesy James D. Julia Auctioneers, Fairfield, Maine; www.JuliaAuctions.com

Tiffany Studios Mosaic Pentray. Inlaid blue decorated Favrile glass. Impressed on the underside "TIFFANY STUDIOS NEW YORK 24336" together with the monogram of the Tiffany Glass & Decorating Co. 7 3/4″ l. Patina may be enhanced. **$8,000**

Photo courtesy Heritage Auction Galleries, Dallas; www.HA.com

Tiffany Studios early experimental Favrile glass vase lamp base, circa 1900, engraved "X103 Louis C. Tiffany-Favrile", 14 3/4″, significant surface scratches along interior, flaw on the body about 1/3 down from rim with some losses. **$3,585**

Photo courtesy James D. Julia Auctioneers, Fairfield, Maine; www.JuliaAuctions.com

Tiffany Studios Red Tulip Table Lamp. The shade depicts the tulip flower in every stage of bloom (second view). The colors used encompass the entire range of the red family from pink to purple. Some blossoms are entirely constructed of the softer colors, while others use striations of light, medium and dark to give a three-dimensional effect. There are other blossoms that used only the deepest colors and represent the flower in its later stage of bloom. This tulip pattern also shows the foliage in most every color of green. Glass used in this shade is also of a wide variety from striated to cat's paw to rippled and finally granular. The shade is completed with three geometric bands of rippled glass in earthen hues of fiery orange with hints of green. The shade is supported by a mock-turtleback base. This three-socket base is complete with riser, wheel and top cap all in a rich patina finish. Shade is signed "Tiffany Studios New York 1596". Base is signed "Tiffany Studios New York 587". Shade is 18″ diameter. Overall 22 1/2″ h. A few tight hairlines in shade. Patina has been enhanced on shade and base. **$109,250**

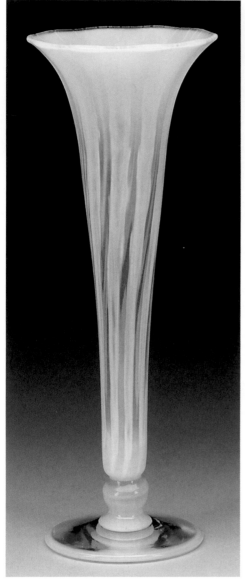

Tiffany Studios Pastel Vase. Clear foot with white opalescent rim. Foot gives way to a white opalescent stem with white opalescent ribs vertically extending to the slightly flaring lip. Interior of the mouth is finished with a rich pastel yellow. Signed on the underside "L.C. Tiffany Favrile 1886". 9 3/4" t. **$1,380**

Tiffany Studios Damascene Table Lamp. Green Favrile shade with a damascene-wave pattern decoration in gold shading to platinum having eight vertical ribs, which give it highlights of blue. The cased lined shade is supported by a patinated single-socket, three-arm bronze base with elongated rib decoration over an ornate root-style foot resting on four ball feet. Lamp is completed with a bronze heat cap. Shade is signed on the fitter rim "L.C.T.". Base is signed "Tiffany Studios New York 431". Shade is 9 1/2" diameter x 3 3/4" fitter. Overall 19 1/2" t. **$6,612**

Tiffany Studios Blue Favrile Vase. Classic Egyptian form with elongated neck and squared shoulder. Vase begins with a platinum iridescence over the neck area that recedes into a medium blue and a cobalt blue at the foot. Signed "L.C. Tiffany Inc. Favrile X1421024". 5 3/4" h. Tiny spot of missing iridescence on shoulder. **$920**

Tiffany Studios Pine Needle Card Case. Constructed of green slag panels with darker striations. These panels are set in a bronze frame with decorative pine-needle decoration overall. Exceptional patina finish. Signed on underside "Tiffany Studios New York 875". 4" x 3" x 1". **$1,495**

Tiffany Studios Favrile Cabinet Vase. Round squat body with pulled handles on each side and a slightly flaring mouth. The gold Favrile finish shows purple and blue highlights at foot and lip. Signed on the underside "L.C. Tiffany-Favrile 4014L". 2" t. **$540**

Photo courtesy James D. Julia Auctioneers, Fairfield, Maine; www.JuliaAuctions.com

Tiffany Studios Tel El Amarna Vase. With applied and decorated collar. Engraved "Exhibition Piece" and "6340N L.C. Tiffany – Favrile" on the underside. 5 3/4" h. Hairline crack to applied rim. **$5,750**

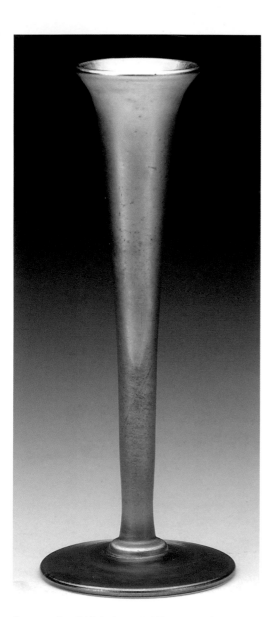

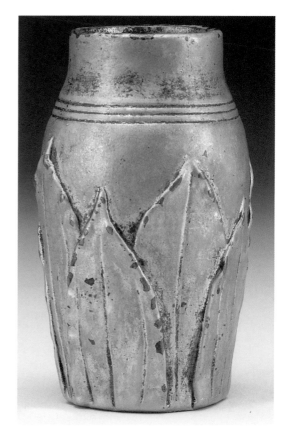

Photo courtesy James D. Julia Auctioneers, Fairfield, Maine; www.JuliaAuctions.com

Tiffany Studios Favrile Lily Vase. Slender body, slightly flaring at the lip with saucer foot. Gold iridescence shows flashes of pink and blue at the foot. Signed on the underside "L.C. Tiffany Inc. Favrile 1504-7408M". 6" t. **$660**

Photos courtesy James D. Julia Auctioneers, Fairfield, Maine; www.JuliaAuctions.com

Tiffany Studios Bronze Pottery Vase. Decorated with an organic overlapping leaf pattern. The finish is basically silver with copper showing through in some areas. Signed on the underside "L.C. Tiffany Favrile Bronze Pottery" as well as "B.P. 249529" as well as "LCT" logo. 4 3/4" h. Minor wear to exterior and tight hairlines to interior glaze that do not penetrate the surface. **$3,910**

Photo courtesy James D. Julia Auctioneers, Fairfield, Maine; www.JuliaAuctions.com

Tiffany Studios Counterbalance Desk Lamp. With pendulous turtleback tile counterweight. Artichoke design stand and blue decorated damascene shade. Shade is signed "L.C.T. Favrile". Base is marked "Tiffany Studios New York". Shade is 8" diameter. Overall 14 1/2" h. Minor chips to three turtleback tiles in the counterweight, one tile with tight hairline, some minor wear to patina. **$32,775**

Photo courtesy James D. Julia Auctioneers, Fairfield, Maine; www.JuliaAuctions.com

Tiffany Studios Bell Shade. Decorated with a translucent green pulled-feather motif with gold trim on an oyster ground. Signed "L.C.T.". 2 1/4" fitter rim x 4 1/2" h. Minor grinding to fitter rim. **$2,530**

Photo courtesy James D. Julia Auctioneers, Fairfield, Maine; www.JuliaAuctions.com

Tiffany Studios Geometric Table Lamp. With leaded "dichroic" glass shade glass (containing multiple micro-layers of metal oxides) that shows colors of green, tan and mauve when unlit. When lit, the glass turns a rich orange. Shade is signed "Tiffany Studios New York 1436" and rests atop an early Tiffany Studios base with an incised and slightly raised wave design. Base is finished with three attached arms to support the shade. Marked on the underside "25778". Shade is 16" diameter. Overall 20" h. A few tight hairlines in the shade. Bottom of font has been drilled. **$15,525**

Photo courtesy James D. Julia Auctioneers, Fairfield, Maine; www.JuliaAuctions.com

Tiffany Studios Pomegranate Table Lamp. Shade has an allover geometric background of green striated glass with hints of blue, yellow and white. The shade is decorated with a single band of pomegranates in fiery mottled yellow and orange glass. Shade is supported by a three-socket, three-armed Grecian urn that is supported by four flaring feet on a pedestal stand. Shade is signed on "Tiffany Studios New York" with a small early tag. Shade is 16" diameter. Overall 20" h. Several spider cracks. **$16,100**

Toys

FUTURE OF THE MARKET: ANTIQUE TOYS

By Catherine Saunders-Watson

How can you accurately gauge the direction of a marketplace sector as vast and heterogeneous as that of antique toys, especially within an economic landscape as topsy-turvy as the one we've been experiencing? Ordinarily I would say it can't be done in an entirely conclusive way, but 2009 proved to be the year in which trends in toy buying would be revealed across the board because of one stellar auction event. Investment-minded toy buyers were able to dip into a golden treasure chest of toys they never dreamed would be sold: the 59 year collection amassed by K B Toys' co-founder Donald Kaufman.

The Kaufman collection's magnitude, depth and maturity positioned it above all others. It contained no duplicates, many one-offs, and every known color variation. In an auction series that debuted March 19-21, 2009, at Bertoia's in Vineland, N.J., its out-of-the-gate performance provided market-watchers with a unique and unprecedented litmus test. It declared in big, round dollar figures exactly which examples savvy collectors seek and how deeply they'd empty their wallets in order to own them.

This breathtaking assemblage of several thousand toys – even Kaufman himself doesn't know how many there are – was extraordinary in its breadth and quality. It took a crew of 10 Bertoia staff member a full week to pack and load the first of the auction goods into three trucks – two of them 26-footers allocated solely to Don's mind-boggling pedal cars and pressed-steel toys.

"To keep it organized, we tried to separate the toys into affinity groupings, and there simply wasn't a weak category anywhere in the collection," recalled Bertoia Auctions associate Rich Bertoia. "Everything Don owns is just incredible. It's the ultimate-upgrade collection."

Because it contained superlative, extremely rare examples from virtually every major toy classification – cast-iron, European and American clockwork, pressed-steel, comic character, et al. – the collection was pure catnip to many investors bitten by Wall Street and seeking the comfort of high-grade tangible assets.

The collection will require two to three years of semi-annual auction events in order to be dispersed in its entirety, so the full story won't be known till the last toy is sold, but the March 2009 Kaufman sale spoke volumes about toy-market trends.

I feel quite comfortable in going on record with these predictions, based on the Kaufman Part I results. These are five categories I like for investment purposes:

Hubley's Royal Circus series – My no. 1 pick for American cast iron is Hubley's series of Royal Circus vans, which depict old-fashioned, wheeled cages used for transporting circus animals. This charming series of toys is a perennial favorite with collectors. En masse, the toys display beautifully in any collection, and I believe their values are going to hold strong in the marketplace, especially for those examples exhibiting fine, original paint. Kaufman owned the most elusive of the Royal Circus vans – a Monkey Cage, complete with figures of impish monkeys and an ingeniously designed mesh interior housing that revolves as the toy is pulled along. Estimated at $30,000-$40,000, it sold for a staggering $97,750.

Marklin tin – The premier brand in European tin toys and trains is Marklin. I see no turning back for this brand. There will always be buyers worldwide for this German maker's beautifully crafted designs. It's not un-

Catherine Saunders-Watson

usual for Marklin toys to top the prices realized in major toy sales, and that's precisely what happened at the Kaufman sale. A rare, hand-painted circa-1909 "Fidelitas" clown-car caravan measuring 37 1/2" long lured not only collectors of European clockwork toys but also collectors of clown toys. (Anytime you have crossover interest from two or more categories, that's like having back-up insurance on your investment.). Estimated at $30,000-$40,000, the Fidelitas handily exceeded expectations to reach top-lot status at $103,500. The buyer was a private collector from Europe.

Early European tin cars – The fascination many of us have for full-size classic cars was grounded in childhood play. Some collectors reclaim their youth by chasing examples of the very toys they actually played with, but serious investment-oriented collectors know the money is in early German, French and Spanish autos. Seven of the top 10 lots sold in Kaufman Part I fell into this category. An extraordinary production by the little-known Barcelona firm Hispania proved to be the connoisseurs' choice. Believed to be the largest of all manufactured toy limousines at 22 1/2" in length, the circa-1907 luxury car was as finely detailed as its full-size counterpart of a century ago. The toy was purchased for $80,500 – probably 80,000 times its original price!

Here are some other prices achieved by European tin cars in the sale: circa 1906-1909 Marklin two-seat open roadster, $57,500; circa-1914 Marklin roadster with spare tire on toolbox trunk, $57,500; circa-1912 Bing luxury taxi, $46,000; and Fischer Father Christmas in open car, $39,100. Other brands we favor for investment are Carette and Gunthermann.

Racers – In more than 20 years of writing about toys, I've never seen a dip in the market for antique tin racers such as the Gordon Bennet cars in the Kaufman sale. With the rule usually being "the larger the racer, the higher the price," this auction made a strong statement when a possibly unique 6 3/4" example zoomed past its $6,000-

$7,500 estimate to cross the finish line at $25,300.

Figural biscuit tins – Here's a wild-card category. Unless you've spent time in the U.K., you may not know what biscuit tins are, but they left quite a few people slack-jawed in the auction room at Bertoia's when they hammered incredible prices. In latter 19th- and early 20th-century Europe, biscuits – or cookies, as we call them in the United States – were packaged in novelty tins that had a second life after the contents were consumed. Quite often the tins were crafted as toys, and with bakeries in ferocious competition for market share, the tins were sometimes nicer than toys available in retail shops. The most desirable biscuit tins are those depicting vehicles, including cars, delivery vans, airplanes, motorcycles, racers and boats. They can run well into the thousands of dollars.

Kaufman's collection held some beauties. An Alfa-Romeo biscuit tin for the Italian company Biscotti Delser was especially rare in that it was outfitted with a clockwork motor. Estimated at $10,000-$12,000, it produced a sweet payday for when it sold for $25,300.

Caution: Sometimes tin toys are represented as biscuit tins when in actuality they are standard manufactured toys of lesser value. I've never seen a case of intentional deceit; it's just that these tins require a particular expertise in order to be properly identified. When buying biscuit tins, it pays to work with a specialty dealer.

Since I've now brought up the subject, I'd like to emphasize that any investor with an inclination to sink their money into old toys should not spend a cent till they've tapped into the toy network and know who the reputable dealers are. Trust is everything when you're buying antique toys.

Nowadays, auctions are the dominant source for investment-grade toys. There are several outstanding auction houses that specialize in toys, including Bertoia's, Morphy Auctions and Noel Barrett Auctions. When you buy from toy auctioneers of this caliber, you know your purchases have been vetted and described by people who really know the toy field.

There's an added bonus to buying at auction that you don't read about very often, if at all: preview scrutiny. At any auction preview, the toys are carefully examined by dealers and collectors who've been at it for many years. If something isn't "right," if it looks like there's a touch of repaint or a replaced part, you may be sure it will be pointed out by someone at the preview and duly noted on the catalog addendum. This can only help in your quest to purchase authentic, original toys, and it's why I recommend buying from auction houses that specialize in toys.

There's another avenue one can take in purchasing toys for investment, and I touched on it earlier. These are the nostalgia toys you may remember from childhood. Because so many of these later toys were mass-produced – even overproduced – during an era in which the collecting phenomenon had already become well entrenched, it takes skill and exceptional market expertise to buy wisely. In this category I would say proceed with caution, as the market is much more fickle than that of antique toys, whose numbers and availability are already well established – there are no more factory finds with the potential of flooding the market when it comes to the antiques, but I wouldn't count out that possibility vis a vis newer toys.

The toys to which I refer when I say "nostalgia" toys are: Star Wars, Star Trek, Transformers, G.I. Joe and other action figures, Barbies and Superheroes. Be sure that if you buy these types of toys for investment, you choose only items you really love because then it won't hurt quite as badly if their values drop.

Personally, my recommendation for boomer-era investment toys would be tin robots of the 1950s and 1960s, preferably mint/boxed; Nightmare Before Christmas rarities, early (Gold and Silver Age) Superhero comics acquired only from experienced, reputable dealers and auction houses, and monster collectibles, which are hotter than ever. Kids loved to be creeped out, and those Saturday matinees with Wolfman and Frankenstein seem to have made a lasting impression on our generation of collectors.

Photo courtesy Bertoia Auctions, Vineland, N.J.; www.BertoiaAuctions.com

Made around 1911 by the German manufacturer Carette, this hand-painted tin luxury limo has beveled glass windows, nickel lamps, fully opening doors, embossed upholstered seating, roof rack, and full running boards. Measuring 16" long, the clockwork toy sold at Bertoia's inaugural auction of the Donald Kaufman collection for **$39,100.**

FUTURE OF THE MARKET: DOOR OF HOPE DOLLS

By Andrew P. Truman
James D. Julia Auctioneers Department Head,
Antique Advertising, Toy & Doll Division

In the decades since their initial creation in the early 1900s, Door of Hope dolls have become an exciting and highly sought-after collectible. Within the last decade particularly, this segment of doll collecting has seen a decided increase in interest, driving up the prices of these Far Eastern treasures. Because of the steady increase in prices, fresh examples have continued to surface. This has kept collectors happy and the market vibrant, but thankfully not enough to flood the market. Of course, as with anything in this present economy, condition is crucial.

Before the Cultural Revolution changed the landscape and lifestyles of modern China, the less fortunate of the country's population of young girls were doomed to a life of illiteracy and hopelessness. That is, until five women from different backgrounds and faiths came together in

Andrew Truman

1901 as missionaries to China with the intention of teaching these unfortunate souls the skills necessary to improve their lives. Rather than a life of prostitution and/or living on the streets, these girls were given a safe haven and an education that included teaching them marketable skills.

Their mission was called the Door of Hope Receiving Home.

Unlike some missionaries of the day — whose agenda was to westernize the culture or to convert them to Christianity — these ladies stressed the importance of upholding and appreciating one's cul-

Photo courtesy James D. Julia Auctioneers, Fairfield, Maine; www.JamesDJulia.com

Door of Hope Child Doll, in colorful costume of rose-colored tunic with magenta vest and green braid trim, plaid trousers, gold hat with red pompom and pale orchid-colored slippers, 7" tall. **$690**

Door of Hope Rice Farmer, Kimport Dolls of Kansas exclusively imported these dolls for many years. The farmer has a most unique outfit of cloth undergarments, and a straw coat and body covering along with his braided straw hat, 12", lacking rake. **$1,265**

tural heritage. The young women learned dressmaking, how to sew, embroider and knit. They were even paid a small sum and given basic money-management skills.

In 1909, a young Pearl Buck, daughter of Presbyterian missionaries and future award-winning author, volunteered at the mission, teaching knitting and embroidery. She later went on to write extensively about the life in China.

As the mission grew, they eventually used nearby expert woodcarvers who honed local pear wood into a wide variety of realistic facial features. The dolls showed a cross section of the various classes and occupations of the

Door of Hope Policeman, a seldom-found figure with wooden hands. Similar to a Policeman of earlier vintage, it is interesting to note the differences that 20+ years makes as far as changes to clothing and facial expressions/ facial carving. Dressed in blue with appliques on his collar. He has a white hat with red fringe, 11 1/2". **$2,875**

citizens of Shanghai where the mission initially resided. Each carved head was unique and was then attached to stuffed-cloth bodies and dressed in the traditional costumes of the Chinese people. The earlier dolls are distinguished by a lack of hands, which then graduated to cloth mitten-type hands. And then by 1914, the dolls evolved to include delicately carved pear wood hands.

By 1940, it is estimated that 25 different dolls were being produced and others were custom made by special order. In that same year, Kimport dolls, an importer, advertised 20 various Door of Hope dolls. These were made mainly for tourists, but many of the Chinese missionaries distributed them to their own countries including England,

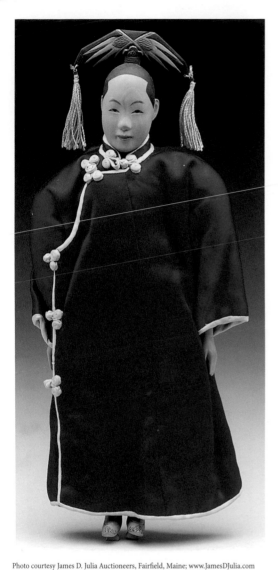

Door of Hope "Manchu Woman", perhaps the most elusive and difficult Door of Hope doll to acquire, this particular example is in all original condition. She features a fanciful red silk long robe (no fading to silk), carved headdress with silk tassels and carved extremities including pedestal/stilt shoes. This doll portrays a rich noblewoman of Manchurian descent. The Manchurians had ruled China from 1644 until the 1911 revolution when Sun Yat-sen succeeded to take power. This doll had been packed away for the last 40+ years. 11 1/4", two minute pinholes to silk on right sleeve. **$8,050**

Door of Hope Amah with child, kindergarten child is perched upon the back of the Amah', who has finely carved wooden hands. The children are perhaps the most desirable with regards to Door of Hope dolls. In all original, untouched condition the child still retaining her decorative skull cap, Amah is 10 1/2", light soiling and some minor fading to Amah's outfit. **$2.070**

Australia, the United States and Africa. The mission was successful in the sense that it was respected and received local support from various charitable groups. The girls were also able to support themselves to some degree, in that the production and sale of these dolls and other needlework pieces greatly contributed to the mission's income. However, Door of Hope did not receive much financial support from local churches or from overseas. In 1949, when the Communists took over China, the Door of Hope mission relocated to Taipei, and doll production declined.

In addition to faithful representations of facial features, the dolls also authentically reflected the behavior of the times. Some of the female dolls exhibit unusually small feet, reflecting the then-current Chinese custom of breaking and binding a girl baby's feet to prevent growth. The practice made the woman's feet similar in shape to a lotus flower, a symbol of potency and wealth. This was a sign of class and beauty among the upper echelons and to separate them from the working class. It was also considered a status symbol, as it suggested the husband could afford a wife that did not need to work.

Other regions of China did not practice this custom. In fact, Manchu women were actually forbidden to bind their feet by a ruling from the emperor in the 1600s. Despite this fact, the rarest and most highly sought after of Door of Hope dolls, the Manchu Woman seems to exhibit the diminutive feet, and is the only one of the line of dolls that features carved shoes. She also features a unique and elaborate carved headdress augmented by tassels, and wears an ornate silk gown. A picture of elegance and extravagance, she invariably steals the spotlight whenever she comes up for sale.

Another characteristic that separates the classes is the choice of materials and colors used for the dolls' costumes. Those representing the upper crust were decked in lavish silk outfits, while those of the working class were clad in cotton. Compare the intricate and vibrant silk attire and finely carved appliqués of the bride to the plain roughhewn tunic of the servant woman (or Amah). The bride is ravishing in her brilliant red court dress, the color in Chinese culture associated with life, happiness, good luck and wealth, while Amah plods along in pale-blue simplicity.

Class distinction was also evident in various occupations, such as a Shanghai Policeman, who comes attired in a deep blue silk uniform with gold buttons and braid. He is often found wearing a silk-covered, cone-shaped hat with red tassels. The Rice Farmer, by comparison, wears a simple blue cotton tunic and trousers under a straw raincoat and a woven coolie hat. He is found barefoot with carved feet, where the higher-ups sport cloth shoes.

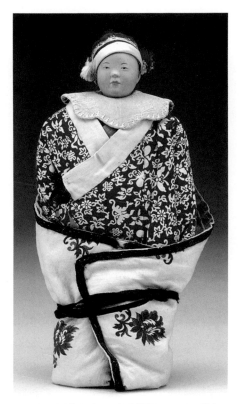

Photo courtesy James D. Julia Auctioneers, Fairfield, Maine; www.JamesDJulia.com

Door of Hope Youth in bunting, with mitt hands, an early example. **$3,220**

Photo courtesy James D. Julia Auctioneers, Fairfield, Maine; www.JamesDJulia.com

Door of Hope female youth, with mitt hands, colorful outfit and an elaborate bonnet, 8 1/2", slight fading to clothing. **$2,875**

Photo courtesy James D. Julia Auctioneers, Fairfield, Maine; www.JamesDJulia.com

Door of Hope Bride and Groom, these dolls were brought back from China in 1913 by Dr. M. Emily Garner, who was a missionary physician in Shanghai from the 1890s to 1913. The dolls had been in the family ever since she returned from Shanghai. The dolls have slips of paper identifying them, that were pinned under the clothes by Garner. Included with each doll is a copy of a 1900 newspaper article discussing woman doctors in Shanghai and a certificate dated Feb. 6, 1913, from the Bureau of Citizenship declaring Garner to be an American citizen for her return passport application. Early examples of the bride and groom, each having mitt hands. The bride has an elaborate and intricate outfit and finely carved appliques to the tightly woven bun on the rear of her head. The groom has a long braided cue, 12" and 10", near mint. **$4,025 pair**

Door of Hope female mourner, features a tight bun with affixed applique, exposed ears, fine wispy bangs and finely carved hands. All original clothing and condition. The small paper pinned to the shirt is the original hand written tag from Rebecca Cloud-Stewart, an American Baptist missionary, 10", light soiling to facial carving. **$1,092**

Door of Hope serving doll, in a muted blue and gray outfit with embroidered vest and velvet hat, this early version has mitt hands, 11", some slight fading/ soiling to outfit, otherwise in untouched condition. **$460**

TOYS

Barbie

Barbie the fashion doll was launched in 1959. The doll is produced by Mattel Inc., founded in 1945 by Harold "Matt" Matson and Elliot Handler. Handler's wife, Ruth, is regarded as the creator of Barbie.

In the early 1950s, Ruth Handler watched her daughter, Barbara, at play with paper dolls, and noticed that she often gave them adult roles. At the time, most children's toy dolls were representations of infants.

During a trip to Europe in 1956 with her children, Barbara and Kenneth, Ruth Handler came across a German doll called Bild Lilli. She purchased three of the adult-figured dolls, gave one to her daughter and took the others back to Mattel.

Ruth Handler redesigned the doll (with help from engineer Jack Ryan) and named her Barbie, after Handler's daughter. The doll made its debut at the American International Toy Fair in New York on March 9, 1959. This date is also used as Barbie's official birthday. Mattel acquired the rights to the Bild Lilli doll in 1964 and production of Lilli was halted.

Barbie's full name is Barbara Millicent Roberts. In a series of novels published by Random House in the 1960s, her parents' names are given as George and Margaret Roberts from the fictional town of Willows, Wis. Her beau, Ken Carson, first appeared in 1961.

Courtesy "Barbie: A Rare Beauty" by Sandi Holder, 2010

Brunette #1 Ponytail Barbie, mint in box (two views). She features all original makeup, a hint of smoky eye shadow, dark pointed eyebrows and orange-red lips. Even skin fading to ivory color. Complete with copper tubes in feet, original stand, booklet, heels and sunglasses. With original box still bearing the price sticker on an end flap. **$13,000+**

Ultra-rare Barbie promotional gift set for Inland Steel Container Co., circa 1967. Designed by Paco Rabanne, the set includes a Silver Ash Blond Standard Barbie doll, with bright blue side-glance eyes and a pink bow in her hair. She came in a special box which has "Barbie Loves the Improvers" (for Inland Steel improving life) stamped on the outside (this doubled as the mailing box). Included are the original liner, gold wire and clear Mod X stand, World of Barbie Fashion booklet #1 and reproduction color copy of the live model wearing this outfit. An Inland Steel pamphlet and insert were originally included but are missing here. Barbie doll comes wearing a cardboard "metal" dress that hangs from a cardboard "metal" neck piece via two silver strings that were made to look like chains. There is a peek-a-boo navel cut-out. Barbie doll is missing her cardboard "metal" cuff. Only a few known to exist. **$2,500+**

An autumn-haze mink stole, one of the most desirable pieces of clothing in Barbie's wardrobe. A Sear's exclusive in 1964, the stole was labeled and had a tan silk laminated lining. It came packaged in a clear box and the outer shipping box was brown corrugate cardboard. **$4,500+**

Courtesy "Barbie: A Rare Beauty" by Sandi Holder, 2010

A #6 Lemon Blond Ponytail Japanese Dressed Box Barbie (two views), wearing a Resort Set (#963) fashion outfit. Pinkish-coral lips, strong eyebrows, blue eyes and blue eyeliner. Hair has original topknot and full, curly bangs. Resort Set ensemble includes charm bracelet and earrings in original cello. The red, white, and blue nautical-themed outfit includes a red sailcloth jacket with middy collar, patch pockets and white trim top, a knit navy/white horizontal-stripe sleeveless shell and white "cuffed" sailcloth shorts. **$8,000+**

Courtesy "Barbie: A Rare Beauty"
by Sandi Holder, 2010

Marketed by Mattel to retailers, this Barbie and Ken Dressed Doll Assortment store display (#909) dates from 1963. The display originally sold as two units, with six dolls each. Each unit was an easel-backed 16" x 31" corrugated display. The dolls came in distinctive striped boxes with acetate cover and were pre-priced for resale. Top row, from left: #6 Redhead Ponytail dressed in Garden Party fashion outfit; Ken in Time for Tennis outfit; Ash Blond Bubblecut Barbie in Nighty Negligee. Bottom row, from left: Brunette Bubblecut Barbie in American Airlines fashion outfit; Ken in Casuals outfit (painted hair, including car keys in booklet cello); and Blond Bubblecut Barbie in Mood for Music fashion outfit. **$18,000+**

Dolls, General

Photo courtesy James D. Julia Auctioneers, Fairfield, Maine; www.JamesDJulia.com

Bebe Mothereau. Most commonly found on composition bodies, this particular example appears to be all original and on a straight-wristed metal body, marked "B4M" on rear of head. She is jointed at shoulders, elbows, knees and hips, but the body has hollow metal construction and strung accordingly. Fine pale bisque with threaded blue paperweight eyes, slight mauve shadow and skin wig. 15 1/2" h. Some wear and flaking of paint to metal body. **$12,650**

A.M. Fany, All original, largest size ever made, character doll contained on the proper chunky composition body with original finish and straight wrists. Marked on rear of the head "231 FANY A. 5 M." he has pale bisque with well defined features such as large ears, arched eyebrows, blue glass sleep eyes and a pouting mouth. 18" h. Some minor wear at fingertips and minute chip at neck socket. **$9,200**

Size 1 Tete Jumeau, Blue paperweight eyes, this cabinet-sized young lady is on a marked straight-wristed Jumeau body. Finely painted features such as eyebrows, eyelashes and mouth. **$5,750**

Cabinet-Sized Bru Jne 4, Brown-eyed bebe on a chevrot body with the hint of a tongue, this young lady features perfect bisque hands, antique aqua outfit and appropriate antique Bru-style shoes. Doll is marked "BRU Jne 4" on head and "BRU Jne 2" on shoulder plate, which is appropriate. Darker brown eyes accented by blonde mohair wig. 13" h. Some minor wear to outfit, kid body slightly soiled. **$12,650**

JDK 206 Character Child, The firm of Kestner made a series of character dolls known as the 200 series. This particular example, a #206, is on a pink ball-jointed composition body with blue glass sleep eyes, flyaway eyebrows and crooked smile. She is wearing a white cotton lace-like dress, antique pink leather shoes, and retains her original mohair wig with right and left braids forming buns over her ears. 12" h. Paint touch-up to right hand, left composition thigh has had extensive repair. **$8,625**

Photo courtesy James D. Julia Auctioneers, Fairfield, Maine; www.JamesDJulia.com

BSW "Wendy" With Original Box. She appears to be all original from head to toe on a pink composition body and contained within a marked BSW box labeled, "Mon Petit Coeur". Peaches-and-cream bisque, pale blue glass sleep eyes, and a fine mohair wig with coiled braids. 14 1/2" h. Near mint original condition. **$17,250**

French Fashion, Contained Within Presentation Box. Swivel neck French fashion on gusseted kid body adorned in a stylish wool outfit and accompanied by a second outfit. Pale bisque with lined blue paperweight eyes and finely detailed facial painting. Outfits appear to be all original with possible exception of shoes. 14 1/2" h. **$1,150**

French Fashion Doll, Cabinet-sized, most likely by the firm of F.G., she is on a straight-legged kid body and dressed in a velvet costume of newer vintage. Finely feathered eyebrows, blue paperweight eyes, and a pursed mouth. 11" h. **$920**

Simon & Halbig, 1294 Character Child With Clockwork Eyes. Most commonly used for store displays, these dolls with side-glancing clockwork eyes were used to draw attention to goods being sold. This particular example has a lifelike expression with an open mouth, mohair wig and when wound, eyes that would move from left to right for several hours before needing to be rewound. Usually found on composition baby bodies, this bisque-headed example is on a ball-jointed composition child body. 31" t. With normal wear and some old repairs at joints. Bisque head appears free of damage. Clockwork mechanism in working order. **$1,265**

Conta & Boehme, China Head Doll. Unusual china head doll from the 1860s-70s. Her hair is drawn into two curls, twirled and made into a bun on the back of her head. Wearing an antique flower print dress affixed to a leather and cloth body. 14" h. Some wear to eyebrows and braids on rear of head. **$540**

Alt Beck & Gottschalk, Victoria Parian Doll. With golden blonde hair, well-defined comb marks and black beaded band in front, pierced ears, circa 1870. She is on an old cloth body with leather upper arms and bisque lower arms. Although old, this body is slightly newer than the head. She is dressed in black taffeta floor-length dress with white lace overlay panels on the front of the skirt and also wears a black beaded necklace and blue enamel drop earrings. 31". Faint hairline on back shoulder plate, small inherent firing flaw on front right shoulder edge. **$747**

Simon-Halbig, "Little Women" Doll. Larger than normally found, glass-eyed shoulder doll, she is incised "S&H 1160-2/0". She has a solid dome head with closed mouth and is on her original cotton-stuffed body with bisque forearms. Costumed in a vertical-striped silk dress with black taffeta cape and antique black leather shoes. Light brown mohair wig is original and is pulled back into four long curls at the neck. 11 1/2". Two finger tips repaired on right hand. **$240**

Shirley Temple Doll, with Original Box. Composition doll portraying the child star with original dress, wig, button and shoes. 19" h. Considerable crazing to face, slightly loose in the joints, otherwise generally good. Box is fair to good with water staining and settling. **$287**

Volland, Beloved Belindy Doll. Stereotype black mammy would accompany Raggedy Ann & Andy on their adventures. In all-original condition with watermelon smile and button eyes. 15" h. Some distress/holes/tear to dress, foot, and right arm area. Minute chip to underside of right eye button. Left side of torso is re-stitched on seam under dress..**$1,035**

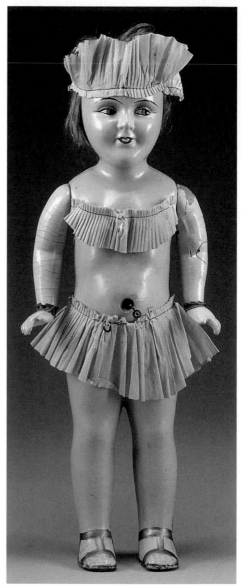

Photo courtesy James D. Julia Auctioneers, Fairfield, Maine; www.JamesDJulia.com

Composition Automated Novelty Doll. Flapper girl dressed in crepe skirt and swimsuit top with matching headpiece. She has painted facial features and sandals. When wound, clockwork mechanism in chest makes her bosom shake. 18" t. Crazing to arms and some scattered chips to body finish, fully functional. **$460**

Photo courtesy James D. Julia Auctioneers, Fairfield, Maine; www.JamesDJulia.com

Clockwork Nodding Santa With Children. Originally on display in the Mary Merritt Doll Museum since the early 1960s, Santa is standing with his basketful of toy treasures and at his feet are two little tots beseeching Santa to remember them on Christmas Eve. Clockwork mechanism within Santa's body is operational, and the children as well as Santa are mounted upon a snow-covered (mica) base with holiday paper trimming on sides. 32" overall h. Some old redressing to figures possible. **$2,300**

Photo courtesy James D. Julia Auctioneers, Fairfield, Maine; www.JamesDJulia.com

Exposition Doll & Toy Co. Raggedy Ann. In as-found, untouched condition, with original and lightly soiled clothing. Exposition Toy Co. produced these dolls beginning in 1934. Perhaps only 20 or so have survived over the last 75 years. 20" h. Thigh joint has some re-enforced stitching. **$4,600**

Photo courtesy James D. Julia Auctioneers, Fairfield, Maine; www.JamesDJulia.com

Circle Dot Bru. Cabinet sized French bebe with amber paperweight eyes, original skin wig (not fully removed) and an original French bebe dress. On a kid body (minor wear) with bisque lower arms, her mouth slightly parted with hint of a tongue, typical of a Circle Dot Bru. 14" h. Hint of whiteness to nose. As typical with early dolls, sometimes some light "dustiness" to bisque is present. Minute chip to bisque at earring hole on underside of right ear and a small patch to kid at shoulderplate on arm. **$11,500**

Dollhouses, Dolls, Accessories

Photo courtesy James D. Julia Auctioneers, Fairfield, Maine; www.JamesDJulia.com

Ten-Room Mystery Dollhouse. Circa 1890. Sold by F.A.O. Schwartz of New York City, this was one of the largest in a series of Mystery Dollhouses sold in the 1890s. The term "Mystery Dollhouse" was given by Flora Jacobs (1918-2006) as the maker has never been identified. This particular house has the gambrel roof and has the carved shingles on the main roof as well as the wing on the right side. Painted a soft cream color with black chamfered wood. There are two entrances; one going into the main part of the house and the other going into the wing. The house has four sections that open to reveal eight rooms. All the rooms have wallpaper, baseboards and raised-panel interconnecting doors. The floors are often referred to as parquet, but are actually scored and hand painted to look like parquet. An elaborate staircase with an alcove is found under the staircase. Additional attic rooms are in the openings on the roof, there is a dormer on the front that opens, a window that opens on the side of the gambrel roof and a window that opens in the back; all having small rooms. Overall house is 39 1/2" t x 59" w x 24 3/4" d. Replaced scalloped trim work at ceiling level of each room, wallpapers in both hallways seem to be original and other rooms appear to have replacement paper. Exterior cream facades are repainted and some trim on interior appears repainted. The small raised-panel door entering the wing is unhinged. **$8,625**

Christian Hacker, Dollhouse With Elevator. German dollhouse with many architectural features, a large front porch and side porch with carved columns, a large front balcony and an elaborate side balcony. The house is painted a cream color with brown timbering decorating the facade of the second story. Although there is repaint on most of the house, it still retains the original design and details. The basement has windows and does open outward to allow storage for a transformer for wiring of electricity. There are painted brackets under the roof and a larger center dormer and balcony on the roof. The roof has lithograph paper that appears to be replaced and also supports a chimney. The house opens from the front and has four large rooms and two hallways for the elevator that moves up and down by a clockwork mechanism. The floors and walls have been re-papered with appropriate papers. All the rooms have their original electrical outlets in the ceiling with beaded chandeliers that do work and provide lighting in the house. 45" t x 44" w x 24" d. The creamy yellow facade may have some touch-up but the brown timbering has been repainted. The blue outlines on the porches and brackets under the roof have been repainted. Gold paint has recently been used on the turned posts and knobs on top of the railings. The doors appear original. The base to the house has been repainted, the back of the house has original brick paper. **$6,900**

Gottschalk, Red-Roof Dollhouse. Circa 1910. Stationary front with both sides and back that are open. The front facade has many architectural features such as curved porches with elaborate railings and columns on both levels, bay windows on both corners, extending from the ground level to the roof, double-door entrances with glass transoms over them at both levels and a set of front steps. On the rooftop is a large dormer with flower boxes and a Dutch gable to accent the house. The exterior of the house is painted a light tan with darker tan trim, cream-colored railings and posts, outline decoration in gray/green. Each side of the house is open, exposing three levels. The rooms have inter-connecting doors and the walls are papered and are angular in shape. One side of the house has an elaborate mahogany staircase that extends all three levels. (There is a small room on the bottom floor that is open.) The back of the house has all three levels open with the addition of railings and posts that enclose the corners of the house. 36" t x 28" w x 28" d. Exterior is repainted, interior repapered but professionally done. **$4,025**

Christian Hacker, Dollhouse With Bay Windows. Two-story house with unusual front, two bays and large dormer on roof and over hanging front porch. House is painted a soft tan with white trim and it has the original lithographed papered roof. Sides of the house have brick paper and the back is painted white. The house opens from the front and has four rooms with interconnecting doors. House is partially furnished with Schneegas furniture. 31" t x 28" w x 19" d. Wallpaper appears to be original; trim work, side brick work and floor papers are possible replacements. One door missing. Front of house has had some restoration. **$2,875**

Homemade, Brown Brick Dollhouse. Circa 1880. Original brown brick facade of double windows, an entrance with a door and skylights and a single window above the doorway. The slanting framed roof is painted black having two chimneys. There are four rooms and two halls with a staircase. There are windows on the front and sides of the house as well as an etched glass window at the top of the stair landing which is on the back of the house. There are also interconnecting doors with porcelain knobs and there is a fireplace in each room. 37" t x 33" w x 16 3/4" d. The floors and the walls have been repapered. **$2,300**

Photo courtesy James D. Julia Auctioneers, Fairfield, Maine; www.JamesDJulia.com

Homemade Dollhouse, With Stained Glass. Exterior of house has been repainted to resemble stucco with a painted dark-red roof having two chimneys. The house opens from the front, a large center hall opens in two parts with a staircase and stained glass windows on the landing of the staircase. There are four large rooms, two large halls with a staircase. The house has a gray stone foundation with matching front steps. The front windows of the house are trimmed with flower boxes. The house has been electrified and a lock and key are found on the front entrance to lock up the entire house. 49" t x 48" w x 21 1/2" d. The interior of the house has been repapered and repainted recently. **$1,150**

Photo courtesy James D. Julia Auctioneers, Fairfield, Maine; www.JamesDJulia.com

Gottschalk, Red Roof Dollhouse. Exterior of the house has been repainted, but the original structure remains intact. It has a light olive-green facade with dark aqua and cream paint. There are cardboard mullions in the windows and doors. The front of the house has three balconies with fancy columns and railing. The house opens from the front to expose six rooms. The wallpapers and floor papers are not original to the house. The house also features side windows, outdoor steps and has been electrified. The roof has been repainted maroon and has two chimneys. 38" t x 31" w x 19" d. **$3,565**

Photo courtesy James D. Julia Auctioneers, Fairfield, Maine; www.JamesDJulia.com

Silber & Fleming Dollhouse, Three-story house, considered a flat-box type; the roof is flat with the front facade rising above the roof, has been over-painted with similar colors to the original surface. The first level has bay windows with paint resembling stone. The two upper levels are painted in a red-orange brick with darker red brick over the windows. The house opens from the front to show six rooms; all wallpapered and three halls with staircases. Each room has a built-in fireplace and each window in the front of the house has lace curtains. There are balconies located on the second floor. 45" t x 34" w x 18 1/2" d. The wallpaper on the back of the large doors that open to the house are original and extends to all levels. The floor papers in all six rooms appear original as they are all the same, the wallpapers in all six rooms may have been replaced. **$2,300**

Photo courtesy James D. Julia Auctioneers, Fairfield, Maine; www.JamesDJulia.com

Doll House Furniture and Accessories. Circa 19th Century. Walterhausen (Boulle) furniture includes six Gothic chairs upholstered in blue cut velvet with gold background, a rectangular marble top dining room table, an upright piano with gold transfer work and depressible keys, a china cabinet with drawers on legs with its original blue interior paper and a fancy wall clock with pendulum and porcelain face. There is a matching pair of ormolu prints made by Erhardt & Sohne, an ornate ormolu mantle clock and a crumber set in ormolu. Largest is 7 3/4" t. **$2,415 all**

Dollhouse Furniture and Accessories, Waltershausen (Boulle) furniture consisting of four-drawer chest with marble top having backsplash, a drop-front desk with carved white front columns and beautiful gold transfer work on the front with the interior having original blue paper and a round marble top table with pedestal base. Accessories include an ormolu cutlery tray with soft metal utensils, vase in ormolu base, soft-metal painted gold metal holder, an ormolu birdcage with wax bird, an Art Nouveau soft-metal clock with paper face, two mantle clocks with one in soft metal painted gold and paper face and the other is ormolu with pendulum and black face, an ormolu coo-coo clock, an amber glass chandelier with soft-metal decoration on the side suspended by a chain, a soft metal compote holder with fishbowl and fish attached, an ormolu holder missing green bowl, an ormolu framed mirror, filigree framed print, a tin painted gold framed print and an ormolu framed print. Desk is 6 3/4" t. Some silver loss to mirror, ormolu clock with pendulum is missing one hand and coo-coo clock is missing string that pulls bird as well as the clock weights...**$2,875 all**

Dollhouse Ormolu Revolving Picture Frame, Circa 19th Century. Each photo is set in a separate ormolu frame, which is attached to a stand. Back of each photo has a foil lining. SIZE: 2 1/4" t. **$3,737**

Two Dollhouse Ormolu Accessories, Circa 19th Century. 1) Fancy ormolu telephone with two cranks on the side of the box with receiver mounted on top. 2) Ormolu floor lamp with white Bristol shade and chimney. Both items were made by Erhard & Sohne; 2 1/4" t and 4 1/2" t...**$2,300 pair**

Artisan Dollhouse Furniture, Eight pieces, seven of which were made by craftsman Renee Isabelle consisting of a flat top highboy, bonnet top highboy, armoire, drop-

front desk (signed by Judith Dunger), corner cabinet, chair, two-drawer chest and small oval table. All are made with scenes in lacquered Japanned designs. Fine detailed pulls, hinges and trim work. In addition there are three original paintings; two larger ones are signed "Whitford"; 2 1/8" to 7 3/4" t. ....**$2,875 all**

Artisan Dollhouse Furniture, Accessories. Six pieces were made by craftsman Renee Isabelle including a linen press, drop front desk, armoire, four-drawer chest, Japanned tall cabinet and round candle stand. These pieces are intricately painted with scenes on back of cupboard doors; doors open to interiors having fine detail and hand painted scenes on backs of doors. Other items include inlaid sideboard, display stand, framed piece of needlework, small boxes with covers by other artists as well as hand-painted portraits framed in gold frames with one being signed "Whitford" and an enameled covered box with jeweled birds on lid; 2 1/2" to 8 1/4" t. ....**$2,185 all**

Artisan Dollhouse Furniture, Consisting of 10 pieces by craftsman Renee Isabelle including two armoires; one on legs with interior scenes on doors and other with hand painted interior drawer, an oval pedestal base with finely painted Japanese motif, two pedestal tables; one topped with a hinged-lid box, a settee upholstered with silk taffeta fabric printed by the artisan, two side chairs upholstered in cream silk with hand-painted flowers and the backs of the chairs have exquisite hand-painted flowers and a demilune cabinet on legs painted in pale gold with swags, scrolls and medallions of various scenes. Includes a sewing table intricately made with a medallion of a country scene hand painted on the lid that opens and a smaller lid of hand-painted scenes that also open with intricate interior space for housing sewing implements which includes a small box with cover. The last piece in the lot is a drop-front secretary with the exterior hand painted in Japan scenes with flower decoration on the front and sides as well as the interior. All edges are painted in gold with serpentine drawers. Included in the lot are four Russian covered boxes all with hand painted decoration, one painting of an 18th Century woman by Whitford housed in a gold frame, a framed black and white image of ballerinas and a large image of a woman in the countryside in gold frame as well as a miniature perfume bottle with lovebirds on lid; 2" to 7 1/4" t. ....**$3,105 all**

Handmade Dollhouse Carpets, 10 rugs from Eastern Europe or India. Copied from original Oriental rugs, these contemporary silk rugs have fine detail. Range from 8 1/2" to 15 1/2" l. ....**$1,495 all**

Dollhouse Furniture And Accessories, Circa 1920s. Set of parlor furniture by Paul Leonhardt made in the 1920's-1930's including a sofa and four side chairs with upholstered seats and backs with gold paint accompanied by a matching marble-top table with four turned legs and a display cabinet with glass on three sides and glass shelves having porcelain dishes. Three additional pieces in cream, including a round table and two side chairs. All are original pieces. Accessories include an ormolu birdcage on legs, two soft-metal framed prints, an Art Nouveau mantle clock painted green with gold decoration and a miniature book with printed pages. Tallest is approx. 8". Parlor set shows slight wear to upholstery, one chair has small piece of decoration missing. ....**$2,875 all**

Antique Dollhouse Dolls, 13 dollhouse dolls; three ladies, one boy and nine men from sizes 5" to 6 3/4" t. Most are redressed and all have painted eyes and molded hair. Remaining dolls are six all bisque children having glass eyes and original dress with a 7 1/2" glass-eyed maid; two sets of twins and the maid appear to be redressed with old fabric. One man has feet broken off, another man has chipped feet. ....**$2,415 all**

Antique Dollhouse Kitchen Accessories, Including a tin Marklin water basin painted white with blue trim with water tank storage on top and a faucet, a blue and white tin onion holder, a six-drawer tin spice holder painted white with blue decoration, two tin brush holders painted blue and white, a large blue and white tin dust pan, early tin kerosene lamp, a blue and white tin cutlery tray, a good tin picnic basket with blue and white Delft photos on each side of the base as well as top with two openings on spring and handle, hanging spice rack with small handled drawers painted white with blue lettering, a tin box that hangs on the wall for brushes and shoe polish painted white with blue lettering, two porcelain-covered boxes with Herring and Asparagus written in German on the lids, a hanging tin shelf with three porcelain canisters with lids and a tin kitchen stove with two open burners with pots and lids that rest inside the burners and a tin plate door on the front. Water basin is 5 1/4" t. ....**$3,565 all**

Antique Dollhouse Accessories, Including a filigree plant stand in soft metal having an asphaltum finish (brown wash) with large circular top holding flower pots and birdcage suspended in center with soft metal flowering tree supporting it and base has fancy scroll design. Marklin tin fireplace having painted brick in soft yellow lined in blue with a grate and fender around it with the trim at the top being tin painted gold, tin birdcage with red roof and bird hanging on a suspended ring, a fancy circular ormolu birdcage on a stand with a wax bird on a swing made by Erhard & Sohne, an ormolu compote with impressed floral design in center, large Art Nouveau hanging mirror with lilies and bellflower in center, an Art Nouveau console mirror which hangs from the wall, a square ormolu birdcage with parrot, an ormolu hanger, an ormolu mantle clock with pendulum and porcelain face, a soft-metal, double-covered inkwell desk set with marble and two ormolu framed prints. Birdcage on stand is approx. 5 1/4" t. Red-roof birdcage having poor repaint and both Art Nouveau mirrors have some dark discoloration. ....**$3,105 all**

Photo courtesy James D. Julia Auctioneers, Fairfield, Maine; www.JamesDJulia.com

Nine Antique Dollhouse Dolls. Four glass-eyed Simon & Halbig ladies wearing evening gowns; two having original dresses and all having original wigs. Five gentlemen with mustaches with four in suits and the other wearing a tuxedo. All men have painted eyes and original limbs. Tallest woman is 8" and the tallest man is 7". Three of the doll's gowns are fragile and are melting, there are no broken or missing limbs. The men's clothing shows wear. **$2,520 all**

Photo courtesy James D. Julia Auctioneers, Fairfield, Maine; www.JamesDJulia.com

Antique Dollhouse Kitchen Furniture and Accessories. Includes two kitchen furniture sets; one set is cream trimmed in blue consisting of a 9 1/2" tall cupboard with matching table and two chairs, a work table and hanging shelf. The second set is mustard trimmed in red consisting of a 9" tall cupboard with matching table and chair as well as a hanging shelf and a workbench having two doors below. A large tin cupboard painted beige and blue in original paint as well as an odd table and two chairs in cream are included. Accessories include a tin egg container with eggs which hangs on the wall, a water basin in mustard trimmed in red with faucet, heavy metal dishes with platters, tureens in tan trimmed in blue. A white tin hanging shelf with canisters labeled with spices having drawers below all trimmed in blue, a tin canister set with four large and four small canisters having lids with four hanging tin containers in tan and blue decoration and a similar wall clock. Two tin hanging utensil racks. Metal clock with movable hands and some treenware plates, bowl, compote and vase in two different patterns. Tallest is 9 1/2". All tin pieces have wear and flaking to paint and some wooden kitchen pieces show minor wear to paint. **$3,737 all**

Ormolu Dollhouse Miniatures, large-scale chandelier with bulbs and shades, console mirror, three-part folding mirror with lithograph scenes on the reverse, a gilt metal three-part picture frame, cruet set, round birdcage as well as three framed prints. Tallest is 7 3/4". Chandelier is missing one bulb. Console mirror is missing tabletop cover. Three-part folding mirror is missing some silvering with slight discoloration at weld points and small amount of lithograph image missing. Cruet set and birdcage show some dark discoloration. ....**$2,185 all**

Four Dollhouse Dolls, 1) Soldier with a red jacket having gold Dresden paper decoration wearing black felt pants and high leather boots. Soldier has rare brown eyes and fine black mustache and hair. 2) Gentleman dressed in a black felt tuxedo with shirt, bow tie and vest. He has painted blue eyes and molded brown hair. 3) Black butler in black felt tuxedo carrying a white towel on his arm with a white shirt, bow tie and vest. He has finely painted eyes, eyebrows and mouth with smooth black hair. 4) Soldier with a red jacket, gold Dresden paper decoration and matching hat as well as a dark velvet jacket on his shoulder complete with a sword at his side and tall leather boots. 7" t each. Black-haired solder has a tiny moth hole in the arm of his jacket. ....**$3,600 all**

Dollhouse Fireplace and Dolls, Circa 19th Century. Large gilt tin fireplace with over-mantel mirror, with hearth area being black tin with a grate and red foil paper to represent a fire. The fireplace has impressed designs around the hearth and on the columns as well as under the mantel. The mantel has a scalloped edge and the over-mantel mirror is divided into three parts with scalloped designs on the outer mirrors and a sunburst in the pediment at the top. Also included are two soldiers with original uniforms; one with red and navy blue having a sword at his side, high black boots, a decorative helmet with gold eagle on the front and tassel on the side. Other soldier has royal blue coat with red decoration, gold buttons with epaulets and he has a sword at his side. Both soldiers have molded hair and mustaches; the soldier in the royal blue jacket has molded black hair and mustache. Fireplace is 8 5/8" t x 6" w. Both soldiers are 7 1/4" t.
....**$3,565 all**

Toys, General

Photo courtesy James D. Julia Auctioneers, Fairfield, Maine; www.JamesDJulia.com

Hathaway's Bread Truck, original condition, a rare version of the Hathaway's truck. Normally found with an advertising decal on the side, this is the rubber-stamped version. Not only is the paint near mint, but the rubber stamping almost totally intact with some minor fading to lettering. International decals along with Arcade decal are intact, 9 1/2". **$8,050**

Photo courtesy Morphy Auctions, Denver, Pa.; www.MorphyAuctions.com

Buddy L, 26" Tank Line truck with original decals. **$5,500**

Photo courtesy Bertoia Auctions, Vineland, N.J.; www.BertoiaAuctions.com

Britains, 17" toy of painted metal features a whimsical hand-painted figure with a striking resemblance to the puppet show character "Punch." The cloth-dressed figure rides in a circle on a two-wheel bicycle attached by a wire support to a heavy base. **$21,850**

Photo courtesy Morphy Auctions, Denver, Pa.; www.MorphyAuctions.com

Louis Marx tin Ring-A-Ling Circus wind-up toy with original pictorial box. **$5,750**

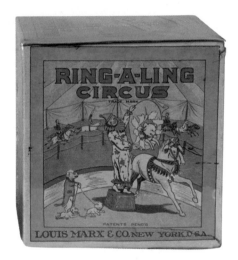

Photo courtesy Heritage Auction Galleries, Dallas; www.HA.com

Hubley "America" cast-iron and aluminum tri-motor airplane, 14" x 17". Turning the wheels causes the propellers to move. Rubber tires. Insignia and markings painted red, engine cylinders painted black. Includes two pilot figures. Modest play wear. **$1,912**

Photo courtesy Morphy Auctions, Denver, Pa.; www.MorphyAuctions.com

Circa-1952 metal Ferrari, made by Toschi (Italy), 21" and in working order. **$5,200**

Photo courtesy Morphy Auctions, Denver, Pa.; www.MorphyAuctions.com

Atom Jet tin friction racecar, Japanese, 25 1/2", all original parts intact. **$15,500**

Photo courtesy James D. Julia Auctioneers, Fairfield, Maine; www.JamesDJulia.com

Arcade White Moving Truck with side mounts. Produced in many different colors, some with store names or advertising logos, this example is mocha colored with deep red highlighting. Dual rear rubber tires with iron hubs and dual side mounts further enhance the appearance of this moving van. In 100% original condition, 13". **$9,775**

Arcade Mack Wrecker Truck. Cast iron with nickel driver figure, dual rear wheels, 12 1/2" x 5" x 4". Retains original paint. **$717**

Marusan (Japan) 1954 friction-drive Chevrolet with original box. **$4,095**

Photo courtesy Morphy Auctions, Denver, Pa.; www.MorphyAuctions.com

1956 Haji (Japan) tin friction Ford Sunliner convertible with original box, 11 1/4". **$7,500**

Photo courtesy Morphy Auctions, Denver, Pa.; www.MorphyAuctions.com

Buddy L Jr., circa 1930 pressed-steel dairy truck, 24" long with opening doors, nickel-plated bumper with headlights, accompanied by six original accessory milk cans. **$11,500**

Photo courtesy Heritage Auction Galleries, Dallas; www.HA.com

Buck Rogers Rocket Pistol XZ-31 (Daisy, 1934). Approximately 9 1/2" long, with a black metal finish, highlighted by chrome barrel attachments. Handle cocks. Light areas of rust are present. No holster or box. **$334**

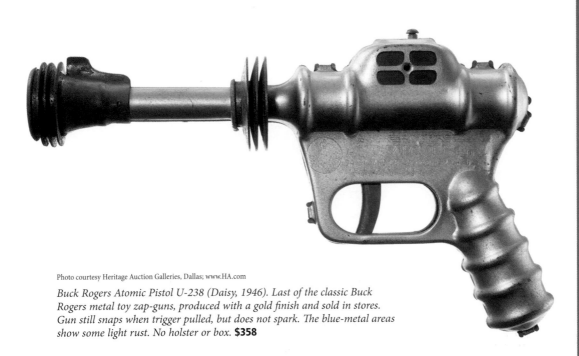

Photo courtesy Heritage Auction Galleries, Dallas; www.HA.com

Buck Rogers Atomic Pistol U-238 (Daisy, 1946). Last of the classic Buck Rogers metal toy zap-guns, produced with a gold finish and sold in stores. Gun still snaps when trigger pulled, but does not spark. The blue-metal areas show some light rust. No holster or box. **$358**

Photo courtesy Bertoia Auctions, Vineland, N.J.; www.BertoiaAuctions.com

Marklin, Circa-1909 Fidelitas clown car caravan. The German hand-painted tinplate toy measures 37 1/2" long and is rarely seen. **$103,500**

Photo courtesy Morphy Auctions, Denver, Pa.; www.MorphyAuctions.com

Harley-Davidson, cast-iron 8 1/2" toy motorcycle replicating a 1930 factory DAH Hill Climber. **$57,500**

Photo courtesy Morphy Auctions, Denver, Pa.; www.MorphyAuctions.com

U.S. Hardware Co., 14" painted cast-iron scull with oarsmen and coxswain. **$11,500**

Photo courtesy Morphy Auctions, Denver, Pa.; www.MorphyAuctions.com

Papier-mache frog ball-toss game on wheeled platform, with original painted-wood balls. **$6,300**

Photo courtesy Mosby & Co. Auctions, Frederick, Md.; www.MosbyAuctions.com

Betty Boop, 9" prewar Japanese celluloid with fur stole. **$2,805**

Photo courtesy Noel Barrett Antiques & Auctions Ltd., Carversville, Pa.; www.NoelBarrett.com

This hand drawn and colored "Monopoly" game, created by John Heap sometime between 1910 and 1917 when his family lived in Altoona, Pa. Charles Darrow's reputation as the inventor of Monopoly has often been disputed, but no more successfully then in a counter suit filed by Ralph Anspach, inventor of the game Anti-Monopoly. Anspach was sued by the General Mills Fun Group for trademark infringement, but the corporation lost their case that went all the way to the Supreme Court, which denied the Darrow claim as inventor. Anspach unearthed a number of earlier versions - what he referred to as "folk art" games. This is the second-oldest such game that Anspach discovered and the oldest with all its playing pieces: handmade money, property cards in color groupings similar to Darrow's version, as well as houses and other "improvement" buildings . Such games and affidavits of those who had played these games well before Darrow's early 1930s "invention" were pivotal in Anspach's ultimate judicial victory. The game is in what appears to be its original frame under glass, 30" square. **$10,350**

Photo courtesy Noel Barrett Antiques & Auctions Ltd., Carversville, Pa.; www.NoelBarrett.com

Gunthermann tinplate clockwork toy depicting a lady with her baby in a spoke-wheeled pram. **$5,175**

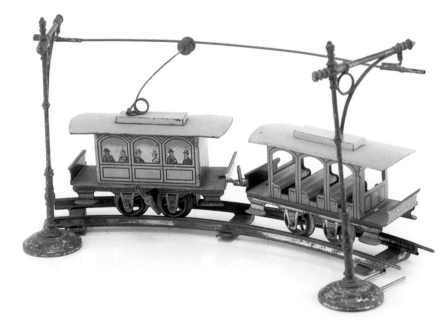

Photo courtesy Noel Barrett Antiques & Auctions Ltd., Carversville, Pa.; www.NoelBarrett.com

Issmayer clockwork tin trolleys, made in Germany for the U.S. market. **$9,200**

Photo courtesy Noel Barrett
Antiques & Auctions Ltd.,
Carversville, Pa.;
www.NoelBarrett.com

Tinplate crank-operated Vielmetter Clown Artist, with four changeable cams enabling the clown to "draw" portraits. **$10,350**

Photo courtesy Noel Barrett
Antiques & Auctions Ltd.,
Carversville, Pa.;
www.NoelBarrett.com

Britains sci-fi figures set, in fine original condition, includes Buck, Wilma, Mekkano Man Robot and three other characters from the Buck Rogers comic strip. **$4,600**

Battery-Operated Mod Monster Blushing Frankenstein in the Original Box, 12 1/2" tall. Operated by two D-size batteries. Made in Japan. Activate a button and Frankenstein's arms move, his pants fall down revealing his red-striped underwear and his face blushes. Monster is in fine condition, no batteries have been stored in the toy. The pictorial box is complete, a bit pushed in on the top panel. **$60**

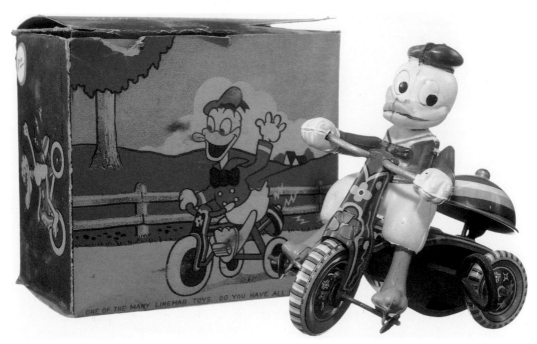

Donald Duck Mechanical Tricycle Wind-up Toy and Box (Line Mar, 1950s). Box shows some minor wear, including a chip missing from the top edge, toy is in NM. **$215**

Photo courtesy Morphy Auctions, Denver, Pa.;
www.MorphyAuctions.com

Nifty Skidoodle tinplate wind-up character auto. **$6,325**

Photo courtesy Noel Barrett Antiques & Auctions Ltd., Carversville, Pa.;
www.NoelBarrett.com

Martin (France) cloth-dressed, painted-tin clockwork Shoeshine Boy, 4 1/2". **$14,950**

Photo courtesy Noel Barrett Antiques & Auctions Ltd., Carversville, Pa.;
www.NoelBarrett.com

Circa-1900 French clown child automaton with bisque head, 20". **$4,600**

Photo courtesy Heritage Auction Galleries, Dallas; www.HA.com

Mickey Mouse Steiff doll with tag (1930s). Plush velvet Mickey standing approximately 7", missing the tail. Includes an orange Steiff tag stamped into the left ear, marked with number 1416. **$507**

Collector's Note: Margarete Steiff (1847-1909) was born in Giengen, Germany. She was a seamstress and confined to a wheelchair due to polio she contracted as a baby. She started making stuffed animals as a hobby in 1880.

These toys began as elephants, based on a design Steiff found in a magazine, and were originally sold as pincushions to her friends. However, children began playing with them, and in the years following she went on to design many other successful animal-themed toys for children, such as dogs, cats and pigs. She designed and made most of the prototypes herself. By 1903, the firm she established with her brother, Fritz, was producing a jointed mohair teddy bear, whose production dramatically increased to more than 970,000 units in 1907. The famed "button in ear" was devised by Margarete's nephew, Franz, in 1904, to keep counterfeits from being passed off as authentic Steiff toys.

Photo courtesy James D. Julia Auctioneers, Fairfield, Maine; www.JamesDJulia.com

Photo courtesy James D. Julia Auctioneers, Fairfield, Maine; www.JamesDJulia.com

Early Steiff Black Coachman's Attendant. With side-glancing glass eyes, he retains his original Steiff button and is in all original, untouched condition with only minor soiling and/or staining to his outfit. 16" t. **$6,900**

Early Steiff Coachman. He has glass eyes, retains his original Steiff button and is in all original, untouched condition with only minor soiling and or staining to his outfit. Some soiling to face, lacking two buttons on vest, sleeves of overcoat torn at seam. **$6,325**

Early Steiff Blacksmith. He shoe button eyes, retains his original Steiff button and is in all original, untouched condition with only minor soiling and or staining to his outfit. 20" h. With soiling and minor staining to face and minor hair loss at top of head. **$4,025**

Early Chocolate 9" Steiff Bear. In as-found, untouched condition, bear retains his button as well as a large amount of his chocolate/cinnamon (?) fur and his felt pads are intact other than a few small moth holes. Shoe button eyes, hump on back, black-stitched nose and a cocked head. Right leg has had amateur old repair at hip by original owner and is stitched back into place. **$1,560**

Photo courtesy Morphy Auctions, Denver, Pa.; www.MorphyAuctions.com

Marx prototype Jiminy Cricket hand-painted tin windup toy with umbrella-twirling action, "1939 Walt Disney Production" mark. **$3,162**

Photo courtesy Noel Barrett Antiques & Auctions Ltd., Carversville, Pa.; www.NoelBarrett.com

French-made Fernand Martin tin wind-up black waiter. **$16,100**

Photo courtesy Morphy Auctions, Denver, Pa.; www.MorphyAuctions.com

Complete boxed set of 12 Peltier marbles, each with a depiction of an early comic character. **$9,200**

Marklin circa-1903 Iowa battleship, 22"
long, painted tin, immaculate condition.
$46,000

Circa-1870s George Brown stenciled tinplate
"Broadway & 42nd Street" horse-drawn trolley.
$6,325

George Brown Excelsior locomotive of painted and stenciled tin, with cast-iron wheels. **$6,300**

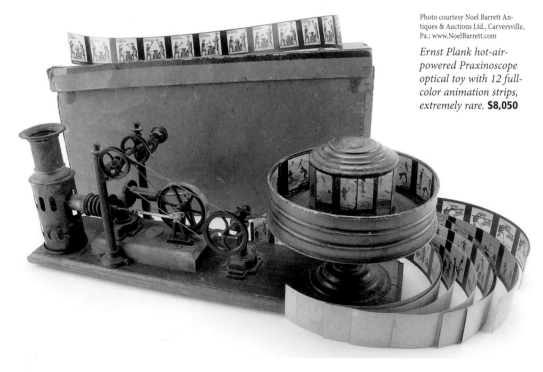

Ernst Plank hot-air-powered Praxinoscope optical toy with 12 full-color animation strips, extremely rare. **$8,050**

Photo courtesy Morphy Auctions, Denver, Pa.; www.MorphyAuctions.com

Masudaya battery-operated Target Robot with original pictorial box and sealed bag of accessories. **$52,900**

Photo courtesy RSL Auction Co., Oldwick, N.J.; www.rslauctions.com

Circa-1865 American clockwork omnibus, painted tin with cast-iron wheels, probably Hull & Stafford. **$47,385**

HOT WHEELS

Hot Wheels is a brand of die-cast toy car, introduced by Mattel on Sept. 7, 1968. It was the primary competitor of Johnny Lightning and Matchbox until 1996, when Mattel acquired rights to the Matchbox brand from Tyco.

Of the first 16 cars (sometimes called the "Sweet 16" by collectors), 10 were based upon customized versions of regular production automobiles of the era, and six were based upon real show cars and cars designed and built for track racing. All of the cars featured "Spectraflame" paint-work, bearings, redline wheels and working suspensions.

Beatnik Bandit, based on Ed "Big Daddy" Roth's show car of the same name. **$50 NM**

Custom Corvette. **$90-$125 NM**

Custom Eldorado. **$65-$100 NM**

Custom Barracuda. **$350 NM**

Custom Camaro. **$125 NM**

Custom Cougar. **$150-$200 NM**

Custom Firebird. **$75-$450 NM**

Silhouette. **$30-$50 NM**

Custom Mustang. **$150-$450 NM**

Hot Heap. **$50-$175 NM**

Custom Fleetside. **$75 NM**

Python. **$30-$175 NM**

Ford J-Car. **$40-$250 NM**

Custom T-Bird. **$150-$700 NM**

Deora. **$65-$85 NM**

Custom Volkswagen. **$55-$275 NM**

Toy Trains

Photo courtesy Noel Barrett Antiques & Auctions Ltd., Carversville, Pa.; www.NoelBarrett.com

Marklin Gauge-I maroon and red American steam-profile clockwork locomotive with tender and three cars (some paint chipping and peeling to boiler); four-wheel tender with rear hinged compartment, No. 21 1000k box car (very good to excellent with some paper residue to high point of roof) and two passenger cars, all with hinged opening lids (passenger cars are fair to very good with one side of car faded, with areas of corrosion and paint loss), engine and tender, 15".
$34,500

Flintstones and Jetsons wind-up Express Trains (Louis Marx Co. Inc., 1962), Hanna-Barbera. The Flintstones' Bedrock Express and the Jetsons' Express trains, with zig-zag action. Joining Fred, the engineer, on the ride are Wilma, Barney, Betty, Dino, detective Perry Gunite, and some of the townsfolk. On the Jetson's train, the whole family, including Jane's mother, are along for the ride. Both in Excellent condition. **$388 pair**

Marklin Gauge-II F&E live steam train, 22" locomotive and tender with 15" long selection of cars. **$32,200**

Photo courtesy Heritage Auction Galleries, Dallas; www.HA.com

Lionel Standard Gauge 347 Model set in the box featuring No. 8E electric locomotive in red, the No. 337 Pullman and the No. 338 observation car in matching red. Each car is in its original box showing only minimal surface scratching and wear. The Pullman has a slight dent on the roof, and the paint on the roof seems discolored. **$239**

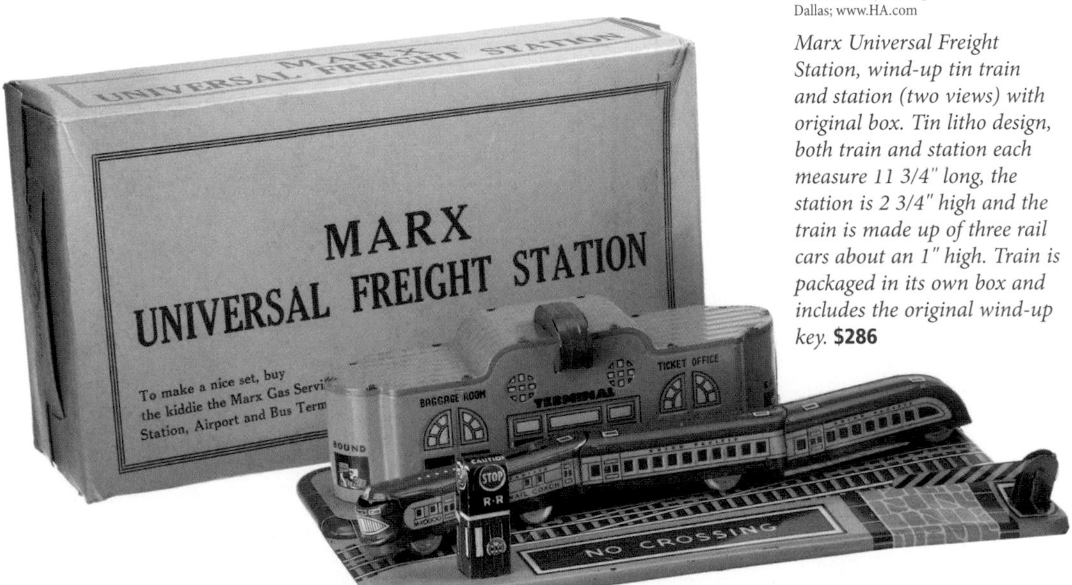

Photo courtesy Heritage Auction Galleries, Dallas; www.HA.com

Marx Universal Freight Station, wind-up tin train and station (two views) with original box. Tin litho design, both train and station each measure 11 3/4" long, the station is 2 3/4" high and the train is made up of three rail cars about an 1" high. Train is packaged in its own box and includes the original wind-up key. **$286**

Photo courtesy Rago Arts and Auction Center, Lambertville, N.J.; www.RagoArts.com

Rare Chilkat Dance Blanket, Northwest Coast: Classic ceremonial garb of hand-woven mountain goat hair, dye with natural pigments, decorated with highly stylized clan symbols and animal forms, mid-19th century. Top edge reinforced with animal hide, woven mountain goat hair and cedar bark. Such blankets were prestigious items for the elite. Fair overall condition, a few small areas of wear and tribal repair. With fringe: 64" x 50". **$22,800**

TRIBAL ARTS

Native American Cultures

Haida Mask, Northwest Coast: Carved wooden face with traditional features, painted in red, black, and green, late 19th-early 20th century. It has been suggested that this mask may have originally been part of a totem pole or house facade. Miniature masks are known to exist, but are very rare. One stress fracture possibly reattached, likely retouched on lips. Mounted on custom display stand. 5 1/4" x 4 3/4". **$2,280**

Otter Potlatch Bowl, Northwest Coast: Elegantly carved wooden bowl with prominently curved tail, inlaid with abalone discs and eyes, 1977. Excellent condition. Indecipherable signature, dated. 4 1/2" x 16". **$1,800**

Athabaskan Shot Pouch With Accoutrements, Alaska: Beaded leather bag and strap on trade cloth with incised powder horn, early 19th century. Fair condition with minor bead loss. 6" x 6 1/2" fold bag, 38" x 3" strap, 8" horn. **$7,800**

Feather Cape, Great Lakes: Exquisite collar of concentric feathers rings sewn together, including peahen, prairie chicken, and guinea fowl, backed and bound in pink woven cloth, mid-19th century. Good condition and color, intact, mounted in a display frame under glass. 12" radius; framed mount 26" x 31". **$1,080**

Chippewa Beaded Shot Pouch, Great Lakes: Overall floral design on black cotton, wool backing, geometric glass bead border, late 19th century. Fair condition, a few minor holes. Including strap, 30 1/4" x 6". **$1,800**

Apache Strike-A-Light, Midwest: Beaded leather pouch fringed with tin cones and four drops, circa 1880. Excellent original condition. 12 1/4" x 4 1/2". **$1,560**

Sioux Tobacco Bag, Midwest: Spider Woman design in quillwork, above quill drops and long leather fringe, accented with tin cones, late 19th century. Remarkably good condition, very minor losses to quill work. With fringe: 38" x 6". **$3,000**

Anasazi Tularosa Vessel, Arizona: Pre-historic black and white jug with zoomorphic lug handle, painted in typical step and swirl designs, AD 1125-1300. Intact with no restoration. 5" x 5 3/4". **$1,080**

Anasazi Tularosa Olla, Arizona: Black and white vessel, AD 1125-1300. Approximately 15-20% restored. 8 3/4" x 12" dia. **$1,800**

Hopi Salako Mana Kachina Doll, Southwest: Painted cottonwood with colorful tabletta, accented with feathers, early 20th century. Good condition, some loss to pigment, overall intact. Mounted on Lucite base. 10" x 6". **$840**

Photo courtesy Rago Arts and Auction Center, Lambertville, N.J.; www.RagoArts.com

Iroquois/Seneca False Face, New York: Exceptional carved wood mask with strong downward mouth, bulging cylindrical eyes, bold red paint, and black horse hair, early 20th century. Worn in healing ceremonies. Interior shows wear and handling consistent with ritual use, several layers of paint evident. 12" x 7 1/2". **$3,360**

Photo courtesy Rago Arts and Auction Center, Lambertville, N.J.; www.RagoArts.com

Hopi Corn Kachina Doll, Southwest: Stout cottonwood figure painted in brilliant polychrome, with attached ears and snout, mid-20th century. Good condition, some loss to pigment. 7" x 3". **$240**

Large Kachina Doll, Southwest: Cottonwood figure topped with a tall tabletta headdress accented with feathers and sweetgrass necklace, its eyes representing profiled faces, frog motif on reverse, early to mid-20th century. Fair condition with reattached legs, loss to foot and repair to other, some decay to pigment. 20 1/2" x 6 1/2". **$720**

Soyal Kachina Doll, Southwest: Carved cottonwood figure accented with feather regalia and long bird-like beak, painted with a pouch and jewelry. The Soyal Kachina, also known as the Return Kachina, is associated with the Third Mesa. His reappearance in late December signals the beginning of a new Kachina season. He tours the village placing prayer feathers at each kiva. These prayer offerings open the way for other Kachinas to return to the village from the spirit world. Good condition. 9" x 2 3/4". **$360**

Hopi Kachina Doll, Southwest: Carved cottonwood with polychrome colors in traditional wrapped shirt and mask, early to mid-20th century. Fair condition with light fading to pigments. 7" x 3 1/4". **$450**

Hopi Flower Kachina, Southwest: Painted cottonwood sculpture with facial tattoos, textile design, and applied comb and beak, early 20th century. Citoto takes part in the Ayavanu water serpent ceremony and in mixed kachina dances. Excellent condition, minimal loss to pigment, original feather regalia removed previously. Mounted on custom metal base. 12 3/4". **$3,000**

Pueblo Clown Mask, Southwest: Painted canvas and textile construction with attached corn husk regalia and applied mouth, early to mid-20th century. Well worn with signs of use, overall intact, mounted on custom wood display stand. 14 1/2" x 8 1/2". **$3,360**

Mela Youngblood, Blackware Vase , New Mexico: Carved vessel from Santa Clara pueblo with cloud, rainbow, and kiva step motif, 1970. Excellent condition. Signed and dated. 3 1/2" x 2 3/4". **$900**

Mound Builder, Feline Effigy Pipe, Ohio: Fort Ancient Culture, carved stone with image of a shaman transforming into a cat, AD 1000-1650. Overall good condition. Custom-mounted on display stand. 2 1/2" x 3 1/2" dia.. .... **$1,200**

Caddo Vessel, Arkansas: Terra cotta bottle form with incised sunflower design, AD 1200-1400. (Provenance: Private collection, Pennsylvania). Completely intact, with no restoration. 7 1/2" x 5 1/4". **$480**

Mississippian, Bell Plain Vessel, Arkansas: Grayware bulbous vessel with four applied faces representing the four directions, AD 800-1200. Restoration to spout, some wear to high points. 8" x 8 1/2". **$720**

Large Caddo Vessel, Arkansas: Terra cotta bottle form, Friendship style, AD 1200-1400. Reassembled from fragments, with approx. 95% original materials. 9 3/4" x 8". **$420**

Crow Parfleche, Fringed Envelope, Montana: Rawhide bag painted with red, yellow, white and indigo pigments in geometric pattern, with red woven wool border and long fringe, early to mid-20th century. Excellent condition. With fringe: 31" x 14". **$420**

Crow Parfleche Envelope, Montana: Rawhide bag painted with red, yellow, white and indigo pigments in geometric pattern, fastened with a leather tie, early 20th century. Fair condition with slight staining and signs of use. 26" x 12".. **$780**

Small Ute Beaded Pouch, Midwest: Leather bag with tin cone fringe and tin button, lazy-stitched bead work, early 20th century. Good condition, minor rust on cones. 7" x 3 1/8". **$480**

Blackfoot, Beaded Knife Sheath And Knife, Montana: Floral design on leather, wood handle on steel blade by Silney R. Baxter & Co., Boston, decorated with brass tack, early 20th century. Excellent original condition, 1/4" loss to bead work. Sheath: 15 1/4" x 3 1/4"; knife: 10 3/4". **$900**

Plains Horse Effigy Mirror, Iowa: Carved wood frame with brass tacks around original mirror, late 19th century. Used as trade goods circa 1890. Overall intact with signs of age. 13" x 7 1/4". **$900**

Iroquois, Beaded Cloth Purse And Hat: Both fully embroidered with polychrome beads in floral patterns: bag, mid-19th century. Fair condition, minor losses consistent with use. Bag: 6 1/2" x 5", hat: 4" x 10 1/2". .... **$780 both**

Ojibwa Bandolier Bag, Great Lakes: Beaded on trade cloth, silk, and red wool, with large glass beads and wool tassels, late 19th century. Fair condition, some losses to silk. 41 1/2" x 10". **$1,200**

Cree, Silk-Embroidered Elk Hide Wall Pocket: Exceptional tulip-shaped pouch of delicate leather, stitched with blossoms in polychrome, lined in silk, 19th century. Overall good condition with light staining from use. 10" x 9 1/4". **$900**

Athabaskan Beaded Medicine Bag, Alaska: Intricately beaded leather pouch with a floral vine on each side, bordered in leather fringe and topped with a leather cord handle, late 19th century. Overall fair condition, with some bead loss and minor stains. 15" x 10 1/2". **$480**

Sioux Doll, Midwest: Cloth body with pressed and stitched leather face accented with glass bead eyes, earrings and necklace and attached human hair, clothed in elk hide garments, late 19th-early 20th century. Fair condition overall with light stains and lost to hair. 12". **$600**

Eastern Woodlands Quilled Leather Case, Northeast: Finely crafted box with intricate porcupine quillwork in floral patterns, embossed design on the bottom and stitched construction, late 19th-early 20th century. An exceptional example. Overall good condition. 3 1/2" x 10 3/4" x 6 1/4"..**$2,160**

Tunxis/Wangunk Lidded Splint Basket, Northeast: Woven black ash rectangular container with separate lid, stained with natural dyes, mid-19th century. Fair condition with signs of use, minor breaks. 12" x 19" x 13". **$2,040**

Inuit Ivory Bracelet, Alaska: Made of carved medallions depicting two polar bears, a seal, and a walrus, joined by contrasting bone tablets, on elastic, 1940s. Perfect condition. 3" x 1 1/8". **$1,560**

Horse Hair Bosal Bridle, Montana: Braided multicolor horse hair reins with bosal nose band decorated with wool in shades of red and brown, and horse hair tassels, circa 1915. Prison-made, likely at a Montana correction facility. Good condition with signs of use, minor split to lining of browband. 18" with 144" reins. **$480**

Sioux Quilled Hair Drop, Midwest: Fully quilled hair extension on leather, in red, purple, and green geometric designs, attached with red dyed hair and feathers capped in tin cones, late 19th century. Excellent condition with minor loss to quill work. 21" x 3". **$960**

Latin American Cultures

Aztec Stone Metate With Carved Relief, Mexico: Ceremonial stone depicting supplicant figure before a seated lord, AD 1200-1500. Excellent condition with no restoration, reverse of stone worn by use. Custom metal display stand. Total: 13" x 15". **$3,240**

Mayan Orangeware Vessel, Mexico: Traditional Mayan pot with painted insect motif, AD 500-700. Excellent condition, intact with root marks and dendrite deposits. 5" x 4 3/4". **$960**

Large Mayan Copador Ceramic Vessel, Honduras: Tall cylinder painted with twin bands of glyphs and images of lords in full regalia, divided by bands of trophy heads, AD 600-900. Minor chipping to rim, a few stabilized hairlines, light wear to surface in some areas consistent with age, in otherwise remarkable state of preservation. 8 1/4" x 6 3/8". **$1,680**

Exceptional Colima Redware Dog, Mexico: Large terra cotta figure with classic plump body and tail spout, incised eyes, mouth and nose, and negative-resist design, 200 BC-AD 250. Intact condition with heavy dendrite deposits and root marks visible. 10 1/2" x 14". **$8,400**

Colima Dwarf Figural Vessel, Mexico: Burnished terra cotta figure with diminutive arms, ear spools and conch shell trumpet, 200 BC-AD 250. Possible professional restoration to the neck, heavy dendrite deposits throughout. 11 1/2" x 7 1/2". **$1,080**

Nayarit Chinesco Painted Female Figure, Mexico: Burnished ceramic idol kneeling with one arm to her abdomen, the other under her breast, 200 BC-AD 250. Adorned with incised plated hair, a nose ring, painted and negative-resist designs, most notably a red hand on her breast. Head has been re-attached and the knees have been restored. 10 1/2" x 6". **$7,800**

Photo courtesy Rago Arts and Auction Center, Lambertville, N.J.; www.RagoArts.com

Sioux Child's Vest, Plains: Lazy-stitched with polychrome beads in geometric design, on animal hide, early 20th century. Excellent condition. 5 3/4" x 8 1/2". **$570**

Photo courtesy Rago Arts and Auction Center, Lambertville, N.J.; www.RagoArts.com

Monumental Colima Shaman Figural Vessel, Mexico: Burnished terra cotta in classic "Admiral" form with stylized shell necklace, traditional top knot, horn hat and spout, 200 BC-AD 250. The shaman tomb guardian protected the deceased in the afterlife. Rare Pre-Columbian indigenous repair evident by two holes to the front and back of the neck, through which sinew or twine would have been wound; such restoration shows particular care for the piece, or for the deceased; heavy dendrite deposits throughout. 16 1/2" x 9". **$10,200**

Nayarit Bichrome Painted Male Warrior, Mexico: Classic image shown with helmet and staff regalia, painted with linear and spot designs, 200 BC-AD 250. Restoration to arm and tip of staff; heavy dendrite deposits throughout. 6 3/4" x 3 1/2". **$360**

Jalisco Mother And Child, Mexico: Early figural ceramic rattle depicting a nursing mother, with remnants of a negative-resist design, adorned with arm bands, nose ring, and necklaces suggesting a person of status, 200 BC-AD 200. Re-assembled from several pieces, appears to be all original. 11" x 7". **$720**

Veracruz Soriente Head Fragment, Mexico: Terra cotta sculpture with serene smiling face related to the Pulque cult, accented with a rare monkey glyph on the headdress, AD 300-600. Stable condition, minor chipping to nose and decay around neck break. Custom metal display stand. 5" x 5". **$840**

Large Mixtec Carved Stone Female Idol, Mexico: Volcanic stone figure wearing a headdress, shown with

hand to breast, archaic face with heart-shaped brow and ear spools, AD 800-1500. Some weathering and chipping to finial. In custom display stand. 24 3/4" x 8 1/4". **$5,100**

Veracruz Stone Hacha, Mexico: Unusual carved volcanic stone image of sacrificial victim relating to the Mesoamerican ball game, featuring a large nose ring and ornate head gear, AD 550-800. Intact with some original pigment remaining. On custom display stand. 8 1/4" x 4". **$3,360**

Veracruz Stone Head, Mexico: Unusually expressive carved head of elongated form, possibly depicting a man with deformity, AD 550-800. Overall good condition. Custom metal display stand. 4 1/2" x 4 1/2". **$660**

Nicoya Jaguar Metate, Atlantic Watershed Culture, Costa Rica: Carved volcanic stone ceremonial implement in feline form, AD 1000-1500. Overall good condition, tail reattached. 4 1/2" x 11" x 5". **$960**

Usulutan Ceramic Flying Shaman, Costa Rica: Burnished terra cotta figural vessel in full reclining posture, holding an owl amphora, AD 300-500. Often referred to as "swimmers", these traditional forms are believed to represent shamans in ritual trance, in flight to the heavens with offerings for the gods. This particular example features an owl vase, relating to the underworld spirits and the night. Restoration to some areas, two well-worn holes suggest loss of original finials long ago. 7 1/4" x 14 1/2". **$1,800**

Quimbaya Terra Cotta Idol, Columbia: Figurine with negative-resist designs and highly stylized facial features, AD 300-1500. Heavy dentrite deposits and small areas of

Photo courtesy Rago Arts and Auction Center, Lambertville, N.J.; www.RagoArts.com

Nicoya Jaguar Mace Head, Atlantic Watershed Culture, Costa Rica: Carved dense green stone featuring the transformation of a shaman into a jaguar, AD 1000-1500. Good condition. Mounted on custom metal stand. Total: 3" x 2 1/4". **$960**

loss, overall intact with no restoration. Custom-mounted to wood base. 8 1/2" x 6 1/2". **$2,400**

Marajo Terra Cotta Vessel, Brazil: Spherical black and white vessel painted with stylized animal form, AD 800-1400. Intact condition with light erosion. 6" x 5 3/4". ...**$900**

Chancay Mummy Mask, Peru: Carved wooden mask with red mineral pigment, accented with woven cotton textile and remains of human hair, AD 1200-1450. Fair condition, with remains of textile imprints on mask, eyes retouched. On display stand. 22 1/2" x 11". **$600**

Inca Terra Cotta Frog Vessel, Peru: Highly stylized zoomorphic vessel with spiraling eyes suggesting a hallucinogenic trance, accented with snake motifs, AD 1450-1550. Overall intact condition with no restoration. 8 1/2" x 6 3/4". **$1,200**

Moche Phase I Stirrup Vessel, Peru: Traditional form vessel painted in a checkerboard pattern in terra cotta on cream slip ground, with a burnished spout, AD 100-300. Completely intact with no restoration, heavy dentrite deposits and root marks present, professionally cleaned and conserved. 8" x 5 1/4". **$900**

Moche Corn God Vessel, Peru: Mold-made ceramic with deity faces and embossed corn motif with cream slip decoration, AD 500-750. Possible restoration to spout and shallow fracture on back of form. 9" x 6". **$300**

Tiwanaku (Tiahuanaco) Ceramic Vessel, Bolivia: Terra cotta jug with painted geometric designs resembling period textiles, AD 300-900. Intact condition with possible restoration to handle. 6 1/2" x 8". **$660**

Taino Ritual Vessel, Caribbean: Carved wood anthropomorphic receptacle with stylized ancestor and traditional geometric motifs, AD 1200-1500. Crystallized residue on interior evidences ceremonial use. 3" x 6 1/2". **$6,000**

Other World Cultures

Bamana Medicine Container, Mali: Carved figural vessel, its lid featuring a classic female ancestor with elaborate headdress and elongated facial features, early 20th century. The incised vessel sits on a star-shaped base. Good condition with slight erosion and signs of ritual use. 23" x 6". **$1,800**

Senufo Kpelie Janus Mask, Ivory Coast: Carved wood with elaborate facial regalia and stylized finial, early to mid-20th century. Images of duality among the tribes of this region often refer to the link between the world of the living and the spirit realm, the moral portrayed is that humans are inextricably connected to the souls of their forebears. Overall good condition. Mounted on custom display stand. 12" x 6 1/2". **$1,920**

Baule Rifle Stock Comb, Ivory Coast: Elegant carved with stylized handle and simple incised linear designs, early 20th century. Fine honey-colored patina, well-worn, loss to three tines. On custom display stand. 10 1/2" x 2 1/2". **$360**

Baule Gong With Carved Handle, Ivory Coast: Hand-forged iron gong with attached wooden handle possibly carved as a cupped hand, early to mid-20th century. A classic percussion instrument used in ceremony and dance. Well-worn handle suggests years of use, some rust and

Photo courtesy Rago Arts and Auction Center, Lambertville, N.J.; www.RagoArts.com

Dan Zakpai Runner Mask, Ivory Coast: Carved wood accented with animal teeth and remains of red textile, early to mid-20th century. Traditionally used in annual races. Well-worn interior showing obvious use. Mounted on custom metal base. 9" x 6". **$2,280**

pitting to gong, overall good condition, clear tone. 22 1/4" x 5 1/4". **$360**

Akan Colonial Figural Comb, Ghana: Carved wood sculptural comb topped by a colonialist wearing coat and hat, linear pattern to base, early to mid-20th century. A rare and superior example, featuring a statuette almost as tall as its tines. Mint condition with lustrous patina. On custom display stand. 6 3/4" x 2". **$1,680**

Ashanti Figural Comb, Ghana: Elegant carved wood example featuring an akuaba fertility doll with traditional facial features accented with kaolin clay, ringed neck with adornment, linear designs to reverse, early 20th century. Excellent condition with signs of use. On custom lucite display stand. 10 1/2" x 2 1/2". **$720**

Kwahu Akan Terra Cotta Memorial Head, Ghana: Ceramic human effigy with abstract and enlarged head on ringed neck, late 19th-early 20th century. Fair condition, some chips around top edge, otherwise intact and stable, permanent display post inserted in base. Mounted on wood block. 7 1/2" x 5 1/8". **$660**

Ashanti Queen Mother Memorial Idol, Ghana: Carved wooden shrine idol adorned with various textiles and strings of glass beads, early 20th century. Complete with infant Akua'ba on her back (daughter of Akua). Intact condition, heavy erosion to bottom of original base, signs of ritual use. Mounted on custom metal display stand. 19" x 5". **$1,140**

Fante Female Shrine Idol, Ghana: Well-handled honey-colored wooden figure accented with red glass beads, mid-20th century. Good condition with losses to feet. Custom-mounted on metal base. 13 1/4" x 3". **$300**

Dan Passport Mask, Ivory Coast: Elegant and classic example, with excised geometric design around the

Photo courtesy Rago Arts and Auction Center, Lambertville, N.J.; www.RagoArts.com

Large Bedu Plank Mask, Togo: Carved wood with abstracted face and stylized bush cow horns, with paint and kaolin on surface, early to mid-20th century. Well-handled surface consistent with field use. 52" x 21 1/2".
$1,140

eyes accented with kaolin, early 20th century. Excellent condition with deep, well-handled patina. On custom display stand. 6" x 3 1/2". **$1,680**

Mende Sowei Mask, Sierra Leone: Carved wooden helmet with stylized coiffure featuring female genetalia finial, early 20th century. Worn exclusively by the women of the Sande society during initiation ceremonies. Good condition with signs of obvious use. 13 3/4" x 8". **$360**

Vai or Gola Helmet Mask, Liberia: Carved wood Borwu (Long-Neck) accented with aluminum elements, early 20th century. Representing female spirit, these masks were used in dance masquerades. Fair condition, heavy use and tribal repairs. 27 1/4" x 9". **$900**

Three Mossi Bigga Dolls, Burkina Faso: Three carved wood dolls, early 20th century. These are used in teaching young girls to care for children, and carried by them until they have children of their own. Overall good condition, signs of handling and use. All mounted on bases. Tallest 15". ....**$420 all**

Jimini Heddle Pulley, Ivory Coast: Uncommon example of a weaving loom implement decorated with a stylized antelope head and incised linear design, early to mid-20th century. Overall good condition, well-handled, area around pulley shows heavy wear. Mounted on custom display stand. 6 1/2" x 2 1/2". **$330**

Two Lobi Bateba Shrine Figures, Burkina Faso: Two carved wood slender female idols, the smaller having unusual treatment of base, early 20th century. Overall good condition with smooth patinas showing years of use. Mounted on custom display stands. 7 1/2" and 5 1/2". ....**$300 both**

Dogon Toguna House Post, Mali: Carved architectural element with stylized female breasts, early 20th century. Used exclusively for men's meeting houses. Obvious erosion to base, wood strong and stable. Mounted on custom metal base. 55" x 17 3/4". **$1,560**

Dogon Sirige Mask, Mali: Classic carved wood mask with superstructure painted in various designs, mid-20th century. Meaning "storied house," the name refers to the family house, and by extension, the lineage of the human family. A dancer would swing the giant superstructure in a circular motion, representing the perceived revolution of the sun around the earth. Fair condition with obvious signs of use. 10' 2 1/2" x 8". **$1,200**

Dagara Phallic Shrine Fetish, Burkina Faso: Tall carved figural ritual object with male and female attributes, early to mid-20th century. Obvious weathering and minor stress fractures, intact and stable. Mounted on custom metal display stand. 26" x 12". **$840**

Nupe Granary Door, Nigeria: Carved wooden panel with geometric designs and spiral motifs. (Provenance: Private collection, New York) Well-worn surface, otherwise intact. Custom metal display stand. 43" x 15". **$420**

Baga Parade Staff, Guinea: Carved wooden female figure shown riding a fish, adorned with a fish finial, mid-20th century. Wear consistent with use, one rattan-wrap tribal repair to fishtail, minor stress fractures throughout. Custom mounted on wood base. 27" x 20". **$1,920**

Chiwara Antelope Headdress, Mali: Carved horizontal wooden finial of crouching animal, its head attached with original leather straps, mid-20th century. Translating to "heart of a lion," chiwara were typically used in agricultural dances honoring hard-working farmers. Excellent condition with signs of use. 11" x 28". **$1,200**

Mossi Terra Cotta Vessel, Burkina Faso: With applied anthropomorphic design under a burnished surface, mid-20th century. Overall good condition, signs of use. 18 1/2" x 17". **$1,080**

Dogon Terra Cotta Vessel, Mali: Highly decorated with incised designs and three spouts around shoulder, mid- to late 20th century. Overall good condition, some minor chipping. 23" x 15". **$360**

Yoruba Ibeji Twin Figures, Nigeria: Carved honey-colored wood male and female shrine objects with elaborate coiffure, classic facial features, adorned with several strands of glass beads, early 20th century. Complete with cowrie shell double garb. Traditionally carved after the death of a twin, these were meant to house the spirit of the deceased, and ritually fed for the remaining lifetime of its owner. The Yoruba have the highest twin birth rate in the world, leading to the creation of a twin cult. Overall good condition with minor stress fractures and signs of use. With robe: 9" x 12". **$480**

Yoruba Osanyin Ritual Staff, Nigeria: Wrought-iron post topped with an elegant avian finial and surrounded with a ring of smaller stylized birds, early to mid-20th century. Used in healing ceremonies. Some rust, overall good condition. On custom metal stand. 30" x 11". **$1,320**

Yoruba Beaded Diviner's Bag, Nigeria: Textile bag adorned with the face of Eshu, various glass beads and large natural seeds, on a long neck strap, early 20th century. Worn during ritual divination as part of the priest's regalia. Overall fair condition with signs of ritual use, mounted on a display board. 35" x 5". **$360**

Yoruba Beaded Coronet, Nigeria: Four-cornered hat with floral designs and avian finial, accented with a band of green and white bias design, early 20th century. Fair condition with signs of heavy use, possible losses to bottom edge. Mounted on custom metal display stand. 13 1/2" x 13 1/2". **$360**

Bini Horned Face Mask, Nigeria: Ekpo society mask carved from a single piece of wood, wearing a serene expression, accented with indigo and white kaolin pigments, early 20th century. Reputed to cleanse the society of disease and protect the village from witchcraft. Overall good condition with signs of handling and use. 11" x 5 3/4". **$960**

Ogoni Articulated Mask, Nigeria: Carved wood with raised scarification, stylized coiffure, attached lower jaw supported with wrapped rattan, painted black and accented with kaolin clay, early to mid-20th century. Overall fair condition with signs of use. On custom display stand. 8 1/2" x 5 1/2". **$480**

Ogoni Antelope Mask, Nigeria: Carved wood accented with red and black paint, and kaolin clay, early to mid-20th century. Well worn condition, several broken attachment holes consistent with years of field use. Mounted on custom display stand. 12 1/2" x 6". **$600**

Ogoni Articulated Mask, Nigeria: Carved wood mask featuring an avian beak, its lower jaw attached with wrapped rattan which, when open, reveals a full set of spindled teeth, the face painted black and red, and accented with kaolin clay, early to mid-20th century. Complete with raised scarification and stylized coiffure. Overall good condition with signs of use. On custom display stand. 8 1/4" x 5"...**$600**

Tiv Imborivungu Cult Fetish, Nigeria: Ritual staff with carved wood male head featuring inlaid glass eyes, scarification of tears, and human hair woven in braids, over a femur bone wrapped with beads, early 20th century. The traditional use of these objects from the only documented cannibal cult in Africa relates to the legend of a Tiv ancestor known as Poor. According to local legend, his original thigh bone was removed so that his memory would be perpetuated. Over time, the original artifact was lost, and was substituted with relics (Imborivungu). Fair condition with some loss to bead work and light decay to hair. Mounted on custom metal display stand. 7" x 2 3/4". **$2,400**

Ibibio Female Marionette, Nigeria: Carved wooden figurine with articulated arms, painted designs, accented with kaolin clay, early to mid-20th century. Fair condition with losses to feet, nose, and hair. 24" x 8". **$480**

Bini Polychrome Mask, Nigeria: Carved wooden mask with stylized coiffure and collar, painted with white and green geometric pattern on a bold burnt-orange ground, early to mid-20th century. Fair condition, loss to collar, obvious handling and wear. Mounted on a custom display stand. 10 1/2" x 6". **$360**

Photo courtesy Rago Arts and Auction Center, Lambertville, N.J.; www.RagoArts.com

Mumuye Horizontal Mask, Nigeria: Abstract form accented with red clay, featuring oversized eyes and flat snout, early 20th century. Well-weathered with signs of heavy use. Mounted on custom display stand. 6" x 7" x 14 1/2". **$4,800**

Photo courtesy Rago Arts and Auction Center, Lambertville, N.J.; www.RagoArts.com

Ibo Helmet Mask, Nigeria: Carved wood with elaborate superstructure featuring ancestors and avian images, early to mid-20th century. With raised scarification on kaolin-covered face and remnants of traditional costume, these represent the spirit of a young deceased maiden, thought of as a protective entity. Fair condition with losses to finial and figures. Mounted on metal display stand. Without costume: 22" x 14". **$1,800**

Ibibio Dance Mask, Nigeria: Carved wooden abstract male face with brilliant yellow natural pigment, traditional scarification and tribal repair, early 20th century. Fair condition with obvious signs of use. On custom display stand. 10 1/2" x 6". **$360**

Ijebu Yoruba Water Spirit Mask, Nigeria: Carved wood fantastical mask with ornate spiral finials, adorned with avian images and archaic human face, mid-20th century. The mirror fragment suggests the reflection of water, domain of the water spirit. Fair condition with several repairs to the finial, and well-weathered surface. 40" x 10 1/2". **$600**

Bamoun Kola Nut Offering Bowl, Cameroon: Highly stylized zoomorphic form, with incised geometric designs, and deeply carved bowl, late 19th-early 20th century. Signs of heavy use, overall intact, with light chipping. 10" x 11 1/2". **$360**

Mboum Headdress, Cameroon: Carved wooden plank mask with stylized cowrie shell images, accented with kaolin and other natural pigments, and adorned with kola nuts, late 19th century. Overall good condition, some minor losses to top of finial. Mounted on custom wood and metal display stand. 34 1/2" x 7". **$1,800**

Ibo Parade Bust, Nigeria: Carved wood ancestor, his fierce features including stylized tattoos and ritual scars, mid-20th century. Fair condition, loss to rear top finial and base. 34" x 12". **$1,200**

Mbundu Mask, Angola: Carved wood with incised linear and geometric design, classic coffee bean eyes, and well defined cheeks, early to mid-20th century. Such masks are worn during the initiation of young men into adulthood. Fair condition with obvious weathering and minor areas of loss, some restoration to stress fractures. 15 1/2" x 11 1/2". **$1,560**

Bembe Female Mukuya Fetish, Democratic Republic Of The Congo: Shown offering a small bird, with classic body scarification and features, her eyes inlaid with ivory, early 20th century. Traditionally thought of as a household protective statue. Overall glossy, well-handled surface; both arms re-attached, loss to part of one arm and both feet. Mounted on custom metal base. 6" x 2 1/2". **$2,280**

Punu Maiden Spirit Mask, Gabon: Classic female face with incised coiffure, accented with red pigment on forehead band, and several layers of kaolin clay, early 20th century. Fair condition, some weathering to one side and signs of handling. Mounted on custom metal display stand. 11 1/2" x 6". **$2,760**

Luba Janus Comb, Democratic Republic Of The Congo: Carved wood with two archaic ancestor heads above incised geometric design, late 19th-early 20th century. Overall good condition with lustrous patina. On custom display stand. 6 1/2" x 3". **$1,920**

Songye Kifwebe Society Mask, Zaire: Carved wood with incised linear designs and tall central crest designating a male mask, painted in bold black and white kaolin pigments, mid-20th century. Attached raffia grass regalia includes sleeves for the wearer. Fair condition with signs of field use. 33" x 12". **$1,020**

Songye Kifwebe Society Mask, Zaire: Boldly carved example with precise linear design, raised finial, protruding four-sided mouth, complete with nose hairs, early to mid-20th century. Very well worn interior, light staining to kaolin, small chip to eye, all consistent with field use. 18" x 7 1/2". **$480**

Kuba Ceremonial Dance Sword, Democratic Republic Of The Congo: Classic painted prestige object incised with design on stylized blade, white and red earthen pigments, early 20th century. Includes original wooden scabbard with woven rattan supports. Custom-mounted on display stand. 25" x 9". **$480**

Fang Figural Comb, Gabon: Small carved wooden comb with ancestral image carved in relief and some linear designs, early 20th century. Excellent condition with well-handled patina. On custom display stand. 6" x 1". **$1,680**

Pende Figural Comb, Democratic Republic Of The Congo: Carved female ancestor adorning hair implement with geometric designs accented in kaolin, early 20th century. Excellent condition with well-handled patina. On custom display stand. 8" x 2". **$1,440**

Yaka Figural Comb, Democratic Republic Of The Congo: Carved wood sculptural comb with classic ancestor face with up-turned nose and large flared ears, adorned with a stylized cap and linear design, early 20th century. Excellent condition with signs of use and wear. On custom display stand. 5 1/2" x 1". **$540**

Luena Mask, Angola: Carved wood with various layers of paint and natural pigment, adorned with a ring of feathers, early 20th century. Used as a dance mask, likely representing the ideal woman. Fair condition with obvious field use. On custom display stand. Total: 9" x 6 1/2". ...**$480**

Pende Munyangi Mask, Zaire: Carved wood Munyangi with strong geometric features, early to mid-20th century. Used in performances associated with youthful energy. Fair condition, some loss to back, showing heavy use. Custom mounted. On base: 13 1/2" x 5 1/2". **$480**

Suku Helmet Mask, Zaire: Carved wooden mask with serene expression, topped by a whimsical animal finial, accented with kaolin clay and natural blue pigment, glass-bead earrings, and grass collar, early to mid-20th century. Stress fracture on forehead, minor chipping, signs of use. 14 1/2" x 11" x 12". **$1,920**

Lega Bwami Society Maskette, Zaire: Carved wood bearing delicate features, the eyes highlighted with kaolin and exposed wood with fine patina, early to mid-20th century. Maskettes were typically worn as armband regalia, or hung around the village as clan totems. Overall good condition with signs of use. Includes a custom metal display stand. 7 3/4" x 3 3/4". **$1,560**

Lwalwa Mask, Democratic Republic Of The Congo: Highly stylized concave human face with large open eyes, and diminutive ears and mouth, the head with remnants of kaolin, mid-20th century. Overall good condition with well-handled surface, minor scrapes, shallow stress fracture on chin. 13" x 9". **$900**

Tabwa Terra Cotta Vessel, Zaire: Shaped as a vessel over a brazier on four feet, decorated with roped medallions, one with an elegant European face, with painted copper details, early to mid- 20th century. Overall good condition, some restoration to rim, one foot re-attached. 15" x 13". **$1,080**

Terra Cotta Vessel, Rwanda: With raised waves accented in red and white pigment, mid-20th century. Overall good condition, with a few minor flecks to high points, consistent with use. 15" x 10 1/2". **$1,560**

Large Shona Terra Cotta Beer Vessel, Zimbabwe: Spherical pot accented with orange and black paint, mid-20th century. Typically used to store millet beer. Some restoration to rim, otherwise intact with signs of use. 14" x 17". **$1,320**

Chewa Animal Mask, Malawi: Carved wood zoomorphic mask with stylized facial features, deep scarification, two bands of glass beads, and evidence of former animal skin regalia, early 20th century. Fair condition with loss to two cowrie shell teeth, signs of heavy ritual use. On custom display stand. 11" x 6 1/2". **$660**

Turkana Male and Female Dolls, Tanzania: Mated pair of carved wood dolls with classic facial features, the female adorned with glass beads and a leather skirt, early 20th century. Overall good condition, chip to back of female's arm. On custom display stands. 16" and 15". ....**$240 pair**

East African Figural Staff: Carved wood with elegant female image, minimal incised design and stylized coiffure, early to mid-20th century. Overall good condition with stable stress fractures, custom metal display stand. 35". **$1,200**

Painted Hide Shield, Nigeria: Geometric red and white designs with animal motifs. Wear consistent with use. 23" dia. **$360**

Photo courtesy Rago Arts and Auction Center, Lambertville, N.J.; www.RagoArts.com

Feather Currency Roll, Santa Cruz, Solomon Islands: Traditional band of wound plant fiber adorned with Myzomela cardinal feathers and strands of shell beads, attached to two bark frames, mid-19th century. Overall good condition, some wear to feathers commensurate with age and use. On custom display stand. Total: 28 1/2" x 29 1/2". **$3,360**

Rapa Nui Moai Kava Kava, Easter Island: Carved wood male ancestor figure, eyes accented with shell and obsidian, mid-19th century. Deified ancestral beings, bearers of knowledge, and dispensers of wisdom, the Kava Kava were worn around the neck of the men who took part in ritual dances. Overall good condition. 24 3/4" x 4 1/2". **$7,800**

Ceremonial Chalice, Trobriand Islands: Highly stylized carved wooden vessel with incised geometric designs accented with kaolin clay, late 19th - early 20th century. Overall good and stable condition, well handled patina with signs of use and two stress fractures. 15" x 5 1/2". **$480**

Wooden Paddle, Austral Island: Elaborately carved with stylized faces and precise geometric design, 19th century. (A very refined example, of a quality seldom found.) Overall excellent condition. On custom stand. Remains of a pre-WWI label. 40" x 6". **$4,200**

Grade Society Fern Figures, Vanuatu: Carved tree fungus with original tree-trunk still evident, early 20th century. Fair condition with heavy erosion to wood, otherwise stable. Male: 80" x 16" x 18", female: 75" x 16" x 17". ....**$3,360 pair**

Marionette Figure, S. Malekula, Vanuatu: Painted tree fern and wood Temes Nevinbur figure, accented with boar's tusks and feathers, early 20th century. Fair condition with losses to natural materials, overall stable. On custom mount, 42 1/2" x 18 1/2". **$1,020**

Baining Fire Dance Mask, New Britain, Papua New Guinea: Light fig tree bark and rattan-frame mask accented with red and black natural pigments, mid-20th century. Excellent overall condition, a few minor holes. On custom display stand. 30 1/2" x 12". **$840**

Root Club, Gilbert Island, Micronesia: Naturally formed spiral staff with woven cane handle, reddish patina of unknown origin, 19th century. Good condition, minor loss to wrap. Mounted on custom metal display. 28" x 4 1/4". **$1,920**

Limestone Memorial Sculpture, Sumba Island, Indonesia: Carved anthropomorphic figure, late 19th - early 20th century. Used locally as markers for sacred sites. Fair condition, erosion consistent with tribal use. Mounted on custom metal stand. 21 1/2" x 7". **$1,560**

Kantu Dayak Hampatong, Borneo: Carved wooden female Padi with stylized top knot and long slender spike carved from a single piece of wood, early 20th century. Used as a protective fetish in fields and granary storage. Fair condition with some erosion. On custom display stand. 18 1/2" x 2"....................**$480**

Dayak Ancestor Hampatong, Borneo: Carved wood female figure of elongated neck and form, with archaic features, 19th century. Traditionally used as protective idols for villages and ceremonial sites. Heavily eroded surface suggesting generations of use. Mounted on custom metal display stand. 21 1/2" x 3 1/2". **$420**

Kayan/Kenyah Dayak Hudoq Mask, Borneo: Classic mask with attached ears and horn-like appendages, bone fangs, and rattan basketry helmet, eyes accented with small mirrors, early to mid-20th century. Typically used in agricultural dances, the painted red, black, and white designs mimic rainforest vines. Fair condition with repairs

Photo courtesy Rago Arts and Auction Center, Lambertville, N.J.; www.RagoArts.com

Dayak Bronze Gong Handle, Borneo/Indonesia: Stylized Aso dragon, early 20th century. Excellent condition. Hanging from custom mount. Handle: 4 3/4" x 3 1/2". **$960**

to ears, horn appendages reglued. Mounted on custom display stand. 20" x 17". **$1,020**

Batak Keris Sword, Sumatra, Indonesia: Iron sword of stylized form topped by an elegant silver-inlaid wood handle, late 19th century. Fits in a carved wooden sheath with scrolled finial. Excellent original condition, slight pitting to blade. Total: 21 3/4". **$480**

Dayak Modang Head-Hunter Mandau Sword, Borneo: Classic iron sword with deer antler handle carved with a stylized head and incised design, 19th century. The unusually decorative blade features an intricately forged edge and is inlaid with copper stars and brass roundels. Fits in a highly ornate carved wooden sheath featuring the dragon Aso among vines. Complete with attached Piso Raout featuring a finely carved antler, missing its small blade. Minor wear to bottom of scabbard, excellent condition. Total: 24". **$840**

Keris Dagger, Sumatra, Indonesia: Fine traditional weapon with ivory handle carved with an abstract form of Garuda, over an iron blade in the Damascus technique, early 20th century. Fits in its original burlwood sheath with repousse metal collar. The confluences of Islam and Hinduism are shown in the depiction of the god Garuda, treated here in its simplest of forms. Small chip and restoration to handle, missing a collar to sheath. Total: 20 1/2" x 6". **$540**

Dragon-Head Sword, Sumatra, Indonesia: Klewang with carved horn handle banded in ivory, above an iron blade chiseled with Islamic script, late 19th century. Complete with contemporary rosewood scabbard. Excellent condition, minor pitting to blade. Sword: 26". **$780**

Dayak Shield, Borneo: Carved wooden shield painted with unusual stylized eyes and mouth, along with traditional tribal motifs in black, ochre and red pigments, two Aso dragons on the reverse, accented with woven rattan bands, early 20th century. Fair condition with minor areas of loss and one fracture. 50" x 14". **$1,920**

Dayak Mualang Iban Altarpiece, Borneo: Carved dark wood figure of ancestor rising from aristocratic burial urn, early 20th century. Overall good condition. 16". **$600**

Tangkhul Naga Architectural Panel, India: Carved wooden facade from a morung (men's meeting house) featuring three archaic mask faces, the central image with feathered headdress, early 20th century. Fair condition with obvious weathering. 46" x 22". **$1,200**

Gunwinggu Bark Painting, Oenpelli, Australia: Traditional painting by George D. Jayngurrnga depicting Mimi spirits, mid-20th century. Good condition. 53 1/2" x 21". **$1,020**

Waksuk Female Idol, Papua New Guinea: Carved wood elongated figure with abstract facial features and incised scarification, red pigment accenting the face, mid-20th century. Good condition with signs of use, custom metal display stand. 54". **$3,120**

Canoe Prow Ornament, Trobriand Islands: Carved wooden finial with classic geometric designs, early 20th century. Intact with signs of use. 19" x 9". **$480**

Skull Rack, Papua New Guinea: Carved wood incised with tribal motifs, accented with two avian images and three trophy heads, with cowrie shell eyes, pierced for hanging, early to mid-20th century. Fair condition with some repairs to finials. 9 1/2" x 43 1/2". **$480**

Hook Mask, Hunstein Mountain, Papua New Guinea: Yam-shaped carved wood with classic curved finials, early to mid-20th century. Kept in the men's cult houses, the hooks or curved beaks relate to the sacred hornbill bird. Overall good condition, one minor chip. 24" x 4 3/8". **$600**

Dani Jade Adze, Papua New Guinea: Braided plant fiber wrap and cassowary bird feathers around a fine speckled jade blade, early 20th century. Most likely used in the preparation of sago, a local food staple. Fair condition with signs of heavy use. On custom display stand. 23" x 12". **$1,320**

Karawari Hook Figure, Papua New Guinea: Carved wooden Yipwon, mid-20th century. Charm used to promote successful hunting. Fair condition with minor loss and short break. On painted wooden base. 23" x 3". **$540**

Basket Hook, Sepik River, Papua New Guinea: Carved wood in figural form, mid-20th century. 22" x 6 1/2". **$420**

Large Abelam Male Figure, Papua New Guinea: Ancestor carved from a single piece of wood, likely an architectural element from a men's meeting house, with

Photo courtesy Rago Arts and Auction Center, Lambertville, N.J.; www.RagoArts.com

Dayak Bidayuh Clan Mask, Borneo: Carved wood face of a shaman, early 20th century. Used in ritual dances. (Seldom comes to market). Excellent condition with signs of use. On custom display stand. 11" x 7 1/2". **$1,200**

headdress and carved arm bands, geometric designs painted in earthen red, yellow, black and white pigment, early to mid-20th century. Fair with obvious erosion, reattached element. 55" x 10". **$600**

Asmat Canoe Prow, Papua New Guinea: Carved openwork finial featuring two ancestors, adorned with cassowary bird feathers and shells, accented in orange and white kaolin clay, mid-20th century. Overall good condition, loss to small piece on edge. 43" x 10". **$780**

Bena Bena Fofona Breast Plate, Eastern Islands, Papua New Guinea: Woven grass adornment accented with various sea shells including two large cowrie shell finials, dyed with natural red and blue pigments with attached neck strap, early to mid-20th century. Overall good condition. 13 1/2" x 13 1/2". **$240**

Conch-Shell Trumpet With Carving, Hawaii: Classic shell instrument with unusual fish hook emblem carved on top, possibly an early signature, 19th century. Well-handled and smooth example, showing much use. 9" x 6 1/2". **$1,200**

Palm Leaf Fan, Hawaii: Classic form in traditional Lauhala weave, late 19th century. In remarkable state of preservation. Professionally conserved in museum wall mounting. Total: 28" x 21 3/4". **$900**

Lava Whetstone, Hawaii: Rare utilitarian object, showing generations of use as a adze stone sharpener, 18th-19th century. Overall good condition with signs of use. 3 3/4" x 16" x 7". **$960**

FUTURE OF THE MARKET: WESTERN MEMORABILIA

Rockmount still sets standard for cowboy couture

By Caroline Ashleigh

From the minute I slipped into my miniature cowgirl ensemble and sashayed onto the playground as a little tyke, I felt, instantly, like a larger-than-life character. Such an outfit has the power to transform you: It was a two-piece bright turquoise gabardine riding outfit, accented with gold leather and rhinestones. It came with a hat, split-fringed skirt, holster, play pistol, belt, bandana, boots, and spurs that went jingle, jangle, jingle. When I wore it, I exuded attitude and style. It seemed to create an aura that made all of the other little buckarettes and buckaroos feel like they were in the presence of the newly crowned Queen of Cowgirl Couture.

Caroline Ashleigh

That's when I fell in love with fancy Western clothes. It turned into a life-long love affair.

Fast forward to the summer of 2009 in Denver, an Antiques Roadshow event drew an unexpected surprise, one that stirred up the cowgirl in me. On a hot, sultry, summer evening in late July, I was invited to attend a private party by Steven E. Weil, president of Rockmount Ranch Wear Manufacturing Co. at his three-generation-owned family business, located in a red brick warehouse in the LoDo district of Denver for over 62 years.

It was there that I had the privilege of meeting Steve, the grandson of the legendary "Papa Jack" Weil, maker of iconic western wear worn around the world, who held the title of the oldest living CEO until his death in 2008, at 107 years of age.

Not unlike my own experience wearing Western wear as a little tyke, Steve began modeling Western wear as an infant in fashion shows. His love for vintage Western wear began in high school when he raided his grandfather's closet for shirts from the 1940s. And that's probably when he fell, cowboy-hat-over-heels, for Western wear, which turned into a lifelong love affair. Today, as president of the company, he is responsible for all design lines and operations, and could easily lay claim to the title as the current King of Cowboy Couture.

As Steve points out in his book titled, *Ask Papa Jack*, "We live and learn from stories in a way far more deeply than any other way short of actual experience." In an era when storytelling is becoming a vanishing art, I was mesmerized listening to Steve talk about his family business that started in the West, and how this original regional market would one day span the globe.

I was fascinated to learn that during the Great Depression in 1935, Papa Jack went into the business of Western wear, and the strategy worked, even in the worst of economic times. Rockmount prospered during the 1940s, as the rural West fared better than large urban areas.

Colleen Long of the Associated Press wrote in a syndicated news story appearing in the Los Angeles Times in 2001, "Rockmount Ranch Wear Ropes in Clients by Bucking Retail Trendiness." Rockmount today is still roping in clients and bucking trends in the second-worst economic downturn since the Great Depression.

Rockmount is the quintessential American success story. Papa Jack proudly stated in an interview with CNN in March 2001, at the age of 100, "We take pride in making it in this country. We would like very much to make it all in this country. It's a philosophy of self-preservation in this country, our way of life. If the people in this country earn their money here, and live here, there's a pretty good chance they will buy some of our products."

Steve adds, "Holding on to our roots at Rockmount became our salvation. Now we are virtually the last guys standing." They are not only the last guys standing, but they are continuing to prosper.

Steve reminisces, "Back in the early '80s, I was browsing through a Los Angeles vintage store on Melrose, and found a brown gabardine shirt that was so old at first I didn't recognize it as Rockmount. It dated from the 1940s and was marked $75, which was twice the price of Rockmount shirts then. I told the retailer it was one of the first Western shirts my grandfather had made. Touched, he told me to take the shirt and send him a couple of new ones for it. Excited by the find, I didn't wait until returning home to tell my grandfather. In those pre-cell-phone days, I found a phone booth and called the office. 'WHAT?' Papa exclaimed, 'you traded two perfectly good new shirts for an old one we sold for $3 forty years ago?'" Fast forward to February 2006. Rockmount shirts that were worn in the movie Brokeback Mountain sell for $101,000 on eBay.

Even though I do not fit the celebrity status as some of Rockmount's clients — such as Elvis Presley, Robert Redford, David Bowie, Bob Dylan and Eric Clapton — after visiting Steve's shop in Denver, there was only one thing I could do. Before sliding up to the bar with my fellow appraisers on Antiques Roadshow in Denver, I got decked out in full Western regalia: my fringed black and silver studded cape, sterling silver snaffle-buckled belt, my rhinestone-encrusted spurred stilettos, and my boldly colored Rockmount shirt with smile pockets, embroidered arrows, piping, enamel snaps, and tiered fringe. And just like that, I was transported back to the playground with all my little buckaroo buddies. I'm still in love with fancy cowboy clothes and spurs that go jingle, jangle, jingle.

Steve Weil points out in his book, *Western Shirts – A*

Above, three generations of the Weil family proudly pose in front of the Rockmount Ranch Wear Manufacturing Co. in Denver. From left, Steve, "Papa Jack" and Jack B.

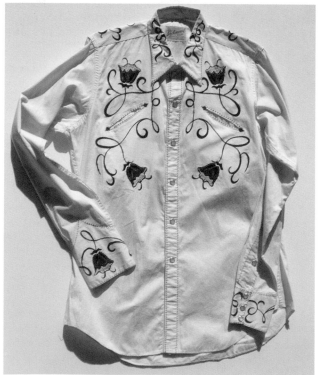

At left is an Art Deco-inspired Rockmount shirt designed by Jack B. Weil in the 1950s. It is highly stylized with chenille embroidery, saddle stitching, special cuff treatment.

Above: Fancy custom red and white parade boots.
$150+

Left: Western shirt designed by Fay Ward Co., cowboy tailors for "The Sundowners," circa 1970.
$300-$400

Below: John Wayne off-white Stetson hat, imprinted "McLintock No.1 — Especially Made for John Wayne".

Elvis Presley studio-stressed Stetson hat imprinted "Charro — Made by Nudies of North California Especially for Elvis Presley."

Gene Autry white Stetson hat imprinted "Made by Stetson for Gene Autry."

Classic American Fashion, there is no consistent standard for pricing vintage clothes. Factors such as demand, condition, rarity, as well as original packaging affect the price. "New/old" is a rarified category highly sought after by collectors. This is the "dead stock" that has escaped the ravages of time. Sometimes it is found in wholesale quantities — forgotten in storage — or it surfaces as a single piece that was put away new and never worn.

The modern-day master tailor who brought mass-media attention and razzle-dazzle to the Western-wear scene was a Russian immigrant by the name of Nuta Kotlyarenko, better known as Nudie Cohn (1902-1984), a.k.a. "Dior of the Sagebrush," and "The Original Rhinestone Cowboy." Cohn influenced the Western-wear industry for nearly 40 years, whipping up costumes for Hank Williams, Hopalong Cassidy, Clayton Moore, Ronald Reagan, Liberace, Elton John, the Rolling Stones and Elvis Presley, among others.

In 1957, he was commissioned to create the most expensive suit he had ever made: a 14k gold lame outfit bejeweled with 10,000 rhinestones. Over the years, Nudie is said to have sold Elvis $100,000 worth of clothes, today worth $400,000-$500,000.

Another immigrant who created a market niche was Nathan Turk from Minsk, Poland. Beginning in the 1930s, movie studios began commissioning Turk to design costumes for Westerns. By the 1940s, Western musicians began frequenting Turk's shop in Van Nuys, Calif. He created the blueprint for most of the successful country bands: a unique ensemble for group leaders to set them apart, with the advertising slogan, "With real western wear from the movies."

The original cost of a Western garment is in direct proportion to the volume produced. Tailor-made shirts by Rodeo Ben and Nudie Cohn were quite expensive and out of the reach of the public when new. These early designs were "one-off" custom makes for celebrities like Roy Rogers and Gene Autry. Later they went to limited production runs but remained much more expensive than production-made garments. By the same token, the more expensive the ready-to-wear garment, the lower the volume in which it was produced. It is not uncommon to find only a single surviving example of the best highly stylized designs.

Generally, today's pricing seems to fall into four ranges:

$300+: extremely fine, rare, ornate shirts.

$100-$300: highly ornate embroideries, pre-1960.

$25-$100: nicely detailed basic shirts in good vintage fabrics, pre-1970.

Less than $25: generic, mass-produced commodity styles, including imports, since 1970s.

Note: Pricing changes along with trends, so these figures have a limited window of accuracy.

Caroline Ashleigh owns Birmingham, Mich.-based Caroline Ashleigh Associates LLC. She is a graduate of New York University in Appraisal Studies in Fine and Decorative Arts and is a board-certified senior member of the Appraisers Association of America. Ashleigh is an internationally known appraiser and regularly appears on the PBS program Antiques Roadshow. Caroline Ashleigh Associates conducts fully catalogued online auctions. Visit www.appraiseyourart.com or www.auctionyourart.com.

Collection of Western ties, circa 1950/1960. **$15-$30 each**

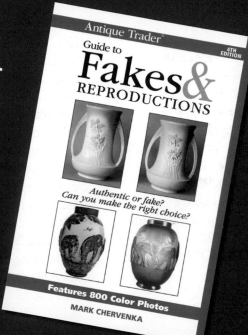

Check Out These Great Products

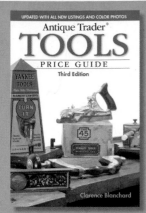
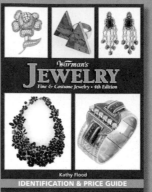